The
A to Z of Edwardian London

With an Introduction by
M. H. Port

Edited by
Ann Saunders

LONDON TOPOGRAPHICAL SOCIETY
Publication No. 166
2007

© London Topographical Society

Publication No. 166 of the
London Topographical Society
3 Meadway Gate, London NW11 7LA

ISBN 0 902087 53 3

PRODUCED IN GREAT BRITAIN BY
OUTSET SERVICES LTD, CLIFFORD, NEAR LEEDS

CONTENTS

Pages numbers stated are to this edition

LONDON 1912

By M. H. PORT

THE Edwardian era, like London itself, is a concept of which the boundaries are indistinct and uncertain: some see it as beginning in the 1880s, when 'society, in the old sense of the term, may be said ... to have come to an end'[i] and Albert Edward, Prince of Wales, assumed the leadership of the new plutocratic society, rather than with his accession to the throne in 1901. Similarly, it is often regarded as lingering on after the king's death in 1910 until the outbreak of war in 1914. Thus, though risking offending the pedantically rigorous chronologist, the Society's Council determined that 'Edwardian London' was the most appropriate title under which to reproduce an atlas published about 1912.

Members will be familiar with Ralph Hyde's account of George Washington Bacon and his atlases of London given in the Society's *The A to Z of Victorian London*, adapted from Bacon's *New Large-Scale Ordnance Atlas of London & Suburbs* of 1888. Here one need do no more than recall that Bacon (1830-1922) was a London printer, publisher, importer and inventor with a particular enthusiasm for publishing large-scale maps of the metropolis, a work in which he had many rivals. The 1888 atlas, however, with its four-inch and nine-inch to the mile maps, was 'in a class of its own'.[ii] The revision of *c*.1912 used for the present volume employs a uniform scale of four inches to the mile (save for special maps displaying various administrative areas and those of the Home Counties), though its index establishes that nine-inch maps were also published in some copies.

To embrace ever-expanding London, 34 four-inch maps were required in 1912, compared with 25 in 1888. The new atlas reached out further than the old, north-west to Harrow and Harrow Weald, south-west to Chessington, south to Cheam, Purley and Selsdon, south-east to Farnborough and Orpington, and to Seven Kings and Chadwell Heath. The great weight of house building in the Edwardian decades, however, fell in those outer districts already included in the 1888 atlas.

Thus we find to the north many new streets in a half-mile radius from Finchley and Muswell Hill stations, in Hornsey and especially in Tottenham and Edmonton; extensively to the north of Walthamstow and north-eastwards to Highams Park; east of Epping Forest in South Woodford; massively from West Ham to Barking and Ilford on the east; and, towards the Thames, north of Victoria Docks. South of the river, there was both infilling and extension in Greenwich (where Booth writes of people from the overcrowded East End 'using the marvellous Blackwall Tunnel roadway [to] go and live in East Greenwich, where there is more room'),[iii] with acres of housing surrounding the great cemeteries further south — Nunhead, Deptford, Lewisham — and marching down to Sydenham and South End; between Streatham Common and Tooting stations; and both north and south of Wimbledon between the Kingston and Croydon railways. Westwards, new streets appear between Ealing and Hanwell, and north of the Great Western Railway at Hanwell, and filling in the salient formed by that line and the Metropolitan District in Acton.

This immense extent of house-building, to meet the needs of a population that in the London County Council area alone increased from 4,228,000 in 1891 to 4,536,000 in 1901, and in the Greater London area from 5,572,000 in 1891 to 7,160,000 in 1911,[iv] was achieved by an army of speculative builders: 1,555 firms in 1881, building in anticipation of demand; few built more than half-a-dozen houses a year. A slump around 1890 weeded out many, but in 1899 small firms still composed about 60 per cent of the total of 614. However, only 17 firms building more than 60 houses a year contributed over 40 per cent of the capital's new housing, the biggest, Watts of Catford, erecting over 400 houses in South-East London in that year.[v]

Related to urban expansion — though how far it was cause, how far effect, is much discussed — was the development of improved forms of mass transportation. The deep-bore 'tube' underground railways of the Central Line (Bank to Shepherds Bush, 1900), Northern Line (Angel-Clapham, 1901; Charing Cross-Golders Green, 1907), and Piccadilly (Kensington-Piccadilly-King's Cross, 1906) appear here, indicated by thin double lines and naming their stations (characterized by shiny ox-blood-red tiled façades). Such developments made little surface change, but a new main line from the Midlands, the Great Central, to a new terminus, Marylebone, wiped out Blandford Square. The heavily-used 'bus and tram routes are clearly marked in orange, with a new down-river crossing available from 1894 over Tower Bridge (Horace Jones and Wolfe-Barry), with its 200 ft opening span to allow ships up river.

But it is not new streets and buildings alone that characterize Bacon 1912. Conspicuous among features of the new suburbs, particularly in the spacious southern outer band, are numerous golf courses. Thus from west to east (sheets 24-8), we find Ditton, Surbiton, Raynes Park, Princes (Mitcham), Tooting Bec, Beckenham, Park Langley, Bromley & Bickley, Orpington, and to the north

of the last (sheet 23) Chislehurst, Sidcup, Eltham, Belmont Park, Sandridge Park, and Elmstead Golf Links. Not as obvious, perhaps, was the proliferation of smaller-scale public parks and recreation grounds: in Ealing, for instance, recreation grounds north and south of Hanwell, at Drayton Green near Pitshanger, and more centrally Walpole Park and Lammas Park, as well as Ealing Common; a football ground at Park Royal, cricket at Green Man Lane and Woodville Gardens, and sports grounds off Haslemere Avenue to the south — none marked on Bacon 1888.

To suggest, however, that new building was confined to the expanding suburbs would be highly misleading. Established in 1889, the new metropolitan local authority, the London County Council, controlled by the Progressives, launched a powerful programme of building improved dwellings for the working classes that should clear away slums. Their Boundary Street Estate of 13 acres in Bethnal Green, to the east of Shoreditch Church, swept away old roads, nests of degradation, to create a circus with radial streets lined by blocks of flats; and on part of the Millbank Penitentiary site built their Arts-and-Crafts Millbank Estate (1897-1902) on an even larger scale and to improved standards. Another scheme, either side of Old Oak Common Lane, Hammersmith (its layout influenced by Hampstead Garden Suburb), begun in 1911, is not marked on Bacon 1912, where the greater part is still Acton Golf Links, and the extension of the Central Line west of Shepherds Bush is unrecorded, as indeed is the 1911 extension of Hampstead Garden Suburb. The expense of inner city sites and new legislation, however, encouraged the LCC to go out of town — to Totterdown Fields (marked as 'Lower Tooting', sheet 20), somewhat monotonously designed cottages on a grid plan (1903-11); and northerly to Old Oak Lane, Tottenham, a 45-acre site of which the southernmost streets, with 781 cottages, completed in 1912, are shown on sheet 2.

The Edwardian era is often associated with opulence, and opulence, grandeur, overwhelming size are the obvious qualities of its architecture. The visitor to London in the new century would have been very conscious of a wave of public building sweeping down Whitehall and Parliament Street to Parliament Square in a succession of colossal office blocks in the imperial Edwardian baroque style: Leeming Brothers' ever-growing Admiralty dominating Horse Guards Parade (1889-1914), William Young's New War Office (1899-1906) overwhelming the Banqueting House, and Brydon's New Public Offices (1899-1915, designed to house the rapidly expanding Boards of Education, Local Government and Trade, but acquired by the Treasury)

challenging the Houses of Parliament across the square.

At the other end of St James's Park, Aston Webb refronted Buckingham Palace in 1913 as a fitting termination for his grand re-planned Mall, the national memorial to Queen Victoria. At its eastern end, he opened the Mall to Charing Cross by a brilliantly designed Admiralty extension over angled triumphal arches, and in front of the palace constructed a *rond-point* with Brock's Queen Victoria Statue in the centre.

Along the Embankment, in place of a putative opera house, Richard Norman Shaw had styled new headquarters for the Metropolitan Police, New Scotland Yard (1889-90), idiosyncratically in red brick (then quite rare for public buildings) with stone dressings. In Parliament Square W. S. Gibson designed a new Guildhall for the Middlesex County Council in an equally idiosyncratic but exquisite version of late Gothic with carvings by Henry Fehr (1906-13). Opposite the Abbey, replacing the Royal Aquarium, rose Lanchester and Rickard's overpowering domed Central Hall in French baroque, for the Wesleyan Methodists (1905-11), while along Millbank W. D. Caröe erected a huge stone-dressed red brick office block for the Anglican Church Commissioners. Similarly dominant blocks spread down Millbank towards the Tate Gallery, built in 1893-7 at sugar-king Sir Henry Tate's expense on the river front of the Millbank Penitentiary site in a Roman baroque manner by Sidney R. J. Smith, and subsequently flanked by an army medical college and an army hospital in red brick and Portland stone.

Greatest of these inner city developments, however, was the construction from 1900 onwards — still incomplete in 1912 — of the major north-south boulevard of Kingsway and its dependant crescent, Aldwych (running north of the Strand, approximately from Waterloo Bridge to St Clement Danes) — a town-planning scheme on the grand scale that took the new powers of the LCC to accomplish. In Regent Street, the Crown Estate entrusted to Norman Shaw the updating of Nash's Quadrant (from 1904), with which was incorporated the baroque Piccadilly Hotel (1905-8).

Yet further west, in South Kensington, Aston Webb completed the South Kensington Museum, renamed the Victoria and Albert (1899-1909), with domed and towered ranges to the Exhibition and Cromwell Roads. On Exhibition Road he designed more strictly classical buildings for the Royal College of Science (1901-6) and the Royal School of Mines (1901-13), thereby completing the overbuilding of the Royal Horticultural Society's gardens between the Royal Albert Hall and Waterhouse's Natural History Museum, on which Collcutt's vast white elephant, the Imperial Institute

(1887-93), had already destroyed the prospect of a grand axial layout embracing the Hall and the Museum.

Returning east, in the City new buildings arose in King Edward Street for the General Post Office (1890-5), and its innovative reinforced-concrete King Edward Building replaced Christ's Hospital (1905-11), both by Henry Tanner of the Office of Works; and on the site of Newgate Prison, a new Central Criminal Court, Old Bailey (1900-7), in a magnificent English baroque by E. W. Mountford.

It was not only public buildings that were changing the topography of inner London. The great financial institutions were demanding huge office blocks. Richard Norman Shaw designed two for Alliance Assurance either side of St James's Street, the first (1883) in red brick, the second (1905) in an unorthodox classicism and Portland stone; Alfred Waterhouse designed dramatic Gothic red brick and terracotta offices for the Prudential Assurance Company in High Holborn (1895-1905) largely on the site of Furnival's Inn. Finsbury Circus saw a new south-west quadrant rise under the Francophile pencil of Davis and Emmanuel (1899-1901), balanced by Gordon and Gunton's baroque London Wall Buildings in the south-east quadrant. In Ludgate Hill Collcutt rebuilt the City of London Bank in terracotta (1890), a material he also used effectively in the Palace Theatre, Cambridge Circus (1888-92), and the Savoy Hotel in the Strand (1885-9, 1903-4). Theatres and hotels were indeed, unsurprisingly, some of the most conspicuous buildings of the Edwardian era, for there the rich could flash their diamonds. Matcham's Coliseum Theatre (1904) in St Martin's Lane, crowned by a revolving globe, is London's largest theatre, but was closely rivalled by the London Opera House (1910, later Stoll Theatre, dem.), off Kingsway. In Piccadilly, the Ritz Hotel (Mewès and Davis, 1906) made history for ingeniously breaking through the prescribed building height, and as the first major steel-framed building in London. The Hotel Cecil (1896, dem. 1930), a leviathan in the Strand (700 bedrooms — some say 1,000, — 200

private sitting rooms, large ball and concert rooms, electric light), said then to be the world's largest hotel, obliterated Salisbury and Cecil Streets and swallowed American tourists; the Great Central fronting Marylebone Station, terracotta by R. W. Edis, likewise with 700 rooms, 1899; Claridges in Brook Street, patronized by royalty, luxuriously rebuilt in red brick (1895-9; rooms, including bath, from 10*s*. 6*d*.); the Carlton (1899, dem. 1957)) composing a block in the Haymarket with Her Majesty's Theatre, by C. J. Phipps ('which expressed the ebullient panache of the Edwardian era better than any other group remaining in Central London')[vi], decorated in Louis Seize style.

Another ostentatious development was the use of 140 acres lying between Wormwood Scrubs and the Uxbridge Road for the Franco-British Exhibition of 1908, adorned by Indian-style pavilions around a lake, the whole layout clearly depicted on sheet 10. The exhibition attracted more than 8,000,000 visitors, and the stadium was then used for the 4th Olympic Games. A Japanese-British Exhibition followed in 1910, but the buildings were not designed to last, and a large part of the site was subsequently acquired for LCC housing. It may be seen as a suitable epitome of the ephemeral panache of Edwardian London, perpetuated on paper.

i   Lady Dorothy Nevill, *Under Five Reigns* (1910), p. 124.
ii   Ralph Hyde, loc. cit.
iii C. Booth, *Life and Labour of the People in London, Third Series: Religious Influences*, 1 (1902), p. 63.
iv   F. Sheppard, *London A History* (Oxford, 1998), app. 2, from the Registrar-General's reports.
v   H. J. Dyos, 'The Speculative Builders and Developers of Victorian London', *Victorian Studies*, XI (1968), pp. 660, 678.
vi   H. Hobhouse, *Lost London* (1971), p. 206.

EDITOR'S NOTE

We have ventured to call this year's publication The A to Z of Edwardian London, even though this edition of Bacon's Large Scale Atlas of London and Suburbs, judging from dating on special maps, could not have been issued before 1912 and Edward VII had died in 1910. We have argued that the additional surveying must have been undertaken in the years previous to

publication, and were anxious to preserve, as far as possible, continuity with the other A to Zs which have already appeared. We have reproduced the maps at almost full size and have retained the colouring of Bacon's original; the copy used was from the library of Roger Cline.

ANN SAUNDERS

BACON'S

LARGE SCALE ATLAS

OF

LONDON AND SUBURBS

(REVISED EDITION)

WITH AN ALPHABETICAL INDEX
OF OVER 20,000 NAMES

NEW ENLARGED AND IMPROVED EDITION

WITH ADDITIONAL ROAD MAPS OF THE HOME COUNTIES AND A SERIES OF
THIRTEEN SPECIAL MAPS SHOWING THE DIFFERENT AREAS
CONTROLLED BY GOVERNMENT DEPARTMENTS, LOCAL AUTHORITIES,
AND SUPPLY COMPANIES HAVING STATUTORY POWERS IN
AND AROUND THE CITY AND COUNTY OF LONDON

EDITED BY
WILLIAM STANFORD

CONTENTS

———•———

MAPS OF THE HOME COUNTIES

SPECIAL MAPS OF LONDON

FOUR-INCH SCALE MAPS

ALPHABETICAL LIST OF DISTRICTS

And the number of the plate on which they can be found.

District	Plate	District	Plate	District	Plate
Acton	9	Finsbury Park	6	Palmer's Green	2
Addington	27, 30a	Foots Cray	23	Peckham	17
Balham	21	Forest Gate	8	Penge	22
Barking	13	Fulham	15	Pentonville	11
Barnes	15	Great Ilford	8	Pimlico	16
Barnsbury	11	Greenwich	17	Pinner	1a
Battersea	15	Hackney	7	Plumstead	18
Bayswater	10	Hackney Wick	7	Poplar	12
Beckenham	22	Hammersmith	10	Pratt's Bottom	30b
Beddington	30	Hampstead	5	Purley	30
Belgravia	11	Hampstead Heath	5	Putney	15
Bermondsey	11	Hampton Court	24	Regents Park	11
Bethnal Green	12	Hanwell	9	Richmond	14
Bickley	28	Harrow-on-the-Hill	1a, 4	Rotherhithe	12
Blackheath	17	Hayes	28, 30a	St. John's Wood	10
Blackwall	12	Hendon	1	Selsdon Hill	30a
Bow	12	Herne Hill	16	Shadwell	12
Brentford	9	Highbury	6	Shepherds' Bush	10
Brixton	16	Highgate	6	Shirley	27
Bromley	12	Holloway	6	Shooters' Hill	18
Bromley (Kent)	23	Hook	28a	Shoreditch	12
Bromley Common	30b	Hornsey	2	Sidcup	23
Brompton	11	Hounslow	14	Somers Town	11
Camberwell	16	Hoxton	11	Southgate	2
Camden Town	6	Isleworth	14	South Kensington	10
Canning Town	12	Islington	6	South Lambeth	16
Carshalton	26	Kennington	16	Southwark	11
Castlenau	15	Kensal Green	10	Stanmore	1a
Catford	22	Kensington	10	Stepney	12
Charing Cross	11	Kentish Town	6	Stoke Newington	6
Charlton	18	Kenton	1a	Stratford	7
Cheam	29	Keston	30b	Streatham	21
Chelsea	15	Kew	14	Sudbury	4
Chelsfield	30b	Kingsland	7	Surbiton	24
Chingford	3	Kingston	19	Sutton	29
Chislehurst	23	Lambeth	16	Sydenham	22
City	11	Lee	17	Teddington	19
Clapham	16	Lewisham	17	Thornton Heath	26
Clapham Junction	16	Limehouse	12	Tooting	21
Clapton	7	Maida Vale	10	Tottenham	3
Claygate	28a	Mayfair	11	Twickenham	19
Clerkenwell	11	Merton	20	Victoria Park	7
Commercial Docks	12	Mitcham	26	Wallington	30
Cricklewood	5	Mile End	12	Walthamstow	3
Crouch End	6	Mill Hill	1	Walham Green	15
Croydon	26	Millwall	12	Walworth	16
Cubitt Town	17	Mortlake	14	Wandsworth	15
Dalston	7	Muswell Hill	2	Wealdstone	1a
Deptford	17	New Cross	17	Wembley	4
Downe	30b	Newington	2	West Ham	12
Dulwich	22	New Southgate	11	Westminster	11
Ealing	9	N. Woolwich	13	W. Norwood	21
East Dulwich	17	Northolt	4	West Wickham	27, 30a
Edgware	1a	Norwood	21	Whitechapel	12
Edmonton	3	Notting Hill	10	Willesden	5
Eltham	18	Nunhead	17	Willesden Green	5
Epsom	28a, 29	Old Ford	12	Wimbledon	20
Esher	24, 28a	Orpington	28	Wood Green	2
Farnborough	30b	Oxshott	28a	Woolwich	18
Finchley	1	Paddington	10		

[6]

Maps of the
Home Counties

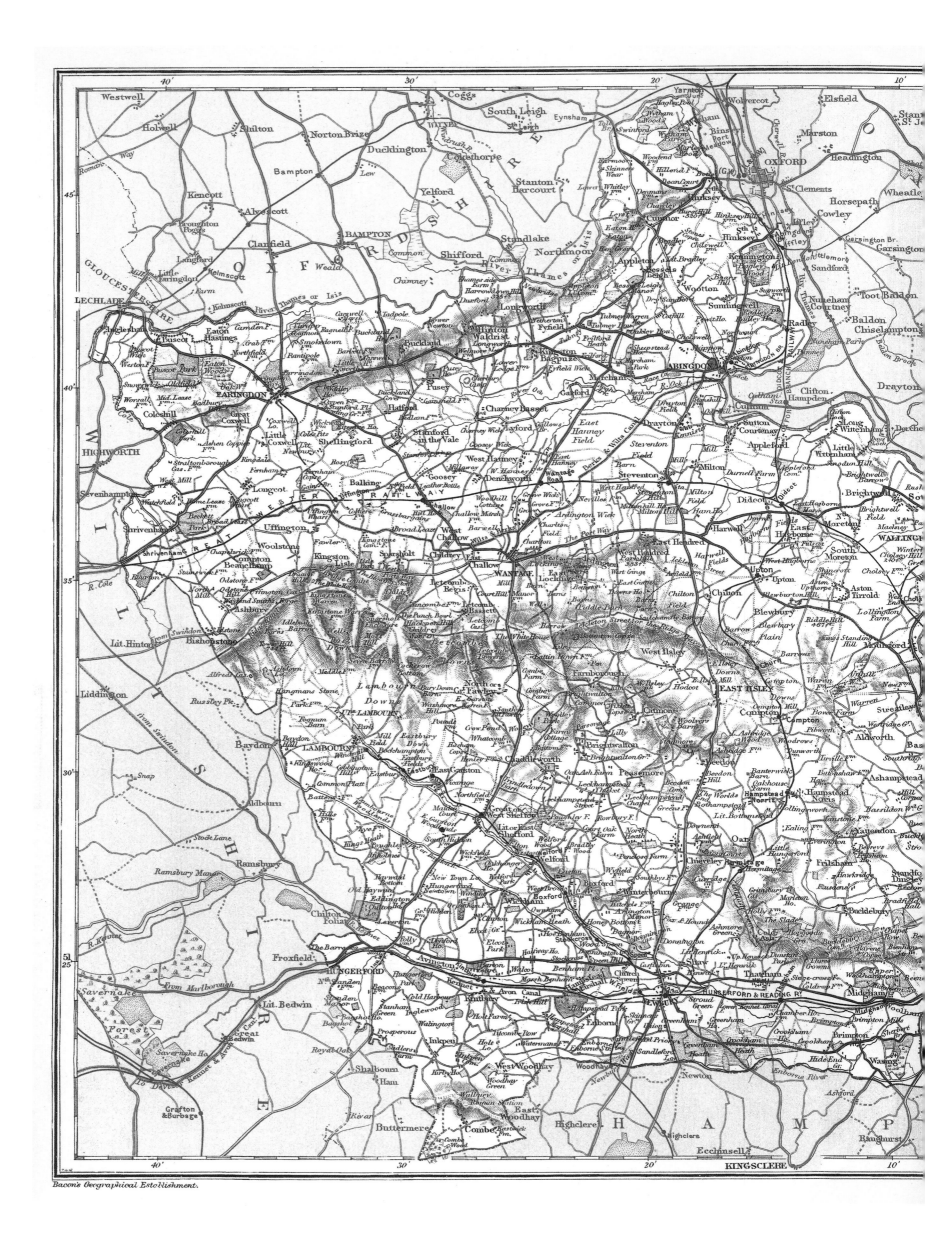

Bacon's Geographical Establishment.

BERKSHIRE.

Scale of Miles

0 1 2 3 4 5 6

EXPLANATION.

Railways and Stations, thus	Fairlop
Main Roads	
Other Roads	
Canals	
Parks and Seats	

Longitude West of Greenwich

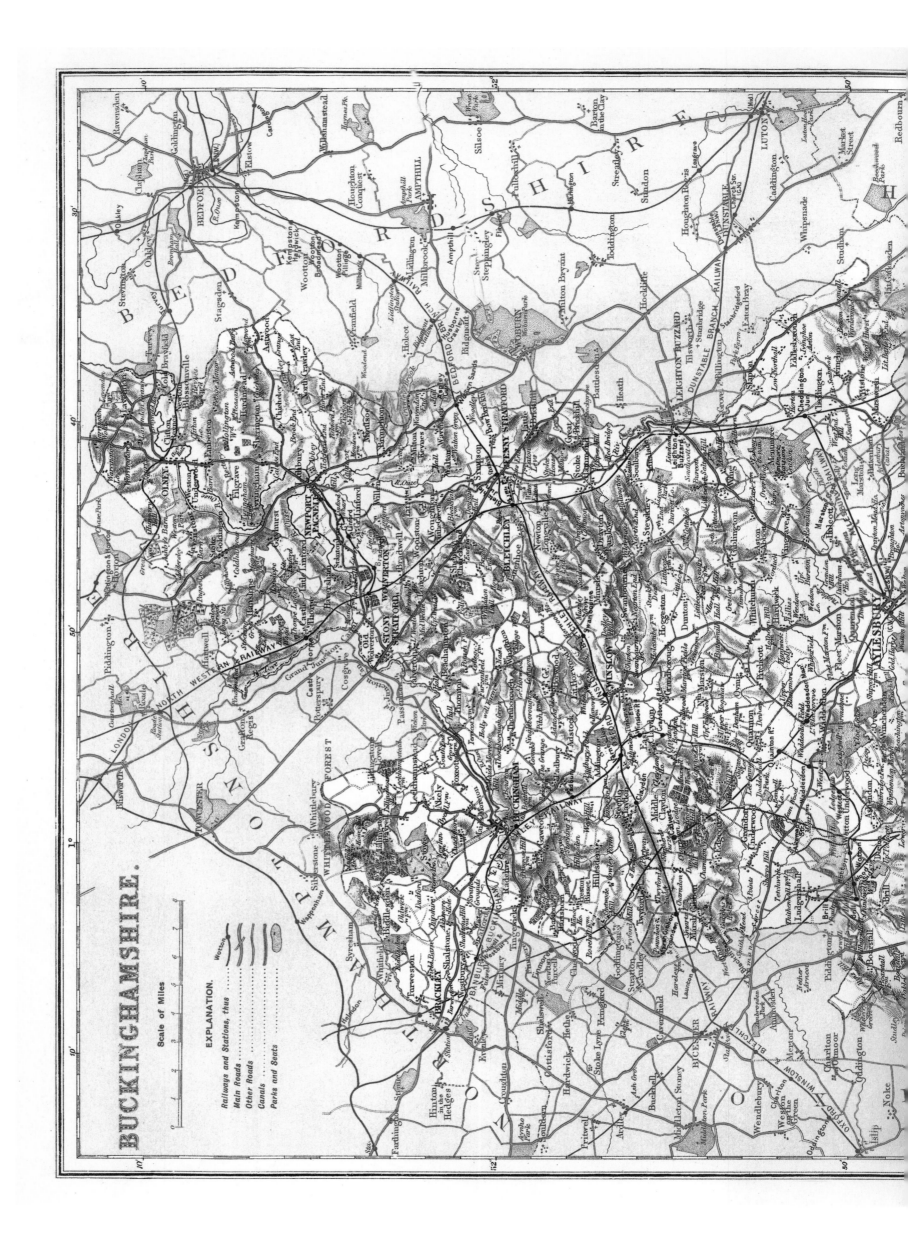

BUCKINGHAMSHIRE.

Scale of Miles

EXPLANATION.

Railways and Stations, thus ......
Main Roads ....
Other Roads ....
Canals ....
Parks and Seats ....

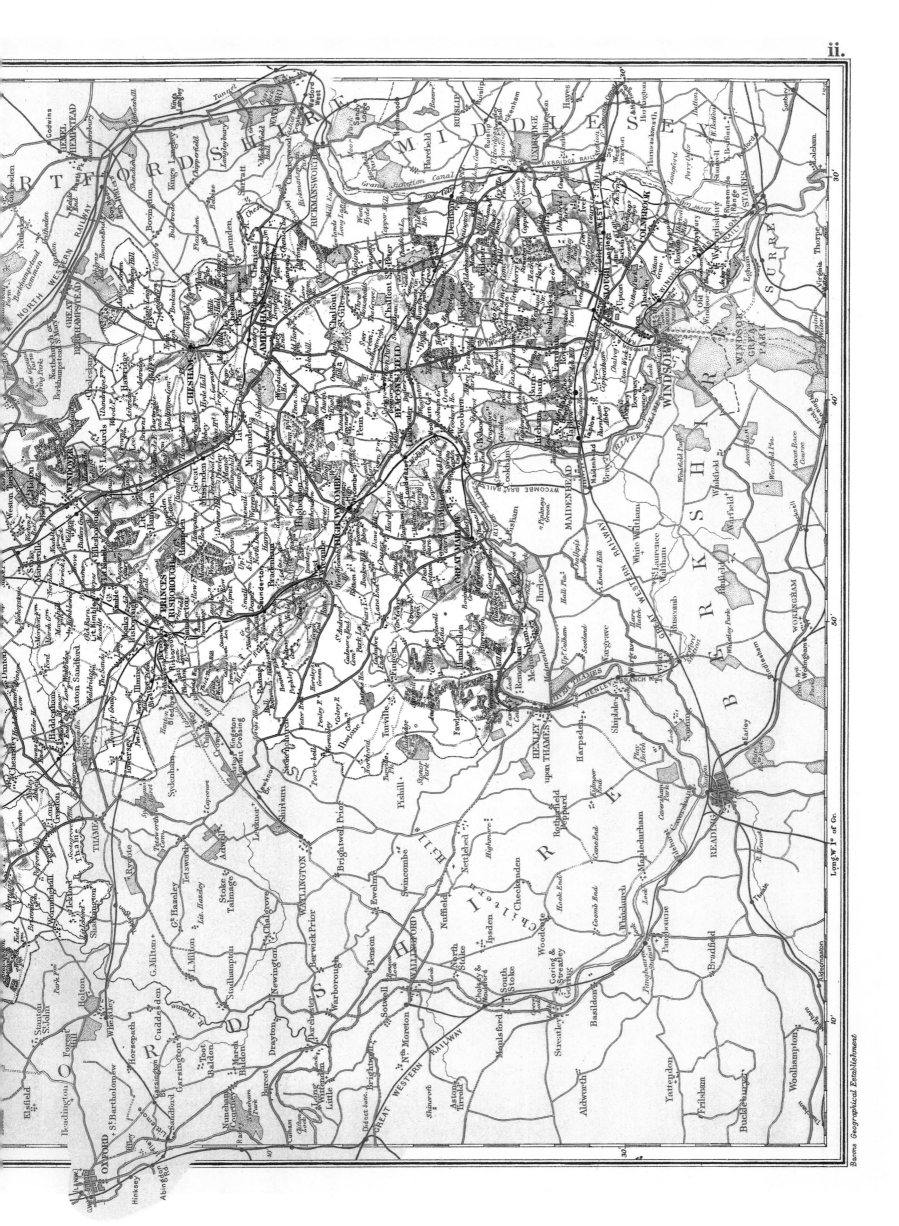

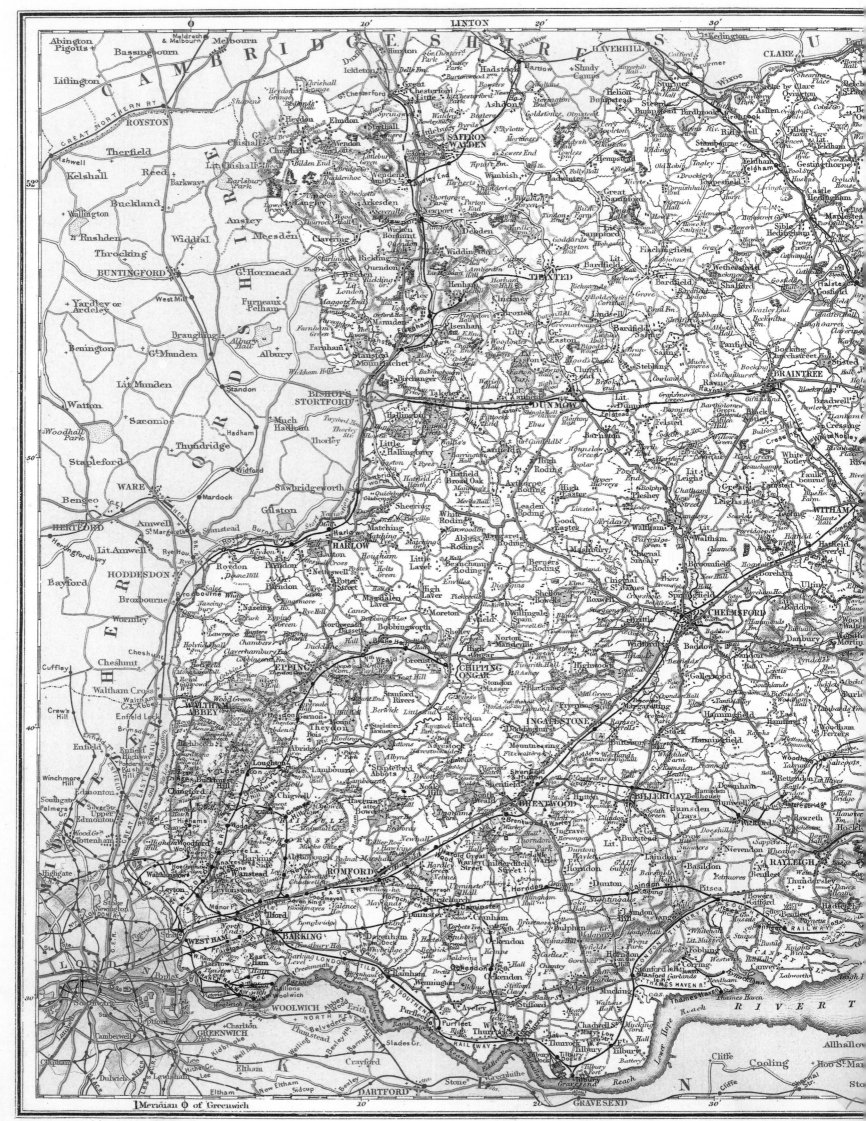

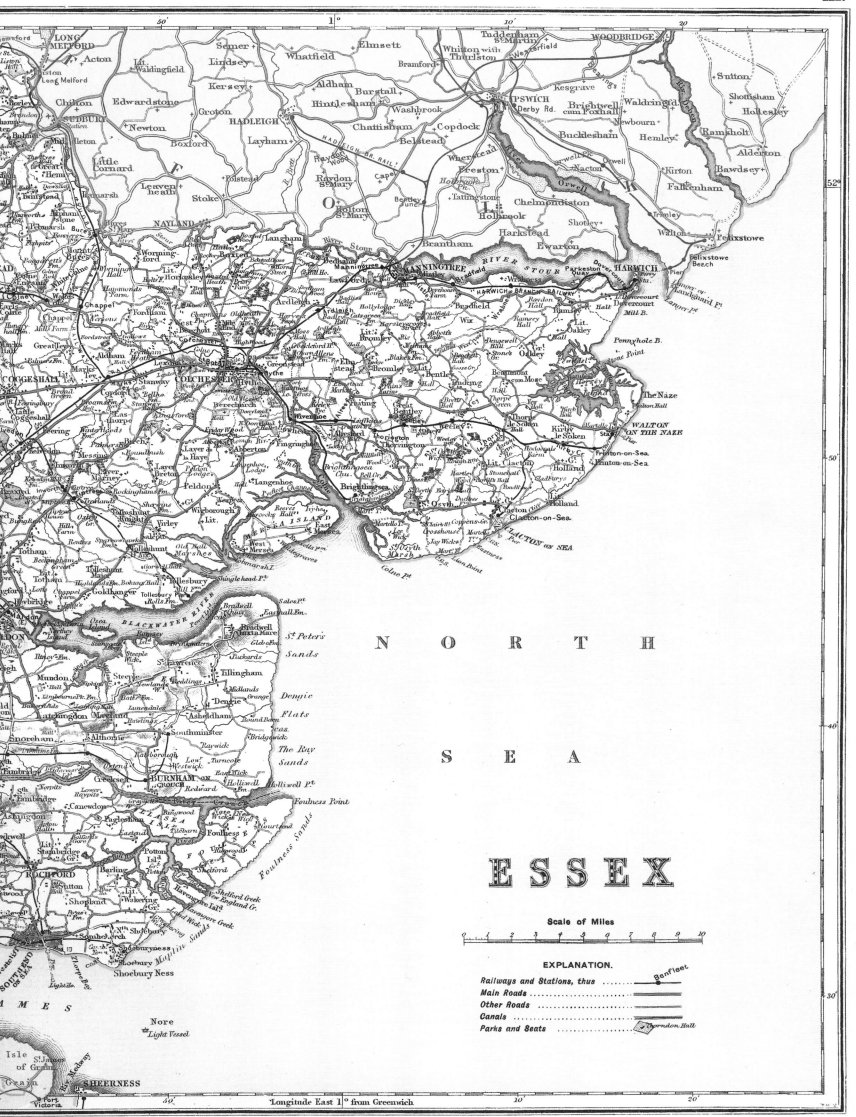

NORTH SEA

ESSEX

Scale of Miles

EXPLANATION.

Railways and Stations, thus .... ●Benfleet
Main Roads ....
Other Roads ....
Canals ....
Parks and Seats .... ◇Thorndon Hall

Longitude East 1° from Greenwich

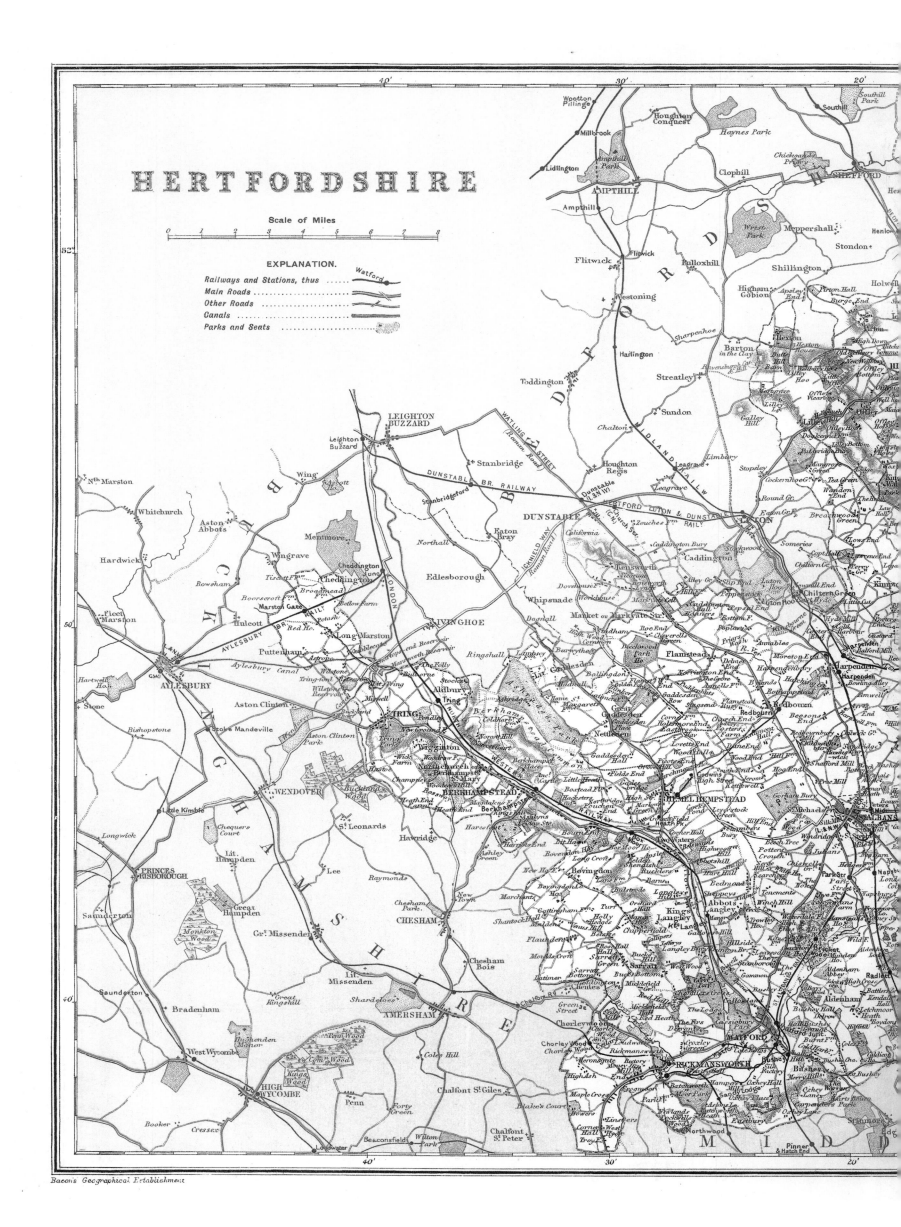

HERTFORDSHIRE

Scale of Miles

EXPLANATION.
Railways and Stations, thus ...... Watford
Main Roads ....
Other Roads ....
Canals ....
Parks and Seats ....

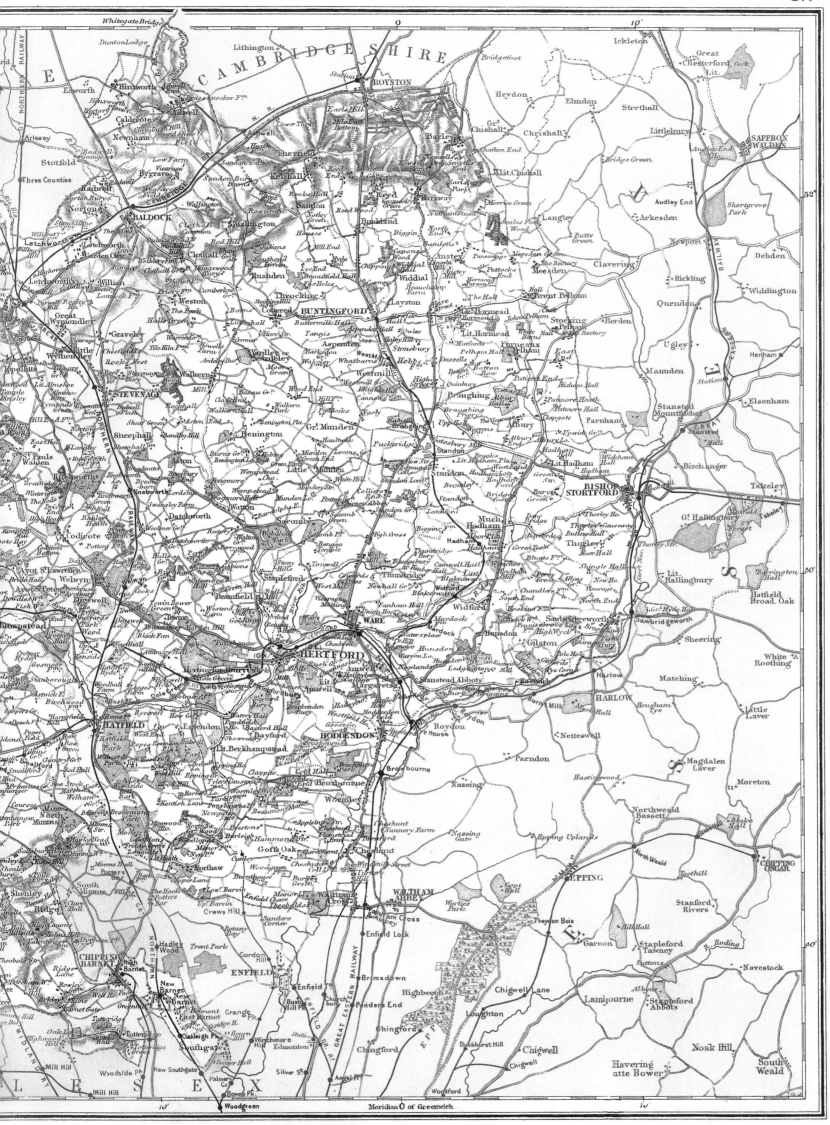

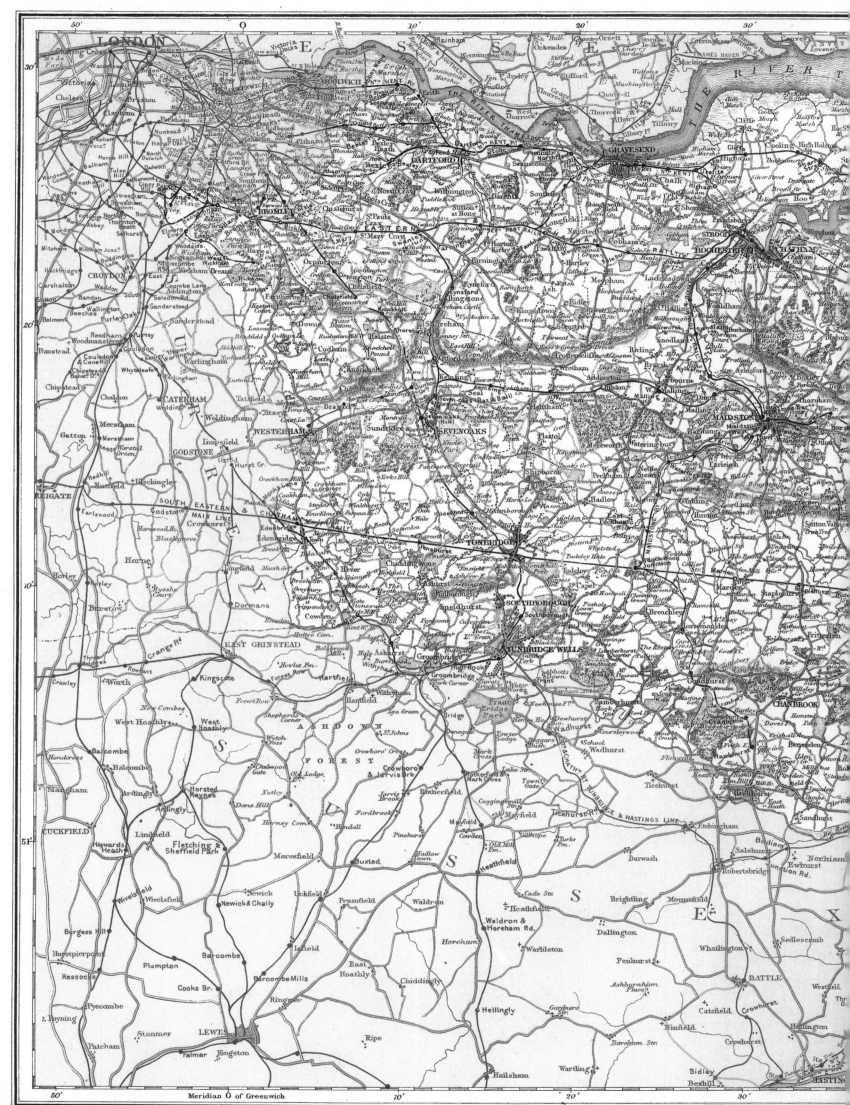

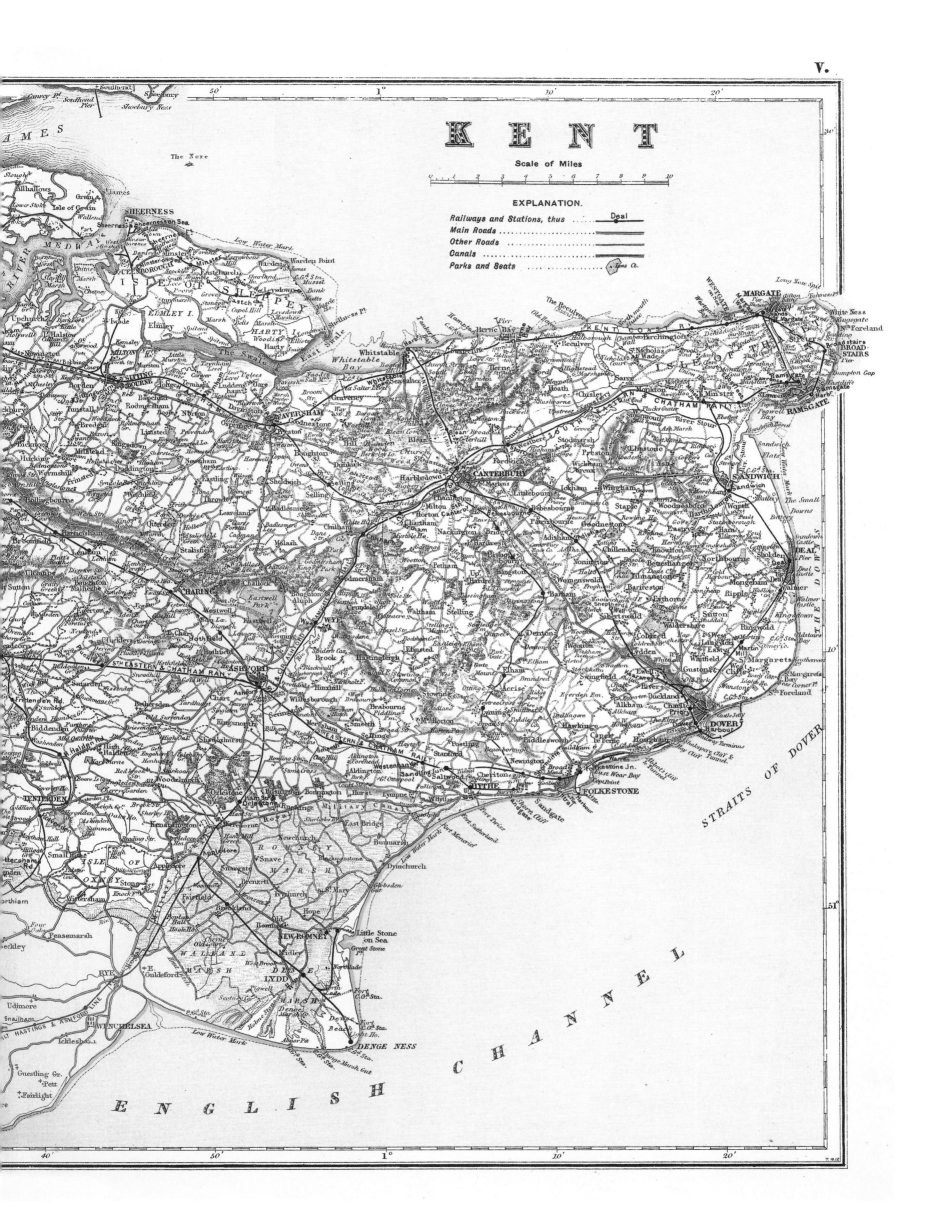

KENT

V.

Scale of Miles

EXPLANATION.

Railways and Stations, thus ..... Deal
Main Roads ....
Other Roads ....
Canals ....
Parks and Seats .... Lees Ct.

[17]

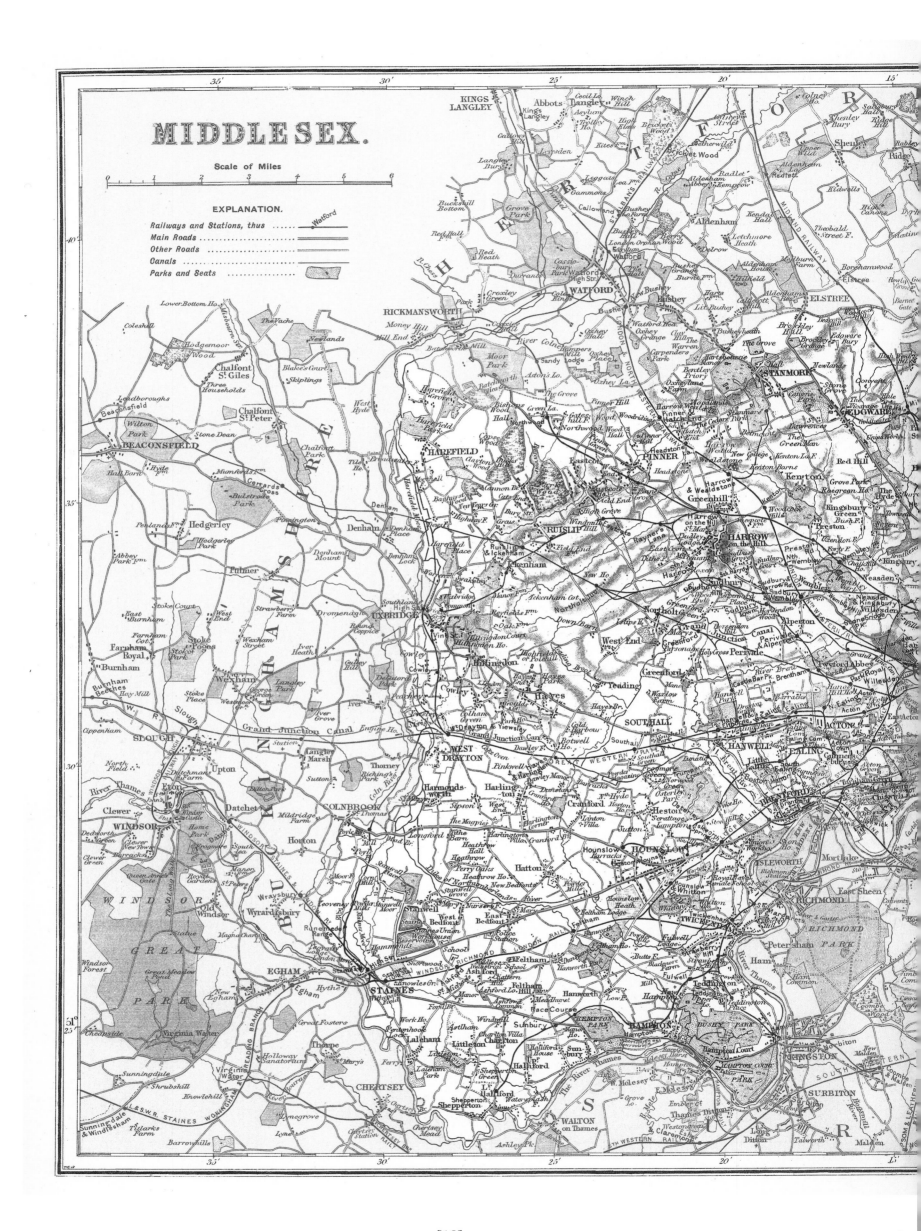

MIDDLESEX.

Scale of Miles

EXPLANATION.

Railways and Stations, thus ...... Watford
Main Roads ....
Other Roads ....
Canals ....
Parks and Seats ....

Meridian 0 of Greenwich

Bacon's Geographical Establishment.

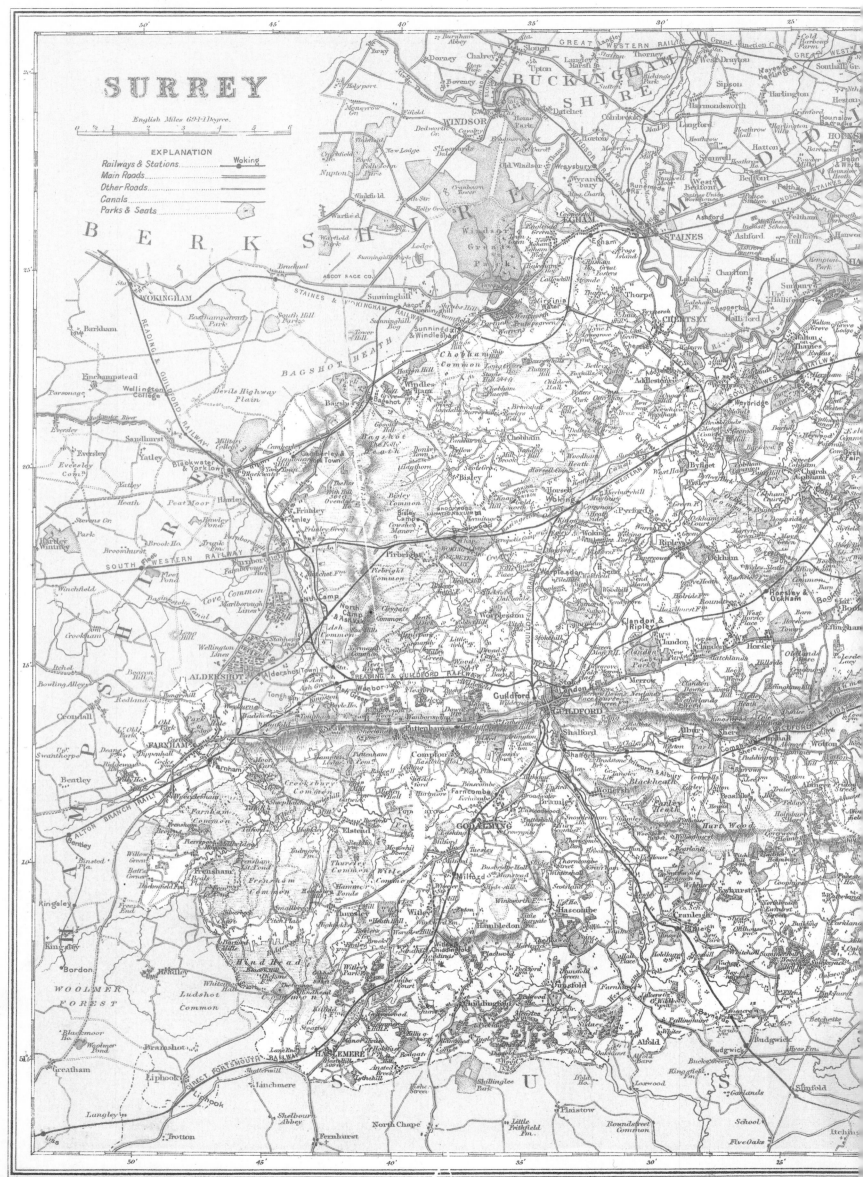

Special Maps
of London

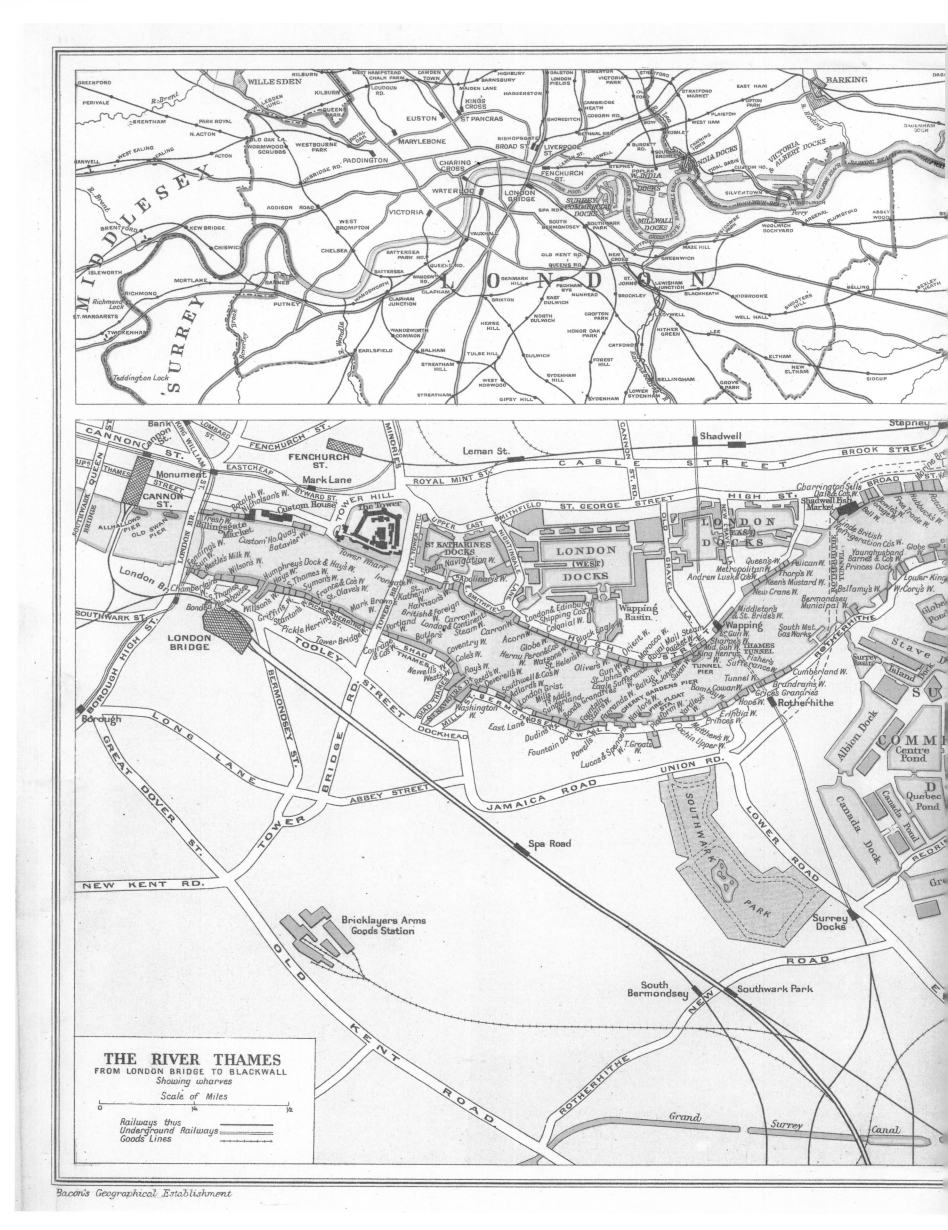

THE RIVER THAMES
FROM LONDON BRIDGE TO BLACKWALL
Showing wharves

Scale of Miles

Railways thus
Underground Railways
Goods Lines

Bacon's Geographical Establishment

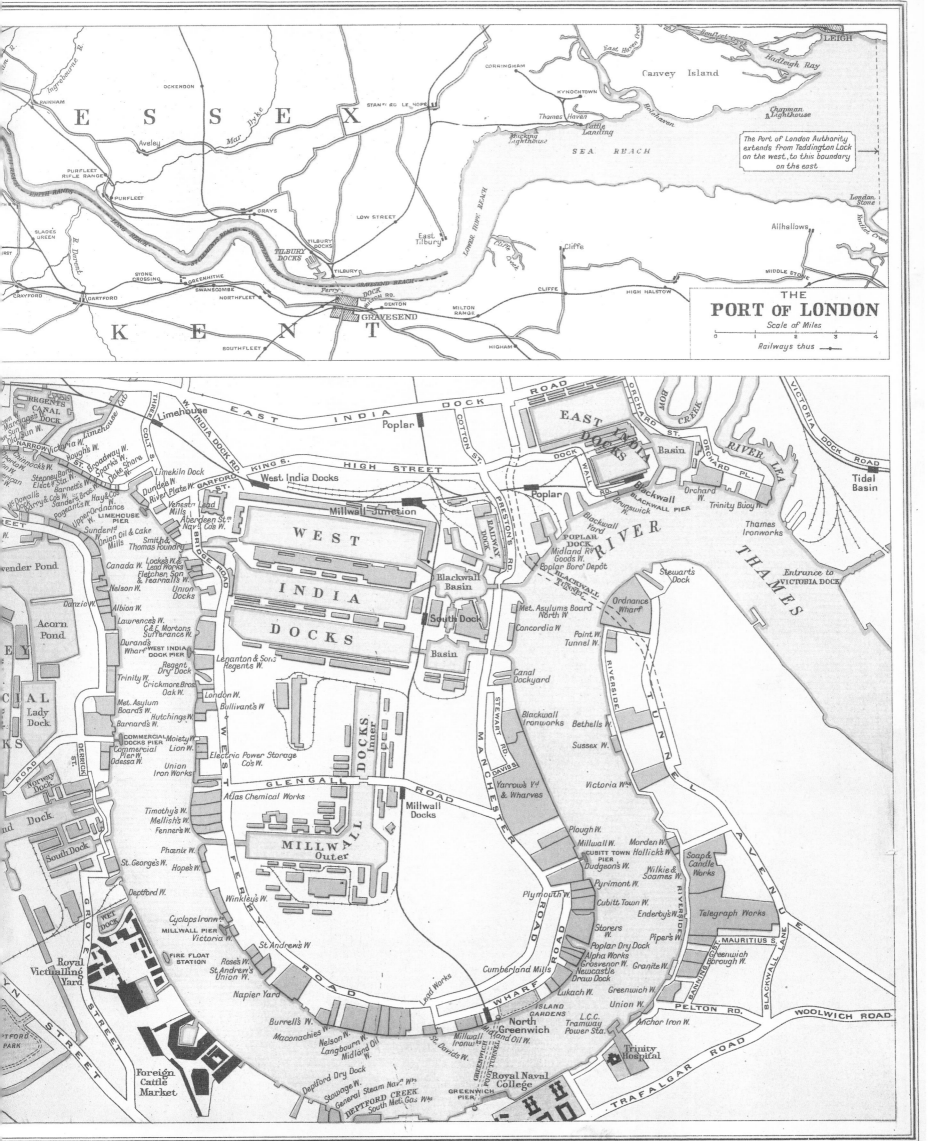

THE
PORT OF LONDON
Scale of Miles
0   1   2   3   4
Railways thus

The Port of London Authority extends from Teddington Lock on the west, to this boundary on the east

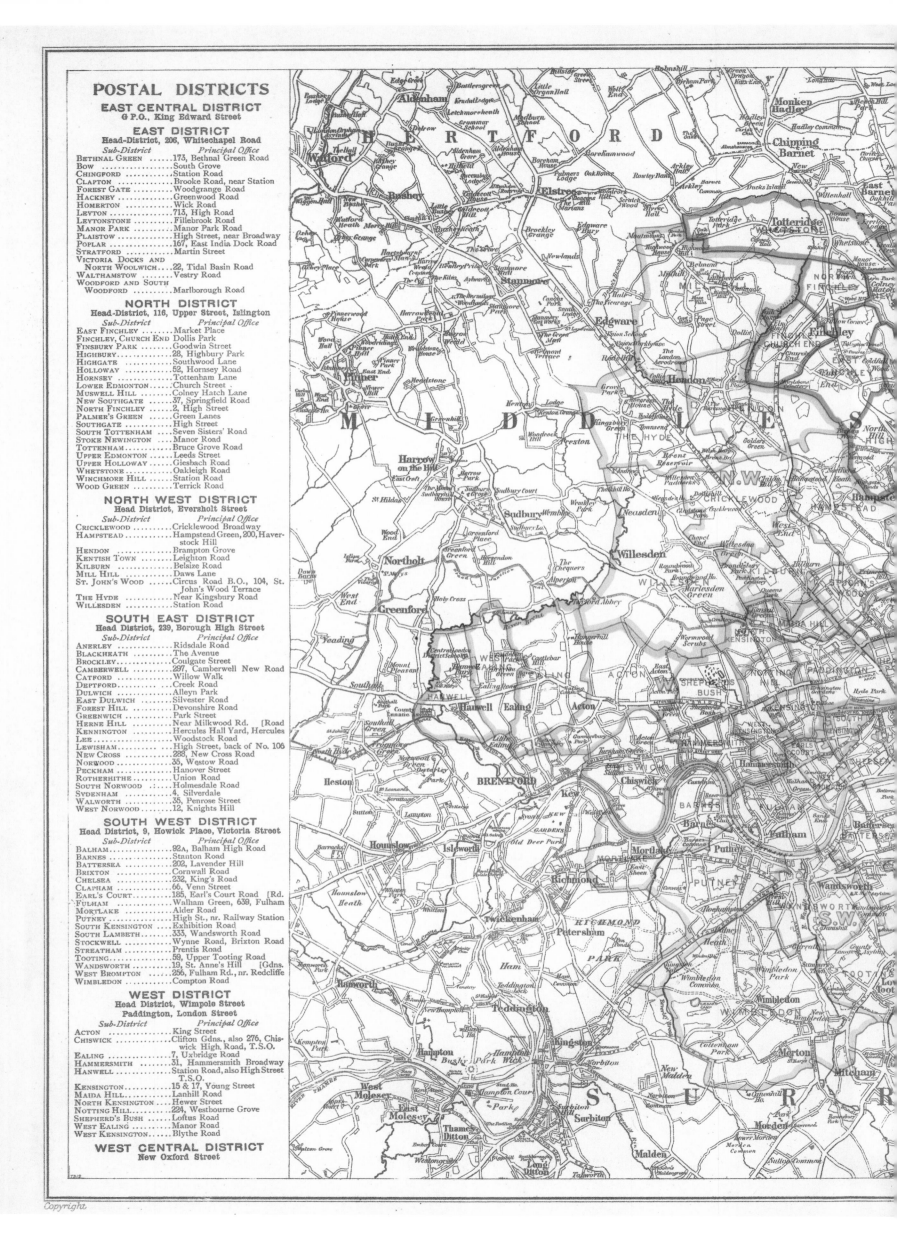

POSTAL DISTRICTS

EAST CENTRAL DISTRICT
G.P.O., King Edward Street

EAST DISTRICT
Head-District, 206, Whitechapel Road

Sub-District	Principal Office
BETHNAL GREEN	173, Bethnal Green Road
BOW	South Grove
CHINGFORD	Station Road
CLAPTON	Brooke Road, near Station
FOREST GATE	Woodgrange Road
HACKNEY	Greenwood Road
HOMERTON	Wick Road
LEYTON	713, High Road
LEYTONSTONE	Fillebrook Road
MANOR PARK	Manor Park Road
PLAISTOW	High Street, near Broadway
POPLAR	167, East India Dock Road
STRATFORD	Martin Street
VICTORIA DOCKS AND NORTH WOOLWICH	22, Tidal Basin Road
WALTHAMSTOW	Vestry Road
WOODFORD AND SOUTH WOODFORD	Marlborough Road

NORTH DISTRICT
Head-District, 116, Upper Street, Islington

Sub-District	Principal Office
EAST FINCHLEY	Market Place
FINCHLEY, CHURCH END	Dollis Park
FINSBURY PARK	Goodwin Street
HIGHBURY	28, Highbury Park
HIGHGATE	Southwood Lane
HOLLOWAY	52, Hornsey Road
HORNSEY	Tottenham Lane
LOWER EDMONTON	Church Street
MUSWELL HILL	Colney Hatch Lane
NEW SOUTHGATE	37, Springfield Road
NORTH FINCHLEY	2, High Street
PALMER'S GREEN	Green Lanes
SOUTHGATE	High Street
SOUTH TOTTENHAM	Seven Sisters' Road
STOKE NEWINGTON	Manor Road
TOTTENHAM	Bruce Grove Road
UPPER EDMONTON	Leeds Street
UPPER HOLLOWAY	Giesbach Road
WHETSTONE	Oakleigh Road
WINCHMORE HILL	Station Road
WOOD GREEN	Terrick Road

NORTH WEST DISTRICT
Head District, Eversholt Street

Sub-District	Principal Office
CRICKLEWOOD	Cricklewood Broadway
HAMPSTEAD	Hampstead Green, 200, Haverstock Hill
HENDON	Brampton Grove
KENTISH TOWN	Leighton Road
KILBURN	Belsize Road
MILL HILL	Daws Lane
ST. JOHN'S WOOD	Circus Road B.O., 104, St. John's Wood Terrace
THE HYDE	Near Kingsbury Road
WILLESDEN	Station Road

SOUTH EAST DISTRICT
Head District, 239, Borough High Street

Sub-District	Principal Office
ANERLEY	Ridsdale Road
BLACKHEATH	The Avenue
BROCKLEY	Coulgate Street
CAMBERWELL	297, Camberwell New Road
CATFORD	Willow Walk
DEPTFORD	Creek Road
DULWICH	Alleyn Park
EAST DULWICH	Silvester Road
FOREST HILL	Devonshire Road
GREENWICH	Park Street
HERNE HILL	Near Milkwood Rd. [Road
KENNINGTON	Hercules Hall Yard, Hercules
LEE	Woodstock Road
LEWISHAM	High Street, back of No. 106
NEW CROSS	288, New Cross Road
NORWOOD	35, Westow Road
PECKHAM	Hanover Street
ROTHERHITHE	Union Road
SOUTH NORWOOD	Holmesdale Road
SYDENHAM	4, Silverdale
WALWORTH	35, Penrose Street
WEST NORWOOD	12, Knights Hill

SOUTH WEST DISTRICT
Head District, 9, Howick Place, Victoria Street

Sub-District	Principal Office
BALHAM	92A, Balham High Road
BARNES	Stanton Road
BATTERSEA	202, Lavender Hill
BRIXTON	Cornwall Road
CHELSEA	232, King's Road
CLAPHAM	66, Venn Street
EARL'S COURT	185, Earl's Court Road [Rd.
FULHAM	Walham Green, 639, Fulham
MORTLAKE	Alder Road
PUTNEY	High St., nr. Railway Station
SOUTH KENSINGTON	Exhibition Road
SOUTH LAMBETH	333, Wandsworth Road
STOCKWELL	Wynne Road, Brixton Road
STREATHAM	Prentis Road
TOOTING	59, Upper Tooting Road
WANDSWORTH	19, St. Anne's Hill [Gdns.
WEST BROMPTON	256, Fulham Rd., nr. Redcliffe
WIMBLEDON	Compton Road

WEST DISTRICT
Head District, Wimpole Street
Paddington, London Street

Sub-District	Principal Office
ACTON	King Street
CHISWICK	Clifton Gdns., also 276, Chiswick High Road, T.S.O.
EALING	7, Uxbridge Road
HAMMERSMITH	31, Hammersmith Broadway
HANWELL	Station Road, also High Street T.S.O.
KENSINGTON	15 & 17, Young Street
MAIDA HILL	Lanhill Road
NORTH KENSINGTON	Hewer Street
NOTTING HILL	224, Westbourne Grove
SHEPHERD'S BUSH	Loftus Road
WEST EALING	Manor Road
WEST KENSINGTON	Blythe Road

WEST CENTRAL DISTRICTS
New Oxford Street

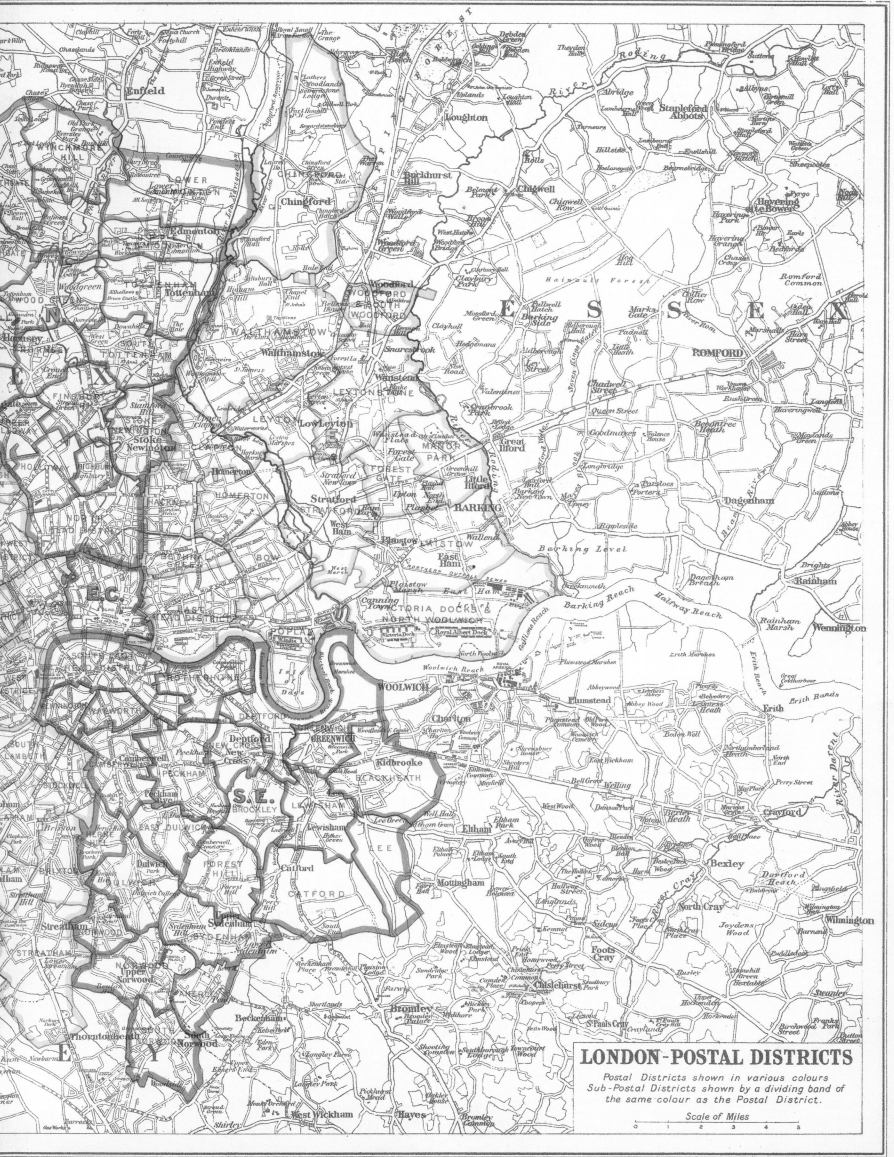

LONDON-POSTAL DISTRICTS

Postal Districts shown in various colours
Sub-Postal Districts shown by a dividing band of
the same colour as the Postal District.

Scale of Miles

Bacon's Geographical Establishment

METROPOLITAN POLICE.

Total Strength of Metropolitan Police (including Dockyard Divisions) Dec., 1910 .. 19,418.
Area of Metropolitan Police District (Greater London) .. .. 699·42 sq. miles.
Population „   „   „   „   „   .. .. 7 to 8 millions.

DIVISION.	Area in sq. miles	Authorised Strength Dec. 1910	SITUATION OF POLICE STATIONS.		
CO or Commissioner's Office	—	—	New Scotland Yard.		
A „ Whitehall ...	1·8	795	Cannon Row, S.W. Wellington Arch.	Rochester Row, S.W.	Hyde Park.
B „ Chelsea	5·1	892	Walton Street. Gerald Road.	Chelsea. South Fulham.	North Fulham.
C „ St. James's ...	0·7	528	Vine Street.	Great Marlborough St.	
D „ Marylebone ...	1·4	578	Marylebone Lane.	John Street.	Tottenham Court Road.
E „ Holborn	0·9	600	Bow Street.	Hunter Street.	Gray's Inn Road.
F „ Paddington ...	3·7	625	Paddington. Kensington.	Notting Hill.	Notting Dale.
G „ Finsbury	1·8	619	King's Cross Road.	Old Street.	City Road.
H „ Whitechapel ...	2·0	624	Leman Street. Commercial Street.	Stepney.	Shadwell.
J „ Hackney	39·1	869	Hackney. Victoria Park. Bethnal Green. Dalston.	Wanstead. Leyton. Leytonstone. Barkingside.	Woodford. Loughton. Claybury.
K „ Bow	37·2	1,161	Limehouse. Poplar. Isle of Dogs. Bow. West Ham.	Forest Gate. East Ham. Plaistow. Canning Town. North Woolwich.	Ilford. Barking. Dagenham. Chadwell Heath. Purfleet Powder Magazine.
L „ Lambeth ...	2·3	541	Kennington Lane. Kennington Road.	Carter Street.	Rodney Road.
M „ Southwark ...	3·4	534	Southwark. Grange Road.	Tower Bridge.	Rotherhithe.
N „ Islington ...	60·4	1,113	Stoke Newington. St. Ann's Road. Islington. Highbury Vale. Tottenham. Edmonton.	Walthamstow. Chingford. Lea Bridge Road. Enfield Highway. Cheshunt. Waltham Abbey.	Goffs Oak. Waltham Abbey (Royal Gunpowder Factory). Enfield Lock (Small Arms Factory).
P „ Camberwell ...	51·5	949	Peckham. Camberwell. East Dulwich. West Dulwich. Knight's Hill.	Norwood. Penge. Lewisham. Catford. Sydenham.	Brockley. Bromley. Beckenham. Farnborough.
R „ Greenwich ...	60·6	969	Blackheath Road. Deptford. Westcombe Park. East Greenwich. Woolwich.	Plumstead. Belvedere. Erith. Bexley. Lee Road.	Eltham. Shooter's Hill. Sidcup. Chislehurst. St. Mary Cray.
S „ Hampstead ...	82·6	951	Albany Street. Portland Town. Hampstead. West Hampstead. Finchley.	Hendon. Whetstone. Barnet. South Mimms. Shenley.	Edgware. Bushey. Elstree. Wealdstone.
T „ Hammersmith ...	70·0	876	Hammersmith. Shepherd's Bush. Chiswick. Bedfont. Harlington.	Staines. Brentford. Hounslow. Isleworth. Norwood Green.	Hampton. Sunbury. Teddington. Twickenham.
V „ Wandsworth ...	65·2	1,121	Wandsworth. Wandsworth Common. Putney. Roehampton. Battersea.	Lavender Hill. Wimbledon. New Malden. Richmond. Barnes.	Kingston. Ditton. Epsom. Surbiton. East Molesey.
W „ Clapham	76·3	1,207	Brixton. Clapham. Battersea Park Road. Balham. Streatham.	Mitcham. Tooting. Sutton. Carshalton. Banstead.	Croydon. Kenley. Thornton Heath. South Norwood.
X „ Kilburn	80·6	937	Harrow Road. Kilburn. Harlesden. Willesden Green. Wembley. Harrow.	Pinner. Greenford. Northwood. Ealing. Acton. Hanwell.	Southall. Uxbridge. Hayes. Harefield. Ruislip.
Y „ Highgate ...	44·4	1,001	Kentish Town. Somers Town. Caledonian Road. Holloway. Upper Holloway.	Highgate. Hornsey. Wood Green. New Southgate. Muswell Hill.	Enfield. East Barnet. Potters Bar. Southgate.
Thames	7·4	240	Wapping. Waterloo Pier.	Barnes.	Blackwall.

CITY POLICE.

Area of City Police District .. .. 673 acres.
Population of City Police District .. .. 26,923 night residents.
Total Strength of City Police .. .. 1,220.

CITY POLICE STATIONS.

Cloak Lane. Moor Lane. Bishopsgate. Minories. Snow Hill. Bridewell Place.

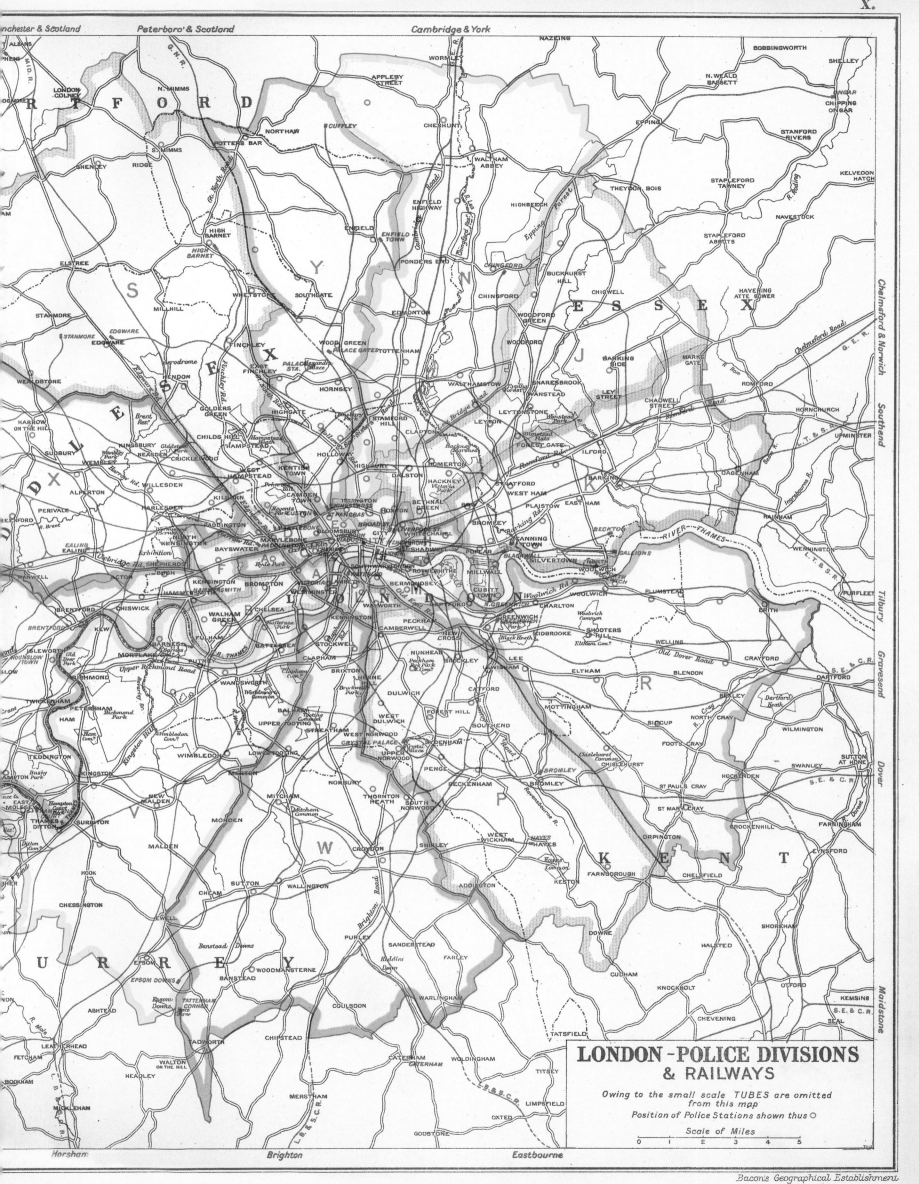

LONDON – POLICE DIVISIONS & RAILWAYS

Owing to the small scale TUBES are omitted from this map

Position of Police Stations shown thus ○

Scale of Miles

Bacon's Geographical Establishment

THE THAMES VALLEY
(3,855 Square Miles).

RAINFALL, STREAM FLOW AND WATER ABSTRACTED.

Month.	General rainfall.	Total volume of water that fell on the area.	Total natural flow of the Thames.	Abstracted by Water Board and Water Companies.
1911.	Inches.	Million gallons.	Million gallons.	Million gallons.
April	1·43	78,910	40,409·1	4,017·9
May	1·95	108,830	31,667·7	4,890·3
June	1·97	110,010	20,091·1	4,631·9
July	·40	22,320	13,523·9	5,273·4
August	1·22	67,730	10,002·9	5,418·4
September	1·33	73,910	10,703·4	4,960·0
Total for summer months, April to September	8·30	462,710	126,398·1	29,191·9
October	2·82	157,550	14,558·7	5,245·1
November	3·48	194,230	25,936·3	5,205·6
December	6·55	365,950	98,438·8	3,237·2
1912. January	4·14	230,980	129,506·0	4,213·8
February	2·28	127,320	97,199·2	5,346·0
March	4·10	228,520	120,269·6	3,776·0
Total for winter months, October to March	23·37	1,304,950	485,908·6	27,023·7
Total for year 1911-12	31·67	1,767,660	612,306·7	56,215·6
Total for year 1910-11	*30·49*	*1,701,760*	*574,648·1*	*49,962·8*
Increase or decrease	+1·18	+65,900	+37,658·6	+6,252·8
Increase or decrease per cent.	+3·870°/₀	—	—	+12,515°/₀

These tables are calculated from the Thames above Teddington.

THE LEE VALLEY
(414 Square Miles).

RAINFALL, STREAM FLOW AND WATER ABSTRACTED.

Month.	General rainfall.	Total volume of water that fell on the area.	Total natural flow of the Lee.	Abstracted by the Water Board.
1911.	Inches.	Million gallons.	Million gallons.	Million gallons.
April	1·07	6,410	3,070·5	1,606·9
May	2·16	12,950	2,545·4	1,687·9
June	2·53	15,170	1,618·1	1,503·6
July	·62	3,720	1,216·3	1,358·5
August	·66	3,960	1,001·3	1,050·7
September	1·34	8,030	1,171·0	890·8
Total for summer months, April to September	8·38	50,240	10,622·6	8,098·4
October	2·87	17,200	1,406·1	1,903·1
November	3·18	19,060	1,963·9	1,980·5
December	4·90	29,370	6,575·8	1,626·5
1912. January	3·42	20,500	9,767·6	1,838·9
February	1·64	9,830	6,257·8	2,040·3
March	3·29	19,720	8,304·6	1,793·1
Total for winter months. October to March	19·30	115,680	34,275·3	10,581·4
Total for year 1911-12	27·68	165,920	44,897·9	18,679·8
Total for year 1910-11	*27·04*	*162,110*	*40,743·4*	*18,531·2*
Increase or decrease	+·64	+3,810	+4,154·5	+149·6
Increase or decrease per cent.	+2·367%	—	—	+·805%

These tables are calculated from the Lee above Feilde's Weir.

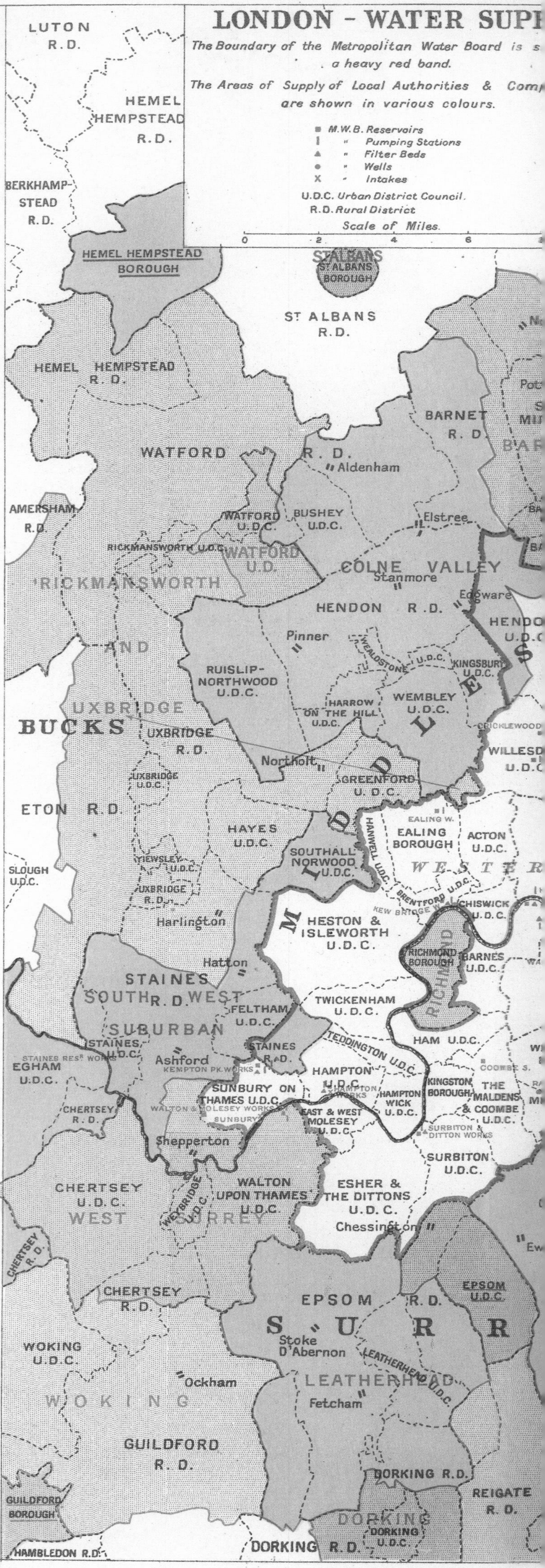

LONDON - WATER SUPP...

The Boundary of the Metropolitan Water Board is s... a heavy red band.

The Areas of Supply of Local Authorities & Comp... are shown in various colours.

- ■ M.W.B. Reservoirs
- I " Pumping Stations
- ▲ " Filter Beds
- ● " Wells
- X " Intakes

U.D.C. *Urban District Council.*
R.D. *Rural District.*

Scale of Miles.

Bacon's Geographical Establishment.

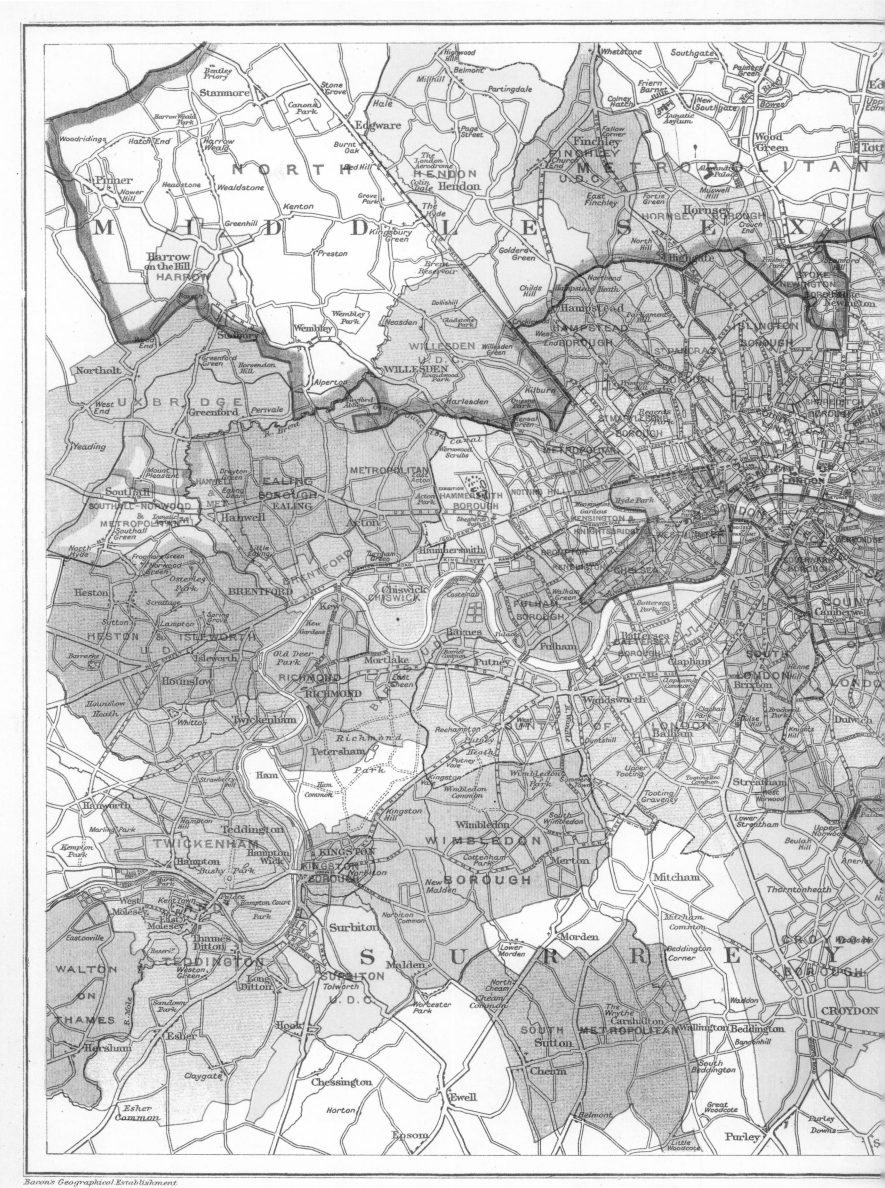

Bacon's Geographical Establishment.

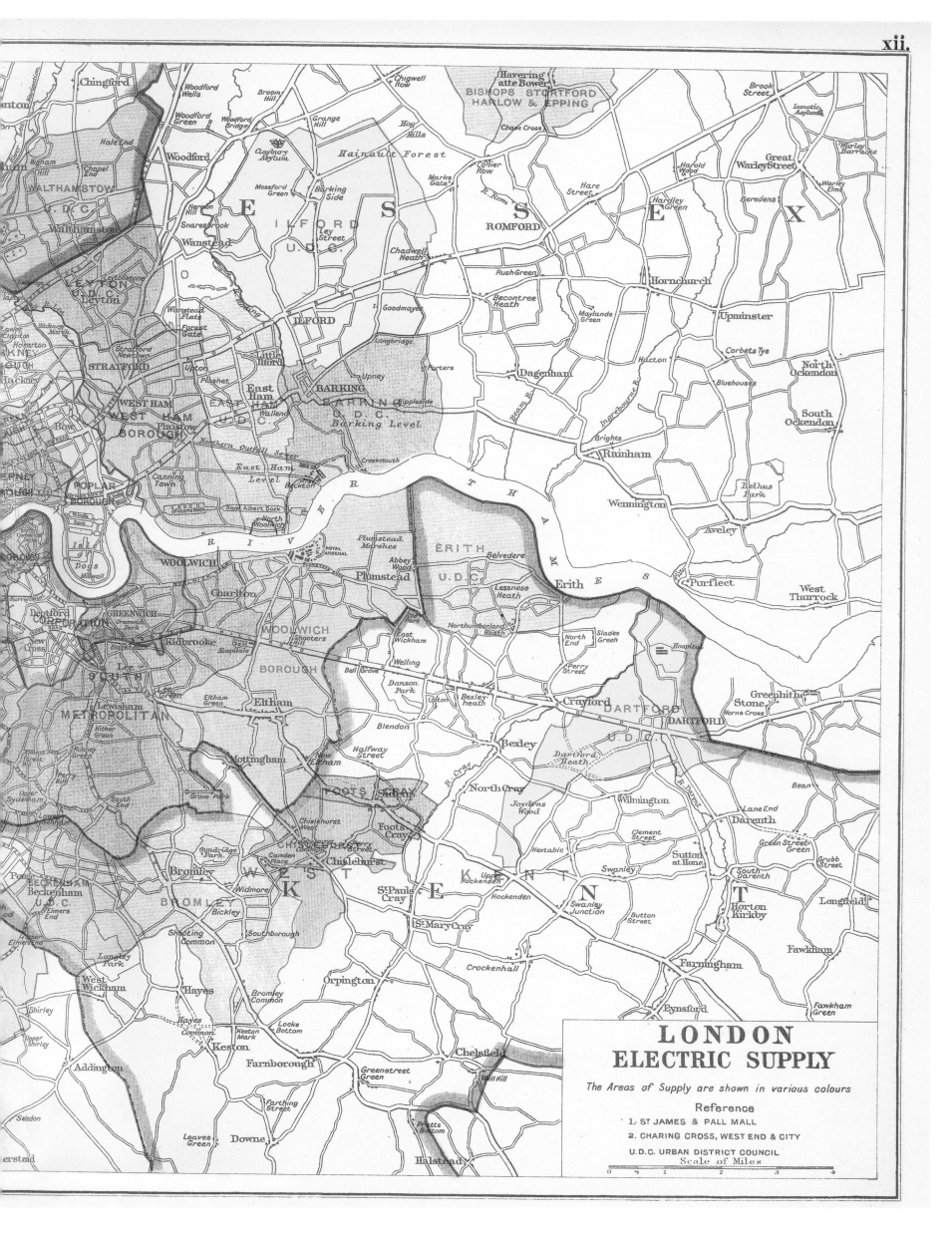

LONDON ELECTRIC SUPPLY

The Areas of Supply are shown in various colours

Reference

1. ST JAMES & PALL MALL
2. CHARING CROSS, WEST END & CITY

U.D.C. URBAN DISTRICT COUNCIL

Scale of Miles

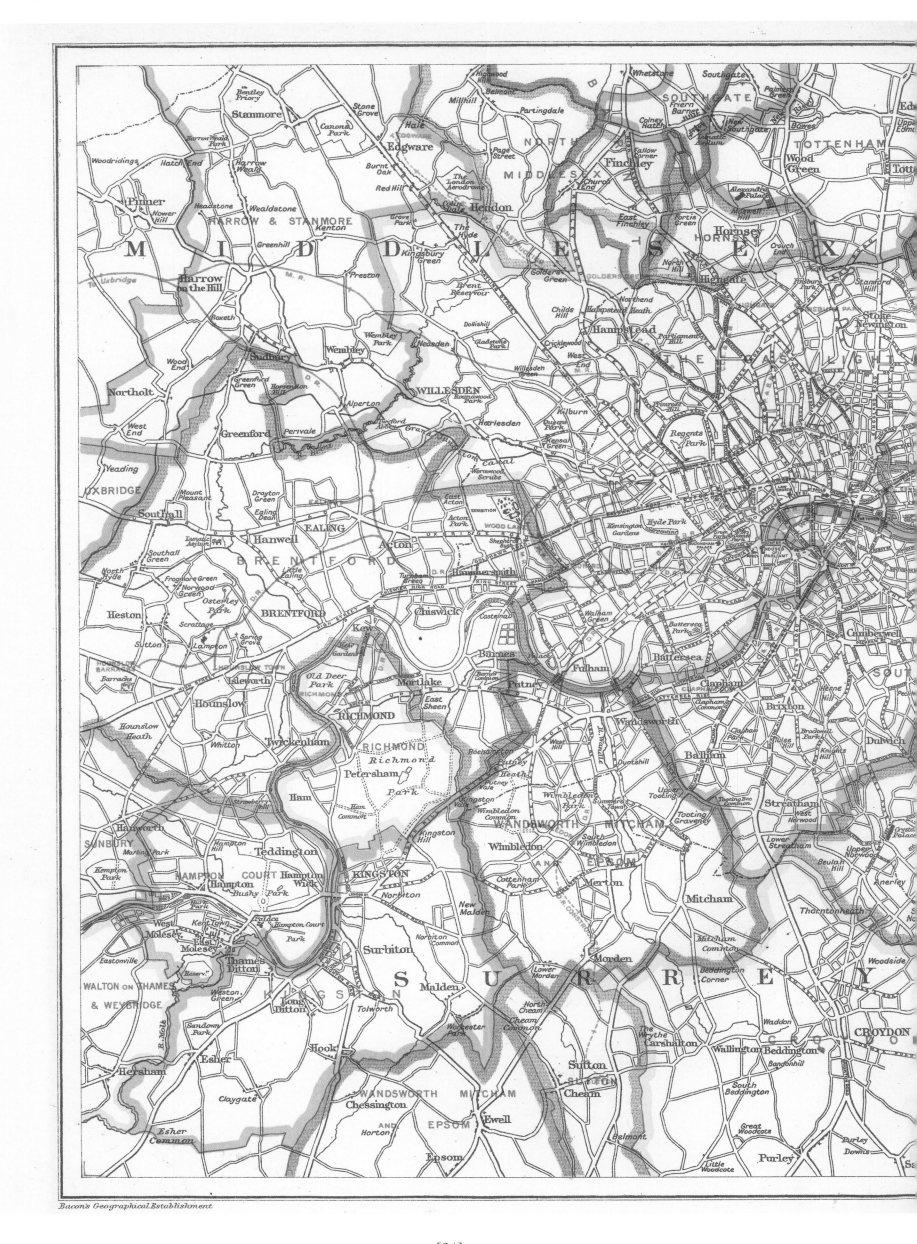

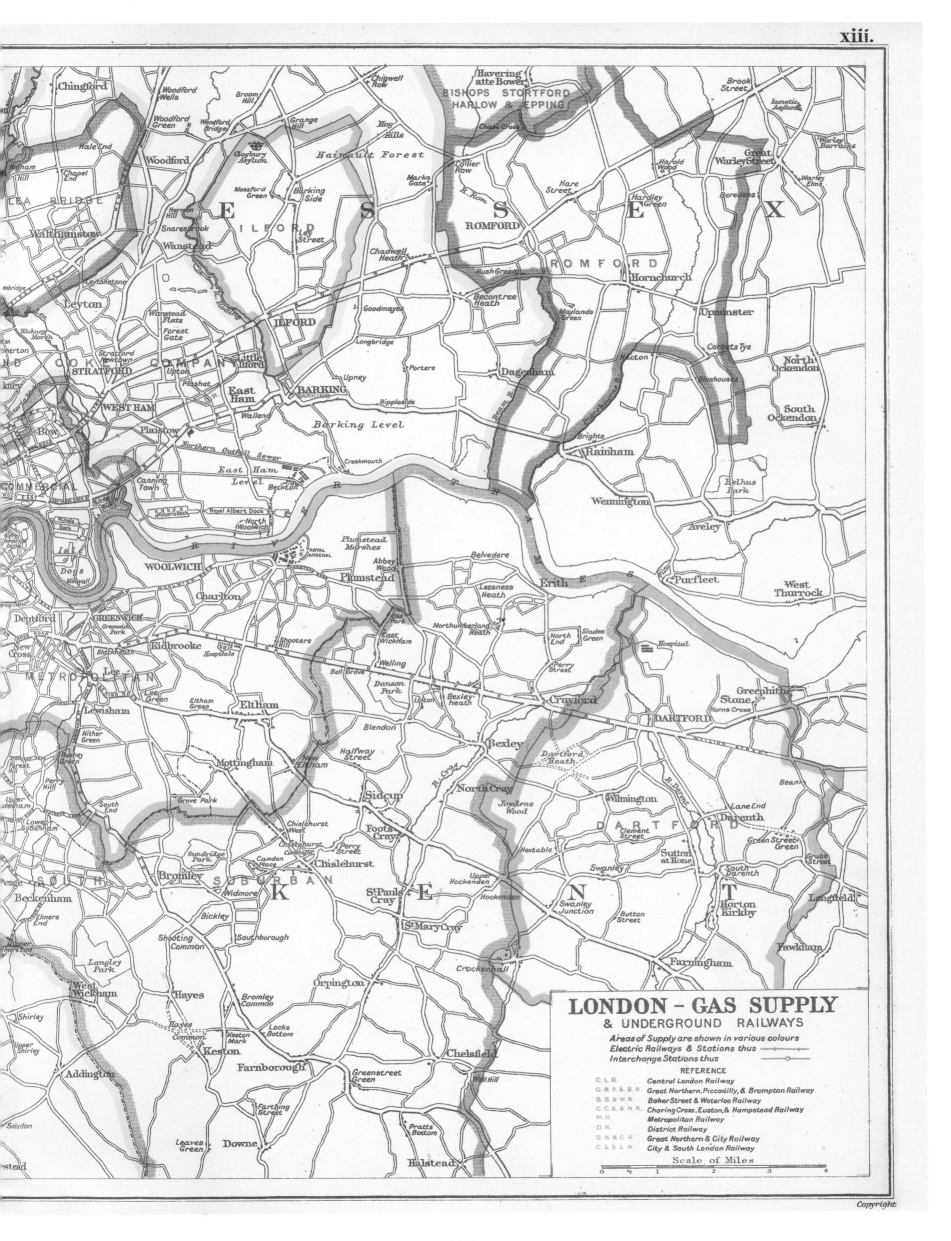

LONDON - GAS SUPPLY
& UNDERGROUND RAILWAYS

Areas of Supply are shown in various colours
Electric Railways & Stations thus ⊣———⊢
Interchange Stations thus ⊣———○———⊢

REFERENCE

C.L.R.	Central London Railway
G.N.P.& B.R.	Great Northern, Piccadilly, & Brompton Railway
B.S.& W.R.	Baker Street & Waterloo Railway
C.C.E.& H.R.	Charing Cross, Euston, & Hampstead Railway
M.R.	Metropolitan Railway
D.R.	District Railway
G.N.& C.R.	Great Northern & City Railway
C.& S.L.R.	City & South London Railway

Scale of Miles
0   ½   1   2   3   4

Copyright

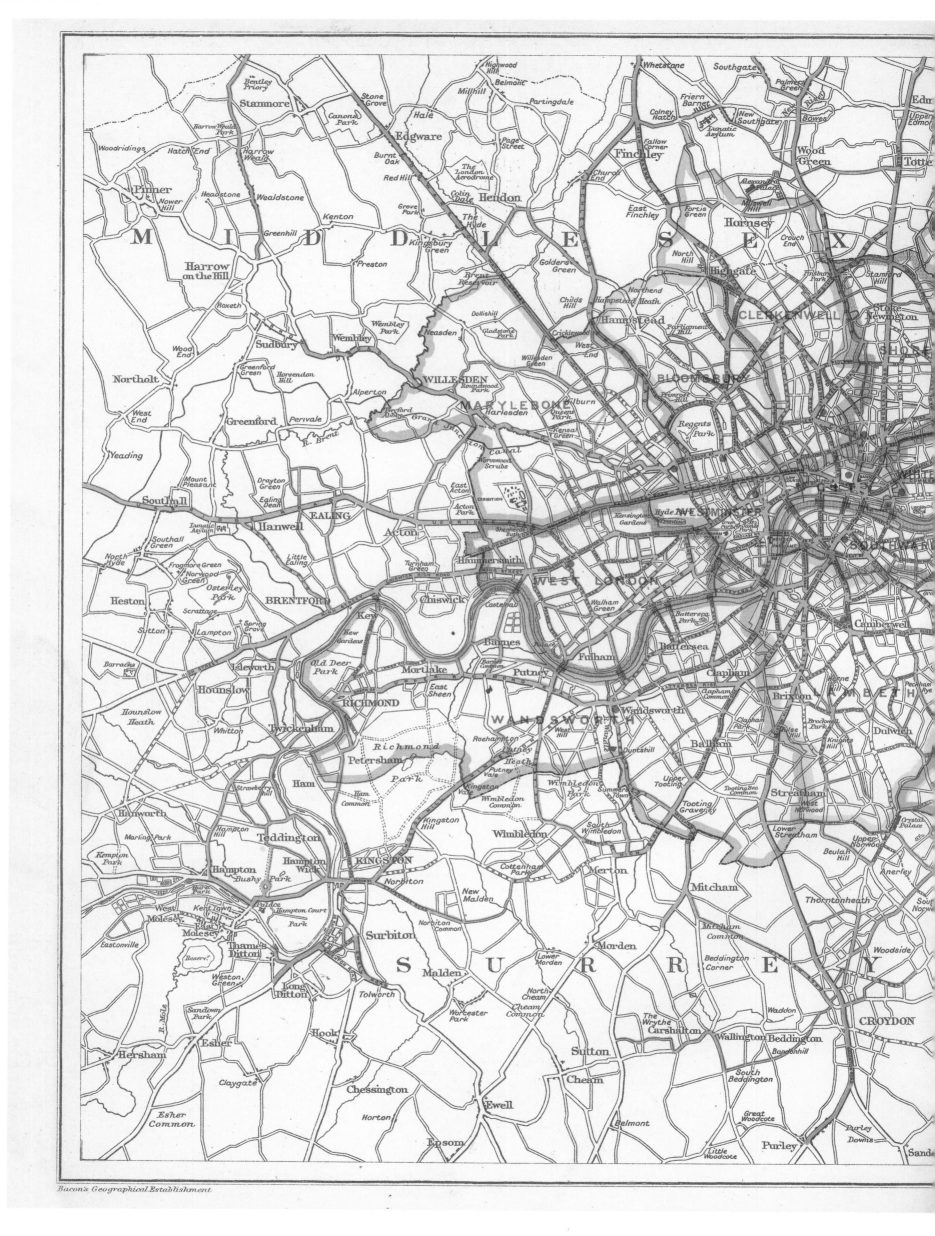

Bacon's Geographical Establishment.

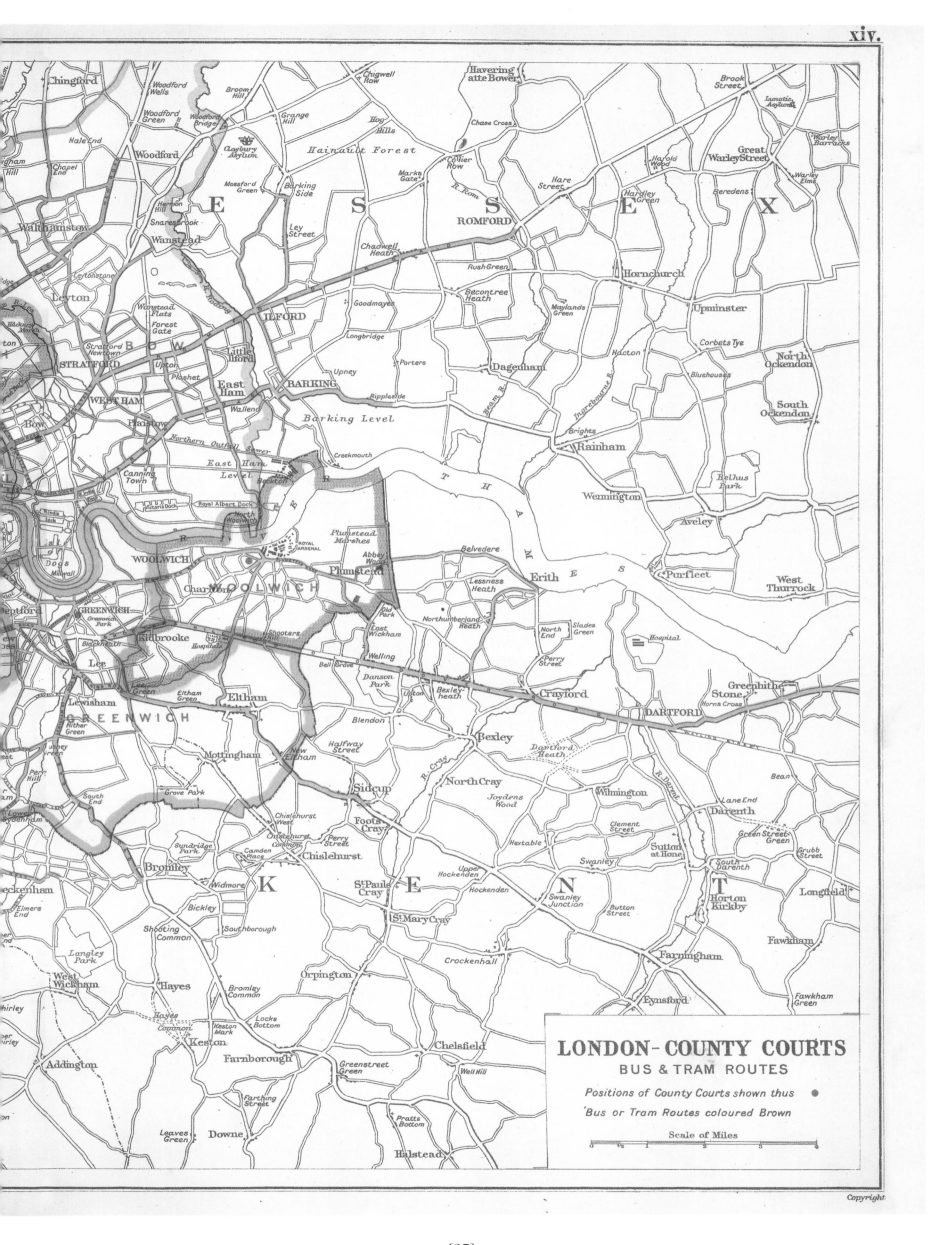

LONDON - COUNTY COURTS
BUS & TRAM ROUTES

Positions of County Courts shown thus ●

Bus or Tram Routes coloured Brown

Scale of Miles

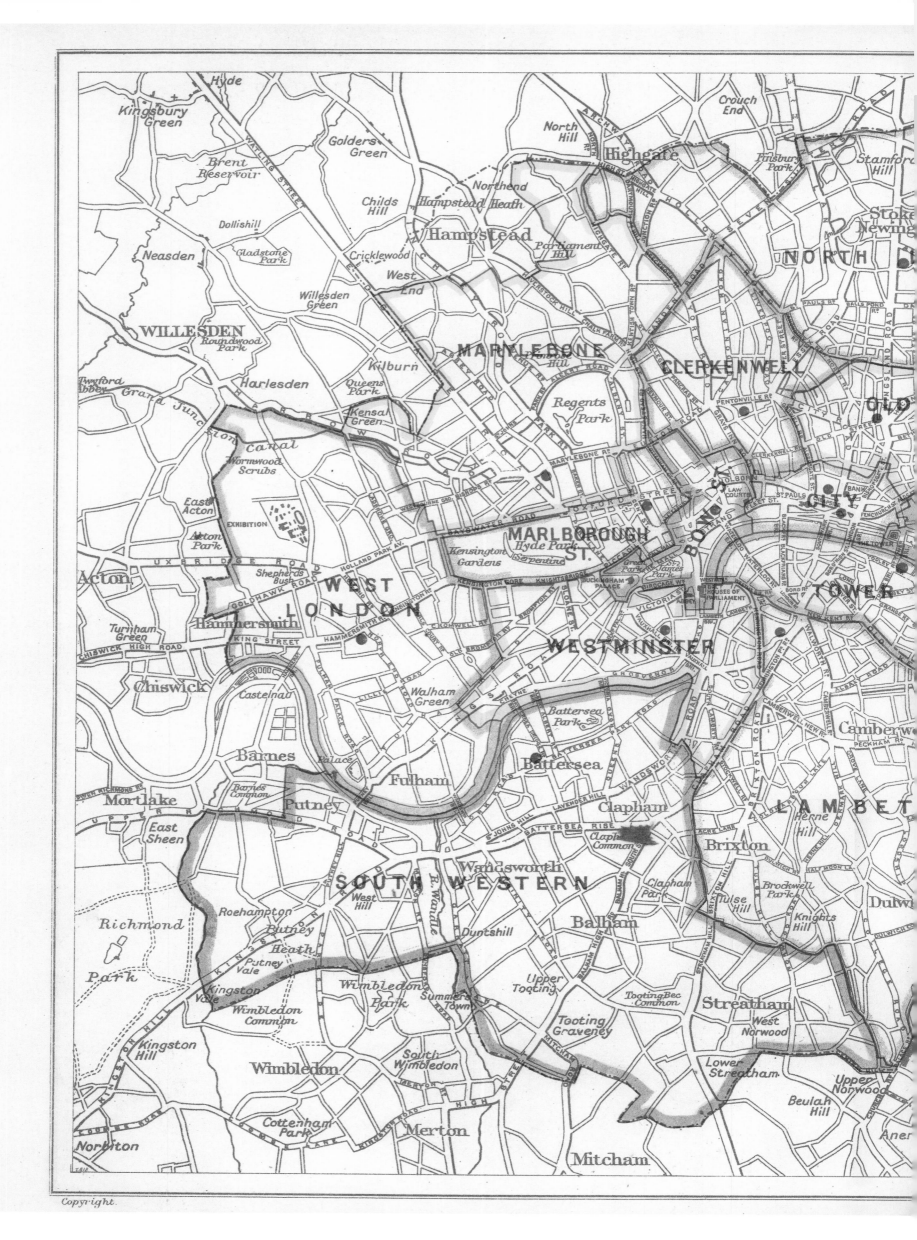

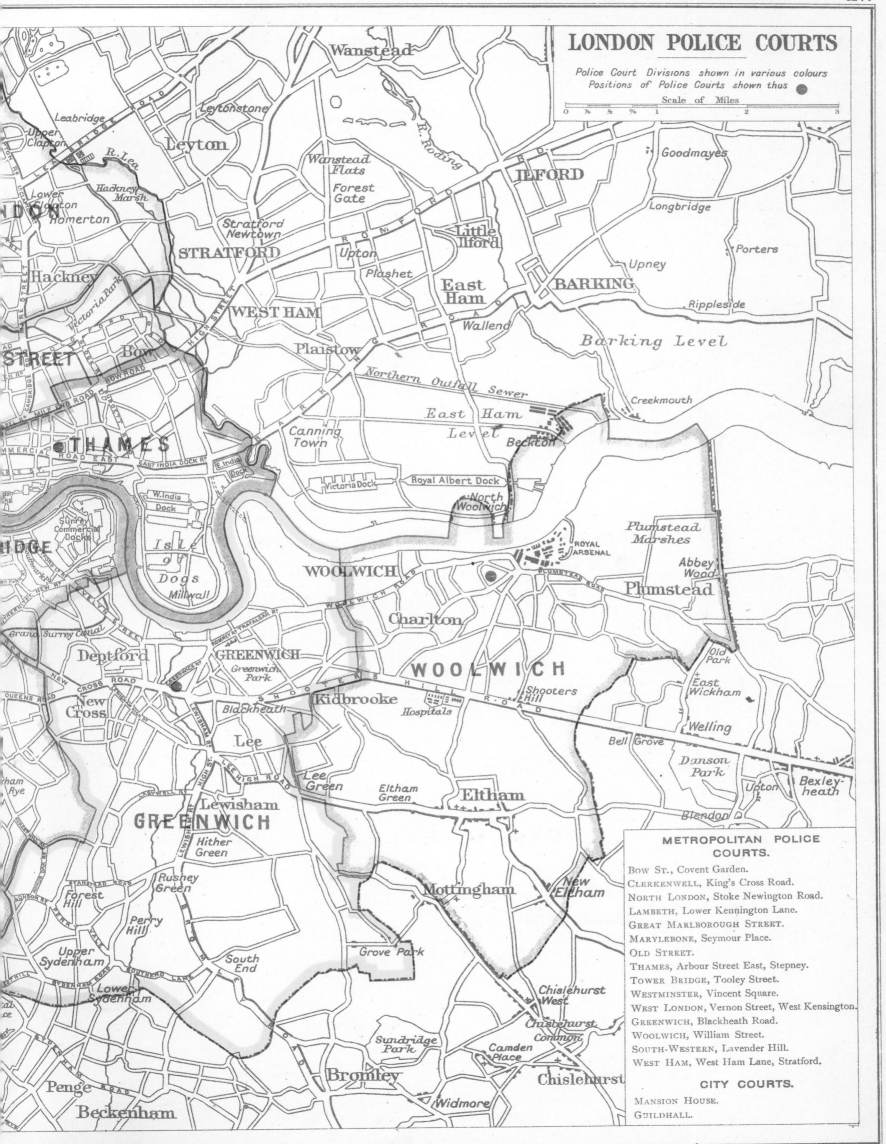

LONDON POLICE COURTS

Police Court Divisions shown in various colours
Positions of Police Courts shown thus ●

Scale of Miles

0 ¼ ½ ¾ 1   2   3

METROPOLITAN POLICE COURTS.

BOW ST., Covent Garden.
CLERKENWELL, King's Cross Road.
NORTH LONDON, Stoke Newington Road.
LAMBETH, Lower Kennington Lane.
GREAT MARLBOROUGH STREET.
MARYLEBONE, Seymour Place.
OLD STREET.
THAMES, Arbour Street East, Stepney.
TOWER BRIDGE, Tooley Street.
WESTMINSTER, Vincent Square.
WEST LONDON, Vernon Street, West Kensington.
GREENWICH, Blackheath Road.
WOOLWICH, William Street.
SOUTH-WESTERN, Lavender Hill.
WEST HAM, West Ham Lane, Stratford.

CITY COURTS.

MANSION HOUSE.
GUILDHALL.

Bacon's Geographical Establishment.

PETTY SESSIONAL BOROUGHS AND DIVISIONS WITHIN AREA OF MAP.

BUCKS.

	Population.	Position of Court House.	Days of Sittings.
Burnham (Beaconsfield Sub-Div.)	} 24,337	Beaconsfield ...	Alternate Mondays.
Burnham (Amersham Sub-Div.)		Burnham ...	Fortnightly on Mondays.
		Amersham ...	Monthly on a Monday.
Chesham	8,129	Chesham ...	Alternate Wednesdays.
Stoke	30,152	Slough ...	Wednesdays.

ESSEX.

	Population.	Position of Court House.	Days of Sittings.
Beacontree ...	399,053	Stratford ...	Daily.
		Walthamstow ...	First Thursday in month.
Brentwood (Brentford Sub-Div.)	} 31,111	Brentwood ...	Alternate Thursdays.
Brentwood (Billericay Sub-Div.)		Billericay ...	Second & Fourth Wednesdays in month.
Chelmsford ...	40,587	Chelmsford ...	First and Third Fridays in month.
Epping (Epping Sub-Div.)	} 37,464	Epping ...	Fridays.
Epping (Waltham Abbey Sub-Div.)		Waltham Abbey ...	Tuesdays.
Harlow	9,584	Harlow ...	Alternate Saturdays.
Ongar	9,474	Chipping Ongar ...	Alternate Saturdays.
Orsett	48,206	Grays...	Fridays.
Rochford ...	31,092	Rochford ...	Alternate Thursdays.
Romford ...	29,773	Romford ...	Thursdays.
East Ham (Borough) ...	133,487	East Ham ...	Daily.
West Ham (Borough) ...	289,080	Stratford ...	Daily.

HERTFORD.

	Population.	Position of Court House.	Days of Sittings.
Hertford (Borough) ...	10,883	Hertford ...	Thursdays.
St. Albans (Borough) ...	18,188	St. Albans ...	Thursdays.
Albury	8,706	Much Hadham ...	Alternate Saturdays.
Barnet	27,790	Barnet ...	Wednesdays.
Bishops Stortford...	12,507	Bishops Stortford ...	Alternate Thursdays.
Cheshunt ...	12,904	Cheshunt ...	Alternate Wednesdays.
Dacorum ...	25,943	Hemel Hempstead ...	Alternate Wednesdays.
Hatfield ...	7,991	Hatfield ...	Alternate Mondays.
Hertford ...	4,928	Hertford ...	Alternate Saturdays.
Hitchin ...	29,439	Hitchin ...	Tuesdays.
St. Albans ...	25,685	St. Albans ...	Saturdays.
Stevenage ...	11,418	Stevenage ...	Second and last Thursdays in month.
Ware	14,377	Ware ...	Alternate Tuesdays.
Watford ...	71,991	Watford ...	Tuesdays.
Welwyn ...	3,593	Welwyn ...	Second Friday in month.

KENT.

	Population.	Position of Court House.	Days of Sittings.
Maidstone (Borough) ...	35,475	Maidstone ...	Tuesdays.
Gravesend (Borough) ...	28,115	Gravesend ...	Mondays, Wednesdays and Fridays.
Rochester (Borough) ...	31,884	Rochester ...	Tuesdays and Saturdays.
Bearsted ...	20,108	Maidstone ...	Mondays.
Bromley ...	103,797	Bromley ...	Mondays.
Dartford ...	107,168	Dartford ...	Fridays.
		Erith ...	Last Wednesday in month.
Malling ...	31,631	West Malling ...	Second and Fourth Mondays in month.
Penge ...	22,988	Anerley ...	Daily.
Rochester ...	129,015	Chatham ...	Tuesdays and Fridays.
		Northfleet ...	Thursdays.
Sevenoaks ...	24,972	Sevenoaks ...	Second and last Fridays in month.
Tonbridge ...	41,835	Tonbridge ...	Tuesdays.

LONDON.

	Population.	Position of Court House.	Days of Sittings.
Blackheath ...	446,812	Greenwich ...	Second Tuesday in month (except April, September and October) and last Tuesday in September.
Finsbury ...	415,870	Clerkenwell ...	Mondays.
Hanover Square ...	69,641	Buckingham Palace Road	Fridays.
Holborn ...	} 113,088	High Holborn ...	Tuesdays.
Holborn (Det.) ...		Rosslyn Hill, Hampstead	Wednesdays.
Kensington ...	529,876	High Street ...	Fridays, and First and Third Tuesdays in month.
Newington ...	1,078,757	Newington, S.E. ...	Monthly on Mondays, January, March, May, July, October and November.
Paddington ...	127,119	Harrow Rd., Paddington	Thursdays monthly (except January, May, August and October).
St. James ...	25,445	Piccadilly ...	Court sits for Licensing matters only in February, April, May, July, December and January.
St. Margarets ...	47,979	Caxton St., Westminster	Licensing Sessions held in January, April, May, July, September, and December.
St. Marylebone ...	117,184	Marylebone Lane...	First Monday in month (except August and September).
St. Pancras ...	218,261	Pancras Road ...	Petty Sessions held about nine times per annum on Wednesdays.
Stoke Newington ...	50,682	Defoe Road, Stoke Newington	Rate Summonses are heard at the Petty Sessional Court House.
Strand ...	14,450	Charing Cross Road	Only on dates fixed as regulated by statute for holding Licensing meetings.
Tower ...	903,289	Old Street, Shoreditch ...	About once monthly, usually on Monday.
		Mare Street, Hackney ...	Alternate Thursdays.
		Bancroft Road, Mile End Old Town	Alternate Fridays.
		Newby Place, Poplar ...	Alternate Tuesdays.
		Cable Street, St. George-in-the-East	Alternate Fridays.
Wandsworth ...	328,404	Garratt Lane, Wandsworth	Special sittings for Petty Sessions are held in March, June, September and December. In other months Petty Sessions are held on days fixed for holding special sessions.

MIDDLESEX.

	Population.	Position of Court House.	Days of Sittings.
Brentford ...	190,989	Brentford ...	Daily.
Edmonton ...	341,534	Tottenham ...	Tuesdays and Thursdays.
Gore ...	93,480	Wealdstone...	Tuesdays.
		Edgware ...	Thursdays.
Highgate ...	138,935	Highgate ...	Daily.
South Mimms ...	2,805	Barnet ...	Wednesdays.
Spelthorne ...	62,897	Feltham ...	Mondays.
Uxbridge ...	39,477	Uxbridge ...	Mondays, and every other week-day if required.
Willesden ...	350,408	Willesden ...	Daily.
		Acton...	Daily.

SURREY.

	Population.	Position of Court House.	Days of Sittings.
Croydon (Borough) ...	169,551	Croydon ...	Daily.
Kingston-upon-Thames (Borough) ...	37,975	Kingston-upon-Thames ...	Wednesdays.
Reigate (Borough) ...	28,502	Reigate ...	Second and Fourth Thursdays.
Richmond (Borough) ...	33,291	Richmond ...	Daily.
Guildford (Borough) ...	28,820	Guildford ...	Mondays.
Chertsey ...	41,483	Chertsey ...	Wednesdays.
Croydon ...	76,767	Croydon ...	Daily.
Dorking ...	18,428	Dorking ...	First and Third Saturdays in month.
Epsom ...	71,498	Epsom ...	Mondays.
		Sutton ...	Alternate Thursdays.
Godstone ...	34,158	Oxted ...	Alternate Mondays.
Guildford ...	37,255	Guildford ...	Fridays.
Kingston ...	66,640	Kingston-upon-Thames ...	Thursdays.
Mortlake ...	90,377	Mortlake ...	Wednesdays.
Reigate ...	19,862	Reigate ...	Tuesdays and Saturdays.
Wimbledon ...	67,904	Wimbledon ...	Wednesdays.
Woking ...	36,762	Woking ...	Saturdays.

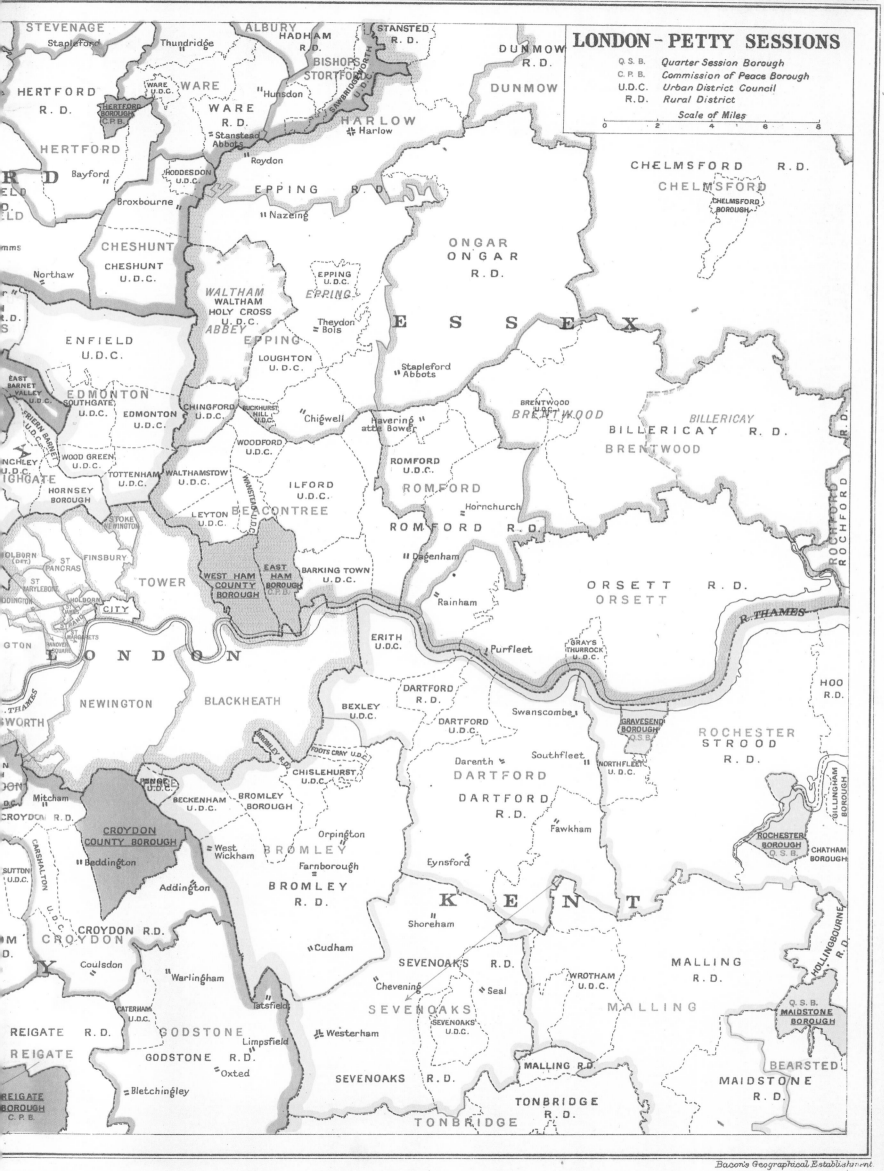

LONDON - PETTY SESSIONS

Q.S.B.	Quarter Session Borough
C.P.B.	Commission of Peace Borough
U.D.C.	Urban District Council
R.D.	Rural District

Scale of Miles

0   2   4   6   8

STEVENAGE
Stapleford

ALBURY
HADHAM R.D.

STANSTED R.D.

DUNMOW R.D.

Thundridge

HERTFORD R.D.

WARE U.D.C.

WARE

BISHOPS STORTFORD

DUNMOW

Hunsdon

HERTFORD

HERTFORD BOROUGH C.P.B.

WARE R.D.

Stanstead Abbots

HARLOW

Harlow

CHELMSFORD R.D.

CHELMSFORD

Bayford

HODDESDON U.D.C.

Roydon

EPPING R.D.

CHELMSFORD BOROUGH

Broxbourne

Nazeing

CHESHUNT

CHESHUNT U.D.C.

Northaw

EPPING U.D.C.

EPPING

ONGAR

ONGAR R.D.

E S S E X

WALTHAM HOLY CROSS U.D.C.

ABBEY

EPPING

Theydon Bois

ENFIELD U.D.C.

LOUGHTON U.D.C.

Stapleford Abbots

EAST BARNET VALLEY U.D.C.

EDMONTON

SOUTHGATE U.D.C.

EDMONTON U.D.C.

CHINGFORD U.D.C.

BUCKHURST HILL U.D.C.

Chigwell

Havering atte Bower

BRENTWOOD U.D.C.

BRENTWOOD

BILLERICAY R.D.

BILLERICAY

FRIERN BARNET U.D.C.

HIGHGATE

WOOD GREEN U.D.C.

WOODFORD U.D.C.

BRENTWOOD

FINCHLEY U.D.C.

HORNSEY BOROUGH

TOTTENHAM U.D.C.

WALTHAMSTOW U.D.C.

ILFORD U.D.C.

ROMFORD U.D.C.

ROMFORD

STOKE NEWINGTON

LEYTON U.D.C.

BEACONTREE

Hornchurch

ROCHFORD R.D.

ROCHFORD

HOLBORN (DET.)

ST PANCRAS

FINSBURY

WANSTEAD U.D.C.

ROMFORD R.D.

ST MARYLEBONE

HOLBORN

TOWER

WEST HAM COUNTY BOROUGH

EAST HAM BOROUGH C.P.B.

BARKING TOWN U.D.C.

Dagenham

PADDINGTON

CITY

ST JAMES

HANOVER SQUARE

ST GEORGES

Rainham

ORSETT R.D.

ORSETT

HOO R.D.

L O N D O N

ERITH U.D.C.

Purfleet

GRAYS THURROCK U.D.C.

R. THAMES

ISLINGTON

R. THAMES

NEWINGTON

BLACKHEATH

DARTFORD R.D.

Swanscombe

GRAVESEND BOROUGH Q.S.B.

ROCHESTER

STROOD R.D.

WANDSWORTH

BEXLEY U.D.C.

DARTFORD U.D.C.

NORTHFLEET U.D.C.

BROMLEY R.D.

FOOTS CRAY U.D.C.

Darenth

Southfleet

GILLINGHAM BOROUGH

CHISLEHURST U.D.C.

DARTFORD

PENGE U.D.C.

Mitcham

BECKENHAM U.D.C.

BROMLEY BOROUGH

DARTFORD R.D.

Fawkham

ROCHESTER BOROUGH Q.S.B.

CHATHAM BOROUGH

CROYDON R.D.

CROYDON COUNTY BOROUGH

Orpington

Beddington

West Wickham

BROMLEY

Farnborough

Eynsford

CARSHALTON U.D.C.

SUTTON U.D.C.

Addington

BROMLEY R.D.

Shoreham

K E N T

HOLLINGBOURNE R.D.

CROYDON R.D.

CROYDON

Coulsdon

Cudham

SEVENOAKS R.D.

MALLING R.D.

Warlingham

WROTHAM U.D.C.

MALLING

CATERHAM U.D.C.

Tatsfield

Chevening

Seal

REIGATE R.D.

GODSTONE

Limpsfield

Westerham

SEVENOAKS

SEVENOAKS U.D.C.

MALLING

Q.S.B. MAIDSTONE BOROUGH

REIGATE

GODSTONE R.D.

Bletchingley

Oxted

SEVENOAKS R.D.

BEARSTED

MAIDSTONE R.D.

REIGATE BOROUGH C.P.B.

TONBRIDGE R.D.

TONBRIDGE

Bacon's Geographical Establishment

LONDON PARLIAMENTARY BOROUGHS

(within the Administrative County.)

No. of Electors

CITY OF LONDON	30,010
BATTERSEA	18,927
BETHNAL GREEN :	
North-East	7,554
South-West	7,103
CAMBERWELL :	
North	11,918
Dulwich	16,478
Peckham	12,341
CHELSEA	11,257
CLAPHAM	22,611
DEPTFORD	15,159
FINSBURY :	
Central (Clerkenwell)	8,094
East	4,855
Holborn	8,608
FULHAM	21,000
GREENWICH	13,153
HACKNEY :	
Central	9,343
North	11,789
South	14,126
HAMMERSMITH	14,362
HAMPSTEAD	12,050
ISLINGTON :	
East	11,118
North	12,677
South	8,268
West	8,544
KENSINGTON :	
North	10,100
South	9,159
LAMBETH :	
Brixton	11,442
Kennington	10,088
North	6,440
Norwood	13,908
LEWISHAM	25,021
MARYLEBONE :	
East	6,759
West	8,576
NEWINGTON :	
Walworth	8,521
West	9,635
PADDINGTON :	
North	10,945
South	6,415
ST. GEORGE'S, HANOVER SQ.	8,954
ST. PANCRAS :	
East	9,487
North	9,977
South	5,536
West	8,589
SHOREDITCH :	
Haggerston	7,936
Hoxton	8,530

London Parliamentary Boroughs—
Continued.

No. of Electors

SOUTHWARK :	
Bermondsey	12,115
Rotherhithe	9,990
West	8,060
STRAND	8,019
TOWER HAMLETS :	
Bow and Bromley	10,330
Limehouse	6,405
Mile End	5,464
Poplar	8,857
St. George's	3,133
Stepney	4,653
Whitechapel	3,986
WANDSWORTH	38,523
WESTMINSTER	7,284
WOOLWICH	18,536

———

COUNTY PARLIAMENTARY BOROUGHS

CROYDON	27,350
WEST HAM :	
North	15,661
South	26,682

———

COUNTY PARLIAMENTARY DIVISIONS

BUCKINGHAMSHIRE :	
Mid or Aylesbury	12,218
South or Wycombe	16,366
ESSEX :	
Mid or Chelmsford	13,314
West or Epping	12,164
South or Romford	52,984
South-East (Tilbury)	24,645
South-West or Walthamstow	39,117
HERTFORD :	
East or Hertford	11,838
Mid or St. Albans	13,929
West or Watford	17,710
KENT :	
North-West or Dartford	21,398
West or Sevenoaks	19,035
MIDDLESEX :	
Brentford	20,701
Ealing	25,073
Enfield	28,571
Harrow	35,379
Hornsey	23,450
Tottenham	29,620
Uxbridge	17,634
SURREY :	
North-West or Chertsey	16,723
Mid or Epsom	18,821
Kingston	19,649
South-East or Reigate	15,636
North-East or Wimbledon	27,810

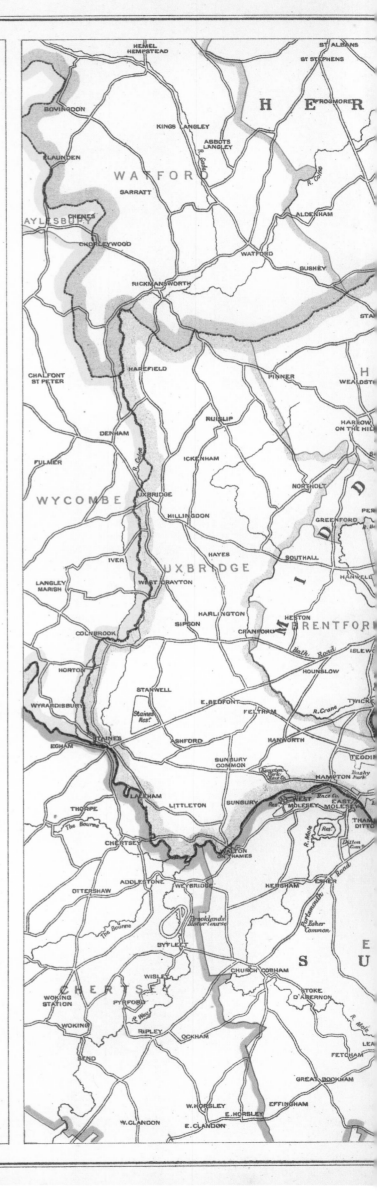

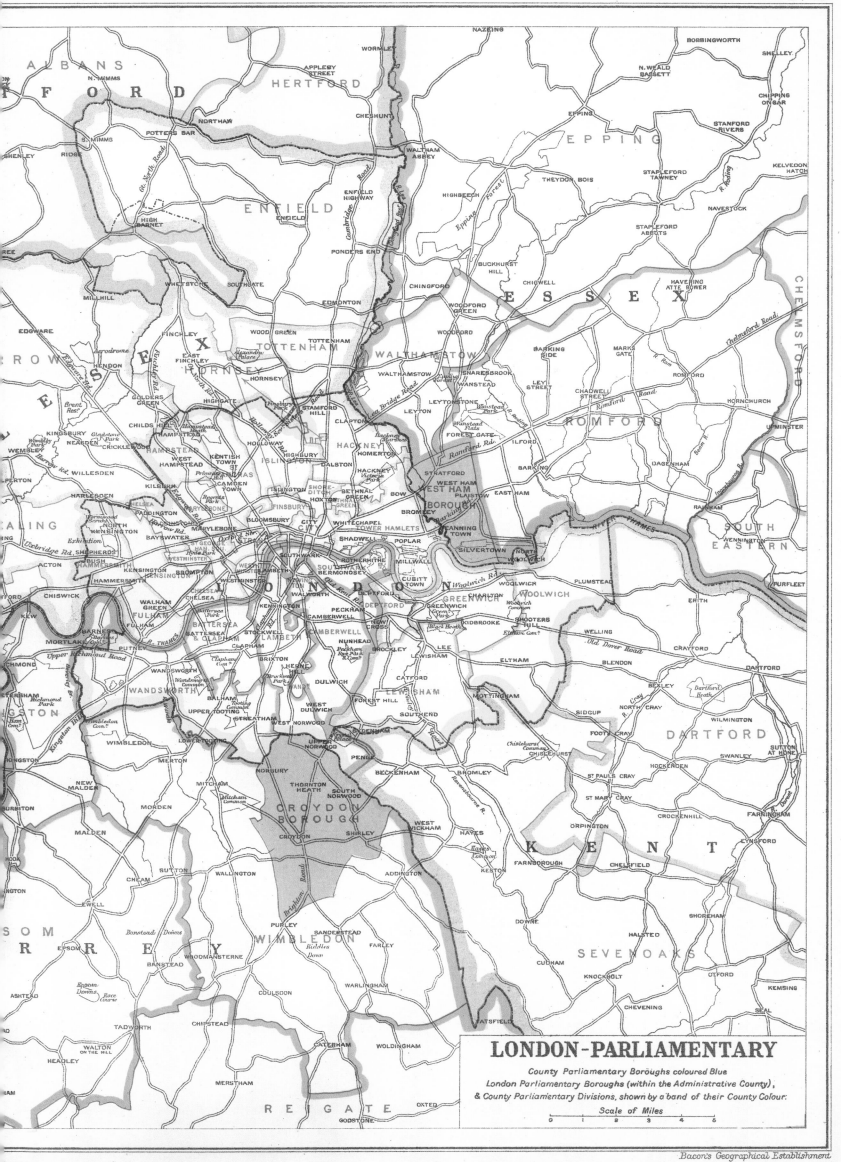

LONDON - PARLIAMENTARY

County Parliamentary Boroughs coloured Blue
London Parliamentary Boroughs (within the Administrative County),
& County Parliamentary Divisions, shown by a band of their County Colour:

Scale of Miles

0 1 2 3 4 5

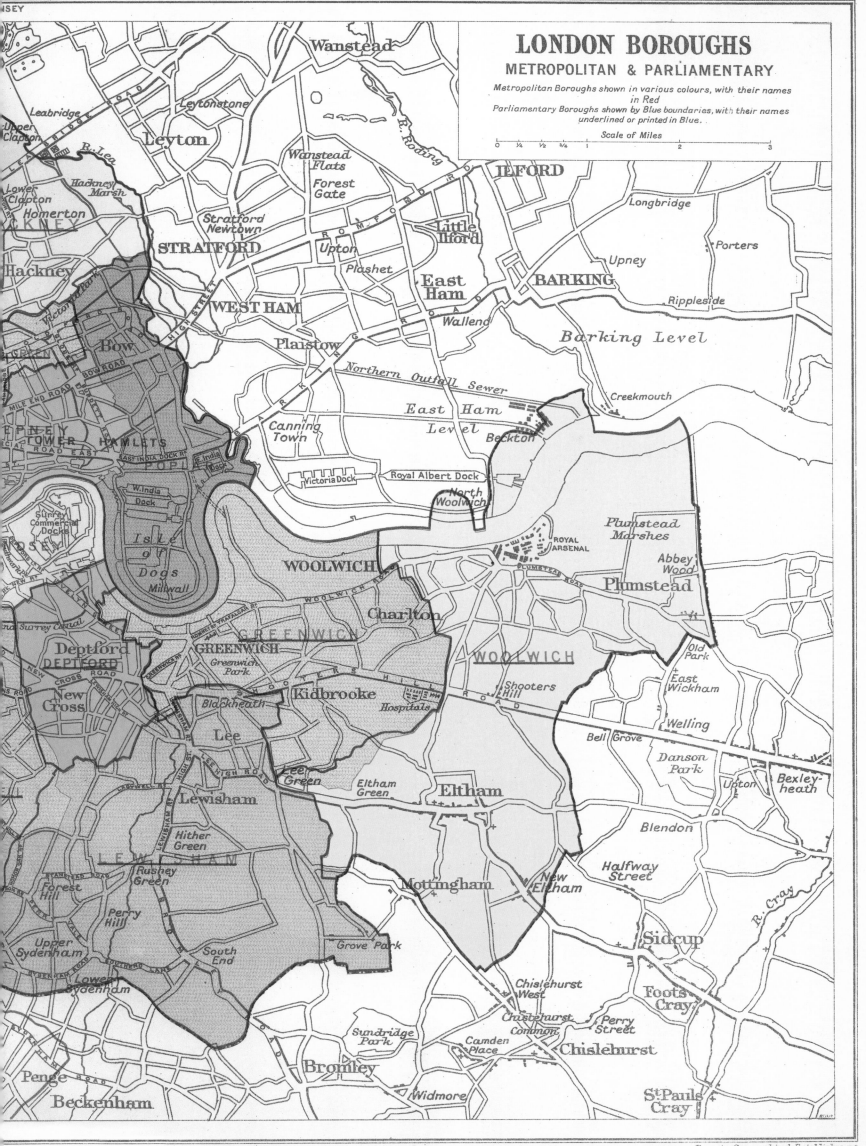

LONDON BOROUGHS
METROPOLITAN & PARLIAMENTARY

Metropolitan Boroughs shown in various colours, with their names in Red
Parliamentary Boroughs shown by Blue boundaries, with their names underlined or printed in Blue.

Scale of Miles

Bacon's Geographical Establishment.

BOROUGHS, URBAN AND RURAL DISTRICTS
That come within the Map, with their Areas and Populations.

BUCKINGHAM:	AREA IN ACRES	POP. IN 1911
URBAN DISTRICT.		
Slough	1,684	14,985
RURAL DISTRICTS.		
Amersham	45,700	18,515
Eton	41,005	23,449

ESSEX:		
COUNTY BOROUGH.		
West Ham	4,683	289,102
MUNICIPAL BOROUGH.		
East Ham	3,324	133,504
URBAN DISTRICTS.		
Barking Town	3,805	31,302
Buckhurst Hill	873	4,887
Chingford	2,808	8,186
Epping	1,420	4,253
Ilford	8,496	78,205
Leyton	2,594	124,736
Loughton	3,961	5,433
Romford	5,630	16,972
Waltham Holy Cross	11,017	6,796
Walthamstow	4,343	124,597
Wanstead	1,679	13,831
Woodford	2,161	18,497
RURAL DISTRICTS.		
Billericay	49,394	21,557
Epping	39,055	13,959
Ongar	47,236	10,647
Orsett	39,939	24,874
Romford	29,720	25,361

HERTFORD:		
MUNICIPAL BOROUGHS.		
Hemel Hempstead	7,184	12,888
St. Albans	997	18,132
URBAN DISTRICTS.		
Barnet	1,510	10,440
Bushey	3,081	6,980
Cheshunt	8,479	12,956
East Barnet Valley	2,644	12,381
Rickmansworth	572	6,288
Watford	2,061	40,953
RURAL DISTRICTS.		
Barnet	10,820	4,969
Berkhampstead	18,383	4,707
Hatfield	23,486	8,592
Hemel Hempstead	19,994	6,565
Hertford	33,835	7,660
St. Albans	38,772	19,469
Ware	33,953	11,466
Watford	31,238	17,779

KENT:		
MUNICIPAL BOROUGH.		
Bromley	4,696	33,649
URBAN DISTRICTS.		
Beckenham	3,890	31,693
Bexley	4,942	15,895
Chislehurst	2,791	8,668
Dartford	4,242	23,609
Erith	3,859	27,755
Foots Cray	2,043	8,494
Penge	770	22,331
Sevenoaks	3,259	9,183
RURAL DISTRICTS.		
Bromley	28,839	21,958
Dartford	37,997	39,910
Sevenoaks	63,336	24,030

LONDON:		
City of London	672	19,657
METROPOLITAN BOROUGHS.		
Battersea	2,160	167,793
Bermondsey	1,500	125,960
Bethnal Green	759	128,282
Camberwell	4,480	261,357
Chelsea	660	66,404
Deptford	1,563	109,498
Finsbury	589	87,976
Fulham	1,704	153,325
Greenwich	3,852	95,977
Hackney	3,288	222,587
Hammersmith	2,286	121,603
Hampstead	2,265	85,510
Holborn	405	49,336
Islington	3,092	327,423
Kensington	2,291	172,402
Lambeth	4,080	298,126

LONDON.—Continued.	AREA IN ACRES	POP. IN 1911
Lewisham	7,014	160,843
Paddington	1,356	142,576
Poplar	2,328	162,449
St. Marylebone	1,473	118,221
St. Pancras	2,694	218,453
Shoreditch	658	111,463
Southwark	1,132	191,951
Stepney	1,766	280,024
Stoke Newington	863	50,683
Wandsworth	9,108	311,402
Westminster	2,502	160,277
Woolwich	8,276	121,403

MIDDLESEX:		
MUNICIPAL BOROUGHS.		
Ealing	2,947	61,235
Hornsey	2,875	84,602
URBAN DISTRICTS.		
Acton	2,305	57,523
Brentford	1,091	16,584
Chiswick	1,249	38,705
Edmonton	3,894	64,820
Enfield	12,601	56,344
Feltham	1,790	5,135
Finchley	3,384	39,425
Friern Barnet	1,304	14,925
Greenford	3,041	1,064
Hampton	2,044	9,221
Hampton Wick	1,306	2,417
Hanwell	1,067	19,131
Harrow-on-the-Hill	2,028	17,076
Hayes	3,311	4,261
Hendon	8,382	38,806
Heston and Isleworth	6,859	43,316
Kingsbury	1,829	821
Ruislip Northwood	6,585	6,217
Southall Norwood	2,575	26,327
Southgate	3,597	33,613
Staines	1,918	6,756
Sunbury-on-Thames	2,659	4,607
Teddington	1,214	17,840
Tottenham	3,014	137,457
Twickenham	2,421	29,374
Uxbridge	868	10,374
Wealdstone	1,061	11,923
Wembley	4,564	10,697
Willesden	4,384	154,267
Wood Green	1,625	49,372
Yiewsley	896	4,321
RURAL DISTRICTS.		
Hendon	11,321	14,161
South Mimms	6,105	2,805
Staines	17,964	21,932
Uxbridge	12,623	9,240

SURREY:		
COUNTY BOROUGH.		
Croydon	9,012	169,559
MUNICIPAL BOROUGHS.		
Guildford	2,593	23,823
Kingston-upon-Thames	1,133	37,977
Reigate	5,994	28,505
Richmond	2,491	33,223
Wimbledon	3,221	54,876
URBAN DISTRICTS.		
Barnes	2,518	30,379
Carshalton	2,926	11,635
Caterham	2,438	10,841
Chertsey	10,777	13,819
East and West Molesey	1,518	6,500
Egham	7,786	12,551
Epsom	4,424	19,156
Esher and The Dittons	5,978	12,518
Ham	1,871	1,435
Leatherhead	3,508	5,491
Merton	1,762	12,938
Surbiton	3,046	17,713
Sutton	1,836	21,275
The Maldens and Coombe	3,220	12,140
Walton-upon-Thames	6,859	12,858
Weybridge	1,371	6,286
Woking	11,826	24,810
RURAL DISTRICTS.		
Chertsey	16,020	9,383
Croydon	21,018	65,136
Dorking	39,525	10,580
Epsom	31,188	29,729
Godstone	49,907	23,317
Guildford	53,336	18,277
Reigate	44,651	21,197

LONDON-BOROUGHS ETC.

County Boroughs coloured Purple
Metropolitan & Municipal Boroughs coloured Blue
Urban Districts coloured Brown
Rural Districts shown by a band of their County colour

Scale of Miles

Bacon's Geographical Establishment

LIST OF UNIONS WITHIN AREA OF MAP,
With their Areas, Populations, and Workhouses.

Unions.	Area in Acres	Pop. in 1911	Workhouse addresses.
LONDON:			
BERMONDSEY	1,500	126,960	Parish Street.—Ladywell.—Tanner Street.
BETHNAL GREEN, ST. MATTHEW	759	128,282	Waterloo Road, E.
CAMBERWELL, ST. GILES	4,480	261,357	Gordon Rd., Peckham, S.E.—Constance Rd., East Dulwich.
CITY OF LONDON	672	19,657	Thavie's Inn—Homerton, N.E.
CHELSEA, ST. LUKE	660	66,404	Arthur Street, Chelsea, S.W.
FULHAM	1,703	153,325	Fulham Palace Road, W.
GREENWICH	3,424	185,688	Greenwich, S.E.—Grove Park, Lee.
HACKNEY	4,151	273,270	Homerton, E.
HAMMERSMITH	2,286	121,603	Ducane Road, Wormwood Scrubs.
HAMPSTEAD, ST. JOHN	2,265	85,510	Hampstead, N.W.
HOLBORN	762	112,247	City Road, E.C.—Mitcham.
ISLINGTON, ST. MARY	3,092	327,423	St. John's Road, Upper Holloway, N.—Cornwallis Road, N.
KENSINGTON, ST. MARY ABBOTS	2,291	172,402	Marloes Road, Kensington, W.—Mary Place, Notting Hill.
LAMBETH	4,080	298,126	Renfrew Road.—Prince's Road, Lambeth.
LEWISHAM	10,774	174,296	Lewisham, S.E.
MILE END OLD TOWN	678	111,375	Bancroft Road, Stepney, E.
PADDINGTON	1,356	142,576	Harrow Road, Paddington, W.
POPLAR	2,328	162,449	High Street, Poplar, E.—Laindon, Essex.—Forest Gate.—Sumpness Farm, Dunton, Essex.
ST. GEORGE-IN-THE-EAST	244	47,101	Raine Street, Old Gravel Lane, E.
ST. GEORGE'S	1,887	117,968	Fulham Rd., S.W.—Buckingham Palace Rd.
ST. GILES-IN-THE-FIELDS AND ST. GEORGE, BLOOMSBURY	232	25,065	Endell Street, W.C.
ST. MARYLEBONE	1,473	118,221	Northumberland Street, W.
ST. PANCRAS	2,694	218,453	King's Road, N.W.—Streatham Hill, S.W.
SHOREDITCH, ST. LEONARD	658	111,463	Reeves Place, Hoxton.—Hazelville Road, N.—The Mansion, Wood Green.
SOUTHWARK	1,132	191,951	Christchurch, Southwark.—Newington.—Mint Street, Southwark, S.E.
STEPNEY	466	53,798	Bromley, E.
STRAND	399	16,858	Edmonton, N.
WANDSWORTH	11,268	479,195	Garratt Lane, Wandsworth.
WESTMINSTER	216	25,451	Poland Street, W.
WHITECHAPEL	378	67,750	South Grove, Mile End Road, E.
WOOLWICH	6,507	127,737	Plumstead.
MIDDLESEX:			
BRENTFORD	20,980	266,932	Brentford.
EDMONTON	47,102	445,960	Edmonton.—Enfield.
HENDON	29,185	93,484	Red Hill, Edgware.
STAINES	24,331	38,430	Stanwell.
UXBRIDGE	26,858	60,740	Hillingdon, Uxbridge.
WILLESDEN	4,384	154,267	494, Acton Lane, N.W.
HERTFORD:			
BARNET	25,767	84,945	Barnet.
BERKHAMPSTEAD	26,854	17,309	Berkhampstead.
HATFIELD	23,486	8,592	Hatfield.
HEMEL HEMPSTEAD	27,178	19,453	Hemel Hempstead.
HERTFORD	34,969	18,044	St. John, Hertford.
ST. ALBANS	41,402	43,774	St. Michael's, St. Albans.
WARE	36,158	22,504	Ware.
WATFORD	36,952	72,000	Watford.
BUCKS:			
AMERSHAM	51,590	29,230	Amersham.
ETON	42,988	41,626	Upton-cum-Chalvey, Slough.
ESSEX:			
BILLERICAY	49,854	28,480	Gt. Burstead.
EPPING	48,117	36,718	Epping.
ONGAR	47,236	10,647	Stanford Rivers, Ongar.
ORSETT	41,298	40,877	Orsett, Grays.
ROMFORD	47,651	151,840	Romford.
WEST HAM	18,784	704,267	Leyton.
SURREY:			
CHERTSEY	43,638	49,621	Chertsey.
CROYDON	32,562	269,964	Croydon.
DORKING	40,864	18,430	Dorking.
EPSOM	43,882	87,286	Epsom.
GODSTONE	52,345	34,158	Bletchingley.
GUILDFORD	65,648	72,731	Guildford.
KINGSTON	24,551	172,637	Kingston-on-Thames.
REIGATE	50,645	49,702	Redhill.
RICHMOND	5,009	63,602	Richmond.
BERKS:			
WINDSOR	21,070	40,602	Old Windsor.
KENT:			
BROMLEY	42,259	104,262	Farnborough.
DARTFORD	51,040	107,169	Dartford.
SEVENOAKS	66,595	33,213	Sundridge, Sevenoaks.

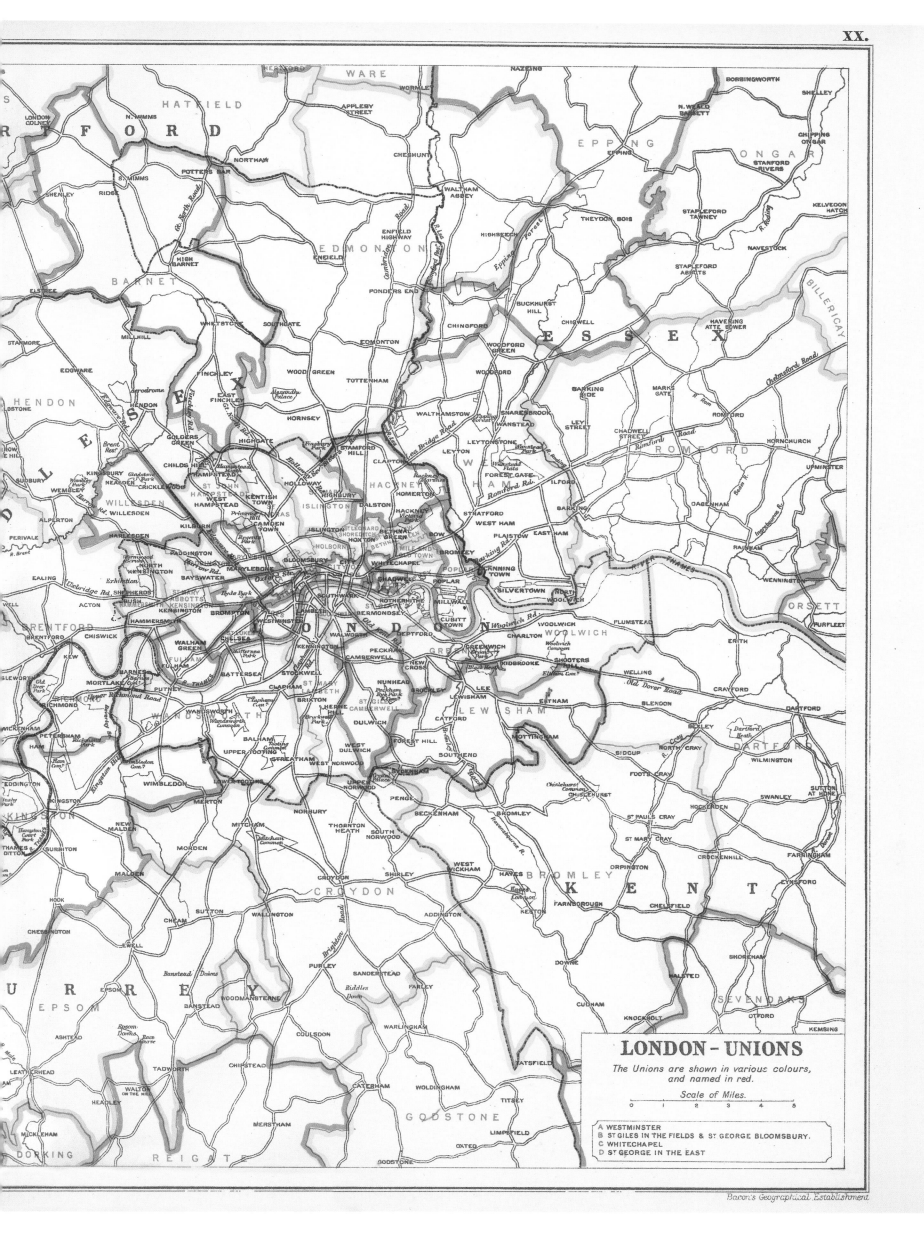

LONDON - UNIONS

*The Unions are shown in various colours,
and named in red.*

Scale of Miles.

0 1 2 3 4 5

A WESTMINSTER
B ST GILES IN THE FIELDS & ST GEORGE BLOOMSBURY.
C WHITECHAPEL
D ST GEORGE IN THE EAST

Bacon's Geographical Establishment

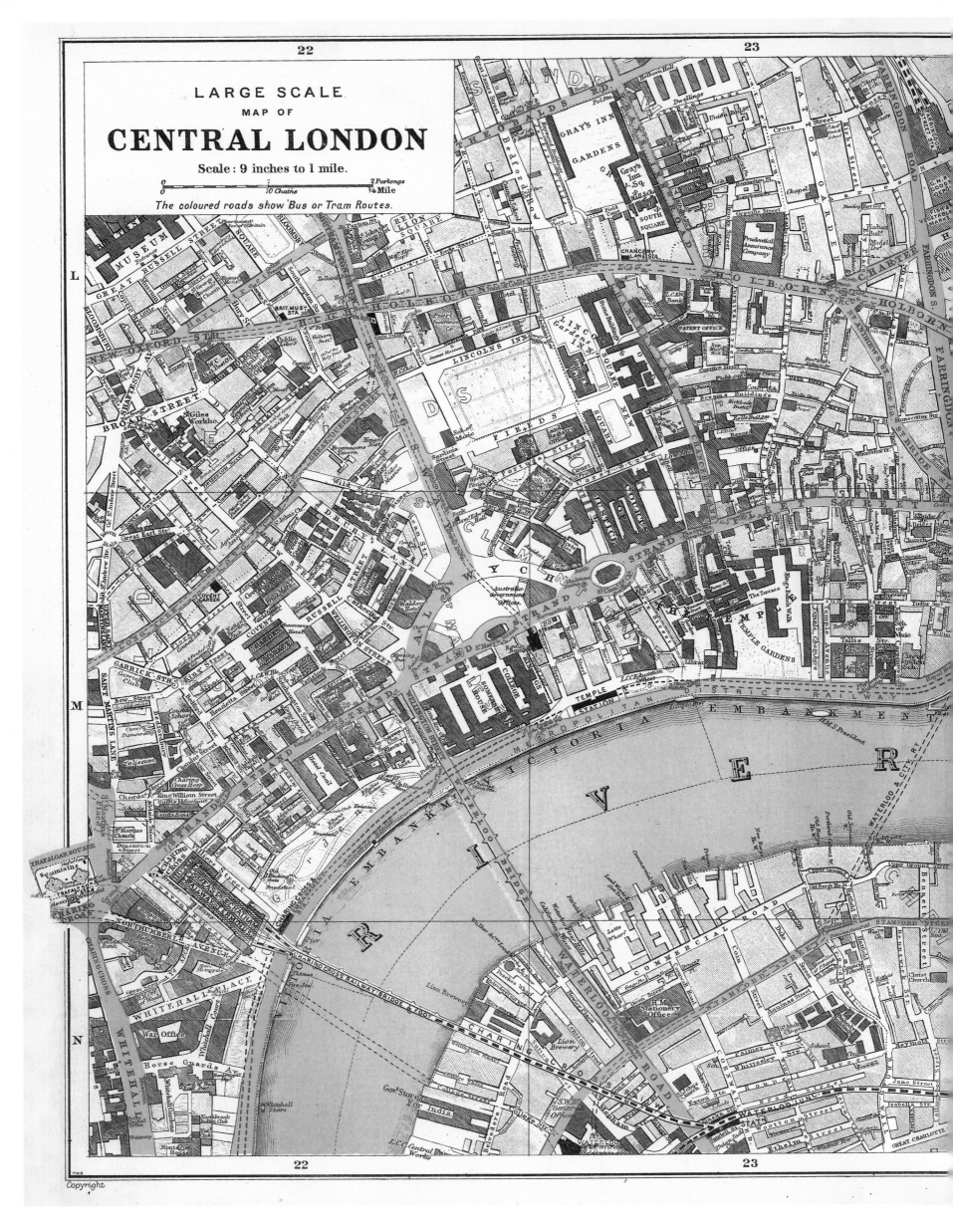

LARGE SCALE
MAP OF
CENTRAL LONDON

Scale: 9 inches to 1 mile.

The coloured roads show Bus or Tram Routes.

Copyright

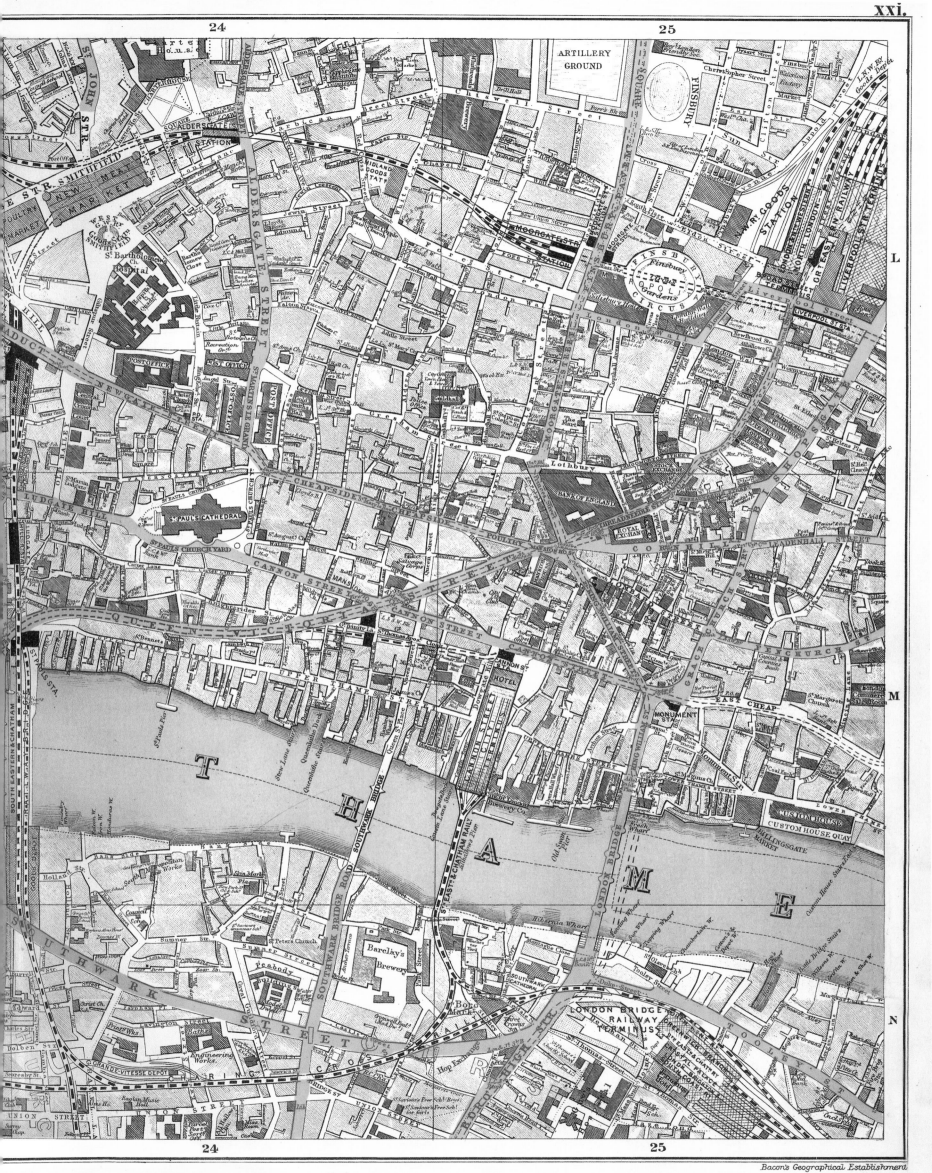

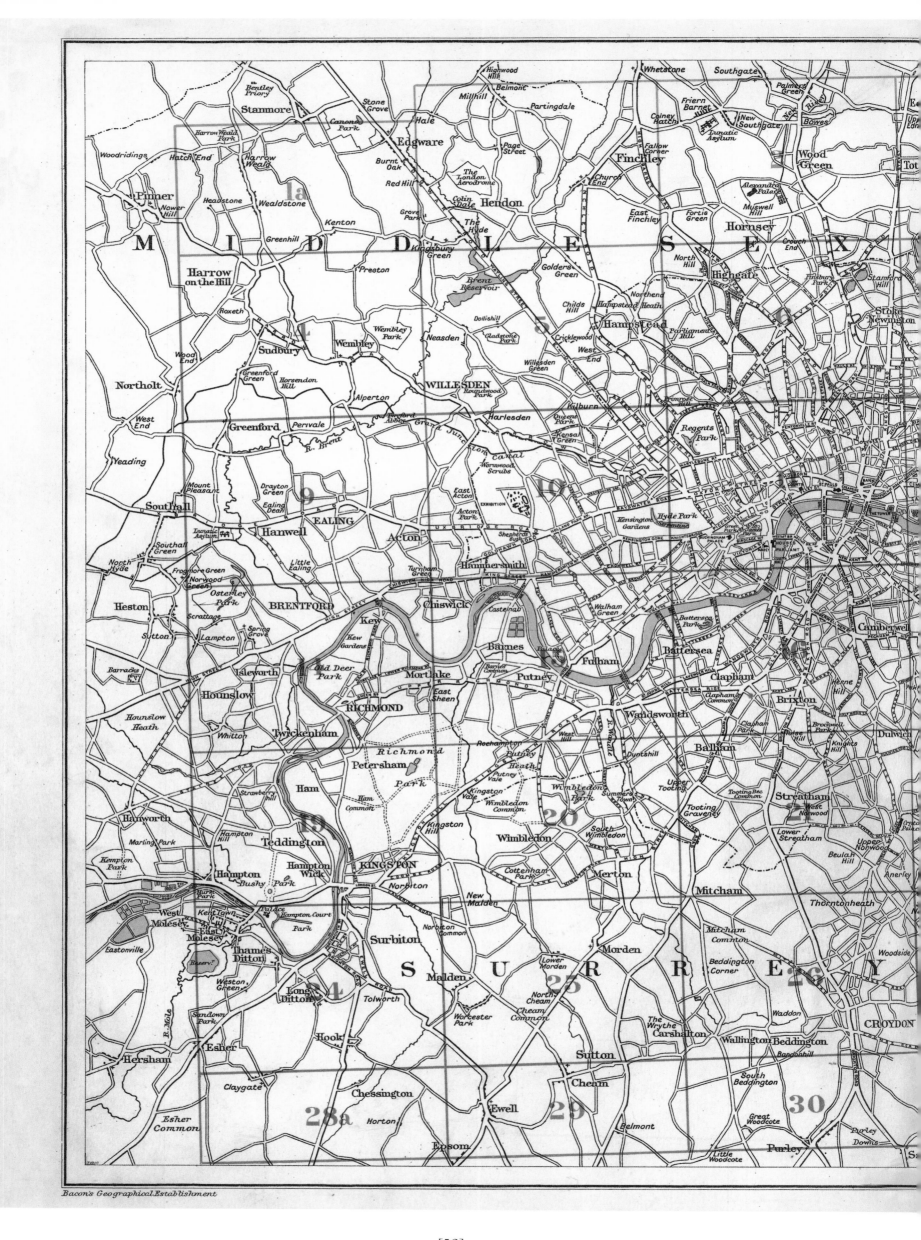

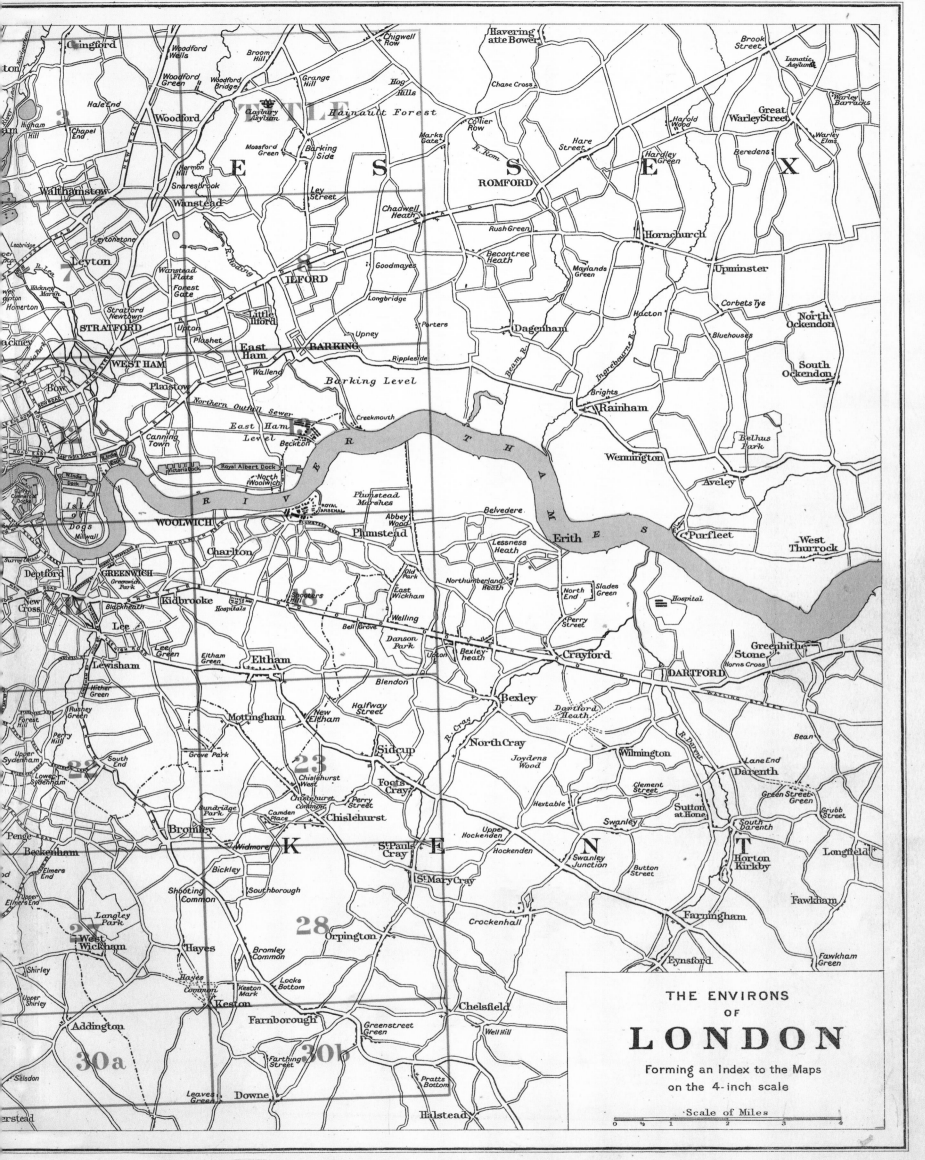

THE ENVIRONS

OF

LONDON

Forming an Index to the Maps
on the 4-inch scale

Scale of Miles

INDEX

TO

STREETS, ROADS, SQUARES, RAILWAY STATIONS, PUBLIC BUILDINGS, Etc.

EXPLANATION.—The figures given in the first column refer to the 4-inch to the mile sheets (Nos. 1 to 30b), the second column figures referring to the 9-inch to the mile sheet (Nos. 31 to 64). The letters and figures in the 3rd and 4th columns refer to the marginal letters and figures shown on the maps; thus, The Abbey, Westminster will be found on sheet 11 of the 4-inch maps and on sheet 53 of the 9-inch maps, in the square opposite the letter O, and under the figure 21.

ABBREVIATIONS.—Ch, church; com, common; cres, crescent; ct, court; gdns, gardens; gr, green; gro, grove; gt, great; ho, house; la, lane; lt, little; pk, park; pl, place; rd, road; sq, square; st, saint; st, street; sta, station; terr, terrace; thea, theatre.

[55]

	4-in. sht.	9-in. sht.	mar.
Artillery-passage, Bishopsg. E	—	46..L	26
,, place, Woolwich	18	—..P	37
,, row, Westminster SW	11	53..O	21
,, street, Bethnal Green	12	47..K	27
,, ,, Tooley-street SE	12	54..N	26
Arundel-gdns, Notting Hill W	10	50..M	15
,, pl, Coventry-st W	11	45..M	21
,, road, Croydon, Surrey	26	—..Z^4	24
,, ,, Ilford	8	—..F	42
,, ,, Stratford E	7	41..G	33
,, square, Barnsbury N	6	37..H	23
,, street, Strand WC	11	45..M	23
,, terrace, Barnes SW	15	58..P	13
Arundell-st, Coventry-st W	11	45..M	21
Ascalon-st, S. Lambeth SW	16	61..R	20
Ascham-st, Kentish Tn. NW	6	36..G	21
Ascot-road, Tottenham N	3	—..C	25
,, st, Canning Town E	12	49..L	33
Ascott avenue, Ealing W	9	—..N	7
Ash-grove, Cricklewood NW	5	—..G	14
,, ,, Hackney E	12	39..J	27
,, ,, Seven Kings, Es.	8	—..F	41
,, rd, Greenstreet Green	30*b*	—..Z^9	40
,, street, Walworth SE	11	54..O	24
Ashbourne, Chiswick W	15	—..P	11
,, gro, E. Dulw. SE	17	—..T	26
,, road, Lower Tooting	21	—..Z^1	19
Ashbridge-rd, Leytonstone E	7	—..D	33
Ashbrook-rd, Up. Holloway N	6	32..E	21
Ashburn-gdns, S. Kens. SW	11	51..O	17
,, pl, S. Kens. SW	10	57..O	17
Ashburnham-gro, Greenw. SE	17	63..R	31
,, road, Canning Town E	13	—..L	34
,, ,, Chelsea SW	15	51..Q	17
,, ,, Greenwich SE	17	63..R	31
,, ,, Kensal Rise NW	10	42..J	13
Ashburton-gro, Holloway N	6	37..G	23
,, rd, Croydon, Surrey	26	—..Z^6	26
Ashbury-road, Battersea SW	16	60..S	19
Ashby-rd, Brockley-rd SE	17	63..S	30
,, ,, Edmonton N	3	—..A	27
,, ,, Essex-road N	6	38..I	25
Ashchurch-gro, Shep. Bush W	10	—..N	12
,, Pk.-villas, Shep. Bu. W	10	—..N	12
,, rd, Croydon, Surrey	26	—..Z^4	26
,, terr, Shep. Bush W	10	50..N	12
Ashcombe-rd, Wimbledon SW	20	—..T	15
,, street, Fulham SW	15	59..S	16
Ashcroft-road, Grove-road E	12	48..K	29
Ashdown-road, Kingston	19	—..Z^1	7
,, st, Kentish Tn. NW	6	36..H	19
Ashen-gro, Wimbledon Pk, SW	20	—..W	15
Ashenden-road, Homerton E	7	40..G	29
Ashfield-la, Chislehurst, Kent	23	—..Z	39
,, road, Tottenham N	7	33..D	25
Ashford-avenue, Hornsey N	2	—..C	22
,, road, Cricklewood NW	5	—..G	14
,, ,, East Ham E	8	—..I	38
,, ,, Walthamstow E	3	—..C	30
,, street, Hoxton N	11	46..K	25
Ashgrove-road, Ilford	8	—..F	41
,, ,, Ravensbourne	22	—..Z^1	32
Ashlake-road, Streatham	21	—..X	21
Ashleigh-road, Mortlake SW	15	—..S	10
Ashley-gdns, Westminster SW	11	52..O	21
,, lane, Hendon NW	1	—..A	14
,, place, Victoria-st SW	11	52..O	20
,, road, Forest Gate E	8	—..I	36
,, ,, Hornsey Rise N	6	32..E	22
,, ,, S. Wimbled. SW	20	—..Y	16
,, ,, Th. Ditt., Surrey	24	—..Z^3	4
,, ,, Tottenham N	3	—..B	27
Ashling-rd, Croydon, Surrey	26	—..Z^5	26
Ashlone-road, Putney SW	15	59..S	13
Ashmead-rd, Deptford SE	17	63..S	30
Ashmill-st, Paddington NW	10	43..K	18
Ashmore-rd, St Peter's Pk. W	10	42..J	15
Ashmount-rd, Up. Hollow. N	6	32..E	21
,, ,, West Gr. N	3	—..C	26
Ashness-rd, Clap. Comm. SW	16	—..T	19
Ashtead-rd, Stamford Hill N	7	33..D	27
Ashton-road, Willesden NW	5	—..I	11
,, street, Poplar E	12	49..M	32
Ashurst-rd, New Southgate N	2	—..A	19
,, street, Battersea SW	16	51..Q	18
Ashville-rd, Leytonstone E	7	—..F	32
Ashwell-rd, Bethnal Green E	12	48..J	29
Ashworth-rd, Maida Vale W	10	43..K	16
Aske-street, Hoxton N	11	46..J	25
Askew-cres, Shep. Bush W	10	—..N	12
,, road, Shep. Bush W	10	—..N	12
,, street, Hackney E	7	39..I	28
Aslett-st, Wandsworth SW	15	—..U	16
Asman's-pl, Hampstead NW	1	—..C	16
Asmun's-hill, Hampstead NW	1	—..C	16
Aspenlea-rd, Hammersm. W	15	58..P	14
Aspinal-road, Brockley SE	4	63 S	29
Aspinden-rd, Rotherhithe SE	17	55..P	27
Asplin-road, Tottenham N	3	—..A	27
Assembly-pass, Mile End-rd E	—	47..L	28
Astbury-road, Peckham SE	17	63..R	28
Astey's-row, Islington N	6	38..I	24
Aston-road, Ealing W	9	—..L	7
,, ,, Raynes Park SW	20	—..Z^1	13
,, st, Limehouse Fields E	12	48..L	29
Astonville-st, Wandswo. SW	20	—..V	15
Asylum-road, Kingston	19	—..Z^1	8
,, ,, Peckham SE	17	55..Q	27
Atbara-road, Teddington	19	—..T	5
Atheldene-rd, Wandswo. SW	20	—..V	61
Athelstane-road, Bow E	12	48..J	30
,, ,, Finsbury Pk. N	6	32..F	23
Athenlay-rd, Peckham SE	17	—..U	28
Atherford-rd, Clapham SW	16	61..S	21
Atherton-rd, Forest Gate E	7	41..H	34
Athlone-road, Brixton SW	21	—..V	22
Athol-rd, Chadwell He., Ess.	8	—..E	42
,, street, Poplar E	12	49..M	32
Atkins-road, Balham SW	21	—..V	20
Atlanta-street, Fulham SW	15	58..Q	14
Atlantic-road, Brixton SW	16	61..T	23
Atley-rd, Old Ford-road E.	12	40..J	30

	4-in. sht.	9-in. sht.	mar.
Atney-road, Putney SW	15	59..S	14
Attenberg-avenue, Ealing W	9	—..N	5
Atterbury-st, Westmin. SW	16	53..P	21
Attneave-st, Clerkenwell WC	11	45..K	23
Atwell-road, Peckham SE	17	62..S	27
,, street, Peckham SE	17	62..S	27
Auberon-st, N. Woolwich E	13	—..N	37
Aubert-pk, Highbury Pk. N	6	38..G	24
Aubrey-rd, Crouch End N	2	—..C	22
,, ,, Kensington W	10	50..N	15
,, walk, Kensington W	10	50..N	15
Auburn-street, Woolwich	18	—..R	40
Aubury-rd, Walthamstow E	3	—..B	31
Auckland-hill, W. Norwood	21	—..X	24
,, road, Battersea SW	16	60..T	18
,, ,, Ilford, Essex	8	—..E	39
,, ,, Leyton E	7	41..F	31
,, ,, Roman-rd E	12	48..J	29
,, ,, Up. Norwood SE	22	—..Z^2	26
,, ,, ,, ,,	21	—..Z^2	25
,, street, Lambeth SE	16	53..P	22
Audley-gdns, Seven Kings, Es.	8	—..F	41
,, road, Hendon NW	5	—..D	13
,, sq, St Audley-st W	11	44..M	20
Augusta-street, Poplar E	12	48..M	31
Augustine-rd, W. Kens. W	10	50..O	14
Augustus-rd, Hammersm. W	10	50..N	13
,, ,, Wimbledon SW	20	—..V	14
,, st, Regent's Pk NW	11	44..J	20
Auley-st, Old Kent-rd SE	17	55..Q	26
Aurelia-rd, Croydon, Surrey	26	—..Z^4	22
Auriol-rd, W, Kensington W	10	58..O	14
Austin-road, Battersea SW	16	60..R	19
,, st, Hackney-road E	12	46..K	26
Austinfriars, Old Broad-st EC	11	46..L	25
Austin Friars-passage EC	—	46..L	25
,, ,, sq, O. Brd.-st EC	11	46..L	25
Austral-st, Southwark SE	11	53..O	23
Australian-av, Aldersg.-st EC	—	46..L	24
,, road, Chingford	3	—..A	33
Autumn-road, Old Ford E	12	48..J	31
Avalon-road, Fulham SW	15	59..R	16
Avarn-road, Tooting SW	20	—..Y	18
Avebury-road, Merton SW	20	—..Z	14
Aveley-rd, Up. Clapton E	7	33..F	28
Aveling Pk.-rd, Chapel End E	3	—..A	31
Ave Maria-la, Ludgate Hill EC	11	46..M	24
Avenell-rd, Highbury N	6	38..F	24
Avenue, The, Harrow, M'sex	1*a*	—..D	3
,, ,, Lee SE	18	—..U	34
,, ,, Norwood SE	21	—..Y	25
,, ,, Pinner M'sex	1*a*	—..A	1
,, ,, Wanstead	8	—..D	35
,, crescent, Acton W	9	—..N	9
,, gdns, Acton W	9	—..N	9
,, ,, East Sheen SW	15	—..T	10
,, ,, Wood Green N	2	—..A	22
,, road, Acton W	9	—..N	9
,, ,, Bow-road E	12	48..J	30
,, ,, Brentford, M'sex	14	—..P	6
,, ,, Camberwell SE	16	54..Q	24
,, ,, Canning Town E	13	—..L	34
,, ,, Carshalton	29	—..Z^9	19
,, ,, Carshalton, Sur.	30	—..Z^9	20
,, ,, Clapton E	7	39..G	27
,, ,, Drayton Gr. W	9	—..M	5
,, ,, Forest Gate E	8	—..G	35
,, ,, Hampton	19	—..Z	1
,, ,, Highgate N	6	32..D	21
,, ,, Kingston	19	—..Z^1	7
,, ,, Lewisham SE	17	64..T	31
,, ,, Stratford E	7	41..G	33
,, ,, New Southgate N	2	—..A	20
,, ,, Norwood SE	26	—..Z^2	26
,, ,, Penge SE	22	—..Z^2	28
,, ,, St John's Wd. NW	5	35..I	18
,, ,, Shep. Bush W	10	50..N	13
,, ,, Spring Grove	14	—..Q	3
,, ,, Teddington	19	—..Y	4
,, ,, Tottenham N	3	—..C	25
,, ,, Upton	18	—..T	43
,, ,, Woodside Pk N	1	—..A	17
,, Park-rd, Tulse Hill	21	—..W	23
,, terr, Forest Gate E	8	—..G	35
,, terr, New Malden	24	—..Z^2	9
Averhill-st, Fulham Pal.-rd W	15	58..Q	14
Avern-rd, W. Moulsey, Surrey	24	—..Z^2	1
Averons-road, Plaistow	13	—..L	34
Avery-hill, Kent	23	—..V	39
,, row, Grosvenor-st W	11	44..M	20
Avignon-rd, Brockley SE	4	63..S	29
Avon-rd, Walthamstow E	3	—..B	32
Avondale-av, W'dside Pk. N	1	—..A	17
Avondale-park, N. Kens. W	10	50..M	14
,, rd, Bromley-road	22	—..Z^1	33
,, ,, Canning Town E	12	49..L	33
,, ,, Croydon, Surrey	30	—..Z^9	24
,, ,, Finchley N	1	—..A	17
,, ,, Leyton-st E	7	—..E	30
,, ,, Mortlake SW	15	—..S	10
,, ,, Mottingham, Kent	23	—..W	36
,, ,, Peckham SE	17	62..S	26
,, ,, Wealdstone M'sex	1*a*	—..A	4
,, ,, Wood Green N	2	—..C	24
,, sq, Old Kent-rd SE	17	55..P	26
Avonley-road, Deptford SE	17	55..Q	28
Avonmore-rd, Hammer.-rd W	10	58..O	15
Avonmouth-st, Newington SE	11	54..O	24
Avonwick-rd, Hounslow	14	—..R	1
Awlfield-av, Tottenham N	2	—..A	25
Axe-street, Barking	13	—..J	39
Aybrook-st, Marylebone W	11	44..L	19
Aycliffe-rd, Shep. Bush W	10	50..M	12
Aylesbury-rd, Bromley, Kent	27	—..Z^2	33
,, st, Clerkenwell EC	11	46..K	23
,, ,, Kingsbury NW	5	—..F	10
,, ,, Walworth SE	17	54..P	25
Aylesford-st, Pimlico SW	16	53..P	21
Aylestone-av, Willesden NW	5	—..J	14
Aylett-rd, Isleworth	14	—..R	3
,, ,, S. Norwood SE	27	—..Z^3	27
Ayliffe-street, Newington SE	11	54..O	24

	4-in. sht.	9-in. sht.	mar.
Aylmer-rd, Shep. Bush W	10	—..N	11
Aylward-rd, Forest Hill SE	22	—..W	29
Aynhoe-rd, W. Kens. W	10	58..O	14
Aynscombe-la, Mortlake SW	14	—..S	9
Aytoun-road, Stockwell SW	16	61..S	22
Azenby-road, Peckham SE	17	62..S	26
Azof-street, Greenwich SE	17	57..P	33

B

	4-in. sht.	9-in. sht.	mar.
Baalbec-road, Highbury N	6	38..H	24
Babbacombe-rd, New Brom.	23	—..Z^1	34
Babington-rd, Hendon NW	1	—..B	13
,, ,, Streatham	21	—..Y	21
Back Ch.-la, Commercl.-rd E	12	47..M	27
,, com, Turnham Gr. W	10	—..O	10
,, hill, Leather-la, EC	11	45..K	23
,, lane, Barking	13	—..J	39
,, ,, Ham	19	—..W	6
,, river, Barking, Essex	8	—..I	38
,, rd, Walthamstow E	3	—..B	32
Baches-street, City-road N	11	46..K	25
Bacon-st, Bethnal Green E	12	47..K	26
Baden-road, Ilford	8	—..H	39
Badlis-rd, Walthamstow E	3	—..B	30
Badminton-road, Balham SW	16	—..U	19
Badsworth-rd, Camberwell SE	16	62..R	24
Baggally-st, Burdett-rd E	12	48..L	30
Bagley's-lane, Fulham SW	15	59..R	16
Bagshot-st, Walworth SE	17	54..P	25
Baildon-street, Deptford SE	4	—..R	30
Bailey-lane, Tottenham	7	—..D	26
Baillie's-walk, Ealing W	9	—..N	7
Bainbridge-st, N. Oxfd.-st WC	11	45..L	21
Baker st, Bethnal Green E	12	47..K	28
,, ,, Commercial-rd E	12	47..L	28
,, ,, Lloyd-square WC	11	45..K	23
,, ,, Brixton-rd SW	16	61..R	23
,, ,, Willesden NW	5	—..I	11
,, ,, W	11	44..L	19
,, ,, ry-sta, Bakerloo-R.	11	44..K	19
,, ,, sta, Met.-R.	11	44..K	19
Baker's-avenue, Leyton E	7	—..D	31
,, Co. Hall, Harp-la EC	—	46..M	25
,, lane, Ealing W	9	—..M	7
,, rents, Rotherhithe SE	12	—..N	29
,, rd, Up. Clapton E	7	33..E	28
,, row, West Ham E	12	41..J	33
Balaam-la, Sutton, Surrey	25	—..Z^6	15
,, street, Plaistow E	13	—..K	34
Balaclava-rd, Bermondsey SE	17	55..P	26
Balaklava-rd, Surbiton, Sur.	24	—..Z^4	5
Balcaskie-road, Eltham	18	—..U	37
Balchien-rd, E. Dulwich SE	17	—..U	27
Balcombe-st, Marylebone NW	11	44..K	18
Balcorne-street, Hackney E	7	39..I	28
Balderton-st, Oxford-st W	11	44..M	19
Baldoc-street, Bow E	12	48..J	31
Baldry-road, Streatham	21	—..Z^1	22
Baldwin-street, City-rd EC	11	46..K	25
Baldwin's-gdns, Gr. In.-rd WC	11	45..L	23
,, pl, Gray's Inn-rd WC	11	45..L	23
Baldwyn-gdns, Acton W	9	—..M	10
Bale-street, Stepney E	12	46..L	29
Balfern-st, Battersea SW	16	60..R	18
Balfour-place, Park-lane W	11	44..M	19
,, road, Acton W	9	—..L	10
,, ,, Bickley	28	—..Z^3	36
,, ,, Ealing W	9	—..N	5
,, ,, Highbury N	6	38..G	24
,, ,, Ilford, Essex	8	—..F	39
,, ,, Merton SW	20	—..Z	16
,, ,, Norwood SE	26	—..Z^3	26
,, ,, Oakleigh Pk N	2	—..A	19
Balgowan-rd, Bechenham, Kt	27	—..Z^2	29
,, street, Plumstead	18	—..P	41
Balham SW	21	—..V	19
,, grove, Balham SW	21	—..V	19
,, high-road, Balham	21	—..W	19
,, hill, Balham SW	16	—..U	20
,, New-rd, Balham	21	—..V	20
,, Park-rd, Balham	21	—..V	19
,, ry-sta, L.B. & S.C. R.	21	—..V	19
Baliol-road, Tottenham N	2	—..A	25
Ball-alley, Lombard-st EC	—	46..M	25
,, st, Kensington W	10	51..N	16
Ballance-rd, Hackney, Wick.	7	40..H	29
Ballantine-st, Wandsw. SW	15	60..T	16
Ballard-rd, Woodside Pk. N	1	—..A	17
Ballard's-lane, Finchley N	1	—..A	16
Ballater-road, Brixton SW	16	61..T	22
,, ,, Croydon, Sur.	30	—..Z^8	26
Ballina-street, Forest Hill	22	—..Y	29
Ballingdon-rd, Battersea SW	16	—..U	19
Balliol-rd, N. Kensington W	10	42..L	13
Balloch-road, Catford SE	22	—..W	32
Ball's Pond-rd, Islington N	7	38..H	26
Balmes-road, Hackney N	7	38..I	25
Balmoral-rd, Forest Ga. E	8	—..H	35
,, ,, Leyton E	7	—..F	31
,, ,, Willesd. Gr. NW	5	—..H	13
Balmore-st, Highgate N	6	—..F	20
Balmuir-road, Putney SW	15	59..T	13
Baltic-st, Golden-lane EC	11	46..K	24
,, yard, Rotherhithe SE	12	55..N	29
Balvernie-gro, Wandsw. SW	20	—..V	15
,, villas, Wimbdn. Pk. SW	20	—..V	15
Balzac-street, Clapham SW	16	61..S	21
Bamford-pl, Barking, Essex	8	—..I	39
Bampton-road, Forest Hill	22	—..W	28
Banbury-ct, Long Acre WC	—	45..M	22
,, road, Hackney E	7	40..I	29
,, st, Battersea SW	16	60..R	18
Bancroft-rd, Mile End-rd E	12	48..K	29
Bandonhill Surrey	30	—..Z^8	21
Bandon-ry-sta, L.B.&S.C.R.	30	—..Z^1	21
,, road, Bethnal Gr. E	12	47..J	28
,, road, Holloway N	6	37..H	22
Bangalore-street, Putney SW	15	59..I	13
Bangor-st, Notting Hill W	10	50..M	14

	4-in. sht.	9-in. sht.	mar.
Banister-street, Homerton E	7	39..H	28
Bank-lane, Norbiton	19	—..T	6
,, of England EC	11	46..M	25
,, railway station EC	11	46..M	25
Bankside, Southwark SE	11	46..M	24
Bankruptcy Ct., Portgl-st WC	11	45..M	23
Bankton-road, Brixton SW	16	61..T	23
Banner-street, St Luke's EC	11	46..K	24
Banning-st, E. Greenwich SE	17	57..P	33
Bannockburn-rd, Plumstead	18	—..P	40
Banstead Downs, Surrey	29	—..Z^{11}	15
,, rd, Purley, Surrey	30	—..Z^{11}	22
,, ,, Sutton, Surrey	29	—..Z^9	17
,, street, Peckham SE	17	63..S	27
Banyard-rd, Bermondsey SE	12	55..O	27
Bara-st, Cubitt Town E	17	57..P	32
Barandon-st, N. Kens. W	10	50..M	14
Barbara-street, Roman-rd N	6	37..H	23
Barbers' Co. Ha, M'kswl-st EC	—	46..L	24
Barbican EC	11	46..K	25
,, court EC	—	46..L	24
Barbot-st, Lr. Edmonton N	3	—..A	27
Barby-av, Hampstead NW	5	—..G	16
Barchard-st, Wandsworth SW	15	60..T	16
Barchester-street, Poplar E	12	48..L	31
Barclay-rd, Croydon, Surrey	26	—..Z^6	24
,, ,, Fulham SW	15	58..Q	15
,, ,, Leytonstone E	7	—..E	33
,, ,, Walthamstow E	3	—..C	32
,, st, Somer's Town NW	11	45..J	21
Barcombe-av, Streatham	21	—..W	22
Bardolph-road, Holloway N	6	37..G	22
Barfett-street, Maida Hill W	10	42..K	15
Barfield-road, Bickley	28	—..Z^2	37
Barforth-road, Peckham SE	17	62..T	27
Barge House-rd, N. Wool. E	13	—..P	38
,, yard, Bucklersbury, EC	—	46..M	25
Bargery-road, Catford SE	22	—..W	31
Barham-rd, Croydon, Surrey	30	—..Z^7	24
,, street, Bermondsey	11	—..N	26
Baring-road, Croydon	27	—..Z^5	27
,, ,, Lee SE	22	—..V	34
,, street, Islington N	7	38..I	25
Bark-place, Bayswater W	10	43..M	16
Barking-rd, Canning Town E	12	49..L	33
,, station, L.T. & S.R.	8	—..I	39
Barkston-gdns, Kens. SW	15	57..P	16
Barkworth-rd, Rotherhithe SE	17	55..P	27
Barlborough-st. Hatcham SE	17	55..Q	28
Barlby-rd, N. Kensington W	10	43..L	13
Barley-lane, Goodmayes, Es.	8	—..E	42
,, place, Cloth Fair EC	—	46..L	24
Barlow-street, Walworth SE	16	54..P	25
Barmeston-road, Catford SE	22	—..W	31
Barmouth-rd, Shirley, Surrey	27	—..Z^6	28
,, ,, Wandsworth SW	15	—..U	17
Barnado-st, Limehouse	12	47..M	28
Barnard-hill, Muswell Hill N	2	—..A	20
,, road, Battersea SW	16	60..T	18
Barnard's Inn, Holborn EC	—	45..L	23
Barnby-st, Somer's Town NW	11	45..J	21
Barnes-common, Barnes SW	15	—..S	12
,, sta, L. & S.W.R., SW	15	—..S	12
,, street, Ratcliff E	12	48..L	29
,, terrace, Barnes SW	15	—..R	11
,, ,, Deptford SE	17	56..P	30
,, Elms Park, Barnes SW	15	—..R	12
Barnet-gro, Bethnal Green E	12	47..J	27
,, road, Oakleigh Park N	2	—..A	20
,, Wd.-rd, Bromley, Kent	28	—..Z^6	35
Barnfield-rd, Castlebar Hill W	9	—..K	6
,, ,, Norwood	21	—..Y	25
,, ,, Plumstead	18	—..Q	38
Barnmead-road, Penge	22	—..Z^2	28
Barnsbury N	6	37..I	23
,, & Cal.-rd ry-sta, N.L. N	6	37..H	23
,, grove, Barnsbury N	6	37..H	23
,, park, Islington N	6	37..I	23
,, road, Islington N	11	37..J	23
,, square, Islington N	6	37..I	23
,, street, Islington N	6	38..I	23
,, terrace, Islington N	6	37..I	23
Barnsdale-rd, Maida Hill W	10	42..K	15
Barnsley-st, Bethnal Green E	12	47..K	27
Barnwell-road, Brixton SW	16	—..T	23
Barnwood-rd, Silvertown E	13	—..N	34
Baron-rd, Canning Town E	12	49..L	33
,, street, Pentonville-rd N	11	45..J	23
,, walk, Mitcham	26	—..Z^2	18
Baroness-rd, Hackney-rd, E	12	47..J	26
Baronet-road, Tottenham N	3	—..A	27
Baron's Ct.-rd, W. Kens. SW	15	58..P	14
,, ,, ry-sta, Picc. R.	15	58..P	14
Baronsfield-rd, Twickenham	14	—..U	5
Baronsmeade-rd, Barnes SW	15	—..Q	12
Baronsmere-rd, E. Finch. N	2	—..C	18
Barrard-rd, Victoria Dock E	13	—..M	34
Barratt-av, Wood Green N	2	—..A	22
Barrett-street, Oxford-st W	11	44..L	19
Barrett's-gro., Stoke New. N	7	38..G	26
Barrington-road, Hornsey N	2	—..C	21
,, ,, Manor Park E	8	—..H	38
,, ,, Stockwell SW	16	61..S	23
Barrow Hill-rd, Portl. T. NW	11	43..J	18
,, road, Streatham SW	21	—..Y	21
Barrowgate-road, Chiswick W	14	—..P	10
Barr's-road, Willesden NW	5	—..H	10
Barry-rd, E. Dulwich SE	17	—..U	26
,, ,, Willesden NW	5	—..I	10
Barsett-road, Peckham SE	17	63..S	28
Barston-road, West Dulwich	21	—..W	24
Barth-road, Plumstead	18	—..P	40
Bartholomew-close EC	11	46..L	24
,, ,, W. Smithfield EC	11	46..L	24
,, lane, Lothbury EC	11	46..L	25
,, place, Kinghorn-st EC	—	46..L	24
,, rd, Kentish Town NW	6	36..H	20
,, square, St Luke's EC	11	46..K	24
,, villas, Kentish Tn. NW	6	36..H	20
Bartle-avenue, East Ham E	13	—..J	37
Bartlett's-bldgs, Holborn EC	—	45..L	23
,, passage, Fetter-lane EC	—	45..L	23

4-*in.* 9-*in.*
sht. *sht.* *mar.*
Bartley-street, Brixton SW 16 —..U 22
Barton-st, W. Kens. SW . 15 58..P 14
,, ,, Westminster SW 11 53..O 21
Bartram-road, Brockley SE 17 —..U 29
Bartripp-street, Homerton E 7 40..H 29
Barwick-rd, Forest Gate E . 8 —..G 35
Basil-street, Chelsea SW . 11 52..O 19
Basildon-road, Plumstead . 18 —..P 42
Basing-rd, Notting Hill W . 10 42..L 15
,, ,, Peckham SE . 17 62..R 26
Basinghall-avenue EC . . 11 46..L 25
,, street, London Wall EC 11 46..L 25
Baskerville-rd, Wandswo. SW 16 —..U 18
Basnet-rd, Lavender Hill SW 16 60..S 19
Bassano-st, E. Dulwich SE 16 —..T 26
Bassant-road, Plumstead . 18 —..Q 40
Bassein Pk.-rd, Shep. Bush. W 10 —..N 12
Bassett-rd, N. Kensington W 10 42..L 14
,, st, Kentish Town NW 6 36..H 19
Bassingham-rd, Wandswo. SW 15 —..U 17
Basterfield-st Finsbury EC 11 46..K 24
Bastion-road, Plumstead . 18 —..Q 44
Bastwick-st, Goswell-rd EC 11 46..K 24
Basuto-road, Fulham SW 15 59..R 15
Batavia-rd, New Cross SE . 17 63..R 29
Bateman-rd, Chingford-rd E 3 —..A 31
,, street, Soho W . . 11 45..M 21
Bateman's-row, H.-st, Sho. E 12 46..K 26
Bath-place, Camberwell SE 17 54..Q 25
,, rd, Chiswick W . 10 —..O 11
,, ,, Mitcham, Surrey 25 —..Z^2 17
,, ,, Stratford E . 7 41..I 33
,, ,, ry-sta, N.&S.W. 10 —..O 11
,, street, City-road EC . 11 46..K 25
,, ,, Poplar, E . . 12 49..M 31
,, ,, Whitechapel E . 12 47..L 27
,, terrace, Newington SE 11 54..O 24
Bathgate-rd, Wimbledon Pk 29 —..W 14
Bathurst-gdns, Ken. Rise NW 10 42..J 13
,, road, Ilford, Essex . 8 —..F 39
,, st, Sussex-sq W . . 11 43..M 17
Batoum-gdns, Hammersm. W 10 50..O 13
Batsford-road, Lewisham SE 17 63..S 31
Battenberg-rd, Richmond . 14 —..R 8
Battersea Bge, Battersea SW 16 51..Q 18
,, ,, rd, Battersea SW 16 60..R 18
,, Cem., Battersea SW . 16 60..T 18
,, New Cem., Mord. Surr. 25 —..Z^4 12
,, Park SW . . . 16 52..Q 19
,, ,, pier . . . 16 52..Q 19
,, ,, rd, Battersea SW 16 60..R 19
,, ,, ry-sta, B'sea SW 16 52..Q 20
,, ,, ry-st, S.E. & C.R. SW 16 61..R 20
,, Rise, Battersea SW . 16 60..T 18
,, ry-sta, Battersea SW 16 60..R 17
Battle Br.-la, Tooley-st SE — 54..N 25
,, ,, rd, King's Cross N 11 54..J 22
Battledean-rd, Highbury N 6 38..G 24
Batty-st, Commercial-rd E 12 47..M 27
Bavant-road, Norbury . 21 —..Z^2 22
,, ,, Denmark Hill SE 16 62..S 24
Bawdale-rd, E. Dulwich SE 17 —..U 26
Bawtree-road, Deptford SE 17 56..Q 29
Baxendale-st, Bethnal Gr. E 12 47..J 27
Baxter-road, Acton NW . 10 —..K 11
,, ,, Canning Town E . 13 —..M 36
,, ,, Edmonton N . 3 —..A 27
,, ,, Essex-road N . 7 38..H 25
,, ,, Ilford . . 8 —..H 39
,, ,, Plaistow E . 13 —..L 35
Bay-street, Dalston E . 7 39..I 26
Bayer-street, Finsbury EC . 11 46..K 24
Bayford-rd, Kensal Gr. NW 10 42..J 14
Bayham-pl, Camden T. NW 6 36..J 21
,, road, Bedford Park W 10 —..N 10
,, st, Camden Town NW 6 36..I 20
Bayley-st, Tott. Court-rd WC 11 45..L 21
Baylin-rd, Wandsworth SW 15 —..U 16
Bayonne-rd, Hammersm. W 15 58..P 14
Bayston-rd, Sto. Newing. N 7 39..F 26
Bayswater-hill, Bays.-rd W 10 43..M 16
,, road W . . . . 10 43..M 17
,, station, Bayswater W 10 43..M 16
,, ter, Bayswater-rd W . 10 43..M 17
Baythorne-st, Stepney E . 12 48..L 30
Bazon-street, Lambeth SE . 11 45..N 23
Beach-rd, Norbury, Surrey 26 —..Z^2 22
Beachcroft-rd, Leytonstone E 7 —..F 33
Beachy-road, Poplar E . 7 40..I 30
Beacon-hill, Islington N . 6 37..G 22
,, road, Lewisham SE . 17 —..U 32
Beaconsfield-rd, Bick. Kent 28 —..Z^2 36
,, rd, Canning Town E . 12 49..K 33
,, ,, Claygate, Surrey 28*a* —..Z^4 3
,, ,, Croydon, Surrey 26 —..Z^8 24
,, ,, Ealing W . . 9 —..N 6
,, ,, E. Greenwich SE 17 —..Q 34
,, ,, Edmonton N . 3 —..A 27
,, ,, Leyton E . . 7 —..F 32
,, ,, New Malden SW 20 —..Z^1 10
,, ,, New Southgate N 2 —..A 20
,, ,, No. Woolwich E 13 —..M 38
,, ,, South Acton W 9 —..O 10
,, ,, Surbiton, Surrey 24 —..Z^4 7
,, ,, Tottenham N . 3 —..C 26
,, ,, Twickenham . 14 —..U 5
,, ,, Walthamstow E 7 —..D 30
,, ,, Willesden NW . 5 34..H 12
Beacontree-av, Forest-rd, E 3 —..A 33
,, rd, Leytonstone E . 7 —..E 34
Beadnell-rd, Forest Hill SE . 22 —..V 28
Beadon-rd, Hammersmith W 10 58..O 13
Beak-street, Golden-sq W . 11 44..M 21
Beal-road, Ilford, Essex . 8 —..F 38
Beale-rd, Old Ford-rd E . 12 40..J 30
,, street, Plaistow E . 13 —..J 34
Bean-road, Welling . . 18 —..U 43
Bear-alley, Farringdon-st EC — 46..L 23
,, lane, Southwk.-st SE . — 46..N 24
,, street, Leicester-sq WC 11 45..M 21
Bearfield-rd, Kingston . 19 —..Z 7
Bearwick-rd, Vic. Docks E 13 —..M 35

4-*in.* 9-*in.*
sht. *sht.* *mar.*
Beatrice-av, Norbury, Surrey 26 —..Z^2 22
,, rd, Bermondsey SE . 17 55..P 27
,, ,, Finsbury Pk N . 6 32..D 23
Beatson-st, Rotherhithe SE 12 —..N 29
Beaucham-rd, W. Moul. Sur. 24 —..Z^2 1
Beauchamp-pl, Bromp.-rd SW 11 52..O 18
,, road, Clapham SW . 16 61..T 18
,, ,, Lav. H. SW. . 16 60..T 18
,, ,, Sutton, Sur. . 29 —..Z^7 15
,, ,, Thornton Heath 21 —..Z^2 24
,, ,, Twickenham . 14 —..U 4
,, ,, Upton E . 8 —..I 35
Beauford-rd, Surbiton, Sur. 24 —..Z^2 6
Beaufort-gdns, Bromp.-rd SW 11 52..O 18
,, rd, Tottenham N . 2 —..C 24
,, street, Chelsea SW . 16 51..Q 17
Beaufoy-rd, Battersea SW . 16 60..S 19
,, ,, Tottenham N . 3 —..A 26
Beaumont-av, Wembley . 4 —..G 6
,, road, Acton W . . 9 —..N 10
,, ,, Hornsey Rise N 6 32..E 22
,, ,, Leyton E . . 7 —..E 31
,, ,, Plaistow E . 13 —..K 35
,, ,, Richmond . 14 —..S 7
,, ,, Southfields . 20 —..V 14
,, ,, W. Kensington W 15 58..P 15
,, square, Mile End E . 12 47..L 28
,, st, Marylebone W . 11 44..K 19
,, ,, Mile End-rd E . 12 47..L 28
Beauval-rd, E. Dulwich SE . 17 —..U 26
Beaverswood-road, Perry-st 23 —..Z 40
Beavor-la, Hammersmith W 15 58..P 12
Beblets, Kent . . . 30*b* —..Z^9 40
Beccles-street, Limehouse E 12 48..M 30
Bechworth-road, Ilford . 8 —..F 40
Beck-rd, Hackney E . . 7 39..I 27
,, ,, West Ham E . 12 41..J 32
Beckenham, Kent . . 22 —..Z^2 30
,, gr, Bromley, Kent . 27 —..Z^2 32
,, Hill-sta, S.E.R. . 22 —..Y 31
,, lane, Beckenham . 22 —..Y 31
,, ,, Bromley . . 22 —..Z^2 33
,, place, Beckenham . 22 —..Z^1 31
,, ,, park, ,, . 22 —..Q^1 31
,, ry-sta, S.E. & C.R. . 22 —..Z^2 30
,, road, Penge SE . . 22 —..Q^1 28
,, ,, W. Wickham . 27 —..Z^5 31
Beckett-av, East Ham E . 13 —..K 38
,, street, Camberwell SE 16 54..Q 24
Beckford-rd, Croydon, Surrey 26 —..Z^4 26
Becklow-rd, Shep. Bush W . 10 —..N 11
Beckton, N. Woolwich E . 13 —..M 39
,, rd, Canning Town E . 13 —..L 34
,, ry-sta, Beckton E . 13 —..L 39
Beckway-st, Walworth SE . 17 54..P 25
Beckwith-rd, Herne Hill SE 16 —..U 25
Becmead-avenue, Streatham 21 —..X 21
Becondale-rd, Up. Norwood 21 —..Y 25
Bective-road, Forest Ga. E . 8 —..G 34
,, ,, Putney SW . 15 59..T 15
Beddington, Surrey . . 26 —..Z^6 21
,, Corner, Surrey . 26 —..Z^4 19
,, gdns, Wallingt., Surrey 30 —..Z^8 19
,, gro, Carshalton, Surrey 30 —..Z^8 21
,, la, Beddington, Surrey 26 —..Z^5 21
,, park, Surrey . . 26 —..Z^6 20
,, ry-sta, Surrey . . 26 —..Z^4 20
,, rd, Golder's Gr NW . 1 —..C 15
Beddome-st, Walworth SE . 16 54..P 24
Bedford-av, Tott.ct-rd WC — 45..L 21
,, court, New North-st WC — 45..L 22
,, gdns, Kensington W . 10 50..N 16
,, hill, Balham . . 21 —..Y 19
,, ,, Tooting Common 21 —..W 20
,, park, Croydon, Surrey 26 —..Z^5 24
,, ,, Chiswick W . 10 —..O 10
,, place, Blackheath SE 18 —..R 34
,, ,, Russell-sq WC . 11 45..L 22
,, rd, Chiswick W . 10 —..O 10
,, ,, Clapham SW . 16 61..S 21
,, ,, Ealing Dean W . 9 —..M 5
,, ,, East Finchley N . 2 —..B 18
,, ,, Harrow, M'sex . 1*a* —..C 3
,, ,, Hornsey N . . 6 32..D 21
,, ,, Ilford, Essex . 8 —..G 39
,, ,, Sidcup . . 23 —..X 40
,, ,, Tottenham N . 3 —..C 25
,, ,, Twickenham . 19 —..W 2
,, ,, Walthamstow E . 3 —..B 31
,, row, Holborn WC . 11 45..L 22
,, ,, Streatham . . 21 —..X 21
,, sq, Bloomsbury WC 11 45..L 21
,, street, Poplar, E . 12 49..M 32
,, ,, Strand WC . 11 45..M 22
,, ,, Walworth SE . 17 54..P 25
,, ,, Whitechapel, E 12 47..L 48
,, terrace, Holloway N . 6 32..F 23
Bedfordbury, Chandos-st WC 11 45..M 22
Bedwardine-rd, Up. Norwood 21 —..Z^1 25
Beech-av, Purley, Surrey . 30 —..Z^{10} 24
,, grove, New Malden . 24 21..Z^1 10
,, rd, Chelsfield, Kent . 30*b* —..Z^9 41
,, ,, New Southgate N . 2 —..A 22
,, street, Barbican EC . 11 46..L 24
,, ,, South Lambeth SW 16 53..Q 22
Beechcroft-av, Gold. Gr. NW 5 —..D 15
,, rd, Upper Tooting SW 20 —..W 18
Beechdale-rd, Brixton SW . 16 —..U 22
Beeches, Carshalton, Surrey 29 —..Z^8 18
Beechfield-rd, Catford SE . 22 —..W 30
,, ,, Tottenham N 7 33..D 25
Beech Hall-rd, Hale End E . 3 —..A 32
Beechhill-road, Eltham . 18 —..U 37
Beech Ho.-rd, Croydon, Sur. 26 —..Z^6 24
Beechmore-rd, Battersea SW 16 60..R 19
Beechnut Tr.-rd, Carsh., Sur. 29 —..Z^9 18
Beecholme-rd, Up. Clapton E 7 39..F 28
Beechwood-avenue, Kew . 14 —..P 8
,, rd, Croydon, Surrey . 30 —..Z^{10} 25
,, ,, Hornsey N . . 2 —..B 22
Beecroft-road, Brockley SE . 17 —..T 29
Beer-la, Gt. Tower-st EC . 12 46..M 26

4-*in.* 9-*in.*
sht. *sht.* *mar.*
Beethoven-st, Kilburn NW . 10 42..J 15
Beira-road, Balham SW . 16 —..U 20
Belfast-rd, S. Norwood SE . 27 —..Z^3 27
,, ,, Stamford Hill N 7 33..F 26
Belgrade-road, Hampton . 19 —..Z 1
Belgrave-dock, Pimlico SW . 16 52..P 20
,, Ms., Belgrave-sq SW . 11 52..O 19
,, M., Belgrave-sq SW . 11 52..N 19
,, pl, Belgrave sq SW . 11 52..O 19
,, rd, Ilford, Essex . 8 —..F 38
,, ,, Leyton E . . 7 —..E 32
,, ,, Norwood SE . 26 —..Z^3 26
,, ,, Pimlico SW . . 16 52..P 20
,, ,, Plaistow E . . 13 —..K 35
,, ,, St John's Wd. NW 5 35..I 17
,, ,, Walthamstow E . 7 —..D 31
,, ,, Wanstead E . 8 —..F 34
,, sq, SW . . . 11 52..O 19
,, st, Belgrave-sq SW . 11 52..O 19
,, ,, Commercial-rd E . 12 —..M 29
,, ,, King's Cross WC . 11 45..J 22
,, walk, Mitcham, Surrey 25 —..Z^2 17
Belham-st, Camberwell SE . 16 62..R 25
Belitha-villas, Islington N . 6 37..I 23
Bell-court, Cornhill EC . — 46..M 25
,, ,, Gray's Inn-rd WC — 45..L 23
,, green, Sydenham SE . 22 —..X 29
,, grove, Welling . . 18 —..S 41
,, lane, Hendon . . 1 —..C 14
,, ,, Spitalfields E . — 46..L 26
,, rd, Hounslow . . 14 —..S 1
,, ,, W. Moulsey, Surrey 24 —..Z^2 2
,, street, Edgware-rd . 11 43..L 18
,, yard, Carey-street WC — 45..L 23
,, ,, Carter-lane EC . — 46..M 24
,, ,, Gracech.st EC . — 46..M 25
,, ,, Strand WC . . 11 45..L 23
,, Gdn-rd, Peckham SE . 17 62..R 27
Bellamy-street, Balham . 21 —..V 19
Bellasis-avenue, Streatham 21 —..W 21
Bell-brook-rd, Gold. Gr. NW 1 —..C 15
Belle Grove-road, Welling . 18 —..S 41
Bellefield-rd, Stockwell SW . 16 61..S 22
Bellenden-road, Peckham SE 17 62..S 26
Belleville-rd, Wandsw. C. SW 16 —..U 18
Bellevue-pk, Thornt. H., Sur. 26 —..Z^2 24
,, road, Barnes SW . 15 —..R 12
,, ,, Castlebar H. W 9 —..K 5
,, ,, Chapel End E . 3 —..A 32
,, ,, Hendon NW . 1 —..C 14
,, ,, N. Southgate N 2 —..A 20
,, ,, Norbiton, Sur. 24 —..Z^2 7
,, ,, Wandsw. Co. SW 20 —..V 18
Bellew-street, Tooting SW . 20 —..X 17
Bellhaven-st, Grove-rd, E . 12 48..K 29
Bellingham-rd, Brom.-rd SE 22 —..X 31
,, sta, S.E. & C.R. . 22 —..X 31
Bellot-st, E. Greenwich SE . 17 57..P 33
Bellwood-rd, Peckham SE . 17 63..T 28
Belmont, Sutton, Surrey . 29 —..Z^{10} 16
Belmont-av, Raynes Park . 25 —..Z^2 12
,, ,, West Green N 2 —..B 24
,, gr, Chiswick W . . 10 —..O 10
,, gro, Lee SE . . 17 64..S 32
,, hill, Lee SE . . 17 64..T 32
,, la, Chislehurst, Kent . 23 —..Y 38
,, ,, Chiswick W . . 9 —..O 10
,, park, Lee SE . . 17 64..T 32
,, ,, rd, Leyton E . 7 —..D 31
,, road, Beckenham, Kent 27 —..Z^2 29
,, ,, Belmont . . 29 —..Z^{10} 15
,, ,, Canning Town E . 12 49..K 33
,, ,, Clapham SW . 16 61..S 21
,, ,, Ilford, Essex . 8 —..G 39
,, ,, Lewisham SE . 17 64..S 32
,, ,, Palmer's Green N . 2 —..A 22
,, ,, S. Norwood SE . 27 —..Z^4 27
,, ,, Tottenham N . 2 —..B 24
,, ,, Twickenham . 19 —..V 2
,, ,, Wallington, Surrey 30 —..Z^8 20
,, sta, L.B.S.C. R. . 29 —..Z^{10} 15
,, st, Kentish Town NW . 6 36..H 19
Belmore-st, S. Lambeth SW 16 61..R 21
Belshaw-st, Homerton E . 7 40..H 29
Belsize-av, Bowes Park N . 2 —..A 23
,, ,, Ealing W . 9 —..N 5
,, ,, Hampstead NW 5 35..H 18
,, cres, Hampstead NW . 5 35..H 18
,, gro, Hampstead NW . 6 36..H 18
,, lane, Hampstead NW . 5 35..H 18
,, park, Hampstead NW 5 35..H 18
,, ,, gdns, Hamp. NW 5 36..H 18
,, ,, sta, Hamp. Tu. R. 5 36..H 18
,, road, Kilburn NW . 5 35..I 16
,, sq, Hampstead NW . 5 35..H 18
,, terr, Hampstead NW . 5 35..H 18
Belton-rd, Forest Gate E . 8 —..I 35
,, ,, Leytonstone E . 7 41..G 33
,, ,, Tottenham N . 3 —..B 26
,, ,, Willesden Gr. NW 5 34..H 12
Beltran-road, Fulham SW . 15 59..R 16
Belvedere-cres, Lambeth SE 11 53..N 22
,, drive, Wimbledon SW 20 —..T 14
,, grove, Wimbledon SW 20 —..T 14
,, road, Lambeth SE . 11 53..N 22
,, ,, Up. Norwood SE 22 —..Z^1 26
,, ,, Wimbledon SW . 20 —..T 14
Belvoir-rd, E., Dulwich SE . 22 —..V 27
Bemerton-st, Islington N . 6 37..I 22
Bemish-road, Putney SW . 15 59..S 14
Bemsted-rd, Walthamstow E 3 —..B 30
Benares-road, Plumstead . 18 —..P 41
Benbow-rd, Hammersmith W 10 50..O 13
Benceo-street, Plaistow E . 13 —..M 34
Bendall-street, Lisson Gr. NW 11 43..L 18
Bendmeer-road, Putney SW 15 59 S 13
Bendon Valley, Wandsw. SW 20 —..V 16
Benedict-rd, Mitcham, Surrey 25 —..Z^2 17
,, ,, Stockwell SW . 16 61..S 22
Benfield-street, Battersea SW 15 60..S 17
Bengal-court, Birchin-la EC — 46..M 25
,, road, Ilford, Essex 8 —..G 38

4-*in.* 9-*in.*
sht. *sht.* *mar.*
Bengeworth-rd, Camberw. SE 16 62..S 24
Benhill-avenue, Sutton . 29 —..Z^7 16
,, road, Peckham SE . 16 62..R 25
,, ,, Sutton, Surrey . 29 —..Z^7 17
,, ,, ,, ,, 25 —..Z^6 17
,, street, Sutton, Surrey 29 —..Z^7 16
,, Wood rd, Sutt., Surrey 25 —..Z^6 16
Benin-street, Lewisham SE . 22 —..V 32
Benington-rd, Tottenham N 2 —..A 25
Benjamin-st, Clerkenwell EC 11 46..L 24
Ben Jonson-rd, Stepney E . 12 48..L 29
Benledi-street, Poplar E . 12 49..M 32
Benndish-rd, East Ham E. . 8 —..I 37
Bennerley-rd, Battersea SW 16 60..T 18
Bennett's-hill, Qu. Vict.-st EC 11 46..M 24
,, park, Blackheath SE . 17 64..S 33
,, street, Blackfriars-rd SE 11 46..N 23
,, ,, Chiswick W . 15 —..P 11
,, ,, Lewisham SE . 17 63..R 31
,, ,, St James' SW . 11 44..N 20
Bennett's Cas.-la, Goodm. Es. 8 —..F 43
Bensham-gr, Thornton Hea. 21 —..Z^2 24
,, lane, Croydon, Surrey 26 —..Z^3 23
,, Manor-rd, Croy., Surrey 26 —..Z^3 24
Benson-av, East Ham E . 13 —..K 36
,, road, Croydon, Surrey 26 —..Z^6 23
,, ,, Forest Hill SE . 22 —..V 28
Bentinck-st, Welbeck-st W . 11 44..L 20
,, terr, Regent's Pk NW 11 36..J 18
Benthall-rd, Stoke Ne. . 7 33..F 27
Bentham-rd, Hackney E . 7 40..H 29
Benton-rd, Ilford, Essex . 8 —..E 40
Benwell-rd, Holloway N . 6 37..G 23
Benworth-street, Bow E . 12 48..K 30
Benyon-rd, Southgate-rd N . 7 38..I 25
,, street, Fulham SW . 15 58..Q 14
Berber-rd, New Wandsw. SW 16 —..T 19
Bere-street, Limehouse E . 12 48..M 29
Berens-rd, Kensal Green NW 10 42..J 14
Beresford-rd, East Finchley N 2 —..B 18
,, ,, Harrow, M'sex . 1*a* —..C 3
,, ,, Highbury N . 7 38..H 25
,, ,, Hornsey N . 2 —..C 23
,, ,, New Malden . 24 —..Z^2 9
,, ,, Norbiton . . 19 —..Z 7
,, ,, Walthamstow E . 3 —..A 31
,, sq, Woolwich . . 18 —..P 38
,, street, Camberwell SE 16 54..Q 24
,, ,, Woolwich . 13 —..O 38
Bereta-rd, New Eltham, Kent 23 —..W 38
Berge-yd, Bucklersbury EC 11 46..M 25
Berger-rd, Homerton E . 7 40..H 29
Bergholt-cr, Stamford Hill N 7 33..D 25
Berkeley-ct, Clerkenwell EC — 46..L 24
,, gdns, Kensington W . 10 43..N 16
,, place, Wimbledon SW 20 —..Z 13
,, road, Crouch End N . 6 32..D 22
,, square W . . . 11 44..M 20
,, street, Clerkenwell EC 11 46..L 24
,, ,, Piccadilly W . 11 44..M 20
Berkhampsted-av, Wembley 4 —..H 8
Berkley-road, East Ham E . 8 —..H 37
Berkshire-road, Hackney E . 7 40..H 30
Berlin-road, Catford SE . 22 —..V 31
Bermondsey SE . . . 12 54..O 25
,, sq, Bermondsey SE . 12 54..O 25
,, st, Bermondsey SE . 12 54..N 25
,, wall, Bermondsey SE . 12 55..N 27
Bernard-avenue, Ealing W . 9 —..N 5
,, gdns, Wimbledon SW . 20 —..T 15
,, road, Carshalton, Surrey 30 —..Z^7 19
,, ,, Tottenham N . 3 —..C 26
,, street, Woburn-pl WC 11 45..K 22
Bernards-road, East Ham . 13 —..J 36
Berner-st, Commercial-rd E 12 47..M 27
Berners-mews, Berners-st W — 45..L 21
,, pl, Oxford-st . . — 45..L 21
,, road, Wood Green N . 2 —..A 23
,, street, Oxford-st W . 11 44..L 21
Berridge-rd, Up. Norwood . 21 —..Y 25
Berry-street, Clerkenwell EC 11 46..K 24
,, ,, Harlesden NW . 5 —..H 11
Berrylands, Surbiton, Surrey 24 —..Z^3 7
,, avenue, Surbiton . 24 —..Z^3 7
,, road, Surbiton, Surrey 24 —..Z^3 7
Berrymead-gdns, Acton W . 9 —..N 9
,, road, Acton W . . 9 —..N 10
Bert-road, Croydon, Surrey 26 —..Z^3 24
Bertal-road, Tooting SW . 20 —..X 17
Berthon-street, Deptford SE 17 56..Q 30
Bertie-rd, Willesden NW . 5 34..H 12
Bertram-road, Hendon NW 5 —..D 12
,, st, Highgate N . . 6 —..F 20
Berwick-road, Plaistow E . 13 —..M 35
,, ,, Walthamstow E 3 —..C 30
,, ,, Wood Green N . 2 —..A 24
,, street, Oxford-st W 11 45..L 21
,, ,, Pimlico SW . 11 52..O 20
Beryl-rd, Hammersmith W . 15 58..P 13
Besley-street, Streatham . 21 —..Z^1 20
Bessborough-gdns, Pimli. SW 16 53..P 21
,, place, Pimlico SW . 16 53..P 21
,, road, Harrow, M'sex. 1*a* —..D 3
,, ,, Little Ilford . 8 —..G 38
,, ,, Putney SW . 20 —..V 12
,, street, Pimlico SW . 16 53..P 21
Bessemer-rd, Denmark Hi. SE 16 62..S 24
Besson-street, New Cross SE 17 63..R 28
Bestwood-st, Deptford SE . 17 56..P 29
Beta-road, Croydon . . 27 —..Z^5 26
Bethel-road, Welling . 18 —..T 43
Bethell-avenue, Ilford . 8 —..E 38
,, ,, Plaistow E . 12 49..K 34
Bethlem Hos., Lambeth-rd SE 11 53..O 23
Bethnal Gr. Junc, G.E.R. 12 47..K 27
,, ,, Mus. Camb.-rd E 12 47..K 28
,, ,, road E . . 12 46..K 26
Bethune-av, Friern Barnet N 2 —..A 19
,, road, Acton NW . 10 —..K 10
,, ,, Stoke Newing. N 7 33..E 25
Betstile-rd, New Southgate N 2 —..A 20
Betterton-st, Drury-lane WC 11 45..L 22

	4-in. sht.	9-in. sht.	mar.
Bettisfield-rd, Charlton	18	—..P	35
Bettridge-rd, Fulham SW	15	59..R	15
Betts-street, Stepney E	12	47..M	27
Beulah-gro, Croydon, Surrey	26	—..Z^4	24
,, hill, Upper Norwood	21	—..Z^2	25
,, road, Leytonstone E	7	—..F	33
,, ,, Merton SW	20	—..Z	15
,, ,, Sutton, Surrey	29	—..Z^7	15
,, ,, Thorn. Hea, Sur.	26	—..Z^2	24
,, ,, E.,Thor.Hea.,Sur.	26	—..Z^2	24
,, ,, Walthamstow E	3	—..C	31
Bevan-st, Islington N	11	38..J	24
Bevenden st, Hoxton N	11	46..J	25
Beverley-gdns, Gold. Gr. NW	5	—..D	15
,, road, Anerley SE	22	—..Z^2	27
,, ,, Barnes SW	15	—..S	11
,, ,, Chiswick W	15	—..P	11
,, ,, New Malden	25	—..Z^2	11
,, ,, Wealdstone	1a	—..A	3
Beversbrook-rd, Up.Hollo.N	6	37..F	21
Beverstone-rd, Croydon,Sur.	26	—..Z^3	23
Bevington-rd, Beckenham	22	—..Z^2	30
,, ,, Notting Hill W	10	42..L	15
Bevis-marks, Houndsditch EC	12	46..L	26
Bexley-road, Eltham.	18	—..U	39
Bianca-road, Peckham SE	17	54..Q	26
,, ,, Peckham SE	17	55..Q	26
Bibbsworth-rd,Church End N	1	—..A	15
Bicester-road, Richmond	14	—..S	8
Bickersteth-rd,Toot.Grave.SW	20	—..Y	18
Bickerton-rd, Up. Hollow. N	6	32..F	21
Bickley, Kent	23	—..Z^1	36
,, crescent, Bickley	28	—..Z^3	36
,, park, Kent	23	—..Z^1	36
,, ,, rd, Bickley,Kent	28	—..Z^2	36
,, road, Bickley	28	—..Z^2	36
,, road, Leyton E	7	—..D	31
,, st,Tooting, Graveney SW	20	—..T	18
Bidborough-st, Euston-rd WC	11	45..K	22
Bidder-st, Canning Town E	12	49..L	33
Biddulph-rd, Croydon,Surrey	30	—..Z^{10}	24
,, ,, Paddington W	10	43..K	16
Big-hill, Up. Clapton E	7	33..E	28
,, Church-hill, Chingford E	3	—..A	31
Biggerstaffe-rd, Stratford E	7	41..I	32
Biggin-hill, Norwood	21	—..Z^1	23
,, road, Norbury	21	—..Z^1	23
Biggindale-rd, Streatham	21	—..Y	21
Biggs-row, Putney SW	15	59..S	14
Bignold-rd, Forest Gate E	8	—..G	34
Bigwood-rd, Hampstead NW	5	—..D	16
Billet-rd, Higham Hill E	3	—..A	30
Billingsgate Mar,L.Tha.-st EC	11	46..M	25
,, st, Greenwich SE	17	57..Q	31
Billington-rd, New Cross SE	17	63..R	29
,, st, New Cross SE	17	63..R	28
Billiter-av, Billiter-street EC	—	46..M	25
,, square ,, ,, EC	—	46..M	25
,, street EC	12	46..M	26
Billson-st, Cubitt Town E	17	57..P	32
Bina-gdns, So. Kens. SW	15	51..P	17
Binden-rd, Shepherd's Bush W	10	—..N	11
Binfield-road, Clapham SW	16	61..R	22
,, ,, Croydon, Surrey	30	—..Z^7	26
Bingfield-street, Islington N	6	37..I	22
Bingham-rd, Crydon SE	27	—..Z^5	27
,, ,, ry-sta,L.B.&S.C.	26	—..Z^5	26
Bingley-rd, Canning Town E	13	—..L	35
,, ,, Plaistow E	13	—..M	35
Binns-road, Chiswick W	15	—..P	10
Birbeck-rd,NbyPk,Ilfd.,Ess	8	—..D	40
Birch-grove, Acton W	9	—..M	8
,, ,, Lee SE	22	—..V	33
,, Wo., Adding., Surrey	30a	—..Z^8	31
Bircham-street, Poplar E	12	49..M	31
Birchanger-rd, Norwood SE	26	—..Z^3	26
Birchdale-rd, Forest Gate E	8	—..H	36
Birchin-lane, Cornhill EC	11	46..M	25
Birchington-rd, Crouch End N	6	32..D	21
,, ,, Kilburn NW	5	35..J	16
Birchlands-rd, Wandsw. SW	15	—..U	16
Birchwood-av, Musw. Hill N	2	—..B	20
,, ,, Sidcup	23	—..X	42
,, lane, Claygate, Surrey	28a	—..Z^9	2
,, road, Streatham	21	—..T	19
Birdcage-walk, Westmin. SW	11	53..N	21
Birdhurst-av, Croyd., Surrey	30	—..Z^7	25
,, gdns, Croydon, Surrey	30	—..Z^7	25
,, rise, Croydon, Surrey	30	—..Z^7	25
,, rd, Croydon, Surrey	30	—..Z^7	25
,, ,, S. Wimbdn. SW	20	—..Z	18
,, ,, Wandsworth SW	15	60..T	17
Bird-in-Bush-rd, Peckham SE	17	55..Q	27
Bird-in-Hand-rd, Bickl. Kent	28	—..Z^2	36
Birkbeck-avenue, Acton W	9	—..L	10
,, place, Streatham	21	—..W	24
,, road, Acton W	9	—..N	10
,, ,, Acton W	9	—..M	10
,, ,, Dalston E	7	39..H	26
,, ,, Hornsey N	2	—..C	22
,, ,, Leytonstone E	7	41..G	32
,, ,, Mill Hill NW	1	—..A	12
,, ,, N. Finchley N	1	—..A	17
,, ,, Penge	22	—..Z^2	28
,, ,, Sidcup, Kent	23	—..X	41
,, ,, Streatham	21	—..W	24
,, ,, Tottenham N	3	—..A	26
,, ,, Wimbledon SW	20	—..Y	16
Birkenhead-av, Kingston	19	—..Z^1	7
Birkhall-road, Catford SE	22	—..W	32
Birley-street, Battersea SW	16	60..S	19
Birnam-rd, Up. Holloway N	6	32..F	22
Birstal-road, Tottenham N	3	—..C	26
Biscay-rd, Hammersmith W	15	58..P	13
Bisham-gdns, Highgate N	6	31..E	20
Bishop King's-rd, W. Kens.W	10	58..O	14
Bishop's-avenue, Fulham SW	15	59..R	14
,, ,, Highgate N	6	31..D	18
,, ct, Chancery-la EC	—	45..L	23
,, ,, Old Bailey EC	—	46..L	24
,, Park-road, Fulham SW	15	59..R	14
,, ,, ,, Norbury	21	—..Z^2	22

	4-in. sht.	9-in. sht.	mar.
Bishop's-P., Chancery-la WC	—	45..L	23
,, road, Bayswater W	10	43..L	16
,, ,, Bethnal Green E	12	39..J	28
,, ,, Croydon, Surrey	26	—..Z^5	23
,, ,, Fulham SW	15	58..Q	15
,, ,, Highgate N	6	31..D	20
,, ,, Paddington W	10	43..L	17
,, Wood, Highgate N	6	31..D	18
,, ,, road, Highgate N	6	31..D	19
Bishopsford, Mitcham, Surr.	25	—..Z^4	18
Bishopsgate EC	11	46..L	26
,, av, Camomile-street EC	—	46..L	25
,, churchyd., Finsbury EC.	11	46..L	25
,, station EC	12	46..K	26
Bishopsthorpe-rd, Sydenh. SE	22	—..X	28
Bismarch-road, Highgate N	6	32..E	21
Bissenden-rd, Croyd., Surrey	26	—..Z^6	25
Bisson-road, West Ham E	12	41..J	32
Bisterne-av, Walthamstow E	3	—..B	32
Black Bird Hill, Kingsb. NW	5	—..F	10
,, Boy-la, Tottenham N	3	—..C	25
,, Horse-rd, ry-sta, M. R.	3	—..C	29
,, ,, yd, Rathb.-pl W	—	45..L	21
,, Raven-ct,Ldnhall-st EC	—	46..M	26
,, Swan-ct, Golden-la EC	—	46..K	24
Blackbrook-la, Brom., Kent	28	—..Z^3	37
Blackett-street, Putney SW	15	59..S	13
Blackfen, Welling	18	—..U	41
,, road, Welling	18	—..U	41
Blackfriars Bridge	11	46..M	23
,, road, SE	11	54..N	23
,, ry-sta, District Ry.	11	45..M	23
Blackheath SE	17	64..S	32
,, av, Greenwich Park SE	17	64..R	32
,, hill, Greenwich SE	17	64..R	31
,, ,, ry-sta, Green. SE	17	63..R	31
,, park, Blackheath SE	17	64..S	33
,, rise, Lewisham SE	4	64..S	31
,, road, Greenwich SE	17	63..R	31
,, ry-sta, Blackhea. SE	17	64..S	33
,, Vale, Blackheath SE	17	64..S	33
Black Horse-la, S. Norwood	27	—..Z^4	26
,, road, Deptford SE	17	56..Q	29
,, rd, Walthamstow E	3	—..C	29
Blacklands, Kent	30b	—..Z^9	38
Black Lion-la, Hammersm. W	15	58..P	12
Blackmore-gdns, Teddington	19	—..Y	4
Black's-rd, Hammersmith W	15	58..P	13
Blackshaw-rd, Toot. Grav.SW	20	—..X	17
Blackstock-rd, Finsb. Pk. N	6	32..F	24
Blackstone-rd, Lond. Fields E	7	39..I	27
Blackthorn-st, Bromley E	12	48..L	31
Blackwall, Poplar E	12	57..N	32
,, basin, Blackwall E	12	57..N	31
,, lane, E., Greenwich SE	17	57..P	33
,, pier E	12	49..M	32
,, ry-station, G.E.R.	12	49..M	32
,, tunnel, Blackwall E	12	57..N	32
Blackwater-rd, Sutton, Surr.	29	—..Z^7	16
,, st, East Dulwich SE	17	—..U	26
Black'd.-street, Walworth SE	17	54..P	25
Blagdon-rd, Catford E	17	—..U	31
,, ,, New Malden	25	—..Z^2	11
Blair-street, Poplar E	12	49..M	32
Blake-rd, Croydon, Surrey	26	—..Z^6	25
,, ,, New Southgate N	2	—..A	21
,, ,, Walham Gr. SW	15	60..R	16
Blakehall-road, Carshalton	29	—..Z^8	18
Blake Hall road, Wanstead	8	—..D	34
Blakemore-rd, Croyd., Surr.	26	—..Z^3	22
,, ,, Streatham	21	—..X	21
Blakenham-rd, Lr. Tooting SW	21	—..X	18
,, ,, Upper Tooting	21	—..X	19
Blakeney-av, Beckenham	22	—..Z^2	30
,, road, Beckenham	22	—..Z^2	30
Blake's-road, Peckham SE	17	54..Q	26
Blakesley-avenue, Ealing W	9	—..L	6
,, street, Stepney E	12	47..M	28
Blanchard-rd, Lond. Fields E	7	39..I	27
Blanche-street, Plaistow E	12	49..L	34
Blandfields-st, Balham SW	16	—..U	19
Blandford-av, Beckenham	22	—..Z^2	29
,, road, Acton W	10	—..N	11
,, ,, Ealing W	9	—..N	7
,, ,, S. Norw., Surrey	27	—..Z	2
,, ,, Teddington	19	—..X	3
,, sq, M'lebone NW	11	44..K	18
,, street, Portman-sq W	11	44..L	19
Blantyre-street, Chelsea SW	16	51..Q	17
Blashford-st, Lewisham SE	22	—..V	32
Blawith-rd, Harrow, M'sex	1a	—..C	4
Blechynden-st, Notting Hill W	10	50..M	14
Bleeding Ht.-yd, Hat. Gdn EC	—	45..L	23
Blegborough-rd, Streatham	21	—..Y	20
Blendon, Welling	18	—..U	43
,, road, Plumstead	18	—..Q	39
Blenheim-ct, Croyd., Surrey	30	—..Z^9	24
,, cres, N. Kensington W	10	50..M	14
,, gdns, Carshalton, Surr.	30	—..Z^8	20
,, ,, Willesden Gr. NW	5	—..H	14
,, grove, Peckham SE	17	62..S	26
,, road, Bickley	28	—..Z^3	36
,, ,, Hornsey N	2	—..B	23
,, ,, Leytonstone E	7	41..G	33
,, ,, Raynes Park SW	25	—..Z^2	12
,, ,, St John's Wd. NW	10	35..J	17
,, ,, Teddington	19	—..X	4
,, ,, Turnham Gr. W	10	—..O	11
,, ,, Up. Holloway N	6	32..F	22
,, ,, Walthamstow E	3	—..B	29
,, street, Chelsea SW	16	52..P	18
,, st, N. Bond-st W	11	44..M	20
,, terr, St John's Wd. NW	10	35..J	17
Blenkarne-road, Battersea SW	16	—..U	18
Blessington-road, Lee SE	17	64..T	32
Blind-la, East Sheen SW	14	—..T	9
,, ,, Hendon NW	1	—..B	14
,, ,, Plumstead	18	—..R	41
,, ,, Wembley, M'sex	4	—..G	7
,, ,, Wood Green N	2	—..A	24
Blissett-st, Greenwich SE	17	64..R	31
Blockhouse-st, Deptford SE	17	55..Q	28

	4-in. sht.	9-in. sht.	mar.
Bloemfontein-av, Shep. Bu.W	10	50..M	12
,, rd, Shep. Bush. W	10	50..M	12
Blomfield-rd, Edgware-rd W	10	43..K	17
,, street, Finsbury EC	11	46..L	25
,, ,, Up. Westb.-ter W	10	43 L	17
Blondel-street, Battersea SW	16	60..R	19
Blonden-street, Bow E	12	48..J	30
Bloom Grove, W. Norwood	21	—..X	23
Bloomfield, Ealing Dean W	9	—..M	25
,, road, Burdett-road E	12	48..L	30
,, ,, Highgate N	6	31..D	20
,, ,, Norbiton, Surrey	24	—..Z^2	7
,, ,, Plumstead	18	—..Q	38
,, terr, Pimlico-rd SW	16	52..P	19
Bloomsbury-ct, Holborn WC	11	45..L	22
,, pl, Bloomsbury WC	11	45..L	22
,, sq, Bloomsbury WC	11	45..L	22
,, street, Bloomsbury WC	11	45..L	22
,, ,, Poplar E	12	49..M	32
Blossom-st, Norton Folgate E	12	46..L	26
Blount-street, Limehouse E	12	48..L	29
Bloxhall-rd, Lea Bridge-rd E	7	—..E	30
Blucher-rd, Camberwell SE	16	62..R	24
Blue Anchor-la, Bermond. SE	12	55..O	27
,, Lion-ct,Aldersgate-st EC	—	46..L	21
Blundell-st, Caledonian-rd N	6	37..H	22
Blunt-road, Croydon, Surrey	30	—..Z^7	24
Blunt's-road, Eltham	18	—..U	37
Blurton-road, Clapton E	7	39..G	28
Blyth-road, Bromley	22	—..Z^2	33
,, ,, Stratford E	7	41..I	32
,, ,, Walthamstow E	7	—..E	30
Blythe-hill, Catford SE	22	—..X	30
,, ,, lane, Catford SE	22	—..Y	30
,, rd, Hammersmith W	10	58..O	14
,, ,, ,, W	10	50..O	13
,, st, Bethnal Green-rd E	12	47..K	27
,, Vale, Catford SE	22	—..W	30
Blythwood-rd, Crouch Hill N	6	32..E	22
,, ,, Seven Kings, Es.	8	—..E	42
Board of Trade, Whiteh. SW	—	53..N	22
,, Agriculture, St J.-sq SW	—	45..M	21
,, street, Greenwich SE	12	57..O	33
Bockhampton-rd, Norbiton	19	—..Y	7
Bodmin-st, Wandsworth SW	20	—..V	16
Bodney-road, Hackney NE	7	39..H	27
Bognor-st, Battersea SW	16	61..R	21
Bohemia-av, Chiswick W	10	—..O	11
Bohn-street, Stepney E	12	48..L	28
Boileau-road, Ealing W	9	—..L	9
Bolan-street, Battersea SW	16	60..R	18
Boleyn-rd, East Ham E	13	—..I	36
,, ,, Forest Gate E	8	—..J I	35
,, ,, Stoke Newing. N	*7	38..G	26
Bolingbroke-gro, Wan. Co. SW	16	—..T	18
,, road, Battersea SW	16	60..R	18
,, ,, Hammersmith W	10	50..O	14
Bollina-rd, Rotherhithe SE	17	55..P	28
Bollo Bridge-rd, Acton W	9	—..N	9
,, lane, Acton W	9	—..N	9
Bolney-st, S. Lambeth SW	16	53..Q	22
Bolsover-st, Oxford-st W	11	44..K	20
Bolt-court, Fleet-street EC	—	45..L	23
Bolton-gdns, Chiswick W	15	—..P	10
,, ,, Queen's Park NW	10	42..J	14
,, ,, S. Kens. SW	15	51..P	16
,, ,, Teddington	19	—..Y	4
,, rd, Chiswick W	14	—..Q	9
,, ,, Edmonton N	3	—..A	26
,, ,, Kilburn NW	5	35..I	16
,, ,, Notting Hill W	10	50..M	15
,, ,, S. Acton W	9	—..O	9
,, ,, Wealdstone M'sex	1a	—..B	3
,, st, Kennington Pk SE	16	53..Q	23
,, ,, Piccadilly W	11	44..M	20
Boltons, W. Brompton SW	15	51..P	17
,, mews, W. Brompton SW	15	51..P	17
Bolwell-st, Lambeth-walk SE	16	53..P	22
Bomore-rd, Notting Hill W	10	50..M	14
Bonamy-st, Bermondsey SE	17	55..P	27
Bonar-road, Peckham SE	17	62..R	26
Bonchurch-rd, Kens. W	9	—..M	5
Bond-court, Walbrook EC	—	46..M	25
,, road, Long Ditton	24	—..Z^5	7
,, ,, Surbiton	24	—..Z^5	7
,, ,, Up. Mitcham SW	20	—..Z^1	18
,, street, Ealing W	9	—..M	6
,, ,, Leytonstone E	7	41..H	33
,, ,, Oxford-st W	11	44..L	20
,, ,, Pentonville	11	38..J	23
,, ,, Vauxhall SW	16	53..Q	22
Bonfield-rd, Lewisham SE	17	64..T	32
Bonham-rd, Brixton SW	16	—..U	22
Bonheur-road, Chiswick W	10	—..N	10
Boniface-st, Westm. Br-rd SE	11	53..N	22
Bonner-rd, Victoria Park E	12	47..J	28
,, st, Bethnal Green E	12	47..J	28
Bonners Hill-road, Kingston	19	—..Z^1	7
Bonnersfield-la, Greenh. M'sex	1a	—..C	5
Bonneville-road, Clapham SW	16	—..U	20
Bonnington-sq, S. Lamb. SW	16	53..Q	22
Bonny Downs-rd, E. Ham E	13	—..K	38
,, st, Camden Town NW	6	36..I	20
Bonser-road, Twickenham	19	—..W	4
Bookham-street, Hoxton N	11	46..J	25
Boone-st, Lee SE	17	64..T	33
Boones-road, Lee SE	17	64..T	33
Boot-street, Hoxton N	11	46..K	25
Booth road, Hendon NW	1	—..B	11
,, st, Spitalfields E	12	47..L	26
Boothby-rd, Up. Holloway N	6	32..E	21
Border-rd, Sydenham SE	22	—..Y	27
Boreham-rd, Wood Gr. N	2	—..A	24
Borgard-road, Woolwich	18	—..P	37
Borland-rd, Peckham Rye SE	17	—..T	28
Borneo-street, Putney SW	15	59..S	13
Borohill-rd, Croydon, Surrey	26	—..Z^6	23
Borough High-st, Southw. SE	12	54..N	25
,, market, Southwark SE	12	54..N	25
,, road, Norbiton	19	—..Z	8
,, ,, Southwark SE	11	54..O	24
Borrett-road, Walworth SE	16	54..P	24

	4-in. sht.	9-in. sht.	mar.
Borrodaile-rd, Wandsw. SW	15	60..U	16
Borthwick-rd, Stratford E	7	41..G	33
Borwick av, Walthamstow E	3	—..B	30
Boscastle-rd, Highgate NW	6	36..F	20
Boscombe-rd, Lr. Tooting SW	21	—..Y	19
,, ,, Merton SW	10	50..N	12
,, ,, Shep. Bush W	20	—..Z	16
Boss-st, Horselydown SE	12	54..N	26
Bostall-heath, Plumstead	18	—..Q	42
,, hill, Plumstead	18	—..Q	42
,, lane, Abbey Wood	18	—..P	42
,, wood, Plumstead	18	—..Q	42
Boston Pk.-rd, Brentf. M'sex	14	—..P	6
,, pl, Dorset-sq NW	11	44..K	18
,, road, Brentford	14	—..P	5
,, ,, Croydon, Surrey	26	—..Z^4	22
,, ,, Hanwell W	9	—..M	4
,, ,, NewBrentf.,M'sex	9	—..O	5
,, ,, Walthamstow E	7	—..D	30
,, street, Dorset-sq NW	11	44..K	18
,, ,, Hackney-rd E	12	39..J	27
Bostonthorpe-rd, Hanwell W	9	—..N	3
Boswell-ct, Devonshire-st WC	—	45..L	22
,, rd, Croydon, Surrey	26	—..Z^3	24
Bosworth-rd, Kensington	10	42..K	15
,, ,, N. Southgate N	2	—..A	22
Botanic-g. (Roy.) Reg. Pk NW	11	44..K	19
Bothwick-rd, Hendon NW	5	—..D	12
Botolph-alley, Botolph-la EC	—	46..M	25
,, lane, Eastcheap EC	11	46..M	25
Boulcott-st, Limehouse E	12	48..M	29
Boulogne-rd, Croydon, Surrey	26	—..Z^4	24
Boulton-road, Bromley E	12	49..L	33
Boundaries-rd, Balham	21	—..W	19
Boundary-la, Camb.-rd SE	16	54..Q	24
,, road, Barking	13	—..J	39
,, ,, Carshalton, Surrey	30	—..Z^8	19
,, ,, Plaistow E	13	—..K	36
,, ,, St John's Wd. NW	5	35..I	17
,, ,, S. Wimb. SW	20	—..Y	17
,, ,, Stoke Newtn. N	2	—..B	24
,, ,, Walthamstow E	7	—..D	30
,, street, Shoreditch E	12	46..K	26
Bounds-gr, New Southgate N	2	—..A	21
Bourdon-st, Berkeley-sq. W	11	44..M	20
Bourke-road, Willesden NW	5	—..H	11
Bourne-rd, Bickley	28	—..Z^3	35
,, ,, Hornsey N	6	32..D	22
Bournemouth-rd, Merton SW	20	—..Z	15
,, ,, Peckham SE	17	62..S	27
Bournvale-road, Streatham	21	—..Y	21
Bousfield-rd, New Cross SE	17	63..S	28
Boutflower-rd, N. Wands. SW	16	60..T	18
Bouverie-road, Harrow	1a	—..D	3
,, ,, Stoke New'ton N	7	33..F	25
,, street, Fleet-st EC	11	45..M	23
,, ,, Paddington W	10	43..L	18
Bovay-st, Holloway-rd N	6	37..G	22
Boveney-rd, Forest Hill SE	22	—..V	28
Bovill-rd, Forest Hill SE	22	—..V	29
Bovingdon-rd, Fulham SW	15	59..R	16
Bow-bridge, Bow E	12	49..J	31
,, churchyd, Cheapside EC	—	46..M	24
,, creek, Blackwall E	12	49..L	32
,, Common-la, Poplar E	12	48..L	30
,, lane, Cheapside EC	11	46..M	24
,, ,, High Barnet	1	—..A	17
,, ,, Poplar E	12	49..M	31
,, road E	12	48..K	30
,, ,, ry-sta, G.E R. E	12	48..K	30
,, ry-sta, N.L.R. E	12	48..K	31
,, st, Covent Garden WC	11	45..M	22
Bowater-pl, Blackheath SE	18	—..R	35
,, road, Woolwich	13	—..O	36
Bowdon, Leyton-street E	7	—..D	31
Bowen-rd, Harrow M'sex	1a	—..D	3
Bower-av, Blackheath SE	17	64..R	33
,, rd, Hackney, Wick. E	7	40..H	30
,, st, Commercial-rd, E	12	47..M	28
Bowerdean-st, Fulham SW	15	59..R	16
Bowes-park, Wood Green N	2	—..A	23
,, ,, ry-sta, G.N.R.	2	—..A	22
,, rd, New Southgate N	2	—..A	21
Bowling Green-la, Farr.-rd EC	11	45..K	23
,, ,, st, Kenn.-rd SE	16	53..Q	23
Bowood-rd, Clapham SW	16	—..T	19
Bowron's-avenue, Wembley	4	—..H	7
Bowton-rd, Woolwich	18	—..Q	39
Box-street, Bromley E	12	48..L	31
,, Ridge-av, Purley, Sur.	30	—..Z^{11}	22
Boxall-rd, Dulwich SE	16	—..U	25
Boxley-rd, Silvertown E	13	—..N	35
Boyce-st, Lambeth SE	—	53..N	23
Boyd-rd, Canning Town E	12	49..M	34
,, ,, S. Wimbledon SW	20	—..Y	17
,, street, St George's E	12	47..M	27
Boyer-road, Plaistow E	13	—..L	35
Boyfield-st, Blackfriars SE	11	54..N	24
Boyle Farm-rd, Th. Ditton	24	—..Z^3	4
,, street, Savile-row W	11	44..M	20
Boyne-road, Lee SE	17	64..S	32
Boyson-rd, Walworth SE	17	54..Q	25
Boyton-road, Hornsey N	2	—..B	22
Brabant-ct, Philpot-la EC	—	46..M	25
Brabazon-street, Poplar E	12	48..L	31
Brabsden-green, Middlesex	4	—..H	4
Bracewell-rd, Wormw. Scr. W	10	42..L	13
Bracey-st, Tollington Park N	6	32..E	22
Brackenbury-rd, E. Finch. N	2	—..B	17
,, ,, Hammersmith W	10	50..N	13
Brackley-road, Beckenham	22	—..Z^1	30
,, ,, Chiswick W	15	—..P	11
,, terrace, Chiswick W	15	—..P	11
Bracknell-gdns, Hampst. NW	5	35..G	16
Brad-street, Lambeth SE	11	53..N	23
Bradbourne-st, Fulham SW	15	59..R	16
Braden-st, Maida Hill W	10	43..K	16
Bradfield-rd, Silvertown E	13	—..N	34
Bradford-av, Red Cross-st EC	11	46..L	24
,, road, Ilford	8	—..F	40
,, ,, Sydenham SE	22	—..X	27
Bradgate-road, Catford SE	22	—..V	31

	4-in. sht.	9-in. sht.	mar.
Brading-rd, Croydon, Surrey	26	—	Z^4 22
Bradiston-rd, St Peter's-pk W	10	42	J 15
Bradley-gdns, Castlebar H. W	9	—	L 5
,, st, Canning Town E .	13	—	L 34
Bradmore-gro, Hammersm. W	10	58	O 13
,, Pk.-rd, Hammersm. W	10	58	O 13
Bradstock-road, Hackney E	7	40	H 29
Bradwell-rd, Mile End E .	12	48	K 29
Brady-st, Bethnal Green E .	12	47	K 27
Braemar-av, Thornton Hth.	26	—	Z^2 23
,, ,, Wimbledon SW .	20	—	W 15
,, ,, Wood Green N .	2	—	A 22
,, rd, Brentford, M'sex .	14	—	P 7
,, ,, Tottenham N .	3	—	C 26
,, st, Barking-road E .	12	49	L 34
Braidwood-rd, Catford SE .	22	—	W 32
Brailsford-rd, Brixton SW .	16	—	U 23
Bramah-road, Brixton SW .	16	61	R 23
Bramber-rd, N. Finchley N .	1	—	A 18
,, ,, W. Kens. SW .	15	58	P 15
Brambledown-rd, Cars., Sur.	30	—	Z^9 20
,, ,, Croy., Sur.	30	—	Z^9 25
Bramblebury-rd, Plumstead	18	—	Q 39
Bramcote-road, Putney SW .	15	59	T 12
,, ,, Rotherhithe SE	17	55	P 28
Bramerton-st, Chelsea SW .	16	51	P 18
Bramfield-rd, Battersea SW	16	—	U 18
,, ,, Wandsworth SW	16	—	U 18
Bramford-rd, Wandsw. SW	15	60	T 17
Bramham-gdns, S. Kens. SW	16	51	P 16
Bramley-hill, Croy., Surrey	30	—	Z^7 24
,, road, Ealing W . .	9	—	N 6
,, ,, Notting Hill W	10	50	M 14
Brampton-gro, Hendon NW	1	—	C 13
,, ,, Highgate N .	2	—	C 19
,, road, Croydon .	26	—	Z^4 25
,, ,, Homerton E .	7	40	H 29
,, ,, Tottenham N .	2	—	C 24
,, ,, Welling . .	18	—	S 43
Bramshill-gdns, Kent.Tn. NW	6	32	F 20
,, road, Harlesden .	10	43	J 11
,, ,, W. Norwood .	21	—	Y 23
,, ,, Willesden NW .	10	—	J 11
Bramshot-avenue, Charlton	18	—	Q 34
Bramwell-st, S. Lambeth SW	16	61	S 20
Brancaster-lane, Purley .	30	—	Z^{10} 24
,, road, Ilford . .	8	—	E 40
,, ,, Little Ilford .	8	—	H 37
,, ,, Streatham .	21	—	X 21
Branch-hill, Hampstead NW	5	35	F 17
Brand-street, Greenwich SE	17	64	R 31
,, ,, Holloway N .	6	37	G 23
Brandenburg-rd, H'smith W	15	58	P 13
Brandenburgh-rd, Chiswick W	14	—	P 9
Brandlehow-rd, Putney SW .	15	59	T 15
Brandon-rd, Brixton SW .	16	—	U 22
,, ,, Islington N .	6	37	I 22
,, ,, Sutton, Surrey	29	—	Z^7 16
,, ,, Walthamstow E	3	—	B 32
,, street, Walworth SE .	16	54	P 24
Brandram-road, Lee SE .	17	64	T 32
Brandreth-rd, Up. Tooting .	21	—	W 19
Brandybottle-hill, Wadd. Sur.	26	—	Z^6 22
Branksome-road, Brixton SW	16	—	T 22
,, ,, Merton SW .	20	—	Z 15
Branscombe-rd, Lewisham SE	17	63	S 31
Branstone-road, Kew .	14	—	R 8
Brantwood-rd, Tottenham N	3	—	A 27
Brassey-sq, N. Wandswth. SW	16	60	S 19
Brathway-rd, Wandswth SW	15	—	U 15
Bravington-rd, Maida Hill W	10	42	J 15
Braxfield-road, Brockley SE	17	63	T 29
Braxted-park, Streatham .	21	—	Z^1 22
Braxton-road, Streatham .	21	—	Y 21
Brayard-rd, Peckham SE .	17	62	S 27
Brayburne-av, Clapham SW	16	61	S 21
Braydon-rd, Stamford Hill N	7	33	E 27
Bread-street, Cannon-st EC	11	46	M 24
,, ,, Cheapside EC .	11	46	M 24
,, ,, hill, Qn. Vic.-st EC	—	46	M 24
Breakspears-rd, Brockley SE	17	63	S 30
Bream-road, Old Ford E .	7	40	J 30
Breamore-road, Ilford .	8	—	F 41
Bream's-bldgs, Fetter-la EC	11	45	L 23
Brechin-pl, S. Kensington SW	16	51	P 17
Brecknock-rd, Holloway N	6	37	G 21
Brecon-road, Fulham SW .	15	58	Q 14
Bredon-road, Camberwell SE	16	62	S 24
,, rd, Croydon, Surrey .	26	—	Z^4 26
Breer-street, Fulham SW .	15	59	S 16
Brenda-rd, Up. Tooting SW	20	—	W 18
Brendon-st, Paddington W .	11	44	L 18
Brent-bridge, Hendon NW .	1	—	C 14
,, green, Hendon NW .	1	—	C 14
,, river, Middlesex .	4	—	I 9
,, ,, NW . . .	5	—	D 14
,, rd, Canning Town E .	13	—	L 34
,, ,, Plumstead .	18	—	R 38
,, street, Hendon NW .	1	—	B 14
,, View-rd, Hendon NW	5	—	D 12
Brentford, Middlesex . .	14	—	P 6
,, Ait	14	—	P 7
,, ry-sta, L. & S.W.R. .	14	—	P 6
,, ,, ,, G.W.R. .	14	—	Q 6
Brentham-way, Castleb. H. W	9	—	K 6
Brenthurst-rd, Willesden NW	5	—	H 12
Brenton-st, Limeh. E . .	12	48	L 29
Brereton-road, Tottenham N	3	—	A 26
Brett-road, Willesden NW .	5	—	I 10
Brettenham-av, Edmonton W	3	—	A 27
,, road, Chapel End E .	3	—	A 30
,, ,, Edmonton N .	3	—	A 27
,, ,, E., Edmonton N	3	—	A 28
Brewer-st, Buck. Pal.-rd SW	11	52	O 20
,, ,, Golden-square W	11	45	M 21
,, ,, Woolwich .	18	—	P 38
,, ,, N., Clerkenwell N	11	45	J 23
Brewers' Co. Hall, Addle-st EC	—	46	L 24
,, lane, Strand WC .	11	45	M 22
,, ,, Up. Thames-st EC	11	46	M 25
Brewery-rd, Bromley, Kent	28	—	Z^5 36
,, ,, Caledonian-rd N	6	37	H 22

	4-in. sht.	9-in. sht.	mar.
Brewery-rd, Plumstead .	18	—	P 40
,, ,, Woolwich .	18	—	P 39
Brewhouse-lane, Putney SW	15	59	S 14
,, Wood, Highgate N .	6	31	D 20
Brewster-gdns, N. Kens. W	10	42	L 13
,, road, Leyton E . .	7	—	E 31
Briant-st, New Cross-rd SE	17	63	R 28
Briar-road, Cricklewood NW	5	—	G 13
,, ,, Twickenham .	19	—	V 3
,, walk, Putney SW .	15	—	T 12
Briarbank-rd, Castleb. Hill W	9	—	L 5
Briardale-gdns, Hampst. NW	5	35	F 16
Briarwood-rd, Clapham SW	16	—	T 21
Brick-court, The Temple EC	—	45	M 23
,, lane, Bethnal Gr.-rd E	12	47	K 26
,, street, Piccadilly W .	11	52	N 20
Brickfield-lane, Carshalton .	29	—	Z^6 18
,, road, Poplar E . .	12	48	K 31
Brickhill-la, Chadw. Hea., Es.	8	—	D 43
,, ,, Up. Thames-st EC	11	46	M 24
Brick Hill-passage, Richmond	14	—	T 7
Bricklayers Arms goods-sta.	12	54	O 25
Brickwood-rd, Croyd., Surr.	26	—	Z^6 25
Bride-ct, New Bridge-st EC	—	46	M 23
,, la, New Bridge-st EC	11	46	M 23
,, street, Islington N .	6	37	H 23
Bridewell-pl, N. Bridge-st EC	11	45	M 23
Bridge-av, Hammersmith W	15	58	P 13
,, lane, Hendon NW .	1	—	C 15
,, road, Beckenham .	22	—	Z^1 29
,, ,, Carshalton, Surrey	30	—	Z^7 20
,, ,, East Ham E .	8	—	I 37
,, ,, E. Moulsey, Surr.	24	—	Z^2 3
,, ,, Hammersmith W	10	58	P 13
,, ,, Isleworth . .	14	—	R 3
,, ,, Leyton-street E	7	—	E 30
,, ,, Millwall E .	12	48	M 30
,, ,, Plaistow E .	13	—	J 35
,, ,, Stratford E .	7	41	I 32
,, ,, Sutton, Surrey .	29	—	Z^8 16
,, ,, Twickenham .	19	—	V 1
,, ,, ,, .	14	—	T 5
,, ,, West Ham E .	12	41	J 33
,, ,, Willesden NW .	5	—	H 11
,, ,, Wood Green N .	2	—	A 22
,, ,, W., Battersea SW	16	60	R 18
,, street, Greenwich SE .	17	57	Q 31
,, ,, Hackney E .	7	39	H 28
,, ,, Hammersmith W	15	58	P 12
,, ,, Mile End-road E	12	48	K 30
,, ,, Westminster SW	11	53	N 22
Bridgefield-gro, Wandsw. SW	15	59	T 16
,, rd, Sutton, Surrey .	29	—	Z^8 15
Bridgend-rd, Wandsworth SW	15	60	T 16
Bridges-road, Merton SW .	20	—	Z 16
Bridgman-rd, Chiswick W .	9	—	O 9
Bridgewater-sq, Barbican EC	11	46	L 24
,, street, Barbican EC .	11	46	L 24
Bridle-lane, Golden-square W	11	45	M 21
,, road, Purley, Surrey .	30	—	Z^{10} 22
Bridport-place, Hoxton N .	11	38	J 25
,, rd, Thornt. Hea., Surr.	26	—	Z^2 23
,, ,, Up. Edmonton N	3	—	A 26
Brierley-rd, Leytonstone E	7	41	G 32
Brigg-street, Cubitt Town E	17	57	P 32
Bright-street, Bromley E .	12	49	L 31
Brightfield-road, Lee SE .	17	—	T 33
Brightling-rd, Brockley SE	17	—	U 30
Brightlingsea-pl, Limehouse E	12	48	M 30
Brighton-rd, Chessing., Surr.	28*a*	—	Z^{10} 5
,, ,, Croydon, Surrey	30	—	Z^8 24
,, ,, East Ham E .	13	—	K 38
,, ,, Hook, Surrey .	24	—	Z^6 6
,, ,, Sto. Newington N	7	38	G 26
,, ,, Surbiton, Surrey	24	—	Z^4 6
,, ,, Sutton, Surrey .	29	—	Z^9 16
,, ,, West Ham E .	12	41	J 33
,, terrace, Brixton SW .	16	61	T 22
Brightside-rd, Lewisham SE	17	—	U 32
Brightwell-cres, Toot., Gra. SW	20	—	Y 18
Brigstock-rd, Croyd., Surrey	26	—	Z^3 23
Brill-street, Fulham SW .	15	60	R 17
Brindley-st, Westbo. Park W	10	43	L 16
Brinkley-road, Malden .	25	—	Z^5 12
Brisbane-avenue, Merton SW	20	—	Z 16
,, road, Ealing Dean W .	9	—	M 5
,, ,, Ilford, Essex .	8	—	E 39
,, ,, Leyton E . .	7	—	F 31
,, street, Camberwell SE	17	54	Q 25
,, ,, Peckham SE .	16	62	R 25
Briscoe-rd, S. Wimbledon SW	20	—	Y 17
Bristol-gdns, Paddington W	10	43	K 16
,, road, Forest Gate E .	8	—	I 36
Bristow-road, Hounslow .	14	—	S 2
,, street, Hoxton N .	11	38	J 25
Britannia-br, Limehouse E .	12	48	M 30
,, road, Fulham SW .	15	51	Q 16
,, ,, Islington N .	6	38	I 24
,, ,, N. Finchley N .	1	—	A 18
,, ,, Surbiton, Surrey	24	—	Z^4 7
,, street, Hoxton N .	11	46	J 25
,, ,, King's Cross WC	12	12	J 22
British-grove, Chiswick W .	15	—	P 11
,, Museum, Bloomsb. WC	11	45	L 21
,, ,, av, Holborn WC	—	45	L 21
,, ,, ry-sta, C.L.R. .	11	45	L 22
,, street, Bow E . .	12	48	K 30
,, ,, Millwall E .	17	56	P 31
Briton-hill, Sanderstead, Sur.	30	—	Z^{11} 25
Britten-street, Chelsea SW .	16	51	P 18
Brixham-rd, Canning Town E	13	—	M 34
,, street, No. Woolwich E	13	—	N 37
Brixton SW	16	61	T 22
,, hill, Brixton SW .	21	—	V 22
,, ,, Brixton SW .	16	—	U 22
,, Prison, Brixton SW .	16	—	U 22
,, road, Brixton SW .	16	61	S 23
Broad-court, Bow-street WC	—	45	M 22
,, gr, Croydon .	26	—	Z^5 23
,, lane, New Hampton .	19	—	Y 1
,, ,, Tottenham N .	3	—	C 27
,, Sanctuary, Westm. SW	11	53	O 21

	4-in. sht.	9-in. sht.	mar.
Broad-street, Bloomsbury WC	11	45	L 22
,, ,, Golden-square W	11	44	M 21
,, ,, Lambeth SE .	16	53	P 22
,, ,, Ratcliff E . .	12	48	M 29
,, ,, Stratford E .	7	41	I 32
,, ,, Teddington .	19	—	Y 3
,, ,, av, Blomf.-st EC	—	46	L 25
,, ,, pl, Blomf.-st EC	—	46	L 25
,, ,, ry-sta EC . .	11	46	L 25
,, walk, Kew . .	14	—	Q 7
,, ,, Notting Hill W	10	43	M 16
,, ,, Regent's Park W	11	44	J 19
,, wall, Lambeth SE .	11	45	N 23
Broadarrow-ct, Milton-st EC	11	46	L 25
Broadfield-road, Catford SE	22	—	W 33
Broadgreen, Croydon, Surrey	26	—	Z^2 23
,, av, Croydon, Surrey	26	—	Z^1 23
Broadhinton-rd, Clapham SW	16	61	S 20
Broadhurst-gdns, Kilburn NW	5	35	H 16
Broadlands-road, Highgate N	6	31	D 19
Broadley-terr, Blandf.-sq, NW	11	44	K 18
Broadwater-rd, Toot., Gra. SW	20	—	X 18
,, ,, Tottenham N .	3	—	A 26
Broadway, Abbey Wood .	18	—	P 43
,, Barking . . .	13	—	J 39
,, Deptford SE . .	17	63	R 30
,, Ealing W . . .	9	—	L 7
,, Eltham . . .	18	—	U 37
,, Hammersmith W .	10	58	O 13
,, Hanwell W . .	9	—	M 3
,, Hornsey N . .	6	32	D 22
,, London Fields E .	7	39	I 27
,, Ludgate Hill EC .	—	46	M 24
,, Plaistow E . .	13	—	K 35
,, Stratford E . .	7	41	I 33
,, Streatham SW . .	21	—	Y 21
,, Sutton, Surrey . .	29	—	Z^7 17
,, Tooting, Graveney SW	20	—	Y 18
,, Twickenham . .	14	—	U 5
,, Westminster SW .	11	53	O 21
,, avenue, Selhurst SE	26	—	Z^3 25
Brock-road, Plaistow E .	13	—	L 35
Brockenhurst-road, Croydon	27	—	Z^5 27
Brockham-st, Newington SE	11	54	O 24
Brocklehurst-st, Deptford SE	17	55	Q 29
,, ,, New Cross-rd SE	17	63	R 29
Brocklesby, S. Norwood SE	27	—	Z^3 27
Brockley SE . . .	17	63	T 29
,, footpath, Brockley SE	17	—	U 29
,, grove, Brockley SE .	17	—	U 30
,, hill SE . . .	22	—	V 29
,, lane ry-sta, Brockley SE	17	63	S 29
,, park, Forest Hill .	22	—	V 29
,, rise, Forest Hill SE .	22	—	V 29
,, road, Brockley SE .	17	63	T 29
,, ry-sta, L. B. & S. C. SE	17	63	S 29
,, villas, Brockley SE .	17	63	S 30
Brockwell-park Herne Hill SE	16	—	U 23
,, ,, gdns, Dulwich SW	21	—	V 23
Brodia-rd, Stoke Newington N	7	33	F 26
Brodrick-rd, Up. Tooting SW	20	—	W 18
Brograve-road, Tottenham N	3	—	B 27
Broke-road, Dalston E .	7	39	I 27
Brokers' Alley, Endell-st WC	—	45	M 22
Bromar-rd, Camberwell SE	17	62	S 26
Bromehead-st, Commer.-rd E	12	47	L 28
Bromell's-road, Clapham SW	16	61	T 21
Bromfelde-road, Clapham SW	16	61	S 21
Bromley-avenue, Bromley .	22	—	Z^2 33
,, crescent, Bromley .	27	—	Z^2 33
,, cemetery, Bromley .	22	—	Z^1 33
,, College, Bromley, Kent	22	—	Z^2 33
,, Common, Bromley, Kent	28	—	Z^3 35
,, gdns, Bromley, Kent	27	—	Z^2 33
,, gr, Bromley, Kent .	27	—	Z^2 32
,, lane, Chislehurst, Kent	23	—	Z 39
,, park, Kent . .	22	—	Z^2 33
,, ry-sta, L.T. & S.R. E	12	49	K 31
,, recr.-gd., Brom., Kent	27	—	Z^2 33
,, road, SE . . .	22	—	W 31
,, ,, Beckenham .	22	—	Z^3 30
,, ,, Leyton E . .	7	—	D 31
,, ,, Tottenham N .	3	—	A 27
,, ,, Walthamstow E	3	—	B 31
,, street, Bromley E .	12	48	L 31
,, ,, Commercial-rd E	12	48	M 29
,, Hall-road, Bromley E	12	49	L 32
,, South, Kent . .	28	—	Z^2 34
Brompton SW . . .	11	51	O 18
,, cemetery, Fulh.-rd SW	15	51	P 16
,, Hospital, Brompton SW	51	—	P 18
,, road, Brompton SW .	11	52	O 18
,, ,, ry-sta, Picc. R.	11	52	O 18
,, sq, Brompton-rd SW .	11	51	O 18
Brondesbury-pk., Bronde. NW	5	34	I 14
,, ,, Willesden Gr. NW	5	—	H 13
,, ,, sta, Hampstead	5	34	J 14
,, road, Kilburn NW .	5	—	I 15
,, ,, sta, Met. Ry. .	5	—	H 15
,, villas, Kilburn NW .	5	—	I 16
Bronsart-road, Fulham SW	15	58	Q 14
Bronson-rd, Raynes Park SW	20	—	Z^1 14
Bronti-pl, Walworth-rd SE	16	54	P 24
Bronze-street, Deptford SE	17	56	Q 30
Brook-green, Hammersm. W	10	50	O 13
,, ,, rd, Hammersm. W	10	58	O 13
,, lane, Welling . .	18	—	U 43
,, Ms., Grosvenor-sq W	11	44	M 20
,, rd, Brentford, M'sex	14	—	P 6
,, ,, Edmonton N .	3	—	A 26
,, ,, Hornsey N .	2	—	B 22
,, ,, Ilford . .	8	—	D 41
,, ,, Twickenham .	14	—	T 4
,, ,, Wood-green N .	2	—	B 23
,, st, Grosvenor-sq W .	11	44	M 20
,, ,, Kennington-rd SE	11	53	O 23
,, ,, Kingston . .	19	—	Z^1 7
,, ,, Limehouse E .	12	48	M 29
,, ,, Ratcliff E . .	12	47	M 28
,, ,, Sussex-square W	11	43	M 18
,, ,, Tottenham N .	3	—	B 26
Brookbank-rd, Lewisham SE	4	63	S 31

	4-in. sht.	9-in. sht.	mar.
Brookdale-rd, Catford SE .	22	—	V 31
,, ,, Walthamstow E	3	—	B 30
Brookdene-rd, Plumstead .	18	—	P 41
Brooke-road, Clapton N .	7	39	F 27
,, ,, Walthamstow E	3	—	C 32
,, street, Holborn EC .	11	45	L 23
Brookfield-av, Waltham. E	3	—	C 32
,, park, Kentish Town NW	6	31	F 20
,, road, Chiswick W .	10	—	N 10
,, ,, Edmonton N .	3	—	A 27
,, ,, S. Hackney E .	7	40	H 29
Brookhill-rd, Woolwich .	18	—	Q 38
Brooklands-rd, Blackheath SE	18	—	S 34
,, ,, S. Lamb. SW .	16	61	R 21
,, st, S. Lambeth SW .	16	61	R 21
Brooklyn-rd, Shep. Bush. W	10	50	N 13
,, ,, S. Norwood SE	27	—	Z^2 27
Brookmill-rd, Deptford SE .	17	63	R 30
Brook's-av, East Ham E .	13	—	L 37
,, lane, Chiswick W .	14	—	P 8
,, road, Plaistow E .	13	—	J 34
Brooksby-st, Islington N .	6	37	I 23
,, walk, Homerton E .	7	40	G 29
Brookscroft-rd, Waltham. E	3	—	A 31
Brookside-rd, Up. Holloway N	6	32	F 21
Brookview-rd, Streatham SW	21	—	Y 20
Brooksville-rd, Queen's Pk. NW	5	—	I 14
Brookville-road, Fulham SW	15	58	Q 15
Brookwood-rd, Wimbl. Pk. SW	20	—	V 15
Broom-road, Teddington .	19	—	Y 5
Brooman-rd, Croydon, Surr.	30	—	Z^9 24
Broomfield-av, Palmer's Gr. N	2	—	A 23
,, lane, Palmer's Green N	2	—	A 22
,, park, Palmer's Gr. N .	2	—	A 22
,, road, Kew . .	14	—	Q 8
,, ,, Surbiton . .	24	—	Z^4 7
,, street, Poplar E .	12	48	L 31
Broomhill-rd, Goodm., Essex	8	—	F 42
,, ,, Wandsworth SW	15	—	U 15
Broomhouse Dock, Fulham SW	15	59	S 15
,, road, Fulham SW .	15	59	R 15
Broomsleigh-st, Hamp. NW	5	—	H 15
Broomwater, Teddington .	19	—	X 5
,, West, Teddington .	19	—	X 5
Broomwood-rd, Battersea SW	16	—	U 18
Broseley-gro, Sydenham SE	22	—	Y 29
Brough-street, Battersea SW	16	60	R 19
Brougham-avenue, Acton W	9	—	L 10
,, road, Dalston E .	7	39	I 27
Broughton-av, N. End, Fin. N	1	—	B 15
,, rd, Croydon, Surrey .	26	—	Z^2 22
,, ,, Ealing Dean W	9	—	M 5
,, ,, Fulham SW .	15	59	R 16
,, ,, Stoke Newing. N	7	38	G 26
,, street, S. Lambeth SW	16	61	R 20
Brouncker-road, Acton W .	9	—	N 9
Brown-st, Edgware-rd W .	11	44	L 18
Brownes-road, Catford SE .	22	—	V 31
Brownhill-road, Catford SE .	22	—	V 31
Browning-road, East Ham E	8	—	H 37
,, ,, Leytonstone E .	7	—	E 34
Brownlow-rd, Croyd., Surrey	30	—	Z^7 25
,, ,, Dalston E .	7	39	I 27
,, ,, Finchley N .	1	—	A 16
,, ,, Forest Gate E .	8	—	G 34
,, ,, New Southgate N	2	—	A 22
,, ,, Willesden NW .	5	—	J 11
,, street, Holborn WC .	11	45	L 22
Brown's-road, Plaistow E .	13	—	J 34
,, ,, Surbiton, Surrey	24	—	Z^4 7
,, ,, Walthamstow E	3	—	B 31
Brownslow-rd, Ealing Dean W	9	—	M 5
Brownswood-rd, Finsb. Pk. N	6	33	F 24
Broxash-road, Battersea SW	16	—	U 19
Broxbourne-rd, Orpington	28	—	Z^5 40
Broxholme-rd, W. Norwood	21	—	X 23
Bruce-green, Tottenham N	3	—	A 26
Bruce Gro.-rd, Tottenham N	3	—	B 26
,, ,, sta, Tottenham N	3	—	B 26
,, road, Bromley E .	12	48	K 31
,, ,, Lower Tooting	21	—	Z^1 19
,, ,, Norwood SE .	26	—	Z^3 25
,, ,, Willesden NW .	5	—	I 10
,, terrace, Tottenham N	3	—	B 26
,, Castle-pk, Tottenham N	3	—	A 26
,, ,, rd, Tottenham N	3	—	A 26
Brund-rd, Rotherhithe SE .	12	55	N 28
Brunn-rd, Walthamstow .	3	—	C 30
Brunner-rd, Castlebar Hill W	9	—	K 6
Brunswick-av, Oakleigh Pk N	2	—	A 20
,, gdns, Kensington W .	10	51	N 16
,, gr, Oakleigh Park N .	2	—	A 20
,, park, Peckham SE .	16	62	R 25
,, place, Hoxton N .	11	46	K 25
,, road, Bromley E .	12	49	L 32
,, ,, Leyton E . .	7	—	E 32
,, ,, Norbiton . .	19	—	Z 8
,, ,, Peckham SE .	16	62	R 25
,, ,, Poplar E . .	12	49	L 32
,, ,, Regent's Park NW	11	44	K 20
,, ,, Sutton, Surrey	29	—	Z^7 16
,, ,, Tottenham N .	2	—	C 26
,, ,, Up. Holloway N	6	32	F 21
,, ,, Upton . .	18	—	T 43
,, square WC . .	11	45	K 22
,, ,, Camberwell SE	16	62	R 25
,, st, Blackfriars-rd SE	—	45	N 23
,, ,, Hackney E .	7	39	H 28
,, ,, Hackney-rd E .	12	39	J 26
,, ,, Poplar E . .	12	49	M 32
,, ,, Walthamstow E	3	—	C 32
Brunton's-pl, Limehouse E	12	48	M 29
Brushfield-st, Spitalfields E	12	46	L 26
Brussels-rd, New Wandsw. SW	15	60	T 17
Bruton-st, Berkeley-sq W .	11	44	M 20
Bryanston-square W . .	11	44	L 19
,, st, Bryanston-sq W .	11	44	M 19
Bryanstone-rd, Crouch End N	6	—	D 22
Bryantwood-rd, Holloway N	6	37	G 23
Brydges-rd, Leytonstone E	7	41	H 33
Bryett-rd, Up. Holloway N	6	32	F 22
Brymer-rd, Camberwell SE	17	54	P 26

Brynmaer-road. INDEX TO STREETS, &c. Carlisle-road.

4-in. 9-in. sht. sht. mar.

Brynmaer-rd, Battersea SW 16 60..R 19
Buccleuch-cotz,Up.Clapton E 7 —..E 27
Buchan-road, Peckham SE. 17 63..S 28
Buchanan-gdns, Kilburn NW 10 42..J 13
Buck-lane, Hendon NW . 1 —..O 10
,, street, Camden Tn. NW 6 36..I 20
,, walk, Walthamstow E 3 —..C 32
Buckhold-rd, Wandsworth SW 15 —..U 16
Buckhurst-st, Bethnal Gr. E 12 47..K 28
Buckingham Gate SW . 11 52..O 21
,, Palace SW . . 11 52..N 20
,, ,, road SW . 11 52..O 20
,, rd, De Beauvoir Tn. N 7 38..H 26
,, ,, Harlesden NW . 10 42..J 12
,, ,, Ilford, Essex . 8 —..F 40
,, ,, Leyton E . . 7 —..F 31
,, ,, Stratford E . 7 41..H 33
,, ,, Wood Green N . 2 —..A 22
,, ,, Woodford, Essex 3 —..A 34
,, street, Strand WC . 11 45..M 22
Buckland-cres, Hampst. NW 5 35..H 17
,, road, Ilford . . 8 —..D 38
,, ,, Leyton E . . 7 —..F 31
,, street, Hoxton N . 11 46..J 25
Buckleigh-rd, Streatham . 21 —..Z[1] 21
Bucklersbury, Cheapside EC 11 46..M 25
Buckley-road, Kilburn NW 5 —..J 15
Buckthorne-rd, Brockley SE 4 —..U 29
Budge-row, Queen Vict.-st EC 11 46..M 25
Buer-road, Fulham SW . 15 59..R 15
Buldank-rd, Thorn. Hea. Sur. 26 —..Z[2] 24
Bulinga-st, Westminster SW 16 53..P 22
Bulkeley-road, Norbury . 21 —..Z[2] 22
Bull-court, Middlesex-st E . — 46..L 26
,, ,, Old-street EC . — 46..K 24
,, lane, Chislehurst . 23 —..Z[1] 39
,, ,, Edmonton N . 3 —..A 26
,, & Gate-yd, Holborn WC — 45..L 22
,, Inn-court, Strand WC — 45..M 22
,, road, West Ham E . 12 41..J 33
Bullen-street, Battersea SW 16 60..R 18
Buller-gdns, Barking, Essex 8 —..H 40
,, rd, Kensal Green NW 10 42..J 14
,, ,, Tottenham N . 3 —..B 27
,, ,, Wood Green N . 2 —..A 23
Bulow-rd, Parsons Gr. SW . 15 59..R 16
Bulstrode-av, Hounslow . 14 —..R 1
,, road, Hounslow . 14 —..R 1
,, st, Welbeck-st W . 11 44..L 19
Bulwer-road, Edmonton N 3 —..A 26
,, ,, Leytonstone E . 7 —..E 33
,, ,, Shep. Bush. W 10 50..N 13
Bungalow-rd, Norwood SE 26 —..Z[3] 25
Bunhill Fields, City-rd EC . 11 46..K 25
,, row, Chiswell-st EC . 11 46..K 25
Bunns-lane, Mill Hill NW . 1 —..A 11
Buntinsbr.-rd, Newb. Pk. Ilf. 8 —..D 40
Bunyan-rd, Walthamstow E 3 —..B 29
Burbage-rd, Herne Hill SE 16 —..U 24
Burcharbro-rd, Abbeywood 18 —..Q 43
Burchell-road, Leyton E . 7 —..E 31
,, ,, Peckham SE . 17 63..R 27
Burdett-rd, Croydon, Surrey 26 —..Z[4] 25
,, ,, Kew . . 14 —..R 8
,, ,, Mile End E . 12 49..K 29
,, ,, ry-sta, G.E.R. E 12 48..L 30
,, street, Bromley E . 12 48..K 31
Burdon-la, Sutton, Surrey 29 —..Z[10] 15
,, road, Sutton, Surrey 29 —..Z[9] 15
Burford-gdns, Palmer's Gr. N 2 —..A 23
,, road, Bickley . . 28 —..Z[3] 36
,, ,, Catford SE . 22 —..W 30
,, ,, Stratford E . 7 41..J 32
Burges-st, Limehouse E . 12 48..L 30
Burgess-hill, Hampstead NW 5 —..G 15
,, road, Stratford E . 8 —..I 37
,, ,, Sutton, Surrey . 29 —..Z[7] 16
Burghill-rd, Sydenham SE . 22 —..X 29
Burghley-rd, Kentish Tn. NW 6 36..G 20
,, ,, Leytonstone E . 7 —..E 33
,, ,, Wimbled. Pk. SW 20 —..X 14
,, ,, Wood Green N . 2 —..B 23
Burgon-st, Carter-lane EC . 11 46..M 24
Burgoyne-road, Bow E . 12 48..J 29
,, ,, Finsbury Park N 6 32..D 24
,, ,, Norwood SE . 26 —..Z[3] 25
,, ,, Selhurst SE . 26 —..Z[3] 25
,, ,, Stockwell SW . 16 61..S 22
Burke-st, Canning Town E 12 49..L 33
Burland-road, Battersea SW 16 —..T 19
Burleigh-street, Strand WC 11 45..M 22
Burley-road, Canning Town E 13 —..L 35
,, ,, Plaistow E . 13 —..L 35
Burlington Arcade, Picc. W 11 44..M 20
,, avenue, Kew . . 14 —..P 8
,, crescent, Chiswick W . 15 —..Q 10
,, gdns, Old Bond-st W 11 44..M 20
,, ,, Chiswick W . 14 —..P 10
,, lane, Chiswick W . 15 —..Q 10
,, road, Fulham SW . 15 59..R 14
,, ,, N. Kensington W 10 42..L 15
,, ,, New Mald., Surr. 25 —..Z[2] 11
,, ,, Thornton Heath 21 —..Z[2] 24
,, ,, Tottenham N . 3 —..A 27
,, street, Regent-street W 11 44..M 20
Burma-rd, Stoke Newing. N 7 38..G 25
Burman-st, London-rd SE . 11 54..O 24
Burmester-road, Tooting SW 20 —..X 17
Burnaby-cres, Chiswick W 14 —..P 9
,, gdns, Chiswick W . 14 —..P 9
,, street, Chelsea SW . 15 51..Q 17
Burnbury-rd, Balham SW . 21 —..V 20
Burne-st, Edgware-rd W . 11 43..L 18
Burnell-rd, Sutton, Surrey 29 —..Z[7] 16
Burney-street, Greenwich SE 17 —..Q 32
Burnfoot-av, Fulham SW . 15 59..R 14
Burnham-rd, Chingford E . 3 —..A 30
,, st, Canning Town E . 12 49..L 33
Burnhill-road, Beckenham 22 —..Z[2] 30
Burnley-rd, Willesden Gr. NW 5 34..G 12
,, Stockwell SW . 16 61..S 22
Burns-road, Battersea SW . 16 60..R 18

Burns-road, Plaistow E . 13 —..M 36
,, ,, Wealdsto., M'sex 1a —..B 4
,, ,, Willesden NW . 5 —..I 11
Burnside-st, Bethnal Gr. E 12 48..K 29
Burnt Ash Hill, Lee SE . 23 —..V 34
,, ,, la, New Bromley 23 —..Y 34
,, ,, road, Lee SE . 17 —..U 33
Burnthwaite-la, Fulham SW 15 58..Q 15
Burntoak-la, Halfway-st Kent23 —..V 41
Burntwood-la, Wand. Com.SW20 —..W 17
Buross-st, Commercial-rd E 12 47..M 27
Burr-road, Wandsworth SW 20 —..V 16
,, st, Lr. E. Smithfield E 12 55..N 26
Burrage-grove, Plumstead . 18 —..P 39
,, road, Plumstead . 18 —..Q 39
Burrard-rd, Hampstead NW 5 35..G 16
Burrell-st, Blackfriars-rd SE 11 46..N 24
Burritt-road, Kingston . 19 —..Z[1] 8
Burroughs-lane, Hendon NW 1 —..C 12
Burrows-rd, Kensal Rise W 10 42..J 13
Burslem-st, St George's E 12 47..M 27
Burstock-road, Putney SW . 15 59..S 14
Burston-road, Putney SW . 15 59..T 14
Burt-street, Silvertown E . 13 —..N 35
Burton-road, Kilburn NW . 5 —..J 15
,, ,, Norbiton . 19 —..Z 7
,, ,, Stockwell SW . 16 61..R 23
,, ,, Streatham SW . 20 —..W 16
,, street, Burton-cres WC 11 45..K 21
Burtonhole-la, Mill Hill NW 1 —..A 15
Burton's-court, Chelsea SW 16 52..P 19
,, lane, New Hampton . 19 —..X 1
Burtonshaw-rd, Thames Dit. 24 —..Z[4] 4
Burwash-rd, Plumstead SE 18 —..Q 39
Bury-court, St Mary Axe EC — 46..L 26
,, road, Wood Green N . 2 —..B 23
,, st, Bloomsbury WC . 11 45..L 22
,, ,, Chelsea SW . 16 51..P 18
,, ,, St James's SW . 11 44..N 21
,, ,, St Mary Axe EC — 46..L 26
Busby-pl, Kentish Town NW 6 37..H 21
,, st, Bethnal Green E . 12 47..K 26
Bush-lane, Cannon-st, EC . 11 46..M 25
,, road, Deptford SE . 17 55..P 29
,, ,, Wanstead . 8 —..E 35
Bushey-road, Plaistow E . 13 —..J 35
,, ,, Sutton, Surrey . 29 —..Z[7] 15
Bushnell-road, Tooting . 21 —..W 20
Bushwood-road, Kew . 14 —..Q 8
,, ,, Leytonstone E . 7 —..E 34
Bushy Down, Up. Tooting . 21 —..X 19
,, Hill-rd, Peckham SE 17 62..R 26
,, park, Middlesex . 19 —..Z 4
,, rd, Teddington . 19 —..Y 5
Butcher-rd, Canning Town E 17 56..Q 30
,, ,, Deptford SE . 13 —..M 34
Butchers' Co. H, B'mew-cl EC — 46..L 24
,, lane, Hendon NW . 1 —..C 13
,, row, Limehouse E . 12 48..M 29
Bute-avenue, Petersham . 19 —..V 7
,, rd, Carshalton, Surrey 30 —..Z[7] 20
,, ,, Croydon, Surrey 26 —..Z[5] 23
,, ,, Ilford . . 8 —..D 39
,, st, S. Kensington SW 11 51..O 17
Butler-avenue, Harrow . 1a —..D 3
,, rd, Harrow, Middlesex 1a —..D 3
,, ,, Thorn. Hea., Sur. 26 —..Z[2] 24
,, street, Milton-street EC 11 46..L 25
Butter Hill, Carshal., Surrey 26 —..Z[6] 19
Buttesland-st, Hoxton N . 11 46..K 25
Buxton-gardens, Acton W . 9 —..M 9
,, road, Barnes SW . 15 —..S 11
,, ,, Croydon, Surrey 26 —..Z[3] 23
,, ,, Stratford E . 7 41..H 33
,, ,, Walthamstow E 3 —..C 30
,, ,, Willesden Gr. NW 5 —..H 13
,, st, Bethnal Green E . 12 47..K 26
Byam-street, Fulham SW . 15 59..S 16
Byegrove-rd, S. Wimble. SW 20 —..Z 17
Byfeld-road, Barnes SW . 15 —..R 12
Byfield-road, Isleworth . 14 —..S 4
,, ,, Walthamstow E 7 —..D 30
Byrgrove-street, Poplar E . 12 48..M 31
Byne-rd, Lr. Sydenham SE 22 —..Y 28
Bynes-rd, Croydon, Surrey 30 —..Z[9] 24
Byng-place, Woburn-sq WC 11 45..K 21
,, street, Millwall E . 12 56..N 30
Byrne-road, Balham . . 21 —..W 20
Byron-av, East Ham E . 8 —..I 37
,, ,, Sutton, Surrey. 29 —..Z[7] 17
,, rd, Harrow, Middlesex 1a —..O 4
,, ,, Leyton-street E 7 —..E 31
,, ,, Walthamstow E 3 —..B 31
,, ,, Wealdst., M'sex 1a —..A 4
,, ,, Wembley . . 4 —..F 6
,, st, Bromley . . 12 47..L 31
Byton-rd, Lower Tooting . 21 —..Y 19
Byward-st, Gt. Tower-st EC 12 46..M 26

C

Cable-street, St George's E 12 47..M 27
,, ,, ry-sta, Shadwell E . 12 47..M 28
Cabul-road, Battersea SW . 16 60..S 18
Cadbury-rd, Bermondsey SE 12 55..O 26
Caddington-rd, Child's Hi NW 5 —..F 15
Cader-rd, Wandsworth SW 15 —..U 17
Cadiz-street, Stepney E . 12 48..L 29
Cadogan-gdns, Chelsea SW . 11 52..O 19
,, place, Chelsea SW . 11 52..O 19
,, rd, Surbiton, Surrey . 24 —..Z[3] 6
,, square, Chelsea SW . 11 52..O 19
,, street, Chelsea SW . 16 52..O 18
,, terrace, Chelsea SW . 11 52..O 19
,, ,, Victoria Park E 7 40..I 30
Cæsar's Camp, Wim. Com.SW 30b —..Z[8] 36
Cahir-street, Millwall E . 17 56..P 31
Cains-street, Islington N . 6 37..I 23
Caird-street W . . . 10 42..K 15
Cairns-road, Battersea SW . 16 60..T 18
Cairo-rd, Walthamstow E . 3 —..C 31
,, ,, Walthamstow E . 43 —..B 29

Caistor-road, Balham . 21 —..V 19
,, Park-rd, West Ham E 12 41..J 34
Caithness-road, Streatham . 21 —..Z[1] 20
,, ,, W. Kens. W . 10 58..O 14
Calabria-road, Highbury N 6 38..H 24
Calais-st, Camberwell SE . 16 62..R 24
Calbourne-road, Balham . 21 —..V 19
Caldecot-rd, Camberwell SE 16 62..S 24
Calderon-road, Leyton E . 7 41..G 32
Calder's-row, Brixton . 21 —..V 22
Caldervale-rd, Clapham SW 16 —..U 21
Caldew-st, Camberwell SE . 17 54..Q 25
Caldwell-yd, Thames-st, EC — 46..M 24
Cale-street, Chelsea SW . 15 51..P 18
Caledon-road, East Ham E 13 —..J 37
,, ,, ,, ,, 8 —..I 38
Caledonia-st, Pimlico SW . 16 52..P 20
Caledonian-rd, Islington N 6 37..H 22
,, ry-sta,G.N.P.&B.Holl.N 6 37..H 22
California-rd, New Malden 24 —..Z[2] 9
Calloway-rd, Shep. Bush. W 10 50..M 12
Calmington-rd, Camberw. SE 17 54..Q 26
Calmont-road, Ravensbourne 22 —..Z[1] 32
Calonne-rd, Wimbledon SW 20 —..X 13
Calthorpe-st, Gray's I.-rd WC 11 45 K 23
Calton-road, Dulwich SE . 16 —..U 25
Calverley-gro, Hornsey Ri. N 6 32..E 21
Calvert-av, Shoreditch E . 12 46..K 26
,, rd, E. Greenwich SE . 17 57..Q 33
Calverton-road, East Ham E 13 —..J 38
Calydon-rd, Old Charlton . 18 —..Q 35
Camac-road, Twickenham . 19 —..V 3
Cambalt-road, Putney SW . 15 59..T 13
Camberwell SE . . . 16 62..R 24
,, Cemetery, E. Dulw. SE 17 —..U 27
,, green, Camberwell SE 16 62..R 24
,, grove, Camberwell SE 16 62..R 25
,, road SE . . . 16 54..Q 24
,, New-road . . . 16 53..Q 23
,, rd ry-sta, S.E. & C. SE 16 62..R 24
Cambole-rd, Lr. Tooting SW 20 —..X 18
Camborne-av, Ealing W . 9 —..N 6
,, road, Sutton, Surrey . 29 —..Z[9] 16
Cambray-road, Balham SW 21 —..V 20
Cambria-rd, Camberwell SE 16 62..S 24
Cambrian-road, Leyton E . 7 —..E 30
,, ,, Richmond . 14 —..U 7
Cambridge-av, Kilburn NW 10 43..J 16
,, ,, New Malden . 25 —..Z[1] 10
,, circus, Char. Cro.-rd WC 11 45..M 21
,, gdns, Kilburn NW . 10 43..J 16
,, ,, N. Kensington W 10 42..L 14
,, Gate, Regent's Pk. NW 11 44..K 20
,, Grove-rd, Kingston . 19 —..Z[1] 8
,, Heath-station E . 12 39..J 27
,, park, Twickenham . 14 —..U 6
,, ,, gdns, Twicken. 14 —..U 6
,, ,, rd, Wanstead E 8 —..D 34
,, place, Paddington W 11 43..L 18
,, ,, Kensington W . 10 51..N 16
,, road, Barking . . 8 —..I 39
,, ,, Barnes SW . 15 —..R 11
,, ,, Battersea SW . 16 60..R 18
,, ,, Blackheath SE . 4 64..R 31
,, ,, Bromley, . . 23 —..Z 34
,, ,, Carshalton . 29 —..Z[7] 18
,, ,, Chiswick W . 14 —..P 9
,, ,, Cottenham Pk SW 20 —..Z[1] 12
,, ,, Croydon, Surrey 26 —..Z[4] 23
,, ,, Hammersmith W 10 58..O 13
,, ,, Ilford . . 8 —..E 41
,, ,, Kilburn NW . 10 43..J 16
,, ,, Kingston . . 19 —..Z[1] 8
,, ,, Lee SE . . 17 —..U 33
,, ,, Mile End E . 12 47..K 28
,, ,, New Mald., Surr. 25 —..Z[2] 10
,, ,, Richmond . . 14 —..U 6
,, ,, Sidcup . . 23 —..X 40
,, ,, S. Norwood SE . 27 —..Z[2] 27
,, ,, Teddington . 19 —..X 4
,, ,, Walthamstow E 7 —..D 30
,, row, Camden Town . 6 37..I 21
,, square, Edgware-rd W 11 43..L 18
,, street, Camberwell SE 16 54..Q 24
,, ,, Edgware-rd W . 11 44..L 18
,, ,, Pimlico SW . 16 52..P 20
,, ,, St Pancras NW . 11 37..J 21
,, terrace, Edgware-rd W 11 43..L 18
,, ,, Regent's Park NW 11 44..K 20
Cambus-rd, Canning Town E 13 —..L 34
Camden-cr, Camden Tn. NW 6 37..H 21
,, grove, Peckham SE . 17 62..R 26
,, ,, N., Peckham SE 17 62..R 26
,, hill, Up. Norwood . 21 —..Y 25
,, park, Chislehurst, Kent 23 —..Z 37
,, ,, rd, Chisleh., Kent 23 —..Z 37
,, ,, ,, Camden-rd NW 6 37..H 21
,, rd, Camden Town NW 6 37..H 21
,, ,, Carshal., Surrey 29 —..Z[7] 18
,, ,, Sutton, Surrey. 29 —..Z[7] 16
,, ,, Walthamstow E 7 —..D 30
,, sq, Camden Town NW 6 37..H 21
,, st, Bethnal Green-rd E 12 47..K 27
,, ,, Camden Town NW 6 36..I 20
,, ,, Islington Gr. N 11 38..J 24
,, ,, Peckham SE . 17 62..R 26
,, Town NW . . . 6 36..I 20
,, ,, sta, Ham. Tu.R 6 36..I 20
,, ,, ,, N.L.R. . 6 36..I 21
Camel-ct, Kensington . — 51..N 16
Camelford-rd, N. Kens. W . 10 42..L 14
Camellia-st, S. Lambeth SW 16 61..R 21
Camelot-st, Southwark SE . 12 54..O 25
Camera-square, Chelsea SW 16 51..Q 17
Cameron-rd, Croydon, Surr. 26 —..Z[4] 23
,, ,, Ilford . . 8 —..F 41
,, st, N. Woolwich E . 13 —..M 38
Camilla-rd, Bermondsey SE 17 55..P 27
Camlet-st, Bethnal Green E 12 46..K 26
Camomile-st, Bishopsg.-st EC 11 46..L 25
Camp-lane, Wimbledon SW 20 —..Y 13
,, street, Canonbury N. 7 38..H 25

Campana-road, Fulham SW 15 59..R 15
Campbell-road, Bow-road E 12 48..K 31
,, ,, Croydon, Surrey 26 —..Z[4] 23
,, ,, East Ham E . 13 —..J 31
,, ,, Hanwell W . 9 —..M 3
,, ,, Holloway N . 6 32..F 23
,, ,, Twickenham . 19 —..V 2
,, ,, Walthamstow E 3 —..C 30
Campdale-rd, Up. Hollow. N 6 37..F 21
Campden-gro, Kensington W 10 51..N 16
,, hill, Kensington W . 10 50..N 15
,, ,, gdns, Kens. W . 10 50..M 15
,, ,, rd, Kens. W . 10 50..N 15
,, ,, square, Kens. W 10 50..M 15
,, House-rd, Kens. W . 10 51..N 16
,, rd, Croydon, Surrey . 30 —..Z[8] 25
,, street, Kensington W 10 50..N 16
Campion-road, Putney SW . 15 —..T 13
Campo-road, Hounslow . 14 —..R 2
Campsbourne-rd, Hornsey N 2 —..B 22
Camrose-street, Plumstead 18 —..P 41
Canada Dock, Rotherhithe SE 12 55..O 28
,, Pond, Rotherhithe SE 12 55..O 29
,, yard, Rotherhithe SE 12 55..O 29
Canal Dockyard, Blackwall E 12 57..N 32
,, road, Kingsland N . 7 38..I 26
,, ,, Mile End E . 12 48..K 29
Canbury, Norbiton . . 19 —..Z 6
,, avenue, Norbiton . 19 —..Z 7
,, Park-road, Norbiton . 19 —..Z 7
,, promenade, Norbiton 19 —..Z 6
Cancell-road, N. Brixton SW 16 61..R 23
Candahar-rd, Battersea SW 16 60..S 18
Candler-road, Tottenham N 7 33..D 25
Candy-street, Bow E . . 7 40..I 30
Canfield-gdns, Kilburn NW 5 35..H 16
Canford-road, Clapham SW 16 —..T 19
Canhall-rd, Leytonstone E . 7 41..G 33
Canham-road, Norwood SE 26 —..Z[2] 25
Canning-cres, Wood Green N 2 —..A 23
,, pl, S. Kensington SW . 10 51..O 17
,, rd, Croydon, Surrey . 26 —..Z[6] 25
,, ,, Highbury N . 6 38..F 24
,, ,, Walthamstow E 3 —..B 30
,, ,, Wealdst., M'sex 1a —..B 4
,, Town E . . . . 12 49..L 33
,, ,, sta, G.E.R. E . 12 49..L 33
Cannon-al, St Paul's-ch'yd EC — 46..M 24
,, hill, Hampstead NW 5 35..G 16
,, ,, lane, Merton SW 20 —..Z[1] 14
,, place, Hampstead NW 5 35..F 17
,, rd, Palmer's Green N 2 —..A 22
,, row, Westminster SW — 53..N 22
,, street EC . . . 11 46..M 25
,, ,, rd, Commer.-rd E 12 47..M 27
,, ,, ry-sta, EC . . 11 46..M 25
Cannonhill-la, Raynes Pk SW 25 —..Z[2] 14
Canon-rd, Bickley, Kent . 28 —..Z[2] 35
,, ,, Hornsey N . 2 —..C 23
Canonbie-rd, Forest Hill SE 22 —..V 28
Canonbury N . . . . 6 38..H 24
,, gr, Islington N . 6 38..I 24
,, lane, Islington N . 6 38..I 24
,, pk, N., Islington N . 6 38..H 24
,, ,, S., Islington N . 6 38..H 24
,, place, Islington N . 6 38..H 24
,, ry-sta, N.L.R. N . 6 38..H 24
,, road, Forest Hill SE . 22 —..V 28
,, ,, Islington N . 6 38..H 24
,, square, Islington N . 6 38..H 24
,, street, Islington N . 6 38..I 24
Canon's-pk, Stanmore, M'sex 1a —..A 8
Canrobert-st, Bethnal Gr.-rd E12 47..K 27
Canterbury-gr, W. Norwood 21 —..X 23
,, road, Ball's Pond-rd N 7 38..H 26
,, ,, Croydon, Surrey 26 —..Z[4] 22
,, ,, Deptford SE . 17 55..Q 28
,, ,, Kilburn NW . 10 42..J 15
,, ,, Leyton E . . 7 —..D 32
,, ,, Stockwell SW . 16 61..S 23
,, terrace, Kilburn NW . 10 42..J 15
,, ,, St John's Wd NW 10 43..J 17
Cantire-st, Camberwell SE . 16 62..R 24
Cantlowes-rd, Camd. Tn NW 6 37..H 21
Canton-street, Poplar E . 12 48..M 30
Cantrell-rd, Bow Common E 12 48..L 30
Cantwell-road, Plumstead . 18 —..R 38
Cape-road, Tottenham N . 3 —..B 27
Capel-ct, Bartholomew-la EC — 46..M 24
,, road, Forest Gate EC 8 —..G 35
Capland-st, Marylebone W . 11 43..K 18
Caple-road, Harlesden NW . 10 —..J 11
Capri-rd, Croydon, Surrey . 26 —..Z[5] 26
Capworth-street, Leyton E . 7 —..E 31
Carbuncle-ditch, Tottenham N 3 —..A 27
Carburton-st, Gt Portl.-st W 11 44..K 20
Carden-road, Peckham SE . 17 62..T 27
Cardigan-road, Bow E . 12 48..J 30
,, ,, Ilford . . 8 —..F 42
,, ,, Richmond . 14 —..U 7
,, street, Lambeth SE . 16 53..P 23
Cardington-st, Hamp.-rd NW 11 44..J 21
Cardross-st, Hammersmith W 10 50..O 12
Cardova-rd, Bethnal Green E 12 48..K 29
Cardozo-rd, Holloway N . 6 37..G 22
Carew-rd, Carshalton, Surrey 30 —..Z[8] 20
,, ,, Ealing W . . 9 —..N 6
,, ,, Thor. Hea., Surr. 26 —..Z[2] 23
,, ,, Tottenham N . 3 —..B 27
Carey-lane EC . . . 46 —..L 24
,, st, Lincoln's Inn WC 11 45..L 23
Cargill-rd, Wandsworth SW 20 —..V 17
Carholme-rd, Forest Hill SE 22 —..W 29
Carisbrook-rd, Waltham. E 3 —..C 29
Carleton-rd, Holloway N . 6 37..G 22
Carlingford-rd, Hampst. NW 5 35..G 18
,, ,, Tottenham N . 2 —..B 24
Carlisle-av, Fenchurch-st EC — 46..M 26
,, pl, Victoria-st SW . 11 52..O 20
,, road, Croydon, Surrey 26 —..Z[6] 21
,, ,, Kilburn NW . 5 —..I 15
,, ,, Leyton E . . 7 —..F 31

	4-in. sht.	9-in. sht.	mar.
Cheltenham-rd, Leyton-st E	7	—..D	32
,, terr, Chelsea SW .	16	52..P	19
Chelverton-road, Putney SW	15	59..T	14
Cheneys-rd, Leytonstone E	7	41..G	33
Chenies-st, Totten. Ct.-rd WC	11	45..L	21
Chepstow-mews, W'brne-gro W	—	43..M	16
,, pl, W'bourne-gro W .	10	43..M	16
,, rise, Croydon, Surrey	26	—..Z^{6}	25
,, rd, Croydon, Surrey .	26	—..Z^{6}	25
,, villas, Notting Hill W	10	43..M	15
Chequer's-gr, Palmer's Gr. N	2	—..A	24
Cherington-road, Hanwell W	9	—..M	4
Cheriton-square, Tooting SW	21	—..W	19
Cherry-gdns Pier, Ro'hithe	12	55..N	27
,, ,, st, Bermondsey SE	12	5..O	27
,, Orchard-rd, Croy., Surr.	26	—..Z^{5}	25
Cherrytree-ct, Aldersg.-st EC	—	46..L	24
,, ,, hill, Highgate N	2	—..C	19
Chertsey-road, Chiswick W	14	—..P	8
,, st, Toot., Graveney SW	21	—..T	19
Chesfield-road, Norbiton .	19	—..Y	7
Chesham-pl, Belgrave-sq SW	11	52..O	19
,, road, Kingston . .	19	—..Z^{1}	8
,, st, Belgrave-sq SW .	11	52..O	19
,, terr, Ealing Dean W .	9	—..M	5
Cheshire-st, Bethnal Green	12	47..K	27
Chesholm-rd, Sto. Newing. N	7	38..F	26
Chesilton-rd, Fulham SW .	15	59..R	15
Chesney-street, Battersea SW	16	60..R	19
Chesnut-av, Walthamstow E	3	—..C	32
,, gr, Balham SW . .	21	—..V	19
,, road, Plumstead SE .	18	—..U	31
,, ,, Raynes Park SW	20	—..Z^{1}	14
,, ,, Tottenham N .	3	—..B	26
Chessington, Surrey . .	28a	—..Z^{8}	6
,, road, Ewell, Surrey .	28a	—..Z^{8}	9
Chesson-rd, W. Kens. SW .	15	58..P	15
Chester-gate, Regent's Pk NW	11	44..K	20
,, mansions, Pimlico SW	11	52..O	20
,, mews, Somers Town W	11	44..K	20
,, pl, Hyde Park-sq W .	11	43..M	18
,, ,, Plumstead .	18	—..P	39
,, road, Canning Town E	12	49..K	33
,, ,, Highgate N .	6	31..F	20
,, ,, Ilford . .	8	—..E	41
,, ,, Regent's Park NW	11	44..K	20
,, ,, Tottenham N .	3	—..B	25
,, ,, Upton E . .	8	—..I	36
,, ,, Walthamstow E	7	—..D	29
,, square, Pimlico SW .	11	52..O	20
,, street, Lambeth SE .	16	53..P	23
,, ,, Leytonstone E .	7	—..F	33
,, ,, Pimlico SW .	11	52..O	20
,, terrace, Chelsea SW .	11	52..O	19
,, ,, Eaton-sq SW .	11	52..O	19
,, ,, Regent's Park NW	11	44..J	20
Chesterfield-gdns, Harringay N	2	—..C	24
,, ,, Hampstead NW	5	35..G	17
,, ,, Mayfair W .	11	44..N	20
,, gro, E. Dulwich SE .	17	—..T	26
,, road, Chiswick W .	15	—..P	10
,, ,, Ewell, Surrey .	28a	—..Z^{9}	9
,, ,, Leyton E . .	7	—..D	32
,, ,, Norbiton . .	19	—..Z	7
,, street, King's Cross WC	11	45..J	22
,, ,, Mayfair W .	11	44..N	20
,, walk, Greenwich SE .	17	64..R	32
Chesterford-rd, Manor Pk. E	8	—..H	38
Chesterton-rd, N. Kens. W	10	42..L	14
,, ,, Plaistow E .	13	—..K	34
,, terrace, Plaistow E .	13	—..K	34
Chestnut-av, Forest Gate E	8	—..G	35
,, ,, Thames Ditton	24	—..Z^{4}	2
,, grove, Balham SW .	21	—..V	19
,, ,, N. Mald., Surrey	24	—..Z^{2}	9
,, road, Norbiton . .	19	—..Z	6
,, ,, Plumstead .	18	—..P	40
,, ,, West Dulwich	21	—..X	24
,, walk, Walthamstow E	3	—..C	32
Chetwode-rd, Up. Tooting .	21	—..W	19
Chetwynd-rd, H'gate-rd NW	6	36..F	20
Cheval-place, Brompton SW	10	52..O	18
,, street, Millwall E .	12	56..O	30
Chevening-rd, E. Greenw. SE	17	57..P	34
,, ,, Queen's Park NW	10	34..J	14
,, ,, Up. Norwood .	21	—..Z^{1}	25
Cheverton-rd, Hornsey Ri. N	6	32..E	21
Chevet-street, Edmonton N	3	—..A	27
,, ,, Homerton E .	7	40..H	29
Cheviot-rd, W. Norwood .	21	—..Y	23
Chewton-rd, Walthamstow E	3	—..C	29
Cheyne-gardens, Chelsea SW	16	52..Q	18
,, row, Chelsea SW .	16	51..Q	18
,, walk, Chelsea SW .	16	51..Q	18
,, ,, Croydon . .	27	—..Z^{6}	26
Chichele-rd, Cricklewood NW	5	—..G	14
Chichester Rents, Chan. la WC	—	45..L	23
,, road, Croydon . .	26	—..Z^{6}	25
,, ,, Kilburn NW .	10	43..J	16
,, ,, Leytonstone E .	7	41..G	33
,, ,, Westbourne-pk W	10	43..L	16
,, street, Pimlico SW .	16	52..P	21
Chicksand-st, Spitalfields E	—	47..L	26
Chiddingstone-st, Fulham SW	15	59..R	16
Chilcot-street, Poplar E .	12	48..M	31
Childebert-road, Tooting SW	21	—..W	20
Childeric-rd, Deptford SE .	4	63..R	29
Childers-st, Deptford SE .	17	56..Q	29
Child's Hill NW	5	—..F	15
Chillerton-road, Tooting SW	21	—..Y	19
Chiltern-road, Bow E . .	12	48..K	31
Chilterton-rd, Lr. Tooting	21	—..T	19
Chilton-st, Bethnal Green E	12	47..K	26
,, ,, Rotherhithe SE	17	56..P	29
Chilver-st, E. Greenwich SE	17	57..P	34
Chilworth-mews, Paddington W	—	43..L	17
,, st, Paddington W	10	43..L	17
China-sq, Lambeth-rd SE .	11	53..O	23
,, walk, Lambeth-rd SE	11	53..O	23
Chinbrook-rd, Grove Pk. SE	23	—..X	35
Chine-rd, Muswell Hill N .	2	—..C	21
Chingford E	3	—..A	31
Chingford Hatch E . .	3	—..A	33
,, lane, Chingford E .	3	—..A	32
,, road, Chingford E .	3	—..A	31
,, ,, Walthamstow E	3	—..B	31
,, Mt. Cemet., Chingf'd E	3	—..A	31
Chip-street, Clapham SW .	16	61..S	21
Chipley-street, Deptford SE	17	56..Q	29
Chippenham-rd, Maida Hill W	10	42..K	15
Chipstead-st, Fulham SW .	15	59..R	16
Chisenhale-rd, Old Ford E .	12	48..J	29
Chish-road, Richmond .	14	—..U	7
Chislehurst, Kent . .	23	—..Z	38
,, av, Finchley N .	1	—..A	17
,, common, Kent . .	23	—..Z	38
,, ry-sta, S.E. & C.R. .	23	—..Z^{1}	37
,, road, Bickley, Kent .	23	—..Z^{1}	36
,, ,, Orpington .	28	—..Z^{5}	41
,, ,, Richmond .	14	—..T	7
,, ,, Sidcup, Kent .	23	—..Y	41
,, West, Kent . .	23	—..Z	38
Chislett-road, Kilburn NW .	5	35..H	16
Chiswell-st, Finsbury EC	11	46..L	25
,, ,, Peckham SE .	16	62..R	25
Chiswick W	15	—..P	11
,, Ait, Chiswick W .	15	—..P	11
,, High-road, Chiswick W	14	—..P	8
,, House, Chiswick W .	10	—..O	11
,, lane, Chiswick W .	15	—..P	11
,, mall, Chiswick W .	15	—..P	11
,, New Town . .	15	—..P	11
,, ry-sta, L. & S.W.R. .	14	—..Q	9
,, ,, ,, Met. R. .	9	—..O	10
,, road, Chiswick Park W	9	—..O	9
,, square, Chiswick W .	15	—..P	11
Chivalry-rd, Battersea SW .	16	60..T	18
Chivers-rd, Chingford E .	3	—..A	31
Choats Manor-rd, Barking .	13	—..L	43
Chobham-rd, Stratf'd N.Tn. E	7	41..H	32
Cholmeley-park, Highgate NE	6	32..E	20
Cholmondley-walk, Richm'd	14	—..T	6
Choumert-gro, Peckham SE	17	62..S	26
,, road, Peckham SE .	17	62..S	26
Chrisp-street, Poplar E .	12	48..M	31
Christ Ch.-rd, Hampstead NW	5	35..F	17
,, ,, ,, Hornsey N	6	32..D	22
,, ,, st, E. Greenw. SE	17	57..P	33
Christch.-av, Brond'bury NW	5	—..H	15
,, ,, N. Finchley N .	1	—..A	17
,, park, Sutton, Surrey	29	—..Z^{8}	16
,, passage, Newgate-st EC	11	46..L	24
,, road, East Sheen SE .	14	—..T	9
,, ,, Ilford, Essex .	8	—..F	39
,, ,, Merton SW .	20	—..Z	17
,, ,, Purley, Surrey .	30	—..Z^{10}	23
,, ,, Tulse Hill .	21	—..V	22
,, street, Chelsea SW .	16	52..P	18
Christian-st, Commercial-rd E	12	47..M	27
Christie-rd, S. Hackney E .	7	40..H	29
Christopher-st, Finsb'y-sq EC	—	46..L	25
Chryssell-road, Brixton SW	16	53..Q	23
Chubworthy-st, Deptford SE	17	56..Q	29
Chudleigh-road, Brockley SE	4	—..U	30
,, ,, Twickenham .	14	—..U	3
Chumleigh-st, Camberwell SE	17	54..Q	25
Church-ap, W. Dulwich SE	22	—..X	25
,, av, Chingford E .	3	—..A	32
,, ,, East Sheen SW .	14	—..S	10
,, ,, Sidcup . .	23	—..Y	38
,, court, Old Jewry EC .	—	46..M	25
,, crescent, Finchley N .	1	—..A	15
,, ,, Muswell Hill N .	2	—..C	20
,, End, Hendon NW .	1	—..B	13
,, entry, Carter-lane EC	—	46..M	24
,, gdns, Ealing W . .	9	—..N	6
,, gro, Hampton, Wick.	19	—..Z	5
,, ,, Lewisham SE .	4	—..T	31
,, hill, Walthamstow E .	3	—..C	31
,, ,, Wimbledon	20	—..Y	15
,, House, Westminster SW	11	53..O	21
,, lane, Battersea SW .	16	60..R	18
,, ,, Beddington, Sur.	26	—..Z^{6}	21
,, ,, Bromley, Kent	28	—..Z^{5}	36
,, ,, Charlton . .	18	—..P	35
,, ,, Chessington, Sur.	28a	—..Z^{8}	7
,, ,, E. Finchley N .	2	—..B	18
,, ,, Hammersmith W	15	58..P	14
,, ,, Kingsbury NW .	5	—..E	10
,, ,, Hornsey N .	2	—..C	23
,, ,, Leytonstone E .	7	—..E	33
,, ,, Merton SW .	20	—..Z^{1}	15
,, ,, Teddington .	19	—..X	4
,, ,, Toot., Grave. SW	21	—..Y	19
,, ,, Tottenham N .	3	—..A	26
,, ,, Wealdst., M'sex	1a	—..A	4
,, ,, Whitechapel E .	12	47..L	27
,, ,, Willesden NW .	5	—..H	11
,, ,, Wimbledon SW	20	—..Z	12
,, passage, Sutton, Surrey	29	—..Z^{7}	16
,, path, Fulham SW .	15	58..Q	14
,, ,, Mitcham, Surrey	25	—..Z^{2}	18
,, ,, Mortlake SW .	14	—..S	10
,, ,, Poplar E . .	12	48..M	30
,, ,, Sto. Newing. N	7	38..G	25
,, ,, Wanstead .	8	—..D	34
,, pl, Gresham-st, EC .	—	46..L	24
,, ,, Kensal Green W	10	42..K	14
,, ,, Peckham SE .	17	55..Q	27
,, road, Acton W . .	9	—..N	9
,, ,, Barking, Essex	8	—..I	39
,, ,, Barnes SW .	15	—..R	11
,, ,, Battersea SW .	15	60..R	17
,, ,, Beckenham .	22	—..Z^{2}	30
,, ,, Beddington, Surr.	26	—..Z^{6}	20
,, ,, Bethnal Green E	12	47..K	27
,, ,, Brixton SW .	16	—..U	22
,, ,, Bromley, Kent	27	—..Z^{2}	32
,, ,, Carshalton .	29	—..Z^{8}	16
,, ,, Claygate, Surrey	28a	—..Z^{8}	3
,, ,, Croydon, Surrey	26	—..Z^{6}	24
,, ,, Essex-road N .	7	38..I	25
,, ,, Ham Common	19	—..X	6
,, ,, Hammersmith W	10	58..O	12
Church-rd, Hampstead NW	1	—..B	13
,, ,, Hanwell W .	9	—..L	3
,, ,, Highgate N .	6	31..D	19
,, ,, Homerton E .	7	40..H	29
,, ,, Ilford . .	8	—..E	40
,, ,, Kent Tn, Surrey	24	—..Z^{2}	2
,, ,, Kingston . .	19	—..Z^{1}	7
,, ,, Leyton E . .	7	—..E	30
,, ,, Long Ditt., Surr.	24	—..Z^{5}	5
,, ,, Malden, Surrey	25	—..Z^{5}	10
,, ,, Manor Park E .	8	—..H	37
,, ,, Merton SW .	20	—..Z^{1}	17
,, ,, Osterley Park .	14	—..Q	3
,, ,, Perry Vale SE .	22	—..W	28
,, ,, Richmond .	14	—..S	7
,, ,, S. Acton W .	9	—..O	10
,, ,, Stoke Newing. N	7	39..F	26
,, ,, Surbiton, Surrey	24	—..Z^{3}	6
,, ,, Teddington .	19	—..X	3
,, ,, Tottenham N .	3	—..A	26
,, ,, Upper Norwood	21	—..Z^{2}	25
,, ,, Up. Park-rd NW	6	36..H	19
,, ,, Walthamstow E	3	—..C	31
,, ,, Willesden NW .	5	—..I	11
,, ,, Wimbledon SW	20	—..Y	14
,, row, Chislehurst, Kent	23	—..Z^{1}	39
,, ,, Hampstead NW	5	35..G	17
,, ,, Fenchurch-st EC	—	46..M	26
,, ,, Limehouse E .	12	48..M	30
,, street, Bethnal Green E	12	46..K	26
,, ,, Canning Town E	12	49..L	33
,, ,, Chelsea SW .	16	51..P	18
,, ,, Chiswick W .	15	—..P	11
,, ,, Croydon, Surrey	26	—..Z^{6}	23
,, ,, Deptford SE .	17	63..R	30
,, ,, Edgware-rd W .	11	43..K	18
,, ,, Fulham SW .	15	59..S	15
,, ,, Greenwich SE .	17	57..Q	32
,, ,, Hampton .	19	—..Z	1
,, ,, Isleworth .	14	—..R	5
,, ,, Islington N .	6	38..I	24
,, ,, Kensington W	10	51..N	16
,, ,, Kingston . .	19	—..Z^{1}	6
,, ,, Lee SE . .	17	64..T	33
,, ,, Mitcham, Surrey	25	—..Z^{2}	18
,, ,, New Cross SE .	4	—..R	30
,, ,, N. Woolwich E	13	—..N	38
,, ,, Paddington W .	11	43..L	18
,, ,, Peckham SE .	16	62..R	25
,, ,, Plaistow E .	13	—..J	34
,, ,, Shoreditch E .	12	46..K	26
,, ,, Soho W . .	11	45..M	21
,, ,, Stoke Newing. N	7	33..F	25
,, ,, Sutton, Surrey	29	—..Z^{7}	16
,, ,, Twickenham .	19	—..V	4
,, ,, West Ham E .	12	41..J	33
,, ,, Woolwich .	13	—..O	37
,, terrace, Lee SE . .	17	64..T	33
,, walk, Child's Hill NW	5	—..F	15
,, ,, Th. Ditt., Surr.	24	—..Z^{3}	3
,, ,, Wandsworth SW	15	60..T	16
Church Fields-rd, Beck'ham	22	—..Z^{2}	29
Churchfield-av, N. Finchley N	1	—..A	18
,, ,, road, Ealing W.	9	—..M	6
,, ,, Welling . .	18	—..T	41
,, ,, East, Acton W .	10	—..M	10
,, ,, West, Acton W .	9	—..M	9
Churchill-rd, Canning Tn. E	13	—..M	35
,, ,, Croydon, Surrey	30	—..Z^{9}	24
,, ,, Homerton E .	7	39..H	28
,, ,, Kentish Tn. NW	6	36..G	20
,, ,, Willesden NW .	5	—..H	13
Church Manor-way, Plumst.	13	—..P	41
Churston-av, Plaistow E	13	—..J	35
Churton-street, Pimlico SW	16	52..P	21
Cibber-rd, Forest Hill SE .	22	—..W	29
Cicada-rd, Wandsworth SW	15	—..U	17
Cintra-pk, Up. Norwood SE	22	—..Z^{1}	26
Circular-rd, Tottenham N .	3	—..B	26
Circus, The, Greenwich SE .	17	64..Q	32
,, place, London Wall EC	—	46..L	25
,, rd, St John's Wood NW	10	43..J	17
,, street, Greenwich SE .	4	64..R	31
,, ,, Marylebone-rd W	11	44..L	18
Cirencester-st, Harrow-rd W	10	43..K	16
Cisburn-road, Hornsey N .	2	—..C	23
Citizen-road, Holloway N .	6	37..G	23
City and Guilds of London Institute, Gresham-st EC	—	46..L	24
City Garden-row, Clerkenw N	—	46..J	24
,, road EC . . .	11	46..J	24
,, ,, Basin EC . .	11	46..J	24
,, ,, ry-sta, C. & S.L.	11	46..J	24
,, of Lond. Cemet., Ilfd E	8	—..G	36
,, ,, Union, Bow E .	12	48..K	30
,, ,, & Tower Hamlet's Cemetery, Bow E .	12	48..K	30
Clack-st, Rotherhithe SE .	12	55..N	28
Clacton-rd, Walthamstow E	7	—..D	29
Clairview-road, Tooting .	21	—..Y	20
Clancarty-rd, Fulham SW .	15	59..S	16
Clandon-road, Ilford . .	8	—..F	41
Clanricarde-gdns, Nott. Hi. W	10	43..M	16
Clapham SW	16	61..S	20
,, Common, Clapham SW	16	60..T	19
,, park, Clapham SW .	16	—..U	21
,, road, Clapham SW .	16	61..S	21
,, Junction ry-sta SW .	16	60..S	18
,, & N. Stkwell ry-sta SW	16	61..S	21
,, Pk.-rd, Clapham SW .	16	61..T	21
,, rd sta, Stockwell SW .	16	61..S	21
Claps Gate-lane, Barking E	13	—..K	39
Clapton E	7	39..F	27
,, Common, Up. Clapton E	7	33..E	27
,, ry-sta, G.E.R. . .	7	33..F	28
,, sq, Lr. Clapton E .	7	39..G	28
Clara-place, Woolwich .	18	—..P	38
Clare-market, Strand WC .	—	45..M	22
,, road, Forest Gate E .	8	—..G	34
,, ,, Willesden Gr. NW	5	34..H	12
,, st, Old Bethnal Gr.-rd E	12	47..J	27
Claremont-av, Finchley N .	1	—..A	17
Claremont-av, Raynes Park	25	—..Z^{2}	12
,, gardens, Ilford . .	8	—..F	40
,, la, Claremont, Surrey	28a	—..Z^{7}	1
,, park, Surrey . .	28a	—..Z^{7}	1
,, road, Bromley, Kent	28	—..Z^{3}	36
,, ,, Claygate, Surrey	28a	—..Z^{8}	3
,, ,, Cricklewood NW	5	—..F	14
,, ,, Croydon, Surrey	26	—..Z^{5}	26
,, ,, Forest Gate E .	8	—..H	35
,, ,, Hornsey N .	6	32..D	21
,, ,, Kilburn W .	10	42..J	15
,, ,, Leyton E . .	7	—..F	32
,, ,, Surbiton, Surrey	24	—..Z^{3}	6
,, ,, Teddington .	19	—..X	4
,, ,, Twickenham .	14	—..U	5
,, ,, Walthamstow E	3	—..B	29
,, ,, Wealdst., M'sex	1a	—..A	4
,, sq, Pentonville-rd N	11	45..J	23
,, st, N. Woolwich E .	13	—..N	38
,, ,, Up. Edmonton N	3	—..A	27
Clarence-avenue, Bickley .	28	—..Z^{3}	36
,, cres, Sidcup, Kent .	23	—..X	41
,, gdns, Regent's-pk NW	11	44..K	20
,, gate, St James's SW .	11	52..N	21
,, lane, Roehampton SW	15	—..U	11
,, place, Clapton E .	7	39..G	28
,, road, Bickley, Kent .	28	—..Z^{2}	36
,, ,, Canning Town E	12	49..L	33
,, ,, Carshalton, Surr.	30	—..Z^{8}	19
,, ,, Chiswick W .	14	—..P	8
,, ,, Clapham-pk SW	16	—..U	21
,, ,, Clapton E .	7	39..H	28
,, ,, Croydon, Surrey	26	—..Z^{4}	24
,, ,, Higham Hill E	3	—..A	29
,, ,, Kentish Tn. NW	6	36..H	20
,, ,, Kew . .	14	—..R	8
,, ,, Kilburn NW .	5	—..I	15
,, ,, Leytonstone E .	7	41..G	33
,, ,, Manor Park E .	8	—..H	36
,, ,, Mott'ham, Kent	23	—..W	36
,, ,, Sidcup, Kent .	23	—..X	41
,, ,, Sutton, Surrey .	29	—..Z^{7}	16
,, ,, Teddington .	19	—..Y	4
,, ,, Tottenham N .	3	—..C	25
,, ,, Wimbledon SW	20	—..Y	16
,, ,, Wood Green N .	2	—..A	22
,, street, Islington N .	11	46..J	24
,, ,, Kingston . .	19	—..Z^{1}	6
,, ,, Rotherhithe SE	12	55..N	28
,, terrace, Hounslow .	14	—..S	1
,, ,, Regent's-pk NW	11	44..K	19
,, villa, Wood Green N .	2	—..A	22
Clarendon-gdns, Ilford, Ess.	8	—..E	38
,, ,, Maida Vale W .	10	43..K	17
,, place, Hyde Park W .	11	43..M	18
,, road, Carshalton, Surrey	30	—..Z^{8}	20
,, ,, Croydon, Surrey	26	—..Z^{6}	23
,, ,, Edmonton N .	3	—..A	27
,, ,, Harrow, M'sex .	1a	—..D	4
,, ,, Hornsey N .	2	—..B	23
,, ,, Lewisham SE .	17	64..T	32
,, ,, Leytonstone E .	7	—..E	32
,, ,, Notting Hill W	10	50..M	14
,, ,, Putney SW .	15	59..S	13
,, ,, Tottenham N .	2	—..C	24
,, ,, Walthamstow E	7	—..D	31
,, sq, Somers Town NW	11	45..J	21
,, street, Maida Hill W .	10	43..K	16
,, ,, Pimlico SW .	16	52..P	20
,, ,, Somers Town NW	11	45..J	21
Clarens-street, Forest Hill SE	22	—..W	29
Clareville-gdns, Hanwell W	9	—..M	4
,, grove, Brompton SW .	10	51..O	17
Clarges-street, Piccadilly W	11	44..N	20
Claribel-road, Brixton SW .	16	61..R	23
Clarissa-road, Ilford . .	8	—..E	43
,, street, Haggerston E .	7	39..I	26
Clark-st, Commercial-rd E .	12	47..L	28
Clarkson-road, Barking .	13	—..J	39
,, ,, Walthamstow E	3	—..B	32
,, st, Canning Town E .	12	49..L	33
Claude-road, Ilford . .	8	—..E	43
,, ,, Leyton E . .	7	—..E	32
,, ,, Peckham SE .	17	62..S	27
,, ,, Plaistow E .	13	—..J	35
,, street, Millwall E .	17	56..P	30
Claughton-road, Plaistow E	13	—..J	36
Claverdale-road, Brixton SW	21	—..V	22
Clavering-rd, Wanstead E .	8	—..F	36
Claverton-street, Pimlico SW	16	52..P	21
Claxton-gro, Hammersmith W	15	58..P	14
Clay-lane, Middlesex . .	1a	—..C	8
Claybrook-rd, Hammersm. W	15	58..P	14
Claygate, Surrey . .	28a	—..Z^{8}	3
,, Common, Surrey .	28a	—..Z^{8}	4
,, road, Ealing W . .	9	—..N	5
,, & Claremont ry-sta	28a	—..Z^{8}	2
Claylands-rd, Clapham-rd SW	16	53..Q	23
Claypit-lane, Grove Park SE	23	—..X	35
Clayponds-la, O. Brent'd, M'x	9	—..O	7
Clayton-avenue, Wembley .	4	—..H	7
,, road, Hook . .	24	—..Z^{7}	6
,, ,, Peckham SE .	17	62..R	27
,, st, Caledonian-rd N .	6	37..I	22
,, ,, Kennington-rd SE	16	53..Q	23
Cleanthus-road, Plumstead	18	—..R	38
Clemence-st, Burdett-rd E .	12	48..L	30
Clement-rd, Beckenham, Kent	27	—..Z^{2}	28
Clement's-ct, Wood-st EC .	—	46..L	24
,, Inn, Strand WC . .	11	45..M	23
,, ,, pass, Strand WC	—	45..M	23
,, la, King William-st EC	—	46..M	25
,, ,, Strand WC .	11	45..M	22
,, road, Bermondsey SE	12	55..O	27
,, ,, East Ham E .	8	—..I	37
,, ,, Ilford, Essex .	8	—..G	39
,, street, Barnsbury N .	6	37..H	23
Clemestina-rd, Lea Bdge-rd E	7	—..E	30
Clensham-la, Sutton, Surrey	25	—..Z^{6}	15
Cleopatra's Needle, Vict. Em.	11	45..M	22
Clephane-road, Islington N	7	38..H	25
Clerkenwell-clo, Clerken. EC	11	46..K	23

Czar-street. INDEX TO STREETS, &c. Dorset-street.

Street	4-in. sht.	9-in. sht.	mar.
Czar-street, Deptford SE .	17	56..Q	30
Dacca-street, Deptford SE.	17	56..Q	30
Dace-road, Bow E . .	7	40..J	30
Dacre-park, Lee SE . .	17	64..T	33
,, road, Plaistow E .	13	—..J	35
,, street, Lee SE . .	17	64..T	33
,, ,, Westmstr SW	11	53..O	21
Dacres-rd, Forest Hill SE .	—	22..W	28
,, ,, Up. Sydenhm SE	—	22..X	28
Dafforne-rd, Up. Tooting .	21	—..W	19
Dagenham-road, Leyton E.	7	—..E	30
Dagmar-av, Wembley, M'x	4	—..G	8
,, rd, Alex. Park N .	2	—..A	22
,, ,, Fins. Park N .	6	32..D	23
,, ,, Norbiton .	19	8..Z	
,, ,, Peckham SE .	16	62..R	25
,, ,, S. Hackney E .	7	40..H	29
Dagnall-rd, Norwood SE .	26	—..Z^3	25
Dagnan-rd, Balham SW .	16	—..U	20
Dahomey-rd, Streatham SW	21	—..Y	20
Dairsie-road, Eltham .	18	—..T	37
Daisy-lane, Fulham SW .	15	59..S	15
Dakins-street, Stepney E .	12	48..L	29
Dalberg-rd, Brixton SW .	16	—..T	23
Dalby-rd, Wands'th SW .	15	60..T	16
,, st, Kentish Tn. NW .	6	36..H	20
Dale-grn, N. Finchley N .	1	—..A	17
,, rd, Canning Town E .	12	49..L	33
,, ,, Kentish Tn. NW .	6	36..G	19
,, street, Chiswick W .	15	—..P	10
,, ,, Mill Hill NW .	1	—..A	14
Dalebury-rd, Up. Toot. SW	20	—..18	W
Daleham-gds, Hamps, SW	5	35..H	17
Daleside-road, Tooting .	21	—..Y	20
Daleview-rd, Stam. Hill N	7	33..D	26
Dalgarno-gds, N. Kens. W	10	43..L	13
Dalgleish-st, Limeh use E .	12	48..M	29
Dalkeith-road, Dulwich .	21	—..V	24
,, ,, Ilford, E .	8	—..G	39
Dallas-road, Sydenham SE	22	—..X	27
Dallin-road, Plumstead .	18	—..R	38
,, ,, Upton .	18	—..T	43
Dalling-rd, Hammersmthw	10	50..O	12
Dalmain-rd, Forest Hl. SE	8	22..	29
Dalmally-rd, Croydon, Sur.	26	—..Z^5	26
Dalmeny-av, Holloway N .	6	37..G	21
,, ,, Norbury .	21	—..Z^2	23
,, rd, Carshal, Sur.	30	—..Z^8	19
,, ,, Malden .	25	—..Z^6	12
,, ,, Tufnell Pk, N	6	37..G	21
Dalmore-rd, W. Dulwich .	21	—..W	24
Dalrymple-rd, Brockley SE	4	—..T	29
Dalston E	7	39..J	26
,, Junction Station .	6	38..H	26
,, lane, Hackney E .	7	39..H	27
Dalton-rd, Hammers. W .	15	58..Q	13
,, st, W. Dulwich SW	21	—..W	24
Dalwood-st, Camber. SE .	16	62..R	25
Dalyell-rd, Stockwell SW .	16	61..S	22
Dame-street, Islington N .	11	38..J	24
Dames-rd, Forest Gate E .	8	—..G	34
Danbrook-rd, Streatham .	21	—..Z^1	21
Danbury-st, Islington N .	11	46..J	24
Danby-street, Peckham SE	17	62..S	26
Dancer-road, Fulham SW .	—	59..R	15
,, ,, Richmond .	14	—..S	8
Dane-av, Herne Hill SE .	16	62..S	24
,, road, Ealing W .	9	—..M	6
,, ,, Ilford .	8	—..H	39
,, ,, Merton SW	20	—..Z	17
,, pl, Roman-rd. E	12	48..J	30
,, st, High Hol. WC	22	45..L	22
Danecroft-rd, Herne H. SE	16	—..T	24
Danemere-st, Putney SW .	15	59..S	13
Daneville-rd, Cambrwell.SE	16	62..R	25
Danson-lane, Welling .	18	—..T	42
,, park, ,, .	18	—..T	42
,, road, ,, .	18	—..U	43
Dante-rd, New. Butts SE .	16	54..P	24
Dantzic-st, Borough-rd. SE	11	54..O	24
Danvers-road, Hornsey N.	2	—..B	21
,, st, Chelsea SW .	16	51..Q	18
Daphne-st, Wands. SW .	15	—..U	16
D'Arblay-street, Soho W .	—	45..L	21
Darell-road, Richmond .	14	—..S	8
Darenth-rd, Stam. Hill N .	7	33..E	26
Darfield-rd, Brockley SE .	4	—..U	29
Darien-rd, Battersea SW .	15	60..S	17
Darkhouse-la, U. T.-st, EC	46	—..M	24
Darlan-rd, Walham Gr. SW	15	59..Q	15
Darlaston-rd, Wimbldn.SW	20	—..Z	14
Darley-rd, Battersea SW .	16	—..U	18
Darling-row, Camb'ge-rd, E	12	47..L	28
Darlington-rd, W. Nor. S .	21	—..Y	24
,, ,, ,, SW	21	—..Y	24
Darnley-road, Hackney E.	7	39..H	28
,, ,, N. Kens. W	10	50..M	14
Darrell-rd, E. Dulwich SE	17	—..U	26
Dartmoor-street, Kens. W	10	43..M	15
Dartmouth-rd, Hendon NW	5	—..D	12
,, ,, Bl'kh'th SE	17	64..R	32
,, ,, Crickle. NW	5	—..H	14
,, ,, Forest H.SE	22	—..W	28
,, st, Westmr. SW	11	53..N	21
,, pk.-av., High-gate NW .	6	36..F	20
,, pk-h, Highgt.N	6	32..E	20
,, pk.-rd, High-gate NW .	6	36..G	20
Dartnell-road, Berm. SE .	17	54..P	26
,, ,, Croydon, Sy.	26	—..Z^4	25
Dartrey-road, Chelsea SW.	15	51..Q	17
Darville-road, St. New. N	7	39..F	26
Darwin-road, Ealing W .	9	—..O	6
,, ,, Wood Gr. N	2	—..A	24
,, st, Walworth SE .	12	54..O	25
Dashwood-rd, Hornsey N .	6	32..D	22
,, ,, S. Lam. SW	16	61..R	21
Dasset-road, W. Norwood	21	—..Y	23
Date-street, Walworth SE .	16	54..P	24
Daubney-road, Clapton E.	7	40..G	29
Dault-rd, Wandsworth SW	15	—..U	17
Davenant-rd, U.HollowayN	6	32..F	22
Davenport-rd, Catford SE	4	—..U	31
Davey-rd, Hackney Wk. E	7	40..J	30
David-st, Stratford E .	7	41..H	33
Davids-rd, Forest Hill SE	22	—..W	28
Davidson-rd, Norwood SE	26	—..Z^4	26
Davies-la, Leytonstone E	7	—..F	33
,, st, Berkeley-sq. W	11	44..M	20
Davis-road, Acton W .	10	—..N	11
,, st, Cubitt Town E .	12	57..O	32
Davisville-rd, Shep. Bsh.W	10	50..N	12
Dawe-road, Fulham SW	15	58..Q	15
Dawlish-road, Leyton E .	7	—..F	31
,, st, S. Lambeth SW	16	53..Q	22
Daws-lane, Mill Hill NW .	—	—..A^1	12
Dawson-pl, Bayswater W .	10	43..M	16
Daylesford-av, Barnes SW	15	—..S	12
Day-place E . . .	12	47..M	27
Days-lane, Eltham .	23	—..V	40
Daysbrook-rd, Streat'm H.	21	—..W	22
Deacon-road, Norbiton .	19	—..	
,, ,, Norbiton .	7	19..Z	7
,, ,, Willesden NW	5	34..H	12
,, st, Walw'th-rd, SE	16	54..P	24
Deal-road, L. Tooting SW.	21	—..Z^1	19
Dealtey-road, Putney SW .	15	—..T	13
Dean-rd, Croydon, Surrey	30	—..Z^7	24
,, ,, Hounslow . .	14	—..T	2
,, ,, Willesden NW .	5	—..H	13
,, st, Fetter lane EC .	11	45..L	23
,, ,, Islington N . .	6	38..J	24
,, ,, Commer.-rd, E .	12	47..M	28
,, ,, Soho-square W .	11	45..L	21
Dean Brad.-st, Westm. SW	—	53..O	22
,, Farrar-st, Westm. SW	—	53..O	21
,, Trench-st, Westm. SW	11	53..O	21
,, Stanley-st, West. SW	—	53..O	22
Deanery-rd, Stratford E .	7	41..J	33
,, st, Park-lane W .	11	44..M	19
Deanhill-rd, E. Sheen SW .	14	—..S	9
Deansbrook-la, Edg, Mid'x	1a	—..A	9
Deans-ct, Old Bailey EC .	46	—..L	24
,, ,, St. Pl's Ch-yd EC	46	—..M	24
,, la, Edgware, Mid'x	1	—..A	10
,, yd, Westmstr. SW .	11	53..O	21
Deansfield-rd, Eltham .	18	—..T	37
Deauville-rd, Clapham SW	16	—..U	21
De Beauvoir-cr, Hack. N .	7	38..J	25
,, ,, rd, Hack. N .	7	38..J	25
,, ,, sq, Hack. N .	7	38..J	26
De Burgh-rd, S. Wimbn SW	20	17..Z	
Decima-st, Long-lane SE .	12	54..O	25
Decoy-av, Golders-gr. NW	1	—..C	15
De Crespigny-pk, Camb. SE	16	62..S	25
Dee-road, Plaistow E .	12	49..K	33
,, street, Poplar E . .	12	49..M	32
Deepdene-rd, Denm. H. SE	16	—..T	24
Deerbrook-rd, Herne H. SE	21	—..V	23
Deer-pk, Morden, Surrey .	25	—..Z^2	17
Deerdale-rd, Herne H. SE	16	62..T	24
Deerhurst-rd, L. Streat-ham SW	21	—..Y	22
Defoe-avenue, Kew . .	—	14..Q	8
,, road, L. Tooting SW	—	20..X	18
,, ,, St. Newington N	7	33..F	26
De Frene-rd, Syden'm SE	22	—..X	29
Dekker-road, Dulwich SE .	16	—..U	25
Delacourt-rd, Black'th SE .	18	—..R	34
Delafield-road, Charlton .	18	—..P	35
Delaford-road, Fulham SW	15	58..Q	15
,, ,, Rothrhithe SE.	17	55..P	27
Delamere-cres, Westb'ne-park W . . .	10	43..L	16
Delamere-rd, Wimble'n SW	20	—..Z^1	13
,, st, Padding'n W	10	43..L	16
,, ter, Padding'n W	10	43..K	16
Delancey-st, Cam. Tn. NW	6	36..J	20
De Laune-st, Kenn'ton SE	16	53..P	23
Delaware-rd, Maida-vale W	10	43..K	16
Delhi-street, Islington N .	6	37..J	22
Delia-st, Wandsworth SW	15	—..U	16
Deloraine-st, Deptford SE	4	63..R	30
Delorme-st, Ful. Pal.-rd. W	15	58..Q	14
Delta-rd, Wor.-pk, Surrey	25	—..Z^6	11
Delverton-rd, Walworth SE	16	54..P	24
Delvin-street, Woolwich .	18	—..Q	38
Delvino-road, Fulham SW.	15	59..R	15
Demesne-rd, S. Bed'n, Sur.	30	—..Z^7	20
De Morgan-rd, Fulham SW	15	59..S	16
Dempsey-st, Com.-rd. E .	12	47..L	28
Dempster-rd, Wands'th SW	15	60..T	17
Den-road, Bromley, Kent.	27	—..Z^2	32
Denbigh-gdns, Richmond .	14	—..T	7
,, pl, Belgr.-rd, SW	16	52..P	20
,, rd, Bow E . .	12	48..J	31
,, ,, Castle'r H. W	9	—..L	6
,, ,, Notting H. W	10	50..M	15
,, ,, Spring-grove	14	—..R	2
,, ,, Willesden NW	5	—..J	11
,, st, Belgr.-rd. SW	16	52..P	20
,, ,, Pimlico SW .	16	52..P	21
Denbridge-road, Bickley .	23	—..Z^1	37
Dendy-street, Balham .	21	—..V	19
Denehurst-gdns, Acton W	9	—..M	9
Denewood-rd, Highgate N	6	31..D	19
Denham-st, E. Greenw. SE	17	57..P	34
Denholme-rd, Kil.-pk. NW	10	42..J	15
Denington-pk-rd, Hamp-stead NW	5	35..H	16
Denison-rd, Castlebar H. W	9	—..K	6
,, ,, S. Wimblen.SW	20	—..Y	17
Denman-rd, Peckham SE .	16	62..R	26
,, st, London Br. SE	—	54..N	25
,, ,, Shaftesb.-av. W	11	45..M	21
Denmark-av, Wimblen. SW	20	—..Z	14
,, gdns, Kil'n NW	10	42..J	15
,, Hill SE . .	16	62..S	25
,, H. st, S.L. Rly.SE	16	62..S	25
,, pl, Ch. Cr.-rd. WC	45	—..L	21
,, rd, Barnsbury N	11	37..J	23
,, ,, Camber. SE .	16	62..R	24
,, ,, Cars'ton, Sur.	25	—..Z^6	18
Denmark-rd, Ealing W .	9	—..M	6
,, ,, Hornsey N .	2	—..B	23
,, ,, Kilburn NW .	10	42..J	15
,, ,, Kingston .	19	—..Z^1	7
,, ,, Peckham SE	17	62..R	26
,, ,, S. Nor. SE .	27	—..Z^3	27
,, ,, Twickenham	19	—..W	2
,, ,, Wimblen. SW	20	—..Y	14
,, st, Barnsbury N	11	37..J	23
,, ,, Cann. Town E	13	—..L	34
,, ,, Ch. Cr.-rd. WC	11	45..L	21
,, ,, Leytonst. E .	7	41..G	33
,, ,, St. George's E	12	47..M	27
,, ,, Tottenham E	3	—..A	27
Denman-rd, L. Ditton, Sur.	24	—..Z^5	7
Dennett-rd, Croydon, Sur.	26	—..Z^5	23
Dennetts-gr, New Cr. SE .	17	63..R	28
,, rd, New Cr. SE .	17	63..R	28
Denning-rd, Hamp'd NW .	5	35..G	18
Dennington-park-rd, West Hampstead NW . .	5	35..H	16
Dennis-rd, W. Moul'y, Sur.	24	—..Z^2	2
,, street, York-road N	11	37..J	22
Denton-rd, Hornsey N .	6	32..D	23
,, ,, Richmond .	14	—..U	6
,, st, Wands'th SW .	15	—..U	16
Dents-rd, Wands. Com. SW	16	—..U	18
Denver-rd, Stamford H. N	7	33..E	25
,, street, Chelsea SW	11	52..O	18
Denzil-road, Willesden NW	5	—..H	11
Deodar-road, Putney SW	15	59..S	14
Deptford SE	17	56..Q	29
,, Bridge, Deptford SE	4	63..R	30
,, Broadwy, Deptfd. SE	17	63..R	30
,, Cattle Mkt, Dptfd. SE	17	56..P	30
,, Cemetery, Br'ckley SE	4	—..T	30
,, Creek, Deptfd SE .	4	63..R	31
,, Ferry-rd, Millwall E .	17	56..P	30
,, Green, Deptford SE .	17	56..Q	30
,, Hosp, Nw Cr'ss-rd SE	17	55..Q	28
,, New Town SE . .	—	63..R	30
,, park, Deptford SE .	17	56..P	29
,, rd Ry St, E. Lon. Ry.	12	55..O	28
,, Sta. S.E. & C.Rly .	17	56..Q	30
Derby-rd, Canning Town E	13	—..L	34
,, ,, Cheam, Surrey .	29	—..Z^8	15
,, ,, Croydon, Surrey	26	—..Z^5	23
,, ,, East Sheen SW .	14	—..S	9
,, ,, Edmonton N .	3	—..A	28
,, ,, Hounslow . .	14	—..S	1
,, ,, Merton SW .	20	—..Z	15
,, ,, Tottenham N .	2	—..C	24
,, st, Forest Gate E .	8	—..H	34
,, ,, Grays Inn-rd WC	11	45..J	22
,, ,, Westminster SW	—	53..N	22
Derbyshire-st, Bethnal Gr.	12	47..K	27
Dering-rd, Croydon, Sur'y	30	—..Z^7	24
,, P.-rd, Croydon, Sur.	30	—..Z^7	24
,, st, Oxford-st, W .	—	44..M	20
Derinton-rd, Upr Tooting	21	—..X	19
Dermody-gar, Lewish'm SE	17	—..T	32
,, rd, Lewisham SE	17	—..T	32
Deronda-rd, Tulse Hill SE .	21	—..V	23
Derrick-st, Rotherhithe SE	12	56..O	29
Dersingham-av, M'n'r Pk E	8	—..G	38
,, rd, Cricklew'd NW	5	—..F	15
Derwent-gr, E. Dulwich SE	17	62..T	26
,, rd, Palmers Gr'n N	2	—..A	22
Derwentwater-rd, Acton W	9	—..M	9
Desart-street, Bromley E .	12	49..M	32
Desenfares-rd, Dulwich SE	16	—..U	25
Desford-road, Plaistow E .	12	49..L	33
Despard-rd, Upr HollowyN	6	32..E	21
Detmold-rd, Upr Clapton E	7	33..F	28
Devas-street, Bromley E .	12	49..K	31
De Vere-gdns, Ilford, Ess'x	8	—..F	38
,, ,, Kens'g'n W	10	51..N	17
Deverell-st, Southwark SE	12	54..O	25
Devereux-court, Strand WC	45	—..M	23
,, rd, Battersea SW	16	—..U	19
Devon-road, Barking .	13	—..J	40
,, ,, Teddington .	3	19..X	—
,, ,, Tottenham N	3	—..B	26
Devonport-rd, Shep. Bsh.W	10	50..N	13
,, st, Comm'l-rd E	12	47..M	28
,, ,, Hyde Pk W	11	43..L	18
Devons-road, Bromley E .	12	48..K	31
Devonshire-av, Sutt'n, Sur.	29	—..Z^9	16
,, gar, Chisw'k W	14	—..Q	9
,, gr, Peckham SE	17	55..Q	27
,, par, Tott'n N .	3	—..A	25
,, pl, Chiswick W	10	—..O	11
,, pl, Maryleb'e W	11	44—K	20
,, rd, Chiswick W	15	—..P	11
,, ,, Croy'n, Sur.	26	—..Z^4	24
,, ,, Ealing W .	9	—..N	6
,, ,, For'st Hl SE	22	—..V	28
,, ,, Gr'nw'h SE	4	63..R	31
,, ,, Hackn'y E	7	39..I	28
,, ,, Hmrsmthw	15	—..P	11
,, ,, Harrw, Mid	1a	—..C	3
,, ,, Holloway N	6	32..F	22
,, ,, Ilford .	8	—..E	40
,, ,, Ilford E .	7	41..G	33
,, ,, Mott'm, Kt	23	—..W	36
,, ,, Palmrs-gr.N	2	—..A	23
,, ,, S. Lamb.SW	16	61..R	21
,, ,, S. WimbsW	18	20..Z	—
,, ,, Vict. Dk. E	13	—..M	35
,, ,, Wal'stow E	7	—..D	31
,, sq, B'gate-st EC	12	46..L	26
,, st, B'gate EC .	—	46..L	26
,, ,, Chiswick W	15	—..P	11
,, ,, Islington, N	11	46..J	24
,, ,, Mile End E	12	47..K	28
,, ,, P'rtl'd-pl W	11	44..L	20
,, ,, Theobalds road WC .	11	45..L	22
,, ter. Padd'n W .	10	43..M	17
Dewar-street, Peckham SE	17	62..S	27
Dewberry-st, Bromley E .	12	49..L	31
Dewey-st, Toot. Gravny.SW	18	20..Y	—
Dewhurst-rd, W. Kens. W	10	50..O	13
Dewsbury-rd, W'den Gr.NW	5	34..G	12
,, st, Camd'n T.NW	6	36..I	20
D'Eynsford, Camb'l SE .	16	62..R	25
Diamond-ter, Greenw'h SE	17	64..R	32
Diana-pl, Euston-rd NW .	—	44..K	20
,, rd, Walthamstow E	3	—..B	30
Dibden-st, Islington N .	6	38..I	24
Dicey-street, Woolwich .	18	—..Q	38
Dickens-rd, East Ham E .	13	—..J	36
,, st, S. Lambeth SW	16	61—R	20
Dickenson-rd, Crouch E. N	6	32..D	22
,, st, Kentish T.NW	6	36..H	20
Dickerage-la, New Malden	9	19..Z^1	—
Dicon-road, New Cross SE .	4	63..R	29
Didcot-st, Battersea SW .	15	60..T	17
Dieppe-st, W. Kens'n SW	15	58..P	15
Digby-rd, Finsbury-pk N	6	33..F	24
,, ,, Homerton E .	7	40..H	29
,, st, Bethnal-green E	12	47..K	28
Dighton-rd, Wands'th SW	15	60..T	16
Dilke-street, Chelsea SW .	16	52..Q	19
Dillwyn-rd, Sydenham SE	22	—..X	29
Dilston-gr, Bermondsey SE	12	55..O	28
Dimsdale-rd, Fulham SW	15	58..Q	15
Dingley-pl, St. Lukes EC	11	46..K	24
,, rd, City-road EC	11	46..K	24
Dingwall-av, Croydon, Sur	26	—..Z^6	24
,, ,, rd, ,, ,,	26	—..Z^5	24
,, ,, Earlsfield SW	17	20..V	—
Dinisdale-rd, Fulham SW	15	58..Q	15
Dinmont-st, Hackney-rd.E	12	47..J	27
Dinsdale-rd, Blackheath SE	17	57..Q	33
Dinsmore-rd, Balham SW	21	—..V	20
Dinton-road, Norbiton .	19	—..Y	7
Dionis-yd, Fenchurch-stEC	46	—..M	26
Dirthouse-wd, Highgate N.	2	—..C	19
Dirty-la, Harrow, Mids'x	1a	—..C	4
Disbrowe-rd, Fulham SW	15	58..Q	14
Disraeli-rd, Ealing W .	9	—..M	6
,, ,, Forest Gate E	8	—..H	34
,, ,, Putney SW .	15	59..T	14
,, ,, Willesden NW .	9	—..J	10
Diss-st, Hackney-road E .	12	47..J	26
Distaff-la, Cannon-st. EC .	—	46..M	24
Distillery-la, Hammer'th W	15	58..P	13
,, rd, Old Brent, Mdx	14	—..P	7
District-rd, Sudbury, Mdx	4	—..G	5
Ditton Common, Surrey .	24	—..Z^5	2
,, rd, Long Ditton, Sy .	24	—..Z^4	7
Dixon-rd, New Cross SE .	17	63..R	29
,, st, Limehouse E .	12	48..M	30
Dock rd, N. Woolwich E .	13	—..N	37
,, st, ,, ,, ,, .	13	—..N	38
,, ,, Stepney E . .	12	47..M	27
Dockhead, Bermondsey SE	12	54..N	26
Dockley-rd, Bermondsy. SE	12	55..O	27
Dockyard-sta, Woolwich .	18	—..P	37
Doctor-st, Walworth SE .	17	54..Q	25
Dod-st, Limehouse E .	12	48..M	30
Dodbrooke-rd, W. Nor. .	21	—..X	23
Doddington-gr, Batter. SW	16	60..R	19
,, grs, Ken.-pkSE	16	54..P	24
Dodson-street, Lambeth SE	11	53..O	23
Dog-lane, Willesden NW .	5	—..H	10
,, knl-hill, Herne Hl. SE	16	62..T	25
Doggett-rd, Catford SE .	22	—..V	30
Dogs-home, Battersea-pk. road SW	16	52..Q	20
Dolben-st, Southwark SE .	11	54..N	24
Dolby-ct, Aldersgate-st. EC	46	—..L	24
Dollis-av, Finchley N .	1	—..A	15
,, lane, Finchley N .	—	—..A^1	15
,, park, Finchley N .	1	—..A	15
,, road, Finchley N .	1	—..A	16
,, hill-av, Willes'n NW	5	—..F	13
,, ,, lane NW . .	5	—..F	12
,, ,, sta, Met. Rail. .	5	34..G	12
Dolphin-ct, Ludgate H. EC	46	—..M	24
,, st, Poplar E .	12	49..M	31
Dominion-rd, Croy. Surr.	26	—..Z^4	26
Donald-road, Plaistow E .	13	—..J	35
,, st, Bromley E .	12	49..K	31
Donaldson-rd, Kilburn NW	5	—..J	15
Donegal-st, Pentonville N .	11	45..J	23
Doneraile-st, Fulham SW .	15	59..R	14
Dongola-rd, Plaistow E .	13	—..K	35
,, ,, Tottenham N	3	—..B	25
Donnington-rd, Harles. NW	5	34..J	12
,, ,, Malden .	25	—..Z^6	12
Donovan-av, Muswell H. N	2	—..B	21
Dora-rd, Wimbledon SW .	15	20..X	—
,, st, Limehouse E .	12	40..L	30
Dorchester-gr, Chiswick W	15	—..P	11
,, st, Shore'ch E .	11	38..J	25
Dordrecht-rd, Acton W .	10	—..N	11
Dore-av, East Ham E .	8	—..H	38
Doria-road, Fulham SW .	—	59..R	15
Dorien-rd, Raynes-pk. SW	20	—..Z^1	13
Doris-st, Lambeth SE .	16	53..P	23
Dorking-rd, Deptford SE .	17	56..Q	29
Dorlcote-rd, Wands'th SW	16	—..U	18
Dormers Wells-la, Southall	9	—..L	1
Dornberg-rd, Blackh'th SE	18	—..R	34
Dornby-rd, Blackh'th SE .	18	—..R	34
Dorncliffe-rd, Fulham SW .	—	59..R	15
Dornfell-st, Hampstead NW	5	—..H	15
Dornton-rd, Balham SW .	21	—..W	20
,, ,, Croydon, Sur	30	—..Z^8	25
,, ,, Tooting .	21	—..W	20
Dorothy-rd, E Sheen SW .	15	—..T	10
,, ,, Lavnder-hi.SW	16	60..S	18
Dorset-rd, Clapham-rd SW	16	53..Q	22
,, ,, Ealing W . .	9	—..N	6
,, ,, Harrow Midd. .	1a	—..C	3
,, ,, Merton SW .	20	—..Z^1	15
,, ,, Mott'gham. Kt.	23	—..W	36
,, ,, Tottenham N .	3	—..C	25
,, ,, Upton E . .	8	—..J	36
,, sq, Marylbne-rd.NW	11	44..K	19
,, st, Baker-st. W .	11	44..L	19
,, ,, Commer.-rd. E .	12	48..M	29

Dorset-street. INDEX TO STREETS, &c. Edgarley-terrace.

Street	4-in. sht.	9-in. sht.	mar.
Dorset-st, Essex-road N .	7	38..	H 25
,, ,, Tudor-street EC	11	45..	M 23
Dorville-road, Lee SE .	18	—..	U 34
Doughty-st, Guilf'd.-st. WC	11	45..	K 22
Douglas-av, Raynes-park .	25	—..	Z^3 12
,, ,, Wembley .	4	—..	H 7
,, rd, Cann. Town E	13	—..	L 34
,, ,, Canonbury N .	6	38..	H 24
,, ,, Chad. Hth, Es	8	—..	E 42
,, ,, Hounslow .	14	—..	S 1
,, ,, Kilburn NW .	5	—..	J 15
,, ,, Lg. Ditt, Surr.	24	—..	Z^5 7
,, ,, Surbiton .	24	—..	Z^5 7
,, ,, Tottenham N .	3	—..	C 25
,, st, Deptford SE .	4	—..	R 30
,, ,, Westm'r SW .	16	53..	P 21
Douro-st, Old Ford-rd. E .	12	48..	J 30
Douro-pl, Kensington W .	10	51..	O 16
Dove-row, Haggerston E .	12	39..	J 27
Dover-rd, Shooters' Hill .	18	—..	S 39
,, Up. Norwood .	21	—..	Z^1 25
,, Wanstead E .	8	—..	F 36
,, st, Piccadilly W .	11	44..	M 20
,, ,, ry-sta,Piccadilly ry	11	44..	M 20
Dovercourt-rd, Dulwich SE	16	—..	U 26
Dowanhill-rd, Catford SE .	22	—..	W 32
Dower-avenue, Carshalton	30	—..	Z^9 20
Dowgate-hill, Cannon-st E	11	46..	M 25
Dowlas-st, Peckham SE .	17	54..	Q 25
Down-lane, Tottenham N .	3	—..	B 27
,, st, Piccadilly W .	11	52..	N 20
,, ,, ry-sta, Piccadilly ry	11	52..	N 20
Downe, Kent . . .	30*b*	—..	Z^{11} 37
,, la, Sanderst'd, Sur	30	—..	Z^{11} 25
Downes-st, Peckham SE .	17	55..	Q 27
Downham-rd, K'gsl'd-rd N	7	38..	I 25
Downhills-la, W. Green N	2	—..	B 24
,, pk, Tottenhm N	3	—..	B 25
,, ,, rd, Tottenhm N	3	—..	B 25
Downing-st, Whitehall SW	11	53..	N 22
Downs-hill, Beckenham .	22	—..	Z^2 32
,, road, Beckenham .	22	—..	Z^2 31
,, ,, Clapton E .	7	39..	G 27
,, pk-rd, Hackney E .	7	39..	G 27
Downsbridge-rd, B'ckh'm	22	—..	Z^2 32
Downsell-rd, Stratford E .	7	41..	G 32
Downsfield-rd, Walth'st'w E	7	—..	D 30
Downshire-hill, Hpstd NW	5	35..	G 18
Downside-cr, Hampst. NW	6	36..	G 18
Downsview-rd, U. Nor. SE	21	—..	Z^1 24
Downton-av, Strhm-hill SW	21	—..	W 22
Dowsett-rd, Tottenham N	3	—..	A 27
Doyle-gdns, Qn's Park NW	10	34..	J 13
,, rd, Up. Tooting SW .	21	—..	W 19
D'Oyley-st, Sloane-sq. SW	—	52..	O 19
Doynton-st,Drmth.-pk-Hl N	6	—..	F 20
Dragon-rd, Peckham SE .	17	54..	Q 25
Drakefell-rd, Brockley SE .	4	63..	S 29
Drakefield-rd, U. Toot. SW	21	—..	W 19
Drant-st, Spitalfields, E .	11	46..	L 26
Draper-st, Newtn Butts SE	11	54..	O 24
Drapers-gs, Th'gm'n-av EC	—	46..	L 25
,, ,, Th'gm'n-av EC	46	—..	L 25
,, Hall,Th'gm'n-st,EC	11	46..	L 25
,, Homes, Mill Hl. NW	1	—..	A 12
Draycot-road, Surbiton .	24	—..	Z^5 7
,, ,, Wanstead E	8	—..	D 35
Draycott-av, Chelsea SW .	11	52..	O 18
,, pl, Chelsea SW .	16	52..	P 19
,, terr, Chelsea SW	11	52..	O 19
Drayton-av, C'tleb'r Hl. W	9	—..	L 5
,, gs, C'tleb'r Hl. W	9	—..	L 5
,, gn, C'tleb'r Hl. W	9	—..	L 5
,, ,, Ealing W .	9	—..	L 4
,, gr, C'tleb'r Hi. W	9	—..	L 5
,, gr, W. Bmptn. SW	15	51..	P 17
,, pk, Highbury N .	6	38..	G 23
,, ,, sta, H'bury N	6	37..	G 23
,, rd, C'tleb'r Hl. W	9	—..	L 5
,, ,, Leytonstone E	7	—..	E 32
,, ,, Tottenham N	3	—..	A 26
,, ,, Willesden NW	5	—..	I 11
,, terr, S. Kens. SW	—	51..	P 17
,, Bg-rd, Dryt'n Gr. W	9	—..	L 4
,, Gr-rd, Ealing Dean W	9	—..	M 5
,, ,, sta, G.W.Ry, Drayton Gr. W	9	—..	L 4
Dreadnought-st, G'nw'h SE	12	57..	O 33
Dresden-rd, H'nsey Rise N	6	32..	E 21
Drew-rd, N. Woolwich E .	13	—..	N 36
Drewstead-rd, Streatham .	21	—..	W 21
Driffield-rd,Romanrd,Bow E	12	40..	J 29
Drive, The, Walth'st'w E .	3	—..	B 31
Drivers-hill, Mill Hill NW .	1	—..	A 13
Dromore-rd, Putney SW .	15	—..	U 14
Drood-yd, St.George's, E .	12	47..	M 27
Droop-st, Kensal Green W	10	42..	K 14
Drovers-rd, Croydon, Sur.	30	—..	Z^8 24
Druce-rd, Dulwich SE .	16	—..	U 25
Drummond-cr, S. Twn NW	11	45..	J 21
,, rd, Rother. SE	12	55..	O 27
,, st, Euston-sq NW	11	45..	K 21
Drury-rd, Harrow, M'sex .	1*a*	—..	D 3
,, lane WC . .	11	45..	L 22
,, la,Th., Russell-st WC	11	45..	M 22
Dry-road, Blackheath SE .	4	64..	R 31
Dryburgh-rd, Putney SW .	15	—..	S 13
Dryden-rd, Croydon, Surr.	26	—..	Z^4 22
,, ,, S. Wimbln SW	20	—..	Y 16
Drylands-rd, Hornsey N .	6	32..	D 22
Drysdale-st, K'gsl'nd-rd N	—	46..	K 26
Ducal-st, Bethnal Green E	12	47..	K 26
Ducane-rd, Shepherd's B.W	10	42..	L 13
Duchess-st, Portland-pl, W	11	44..	L 20
Duchess of Bedford's Wlk, Kensington W . .	10	50..	N 15
Ducie-st, Brixton SW .	16	61..	T 22
Duck-la, Wardour-st, W .	45	—..	M 21
Duckett-rd, Harringay N .	6	—..	D 24
,, st, Stepney E .	12	48..	L 29
Duck's Foot-la, U. T.-st EC	46	—..	M 25
Dudding-hill-la, Willes. NW	5	34..	G 12

Street	4-in. sht.	9-in. sht.	mar.
Dudley-gdns, Ealing W .	9	—..	N 5
,, rd, Ilford, Essex .	8	—..	G 39
,, ,, Kew . .	14	—..	R 8
,, ,, Kingston .	19	—..	Z^1 7
,, ,, Wimble'n SW	20	—..	T 15
Dudlington-rd, Clapton E .	7	33..	F 28
Duff-street, Poplar E .	12	49..	M 32
Dufferin-st, Bunhill-row EC	11	46..	K 25
Duffield-st, Battersea SW .	16	60..	S 18
Duke-st, Adelphi WC .	—	45..	M 22
,, Aldgate-st EC .	11	46..	M 26
,, Grosvenor-sq, W	11	44..	M 19
,, Kensington W .	10	51..	N 16
,, Lambeth SE .	11	45..	N 23
,, Lisson-grove W .	11	44..	K 18
,, Manchester-sq, W	11	44..	L 19
,, Richmond . .	14	—..	T 6
,, St. James's W .	11	44..	M 21
,, Southwark SE .	12	54..	N 25
,, Spitalfields E .	12	46..	L 26
Duke-st, W. Smithfield EC	11	46..	L 24
Dukes-av, Chiswick W .	15	—..	P 10
,, ,, Finchley N .	1	—..	A 16
,, ,, Muswell Hill N .	2	—..	B 21
,, ,, New Mal. Sur. .	25	—..	Z^2 10
,, rd, Chiswick W .	15	—..	P 10
,, ,, East Ham E .	13	—..	J 38
,, ,, Euston-rd. NW .	11	45..	K 21
Dukethorpe-rd, Sy'nh'm SE	22	—..	X 28
Dulka-road, Battersea SW .	16	—..	U 19
Dulwich	21	—..	V 25
,, College, Dulwich	21	—..	W 25
,, Common, Dul. .	21	—..	W 25
,, com.-la, Dul. SE	22	—..	V 26
,, pk, Dulwich SE .	22	—..	S 26
,, rd, Herne H. SE .	16	—..	U 23
,, ry-sta, S E & C ra.	21	—..	W 25
,, wood-pk, Nor. SE.	21	—..	X 25
Dumbarton-rd, Brix. H SW	16	—..	U 22
Dumbreck-road, Eltham .	18	—..	T 37
Dumont-rd, St. New'ton N	7	33..	F 26
Dunbar-av, Norbury, Sur.	26	—..	Z^2 23
,, ,, New Malden .	24	—..	Z^2 9
,, ,, Upton-lane E .	8	—..	J 34
,, ,, Wood-green N	2	—..	A 24
,, st, W. Norwood .	21	—..	X 24
Duncan-rd,London-fields E	39	—..	I 27
,, ,, Richmond .	14	—..	S 7
,, st, Islington N .	11	38..	J 23
,, ,, Whitechapel E	12	47..	M 26
,, terr, Islington N .	11	46..	J 23
Duncannon-st, Strand WC	11	45..	M 22
Duncombe-hill, Forest Hill	22	—..	V 29
,, rd, Hrnsy. Rs. N	6	32..	E 21
Duncrievie-rd, Lewis'm SE	17	—..	U 32
Dundalk-rd, Brockley SE .	4	63..	S 29
Dundas-rd, Peckham SE .	17	63..	S 28
Dundee-rd, Plaistow E .	13	—..	K 35
,, ,, S. Norwood SE	27	—..	Z^3 27
,, street, Wapping E	12	55..	N 27
Dundonald-rd, Wimb'n SW	20	—..	Z 14
,, ,, Willes'n NW	5	—..	J 14
,, st, Westmr SW	16	53..	P 21
Dunedin-road, Ilford .	8	—..	F 39
,, ,, Leyton E .	7	41..	F 31
Dunford-road, Holloway N	6	37..	G 23
Dungarvan-av, Barnes SW	15	—..	S 12
Dunheved-rd, Croy, Sur. .	26	—..	Z^4 23
Dunk-st,Ml.-End New Tn.E	12	47..	L 27
Dunkeld, Ilford . .	8	—..	F 43
,, rd, Norwood SE .	26	—..	Z^2 25
,, st, Poplar E .	12	49..	M 32
Dunlace-rd, Clapton E .	7	39..	G 28
Dunloe-st, Hackney E .	12	47..	J 26
Dunmore-rd, Q'ns-pk NW .	5	—..	J 14
,, ,, Wimb'n. SW	20	—..	Z^1 13
Dunmow-rd, Stratford E .	7	41..	G 33
Dunn-street, Kingsland E ,	7	39..	G 26
Dunollie-rd, Kentish T. NW	6	—..	G 21
Dunoon-rd, Forest Hl. SE	22	—..	V 28
Dunraven-rd, Shep. Bh. W	10	50..	M 12
Dunsany-rd, Hmsmith. W .	10	50..	O 13
Dunsford-cr, Wands'th SW	15	—..	U 15
Dunsmore-rd, Balham .	21	—..	V 20
,, ,, Stam. H. N	7	33..	E 26
Dunstable-villas, Richmd.	14	—..	T 7
,, rd, ,,	14	—..	T 7
Dunstan-rd, Dulwich SE .	22	—..	V 27
Dunstans-rd, E. Dulw. SE .	17	—..	U 27
Dunster-ct, Mincing-la, EC	—	46..	M 25
,, gdns, Kilburn NW	5	—..	J 15
Dunston-rd, Kingsl'd-rd. E	7	38..	J 26
,, st, Kingsl'd-rd. E	7	38..	J 26
Dunton-road, Leyton E .	7	—..	D 31
Duntshill-rd, Earlsfield SW	20	—..	V 16
Dunvegan-gdns, Eltham .	18	—..	T 37
,, road, ,, .	18	—..	T 37
Dupont-rd, Raynes-pk SW	20	—..	Z^1 13
,, street, Stepney E .	12	48..	L 29
Duppas-hill, Croydon, Sur.	30	—..	Z^7 23
,, ,, la, Croy. Sur.	30	—..	Z^6 23
,, ,, rd, ,, ,,	30	—..	Z^7 23
Dupree-road, Charlton .	18	—..	P 34
Durand-gdns, Brixton SW	16	61..	R 22
Durban-rd, Becken'm, Kt.	27	—..	Z^2 29
,, ,, West Ham E .	12	49..	K 33
,, ,, W. Norwood .	21	—..	X 24
Durham-av, Bromley, Kt.	27	—..	Z^3 33
,, grove, Hackney E.	7	39..	H 28
,, rd, Cann. Town E	12	49..	L 33
,, ,, Cotten'm-p. SW	20	—..	Z 12
,, ,, E. Finchley N .	2	—..	B 19
,, ,, Holloway N .	6	32..	F 23
,, ,, Manor-park E .	8	—..	H 36
,, ,, S. Ealing W .	9	—..	O 6
,, ,, Sidcup . .	23	—..	Y 42
,, ,, Tottenham N .	3	—..	B 25
,, ,, Wimble'n-p SW	20	—..	X 14
,, ,, Woolwich .	18	—..	P 39
,, row, Stepney E .	—	48..	L 29
,, st, Kenn'ton-la. SE	16	53..	P 22
,, ,, Kensington W .	10	50..	N 15

Street	4-in. sht.	9-in. sht.	mar.
Durham-terr, Bayswater W	10	43..	L 16
,, vil, Kensing'ton W	10	51..	N 16
Durnsford-av, Wimb'n SW	20	—..	W 15
Durham-house-st, Str. WC	—	45..	M 22
,, rd, Bowes-pk. N	2	—..	A 21
,, ,, Earlsfield SW	20	—..	W 16
,, ,, Wimb'n SW	20	—..	X 16
Durley-rd, Stamford H. N	7	33..	E 26
Durlston-road, Clapton E .	7	33..	F 27
,, ,, Kingston	19	—..	Y 7
Durrell-road, Fulham SW .	15	59..	R 15
Durrington-rd, Hom'ton E	7	40..	G 29
Durward-st, Whitechapel E	12	47..	L 27
Dutton-st, Greenwich SE .	4	64..	R 31
Duval-st, Spitalfields E .	12	46..	L 26
Dye House-la, Old Ford E	12	48..	J 31
Dyers-bldgs, Holborn EC .	45	—..	L 23
,, ct, Aldermanbury EC	46	—..	L 24
,, Hall,10Dowg'te-hl,EC	11	46..	M 25
,, ,, rd, Leytonst. E	7	—..	F 33
,, ,, Wharf, Upper Thames-st, EC	—	46..	M 25
,, lane, Putney SW .	15	—..	S 12
Dymock-st, Fulham SW .	15	59..	S 16
Dyne-road, Kilburn NW .	5	—..	I 15
Dynevor-rd, Richmond .	14	—..	T 7
,, ,, Stoke New. N	7	38..	F 26
Dynham-rd, Kilburn NW .	5	35..	H 16
Dyott-st, New Oxf.-st, WC	11	45..	L 22
Dysart-street, Finsbury EC	46	—..	L 25
Dyson-rd, Leytonstone E .	7	—..	D 33
,, ,, Stratford E .	7	—..	I 34
Dyson's-road, Edmonton N	3	—..	A 28

E

Street	4-in. sht.	9-in. sht.	mar.
Eade-rd, Finsbury-park N	6	33..	D 24
Eagle-av, Tottenham N .	3	—..	B 26
,, -hill, Upper Nor. SE .	21	—..	Z^1 25
,, place, Piccadilly SW	—	45..	M 21
,, road, Wembley .	4	—..	H 7
,, street, Holborn WC ,	11	45..	L 22
,, Wharf-rd, Hoxton N	11	38..	J 25
Eaglesfield-rd, Shooters-hill	18	—..	R 38
Eaglewood-rd, Balham SW	16	—..	U 20
Eagling-road, Bow E .	12	48..	K 31
Ealing, Middlesex W . .	9	—..	M 7
,, Common, Ealing W	9	—..	M 7
Ealing Common & West Acton Sta., Met. Dist. Rly, Ealing W . .	9	—..	M 8
Ealing Dean, Middlesex W	9	—..	M 5
,, Green, Ealing W ,	9	—..	M 6
,, rd, Brentford, Mid.	14	—..	P 7
,, ,, Sudbury, Mid. .	4	—..	H 7
,, ,, sth, Ealing W .	9	—..	N 6
Ealing Sta., G.W. & Met. Dis. Rlys, Ealing W .	9	—..	L 7
Ealing-pk-gds, S. Ealing W	9	—..	O 6
Eamont, New Cross SE .	4	63..	R 29
,, st, S.John's W.NW	11	36..	J 18
Eardley-cres, Earl's-ct. SW	15	51..	P 16
,, rd, Streatham .	21	—..	Y 20
Earl-rd, Bermondsey SE .	17	55..	P 26
,, st. Finsbury EC .	11	46..	L 25
,, ,, Lisson-grove NW .	11	43..	K 18
,, ,, Stratford E . .	7	41..	J 32
,, ,, London-road SE .	11	54..	O 24
,, ,, Westminster SW .	11	53..	O 21
,, ,, Woolwich . .	18	—..	P 39
Earldom-rd, Putney SW .	15	59..	S 13
Earlham-gr, Forest Gate E	8	41..	H 34
,, ,, Wood Gr'n N	2	—..	A 23
Earl's-court, SW . .	15	51..	P 16
Earl's-ct. ex., Warw.-rd, SW	15	58..	P 15
,, ,, gds, E.-ct.-rd,SW	15	51..	P 16
,, ,, gr, Earl's-ct, SW	15	58..	P 16
,, ,, rd, Kensingt'n W	10	51..	O 16
,, ,, Ry. Sta, Dist. R.	15	51..	P 16
,, ,, sq, Earl's-ct, SW	15	51..	P 16
Earlsfield-rd, Earlsfield SW	—	20..	V 17
Earlsfield Station, S.W.R., Earlsfield SW . .	20	—..	V 16
Earlshall-rd, Eltham .	18	—..	T 37
Earlsmead-rd, Q'ns-pk NW	10	42..	J 13
,, ,, W. Green N	3	—..	C 26
Earlsthorpe-rd, Syd'n'm SE	—	22..	X 28
Earlswood-st, E. Green. SE	17	57..	P 33
Earlton-rd, Earlsfield SW	20	—..	V 16
Eartham-rd, Bowes-park N	2	—..	A 23
East-av., East Ham E .	8	—..	I 37
,, ,, Walthamstow E .	3	—..	C 31
,, Bank, Stoke New. N .	7	33..	E 26
,, Hill, Bickley, Kent	28	—..	Z^2 37
,, ,, Wandsworth SW	15	60..	T 17
,, ,, ,, ,,	15	—..	T 16
,, lane, Bermondsey SE	12	55..	O 27
,, ,, Sudbury, Mid. .	4	—..	F 6
,, ,, Wembley . .	4	—..	F 7
,, passage, Long-lane EC	46	—..	L 24
,, rd, Edgware, Mid. .	1*a*	—..	A 10
,, ,, Hounslow . .	14	—..	T 1
,, ,, Hoxton N . .	11	46..	J 25
,, ,, Norbiton . .	19	—..	Z 7
,, ,, Plaistow E . .	13	—..	J 34
,, ,, ,, ,, .	13	—..	J 35
,, ,, S. Wimbledon SW	20	—..	Z 17
,, Row, Kensal-green W	10	42..	K 14
,, Square, Woolwich .	18	—..	P 37
,, st, Baker-street W .	11	44—	L 19
,, ,, Barking . .	13	—..	J 39
,, ,, Barnsbury N .	6	37..	I 22
,, ,, Epsom, Surrey .	29	—..	Z^{11} 10
,, ,, Lambs Cond.-st WC	11	45..	L 22
,, ,, Walworth-rd SE .	17	54..	P 25
,, ,, Woolwich E . .	13	—..	O 36
,, Acton, Middlesex W .	10	—..	M 11
,, ,, -lane, Acton W	10	—..	M 10
,, Arbour-st, Stepney E	12	47..	L 28
,, Brixton ry-st, Brix.SW	16	61..	T 23

Street	4-in. sht.	9-in. sht.	mar.
East Chapel-st, Mayfair W	—	44..	N 20
,, Croydon railway sta., L.B.& S.C. Railway	26	—..	Z^6 25
,, Down-pk, Lewis'm SE	17	64..	T 32
,, Dulwich, E. Dul. SE	17	62..	T 26
,, ,, -gr, E.Dul. SE	17	62..	T 26
,, ,, ,, ,, ,,	16	—..	U 25
,, ,, road SE .	17	62..	T 26
,, ,, ry station, Dulwich SE .	17	62..	T 26
,, End-rd, E.Finchley N	2	—..	B 18
,, ,, ,, ,, ,,	2	—..	B 17
,, ,, ,, Finchley N .	1	—..	A 16
,, Ferry-rd, Isle Dogs E	12	57..	O 31
,, Finchley N . .	2	—..	B 18
,, ,, sta, East Finchley N	2	—..	C 18
,, Greenwich, E.Gr'n. SE	17	57..	P 33
,, Ham E . . .	13	—..	K 37
,, Ham Manor Way, North Woolwich E .	13	—..	N 38
,, Ham sta, L.T. & S.R.	8	—..	I 37
,, Harding-st, Fet'r-la EC	45	—..	L 23
,, Heath-rd, Hamp. NW	5	—..	F 17
,, India-av, Lead.-st. EC	—	46..	M 25
,, ,, Dk.-rd, Poplar E	12	48..	M 31
,, ,, ,, ,,	12	49..	M 32
,, ,, Dks, Poplar E .	12	49..	M 32
,, India Dock Wall-rd, Blackwall E . .	12	49..	M 32
,, Lon. Cemet., W.Hm E	12	49..	K 34
,, Moulsey, Surrey .	24	—..	Z^2 3
,, Mount-st, Whitech.R.E	12	47..	L 27
,, Putney ry sta, Put.SW	15	59..	T 14
,, Sheen SW . . .	14	—..	T 9
,, ,, -av, E. Sheen SW	15	—..	T 10
,, Surrey-gds, Peck'm SE	17	54..	Q 26
,, Wickham, Kent .	18	—..	S 41
Eastbank-rd, N'w H'mpton	19	—..	X 2
Eastbourne-rd, Brntfd, Md.	14	—..	P 6
,, ,, E. Ham, E	13	—..	K 38
,, ,, L.Tootg SW	21	—..	Z^1 19
,, ,, W. Ham E	12	41..	J 33
,, ,, Tottenm N.	7	33..	D 26
,, ter., Pr'd-st W	10	43..	L 17
Eastbrook-rd, Bl'khth, SE.	18	—..	R 35
Eastbury-gve, Ham'rs'th W	15	—..	P 11
,, rd, Norbiton .	19	—..	Z 6
Eastcheap, EC . . .	11	46..	M 25
Eastcombe-av, Charlton .	18	—..	Q 34
Eastcote, S. Harr'w, Mdx	4	—..	F 2
,, st, Stockwell SW	16	61..	S 22
Eastdown, Lewisham SE .	17	—..	T 32
,, pk, Lewish. SE.	17	64..	T 32
Eastern rd, Brockley, SE .	17	63..	I 30
,, ,, Ladywell SE .	17	63..	T 30
,, ,, Muswell-hill N .	2	—..	B 19
,, ,, Wood-green N .	2	—..	A 22
,, Fever Hos., Hom.E	7	40..	G 29
Eastfield-rd, Waltham'w E	3	—..	C 31
,, st, Stepney E .	12	48..	L 29
Eastfields rd, Acton, W .	9	—..	L 10
Eastlake-rd, Camb'rw'll SE	16	62..	S 24
Eastlands, E. Dulwich SE .	17	—..	U 26
Eastmearn-road, Dulwich .	21	—..	W 24
Eastney-st, Greenwich .	17	—..	Q 32
,, ,, ,, .	17	64..	Q 32
Easton-st, Clerkenwell WC.	11	45..	K 23
Eastward-st, Bromley E .	12	48..	L 31
Eastwood-rd, Gdmay's.Esx	8	—..	E 42
,, ,, Victoria D. E	13	—..	N 34
,, st. Streatham .	21	—..	Z^1 20
Eatington-rd, Walth'w E .	3	—..	C 32
Eaton-grove, Lee SE .	17	64..	T 33
Eaton-pl, Eaton-sq. SW .	11	52..	O 19
,, rd, Castlebar-hill W	9	—..	L 6
,, ,, Croydon, Surrey	26	—..	Z^5 23
,, ,, Ilford, Essex .	8	—..	H 39
,, ,, Sutton, Surrey .	29	—..	Z^8 17
,, square, SW . .	11	52..	O 19
,, terr, Eaton-sq. SW .	11	52..	O 19
,, ,, S.Johns-wd NW	11	35..	J 18
Eatonville-rd, Uppr Toot.	21	—..	W 19
Ebbsfleet-rd, Cricklewd.NW	5	—..	G 14
Ebner-st. Wandsworth SW	15	59..	T 16
Ebsworth-st, Brockley SE .	8	22..	29
Ebury-br, Pimlico-rd, SW .	16	52..	P 20
,, sqr, Pimilico SW .	—	52..	P 20
,, st. Pimlico SW .	16	52..	P 19
Ecclesbourne-rd, Croy. Sur	26	—..	Z^3 24
,, ,, Isling. N.	6	38..	I 24
Eccles-road, Battersea SW	16	60..	T 18
Eccleston-br, Pimlico SW .	11	52..	O 20
,, pl, Pimlico SW .	11	52..	O 20
,, rd, Hanwell W .	9	—..	M 4
,, sq, Belgr.-rd.SW	16	52..	P 20
,, st. Pimlico SW .	11	52..	O 20
Ecclestone-pl, Wembley .	4	—..	G 8
Eckstein-rd, Battersea SW.	16	60..	T 18
Eclipse-rd, Canning T. E .	13	—..	L 34
,, ,, Plaistow E .	13	—..	L 34
Edale-rd, Rotherhithe SE .	17	55..	P 28
Edbrooke-rd, S.Peters-pk.W	10	43..	K 16
Eddystone-rd, Brockley SE	4	—..	U 29
Eden-grove, Holloway N .	6	37..	H 23
,, prk, Beckenh'm Kent	27	—..	Z^3 29
,, rd, Croydon, Surrey	30	—..	Z^7 24
,, ,, Elmers End, Sur.	27	—..	Z^3 29
,, ,, Walthamstow E	3	—..	C 31
,, ,, W. Norwood SE .	21	—..	Y 24
,, st, Hamp'd-rd NW .	—	44..	K 21
,, ,, Kingston . .	19	—..	Z^1 6
,, Pk Ry Sta, S.E.& C.R.	27	—..	Z^4 30
Edeboro-rd, Limehouse E .	12	48..	L 30
Edenhurst-av, Fulham SW	15	59..	S 15
Edensor-road, Chiswick W.	15	—..	Q 11
Edenvale-st, Fulham SW .	15	59..	S 16
Ederline-rd, Norbury, Sur.	26	—..	Z^2 22
Edgar-road, Bromley E .	12	48..	K 31
,, ,, Ilford . .	8	—..	E 43
,, ,, Purley, Surrey	30	—..	Z^{10} 24
Edgarley-ter, Fulham SW .	15	59..	R 14

Edge-hill. INDEX TO STREETS, &c. Euston-buildings.

	4-in. sht.	9-in. sht.	mar.
Edge-hill, Wimbledon SW .	—	20	Z 13
,, rd, Cstlebr-hill W	9	—	L 6
,, ,, Purley .	30	—	Z^1 23
Edge-st, Kensington W .	10	43	M 16
Edgel-st, Wandsworth SW	15	59	T 16
Edgington-rd, Strthm. .	21	—	Z^1 21
Edgware-rd, W . .	10	44	L 18
,, ,, Cricklewd NW	5	—	G 14
Edgware-road rlwy.-stat, Bakerloo-rlwy. NW . . .	11	43	L 18
Edgware-sta, G.N.R. Mdx.	1a	—	A 9
Edinburgh-rd, Edmont. N.	3	—	A 27
,, ,, Sut, Surr. .	25	—	Z^6 17
,, ,, Walth'w E .	7	—	D 30
Edison-rd, East Wickham.	18	—	R 41
Edith-gr, Fulham-rd, SW .	15	51	Q 17
,, rd, Bounds-gr.-rd, N	2	—	A 22
,, ,, Farnborough .	30b	—	Z^8 41
,, ,, Leyton E . .	7	41	H 32
,, ,, Peckham SE .	17	63	S 28
,, ,, Upton E . .	8	—	I 36
,, ,, Tottenham N .	3	—	B 27
,, ,, W. Kensing. SW.	15	58	P 14
,, street, Hackney E .	12	39	J 26
,, vils, W. Kensing. SW	15	58	P 15
Edithna-st, Stockwell SW .	16	61	S 22
Edmond-road, Mitcham .	26	—	Z^2 18
Edmonton N	3	—	A 27
,, marsh N .	3	—	A 29
Edmund-pl, Aldersg.-st EC	46	—	L 24
,, -road, Mitcham	25	—	Z^2 18
,, ,, Welling	18	—	T 41
,, st. Camberwell SE	17	54	Q 25
Edna-rd, Raynes-pk. SW .	20	—	Z^1 13
,, st, Battersea SW .	16	60	R 18
Edric-road, Deptford .	17	55	Q 28
Edscote-road, Hendon NW	1	—	C 13
,, ,, Hendon NW	1	—	C 13
Education Offices L.C.C. Victoria-embankmt. WC.	11	45	M 23
Edward-rd, Croy. Surrey .	26	—	Z^4 25
,, ,, New Hampton	19	—	X 2
,, ,, New Mald, Sur	25	—	Z^3 11
,, ,, Penge SE .	22	—	Q^1 28
,, ,, Waltham. E .	3	—	C 29
,, ,, Willesden NW.	10	—	K 10
,, sq, Islington N .	—	37	J 22
,, st, Canning Tn. E	13	—	L 34
,, ,, Deptford SE .	17	56	Q 30
,, ,, Islington N .	17	46	J 24
,, ,, Soho W . .	—	45	M 21
,, ,, Regents-pk NW	11	44	J 20
Edwardes-sq, Kensing. W.	10	50	O 15
Edwards-rd, Mile-end-rd. E	12	48	K 30
Edwin-st, Canning Tn. E .	13	—	L 34
Eel-brook-com, Fulham SW	15	59	R 16
Eel-pie-island, Twicken'm.	19	—	V 5
Effie-road, Fulham SW .	15	51	Q 16
Effingham-rd, Hornsey N .	2	—	C 23
,, ,, Lee SE .	17	—	U 33
,, st. Pimlico SW	—	52	P 20
Effort-st, Low. Tooting SW	21	—	Y 18
Effra-parade, Brixton SW .	16	—	U 23
Effra-road, ,, SW .	16	—	T 23
,, ,, Wimbledon SW.	20	—	Y 16
Egbert-st, Regents-pk. NW	6	36	I 19
Egerton-cres, Brompt. SW.	11	51	O 18
,, gds, Brompt.-rd.SW	—	51	O 18
,, gardens, Castlebar Hill W . .	9	—	L 5
,, gdns, Hendon NW	1	—	C 13
,, rd, Greenwich SE	4	63	R 31
,, ,, Norwood SE .	26	—	Z^2 25
,, ,, Stamford H N	7	33	D 26
,, ter, Brompt. SW .	11	51	O 18
Egham-road, Plaistow E .	13	—	E 35
Eglantine-rd, Wands. SW .	15	—	U 16
Egleton-rd, Bromley E .	12	48	K 31
Eglinton-road, Bow E .	12	48	J 30
,, ,, Plumstead .	18	—	Q 38
Egliston-road, Putney SW	15	—	G 13
Egmont-rd, L. Ditt. Surr.	24	—	Z^5 7
,, ,, Sutton Sur.	29	—	Z^9 16
,, st, New Cross SE.	17	63	R 29
Egremont-rd, W. Norw'd SE	21	—	X 23
Eighth-av, Manor-pk. E .	8	—	G 37
Eileen-road, Norwood SE .	26	—	Z^3 25
Elaine-gr, Kentish Tn. NW	6	36	G 19
Elam-st, Camberwell SE .	16	62	S 24
Eland-rd, Lavender H. SW	16	60	S 19
,, ,, Croydon, Sur. .	26	—	Z^6 23
Elbe-street, Fulham SW .	15	60	R 17
Elborough-st, Wands. SW .	20	—	V 15
Elder-av, Crouch-end N .	2	—	C 22
,, rd, Sydenham SE .	22	—	X 29
,, ,, W. Norwood .	21	—	Y 24
,, st, Norton Fol. E.	12	46	L 26
Elderfield-rd, Clapton E .	7	39	G 28
,, ,, Clapton E .	7	40	G 29
Elderslie-road, Eltham .	18	—	U 38
Eldon-pk, S. Norwood SE .	27	—	Z^2 27
,, rd, Hampstead NW	5	36	G 18
,, ,, Kensington W .	10	51	O 16
,, ,, Walthamst'w E	3	—	C 30
,, ,, Wood Green N .	2	—	A 24
,, street, Finsbury EC.	11	46	L 25
Eldred-road, Barking .	13	—	J 40
Eleanor-grove, Barnes SW	15	—	S 11
,, rd, Bowes-park N.	2	—	A 22
,, ,, Hackney E .	7	39	H 27
,, ,, Plaistow E .	13	—	J 34
,, ,, Stratford E .	7	—	I 34
,, ,, Woolwich .	18	—	P 38
,, street, Bow E .	12	48	K 30
Electric-av. Brixton SW .	16	61	T 23
Elephant & Castle, New. SE	11	54	O 24
,, ,, Station New Kent-rd, SE	11	54	O 24
,, rd,N. Kent-rd,SE	11	54	O 24
,, yd, Fore-st, EC .	46	—	L 24
Elers-road, Ealing W .	9	—	N 6
Elfindale-rd, Herne H. SE	16	—	W 24
Elfort-road, Highbury N .	6	38	G 23
Elgar-st, Rotherhithe SE .	12	56	O 29
Elgin-av, Maida Vale W .	10	43	K 16
,, -cres, Notting Hill W	10	50	M 14
,, rd, Alexandra-pk N .	2	—	A 21
,, ,, Carshalton, Surr.	30	—	Z^8 20
,, ,, Croydon, Surrey	26	—	Z^6 26
,, ,, Ilford, Essex .	8	—	E 41
,, ,, Sutton, Surrey .	25	—	Z^6 17
,, ter, Maida Hill W .	10	43	J 16
Elibank-road, Eltham .	18	—	T 37
Eliot Bank, Forest Hill SE	22	—	W 27
,, hill, Lewisham SE .	17	64	S 32
,, pl, Blackheath SE .	17	64	S 32
,, Vale, Blackheath SE	17	64	S 32
Elizabeth-br, S G'ges-rd,SW	16	52	P 20
,, pl, Poplar E .	12	48	M 31
,, ,, Wh.Cross-st,EC	46	—	K 24
,, rd, Plaistow E .	8	—	I 36
,, ,, Plaistow E .	13	—	L 35
,, ,, Tottenham N	3	—	C 26
,, st, N. WoolwichE	13	—	N 37
,, ,, Eaton-sq, SW	11	52	O 19
,, ,, Walworth SE	17	54	Q 25
Elkington-rd, Plaistow E .	13	—	L 35
Ella-rd, Hornsey N . .	6	32	D 22
Ellaline-rd, Hmrsmth. W .	15	58	Q 13
Elland-road, Peckham SE .	17	63	T 28
Ellen-st, St. George's E. E	12	47	M 27
Ellenboro-rd, Wood Gr. N	2	—	A 24
Elleray-rd, Teddington .	19	—	T 4
Ellerby-st, Fulham SW .	15	59	R 14
Ellerdale-rd, Hmpstd. NW	5	35	G 17
,, st, Lewisham SE	4	63	T 31
Ellerker-gdns, Richmond .	14	—	T 7
Ellerslie-rd, Brixton SW .	16	—	T 21
,, ,, N. Kens. W .	10	50	M 13
,, ,, Shepherd's B. W	10	50	M 12
Ellerthorp-street, Poplar E	12	48	M 31
Ellerton-rd, L. Ditt., Surr.	24	—	Z^5 7
,, ,, Wands'th SW .	20	—	V 17
Ellery-st, Peckham SE .	17	62	S 27
Ellesborough-rd, W. Gr. N	2	—	A 22
Ellesmere-rd, Chiswick W .	14	—	P 10
,, ,, Poplar E .	12	48	L 31
,, ,, Roman-rd E	12	40	J 29
,, ,, Victoria D. E	13	—	N 34
,, ,, Willes. Gr. NW	5	—	G 12
Ellingfort-rd, Hackney E .	7	39	I 28
Ellingham-rd, St'f'd, N.T. E	7	41	G 32
Ellington-rd, Muswell Hi. N	2	—	C 20
,, st, Holloway N .	6	37	H 23
Elliot-road, Bickley . .	28	—	Z^3 35
Elliott-rd, Chiswick W .	10	—	O 10
,, ,, N. Brixton SW .	16	61	R 23
,, ,, Th'nt'n H., Sur.	26	—	Z^3 23
Elliotts-row, Lambeth SE .	11	54	O 24
Ellis-st, Sloane-st, SW .	11	52	O 19
Elliscombe-rd, Old Ch'lton	18	—	Q 35
Ellison-rd, Streatham .	21	—	Y 21
Ellora-road, Streatham .	21	—	Y 21
Elm-court, The Temple EC.	45	—	M 23
,, crescent, Norbiton .	19	—	Z 7
,, gdns, Hammers'th W .	10	58	O 13
,, gro, Cricklewood NW .	5	—	G 14
,, ,, Hammers'th W .	10	58	O 13
,, ,, Hornsey N . .	6	32	D 22
,, ,, Norbiton . .	19	—	Z 7
,, ,, Peckham SE .	17	62	S 26
,, ,, Plumstead . .	18	—	Q 40
,, ,, Wimbledon SW .	20	—	Z 14
,, ,, rd, Barnes SW .	15	—	R 12
,, ,, ,, Ealing W .	9	—	M 7
,, ,, ,, Ealing W .	9	—	N 7
,, lane, Catford SE .	22	—	W 30
,, pk, Brixton SW . .	16	—	U 22
,, ,, Brixton SW . .	21	—	V 22
,, pl, S. Kensington SW	—	51	P 17
,, rd, Beckenham . .	22	15	Z^2 29
,, ,, Camden Town NW	6	37	I 21
,, ,, Chelsfield, Kent .	30b	—	Z^9 40
,, ,, Croydon, Surrey .	26	—	Z^3 24
,, ,, Ewell . .	29	—	Z^8 11
,, ,, Hackbridge, Surr.	26	—	Z^5 19
,, ,, Hook . .	24	—	Z^7 6
,, ,, Leyton E . .	7	—	F 32
,, ,, Mortlake SW .	14	—	S 9
,, ,, New Malden .	25	—	Z^2 10
,, ,, NewMalden,Surrey	25	—	Z^2 10
,, ,, Norbiton .	19	—	Z 7
,, ,, Sidcup, Kent .	23	—	Y 41
,, ,, Sudbury, Mid'sex	4	—	G 7
,, ,, Walthamstow E .	3	—	C 32
,, st, Grays Inn-rd, WC .	11	45	K 23
,, ,, Woolwich . .	18	—	P 39
,, Bank-gdns, Barnes SW	15	—	R 11
,, pk-gdns, Chelsea SW .	16	51	P 17
,, ,, rd, Chelsea SW .	16	51	P 17
,, ,, ,, Finchley N .	1	—	A 15
,, ,, ,, Lea Brge-rd, E	7	—	E 30
,, ,, ,, Stamford Hi. N	7	—	D 27
,, Tree-av, Th. Ditton .	24	—	Z^4 2
,, ,, rd, S John's W. NW	10	43	J 17
Elmar-rd, Tottenham N .	3	—	C 25
Elmbourne-rd, Tooting .	21	—	X 19
Elmcroft-cres, Hendon NW	5	—	D 14
,, rd, Clapton E .	7	39	G 28
,, ,, Orpington .	28	—	Z^5 41
Elmdale-rd, Bowes Park N	2	—	A 23
Elmer-rd, Catford SE .	22	—	Y 31
Elmers-av, Surbiton, Surr.	24	—	Z^3 6
,, End-rd, Elmers E. Kt.	27	—	Z^2 28
,, ,, ,, Penge SE .	22	—	Z^2 27
,, ,, Ry Sta, S.E.&CR	27	—	Z^3 28
Elmfield-av, Teddington .	19	—	X 4
,, pl, Bickley, Kent	28	—	Z^2 34
,, road, Balham .	21	—	W 19
,, ,, Bickley, Kent	28	—	Z^2 34
,, ,, Walth'mst'w E	7	—	D 29
Elmhurst-rd, Forest-ga. E .	8	—	J 35
Elmhurst-rd, Tottenm. N .	3	—	A 26
,, st, Clapham SW .	16	61	S 21
Elmington-terr, Peckm. SE	16	62	R 25
Elmira-street, Lewisham SE	4	63	S 31
Elmore-road, Leyton E .	7	41	G 32
Elmore-st, Essex-road N .	7	38	J 25
Elms-av, Muswell Hill N .	2	—	B 20
,, lane, Sudbury . .	4	—	F 5
,, road, Clapham SW .	16	—	U 21
,, ,, Dulwich SE .	16	—	U 25
Elmsdale-rd, Walthamst. E	3	—	C 30
Elmsleigh-rd, Twickenham	19	—	V 3
,, ,, Wands. SW .	15	60	T 17
Elmstead-lane, Kent .	23	—	Z 36
,, road, Ilford .	8	—	F 41
,, Wood, Kent .	23	—	Y 36
,, Woods, S. E. & C. R.-rail-sta.	23	—	Z 36
Elmstone-rd, Fulham SW .	—	59	R 15
Elmsworth-rd, Hounslow .	14	—	R 1
,, ,, Mitcham .	25	—	Z^2 18
,, rd, Croydon, Sur	26	—	Z^4 23
,, ,, Herne H. SE	16	—	U 25
,, ,, Mitcham .	26	—	Z^2 18
Elmswood-rd, Chiswick W	14	—	P 9
Elmwood-avenue, Greenhill	1a	—	C 5
Elphenstone-rd, Chpl Ed. E	3	—	A 30
Elphicke-st, Cann. Town E	13	—	M 34
Elsa-road, East Wickham .	18	—	T 42
,, street, Stepney E .	12	48	L 29
Elsdale-street, Hackney E .	7	39	J 28
Elsden-road, Tottenham N	3	—	A 26
Elsenham-road, Manor-pk.	8	—	H 38
,, st, Wands. SW .	20	—	15 V
Elsham-rd, Leytonstone E	7	41	G 33
,, ,, W. Kenstn. W	10	50	N 14
Elsie Maud-st, Brockley SE	4	—	U 30
Elsinore-rd, Forest Hill SE	22	—	W 29
Elsley-rd. E. Battersea SW	16	60	S 19
,, ,, W. ,, ,,	16	60	S 19
Elslie-rd. E. Dulwich SE .	17	62	T 26
Elspeth-rd, Battersea SW .	16	60	T 19
,, ,, Sudbury, Mdx	4	—	G 7
Elsted-street, Walworth SE	17	54—	P 25
Elswick-rd, Lewisham SE .	4	63	S 31
Elsworthy-rd, Hampst. NW	5	35	J 18
Eltham-bridge, Eltham SE	18	—	U 35
,, common, ,, .	18	—	S 37
,, green, Eltham SE .	18	—	U 35
,, hill, Eltham .	18	—	V 36
,, park, Eltham .	18	—	T 38
,, road, Lee SE .	18	—	U 34
,, st, Walworth SE .	17	54	P 25
,, & Mottingham S. E. & C. R. ra. sta. .	23	—	W 36
Elthiron-road, Fulham SW.	15	59	R 16
Elthorne-av, Hanwell W .	9	—	N 4
,, rd, Hornsey R. N	6	32	E 21
,, pk-rd, Hanwell W	9	—	N 4
Elthruda-rd, Lewisham SE	17	—	U 32
Eltisley-road, Ilford, Essex	8	—	G 38
Elton-road, Norbiton .	19	—	Z 7
,, street, Kingsland N .	7	38	H 26
Eltringham-st, Wands. SW	15	60	T 17
Elvaston-pl, S. Knes. SW .	10	51	O 17
Elvendon-rd, Nw. S'gate N	2	—	A 22
Elverson-rd, Deptford SE .	4	63	S 31
Elwell-road, Clapham SW .	16	61	R 21
Elwill-way, Bromley . .	27	—	Z^3 31
Elwood-st, Highbury N .	6	38	F 24
Ely-pl, Holborn-circus EC	—	45	L 23
,, ,, Tottenham N .	2	—	C 24
,, road, Leyton-st, E .	7	—	D 32
,, ,, Thorn. Hth, Sur.	26	—	Z^3 25
,, terr, Mile End-road E	12	48	K 29
Elyne-rd, Stroud-green N .	6	32	D 23
Emanuel-avenue, Acton W	9	-	L 10
Embankment, Putney SW	15	59	S 14
,, r-sta, Bakerloo r.	11	45	M 22
Embercourt-rd, Th.Ditton, Surrey . . .	24	—	Z^3 2
Ember-pk-rd, Th. Ditton .	24	—	Z^4 2
Embleton-rd, Lewishm. SE	4	63	T 31
Emerald-st, Theo'ds-rd WC	11	45	L 22
Emerson-st, Bankside SE .	11	46	N 24
Emery-hill-st, Westmr. SW	—	52	O 21
Emily-st, Canning Town E	12	49	M 33
Emlyn-road, Shep. Bush W	10	—	N 11
Emmanuel-rd, Balham SW	21	—	W 20
Emma-road, Plaistow E .	12	—	K 34
,, street, Hackney E .	12	39	J 27
,, ,, Silvertown E .	13	—	N 36
Emmett-street, Poplar E .	12	48	M 30
Emmott-street, Mile End E	12	48	K 29
Emperors-ga, S. Kens. SW	10	51	O 16
Empress-av, Chapel End E	3	—	A 31
,, ,, Ilford, Essex	8	—	F 38
,, ,, Wanstead E .	8	—	F 36
,, ,, Walwh-rd, SE	16	54	Q 24
Empson-street, Bromley E	12	49	K 31
Emsworth-st, Streatm. Hi.	21	—	W 22
Emu-road, Battersea SW .	16	61	S 20
Ena-road, Norbury, Surrey	26	—	Z^2 22
Enbrook-st, Kensal-gr. W .	10	42	K 14
Endell-st, Long acre WC .	11	45	L 22
Endive-st, Limehouse E .	12	40	L 30
Endlesham-rd, Balham SW	16	—	U 19
Endsleigh-gdns, Eus-rd,NW	11	45	K 21
,, gdn, Ilford, Ess.	8	—	F 38
,, road, Hanwell W	9	—	M 4
,, street, WC .	11	45	K 21
Endwell-road, Brockley SE	4	63	S 29
Endymion-rd, Brixton SW	16	—	U 22
,, ,, Fins.-pk. N	6	32	D 24
Enfield-rd, Acton W . .	9	—	N 9
,, ,, Brentford,Mdx	14	—	P 6
,, ,, Hornsey N .	2	—	C 22
,, ,, Kingsland-rd N	—	38	I 26
Engadine-st, Wandsth SW .	20	—	V 15
Engate-st, Lewisham SE .	4	64	T 31
Engineer-rd, Woolwich,Kt	18	—	Q 38
Englands-lane, Hmpstd.NW	6	36	H 19
Englefield-rd, Essex-rd N .	7	38	J 25
Engleheart-rd, Catford SE	22	—	V 31
Englewood-rd, Balham SW	16	—	U 20
Enid-st, Bermondsey SE .	12	53	O 26
Enmore-road, Putney SW .	15	59	T 13
Ennerdale-road, Kew. .	14	—	R 8
Ennersdale-rd, Lewshm SE	17	—	U 32
Ennis-rd, Finsbury-park N	6	32	E 23
,, ,, Plumstead .	18	—	Q 39
Ennismore-gdns, Kensington-rd, SW . .	11	52	O 18
Enslin-rd, Eltham, Kent .	23	—	V 37
Epple-road, Fulham SW .	15	59	R 15
Epping Forest . . .	3	—	C 33
Epsom, Surrey . .	29	—	Z^{10} 11
,, rd, Epsom, Surrey.	—	—	Z^1 11
,, ,, Croydon, Sury .	30	—	Z^7 22
,, Ry. Sta. C. B. & S. C. Ry.	28	—	Z^{11} 9
Erasmus-st, Westmr. SW .	16	53	P 21
Eresby-road, Kilburn NW .	5	35	J 16
Eric-road, Willesden NW .	5	—	H 11
,, st, Mile End-road E .	12	48	K 30
Eridge-rd, Bedford-pk W .	10	—	N 10
,, ,, Croydon, Sur.	26	—	Z^3 23
Erlam-rd, Rotherhithe SE	17	55	P 28
Erlanger-rd, New Cross SE	17	63	R 28
Ermine-rd, Lewisham SE .	4	63	T 31
Ernest-rd, Canning Town E	12	49	L 33
,, ,, Forest Gate E .	8	—	G 34
,, st. Bermondsey SE.	12	35	O 26
,, ,, Stepney E .	12	48	M 29
,, ,, W. Norwood .	21	—	X 24
Erpingham-rd, Putney SW	15	59	G 13
Erridge-raad, Merton SW .	20	—	Z^1 15
Errington-rd, Maida-hill W	10	42	K 15
Errol-st, Bunhill-row EC .	11	46	K 25
Erskine-hill, Hampst'd NW	1	—	C 16
,, rd, Regents pk NW	6	36	J 19
,, ,, Walthamst'wE	3	—	C 30
Esher, Surrey . . .	24	—	Z^6 1
,, green, Esher, Surrey	24	—	Z^6 1
,, lane, E. Moulsey, Sur	24	—	Z^2 2
,, rd, E. Moulsey, Sury.	24	—	Z^3 2
,, ,, Ilford . .	8	—	G 41
,, st, U. Kenningn-la.SE	16	53	P 23
,, & Claremont L. & S. W. Railway Sta. .	24	—	Z^5 2
,, park-avenue, Esher .	24	—	Z^7 1
Esmeralda-rd,Bermdsy.SE.	55	—	P 27
Esmond-rd, Acton-green W	10	—	O 10
,, ,, Kilburn, NW .	5	—	J 15
,, street, Putney SW.	15	59	T 14
Esparto-street, Wands. SW	15	—	U 16
Essendine-rd, Elgin-av. W	10	43	K 16
Essendon-rd, Croydon, Sur	30	—	Z^9 25
Essex-ct, The Temple EC .	45	—	M 23
,, gr, Up. Norwood SE	21	—	Z^1 25
,, ,, Walthamstow E.	3	—	C 29
,, pk-mews, Acton W .	10	—	N 11
,, place, Chiswick W .	9	—	O 10
,, rd, Acton W . .	9	—	L 9
,, ,, East Ham E .	8	—	H 37
,, ., Goodmayes, Es .	8	—	E 43
,, ,, Islington N	6	38	J 24
,, ,, Sta. Islington N	6	38	I 24
,, ,, Leyton E . .	7	—	D 32
,, ,, Walthamstow E	7	—	D 29
,, ,, Willesden NW .	5	—	H 11
,, st, Bethnal-green E	12	47	K 28
,, ,, Bouverie-st. EC .	45	—	M 23
,, ,, Dalston E .	7	39	J 27
,, ,, Forest-gate E .	8	—	H 43
,, ,, Kensington W .	10	50	N 15
,, ,, Kingsland-rd N	12	46	J 26
,, ,, Strand WC. .	11	45	M 23
,, villas, Kensington W	10	51	N 16
Estcourt-rd, Fulham SW .	15	58	Q 15
,, ,, S. Norwood SE	27	—	Z^4 27
Este-road, Battersea SW .	16	60	S 18
Estella-avenue Raynes-pk.	25	—	Z^2 12
Estelle-rd, Hampstead NW	6	36	G 19
Esther-rd, Leytonstone E .	7	—	D 33
Estreham-rd,Streatham SW	21	—	Y^1 21
Eswyn-rd, Toot. Grvny SW	20	—	X 18
Etchingham-rd, Leyton E	7	41	G 32
,, pk-rd, Finch N	1	—	A 17
Ethel-road, Plaistow E .	13	—	K 34
,, ,, Victoria Dk . E	13	—	M 35
Ethelbert-rd, Wimble. SW	20	—	Z^1 13
,, street, Tooting .	21	—	V 20
Ethelburga-st, Battersea S	16	60	R 18
Ethelden-rd, Shep. Bush W	10	50	M 13
Etheldene-av. Muswell-hi. N	2	—	C 21
Ethelred-st, Lambeth SE .	16	53	P 23
Etherley-rd, Tottenham N	2	—	C 24
Etherow-st, E. Dulwich SE	21	—	V 26
Ethnard-rd, O. Kent-rd SE.	17	35	Q 27
Etloe-road, Leyton E .	7	40	F 30
Eton-avenue, Finchley N .	1	—	A 17
,, ,, Hmpstd. NW	5	35	H 18
,, ,, New Malden	—	25	Z^2 10
,, ,, Wembley .	4	—	G 6
,, pl, Hampstead NW .	5	36	J 18
,, rd, Haverstk hi. NW	6	36	H 19
,, ,, Plumstead. .	—	18	P 39
,, st, Regents-pk. NW	6	36	I 19
,, ,, Woolwich . .	18	—	P 39
,, vil. Haverstk.-hi. NW	6	36	H 19
Etruria-st, S. Lambeth SW	16	61	R 21
Etta-st, Deptford SE .	17	56	Q 29
Ettrick-street, Poplar E .	12	49	M 32
Eugenie-road, Rother. SE .	17	55	P 28
Eureka-road, Kingston .	19	—	Z^1 8
Eustace-road, Fulham SW	15	58	Q 15
Euston-bgs, Euston-sq NW	—	45	K 21
,, gro, Euston-sq NW	11	45	K 21
,, road, NW . .	11	45	K 21
,, ry. st, L. & N.W.Ry.	11	45	J 21
,, sq, Euston-rd NW .	11	45	K 21
,, sq Sta, Hmpstd.Ry	11	45	K 21
,, st, Euston-sq NW .	11	45	K 21

Evandale-road. INDEX TO STREETS, &c. **Foreign-street.**

4 in. sht. 9-in. sht. mar.

Evandale-rd, Brixton SW . 16 61..R 23
Evangel-ct, Pilgrim-st EC . — 46..M 24
Evangelist-rd, Ksh. Tn. NW 6 36..G 20
Eve-road, Isleworth . 14 —..S 4
„ „ Leytonstone E . 7 41..G 33
„ „ Sudbury, Msex. 4 —..H 7
„ „ Tottenham N . 3 —..B 26
„ „ West Ham E . 12 41..J 33
Evelina-rd, Peckham SE . 17 63..S 28
„ „ Penge SE . 22 —..Q¹ 28
Evelyn-gdns, S. Kens. SW 15 51..P 17
„ „ Richmond . 14 —..S 7
„ „ S. Acton W . 9 —..O 10
„ „ Victoria Dcks E 13 —..N 34
„ „ Walthamstow E 3 —..C 32
„ „ Wimbledon SW 29 —..Y 16
„ st, Deptford SE . 17 56..Q 30
„ „ Hoxton N . 11 46..J 25
Everest-road, Eltham . 18 —..U 36
Evering-road, Clapton E . 7 33..F 27
Everington-st, Fulham SW 15 58..Q 14
Everitt-st, Nine Elms SW . 16 53..Q 21
Eversford-road, Kew . 14 —..R 7
Evershot-rd, Finsb'y Pk. N 6 32..E 23
Eversholt-st, Cdn. Tn. NW 11 36..J 21
Eversleigh-rd, Battersea SW 16 60..S 19
„ „ Edmonton N . 3 —..A 26
„ „ Finchley N . 1 —..A 16
„ „ Plaistow E . 13 —..J 36
Eversley-cr, Osterley, M'x 14 —..Q 3
„ rd, Charlton . 18 —..Q 34
„ „ U. Norwood . 21 —..Z¹ 24
Everton-rd, Croydon, Sur. 26 —..Z² 26
Evesham-rd, Chapel End E 3 —..A 31
„ „ Stratford E . 7 41..J 33
Ewald-road, Fulham SW . 15 59..R 15
Ewart-gro, Wood Green N 2 —..A 23
„ road, Brockley SE . 22 —..V 29
Ewell, Surrey . . 29 —..Z⁸ 11
„ gro, Ewell, Surrey . 29 —..Z⁸ 11
„ rd, Surbiton, Surrey 24 —..Z⁴ 7
„ sta, L. & S.W. Ry . 29 —..Z⁸ 10
Ewelme-rd, Forest Hill SE 22 —..V 28
Ewhurst-rd, Brockley SE . 17 —..U 30
Ewing-road, Mile End E . 12 48..K 29
Exbury-road, Catford SE . 22 —..W 30
Excelsior-road, Kingston . 19 —..Z¹ 7
Exchange-court, Strand WC — 45..M 22
Exeter-rd, Brondesbury NW 5 —..H 14
„ „ Croydon, Surrey 26 —..Z⁴ 25
„ „ Walthamstow E 3 —..C 30
„ st, Marylebone W . 11 43..K 18
„ „ Strand WC . 11 45..M 22
Ethelm-st, Lambeth SE . 11 53..N 23
Exhibition-rd, S. Kens. SW 11 51..N 18
Exmoor-street, N. Kens. W. 10 42..K 14
„ place, Hackney E 7 39..I 27
Exmouth road, Waltham. E 3 —..C 30
„ st, Com.-rd, E . 12 47..L 28
„ „ Euston-sq NW 11 44..K 21
„ „ Farring.-rd EC 11 45..K 23
Exning-rd, Canning Tn E . 12 49..L 33
Exton-st, Waterloo-rd SE . 11 53..N 23
Eynella-rd, E. Dulwich SE 21 —..V 26
Eynham-street, N. Kens. W 10 42..L 13
Eyot-gdns, Hmsmth. W . 15 —..P 11
Eyre-road, Hampstead NW 5 35..G 17
Eythorn-rd, N. Brixton SW 16 61..R 23
Ezra-street, Hackney E . 12 47..J 26

F

Fabian-road, Fulham SW . 15 58..Q 15
„ street, East Ham E. 13 —..L 37
Factory-road, Silvertown E 13 —..N 37
Fair-st, Tooley-street SE . 12 54..N 26
Fairbourne-rd, Totten. N . 3 —..B 25
Fairbridge-rd, U. Norwood 6 32..F 21
Fairbridge-road, U. Hlwy. N 6 32..F 21
Fairchild-pl, Shoreditch EC. — 46..K 25
„ st, Shoreditch EC. 12 46..K 25
Fairclough-st, S. Gges. E. E 12 47..M 27
Fair Cross, Ilford, Essex . 8 —..H 40
Faircross-av, Barking, Esx. 8 —..I 39
Fairfax-rd, Hornsey N . 2 —..C 23
„ „ Kilburn NW . 5 35..I 17
„ „ Teddington . 19 —..Y 4
„ „ Turnham Gr. W 10 —..O 11
Fairfield, Kingston . 19 —..Z¹ 7
„ North, Kingston 19 —..Z¹ 7
„ pl, Kingston . 19 —..Z¹ 7
„ rd, Beckenham . 22 —..Z² 30
„ „ Bow E . . 12 48..J 30
„ „ Charlton . 18 —..O 36
„ „ Croydon, Sur. 26 —..Z⁶ 24
„ „ Croydon, Surr. 26 —..Z⁶ 25
„ „ Edmonton N . 3 —..A 27
„ „ Grove Park SE 23 —..X 35
„ „ Grove Park SE 23 —..X 35
„ „ Hornsey N . 2 —..C 22
„ „ Ilford, Essex . 8 —..H 39
„ „ Kingston . 19 —..Z¹ 6
„ „ New Bromley 22 —..Z 33
„ South, Kingston . 19 —..Z¹ 7
„ st, Wandsworth SW 15 59..T 16
„ West, Kingston . 19 —..Z¹ 7
Fairholme-rd, Croydon, S . 26 —..Z³ 23
Fairfoot-road, Bow E . 12 48..K 30
Fairhazel-gdns, Hamp. NW 5 35..H 17
„ „ Harrow, M'x 1a —..C 4
„ „ W. Kens. SW 15 58..P 15
Fairholt-rd, St. Newing. N 7 33..E 25
Fairland-road, Stratford E 7 41..I 34
Fairlawn-av, Chiswick-pk W 9 —..O 9
„ gro, Chiswick-pk W 9 —..O 10
„ pk, Chiswick-pk W 9 —..O 9
„ „ Sydenham SE 22 —..Y 29
„ road, Merton SW 15 20..Z 15
„ villas, Merton SW 20 —..Z¹ 15
Fairlight-av, Harlesden NW 10 —..J 11

4-in. sht. 9-in. sht. mar.

Fairlight-rd, Streatham SW 17 20..X 17
Fairlop-rd, Leytonstone E 7 —..E 32
Fairmead-road, Holloway N 6 37..F 22
Fairmile-av, Streatham SW 21 —..Y 21
Fairmount-rd, Brixton SW 16 —..U 22
Fairthorn-rd, Nw Charlton 18 —..P 34
Fairview-rd, Norbury . 21 —..Z² 22
„ „ Sutton, Surry. 29 —..Z⁸ 17
„ „ Tottenham N 7 —..D 26
Fakenham-street, N . . — 37..H 22
Falcon-av, Aldersg'te-st, EC — 46..L 24
„ „ „ „ — 46..L 24
„ gr, Battersea SW . 16 60..S 18
„ rd, Battersea SW . 16 60..S 18
„ sq, Aldersgte-st, EC 11 46..L 24
„ st, Aldersg'te-st, EC 11 46..L 24
„ „ Plaistow E . 12 —..K 34
„ terr, Battersea SW . — 60..S 18
Falkirk-st, Kingsl'nd-rd, N 12 46..J 26
Falkland-rd, Hornsey N . 2 —..C 23
„ „ Kentish T. NW 6 36..G 21
„ Way, Beckenh'm 27 —..Z² 30
Fallow-ct-av, Finchley N . 1 —..A 17
Fallsbrook-rd, Streatham . 21 —..Z¹ 20
Falmer-rd, Walthamstow E 3 —..B 31
„ „ West Green N . 2 —..C 25
Falmouth-rd, N.Kent-r. SE 11 54..O 24
Fambridge-rd, L.Sydnhm SE 22 —..X 30
Fann-st, Aldersgate-st, EC — 46..K 24
Farmdale-rd, E.Greenw. SE 18 —..P 34
Fanny-road, Castelnau SW . 15 58..P 12
Fanshaw-av, Barking, Ess. 8 —..I 39
„ st, Hoxton N . 11 46..J 25
Fanthorpe-st, Putney SW . 15 59..S 13
Faraday-rd, Acton W . 9 —..L 10
„ „ N. Kens'n W . 10 42..L 14
„ „ Wimbledon SW 20 —..Y 16
„ st, Walworth SE . 17 54..P 25
Farleigh-rd, Stoke New. N . 7 39..G 26
Farley-road, Catford SE . 22 —..V 31
„ „ Norwood SE . 26 —..Z³ 26
Farlow-road, Putney SW . 15 59..S 13
„ street, Walworth SE 17 54..P 25
Farm-avenue, Streatham . 21 —..X 21
„ lane, Fulham SW . 15 51..Q 16
„ street, Berkeley-sq, W 11 44..M 20
Farmer-rd, Leyton-st, E . 7 —..E 31
„ st, Notting Hill W 10 43..M 16
Farmers-rd, Camberw'll SE 16 54..Q 23
Farmilo-rd, Waltham'w E 7 —..D 30
Farnaby-road, Beckenham 22 —..Z¹ 32
Farnan-av, Walthamst'w E 3 —..B 31
„ road, Streatham . 21 —..Y 22
Farnborough, Kent . . 30b —..Z⁸ 38
„ Com'n, Kent 30b —..Z⁸ 36
Farncombe-st, Berm'sey SE 12 55..O 27
Farningham-rd, Tott'n'm N 3 —..A 27
Farnley-road, Norwood SE 26 —..Z³ 25
Farnold-av, East Ham E . 13 —..J 37
Faroe-rd, W. Kensing'n W 10 50..O 14
Farquhar-rd, Norwood SE 22 —..Y 26
„ „ Wimb.-pk. SW 20 —..W 15
Farquharson-rd, Croy., Sur. 26 —..Z⁴ 24
Farrance-st, Limehouse E . 12 48..M 30
Farrant-av, Wood Green N 2 —..A 24
„ st, Kensal Gr'n W 10 42..K 14
Farrer-road, Hornsey N . 2 —..C 21
Farringdon-av, Farr.-st, EC 11 45..L 23
„ rd, EC . . 11 45..K 23
„ „ Stratford E 7 41..I 33
„ street, EC . 11 45..L 23
„ st. ry sta., Met. Railway, EC. 11 46..L 23
Farwell-road, Sidcup . 23 —..X 42
Farwig-lane, Bromley . 22 —..Z² 33
Fashion-st, Spitalfields E . 12 47..L 26
Fashoda-road, Bickley . 28 —..Z² 35
Fassett-rd, Surbiton, Surr. 24 —..Z⁴ 6
Faulkner's-alley, Far.-rd, EC — 46..L 24
Faustin-pl, Rotherhithe SE 12 56..N 29
Favant-road, Fulham SW . 15 59..R 15
Faversham-rd, Beckenham 22 —..Z² 30
„ „ Catford SE . 22 —..V 30
Favilla-road, Isleworth . 14 —..R 3
Favonia-street, Bromley E 12 49..K 31
Fawcett-rd, Croydon, Surr. 26 —..Z⁶ 24
„ „ Rotherhithe SE 17 55..P 28
„ st, W.Bromptn.SW 15 51..Q 16
Fawe-park-rd, Putney SW 15 59..T 15
Fawley-rd, Hampstead NW 5 35..H 16
„ „ Tottenham N . 3 —..C 27
Fawnbrake-av, Herne-hl.SE 16 —..T 24
Faygate-rd, Streatham-hill 21 —..W 22
Fayland-avenue, Streathm 21 —..Y 20
Fearnley-rd, Peckham SE . 16 62..S 25
Featherbed-la, Adgtn, Sur. 30a —..Z⁹ 29
Featherstone-bldgs, Hol.WC 11 45..L 22
„ „ „ 11 45..L 22
„ st, City-rd, EC 11 46..K 25
Federation-rd, Abbey W'd 13 —..P 42
Felbrigg-rd, E.Dulwich SE 17 —..U 26
„ st, Bethnal Gr'n E 12 47..K 27
Felday-road, Catford SE . 4 —..U 31
Felden-street, Fulham SW . 15 59..R 15
Felix-rd, Drayton Green W 9 —..M 5
„ „ Hanwell W . 9 —..M 4
„ st, Old Beth.-gr.-rd, E 12 47..J 27
„ „ Westmr.-bge-rd.SE 11 53..N 22
Felixstowe-rd, Edmonton N 3 —..A 27
„ „ Quns.-pk, NW 10 42..J 13
Fell-road, Croydon, Surrey 26 —..Z⁴ 24
„ street, Wood-street, EC — 46..L 24
„ „ „ — 46..L 24
Fellbrigg-rd, E.Dulwich SE 17 —..U 26
Fellows-rd, Hampstead NW 5 36..H 18
„ „ Hackney E . 12 39..J 26
Felmingham-rd, S.Norw.SE 27 —..Z³ 27
Felsham-road, Putney SW 15 59..S 13
Felstead-road, Hackney E 7 40..H 30
„ „ Wanstead E 8 —..E 35
Feltham-road, Mitcham . 21 —..Z² 19
Felton-street, Hoxton N . 7 38..I 25

4-in. sht. 9-in. sht. mar.

Fen-court, Fenchurch-st, EC — 46..M 25
Fen-ct, Fenchurch-st, EC . — 46..M 25
Fenchurch-av, Lime-st, EC — 46..M 25
„ buildings EC . 46 —..M 26
„ street EC . . 12 46..M 26
„ „ sta, GER EC 12 46..M 26
Fendall-st, Bermondsey SE 12 54..O 26
Fenelon-rd, Kensington SW 15 58..P 15
Fenham-road, Peckham SE 17 62..R 27
Fenner-rd, Bermondsey SE 12 55..O 27
Fenstanton-av, N. Finch. N 1 —..A 18
Fentiman-rd, S. Lambh. SW 16 53..Q 22
Fenton's-av, Plaistow E . 13 —..K 34
Fenwick-pl, Stockwell SW . — 61..S 21
„ rd, Peck'm Rye SE 17 62..S 27
„ street, Woolwich 18 —..Q 38
Ferdinand-pl, Chalk-farm-road NW . 6 36..H 20
„ st, Chalk-farm-road NW . 6 36..H 20
Fergus-rd, Canonbury N . 6 38..H 24
Ferme-park-rd, Hornsey N 6 32..C 22
Fermor-rd, Forest Hill SE . 22 —..W 29
Fermoy-road, Maida Hill W 10 42..K 15
Fern-road, Stratford E . 7 41..I 33
„ street, Bromley E . 12 48..L 31
Fernbank-avenue, Sudbury — 4..G 4
Fernbrook-road, Lee SE . 17 —..U 33
Ferncliff-road, Dalston E . 7 39..G 27
Ferncroft-av, Gold's-gr. NW 5 —..D 15
„ „ Hampstd.NW 5 35..G 16
Ferndale-av, Walthamstw. E 3 —..C 32
„ rd, Clapham SW . 16 61..T 21
„ „ Leytonstn. E 7 —..F 33
„ „ S. Norwd. SE 27 —..Z³ 27
„ „ Tottenham N 7 —..D 26
„ „ Upton E . 8 —..I 35
„ st, N. Woolw. E 13 —..M 38
„ ter, Wealdst. Mx 1a —..B 4
Ferndene-rd, Herne Hl. SE 16 62..T 24
Fernham-rd, Thornth. Hth Surrey . . . 26 —..Z² 24
Fernhead-rd, Kilburn NW . 10 42..J 15
Fernhill-road, N. Woolw. E. 13 —..N 37
Fernholme-rd, Peckham SE 17 —..T 28
Fernhurst-road, Croydon . 27 —..Z⁶ 27
„ „ Fulham SW . 15 58..Q 14
Fernlea-road, Balham SW . 21 —..V 20
Fernsbury-st, Clrknwll. WC 11 45..K 23
Fernshaw-rd, Ful.-rd, SW . 15 51..Q 17
Fernside-road, Balham . 21 —..V 19
Fernthorpe-rd, Streatham 21 —..Y 20
Ferntower-rd, Highbury N 7 38..G 25
Fernood-av, Streatm. SW 21 —..X 21
Ferrers-road, Streatham . 21 —..Y 21
Ferrier-st, Wandsworth SW 59 —..T 16
Ferris-rd, East Dulwich SE 17 62..T 27
Ferry-lane, Castelnau SW . 15 —..Q 12
„ „ Deptford E . 17 —..C 27
„ „ Kew . . 14 —..P 8
„ „ Tottenham N . 3 —..B 27
„ road, Teddington . 19 —..X 5
„ st, Cubitt Town E . 17 57..P 31
Festing-road, Putney SW . 15 59..S 13
Fetter-lane, Fleet-st, EC . 11 45..L 23
Field-court, Grays Inn WC. 45 —..L 23
„ road, Forest-gate E . 8 —..G 34
„ „ Hmersmth. SW 15 58..P 14
Fieldgate-la, Mitcham, Sur. 25 —..Z¹ 18
„ st, Whitech-rd. E 12 47..L 27
Fielding-road, Chiswick W. 10 —..N 11
Fieldway-cres, Highbury N 6 37..H 23
Fife-road, Canning Town E 13 —..L 34
„ „ East Sheen SW . 14 —..T 9
„ „ Kingston . . 19 —..Z¹ 6
Fifth-av, Kensal-green W . 10 42..K 14
„ „ Manor-park E . 8 —..G 37
„ cr-rd, Twickenham . 19 —..V 2
Figtree-ct, The Temple EC 45 —..M 23
Filbrigge-rd, Seven Kings, Essex . . . . 8 —..F 41
Filey-av, St. Newington N 7 33..E 27
Fillebrook-rd, Leytonst. E 7 —..E 33
Filmer-road, Fulham SW . 15 58..Q 15
Finboro-rd, W. Brompn SW 15 51..P 16
Finborough-rd, Tooting, Graveney SW . . 20 —..Z 18
Finch-lane, Cornhill EC . 11 46..M 25
„ st, Whitechapel E . 12 47..L 26
Finchley N . . . 1 —..A 17
„ av, N. End, Fin.N 1 —..B 15
„ lane, Hendon NW 1 —..B 14
„ pk, N. Finchley N 1 —..A 18
„ pl, S.Jhn's-wd NW 10 35..I 17
„ rd, Hampstd. NW 1 —..C 15
„ „ NW . . 5 35..F 16
„ „ S. Jhns-wd. NW 5 35..I 17
„ „ Walworth SE 16 54..Q 24
„ sta, G. N. R. N . 1 —..A 16
„ „ Met. Railway 5 35..H 17
„ „ station N . 5 35..H 17
Finden-st, Forest Gate E . 8 —..H 35
Findhorn-street, Bromley E 12 49..L 32
Findon-road, Shep. Bush W 10 50..N 12
Fingal-st, E. Greenwich SE 17 57..P 33
Finland-road, Brockley SE. 17 63..T 29
Finley-street, Fulham SW . 15 59..R 14
Finsbury-av, Finsbury EC 11 46..L 25
„ cir, Finsbury EC 11 46..L 25
„ mkt, Finsbury EC — 46..L 25
„ park N . . 6 32..E 23
„ pavmnt, Fins. EC 11 46..L 25
„ road, Wood-gr. N 2 —..A 22
„ sq, Finsbury EC . 11 46..L 25
„ st, Finsbury EC . 11 46..L 25
„ pk-rd, Fins-pk. N 6 32..F 24
„ „ sta, G. N. R. N 6 32..F 23
Finsen-rd, Camberwell SE . 16 —..S 24
Finstock-rd, N. Kensin. W 10 42..L 14
Fir-walk, Cheam, Surrey . 29 —..Z⁸ 13
Fircroft-rd, Up. Tooting SW 21 —..W 19
Firs-av, Muswell Hill N . 2 —..B 20

4-in. 9-in. sht. sht. mar.

Firsby-rd, St. Newington N 7 33..E 27
First-avenue, Acton W . 10 —..M 11
„ „ Barnes SW . 15 —..S 10
„ „ Maida-hill W . 10 42..K 15
„ „ Manor-park E . 8 —..H 37
„ „ Plaistow E . . 13 —..K 34
„ „ Walthamstow E . 3 —..C 31
„ av-rd, Hendon NW . 1 —..B 14
„ cr-rd, Twickenham . 19 —..3 V
„ road, Woolwich . 18 —..P 37
First-street, Chelsea SW . 11 52..O 18
Fish-mkt, W. Smith'ld EC 11 46..L 24
„ st-hi, Eastcheap EC . 11 46..M 25
Fisher-st, Canning Town E 13 —..L 34
„ „ Red Lion-sq, WC — 45..L 22
Fishers-lane, Chiswick W . 10 —..O 10
Fishmers.-hil, Lon.-brg. EC — 46..M 25
„ „ „ 11 46..M 25
Fitchetts-ct, Noble-st, EC . 46 —..L 24
Fitzallan-rd, Finchley N . 1 —..B 15
Fitzalan-st, Kenntn-rd, SE 11 53..O 23
Fitzgerald-rd, Th. Ditton . 24 —..Z³ 4
Fitzgeorge-av, W. Kens. W 10 58..O 14
Fitzjames-av, W. Kens. W 10 58..O 14
Fitzjohns-av, Hampst. NW 5 35..H 17
Fitzroy-park, Highgate N . 6 31..E 17
Fitzroy-place, Fitzroy-sq W 11 44..K 20
„ rd, Regent's-pk NW 6 36..I 19
„ square W . . 11 44..K 20
„ street, Fitzroy-sq W 11 44..K 20
Fitzwarren-gds, Highgate N 6 —..E 21
Fitzwilliam-avenue, Kew . 14 —..R 7
„ rd, Claphm SW 16 61..S 20
Fladbury-rd, Tottenh'm N 7 33..D 25
Fladgate-rd, Leytonstone E 7 —..D 33
Flamborough-st, Com.-rd E 12 48..M 29
Flanchford-rd, Shep. B. W 10 —..O 11
Flanders-rd, Tnham.-gr. W 10 —..O 11
Flask-walk, Hampst. NW . 5 35..G 17
Flavell-rd, Wandswth. SW 15 60..T 17
Flaxman-road, Camber. SE 16 62..S 24
Flaxton-road, Plumstead . 18 —..Q 40
Fleece-rd, L. Ditton, Sur. 24 —..Z⁴ 5
„ „ Surbiton . . 24 —..Z⁴ 5
Fleet-lane, Old Bailey EC . 11 46..L 24
„ road, Hampstead NW 5 36..G 18
„ street EC . . 11 45..M 23
Fleetwood-rd, Will. Gr. NW 5 34..G 12
Fleming-rd, Walthmstw. E 3 —..B 30
„ „ Walworth SE . 16 54..Q 24
„ st, Kingsl'd-rd, N 12 46..J 26
Fletcher-road, Acton W . 9 —..N 10
Fletching-road, Clapton E. 7 39..G 28
Fletton-rd, Bowes-park N 2 —..A 22
Fleur-de-Lis-ct, Fet.-la EC — 45..L 23
Fleuer-de-Lis-st, Spital. E . 12 46..L 26
Flint-street, Poplar E . 12 48..L 31
„ „ Walworth SE . 17 54..P 25
Flinton-st, Bermondsey SE. 17 54..P 25
Flockton-st, Bermond. SE. 12 55..O 27
Flodden-rd, Camberwell SE 16 62..R 24
Flood-street, Chelsea SW . 16 52..P 18
Flora-gdns, Hmsmth.W . 10 58..O 12
Floral-st, Covent-grdn WC 11 45..M 22
Florence-rd, B'ckh'm, Kent 27 —..Z² 29
„ „ Deptford SE . 4 63..R 30
„ „ Ealing W . 9 —..M 7
„ „ Edmonton N . 3 —..A 28
„ „ Finsbury-pk N 6 32..E 23
„ „ Leytonstone E 7 —..F 32
„ „ Norbiton . 19 —..Z 7
„ „ Plaistow E . 13 —..J 36
„ „ Purley, Surrey 30 —..Z¹ 24
„ „ Wmbldn. SW 20 —..Y 16
„ st, Plaistow E . 12 49..K 33
„ „ Islington N . 6 38..I 24
Florian-road, Putney SW . 15 59..S 14
Florida-st, Beth. Gr.-rd E . 12 47..K 27
Floss-street, Putney SW . 15 59..S 13
Flower-lane, Mill Hill NW . 1 —..A 12
„ & Dean-st, Sptlfds E 12 47..L 26
Floyd-road, Woolwich . 18 —..P 35
Fly-lane, Ewell, Surrey . 28a —..Z⁹ 8
Foley-place, Clapham SW . 16 61..S 20
„ rd, Claygate, Surrey 28a —..Z⁷ 3
„ st, Gt.Titchfield-st W 11 44..L 20
Folkestone-gds, Deptfrd. SE 17 56..Q 29
„ rd, East Ham E 13 —..K 38
„ „ Edmonton N 3 —..A 27
„ „ Waltham. E 3 —..C 31
„ „ W. Ham E 12 41..J 33
Follett-street, Bromley E . 12 49..M 31
Folly-lane, Chingford E . 3 —..A 30
Fontaine-rd, L. Streat. SW 21 —..Z¹ 22
Fontarabia-rd, Lav. Hl. SW 16 60..T 19
Fontenoy-rd, Balham SW . 21 —..W 20
Fonthill-rd, Finsbury-pk N 6 32..E 23
Foots Cray, Kent . . 23 —..Z 42
„ „ lane, Kent . 23 —..W 42
„ „ rd, N Elt. Kent 23 —..W 38
Forburg-rd, S. Newington N 7 33..E 27
„ rd, Roman-rd, Bow E 12 48..J 29
„ st, Canning Town E . 12 49..M 33
„ „ Bow E . . 12 40..J 29
„ „ Roman-road E . 12 40..J 29
Fordcroft, Orpington . 28 —..Z⁴ 41
Ford-croft, S. Mary C. Kent 28 —..Z⁴ 41
Fordel-road, Lewisham SE 22 —..V 32
Fordham-st, Whitechapel E 12 47..L 27
Fordingley-rd, St.Ptr's Pk.W10 42..K 16
Fordington-rd, Mus. Hill N 2 —..C 19
Ford's Park-rd, Plaistow E 13 —..L 34
Fords-place, Battersea SW 16 51..Q 18
Fordwych-rd, Crickle. NW 5 —..H 15
Fordyce-rd, Lewisham SE 4 —..U 31
Fore-street, Cripplegate EC 11 46..L 24
„ „ Edmonton N . 3 —..A 27
„ „ avenue, Fore-st EC — 46..L 25
Foreign Cattle Market, Deptford SE . 17 56..Q 30
„ **Off., Downg-st** SW 11 53..N 21
„ **st, Camberwell** SE . 16 62..S 24

	4-in. sht.	9-in. sht.	mar.
Gladstone-st, Lambeth SE	11	54..O	23
,, ter, Battersea SW	16	61..R	20
Gladwell-road, Hornsey N.	6	32..D	22
,, ,, New Bromley	23	—..Z	34
Gladwyn-road, Putney SW	5	59..G	13
Gladys-road, Kilburn NW .	5	35..H	16
,, ,, Low Leyton E .	7	—..R	30
Glamis-road, Shadwell E .	12	47..M	28
Glamorgan-rd, H'pt'n Wick	19	—..Z	6
,, st, Pimlico SW	16	52..P	20
Glaserton-rd, Stamfd. Hi. N	7	33..E	26
Glazbury-rd, W. Kens. W .	—	58..P	14
Glasford-st, L. Tooting SW	20	—..T	18
Glasgow-rd, Edmonton N .	3	—..A	27
,, ,, Plaistow E .	13	—..J	35
Glaskin-road, Hackney E .	7	39..I	28
Glasshouse-st, Regent-st W	11	44..M	21
,, ,, Vxhall-wk SE	16	53..P	22
,, ,, U. E. Smthfld	12	47..M	26
,, flds-st, Shadwl E	12	47..M	28
Glass-house-yard, Aldersgate-street EC . .	46	—..L	24
Glasslyn-road, Crouch E. N	2	—..C	21
Glaucus-street, Bow E .	12	48..L	31
Glebe, The, Camberwll SE	17	62..S	25
,, ,, Lee SE . .	17	64..S	33
,, Mitcham, Surrey .	25	—..Z^2	18
,, path, Mitcham .	25	—..Z^2	18
,, place, Chelsea SW .	16	51..P	18
,, rd, Barnes SW .	15	—..R	12
,, ,, Hornsey N .	2	—..C	22
,, ,, Sutton, Surrey .	25	—..Z^6	16
,, street, Chiswick W.	15	—..P	10
Glebelands, Mitcham, Sur.	25	—..Z^2	17
Gledhow-gdns, Kensng. SW	—	51..P	18
,, terr, S. Kens. SW	15	51..P	17
Gledstanes-rd, W. Kens. SW	15	58..P	14
Glen-avenue, Muswell Hill N	2	—..C	21
,, road, Plaistow E .	13	—..K	35
Glenarn-road, Clapton E .	7	39..G	28
Glenavon-rd, Stratford E .	7	41..I	33
Glenbuck-rd, Surbiton, Sur	24	—..Z^3	6
Glenburnie-rd, U. Toot. SW	20	—..W	18
Glencairn-road, Streatham	21	—..Z^1	21
Glencoe-av, Ilford, Essex .	8	—..E	40
,, street, Bromley E	12	49..L	32
Glendale-av, Wood Gr. N .	2	—..A	23
Glendarvon-st, Putney SW	15	59..S	14
Glendish-rd, Tottenham N	3	—..A	27
Glendower-pl, S. Kens. SW	15	51..O	17
,, rd, E. Sheen SW	14	—..S	10
Gleneagle-road, Streatham	21	—..Y	21
Gleneldon-rd, Streatham .	21	—..X	22
Glenelg-road, Brixton SW .	16	—..T	22
Glenesk-road, Eltham .	18	—..U	38
Glenfarg-road, Catford SE .	22	—..V	32
Glenfield-road, Ealing W .	9	—..N	5
,, ,, Balham .	21	—..V	21
,, ,, Walthstw E	3	—..C	30
,, ter, Ealng Dean W	9	—..M	5
Glenforth-st, E. Grnwch SE	17	57..P	33
Glengall-road, Kilburn NW	5	—..I	15
,, ,, Millwall E .	12	56..O	31
,, ,, O. Kent-rd SE	17	55..Q	26
Glengarry-rd, E. Dulwch SE	17	—..T	26
Glenhouse-road, Eltham .	18	—..U	37
Glenhurst-rd, Brntfd, Mdx	14	—..P	6
Glenilla-rd, Hampstead NW	5	35..H	18
Glenister-rd, E. Gnwch SE	—	57..P	33
,, st, N. Woolwch E	13	—..N	38
Glenlea-road, Eltham .	18	—..U	37
Glenloch-rd, Hampsted NW	5	36..H	18
Glenluce-rd, Blackheath SE	18	—..Q	34
Glenmore-rd, Hampst. NW	5	36..H	18
Glennie-road, W. Norwood	21	—..X	23
Glenny-rd, Barking, Essex	8	—..I	39
Glenparke-rd, Forest Gt. E	8	—..H	35
Glenrosa-street, Fulham SW	15	59..R	16
Glenroy-st, Hammersmith W	10	42..L	13
Glensdale-rd, Brockley SE	4	63..T	30
Glenshiel-road, Eltham .	18	—..U	38
Glenside-road, Plumstead .	18	—..P	40
Glentham-rd, Castlenau SW	15	58..P	12
Glenthorn-rd, Norbitn, Sur	24	—..Z^2	7
Glenthorne-rd, Hmsmth. W	10	58..O	13
,, ,, N. Sthgte N	2	—..A	19
,, ,, Wlthmtw. E	3	—..C	29
Glenton-road, Lee SE .	17	64..I	32
Glentrammon-rd, Farnbrgh	30*b*	—..Z^9	40
Glentworth-st, Dorset-sq W	11	44..K	19
Glenure-road, Eltham .	18	—..U	38
Glenview-rd, Lewisham SE	17	—..U	32
Glenwood-road, Catford SE	22	—..V	30
,, ,, Tottenham N	2	—..C	24
Gliddon-rd, W. Kens. SW .	15	58..P	14
Globe-alley, Limehouse E	12	48..M	29
,, cr, Leytonstone E .	7	41..H	33
,, pond, Rotherhthe SE	12	56..N	29
,, rd, Mile End E .	12	47..K	28
,, ,, Sta. Ry. Mile E E	12	47..K	28
,, st, Gt. Dover-st SE .	—	54..O	25
Glossop-rd, Croydon, Surr.	30	—..Z^9	24
Gloucester-cr, Rgts Pk. NW	6	36..I	20
,, gds, Padding. W	10	43..L	17
,, gt, Reg. Pk. NW	11	36..J	20
,, gr, Brmpton SW	11	51..O	17
,, pl, Prtmn.-sqW.	11	44..L	19
,, ,, Greenw'ch SE	17	—..Q	32
,, rd, Acton W .	9	—..N	10
,, ,, Camber. SE	17	54..Q	25
,, ,, N. Hmptn .	19	—..Y	1
,, ,, Reg. Pk NW	6	36..I	20
,, ,, Croydon, Sur.	26	—..Z^4	25
,, ,, Ealing W .	9	—..N	6
,, ,, Edmont'n N	3	—..A	26
,, ,, Finsb'y-pk N	6	32..E	24
,, ,, Higham-hil E	3	—..A	29
,, ,, Holloway W	6	37..F	22
,, ,, Homert'n E	7	40..H	29
,, ,, Kew . .	14	—..Q	8
,, ,, Kingston .	19	—..Z^1	8
,, ,, Camber. SW	16	54..Q	25

	4-in. sht.	9-in. sht.	mar.
Gloucester-rd, Norbiton .	19	—..Z	8
,, ,, Reg. pk. NW	6	36..J	19
,, ,, Reg. pk. NW	6	36..J	19
,, ,, S. Kens. SW	10	51..O	17
,, ,, Teddington	19	—..X	3
,, ,, Tottenh'm N	3	—..B	25
,, ,, ry. sta., Dist. Ry	10	51..O	16
,, ,, ry. sta., Dist. Ry	10	51..O	17
,, sq, Hyde pk W	11	43..M	18
,, st, Clerken. EC .	11	45..K	23
,, ,, Myd't'n-st EC	11	45..K	23
,, ,, Pimlico SW .	16	52..P	20
,, ,, P'rtm'n-sq W	11	44..L	19
,, ,, Theo.-rd WC	11	45..L	22
,, ter, Hyde-pk W	10	43..L	17
,, ,, B'yswtr W	10	43..L	16
,, ,, Reg.-pk NW	11	36..J	20
,, ,, S. Kens. SW	—	51..P	17
,, walk, Kens. W .	10	51..N	16
Glove-street, Plaistow E .	13	—..L	34
Glover-st, Shoreditch EC .	—	46..K	25
Glycena-rd, Battersea SW .	16	60..S	19
Glyn-road, Clapton E .	7	40..G	29
Glynde-road, Upton .	18	—..T	43
,, st, Brockley SE .	4	—..U	30
Glyndow-rd, Plumstead .	18	—..P	39
Glynfield-rd, Harlesden NW	5	—..J	11
Goat-rd, Mitcham, Surrey	26	—..Z^4	19
Goda-street, Lambeth SE .	16	53..P	23
Goddington, Orping., Kent	28	—..Z^6	42
Godfery-hill, Woolwich .	18	—..P	37
Godfrey-st, Chelsea SW .	16	52..P	18
,, ,, West Ham E .	12	41..J	32
Goding-st, Vauxhall SE .	16	53..P	22
Godliman-st, Q. Vict.-st EC	—	46..M	24
Godman-rd, Peckham SE .	17	62..S	27
Godolphin-rd, Shep. B. W .	10	50..N	12
Godson-rd, Croydon, Sur.	26	—..Z^6	23
Godstone-rd, Purley, Sur.	30	—..Z^{11}	23
Godwin-road, Bickley .	28	—..Z^2	35
,, rd, Forest Gate E .	8	—..G	35
Golborne-rd, N. Kens. W .	10	42..L	15
Gold-street, Stepney E .	12	47..L	28
Golden-lane, Barbican EC .	11	46..K	24
,, manor, Hanwell W	9	—..M	3
,, sq, Hampstead NW	—	35..F	17
,, ,, Regent-st W .	11	44..M	21
Golders-gdns, Golders-gr NW	5	—..D	15
,, green, Hendon NW	5	—..E	15
,, gr, Crematorium NW	5	—..D	16
,, ,, cres, Golder's green NW .	5	—..D	16
,, ,, rd, Hendon NW	5	—..D	14
,, ,, ry. sta, Hamp ry	5	—..E	16
Goldershaw-rd, Eal'ng D'nW	9	—..M	5
Golders-hill, Hampstead NW	5	—..E	16
Golding-ter, St. George's E	12	47..M	27
Godhawk-rd, Hmsmth. W .	10	—..O	11
Goldhawk-rd, Shep. B. W .	10	50—N	12
Goldhurst-gdns, Kilburn NW	5	35..J	16
,, ter, Kilburn NW	5	35..J	17
Goldington-cr, S. P'ncr's NW	11	37..J	21
,, st, P'nc's-rd NW	11	45..J	21
Goldney-rd, Harrow-rd W .	10	43..K	16
Goldsborough-rd, S. Lam. SW	16	61..R	21
Goldsmith-av, Acton W .	9	—..M	10
,, ,, Manor-pk E	—	—..H	37
Goldsmiths-hill, Foster-la. EC	11	46..L	24
,, road, Acton W .	9	—..M	10
,, ,, Leyton E	7	—..F	31
,, rd, Peckham SE	17	62..R	27
,, ,, N. S'thg'te N	2	—..A	19
,, ,, Waltham. E	3	—..B	29
,, row, Hackney E	12	39—J	27
,, st, Drury la WC	—	45..L	22
,, ,, Wood-st EC .	—	46..L	24
,, ,, Wood-st EC .	—	46..L	24
Goldwell-rd, Norbury, Sur.	26	—..Z^2	22
Golf-road, Ilford . .	8	—..G	40
Gondar-gdns, Hampst'd NW	5	—..G	15
Gonsalva-rd, S. Lamb'th SW	16	61..R	20
Gonville-rd, Croydon, Sur.	26	—..Z^3	22
Goodall-rd, Leytonstone E	7	41..G	32
Goode-st, Clerkenwell EC .	11	45..K	23
Goodenough-rd, Wimble. SW	20	—..Z	14
Goodge-st, Tott.-ct.-rd WC	11	45..L	21
,, ,, ry. sta, Hampstead Ry. WC	11	45..L	21
Goodinge-rd, Islington N .	6	37..H	22
,, ,, Holloway N	6	37..H	22
Goodman's Fields, E .	—	47..M	26
,, yd, Gdmns flds E	12	47..M	26
Goodmayes-av, Gdmys. Es	8	—..F	42
,, la, Gmdys. Es.	8	—..G	42
,, rd, Gdmys. Es.	8	—..F	42
,, ry-sta, G.E.R.	8	—..F	42
Goodmead-road, Orpington	28	—..Z^5	41
Goodrich-rd, E. Dulwich SE	17	—..U	26
Goodson-rd, Harlesden NW	5	—..H	11
Goodwin-rd, Shep. B. W .	10	50..N	12
,, st, Finsbury-pk N	6	32..F	23
Goodwins-ct, S Mrtn's-la WC	—	45..M	22
Goodwyns-rd, Musw'll-hl N	2	—..A	20
Goose Green, E. Dulwich SE	17	62..T	26
Gooseley-la, East Ham E .	13	—..K	38
Gopsall-street, Hoxton N .	11	38..J	25
Gordon-av, Stanm're, M'x	1*a*	—..A	5
,, ,, Twickenham .	14	—..T	5
,, gr, Camberwell SE	16	62..S	24
,, pl, Gordon-sq WC .	—	45..K	21
,, ,, Kensington W .	—	51..N	16
,, rd, Barking . .	13	—..J	40
,, ,, B'ckenh'm, Kent	27	—..Z^2	28
,, ,, Carshalton, Sur.	29	—..Z^8	18
,, ,, Castlebar Hill W	9	—..L	6
,, ,, Chiswick W .	14	—..P	9
,, ,, Ealing W . .	9	—..L	6
,, ,, Finchley N .	1	—..A	15
,, ,, Hornsey N .	2	—..C	23
,, ,, Hounslow .	14	—..S	2

	4-in. sht.	9-in. sht.	mar.
Gordon-rd, Ilford, Essex .	8	—..G	40
,, ,, Kew . .	14	—..R	8
,, ,, Kingston . .	19	—..Z	7
,, ,, Leyton E . .	7	41..G	32
,, ,, New Southg'te N	2	—..A	21
,, ,, Peckham SE .	17	62..S	27
,, ,, St. Newington N	7	38..G	26
,, ,, Surbiton .	24	—..Z^4	7
,, ,, Wealdstone, M'x	1*a*	—..B	4
,, sq, Bloomsbury WC	11	45..K	21
,, st, Gordon-sq WC .	11	45..K	21
,, , Islington N .	11	46..J	24
,, ,, Plaistow E .	13	—..K	34
Grodonbrock-st, Brockley SE	4	—..U	30
Gordondale-rd, Earlsfi'ld SW	20	—..W	16
Gordon Hse-rd, Kent. T. NW	6	36..G	20
Gore-rd, Raynes-park .	20	—..Z^1	13
,, ,, Raynes-park SW .	20	—..Z^1	13
Gore-rd, Victoria-park E .	12	39..J	28
,, st, S. Kensington SW	10	51—O	17
Goring-road, Wood Gr'n N	2	—..A	22
,, st. Hackney E .	7	39..J	27
,, ,, St. Mary Axe EC	—	46..L	26
Gorschill-st, Streatham .	21	—..T	20
Gorst-rd, Battersea SW .	16	—..U	18
Gorsuch-st, Shoreditch E .	12	47..J	26
Gosberton-road, Balham .	21	—..V	19
Gosbury-hill, Hook . .	24	—..Z^7	6
Gosfield-st, Langham-st, W	11	44..L	20
Gospel Oak-rd, Kent. T. NW	—	36..G	19
,, ,, rly sta. N.L.R.	6	36..G	19
Gosport-rd, Walthamst'w E	7	—..D	30
Gossett-st, Bethnal G. rd. E	12	47..K	27
Gosterwood-st, Deptford SE	17	56..Q	29
Goswell-road, EC . .	11	46..J	24
Gothic-rd, Twickenham .	19	—..V	2
Gough-square, Fleet-st, EC.	11	45..L	23
,, st, Calthorpe-st. WC	11	45..K	23
,, ,, Poplar E . .	12	48..M	30
,, ,, Woolwich . .	13	—..O	38
Goulston-st, Whitechapel E	11	47..L	26
Goulton-road, Clapton E .	7	39..G	28
Gouim-rd, Rotherhithe SE .	12	55..O	28
Gould-road, Twickenham .	19	—..V	3
Goulden-st, Battersea SW .	16	60..R	18
Goulston-street, Aldgate E	12	46..L	26
Goulton-road, Clapton E .	7	39..G	28
Gourock-road, Eltham .	18	—..U	37
Gowan-av, Fulham SW .	15	59..R	14
Gower-pl. Euston-rd. WC .	11	45..K	21
,, rd, Forest Gate E .	8	—..J	34
,, st, Bedford-sq. WC .	11	45..K	21
,, ,, rly. Station NW	11	45..K	21
Gowers-wlk, Com'cial-rd. E	12	47..M	27
Gowland-rd, Beckenham, K	27	—..Z^2	29
Gowlett-road, Peckham SE	17	62..T	26
Gowrie-rd, Lavender-hl. SW	16	60..S	19
Grace-rd, Croydon Surrey .	26	—..Z^4	24
,, ,, Stratford E. .	7	41..J	32
,, street, Bromley E .	12	48..K	31
Gracechurch-street, EC .	11	46..M	25
Gracedale-rd, Streatham SW	21	—..T	20
Graces-rd, Camberwell SE .	16	62..R	25
Graemesdyke-av, Mort. SW	14	—..S	9
Grafton-cr, Kentsh T'n NW	6	36..H	20
,, pl, Euston-sq. NW	—	45..K	21
,, road, Acton W .	9	—..M	10
,, rd, Croydon, Sur.	26	—..Z^5	23
,, ,, Harrow, Mdsx .	1*a*	—..C	3
,, ,, Holloway N .	6	37..F	22
,, ,, Kentish T'n NW	6	36..H	20
,, ,, N. Malden, Sur.	25	—..Z^2	10
,, ,, Plaistow E .	13	—..J	34
,, ,, Worc'r-pk. Sur.	25	—..Z^6	11
,, sq. Clapham SW .	16	61..S	21
,, st, Mile End E .	12	48..K	29
,, ,, N. Bond-st. W.	11	44..M	20
,, ,, Tothm C.-rd WC	11	45..K	21
,, ter, Hampstead NW	6	36..H	19
Graham-avenue, Ealing W	9	—..N	5
,, av. Uppr Mitcham	21	—..Z^2	19
,, gdns, Hanwell W .	9	—..L	4
,, road, Acton W .	9	—..N	10
,, ,, Dalston E .	7	39..H	27
,, ,, Merton SW	20	—..Z	15
,, ,, New Malden	25	—..Z^2	10
,, ,, Plaistow E .	13	—..K	34
,, ,, Up. Mitch'm	21	—..Z^2	19
,, ,, Wealdstone	1*a*	—..A	4
,, ,, WldstneMid	1*a*	—..A	4
,, ,, West Green N	2	—..W	13
,, street, City-rd. N .	11	46..J	24
,, ,, Pimlico SW .	16	52..P	19
Granard-road, Balham SW	16	—..U	18
Granby-st, Hamp'd-rd. NW	11	44..J	20
Grand-av, Muswell-hill N .	2	—..B	20
,, Depot-rd, Wool'ch .	18	—..P	38
,, Drive, Raynes-pk. SW	25	—..Z^2	13
,, Parade, Hampstd NW	5	35..H	17
,, Junction Canal W .	9	—..N	3
,, Junc. Cnl, Willsdn NW	10	—..K	12
,, Surrey Canal . .	17	55..P	27
,, View-rd, Farnbo'gh	30*b*	—..Z^8	40
Grandison-rd, Battersea SW	16	—..T	19
Grange, The, Wimbledon SW	20	—..Y	14
,, court, Carey-st. WC	—	45..M	23
,, hill, Uppr. Norw'd	21	—..Z^2	25
,, park, Ealing W .	9	—..M	7
,, rd, Barnes SW .	15	—..R	11
,, ,, Bermondsey SE	12	54..O	25
,, ,, Camden Twn NW	6	36..J	20
,, ,, Canonbury-N .	6	38..H	24
,, ,, Chiswick W .	14	—..P	9
,, ,, Clapham, SW .	16	61..S	20
,, ,, Ealing W. .	9	—..M	7
,, ,, Highgate N .	6	31..D	19
,, ,, Ilford, Essex .	8	—..G	39
,, ,, Kentish Twn NW	6	36..J	20
,, ,, Kingston .	19	—..Z^1	7
,, ,, Leyton E. .	7	—..E	31
,, ,, Plaistow E .	12	49..K	33
,, ,, Stoke New'gn N	7	33..E	25

	4-in. sht.	9-in. sht.	mar.
Grange-rd, Sutton, Surrey	29	—..Z^9	15
,, ,, Thornt'nH. Sur	26	—..Z^2	25
,, ,, Upper Norwood	21	—..Z^2	25
,, ,, W. Moulsey, Sur	24	—..Z^2	1
,, ,, Willesden G. NW	5	—..H	13
,, street, Hoxton N .	11	38..J	25
,, vale, Sutton, Sur. .	29	—..Z^8	16
,, walk, Bermond. SE	12	54..O	26
,, yard, Bermond. SE	12	54..O	26
Grangecourt-rd, St. New. N	6	33..E	25
Grangehill-road, Eltham .	18	—..T	37
Grange Park-rd, Leyton E.	7	—..F	31
,, ,, Thornton Heath Surrey	—	26..Z^2	24
Granger-rd, Wood Green N	2	—..A	24
Gransden-rd, Ilford, Essex	8	—..E	40
Grant-rd, Battersea SW .	16	60..S	18
,, ,, Croydon, Surrey	26	—..Z^5	26
,, ,, Wealdstone Mdx	1*a*	—..A	4
Grantbridge-st, Islington N	11	46..J	24
Grantham-pl, Park-lane W	—	52..N	20
,, rd, Chiswick W	15	—..Q	11
,, ,, Great Ilf'd E	8	—..G	38
,, ,, Stockwell SW	16	61..S	22
Grantully-rd, Maida-hill, W	10	43..K	16
Granville-av, Finchley N .	1	—..A	17
,, ,, Lr. Edmon. N.	3	—..A	28
,, gdns, Ealing W	9	—..M	8
,, pk, Lewisham SE	17	64..S	32
,, pl, Portman-sq. W	11	44..M	19
,, rd, Canning Tn E	13	—..L	34
,, ,, Childs-hill NW	5	—..F	15
,, ,, Finchley N .	1	—..A	17
,, ,, Golders G. NW	5	—..E	15
,, ,, Hornsey N .	6	32..D	23
,, ,, Ilford, Essex	8	—..F	39
,, ,, Kilburn NW .	10	43..J	16
,, ,, Lewisham SE	17	64..S	32
Granville-rd, Putney SW .	15	—..U	15
,, ,, Sidcup, Kent	23	—..X	41
,, ,, Waltham. E .	7	—..D	31
,, ,, Wandsth. SW	15	—..U	15
,, ,, Welling .	18	—..T	43
,, ,, Wood-gr, N .	2	—..A	24
,, sq, Pent'ville WC	11	45..K	23
Grasmere-rd, Alex.-park N.	2	—..A	20
,, ,, Bromley .	22	—..Q^1	33
,, ,, S. Nrwood SE	27	—..Z^4	27
Gravel-hill, Church-end N .	1	—..A	15
,, lane, Houndsditch E	46	—..L	26
,, ,, Southwark SE.	11	54..N	24
,, rd, Bromley, Kent	28	—..Z^6	36
,, ,, Hanwell W .	9	—..N	4
,, ,, Twickenham .	19	—..V	3
,, pit-lane, Eltham .	18	—..U	39
Graveney-rd, Tooting SW .	20	—..X	18
,, river, Tooting .	21	—..Y	19
Gray-st, Blackfriars-rd, SE	11	53..N	23
,, ,, Poplar E . .	12	49..M	32
,, ,, Marylebone W .	11	44..L	19
,, ,, Southwark SE .	11	54..N	23
Graylands-rd, Peckham SE	17	54..Q	26
Grayling-rd, S. Newing. N.	7	33..F	25
Grays-inn, Holborn WC .	11	45..L	23
,, ,, pla, Holborn EC	45	—..L	23
,, ,, road, WC . .	11	45..K	22
,, ,, sq, Grays-inn WC	11	45..L	23
Grayshot-rd, Lav.-hill SW	16	60..S	19
Graystoke-pl, Fetter-la, EC	45	—..L	23
Grazebrook-rd, St. New. N	7	33..F	25
Gt. Alie st, Whitechapel E	12	47..M	26
,, Arthur-st, Goldn.-la, EC	11	46..K	24
,, av, Malden, Surrey .	25	—..Z^5	11
,, Bath-st, Clerkenwell N	11	45—K	23
,, Bell-al, Morgate-st, EC	46	—..L	25
,, Bland-st, Southwrk. SE	12	54..O	25
,, Cambridge-st, Hackney road E . . .	12	39..J	26
,, Castle-st, Regent-st, W	11	44..L	20
,, Central ra.-sta, Bakerloo Railway . .	11	44..K	18
,, Central-st, Mylbn. NW	—	44..K	19
,, Chapel-street, Soho W	11	45..L	21
,, Charlotte-street, Blackfriars-road, SE . .	11	54..N	23
,, Chart-st, Hoxton N .	11	46..K	25
,, Chesterfield-st, Mylbn W	—	44..L	20
,, Church-la, Hammer. W	15	58..P	13
,, College-st, Cam. T. NW	6	37..I	21
,, ,, ,, Westmr. SW	11	53..O	22
,, Cross-av, Greenwich SE	17	64..R	32
,, Cumberland-p, Ox.-s, W	11	44..L	19
,, Dover-st, Southwrk SE	12	54..O	25
,, Earl-st, Seven Dls. WC.	11	45..M	22
,, Eastern-rd, Stratford E	7	41..I	32
,, Eastern Sta, Shordh. E	12	46..K	26
,, Easter-st, Shrdth. EC .	12	46..K	26
,, Elms-rd, Bromley, Kt.	28	—..Z^3	35
,, Garden-st, Whitech. E.	12	47..L	27
,, George-st, Westmr. SW	11	53..N	21
,, Guildford-st, Southwkbridge-road SE. .	11	46..N	24
,, Hermitage-st, Wapng E	12	55..N	27
,, James-st, Hoxton N .	11	46..J	25
,, ,, ,, Lisson-gr. NW	11	44..L	18
,, ,, ,, Theo.-rd, WC	11	45..K	22
,, Marlborough-street, W	11	44..M	21
,, Maze-pd, Bermond. SE	11	54..N	25
,, ,, yd, Southwrk SE	12	54..N	25
Gt. New-st, Fetter-lane EC	11	45..L	23
,, Newport-st, L.-acre WC	11	45..M	21
,, Northern Cemety, Oakleigh-park N . .	2	—A	20
,, Northern Potato Market, King's Cross N.	11	37..I	22
,, Ormond-st, Qn.-sq, WC	11	45..K	22
,, Pearl-st, Commer.-st, E	12	47..L	26
,, Percy-street, WC . .	11	45..J	23
,, Peter-st, Westmr. SW .	11	53..O	21
,, Portland-street, W .	11	44..L	20
,, Prescott-st, S. George E	12	47..M	26
,, Pulteney-st, Gold.-sq W	11	45..M	21

Hammersmith Pier. INDEX TO STREETS, &c. **Hendon-avenue.**

	4-in. sht.	9-in. sht.	mar.
Hammersmith Pier . .	15	58..P	12
,, road W .	10	58..O	14
,, ry-st, Dis.R.	10	58..O	13
,, ,, Met.R.	10	58..O	13
,, railwy sta, N.& S.W. Junc. Railwy.	10	—..O	11
Hammersmith-ter, W .	15	—..P	12
Hammond-st, Kent.Tn. NW	6	36..H	21
Hampden-rd, Beck'm, Knt	27	—..Z^2	29
,, ,, Hornsey N .	2	—..C	23
,, ,, Kingston .	19	—..Z^1	8
,, ,, N.Southg'e N	2	—..A	20
,, ,, Tottenhm. N	3	—..A	27
,, ,, Up. Hlwy. N	6	32..F	21
,, st, Somers T. NW	11	45..J	21
,, ,, Westb.-pk W	10	43..L	16
Hampshire-st, Kent.Tn. NW	6	37..H	21
Hampstead NW . .	5	35..G	17
,, Cemetery NW .	5	—..G	15
,, Heath NW .	5	31..F	17
,, la, Highgate N	6	31..E	18
,, sq, Hamps. NW	—	35..F	17
,, road, NW .	11	44..K	21
,, sta, Hampstd Tube Raily.	5	35..G	17
,, Way, Golders Green NW .	5	—..D	16
,, Gdn Sub'rb NW	1	—..C	16
,, Hth-sta, N.L.R.	5	36..G	18
,, hi-gds, Ham. NW	5	35..G	18
Hampton, Middlesex .	19	—..Z	1
,, bridge . .	24	—..Z^2	3
,, gds, Twicken'm	19	—..W	2
,, rd, Alex'dra-pk N	2	—..A	21
,, ,, Chingford E	3	—..A	30
,, ,, Croydn, Sur.	26	—..Z^4	24
,, ,, Forest Gte E	8	—..H	35
,, ,, Ilford, Essex	8	—..G	39
,, ,, Teddington .	19	—..X	3
,, ,, Twickenham	19	—..W	3
,, st, Walw'th-rd SE	16	54..P	24
,, Wick, Middlesex	19	—..Z	5
,, Court-Pal, Mid.	24	—..Z^2	4
,, ,, park, Mid.	24	—..Z^2	4
,, ,, rd, B'y-pk.	19	—..Z^1	5
,, ,, ,, Hamp.	19	—..Z^1	2
,, ,, raily-sta., L.&S.W.R.	24	—..Z^2	3
,, Wick station, L.&S.W.R. Hamp. Wick.	19	—..Z	6
Hamsell-street, Jewin-st, EC	—	46..L	24
Hanbury-rd, Acton W .	9	—..N	9
,, ,, Battersea SW	16	60..S	19
,, ,, Hornsey N .	2	—..C	23
,, ,, Tottenham N	3	—..A	27
,, st, Spitalfields E	12	47..L	26
Hancock-rd, Bromley E .	12	49..K	31
Hand-court, Holborn WC .	—	45..L	23
,, & Pen-ct, Lead.-st. EC	..	46..M	26
Handcroft-rd, Croydn, Sur.	26	—..Z^5	23
Handel-st, Brunsw'k-sq, WC	11	45..K	22
,, ,, Wandsw'th SW	15	59..T	16
Handen-road, Lee SE .	17	—..U	33
Handforth-rd, Brix.-rd, SW	16	53..Q	23
Handley-rd, Hackney E .	7	39..I	28
Handsworth-av, Hale E. E	3	—..A	32
,, rd, Tott'm N	3	—..B	25
Hanger-hill, Ealing W .	9	—..K	8
,, lane, Ealing W .	9	—..K	8
,, vale, Ealing W .	9	—..L	8
,, hill Crest Park, Castlebar-hill W .	9	—..K	7
Hanging Wood-la, Charltn	18	—..P	36
,, sword-alley, Whitefrairs-st. EC .	—	45..M	23
Hanley-rd, Finsbury Pk. N	6	32..E	22
Hanlon-street, Deptford SE	17	56..P	29
Hannell-road, Fulham SW	15	58..Q	14
Hannibal-rd, Step. gr-rd. E	12	47..L	28
Hanning-street, Stepney E	12	48..L	29
Hanover-bdgs, Tooley-st SE	12	54..N	26
,, crt, Long acre WC	—	45..M	22
,, park, Peckham SE	17	62..R	27
,, rd, Spring gr. Mx.	14	—..Q	3
,, ,, Tottenham N	3	—..C	26
,, ,, Willesden NW	5	—..I	13
,, ,, Woolwich .	18	—..Q	38
,, square, W . .	11	44..M	20
,, st, Hanover-sq W	11	44..M	20
,, ,, Islington N .	11	46..J	24
,, ,, Kentish T. NW	6	36..G	19
,, ,, Peckham SE .	17	62..R	26
,, ter, Notting Hl. W	10	50..M	15
,, ,, Reg. Park NW	11	44..K	18
Hans-cres, Sloane-st SW .	11	52..O	19
,, place, Sloane-st SW .	11	52..O	19
,, rd, Brompton-rd SW	11	52..O	18
,, street, Sloane-st SW .	—	52..O	19
Hansol-road, Upton . .	18	—..U	43
Hanster-gro, W. Moulsey, Surrey . .	24	—..Z^2	2
,, rd, E. Dulwich SE	17	—..T	26
Hanway-pla, Oxford-st W	45	—..L	21
,, st, Oxford-st W .	11	45..L	21
Hanwell, Middlesex W .	9	—..M	4
,, bridge, Hanwell W	9	—..M	3
,, park, Hanwell W .	9	—..L	4
,, sta, G.W. Railway, Hanwell W .	9	—..M	4
Hanworth-road, Hounslow	14	—..T	1
,, ,, N. Hampton	19	—..X	1
Harberson-rd, West Ham E	12	41..J	34
Harberton-rd, Up. Holl. N	6	32—E	21
Harborough-rd, Streatham	21	—..X	22
Harbut-rd, Battersea SW .	15	60..T	17
Harcombe-rd, S. Newing. N	7	38..F	26
Harcourt-av, Manor Pk E .	8	—..H	37
,, rd, Alexr. Park N	2	—..A	21
,, ,, Brockley SE .	4	63..T	29
,, ,, Carshal. Sur.	30	—..Z^7	20
,, ,, West Ham E	12	41..J	33
,, st, Mrylb.-rd. W .	11	44..L	18
Harcourt ter, W. Bmptn SW	15	51..P	16
Hardcastle-st, Peckham SE	17	62..R	27
Hardens Manor-way, Wool.	13	—..O	36
Harder-road, Peckham SE	17	62..R	27
Hardinge-street, Com.-rd E	12	47..M	28
Hardings-lane, Penge SE .	22	—..Z^1	28
Hardington-st, Edgw.-rd W	11	43..K	18
Hardman-road, Woolwich	18	—..P	34
Hardwick-street, Barking	13	—..J	39
,, ,, Clrkenwl. EC	—	45..K	23
Hardwicke-rd, N. Sthgte N	2	—..A	22
Hardy-rd, Blackheath SE .	17	57..Q	33
,, ,, Merton SW .	20	—..Z	16
Hare-court, The Temple EC	—	45..M	23
,, st, Bethnal Green E .	12	47..K	26
,, ,, Woolwich . .	13	—..O	38
Haredale-rd, Herne Hill SE	16	62..T	24
Harefield-road, Brockley SE	4	63..S	30
,, ,, Hornsey N .	2	—..C	21
,, ,, Tottenham N	7	33..D	25
Harclane, Surrey . .	28*a*	—..Z^7	2
,, gr, Harclane, Sur.	28*a*	—..Z^7	2
Harewood-av, Mybne-rd NW	11	44..K	18
,, pl, Hanover-sq W	—	44..L	20
,, rd, Croydon, Sur.	30	—..Z^8	25
,, ,, Tooting SW .	18	20..Z	18
Harford-street, Stepney E	12	—..L	29
Hargor-rd, Plumstead SE .	18	—..Q	39
Hargrave-pk, Up. Hlwy. N	6	32..F	21
,, rd, Up. Hlwy. N.	6	23..F	21
Hargwyne-st, Stockwell SW	16	61..S	22
Harringay-park, Hornsey N	6	—..D	22
Harlech-rd, Palmers Grn N	2	—..A	22
Harelscott-rd, Peckham SE	17	63..T	28
Harlesden-gdns, Willes. NW	5	—..I	11
,, gr, Harlesden NW	10	—..J	12
,, rd, Willesden NW	5	34..I	12
,, ,, Willesden NW	5	34..H	12
Harley-gdns, W. Brptn SW	15	57..P	17
,, road, Willesden NW	10	—..J	11
,, ,, Leytonstone E	7	—..E	34
,, ,, S. Jns. Wd. NW	5	35..I	18
,, st, Bow E . .	12	48..K	30
,, ,, Cavendish-sq W	11	44..K	20
Harleyford-st, Kensing. SE	16	53..Q	23
,, rd, Vauxhall SE	16	53..P	22
Harlington-rd, Totten. N .	3	—..A	27
,, ,, Walthstw E	7	—..D	29
Harman-st, Kingsland-rd N	12	46..J	26
Harmood-st, Chalk Farm-road NW . .	6	36..I	20
Harmsworth-st, Kens. SE .	16	53..P	23
Harold-rd, Hornsey N .	2	—..C	22
,, ,, Leytonstone E	7	—..F	33
,, ,, Plaistow E .	13	—..J	35
,, ,, Sutton, Surrey	29	—..Z^7	17
,, ,, Tottenham N .	3	—..C	26
,, ,, Norwood .	21	—..Z^1	25
Harlodstone-rd, Walthstw E	3	—..C	29
Haroman-road, Kingston .	19	—..Z^1	7
Harp-alley, Farring.-st EC	46	—..L	23
,, crt, Milton-street EC	46	—..L	25
,, la, L. Thames-st EC .	11	46..M	25
Harpenden-rd, Tulse Hill .	21	—..W	23
,, ,, Wanstead E	8	—..F	35
Harper-st, New Kent-rd SE	11	54..O	24
Harpour-rd, Barking, Esx.	8	—..I	39
Harpur-st, Theoblds-rd WC	11	45..L	22
Harringay-gro, Hornsey N	2	—..B	23
,, park, Hornsey N	6	32..D	22
,, rd, Hornsey N .	2	—..C	22
,, ,, Tottenham N	2	—..C	24
,, sta, G.N.Ry. N	6	32..D	23
,, Pk sta, T. & H. Ry, Finsbury Park N .	6	32..D	24
Harrington-gns, S Kens. SW	15	51..P	16
,, rd, Leytnstn. E	7	—..E	33
,, ,, S Kens. SW	10	51..O	17
,, ,, S. Norwd SE	27	—..Z^3	27
,, sq, Hpstd-rd NW	—	36..J	21
Harris-rise, Croydon Surrey	26	—..Z^6	23
,, st, Camberwell SE .	17	54..Q	25
,, ,, Walthamstow E	7	—..E	30
Harrison-st, Grays Inn-rd WC	11	45..K	22
Harrow, Middlesex . .	4	—..E	4
,, green, Leytnstne E	7	41..G	33
,, place, Midsx-st. E.	—	46..L	26
,, road, Paddington W	10	43..L	17
,, road, Battersea SW	15	60..R	17
,, ,, East Ham E	13	—..J	37
,, ,, Harlesd'n NW	10	42..J	12
,, ,, Kensal G. W	10	42..K	14
,, ,, Leytonstone E	7	41..F	33
,, ,, New Malden	24	—..Z^2	9
,, ,, Sudbury, Mdx	4	—..G	6
,, ,, Wembley .	4	—..H	9
,, sta., L.& N.W.R.	1*a*	—..B	4
,, st, Lisson Gr. NW.	11	43..L	18
,, View, Wealdstn Mx	1*a*	—..B	3
,, Manor Way, Plumd	13	—..O	43
,, on-the-Hill Sta. Met. Railway .	1*a*	—..D	4
,, View-rd, Castlebar Hill W . .	9	—..K	6
,, Weald-pk, Harrow Weald, Middlesex	1*a*	—..A	3
Harrowdene-rd, Wembley Middlesex .	4	—..F	6
Harrowgate-rd, S. Hack. E	7	40..I	29
Hart-grove, Acton W. .	9	—..M	8
,, street, Bloomsbry WC	11	45..K	22
,, ,, Mark-lane EC	12	46..M	26
,, ,, Wood-street EC	—	46..L	24
Hartfield-cres, Wmbledn SW	20	—..Z	15
,, road, Wmbledn SW	20	—..Z	15
Hartham-rd, Holloway N .	6	37..G	22
,, rd, Spring-grove	14	—..Q	4
,, ,, Tottenm N	3	—..A	26
Hartland-road, Isleworth .	14	—..R	5
,, ,, NW . .	6	36..I	20
,, ,, Kilburn NW	10	34..J	15
Hartland-road, Stratford E	7	41..I	33
Hartley-avenue, E. Ham E	13	—..J	37
,, rd, Croydon, Sur. .	26	—..Z^4	24
,, st, Bethnal Green E	12	47..J	28
Hartington-rd, Cann.Twn. E	13	—..M	35
,, ,, Chiswick W	14	—..Q	9
,, ,, Ealing Dn. W	9	—..M	5
,, ,, S.Lmbth SW	16	61..R	21
,, ,, Twickenham	14	—..U	5
Hartismere-rd, Fulham SW	15	58..Q	15
Hartnoll-st, Holloway N .	—	37..G	23
Harton-street, Deptford SE	4	63..R	30
Harts-lane, New Cross SE .	17	63..R	29
Hartshorn-al, Ldnhll-st, EC	—	46..M	26
Hartswood-rd, Shep.Bsh. W	10	—..N	11
Hartville-road, Plumstead	18	—..P	40
Harvard-rd, Spring-grove .	14	—..R	3
,, ,, Chiswick W .	14	—..P	9
,, ,, Lewisham SE	17	—..U	32
Harvey-road, Hornsey N .	2	—..C	23
,, ,, Ilford, Essex	8	—..H	39
,, ,, L'yst'nst'ne E	7	—..E	33
,, ,, Peckham SE.	16	62..R	25
Harvist-road, Holloway N .	6	37..G	23
,, ,, Queens-pk, NW	10	42..J	14
Harwood-road, Fulham SW	15	51..Q	16
,, ter, Fulham SW .	15	59..R	16
Haselbury-rd, Edmonton N	3	—..A	26
Haselrigge-rd, Claphm SW.	16	61..T	21
Haseltine-rd, L.Syden. SE .	22	—..X	29
Haselmere-road, Hornsey N	6	32..D	22
Hasker-street, Chelsea SW .	11	52..O	18
Hasledene-road, Chiswick W	14	—..P	9
Haslemere-aven, Ealing W	9	—..N	5
,, rd, Croyd. Sur.	26	—..Z^3	23
,, ,, Seven Kings, Essex . .	8	—..F	41
Haslitt-rd, W. Kensing. W	10	50..O	14
Hassard-st, Hackney-rd, E	12	47..J	26
Hassendean-rd, Blackth SE	18	—..Q	34
Hassett-road, Homerton E	7	40..H	29
Hassop-rd, Cricklewood NW	5	—..G	14
Hastings-road, Croyd. Sur.	26	—..Z^5	25
,, ,, Ealing W .	9	—..M	5
,, ,, West Ham E	12	41..J	33
,, st, C'rtwr't-gds, WC	11	45..K	22
Hatch End, Pinner Midsx.	1*a*	—..A	2
,, lane, Ilford, Es. .	8	—..D	40
,, road, Norbury .	21	—..Z^2	21
Hatcham, SE . . .	17	63..R	28
,, rd, O. Kent.rd, SE	17	53..Q	28
,, park-road, SE .	4	63..R	29
Hatchard-rd, Upp. Hlwy. N	6	32..F	22
Hatfield-road, Acton W .	10	—..N	10
,, st, Goswell-rd, EC	—	46..K	24
,, ,, Finsbury EC .	11	46..K	24
,, ,, Southwark SE .	11	45..N	23
Hathaway-rd, Croyd. Sur.	26	—..Z^5	23
Hatherley-rd, Sidcup, Kent	23	—..X	41
,, ,, Walthmstw E	3	—..C	30
,, ,, Wood Grn N	2	—..A	24
Hatherstone-road, Kew .	14	—..R	8
Hatley-road, Finsbury-pk. N	6	32..F	23
Hatton-gdn, Holborn EC .	11	45..L	23
,, Wall, Leather-la. EC	11	46..L	23
,, yd, Hatton-gdn EC	—	45..L	23
Havanah-rd, Earlsfield SW.	20	—..W	16
Havannah-street, Milwall E	12	56..O	30
Havant-road, Wlthmstw. E	3	—..B	32
Havelock-road, Hackney E	7	39..I	28
Haven-green, Ealing W .	9	—..L	7
,, lane, Ealing W .	9	—..L	7
Havelock-rd, Bromley, Knt	28	—..Z^3	35
,, ,, Croydon, Sur.	26	—..Z^6	26
,, ,, Hackney E .	7	39..I	28
,, ,, Tottenham N	3	—..A	27
,, ,, Weald. Mdsx.	1*a*	—..A	4
,, ,, W. Kens. W .	10	50..O	14
,, ,, Wimbled'n SW	20	—..Y	16
,, street, Islington N	6	37..I	22
,, ter, Battersea SW	16	61..R	20
Haverford-green, Kew .	14	—..Q	8
Haverhill-rd, Balham SW .	21	—..Y	20
Havering-st, Com'cial-rd E	12	47..M	28
Haverstock-hl, Hamp. NW.	5	35..G	18
,, rd, Kent.Twn NW	6	36..G	19
,, st, City-rd, N .	11	46..J	24
,, hl. sta. Mid. R.	6	36..G	19
Havil-st, Camberwell SE .	16	62..R	25
Hawarden-green, Dulwich	21	..—V	24
,, rd, Wlthstw. E	3	—..C	29
Hawes-la, West Wickham	27	—..Z^6	32
Hawgood-street, Brom. E .	12	48..L	31
Hawke-road, Norwood .	21	—..Y	25
Hawkeslade-rd, Nunh'd SE	17	—..U	28
Hawkesley-rd, Waltham. E	3	—..C	29
Hawkins-street, Mile End E	12	47..L	28
Hawks-road, Kingston .	19	—..Z^1	7
Hawksley-rd, St. Newgtn. N	7	38..F	25
Hawkstone-rd, Rother. SE	17	55..P	28
Hawkwood-la, Chislehurst	23	—..Z^1	39
Hawley-cr, Kent. Twn. NW	6	36..I	20
,, rd, Kent. Twn. NW	6	36..I	20
,, st, Kent. Twn. NW	6	36..I	20
Hawthorn-rd, Hornsey N	2	—..B	22
,, ,, Sutton Sur.	29	—..Z^6	17
,, ,, U.Edmonton N	3	—..A	26
,, ,, Willesden NW	5	34..H	12
Hawthorne-gr, Anerley SE	22	—..Z^2	27
,, rd, Bickley K.	28	—..Z^2	36
,, ,, C'rsh'ltn Sur	30	—..Z^9	19
Hay-hl, Berkeley-square W	11	44..M	20
,, lane, Kingsbury NW .	1	—..B	10
Haycroft-rd, Brixton SW .	16	—..U	22
Hayday-road, Plaistow E .	13	—..L	34
Haydock-road, Deptford SE	17	55..P	28
Haydon-rd, Wimbledon SW	20	—..Y	16
,, square Minories E	11	47..M	26
,, street, Minories E.	12	47..M	26
,, street, Highgate N	6	—..F	20
Haydons-rd, Wimbledn SW	20	—..Y	16
,, pk.-rd, Wimble. SW	20	—..Y	16
Haydons-rd. sta. Wimble. SW . .	20	—..Y	16
Hayes, Kent . . .	18	—..Z^5	34
,, Common, Kent .	30*a*	—..Z^7	34
,, cr, Golders Green NW	1	—..C	15
,, grove, Hayes, Kent	28	—..Z^6	34
,, la, Bromley, Kent .	27	—..Z^3	32
,, ,, Bromley, Kent.	28	—..Z^3	34
,, ,, Tooley-street, SE	12	54..N	25
,, ry. sta., S.E. & C.R.	27	—..Z^5	33
,, Way, Bromley .	27	—..Z^3	31
Hayles-st, St.Georges-rd, SE	11	54..O	23
Haymarket, The, SW. .	11	45..M	21
Haymerle-rd, Peckham SE.	17	55..Q	26
Hayne-road, Beckenham .	22	—..Z^2	29
Haysleigh-gds, S.Norwd. SE	27	—..Z^2	27
Hayter-road, Brixton SW .	16	—..T	22
Haywood-road, Bickley .	28	—..Z^3	35
Hazel-rd, Kensal Green NW	10	42..J	13
Hazelbank-rd, Catford SE .	22	—..W	32
Hazlebourne-rd, Balham SW	16	—..U	20
Hazelbury-rd, Fulham SW	15	59..R	16
Hazeldean-rd, Willes. NW	5	—..I	10
Hazeldene-rd, Croydon, Sy	26	—..Z^6	25
,, ,, Goodmayes, Essex . .	8	—..F	42
Hazeldon-road, Brockley SE	4	—..U	29
Hazelhurst-road, Toot. SW	20	—..X	17
Hazelmere-rd, Kilburn NW	5	—..I	15
Hazelwell-road, Putney SW	15	—..T	13
Hazelwood-cr, Maida-hi. W	10	42..K	15
,, la, Palmers G. N	2	—..A	23
,, rd, Walthmstw E	3	—..C	29
Hazelville-rd, Hornsey-rise N	6	32..E	21
Hazelbury-rd, Fulham SW	15	59..R	16
Hazlit-rd, W. Kensington W	10	50..O	14
Headcorne-rd, Norb'y Sur.	26	—..Z^2	22
Heading-street, Hendon NW	1	—..B	13
Headstone-drive, Weald., Middlesex .	1*a*	—..B	3
,, la, Pinner Mdx.	1*a*	—..A	2
,, rd, Harrow Mdx	1*a*	—..C	3
Headworth-rd, Wands. SW	20	—..X	16
Healey-st, Kent. Twn NW	6	36..H	20
Hearn-street, Curtain-rd EC	12	46..K	26
Hearnville-road, Balham .	21	—..V	19
Heath-av, Golders Grn NW	5	—..E	16
,, drive, Hampstd NW	5	35..G	16
,, gdns, Twickenham .	19	—..V	4
,, pk, Willesdn.G. NW	5	—..H	13
,, rd, Harrow, Mdsx .	1*a*	—..D	3
,, ,, Hounslow .	14	—..S	2
,, ,, S. Lambeth SW .	16	61..S	20
,, ,, Thornton H. Sur	26	—..Z^2	24
,, ,, Twickenham .	19	—..V	4
,, street, Barking .	13	—..J	39
,, st, Com'cial-rd, E .	12	48..M	29
,, ,, Hampstead NW .	5	35..G	17
Heathcote-rd, Twickenham	14	—..T	5
,, st, Grays Inn-road, WC . .	11	45..K	22
Heathdene-rd, Crshltn, Sur.	30	—..Z^9	19
,, ,, L. Streat. SW	21	—..Z^1	22
Heather-road, Lee SE .	23	—..W	34
Heatherley-st, St. Newg E	7	39..G	27
Heatherside-rd, Ewell, Sur.	28*a*	—..Z^9	9
Heathfield-av, Wands. SW	15	—..U	17
,, gds, Chiswick W	14	—..P	9
,, N. Twickenham	14	—..U	4
,, pk, Willes.-Gr. NW	5	34..H	13
,, rd, Acton W .	9	—..N	9
,, ,, Bromley .	22	—..Q^1	33
,, ,, Croydon Sur.	30	—..Z^7	24
,, ,, Wans. SW .	15	—..U	17
,, S. Twick'ham	14	—..U	4
,, ter, Chiswick W	14	—..P	10
,, ,, gds, Chis. W	13	—..P	9
Heathgate, Hampstead NW	5	—..D	16
Heathland-rd, Stk. New. N.	7	33..E	25
Heathurst-rd, Croydon Sur.	30	—..Z^1	25
,, rd, Hamp. NW .	5	35..G	18
Heathville-rd, Fins.-pk. N .	6	32..E	22
Heathwall-st, Battersea SW	16	60..S	19
Heathwood-gds, Charlton .	18	—..P	36
Heaton-pl, Stratford-rd. E	7	41..H	32
Heaton-road, Lwr Tooting	21	—..Z^1	19
,, ,, Peckham SE .	17	62..S	27
Heaver-road, Battersea SW	16	60..S	18
Heavitree-road, Plumstead	18	—..Q	39
Heber-rd, Cricklewood NW	5	—..G	14
,, ,, E. Dulwich SE .	17	—..U	26
Heckfield-pl, Fulham SW .	15	58..Q	15
Heddon-street, Regent-st W	—	44..M	20
Hedge-la, Edmonton N .	3	—..A	25
,, ,, Palmers-green N	2	—..A	24
Hedgers-gr, S. Hackney E	7	40..H	29
Hedgley-street, Lee SE .	17	—..U	33
Heigham-road, E. Ham E .	8	—..I	36
Helena-rd, Ealing W . .	9	—..K	7
,, ,, Walthamst'w E	7	—..D	30
Helix-gdns, Brixton SW .	16	—..U	22
,, road, Brixton SW .	16	—..U	22
Helmet-ct, Wormw'd-st, EC	—	46..L	25
,, row, Old-street, EC	11	46..K	24
Helvetia-st, Forest-hill SE	22	—..W	29
Hemans-st, Nine Elms SE .	16	53..Q	21
Hemberton-rd, Claphm. SW	16	61..S	22
Heming-rd, Edgware, Mid.	1*a*	—..A	9
Hemingford-rd, Barns'y N	6	37..I	23
,, ,, Ch'm, Sur.	29	—..Z^7	13
Hemington-av, N.Sthgte N	2	—..A	19
Hemming-st, Bethnal-gr'n	12	47..K	27
Hempstead-rd, Wlthstw. E	3	—..B	32
Hemstal-rd, Kilburn NW .	5	35..H	16
Hemsworth-st, Cann. Tn. E	12	49..L	34
,, ,, Hoxton N .	11	38..J	25
Henderson-rd, Wandsw. SW	16	—..U	18
,, ,, Croy'n, Sur.	26	—..Z^4	24
,, ,, Forest Ga. E	8	—..H	35
Hendham-rd, U.Tooting SW	20	—..W	18
Hendon NW . . .	1	—..B	13
,, av, Church End N	1	—..A	15

	4-in. sht.	9-in. sht.	mar.
Hendon-lane, Finchley N .	1	—	B 15
,, pk-cemet, Hen. NW	1	—	A 14
,, sta, Mid. Rly, NW	5	—	D 12
Hendrick-av, Balham SW .	16	—	U 19
Heneage-la, Bevis Mrks EC	—	46	M 26
,, st, Spitalfield E .	12	47	L 23
Henfield-road, Merton SW	20	—	Z^{1} 15
Hengrave-rd, Forest-hil SE	22	—	V 28
Henley-rd, Edmonton N .	3	—	A 26
,, ,, Ilford, Essex .	8	—	H 39
,, ,, N. Woolwich E	13	—	O 37
,, ,, Willesden NW .	5	—	I 13
,, st, Battersea SW .	16	60	R 19
Henniker-rd, Stratford E .	7	41	H 32
Henning-st, Battersea SW .	16	60	R 18
Henrietta-st, Covent-gn WC	11	45	M 22
,, ,, Cavend.-sq. W	11	44	L 20
Henry-road, East Ham E .	13	—	J 37
,, ,, Tottenham N .	7	—	D 25
,, st, Battersea SW .	16	60	R 18
,, ,, Grays-inn-rd, WC	11	45	K 22
,, ,, Kenningtn-la, SE	16	53	P 22
,, ,, Old-street, EC .	—	46	K 25
,, ,, S. John's W. NW	11	35	J 18
,, ,, Woolwich . .	18	—	P 37
Henryson-st, Brockley SE .	4	—	U 30
Henshaw-st, Walworth SE	12	54	O 25
Henslowe-rd, E. Dulw'h SE	17	—	U 27
Henstridge-p, S.J'ns W. NW	11	35	J 18
Hepscott-rd, Hack. Wick. E	7	40	I 30
Hepworth-rd, Streatham	21	—	Z^{1} 21
Herbaceous-road, Purley .	30	—	Z^{11} 21
Herbert-cres, Chelsea SW .	—	52	O 19
,, gds, Kens. Rise NW	10	42	J 13
,, rd, Bickley . .	28	—	Z^{3} 36
,, ,, Bowes-park N	2	—	A 22
,, ,, East Ham E .	8	—	H 37
,, ,, Hendon NW .	5	—	D 12
,, ,, Ilford, Essex .	8	—	F 40
,, ,, Merton SW .	20	—	Z 15
,, ,, Plaistow E .	13	—	K 34
,, ,, Stockwell SW .	16	61	S 22
,, ,, Tottenham N .	3	—	C 26
,, ,, Walthamstw E	7	—	D 30
,, ,, Wimbledon SW	20	—	Z 15
,, ,, Woolwich .	18	—	Q 38
,, street, Hoxton N .	11	46	J 25
Herbrand-st, Bern'd-st, WC	11	45	K 22
Hercules-road, Holloway N	6	37	F 22
,, ,, Lambeth SE	11	53	O 23
Hereford-gds, Hyde-park W	11	44	M 19
,, rd, Acton W .	9	—	L 9
,, ,, Bayswater W	10	43	L 16
,, ,, Lit. Ealing W	9	—	O 6
,, sq, S. Kens'n SW	15	51	P 17
,, st, Bethnal-grn E	12	47	K 27
,, ,, Lisson-gr. NW	11	44	L 18
Hereward-rd, Tooting SW .	20	—	X 18
Herga-rd, Wealdst'ne, Mid.	1*a*	—	B 4
Heriot-road, Hendon NW .	1	—	C 14
Hermit-rd, Canning Twn E	12	49	K 33
Hermitage-la, Childs-hi. NW	5	—	F 16
,, ,, Croydn, Sur.	26	—	Z^{4} 26
,, rd, Finsby-pk N	6	33	D 24
,, ,, Norwood .	21	—	Z^{1} 24
Herndon-rd, Wandswth SW	15	—	T 16
Herne-hill SE . . .	16	62	T 24
,, place, Herne-hill SE	16	—	U 23
,, st, Canning Town E	12	49	M 33
,, hill-rd, Herne-hi. SE	16	62	S 24
,, ,, sta, S.E.& C.R. Herne-hill SE . .	16	—	U 24
Heron-rd, Herne-hill SE .	16	62	T 24
,, ,, Twickenham .	14	—	T 5
,, ,, Willesden NW .	5	—	H 11
Herondale-av, Wands. C. SW	20	—	V 18
Herongate-rd, Manor Pk E	8	—	F 36
Herrick-road, Highbury N	6	38	F 24
,, st, Westminster SW	16	53	P 21
Herries-st, Maida Hill W .	10	42	J 15
Herring-st, Camberwell SE	17	54	Q 26
Hertford-rd, E. Finchley N	2	—	B 18
,, ,, East Ham E .	8	—	I 38
,, ,, Ilford . .	8	—	D 40
,, ,, De Beauv. T N	7	38	I 26
,, street, Mayfair W	11	52	N 20
Hertslet-rd, Holloway N .	6	32	F 22
Hervey-rd, Blackheath SE	18	—	R 34
,, pk-rd, Walthmstw E	3	—	C 29
Hesketh-rd, Forest Gate E	8	—	G 34
Heslop-road, Balham .	21	—	V 19
Hessel-road, Ealing W .	9	—	N 5
,, st, Commer.-rd E .	12	47	M 27
Hestercombe-av, Ful. SW .	15	59	R 14
Heston-road, Osterley, Mdx	14	—	Q 1
,, Hounslow Station Rly., Hounslow .	14	—	R 1
Hetherington-rd, Clphm SW	16	61	T 21
Hethpool-st, Paddington W	10	43	K 17
Hetley-rd, Shepherd's B. W	10	50	N 12
Hewer-st, N. Kensington W	10	42—	K 14
Hewett-st, Curtain-rd EC .	—	46	K 26
Hewitt-av, Wood Green N	2	—	A 24
,, road, Hornsey N .	2	—	C 23
Hewlett-rd, Roman-road E	12	40	J 29
Heybridge-av, Streatham .	21	—	Z^{1} 22
Heygate-st, Walworth-rd SE	16	54	P 24
Heymer-st, Pentonville N .	11	45	J 23
Heysham-rd, Tottenham N	7	33	D 25
Heythorp-st, Southfields SW	20	—	V 15
Heyworth-road, Clapton E	7	39	G 27
,, rd, Stratford E	7	41	H 33
Hexham-rd, W. Dulwich SE	21	—	W 24
,, ,, W. Dulwich SW	21	—	W 24
Hibbert-rd, Walthmstw E	7	—	E 30
,, st, Battersea SW .	15	60	S 17
Hibernia-road, Hounslow .	14	—	S 1
Hichisson-rd, Peckham SE	17	—	T 28
Hickling-road, Ilford .	8	—	H 39
Hickmans Folly, Dckhd SE	12	54	N 26
Hide-place, Westmnstr SW	16	53	P 21
,, rd, Wealdstone, Mdx	1*a*	—	B 3
High Holborn WC . .	11	45	L 22
,, lane, Hanwell W .	9	—	L 3
,, path, Merton SW .	10	—	Z 16
,, rd, Bowes Park N .	2	—	A 23
,, ,, Chadwell Hth, Ex.	8	—	E 43
,, ,, E. Finchley N .	2	—	A 18
,, ,, Kilburn NW .	5	—	I 15
,, ,, Lee SE . .	17	64	T 33
,, ,, Leyton E . .	7	—	D 31
,, ,, Leyton E . .	7	—	F 32
,, ,, Leytonstone E .	7	41	F 33
,, ,, North Finchley N	2	—	A 17
,, ,, Streatham . .	21	—	X 21
,, ,, Tottenham N .	3	—	A 26
,, ,, Tottenham N .	3	—	C 26
,, ,, Willesden NW .	5	34	H 12
,, ,, Wood Green N .	2	—	A 23
,, st, Acton W . .	9	—	M 9
,, ,, Aldgate E . .	—	46	M 26
,, ,, Alperton, Mdx	4	—	I 7
,, ,, Barnes SW . .	15	—	R 11
,, ,, Battersea SW .	16	60	R 18
,, ,, Beckenham .	22	—	Z^{2} 30
,, ,, Bickley, Kent	28	—	Z^{2} 34
,, ,, Borough SE .	11	54	N 25
,, ,, Brentford, Mdx .	14	—	Q 6
,, ,, Bromley E . .	12	48	K 31
,, ,, Bow E . .	12	48	J 31
,, ,, Camden Town NW	6	36	I 20
,, ,, Carshalton, Sur. .	30	—	Z^{7} 19
,, ,, Cheam, Surrey .	29	—	Z^{8} 14
,, ,, Child's Hill NW .	5	—	F 15
,, ,, Clapham SW .	16	61	T 21
,, ,, Croydon, Surrey .	26	—	Z^{6} 24
,, ,, Deptford SE .	4	63	R 30
,, ,, Dulwich SE .	16	—	U 25
,, ,, Deptford E . .	17	63	R 30
,, ,, Ealing W . .	9	—	M 6
,, ,, Ealing W . .	9	—	M 6
,, ,, East Ham E .	13	—	J 37
,, ,, Eltham . .	18	—	U 37
,, ,, Esher, Surrey .	24	—	Z^{6} 1
,, ,, Fulham SW . .	15	59	R 14
,, ,, Hampstead NW .	5	35	G 17
,, ,, Hampton . .	19	—	Z 2
,, ,, Hampton Wick .	19	—	Z 6
,, ,, Hanwell W . .	9	—	M 3
,, ,, Harlesden NW .	10	—	J 12
,, ,, Harrow, Midlex .	4	—	E 4
,, ,, Highgate N . .	6	31	E 20
,, ,, Homerton E .	7	39	H 28
,, ,, Hornsey N .	2	—	B 22
,, ,, Hounslow . .	14	—	S 1
,, ,, Ilford, Essex .	8	—	G 38
,, ,, Islington N . .	11	38	J 23
,, ,, Kensington W .	10	51	N 16
,, ,, Kingsland N .	7	38	H 26
,, ,, Kingston . .	19	—	Z^{1} 6
,, ,, Lambeth SE .	11	53	O 22
,, ,, Lewisham SE .	4	64	T 31
,, ,, Marylebone W .	11	44	L 19
,, ,, Merton SW . .	20	—	Z 16
,, ,, Mortlake SW .	15	—	S 10
,, ,, New Hampton .	19	—	X 2
,, ,, N. Finchley N .	1	—	A 17
,, ,, North Woolwich E	13	—	N 38
,, ,, Norwood SE .	26	—	Z^{3} 26
,, ,, Notting Hill W .	10	50	M 15
,, ,, Peckham SE .	17	62	R 26
,, ,, Pentonville N .	11	45	J 23
,, ,, Plaistow E . .	13	—	J 34
,, ,, Plumstead . .	18	—	P 39
,, ,, Poplar E . .	12	49	M 31
,, ,, Putney SW . .	15	59	S 14
,, ,, Roehampton SW .	15	—	U 12
,, ,, Sidcup . .	23	—	Y 38
,, ,, St. Giles' WC .	11	45	L 21
,, ,, S. John's Wood NW	11	35	J 18
,, ,, Shadwell E . .	12	47	M 28
,, ,, Shoreditch E . .	12	46	K 26
,, ,, Wimbledon SW .	20	—	Z 17
,, ,, Stepney E . .	12	48	L 29
,, ,, Stoke Newing. N .	7	39	G 26
,, ,, Stratford E . .	7	41	I 32
,, ,, Sutton, Surrey .	29	—	Z^{7} 16
,, ,, Teddington .	19	—	X 4
,, ,, Th. Ditton, Sur. .	24	—	Z^{3} 4
,, ,, Thrntn Hth, Sur.	26	—	Z^{2} 24
,, ,, Tooting SW . .	20	—	Y 18
,, ,, Sydenham SE .	22	—	X 27
,, ,, Walthamstow E .	3	—	C 30
,, ,, Wandsworth SW .	15	—	T 16
,, ,, Wanstead E. .	8	—	D 35
,, ,, Wapping E . .	12	55	N 27
,, ,, Wealdstone, Mdx.	1*a*	—	B 4
,, ,, Welling . .	18	—	T 42
,, ,, West Norwood .	21	—	X 24
,, ,, W. Wickham, Kt.	27	—	Z^{5} 31
,, ,, Whitechapel E .	12	47	L 26
,, ,, Wimbledon SW .	20	—	Y 14
,, ,, Woolwich SE .	13	—	O 38
,, ,, north, E. Ham E	13	—	J 37
,, ,, south, ,, ,,	13	—	K 37
,, Barnet-road, N .	1	—	A 18
,, Cross-road, Totten. N	3	—	B 26
,, hill-ferry, U. Claptn. E	7	33	E 28
,, park-road, Kew .	14	—	R 8
,, Timber-s, U. Tms. st EC	—	46	M 24
,, view-rd, Sidcup, Kt .	23	—	X 42
Higham-hill, Walthamw. E	3	—	A 29
,, rd, Tottenham N .	3	—	B 25
,, st, Walthamstw. E	3	—	B 29
,, hill-rd, Wlthmw. E	3	—	A 29
,, pk. & Hale-end ry sta, Chingrd. E	3	—	A 32
,, sta.-av, Walthamstow. E . .	3	—	A 31
Highan-rd, Leytonstone E.	7	41	H 33
Highbarrow-rd, Croydn. S.	26	—	Z^{5} 26
Highbury, N	6	37	H 24
,, av, Thornton H.	26	—	Z^{2} 23
,, cres, Highbury N	6	38	H 23
Highbury-fields, Highby. N	6	38	G 24
,, gardens, Ilford .	8	—	F 40
,, gr, High.-pk, N .	6	38	G 24
,, grove, Highbry. N	6	38	G 24
,, hill, Highbury N	6	38	G 23
,, pk, Highbury N.	6	38	G 24
,, pl, Highbury N .	6	38	H 24
,, Quadrant, Highbury New-pk, N	6	38	F 24
,, rd, Wimble. SW.	20	—	Y 14
,, ter, Highbury N	6	38	G 24
,, & Islington ry. sta, N.L. Rwy.	6	38	H 23
,, New-park, N .	6	38	G 24
Highclere-rd, New Malden	24	—	Z^{2} 9
,, st, Sydenham SE	22	—	X 29
Highcroft-rd, Hornsy. R, N	6	32	E 22
Highfield-av, Hendon NW .	5	—	D 14
,, hill, Norwood .	21	—	Z^{1} 25
,, rd, Bromley, Kt.	28	—	Z^{3} 36
,, ,, Carshalton, S.	29	—	Z^{7} 18
,, ,, Hendon NW .	5	—	D 15
,, ,, Purley . .	30	—	Z^{10} 22
,, ,, Spring-grove.	14	—	Q 4
Highgate, N	6	31	E 19
,, Archwy N . .	6	32	E 21
,, av, Highgate N .	4	31	D 20
,, Cemety, High. N.	6	31	E 20
,, hill, N . . .	6	32	E 21
,, rd, Kentish T. NW	6	—	F 20
,, Wood, Highgate N	2	—	C 19
,, Wood, Mus. H. N	2	—	C 20
,, rd. sta, Mid. Ry.	6	36	G 20
,, sta, H. & L. Rly, Highgate N .	6	31	D 20
Highland-road, Bromley .	22	—	Z^{2} 33
,, ,, U. Norwood	21	—	Y 25
,, street, Bromley E	12	49	L 32
Highlands-avenue, Acton W	9	—	M 9
,, gds, Ilford, Ess.	8	—	E 37
Highlever-rd, N. Kens. W .	10	42	L 13
Highmore-road, Greenwich	17	64	Q 33
Highview-rd, Castlebr. H. W	9	—	L 5
,, ,, Norwood SE.	21	—	Z^{1} 25
Highweek-rd, Tottenham N	3	—	C 26
Highworth-rd, N South. N.	2	—	A 22
Hilda-road, East Ham E .	8	—	I 36
,, ,, Plaistow E .	12	49	K 33
,, vale-rd, Farnboro', Kt	30*b*	—	Z^{7} 37
Hilder-st, Croydon, Surrey	30	—	Z^{8} 24
Hilderton-cres, Hendon NW	1	—	C 13
Hildersdown-vi, Barnes SW	15	—	R 12
Hildridge-wd, Highgate N.	2	—	C 19
Hilgrove-rd, Finchly-rd. NW	—	35	I 17
Hill-brow, New Malden .	25	—	Z^{2} 11
,, ,, Widmore . .	23	—	Z^{2} 36
,, rise, Richmond . .	14	—	U 7
,, rd, Carshalton, Surrey	29	—	Z^{8} 18
,, ,, L. Streatham SW .	21	—	Z^{1} 20
,, ,, Purley, Surrey .	30	—	Z^{11} 22
,, ,, S. Johns Wood NW	10	43	J 17
,, st, Berkeley-square W	11	44	M 20
,, ,, Finsbury EC . .	11	46	K 25
,, ,, Knightsbridge SW .	11	52	N 18
,, ,, Peckham SE . .	17	62	R 26
,, ,, Richmond . .	14	—	T 6
,, ,, Victoria Dock E .	13	—	M 34
,, ,, Woolwich . .	18	—	R 37
,, house-rd, L. Streat. SW	21	—	Y 22
,, place-street, Poplar E.	12	48	L 31
,, view-road, Orpington.	28	—	Z^{6} 40
,, ,, ,, Sutton, Sy.	25	—	Z^{6} 17
,, ,, ,, Twickenhm	14	—	U 4
Hillbury-rd, Tooting. cn. SW	21	—	W 20
Hillbrow-road, Esher .	24	—	Z^{6} 1
Hillcrest-road, Acton W .	9	—	M 9
,, ,, Chapel-end E	3	—	A 32
,, ,, Sydenm. SE.	22	—	Y 26
Hillcroft-avenue, Ealing W	9	—	L 7
Hillcroome-rd, Sutton, Sur	29	—	Z^{8} 17
Hilldown-rd, L. Streat. SW	21	—	Z^{1} 22
Hilldrop-cres, Holloway N.	6	37	H 21
,, road, Holloway N	6	37	G 21
,, ,, N. Bromley.	23	—	Z 34
Hillfield-avenue, Hornsey N	2	—	C 22
,, gds, Barking, Ess.	8	—	I 40
,, road, Kilburn NW.	5	—	G 15
Hillgrove-road, Kilburn NW	—	35	I 17
,, road, Kilburn NW .	5	—	G 15
Hilliards-court, Wapping E	12	55	N 28
Hillier-rd, N. Wands. SW .	16	—	U 19
Hillingdon-st, Walworth SE	16	54	Q 24
Hillmarton-rd, Caled'n-rd. N	6	37	G 22
Hillmore-gr, Lr. Sydnhm SE	22	—	Y 29
Hillsborough-rd, E. Dul. SE	16	—	U 25
Hillside, Wimbledon SW .	14	20	Z 14
,, gds, Carshalton .	30	—	Z^{9} 20
,, ,, Highgate N .	6	31	D 20
,, rd, Ealing-hill W .	9	—	L 7
,, ,, Tulse-hill .	21	—	W 22
,, ,, Tottenham N .	7	33	D 26
Hills-place, Oxford-st. W .	—	44	L 20
Hillsleigh-rd, Kensington W	10	50	M 15
Hilltop-road, Kilburn NW .	5	35	H 16
Hilly Fields-cr, Brockley SE	4	63	T 30
,, pk, Brock'y SE	4	63	T 30
Hilmer-st, W. Kensing. SW	15	58	P 15
Hilsea-street, Clapton E .	7	39	G 28
Hilton-av, N. Finchley N .	1	—	A 18
Himley-road, L. Tooting SW	20	—	Y 18
,, ,, Tooting SW .	21	—	Y 18
Hinckley-rd, Peckham SE .	17	62	T 26
Hind-court, Fleet-street EC	—	45	L 23
,, street, Poplar E .	12	48	M 30
Hinde-st, Manchstr-sq. W .	11	44	L 19
Hindes-rd, Harrow, Mdsx	1*a*	—	C 4
Hindleys-pl, Lewisham SE	22	—	W 28
Hindmans-rd, E. Dul. SE .	17	—	U 26
Hinstock-road, Plumstead.	18	—	Q 39
Hinton-rd, Carshalton, Sur.	30	—	Z^{8} 10
,, ,, Herne-hill SE .	16	62	S 24
Hippodrome, Cr'nb'ne-st. WC	11	45	M 21
His Majesty's Theatre, Haymarket SW . .	—	45	K 21
Hitcham-rd, Waltham'w E	7	—	E 30
Hither-green, SE . .	17	—	U 32
,, ,, Cemetery SE	22	—	W 33
,, ,, Junc. Sta. D. Rly, Lewisham SE.	17	—	U 32
Hither-green-la, Lew. SE .	4	—	T 31
Hitherfield-rd, Streatm-hi.	21	—	W 22
Hobart-place, Pimlico SW .	11	52	O 20
Hobman-st, Rotherhithe SE	12	56	O 29
Hocker-st, Bethnal Green E	—	47	K 26
Hockley-av, East Ham E .	13	—	J 37
Hodford-rd, Golders Gr. NW	5	—	E 15
Hoe-street, Walthamst'w E	3	—	C 30
,, ,, ry. sta. G.E. Ry.	3	—	C 31
Hogarth-lane, Chiswick W	15	—	P 10
,, place, Chiswick W	15	—	P 10
,, rd, Earls Court SW	10	51	O 16
Hogsmill river, Surrey .	28*a*	—	Z^{7} 9
,, ,, ,, .	24	—	Z^{3} 9
Holbeach-rd, Catford SE .	22	—	Y 30
Holbein-pl, Sloane-sq. SW .	—	52	P 19
Holborn EC . . .	11	45	L 23
,, buildings, EC .	—	45	L 23
,, circus, EC . .	11	45	L 23
,, pl, Holborn WC .	—	45	L 22
,, road, Plaistow E .	13	—	L 35
,, Ry. Sta. Pica. Ry.	11	45	L 22
,, viaduct EC . .	11	46	L 23
,, ,, Ry. Sta. S.E. & C. R. .	11	46	L 24
Holbrook-la, Chisleh't, Kent	23	—	Z 39
,, rd, W. Ham E .	12	41	J 33
,, wd, Per'y-st, Knt	23	—	Z^{1} 40
Holcombe-hill, Mill-hill NW	—	—	A^{1} 12
,, road, Ilford .	8	—	E 38
,, ,, Totten. N	3	—	B 27
Holcroft-road, Hackney E	7	39	I 28
Holden-av, Woodside-pk. N	1	—	A 17
,, road, Bow . .	12	48	K 31
,, ,, N. Finchley N	1	—	A 17
,, ,, Woodside-pk. N	1	—	A 17
,, st, N. Wands. SW .	16	60	S 19
Holdenby-rd, Brockley SE	4	—	U 29
Holdenhurst-av, Finch. N .	1	—	A 17
Holdernesse-rd, Up. Toot..	21	—	W 19
Holford-rd, Hampstead NW	5	35	F 17
,, sq, Clerkenwell EC	11	45	J 23
Holland-av, Sutton, Surrey	29	—	Z^{9} 15
,, grove, Brixton SW	16	53	Q 23
,, house, Kensing. W	10	50	N 15
,, pk, Notting-hill W	10	50	N 15
,, rd, East Ham E .	13	—	J 37
,, ,, Finsbury-pk. N	6	32	E 22
,, ,, Harlesden NW	10	34	J 12
,, ,, Kensington W	10	50	N 14
,, ,, S. Norwood SE	27	—	Z^{3} 27
,, ,, Stockwell SW .	16	62	S 23
,, ,, Sutton, Surrey	29	—	Z^{8} 17
,, ,, West Ham E .	12	49	K 33
,, st, Kensington W	10	51	N 16
,, ,, Brixton SW .	16	61	R 23
,, ,, Southw'rk-st. SE	11	46	M 24
,, ter, Crouch End N	6	32	D 22
,, walk, Kensing. W.	10	50	N 15
,, pk-av, Nott'g-hi. W	10	50	N 12
,, ,, gds, Adsn.-rd. W	—	50	N 14
,, ,, rd, Adsn.-rd. W	10	50	O 15
,, villas-rd, Kens. W	10	50	N 14
Holles-street, Oxford-st. W	11	44	L 20
Holligrave-rd, N. Bromley	23	—	Z^{1} 34
Hollingbourn-gds, Castle-bar-hill W . . .	9	—	L 5
Hollingbourne-rd, Herne-hill SE . . .	16	—	U 24
Hollingsworth-rd, Isling. N	6	37	H 23
Hollington-rd, Tottenhm N	3	—	A 27
,, st. Cam'rw'll SE	16	54	Q 24
Hollow walk, Kew . .	14	—	Q 7
Holloway	6	37	F 22
,, down, Leyt'ne E	7	41	G 33
,, Prison, Holloway N	6	37	G 22
,, road, N . .	6	37	G 23
,, ,, East Ham E	13	—	K 37
,, ,, Leytnstne E	7	41	G 33
,, sta., G. N. Ry. N	6	37	G 23
,, st, Hounslow .	14	—	R 2
,, ,, Whitechapel E	12	47	L 27
Holly-hill, Hampstead NW	5	35	G 17
,, lane, Willesden NW .	5	—	H 11
,, park, Finsbury-pk. N	6	32	E 22
,, ,, Crouch-hill N	1	—	B 16
,, rd, Chelsfield, Kent	30*b*	—	Z^{9} 41
,, ,, Chiswick W .	10	—	O 10
,, ,, Finsbury-pk. N .	6	32	E 22
,, ,, Hounslow . .	14	—	S 2
,, ,, Leytonstone E .	7	—	E 34
,, ,, New Hampton .	19	—	Y 2
,, ,, Twickenham .	19	—	V 4
,, street, Dalston E .	7	39	J 26
,, Bush-hill, Hamp. NW	5	35	G 17
,, pk-gdns. North End Finchley N . .	1	—	B 16
,, ,, rd, Hanwell W .	9	—	M 4
,, ,, ,, N'wSouthgte N	2	—	A 20
,, ,, ,, N'wSouthgte N	2	—	A 20
Hollybush-gdns, Bethnal Green-road E	12	47	K 27
,, st, Plaistow E .	13	—	K 35
Hollycroft-av, Hamp. NW	5	35	F 16
Hollydale-rd, Peckham SE	17	63	S 28
Hollywell-la, Curtain-rd EC	12	46	K 26
Hollywood-rd, Ful.-rd. SW	15	51	P 17
Holman-rd, Battersea SW .	15	60	S 17
Holmbush-road, Putney SW	15	—	U 14
Holmdale-rd, Kilburn NW	5	35	G 16
Holmdene-av, Herne-hi. SE	16	—	W 24
Holme-road, East Ham E .	13	—	J 37
Holmes-rd, Kentish Twn NW	6	36	H 20
,, ,, Twickenham .	19	—	V 4
Holmesdale-av, Mortlake SW	14	—	S 9

John-street. INDEX TO STREETS, &c. Kirkstall road.

4-in. sht. 9-in. sht. mar.
John-st, Grays-inn-rd, WC. 11 45..K 22
,, ,, Hendon NW. . 1 —..B 13
,, ,, Hanway-street, W — 45..L 21
,, ,, Minories EC . 12 46..M 26
,, ,, West Ham E . 12 41..J 33
,, Campbell-rd, Stoke Newington N . 7 38..H 26
,, Carpenter-st, Tudor-street, EC . . — 45..M 23
,, Penn-st,Lewism-.rd,S 4 63..R 31
Johns-road, Tottenham N 7 33..D 25
Johnson-rd, Bromley, Knt. 28 —..Z^3 35
,, ,, Croydon, Sy . 26 —..Z^4 24
,, st, Commrcl-rd.E. 12 47..M 28
,, ,, Cubitt Town E 17 57..P 32
,, ,, Notting-hill W 10 43..M 15
,, ,, Somers Tn. NW 11 45..J 21
Johnsons-court, Fleet-st,EC — 45..L 23
Jonathon-st,Vauxhll-wk.SE 16 53..P 22
Joscelyn-st, Peckham SE . 17 62..R 26
Joseph-street, Limehouse E 12 48..L 30
Josephine-av, Brixton SW 16 —..U 22
Joshua-street, Poplar E . 12 49..L 31
Joubert-st, Battersea SW . 16 60..R 19
Jubilee-place, Chelsea SW . 16 52..P 18
,, rd, Cheam, Surrey. 29 —..Z^8 14
,, street, Stepney E . 12 47..L 28
Judd-st, Brunswick-sq,WC 11 45..K 22
Juer street, Battersea SW . 16 —..Q 18
Julian-avenue, Acton W . 9 —..M 9
,, rd, Little Ealing W. 9 —..O 6
Junction-road, Acton W . 9 —..O 9
,, rd, Croydon, Sy . 30 —..Z^8 24
,, ,, Ealing W . 9 —..O 6
,, ,, Leytonstone . 7 41..H 33
,, ,, Tottenham N 3 —..B 27
,, ,, U.Hollowy N. 6 32..F 21
,, ,, ry.-sta, Mid. Railway N . 6 36..F 21
,, st, Canning Tn.E 12 49..L 33
Juniper-street, Shadwell E. 12 47..M 28
Jupp-road, Stratford E . 7 41..I 32
Jupps-rd, Bethnal-green E 12 48..K 29
Jutland-road, Catford SE . 22 —..V 31
Juxon-st, Lambeth-wlk.SE 11 53..O 22

K

Kambala-rd, Battersea SW 16 60..S 18
Kangley-br.-rd, L. Sydm. S 22 —..Y 29
Kashgar-road, Plumstead . 13 —..P 41
Kate-street, Balham . 21 —..V 19
Katherine-rd, East Ham E 8 —..I 36
,, ,, Plaistow E . 13 —..J 36
,, ,, Twickenham 14 —..U 4
,, ,, Upton E . 8 —..I 36
,, st, Croydon, Sy. 26 —..Z^6 24
,, ,, Silvertown E 13 —..N 36
Kathleen-rd, Battersea SW 16 60..S 18
Kay-road, Stockwell SW . 16 61..S 22
,, street, Hackney-rd, E 12 47..J 27
Kean-street, Drury-la, WC. 11 45..M 22
Keats-grv, Hampstead NW 5 35..G 18
Keble-street,Streatham SW 20 —..X 17
Keeley-rd, Croydon, Surry 26 —..Z^6 24
,, st, Kingsway WC . 45 —..L 22
Keens-rd, Croydon, Surrey 30 —..Z^7 24
Keetons-rd, BermondseySE 12 55..O 27
Keildon-rd, Battersea-ri.SW 16 60..T 18
Keith-gr, Shepherds Bh. W 10 50..N 12
,, road, Barking . 13 —..J 39
Kelday-rd, S. Hackney E . 7 40..I 30
Kelfield-gds, N. Kenstn. W 10 42..L 14
Kelland-road, Plaistow E . 13 —..K 34
Kellerton-rd, Lewisham SE 17 —..U 32
Kellett-road, Brixton SW . 16 61..T 23
Kelloway-st, Brixton SW . 16 61..T 21
Kelly-rd, Canning Town E. 13 —..L 34
,, st, Kentish Town NW 6 36..H 20
Kelmore-grv, E.Dulwich SE 17 62..T 26
Kelmscott-rd, BatterseaSW 16 —..U 18
Kelcross-road, Highbury N 6 38..G 24
Kelsey-road, Beckenham . 22 —..Z^2 30
,, pk.-av, Beckhm, K. 27 —..Z^2 31
Kelso-place, Kensington W — 51..O 16
Kelson-road, Ealing W . 9 —..M 7
,, ,, Kilburn NW . 5 —..H 15
Kelvedon-road,Fulham SW 15 58..Q 15
Kelvin-avenue, Bowes-pk.N 2 —..A 23
,, road, Highbury N . 6 38..G 24
Kemble-rd, Croydon, Sury 26 —..Z^6 23
,, ,, Forest-hill SE . 22 —..W 29
,, ,, Tottenham N . 3 —..A 27
,, st, Drury-lane WC 11 45..M 22
Kemerton-rd, Beckhm, Kt. 27 —..Z^2 31
,, ,, Croydon, Sy 26 —..Z^5 26
,, ,, Herne-hll.SE 16 62..S 24
Kemnal-rd, N. Eltham,Kt. 23 —..X 39
Kemoor-street, Woolwich . 16 —..Q 38
Kempe-rd, Queens-pk, NW 10 42..J 14
Kemplay-rd, Hampstd. NW 5 35..G 18
Kemps-ct, Berwick-st, W . 45 —..M 21
Kempsford-gds, Earls-C.SW 15 57..P 16
,, rd, Kenning.SE 16 53..D 23
Kempshott-road, Streathm 21 —..Z^1 21
Kempton-rd, East Ham E. 13 —..J 37
Kemsing-rd, E. Grnwch. SE 18 —..P 34
Ken Wood, Hampstead N . 6 31..E 18
Kenbury-st, Camberwll.SE 16 62..R 24
Kendal-avenue, Purley . 30 —..Z^1 24
,, road, Neasden NW . 5 —..G 12
Kendall-place, Beckenham 22 —..Z^2 29
,, road, Beckenham. 22 —..Z^2 29
Kender-st, New Cross SE . 17 63..R 28
Kemlford-road, Balham . 21 —..V 20
Kenilworth-av, Wlthmw. E 3 —..B 31
,, ,, Wmbln. SW 20 —..X 15
,, gds,S.Kngs,Ex 8 —..F 41
,, rd, Ealing W . 9 —..M 7
,, ,, Kilburn NW 5 —..I 15

4-in. sht. 9-in. sht. mar.
Kenilworth-rd, Roman-rdE 12 48..J 29
,, st, N. Kens. W 10 50..M 14
Kenley-rd, Brentford, Mx. 14 —..P 7
,, ,, Notting Hill W 10 50..M 14
,, ,, Twickenham . 14 —..U 5
,, st, Notting-hill W 10 50..M 14
Kenlor-rd, S. Wimbldn SW 20 —..Y 17
Kenmont-gdns, Col.-pk NW 10 42..J 12
Kenmure-road, Hackney E 7 39..H 27
Kennard-rd, New Sthgte N 2 —..A 19
,, st, N. Woolwch E 13 —..N 37
Kennedy-road, Barking . 13 —..J 40
Kenninghall-rd, Clapton E 7 39..F 27
Kenningham-rd, Edmtn. N 3 —..A 28
Kennington SE . . 16 53..P 23
,, oval SE . . 16 53..Q 23
,, park SE . . 16 53..Q 23
,, park-road SE . 16 53..P 23
,, road SE . . 11 53..O 23
,, ter, Ken.-pk SE 16 53..Q 23
Kenrick-place W . . 11 44..L 19
Kensal-grn, Middlesex NW 10 42..K 14
,, rise ry. sta, Hampst. Jct. Rly., Mx. NW 10 42..J 14
,, rd, Kensal-green W 10 42..K 14
,, grn. cem. Ksl.-gr.W 10 42..K 13
Kensington W . . 10 51..N 16
,, av, E. Ham E . 8 —..I 37
,, ,, Norbury . 21 —..Z^2 23
,, ct, Kens., High-street W . 10 57..N 16
,, cres, Kens.-rd W — 58..O 15
,, gds, Ilford, Esx 8 —..F 37
,, ,, Kensgtn W 10 43..M 17
,, gte, Kensgtn W 10 51..O 18
,, gore, Kens.-rd — 51..N 17
,, Palace W . . 10 51..N 16
,, pl, Kensngtn W 10 43..M 16
,, road W . . 10 50..O 15
,, sq, Kensngtn W 10 51..N 16
,, Addison-rd ry. sta, Dist. Ry. 10 50..O 14
,, ct.-pl, Kens. W 10 51..O 16
,, gardens-sq. W . 10 43..M 16
,, High-st, Kns. W 10 51..N 16
,, ,, ry. sta, Dist. Railwy 10 51..N 16
,, pal.-gds, Kns. W 10 43..M 16
,, pk-gds, Kens. W 10 50..M 15
,, park-road W . 10 50..M 15
Kent-av, Castlebar-hill W . 9 —..K 5
,, gardens, Ealing W . 9 —..K 5
,, road, Kew . . 14 —..Q 8
,, ,, W. Moulsey, Sy 24 —..Z^2 2
,, ,, W. Wickham . 27 —..Z^5 31
,, street, Hackney E . 12 39..J 26
,, ,, Plaistow E . 13 —..K 35
,, ter, Regent's-pk. NW 11 44..K 18
,, Town, Surrey . . 24 —..Z^2 2
,, house-la, Sydnhm. SE 22 —..Z^1 29
,, ,, rd, Sydnhm. SE 22 —..Z 29
,, hse.-ry sta, S.E. & C. Ry. . . . 22 —..Z^2 29
Kentish Town NW . . 6 36..H 20
,, ,, sta, Hampstd. Tube Railway 6 36..H 20
,, ,, ,, Mid. Ry. . 6 36..H 20
,, ,, ,, N.L.R. . 6 36..H 20
Kentmerch-rd, Plumstead 18 —..P 40
Kenton, Middlesex . . 1a —..C 7
,, la, Kenton, Mdsx. . 1a —..A 6
,, rd, Harrow, Mdsx . 1a —..D 4
,, ,, Homerton E . 7 40—H 29
,, st, Brunswck-sq. WC 11 45..K 22
Kenway-rd, Cromwll-rd. SW 10 51..O 16
Kenwyn-rd, Clapham SW . 16 61..T 21
,, ,, Cotnhm-pk SW 20 —..Z^1 13
Kenyon-st, Fulham SW . 15 58..Q 14
Keogh-road, Stratford E . 7 41..H 33
Keppell-st, Chelsea SW . 11 52..O 18
,, ,, Russell-sq. WC . 11 45..L 21
Kerbela-st, Beth.-Grn-rd. E 12 47..K 26
Kerbey-street, Poplar E . 12 48..M 31
Kerrison-rd, Battersea SW 16 60..S 18
Kerry-road, Deptford SE . 17 56..Q 29
Kersfield-road, Putney SW 15 —..U 14
Kersley-rd, St. Newing. N 7 33..F 26
,, st, Battersea SW . 16 60..R 18
Keslake-rd, Kensal-rise NW 10 42..J 14
Keston, Kent . . 30b —..Z^7 35
,, avenue, Keston . 30b —..Z^8 35
,, common, Kent . 30b —..Z^8 35
,, mark, Kent . . 30b —..Z^7 36
,, rd, E. Dulwich SE 17 62..T 26
,, ,, West-green N . 3 —..B 25
Kestrel-av, Herne Hill SE . 16 —..T 24
Keswick-road, Orpington . 28 —..Z^5 41
,, ,, Putney SW . 15 59..U 14
Kettering-street, Streatham 21 —..Z^1 20
Kettino-st, L. Tooting SW 20 —..X 18
Kettlebaston-rd, Lea-bdge road E . . . 7 —..E 30
Kew . . . . 14 —..Q 8
,, green, Surrey . . 14 —..Q 8
,, palace, Surrey . . 14 —..Q 7
,, road, Richmond . 14 —..S 7
,, bridge . . . 14 —..P 8
,, ,, rly. station . 14 —..P 8
,, foot-la, Richmond . 14 —..S 7
,, gardens-road, Kew . 14 —..Q 8
,, gds sta, S.W. Ry, Kew 14 —..R 8
Keyes-road, Cricklewd. NW 5 —..G 14
Keymer-rd, Streatham-hill 21 —..W 22
Keystone-cres, Kgs Cross N 11 45..J 22
Khartoum-rd, Ilford, Essx 8 —..H 39
,, ,, Plaistow E . 13 —..K 35
,, ,, Tooting SW 20 —..X 17
Khedive-rd, Forest Gate E 8 —..I 35
Khoma-st, Lowr Toot. SW 21 —..X 18
Khyber-road, Battersea SW 16 60..S 18
Kibworth-st, S. Lambth SW 16 53..Q 22
Kidbrook-gdns, BlackhthsE 18 —..R 34

4-in. sht. 9-in. sht. mar.
Kidbrook-grn, Blckth. SE . 18 —..S 35
,, gro, Blckth. SE . 18 —..R 34
,, la, Bl'ckh'th SE 18 —..T 36
,, ry-sta, Bl'k'th SE 18 —..T 35
,, pk-rd, Bl'k'th SE 18 —..S 35
Kidd-street, Woolwich . 18 —..P 37
Kidderminster-rd, Cryn, Sy 26 —..Z^5 23
Kidderpore-av, Hampst.NW 5 35..G 16
,, gds, Hamp. NW 5 35..G 16
Kilburn NW . . . . 5 —..I 15
,, la, Kensal-green W 10 42..I 14
,, priory, Kilburn NW 5 —..I 16
,, ry sta, L. & N.W.R. 5 35..I 16
,, sq, Kilburn NW . 5 —..I 16
,, vale, Kilburn NW — 35..I 16
,, and Brondesbury sta, Met. Ry. . 5 —..H 15
Kilburn-pk.-rd, Kilbrn. NW 10 43..J 16
Kildare-gds, Bayswater W. 10 43..L 16
,, ter, Bayswater W . 10 43..L 16
Kildoran-road, Brixton SW 16 —..T 22
Kildown-road, Ilford. Esx. 8 —..F 42
Kilgour-street, Brockley SE 4 —..U 29
Kilkie-street, Fulham SW . 15 59..S 16
Killarney-rd, Wands. SW . 15 —..U 17
Killearn-road, Catford SE . 22 —..W 32
Killeser-avenue, Streatham 21 —..W 21
Killyon-rd, S. Lambeth SW 16 61..S 21
Kilmain-road, Fulham SW. 15 58..Q 14
Kilmarsh-rd, Hmsmth. W . 10 58..O 13
Kilmartin-av, Norbury, Sy. 26 —..Z^2 22
Kilmorie-rd, Forest-Hill SE 22 —..W 29
Kilravock-st, Kensal Gr. W 10 42..J 14
Kilton-street, Battersea SW 16 60..R 19
Kimbell-gdns, Fulham SW. 15 59..R 14
Kimber-road, Penge . . 22 —..Z^2 28
Kimberley-av, Ilford, Esx. 8 —..E 40
,, ,, Plaistow E . 13 —..J 36
,, gds, Fins.-pk.N 2 —..C 24
,, rd, Croydon, Sy 26 —..Z^4 23
,, ,, Edmonton N 3 —..A 28
,, ,, Kilburn NW 5 —..I 15
,, ,, Peckham SE 17 63..S 27
,, ,, Stockwell SW16 61..S 22
,, ,, Tottenbm N 3 —..B 27
Kinburn-st,Rotherhithe SE 12 55..N 28
Kinfauns-rd, Goodmys, Ex. 8 —..F 42
,, ,, Tulse-hill . 21 —..W 23
King-street, Baker-street W 11 44..L 19
,, ,, Camden T. NW 11 38..J 20
,, ,, Cheapside EC 11 46..L 25
,, ,, Chelsea SW . 16 51..P 18
,, ,, Covent-gdn.WC 11 45..M 22
,, ,, Hmsmth. W . 10 58..O 12
,, ,, Kensington W 10 51..N 16
,, ,, Leyton E . 7 —..E 31
,, ,, Mile End E . 12 47..K 28
,, ,, Plaistow E . 13 —..L 34
,, ,, Poplar E . 12 48..M 30
,, ,, Richmond . 14 —..T 6
,, ,, St. James's SW 11 44..N 21
,, ,, Tottenham N 3 —..A 26
,, ,, Tower-hill E . 12 47..M 26
,, ,, Twickenham . 19 —..V 4
,, ,, Victoria Dck E 13 —..M 34
,, ,, Walthamw. E 7 —..D 29
,, ,, W. Smithfd. EC 11 46..L 24
King & Queen-st, Wlwth.SE 16 54..P 24
,, Arthur-st, Peckhm SE 17 63..R 28
,, Charles-rd, Surbtn, Sy. 24 —..Z^3 7
,, ,, st, Westmr SW 11 53..N 21
,, David-la, Shadwell E 12 47..M 28
,, Edward-gds, Ealing W 9 —..M 8
,, ,, rd, Hacky. E 7 39..I 28
,, ,, ,, Leyton E 7 —..E 32
,, ,, ,, Walthw. E 3 —..B 29
,, ,, st, Lambeth-rd, SE 11 53..O 23
,, ,, ,, Mile End E 12 47..L 27
,, ,, ,, Newgate-st. EC. 11 46..L 24
,, Edwards-gr, Tedgtn. 19 —..Y 5
,, ,, rd,Bark'g E 13 —..J 40
,, George-av, Plaistow E 13 —..M 36
,, ,, st, Grnwch.SE 17 64..R 32
,, Henry-st, Sk. Newn.N 7 38..H 26
,, Henry's-rd, Hamp.NW 5 35..I 18
,, ,, wk,Mildmay-park N . 7 38..H 25
,, James-st, Boro'-rd,SE 11 54..O 24
,, John's-la, Elthm, Knt 23 —..V 36
,, William-street, EC . 11 46..M 25
,, ,, st,Grnwch SE 17 57..Q 32
,, ,, ,, StrandWC 11 45..M 22
Kingdon-rd, Kilburn NW . 5 35..H 16
Kinghorn-st, Long-lane EC — 46..L 24
Kinglake-st, O. Kent-rd,SE 16 54..P 26
,, ,, Bermond. SE. 17 54..P 32
Kingly-st, Regent-street W 11 44..M 20
Kingmead-road, Tulse-hill 21 —..W 23
King's-av, Bromley-road . 22 —..Q^1 33
,, ,, Clapham SW . 16 —..U 21
,, ,, Ealing W . 9 —..L 7
,, ,, Greenford. . 9 —..L 2
,, ,, Muswell-hill N . 2 —..B 20
,, ,, Streatham . 21 —..V 21
,, Cross WC. . . 11 45..J 22
;,, drive, Thames Dit.. 24 —..Z^4 4
,, highway, Plum. SE 13 —..Q 41
,, la, Sutton, Surrey . 29 —..Z^7 17
,, road, Barking, Essx. 8 —..I 39
,, ,, Brownswd-pk.N 6 33..F 24
,, ,, Camden T. NW 6 37..I 21
,, ,, Chelsea SW . 16 51..P 18
,, ,, Ealing W. . 9 —..L 7
,, ,, Edmonton N . 3 —..A 27
,, ,, Finsbury-pk. N 6 33..F 24
,, ,, Fulham SW . 15 51..Q 16
,, ,, Kentish T'n.NW 6 36..H 20
,, ,, Leytonstone E 7 —..E 33
,, ,, Long Ditton . 24 —..Z^4 5
,, ,, Mitcham, Sur. 26 —..Z^2 19

4-in. sht. 9-in. sht. mar.
King's-road,Mortlake SW . 15 —..S 10
,, ,, N. Malden, Sy. 25 —..Z^2 11
,, ,, Norbiton. . 19 —..Z 8
,, ,, ,, . 19 —..Z 7
,, ,, Orpington . 28 —..Z^7 40
,, ,, Peckham SE . 17 63..R 27
,, ,, Plaistow E . 13 —..J 35
,, ,, Plaistow E . 13 —..J 36
,, ,, Richmond . 14 —..S 7
,, ,, S. Norwood SE 27 —..Z^2 27
,, ,, Sutton, Surrey 29 —..Z^{10} 15
,, ,, Teddington . 19 —..X 2
,, ,, Tottenham N . 3 —..A 26
,, ,, Twickenham . 14 —..U 5
,, ,, Willesden NW . 5 34..I 12
,, ,, Wimbledon SW 15 20..Y 15
,, ,, Wood Green N 2 —..A 23
,, sq, Goswell-road EC 11 46..K 24
,, Arms-yd,Mrgte-st.EC — 46..L 25
,, Bench-wk,Tmple EC — 45..M 23
,, College-rd, Hmp.NW 5 35..I 18
,, Cross-road WC . 11 45..J 22
,, ,, ra. st,Met.R.11 45..J 22
,, ,, ,, ,, G.N.R. 11 45..J 22
,, Down-av,Croyn.,Sy. 30 —..Z^{10} 23
,, Head-ct, Bow-st.WC — 45..M 22
,, ,, HolbornEC — 45..L 23
,, ,, Shoe-la. EC — 45..L 23
Kingsbridge-rd, N. Kens.W 10 42..L 13
Kingsbury NW . . . 5 —..F 10
,, green NW. . 1 —..C 10
,, rd, B.Pond-rd N 7 38..H 26
,, ,, Kngsbry NW 1 —..C 11
,, and Neasden sta. Met. Ry. . 5 —..G 11
Kingscliffe-gds,Wim.-pk,SW 20 —..V 15
Kingscote-road, Croydon . 27 —..Z^5 27
,, ,, N. Malden. 25 —..Z^2 10
,, ,, S. Acton W 9 —..O 10
,, st, Tudor-st, EC — 46..M 23
Kingscourt-road, Strethm. 21 —..X 21
Kingsdale-road, Penge SE . 22 —..Z^1 28
,, ,, Plumstead 18 —..Q 40
Kingsdown-rd, Ealing W . 9 —..N 5
,, ,, Leytonst. E 7 41..G 33
,, ,, Surbiton, S. 24 —..Z^4 7
,, ,, U.Hollwy.N 6 32..F 22
Kingsford-st, Cubitt Tn. E 17 57..P 32
Kingsgate-rd, Kilburn NW. 5 35..H 16
Kingshall-road, Beckenhm. 22 —..Z^1 29
Kingsland, N . . . . 7 38..H 25
,, grove,Kingslnd. High-street, N 7 38..H 26
,, gr, Kingsland N 7 38..H 26
,, High-street E . 7 38..H 26
,, road, N . . 12 38..J 26
,, ,, Plaistow E 13 —..K 35
Kingsley-av,Castlebar-h, W 9 —..L 5
,, ,, Sutton, Surry. 29 —..Z^7 17
,, rd, Farnborough. 30b —..Z^9 40
,, ,, Harrow . 4 —..F 2
,, ,, Hounslow . 14 —..R 2
,, ,, Kilburn NW 5 —..I 15
,, ,, Palmers-gr, N 2 —..A 24
,, ,, Walthamw. E 3 —..B 32
,, ,, Wimbledn. SW 20 —..Y 16
,, st, Battersea SW 16 60..S 19
Kingsman-st, Woolwich . 18 —..P 37
Kingsmead-av, Malden . 25 —..Z^6 12
Kingsthorpe-rd, Sydnm. SE 22 —..X 28
Kingston, Surrey . . 19 —..Z^1 7
,, bridge, Kingston 19 —..Z^1 6
,, cemery,Kingston 19 —..Z^1 8
,, common, Surrey. 24 —..Z^5 6
,, hill, Surrey . 19 —..Y 9
,, lane, Teddington 19 —..Y 4
,, rd, Ewell, Surrey 29 —..Z^7 10
,, ,, Ilford, Essex 8 —..G 39
,, ,, Leytonstone E 7 41..G 33
,, ,, Merton SW . 20 —..Z^1 14
,, ,, N.Malden,Sy 24 —..Z^2 9
,, ,, Putny-hth.SW 20 —..V 12
,, ,, Raynes-pk,SW 20 —..Z^1 13
,, ,, Teddington . 19 —..Y 5
,, vl,Rchmd.-pk.SW 20 —..W 10
,, hall-rd,Kingston 19 —..Z^1 7
,, hl.-rd,Kingstn.-hl 19 —..Y 9
,, ry.-sta,L. & S.W. Rly, Kingston . 19 —..Z 7
,, vale, Putney SW. 20 —..X 10
,, st, Regnts-pk, NW 6 36..I 19
Kingsway WC . . . 11 45..L 22
,, , Mortlake SW . 14 —..S 9
Kingswood-av,Qns.-pk,NW 10 34..J 15
,, rd, Acton W. 9 —..N 9
,, ,, Balham SW 16 —..U 21
,, ,, Bromley,K. 27 —..Z^2 32
,, ,, Dulwich SE 22 —..X 26
,, ,, Goodmys.E 8 —..E 42
,, ,, Merton SW. 20 —..Z 15
,, ,, NorwoodSE 22 —..X 25
,, ,, Penge SE . 22 —..Z^1 28
Kingthorpe-rd, Willsdn. SW 5 —..H 10
Kingwood-av, Qns.-pk.NW 5 —..I 14
,, road, Fulham SW 15 58..Q 14
Kinnaird-av, Nw. Bromley 22 —..Z^1 33
Kinnears-rd,Shephds.Bh.W 10 —..N 11
Kinnerton-st, Knightsb.SW 11 52..O 19
Kinnoul-rd, Hammersth.W 15 58..P 14
Kinveachy-gds, Charlton . 18 —..P 36
Kinver-rd, U. Sydenhm.SE 22 —..X 28
Kipling-street, Long-la, SE 12 54..N 25
Kirby-st, Hatton-grdn. EC 11 45..L 23
,, ,, Southwark SE. 12 54..N 25
Kirchen-rd, Drayton-gr, W 9 —..M 5
Kirk-lane, Plumstead SE . 18 —..Q 39
Kirkdale, Sydenham SE . 22 —..X 27
,, rd, LeytonstoneE 7 —..E 33
Kirkham-street, Plumstead 18 —..Q 40
Kirkley-road, Merton SW . 20 —..Z 15
Kirkside-road, Charlton SE 18 —..Q 34
Kirkstall-road, Streatham. 21 —..V 21

Kirkwood road. INDEX TO STREETS, &c. **Lennox-gardens.**

	4-in. sht.	9-in. sht.	mar.
Kirkwood-rd, Peckham SE	17	63..S	27
Kirtley-rd, Sydenham SE	22	—..X	29
Kirtling st, Battersea SW	16	52..Q	20
Kirton-road, Plaistow E	13	—..J	35
Kitchener-rd, Chapel End E	3	—..A	31
,, ,, E. Finchley N	2	—..B	18
,, ,, Thorn.Hth.S	26	—..Z^2	24
,, ,, Upton E	8	—..I	35
Kitson-road, Barnes SW	15	—..R	12
Kitto-road, New Cross SE	17	63..S	28
Klea-avenue, Clapham SW.	16	—..U	20
Knapp-road, Bromley E	12	48..K	30
Knaresborough-pl, Cromwll. road SW.	10	51..O	16
Knatchbull-rd, Cmbrwll. SE	16	62..R	24
,, ,, Willesdn NW	5	—..I	10
Knee-hill, Abbey Wood	13	—..P	43
Knightland-rd, Clapton E	7	33..F	27
Knighton-rd, Forest-gt, E.	8	—..G	34
,, pk.-rd, L.Sydm SE	22	—..Y	29
Knightrider-st, Doctrs.-c. EC	11	46..M	24
Knights-hill, Dulwich	21	—..V	24
,, ,, W. Norwood	21	—..Y	23
,, la, L.Edmontn. N.	3	—..A	27
,, park, Kingston	19	..—Z^1	7
,, rd, Victoria Dk. E	13	—..N	34
Knightsbridge SW	11	52..N	18
Knightsbridge raily.-statn, Piccadilly Railway	11	52..N	19
,, gr, Kntb. SW	—	52..N	19
Knivett-rd, Fulham SW	15	58..Q	15
Knoll-rise, Orpington	28	—..Z^6	40
,, road, Sidcup	23	—..Y	42
Knollys-rd, Streatham SW.	21	—..X	23
Knott-street, Deptford SE.	17	56..Q	31
Knotts-green, Leyton E	7	—..D	32
,, ,, rd, Leyton E	7	—..D	31
Knowle-road, Brixton SW	16	61..S	23
Knowles-hl-crs, Lewishm SE	17	—..U	32
Knowsley-rd, Battersea SW	16	60..S	18
Knox-road, Battersea SW	15	60..S	17
,, st, Marylebne.-rd. W.	11	44..L	19
Knoyle-street, Deptford SE	17	56..Q	29
Knutsford-st, Battersea SW	16	61..R	21
Kohat-rd, Wimbledon SW	20	—..Y	16
Koundell-st, Clapham SW	16	61..S	20
Kremlin-av, Thornton-hth.	26	—..Z^2	23
Kylemore-rd, Hampstd. NW	5	35..H	16
Kymberley-rd, Harrow Mx.	1a	—..C	4
Kynance-pl, S.Kensingtn SW	10	51..O	17
Kynaston-rd, Croydon, Sy.	26	—..Z^3	24
,, ,, Stk.Nwng. N	7	38..F	26
Kyrle-rd, Battersea SW	16	—..U	19
Kyverdale-rd, Stoke New. N	7	33..E	26

L

	4-in. sht.	9-in. sht.	mar.
La Belle Sauvage-yard, Ludgate-hill EC	—	46..M	24
Laburnum-rd, S. Wimb. SW	20	—..Z	17
,, st, Kingsld.-rd, E	12	39..J	26
Lacey-street, Bow E	12	48..J	30
Lacon-road, E. Dulwich SE	17	—..T	26
Lacey-road, Putney SW	15	59..S	14
,, ,, ,, ,,	15	59..S	14
Ladas-road, W. Norwood	21	—..Y	24
Ladbroke-gds, Nott.-hill W	10	50..M	15
,, gr, Nottg.-hill W	10	42..K	14
,, rd, Nottg.-hill W	10	50..M	15
,, sq. Nottg.-hill W	10	50..M	15
,, ter, Nottg.-hill W	10	50..M	15
Ladbrook-rd, Norwood SE	26	—..Z^2	25
Lady Dock, Rotherhithe SE	12	56..O	29
,, Margaret-rd, Ken.T. N	6	37..G	21
,, Somerset-rd, Kn.T. NW	6	36..G	20
Ladysmith-av, Plaistow E	13	—..J	36
,, ,, Seven Kgs., Ilford, Essex	8	—..E	40
,, rd, Cann. Tn. E	12	49..K	33
,, ,, Edmontn N	3	—..A	28
,, ,, Eltham, Kt	23	—..V	37
,, ,, Tottenhm N	3	—..B	27
Ladywell, Lewisham SE	4	—..U	30
,, Cemet., Brckly. SE	4	—..T	30
,, pk, Lewisham SE	4	—..T	31
,, rd, Lewisham SE	4	—..T	30
,, sta, Lewisham SE	4	—..U	31
Lafone-st, Southwark SE	12	55..N	26
Lahore-rd, Croydon, Surry	26	—..Z^4	25
Lainson-st, Wandswrth SW	20	—..V	15
Laitwood-rd, Balham	21	—..Y	20
Lake-house-rd, Wanstead E	8	—..F	34
,, rd, The, Wimbdn SW	20	—..Y	15
,, street, Ratcliff E	12	47..M	28
Lakedale-rd, Plumstead	18	—..P	40
Lakefield-rd, Wood-green N	2	—..B	24
Lakehall-rd, Croydon, Sur.	26	—..Z^3	23
Lakes-road, Keston	30b	—..Z^8	35
Lakeside, Beckenham	27	—..Z^2	31
,, rd, Palmers-gr. N	2	—..A	23
Laleham-rd, Catford SE	22	—..V	31
Lalor-street, Fulham SW	15	59..R	14
Lamb-lane, Hackney E	7	39..I	27
,, street, Spitalfields E	12	46..L	26
Lambden-rd, Wandsw. SW	15	60..U	16
Lambert-rd, Brixton SW	16	—..U	22
,, ,, N. Finchley N	1	—..A	18
,, ,, Victoria Dk. E	13	—..M	35
Lamberts-rd, Surbiton, S'y	24	—..Z^3	7
Lambeth. SE	11	53..O	22
,, Bridge	11	53..O	22
,, Cemet, L.Toot. SW	20	—..Y	17
,, hill, Q.Vict.-st. EC	11	46..M	24
,, Lwr. Marsh SE	11	53..N	23
,, Palace, SE	11	53..O	22
,, rd, Lambeth SE	11	53..O	23
,, st, Commcl-rd, E	12	47..M	27
,, walk, Lambth SE	11	53..O	23
,, pal-rd, SE	11	53..O	22
Lamble-st, Kentish Tn. NW	6	36..G	19
Lambolle-pl, Hampstd. NW	5	36..H	18
,, rd, Hampstd. NW	5	36..H	18
Lambourne-rd, Claphm SW	16	61..S	20
,, ,, Ilford	8	—..F	41
Lambrook-ter, Fulham SW	15	59..R	14
Lamb's Conduit-street, Theobalds-rd, WC	11	45..K	22
,, pas, Finsbury EC	11	46..L	25
Lambton-rd, Cott'm-pk. SW	20	—..Z^1	13
,, ,, Finsb'y-pk. N	6	32..E	22
,, ,, Raynes-pk. SW	20	—..Z^1	13
Lamer-rd, Lewisham SE	17	—..U	32
Lamerton-st, Deptford SE	17	56..Q	30
Lammas-park, Ealing W	9	—..N	6
,, rd, S. Hackney E	7	40..I	29
,, pk-rd, Ealing W	9	—..M	6
Lammermoor-rd, Balham	21	—..V	20
Lamont-street, Chelsea SW	15	51..Q	17
Lamp Mead-road, Lee SE	17	—..T	33
Lamprell-street, Bow E	7	40..I	30
Lampton, Middlesex	14	—..Q	2
,, par, Hounslow	14	—..R	1
Lanark-villas, Maida Vle W	10	43..K	17
Lanbury-road, Nunhead SE	17	63..T	28
Lancaster-av, Ealing W	9	—..N	5
,, gds, Hyde-pk. W	10	43..M	17
,, gate, Hyde-pk. W	10	43..M	17
,, park, Richmond	14	—..T	7
,, pl, Hampst'. NW	5	35..H	18
,, ,, Strand WC	11	45..M	22
,, rd, Edmonton N	3	—..A	26
,, ,, Finsby-pk. N	6	32..E	23
,, ,, Hampstd. NW	5	35..H	18
,, ,, Leytonstne E	7	—..F	33
,, ,, Neasden NW	5	34..G	12
,, ,, N. Southg. N	2	—..A	22
,, ,, Norwood SE	26	—..Z^2	26
,, ,, Notting-hi. W	10	42..L	14
,, ,, E. Ham E	8	—..I	39
,, ,, Upton E	8	—..I	34
,, ,, Walthamst. E	3	—..B	29
,, ,, W. Norwood	21	—..W	24
,, ,, Wimbln. SW	20	—..T	14
,, st, Boro'-rd, SE	11	54..O	24
,, ,, Hyde-pk. W	—	43..M	17
,, ter, Reg.-pk. NW	—	36..I	19
,, Gate raily-sta, Cent. Lond. Ry	10	43..M	17
,, Gate-ter, H.-pk. W	10	43..M	17
Lance-rd, Harrow, Middsx.	1a	—..D	3
Lancefield-st, Queens-pk. W	10	42..J	15
Lancelot-rd, Sudbury, Mid.	4	—..G	7
,, st, Knightbr. SW	11	52..N	18
Lanchester-rd, Musw.-hi. N	2	—..C	19
Lancing-st, Euston-sq, NW	11	45..K	21
Landcroft-rd, E. Dulw. SE	17	—..U	26
Landells-rd, E. Dulwich SE	17	—..U	26
Landford-road, Putney SW	15	59..T	13
,, st, Stoke New. E	7	39..G	27
Landor-road, Stockwell SW	16	61..S	22
Landridge-rd, Fulham SW	15	59..R	15
Landrock-rd, Hornsey N	6	32..D	22
Landsdowne-rd, Finchly N	1	—..A	16
,, ,, Wimb. SW	20	—..Z	13
Landseer-av, Manor-park E	8	—..H	38
,, rd, Bow E	—	48..K	30
,, ,, Sutton, Surry	29	—..Z^8	15
,, ,, U. Hol'way N	6	32..F	22
,, st, Battersea SW	16	60..R	19
Landway-rd, E. Wickham	18	—..S	42
Lanefield-st, Maida-hill W	10	42..J	15
Lanercost-road, Tulse-hill	21	—..W	23
Lanfranc-st, West.-br.-r. SE	11	53..O	23
Langdale-avenue, Mitcham	26	—..Z^2	19
,, rd, Croydon, Sur.	26	—..Z^3	23
,, st, St. George's E	12	47..M	27
Langdon-pk, Highgate N	6	32..D	21
,, road, Bromley	28	—..Z^2	34
,, ,, E. Ham E	13	—..J	38
,, ,, Highgate N	6	—..F	20
,, ,, U. Hol'wy N	6	32..F	21
Langdon-pk-rd, Highgate N	6	32..D	20
Langford-pl, S. Jns Wd. NW	10	35..J	17
,, rd, Fulham SW	15	59..R	16
Langham-pl, Reg.-street W	11	44..L	20
,, rd, Teddington	19	—..Y	5
,, ,, Tottenham N	2	—..B	24
,, ,, W. Green N	2	—..B	24
,, ,, Willesden NW	5	—..F	13
,, ,, Wimbldn SW	20	—..Z^1	13
,, st, Mrylebne W	11	44..L	20
Langland-gds, Hampst. NW	5	35..G	17
Langler-rd, Kensal-grn NW	10	42..J	13
Langley-av, L. Ditton, Sur.	24	—..Z^4	6
,, ,, Nw Malden SW	20	—..Z^1	10
,, crt, Long Acre WC	—	45..M	22
,, la, S. Lam.-rd SW	16	53..Q	22
,, pk, Bcknhm, Kent	27	—..Z^4	31
,, ,, Mill Hill NW	1	—..A	11
,, rd, Elmers-end, Sy	27	—..Z^3	23
,, ,, L. Ditt., Sur.	24	—..Z^4	7
,, ,, Merton SW	20	—..Z^1	15
,, st, Long acre WC	11	45..M	22
,, pk-rd, Sutton, Su.	29	—..Z^8	17
Langroyd-rd, Up. Toot. SW	20	—..W	18
Langside-av, Barnes SW	15	—..S	12
Langthorne-ct, Cpthl-av, EC	—	46..L	25
,, st, Fulham SW	15	58..Q	14
,, ,, W. Ham E	7	41..J	33
Langton-av, East Ham E	13	—..K	38
,, rd, Dulwich SE	22	—..V	27
,, ,, W. Moulsey, Sy	24	—..Z^2	1
,, st, Chelsea SW	15	51..Q	17
Lanhill-rd, Maida Hill W	10	43..K	16
Lanier-rd, Lewisham SE	17	—..U	32
Lanodale-road, Mitcham	25	—..Z^2	19
Lanrick-rd, Canning Tn. E	12	49..L	33
Lansdell-road, Mitcham	21	—..Z^2	19
Lansdown-rd, Alex. Pk. N	2	—..A	21
,, ,, Cann. Tn. E	12	49..M	34
,, ,, Lee SE	17	64..T	33
Lansdowne-cres, Not. Hl W	10	50—M	15
Lansdowne-gds, S. Lam. SW	16	61..R	22
,, gro, Neasden NW	5	—..G	11
,, hl, W. Norwd.	21	—..X	23
,, rd, Charlton	18	—..Q	36
,, Croydon, Sur.	26	—..Z^5	24
,, Dalston E	3	39..J	27
,, Edmonton N	3	—..A	26
,, Leytonstone E	7	—..F	33
,, Notting Hl. W	10	50..M	15
,, Sev. K'gs, Es.	8	—..E	41
,, Sidcup, Kent	23	—..X	42
,, S. Lambeth SW	16	61..R	22
,, Tottenham N	3	—..A	27
,, Upton E	8	—..J	35
,, Walthmstw E	7	—..D	30
,, Wimbldn SW	20	—..Z	13
Lant-street, Borough SE	11	54..N	24
Larch-road, Balham	21	—..W	19
,, ,, Cricklewd NW	5	—..G	14
Larcom-st, Walworth SE	16	54..P	24
Larden-road, Acton W	10	—..N	11
Lark-row, Victoria-pk. E	12	39..J	28
Larkbere-rd, Sydenham SE	22	—..X	29
Larkfield-road, Richmond	14	—..S	7
Larkhall-la, Clapham SW	16	61..S	21
,, rise, Clapham SW	16	61..S	21
Larks-wood, Chingford E	3	—..A	32
Larnaca-st, Bermondsy SE	12	54..O	26
Larpent-av, Putney SW	15	—..T	13
Lascelles-rd, Leytonstone E	7	—..F	33
Lascotts-rd, Bowes-pk. N	2	—..A	23
Lassa-road, Eltham	18	—..U	36
Lastfield-rd, Hornsey N	2	—..B	22
Latchmere-gro, Batrsea SW	16	60..S	18
,, lane, Norbiton	19	—..Y	7
,, rd, Battersea SW	16	60..R	18
Lateward-rd, Brentfrd, Mx	14	—..P	6
Latham-street, Poplar E	12	48..L	30
,, rd, Twickenham	14	—..U	4
Lathom-rd, East Ham E	8	—..J	37
Latimer-av, East Ham E	13	—..J	37
,, rd, Battersea SW	16	60..S	18
,, ,, Forest Gate E	8	—..G	35
,, ,, Merton SW	20	—..Z	16
,, ,, N. Kensgtn W	10	50..M	14
,, ,, Teddington	19	—..X	3
,, ,, sta, G.W. Rly., N. Kensgton W	10	50..M	14
,, street, Stepney E	12	48..L	29
Latona-rd, Peckham SE	17	55..Q	26
Laud-st, Croydon, Surrey	30	—..Z^7	24
Lauderdale-ct, Aldersgate-street EC	—	46..L	24
Lauderdale-rd, Maida V. W	10	43..K	16
Launceston-pl, Kens. SW	10	51..O	17
Launch-st, Isle of Dogs E	12	57..O	32
Laundry-rd, Fulham SW	15	58..Q	14
Launton-rd, Muswell Hl. N	2	—..C	19
Laura-rd, Low Leyton E	7	—..F	30
Lauradale-rd, Muswell Hl. N	2	—..B	19
Laural-av, Twickenham	19	—..V	4
Laurel-gdns, Hanwell W	9	—..M	3
,, gr, L. Sydenhm SE	22	—..Y	29
,, ,, Penge SE	22	—..Z^1	27
,, rd, Cottenhm-pk. SW	20	—..Z	12
,, ,, Barnes SW	15	—..R	12
,, street, Dalston E	7	39..H	26
,, ter, Tottenham N	3	—..A	27
Laurence Pountney-hill, Cannon-street EC	11	46..M	25
Laurence Pountney-lane, Cannon-street EC	11	46..M	25
Laurie-gro, New Cross SE	4	63..R	29
Laurier-rd, Croydon, Sur.	26	—..Z^4	26
Lauriston-rd, S. Hackney E	7	39..J	28
,, ,, Wimbldn SW	20	—..Y	13
Lausanne-rd, Hornsey N	2	—..C	23
,, ,, Peckham SE	17	63..R	28
Lavender-gds, Batt'rsea SW	16	60..T	19
,, gro, Dalston E	7	39..J	27
,, hill, Battersea SW	16	60..S	19
,, la, Battersea SW	16	60..T	18
,, pnd, Rother. SE	12	56..N	29
,, rd, Battersea SW	15	60..S	17
,, ,, Carshal., Sur.	30	—..Z^7	19
,, ,, Carshal., Sur.	29	—..Z^7	17
,, swp, Battersa SW	16	60..T	18
,, ter, Battersea SW	16	60..S	18
,, vle, Carshal., Sur.	30	—..Z^8	21
,, yd, Rother. SE	12	—..N	29
Lavengro-rd, W. Dlwch SW	21	—..W	24
Lavenham-rd, Wim.-pk. SW	20	—..V	15
Lavers-rd, St. Newington N	7	38..F	26
Lavington-rd, Beddington	30	—..Z^7	22
,, ,, Eal'g Dean W	9	—..M	5
Lavington-st, Sthwk.-st. SE	11	54..N	24
Law-street, Bermondsy. SE	12	54..O	25
Lawford-rd, Kentsh Tn. NW	6	36..H	20
Lawfrance-rd, Roman-rd. Bow E	12	48..J	29
Lawin-road, Twickenham	19	—..V	3
Lawn-crescent, Kew.	14	—..R	8
,, gardens, Hanwell W	9	—..M	3
,, la, S. Lambeth-rd. SW	16	53..Q	22
,, road, Beckenham	22	—..Z^1	30
,, ,, Hampstead NW	6	36..H	19
,, ter, Blackheath SE	17	64..S	33
Lawrence-av, Manor-pk. E	8	—..G	38
,, la, Cheapside EC	11	46..M	24
,, rd, Ealing W	9	—..O	6
,, ,, Edmonton N	3	—..A	27
,, ,, Norwood SE	26	—..Z^3	26
,, ,, Plaistow E	13	—..J	35
,, ,, Tottenham N	3	—..B	25
,, st, Canning T. E	12	49..L	33
,, ,, Chelsea SW	16	51..Q	18
,, ,, Malmesbury-road, Bow E.	12	48..J	30
,, ,, Mill-hill NW	1	—..A	12
Lawrie-pk.-av, Sydnhm SE	22	—..Y	27
,, gds, Sydnhm SE	22	—..Y	27
,, rd, Sydenhm SE	22	—..Y	27
Lawson-st, Gt.Dover-st. SE	12	54..O	25
Lawstead-rd, Lewisham SE	4	—..U	31
Lawton-rd, Leyton-st. E	7	—..E	32
,, ,, Mile End E	12	48..K	29
,, ,, Wood Green N	2	—..B	23
Laxey-road, Farnborough	30b	—..Z^9	40
Layard-rd, Bermondsey SE	12	53..O	27
Layer-gardens, Ealing W	9	—..M	8
Layfield-place, Bromley E	12	49..L	31
Layton-rd, Brentford, Mx.	14	—..P	6
,, ,, Hounslow	14	—..S	1
Lea Bridge E.	17	64..T	32
,, River	12	49..L	32
,, ,,	40	—..G	30
,, Bridge-road E	7	40—F	29
,, ,, ry. sta. G.E. Ry.	7	—..E	29
,, Hall-road, Leyton E	7	—..E	31
Leabon-street, West Ham E	12	41..J	33
Leabourne-rd, Stam. Hl. N.	7	33..D	27
Leadenhall Market EC	11	46..M	25
,, pl, Lime-st. EC	—	46..M	25
,, street EC	11	46..M	25
Leader-street, Chelsea SW	16	51..P	18
Leading-street, Shadwell E	12	47..M	28
Leage-street, City-road EC	11	46..K	25
Leahurst-road, Lee SE	17	—..U	33
,, ,, Lwsham SE	17	—..U	32
Lealand-road, Tottenham N	7	—..D	26
Leamington-park, Acton W	9	—..L	10
,, road, Ilford	8	—..F	41
,, ,, villas, Wst-bourne-pk. W	10	42..L	15
Leander-road, Brixton SW.	16	—..U	22
,, ,, Norbury, Sy	26	—..Z^3	22
Leaside-av, Muswell-hill N	2	—..B	20
,, rd, Up. Clapton E.	7	—..E	28
Leasowes-road, Leyton E	7	—..E	31
Leathersellers Hall, St. Helens-pl. EC	12	46..L	25
Leather-lane, Holborn EC	11	45..L	23
,, Mkt, Bermond. SE	12	54..O	25
Leatherdale-st, Mile End E	12	47..K	28
Leathwaite-rd, Battersea-rise SW	16	60..T	19
Lebanon-gds, Wands. SW	15	—..U	15
,, pk, Twickenham.	14	—..U	5
,, rd, Croydon, Sur.	26	—..Z^5	25
,, ,, Wndswth. SW	15	—..U	15
Lechmere-rd, Willes.-gr. NW	5	—..H	13
Leconfield-rd, Highbury N	7	38..G	25
Ledbury-rd, Croydon, Sur.	30	—..Z^7	24
,, ,, Notting-hill W	10	42..L	15
Lee SE	17	64..T	33
,, bridge, Lewisham SE	17	64..T	32
,, green, Lee SE	18	—..T	34
,, park, Blackheath SE	17	64..T	33
,, place, Sutton, Surrey	29	—..Z^7	16
,, road, Blackheath SE	17	64..T	33
,, station, Lee SE	18	—..U	34
,, street, Kingsland-rd. N	7	39..I	26
,, ,, Limehouse E	12	48..L	30
,, ,, Plumstead	18	—..Q	39
,, terrace, Blackheath SE	17	64..S	33
,, High-road, Lee SE	17	64..T	33
Leeds-road, Ilford	8	—..F	40
,, street, Edmonton N	3	—..A	27
Leeke-st, Kings Cross WC	11	45..J	22
Lefevre-rd, Old Ford-rd, E	12	40..J	30
Leffern-rd, Shepherds B. W	10	50..N	12
Lefroy-rd, Shepherds B. W	10	—..N	11
Leghorn-rd, Harlesden NW	10	34..J	12
,, ,, Plumstead	18	—..Q	40
Leicester-pl, Leicestr-sq. WC	—	45..M	21
,, rd, Croydon, Sy.	26	—..Z^5	25
,, ,, E. Finchley N	2	—..B	18
,, ,, Harlesden NW	5	—..H	10
,, square WC	11	45..M	21
,, ,, ry. sta. Piccadilly Ry.	11	45..M	21
,, st, Leicester-sq. WC	—	45..M	21
,, ,, Poplar E.	12	49—M	32
Leigh-pl, Leather-lane EC	—	45..L	23
,, road, East Ham E	8	—..I	38
,, ,, Highbury N	6	38..G	24
,, ,, Leyton E	7	—..E	32
,, ,, Walthamstw. E	3	—..B	32
,, st, Cartw'ght-gds. WC	11	45..K	22
Leigham-vale, Tulse-hill	21	—..W	23
,, av, Streatham	21	—..X	21
,, ct.-rd, Streatm-hl.	21	—..X	22
Leighton-cres, Kent.Tn. NW	6	37..G	21
,, gds, Knsl.-rise NW	10	34..J	13
,, gr, Kent.Tn. NW	6	37..G	21
,, rd, Ealing W	9	—..N	5
,, ,, Kent. Tn. NW	6	37..H	21
,, st, E. Croyd. Sur.	26	—..Z^5	23
Leinster av, E. Sheen SW	14	—..S	9
,, gds, Bayswater W	10	43..M	17
,, rd, Kilburn NW	10	43..J	15
,, ,, Muswell-hill N	2	—..C	20
,, sq, Bayswater W	10	43..M	16
,, ter, Bayswater W	10	43..M	17
Leipsic-rd, Camberwell SE.	16	62..R	24
Leith-road, Wood-green N.	2	—..A	24
Leitrim-gr, Battersea SW	16	60..R	19
Leman-st, Whitechapel E	12	47..M	26
,, ,, rlwy station E	12	47..M	27
Lemna-rd, Leytonstone E	7	—..E	33
Lemons-lane, Epsom.	29	—..Z^{11}	10
Lemnel-st, Wansdworth SW	15	—..U	16
Lena-gds, Hammersmith W	10	50..O	13
Lenelby-road, Surbiton	24	—..Z^5	8
Lenham-rd, Lee SE	17	—..T	33
,, ,, Sutton, Surrey	29	—..Z^7	16
,, ,, Thorntn.Hth.S	26	—..Z^2	25
Lennard-rd, Beckenham	22	—..Z^1	29
,, ,, Croydon, Sury	26	—..Z^5	24
,, ,, Penge SE	22	—..Z^1	28
Lennox-gds, Chelsea SW	11	52..O	18
,, ,, Ilford, Essex	8	—..E	37
,, rd, Finsbury-pk, N	6	32..E	23
,, ,, Walthamstw. E	7	—..D	30

Lensden-place. INDEX TO STREETS, &c. Lorrimore-road.

	4-in. sht.	9-in. sht.	mar.
Lensden-pl, Golden-laneEC	—	46..L	24
Lenthall-road, Dalston E .	7	39..J	26
Lenthorp-rd, E. Greenw.SE	17	57..P	33
Lenton-road, Edmonton N	3	—..A	26
Leo-street, Peckham SE .	17	55..Q	27
Leonard-road, Chingford E	3	—..A	31
,, rd, Forest-gate E.	8	—..G	34
,, ,, N.Woolwich E	13	—..N	37
,, street, City-rd, EC	11	46..K	25
Leopold-av, WimbledonSW	20	—..Y	15
,, rd, Ealing W .	9	—..M	8
,, ,, E. Finchley N.	2	—..B	18
,, ,, Edmonton N	3	—..A	28
,, ,, Harlesden NW	5	—..J	11
,, ,, Wimbledon SW	20	—..X	15
,, street, Bow E .	12	—..L	30
Leppoc-road, Clapham SW.	16	—..T	21
Leroy-st, Bermondsey SE .	12	54..O	25
Lesley-st, Roman-rd, N .	6	37..H	22
Leslie-gr, Croydon, Surrey	26	—..Z^5	25
,, rd, Canning Town E	13	—..M	35
,, ,, E. Finchley N .	2	—..B	18
,, ,, Leyton E . .	7	41..G	32
,, pk.-rd, Croydon, Sy.	26	—..Z^5	25
Lessada-st, Bethnal-gr, E .	12	48..J	29
Lessar-av, Clapham SW ,	16	—..U	20
Lessing-st, Honor Oak SE .	22	—..Y	29
Lessingham-av, U.Tooting	21	—..X	19
Leswin-rd, S. Newingtn N.	7	39..F	26
Letchford-gds, HarlesdnNW	10	42..J	12
Letchworth-st, Tooting SW	20	—..X	18
Lethreullier-rd, Barking,Ex	8	—..J	40
Lett-road, Stratford E .	7	41..J	—
Lettsom-st, Camberwell SE	16	62..S	25
Leucka-rd, Walthamstw. E	3	—..C	29
Leven-road, Poplar E .	12	49..L	32
Levendale-rd, Forest-hl.SE	22	—..W	29
Lever-st, Goswell-road, EC	11	46..K	24
Leverett-sreet, Chelsea SW	11	52..O	18
Leverson-street, Streatham	21	—..Z^1	20
Leverton-st,Kentish T.NW.	6	36..G	20
Levett-road, Barking, Esx	8	—..J	40
Levingstone-rd, B'sea. SW	15	60..S	17
Levington-rd, Hendon NW	5	—..D	13
Lewes-rd, New Bromley,K	23	—..Z^1	35
Leweston-pl,Stamfd-hl. N .	7	33..E	26
Lewin-road, Mortlake SW .	15	—..S	10
,, ,, Streatham .	21	—..Y	21
Lewis-gr, Lewisham SE .	17	64..T	32
,, rd, Camberwell SE .	16	62..S	24
,, ,, Merton SW .	20	—..Z^1	17
,, ,, Sutton, Surrey .	29	—..Z^7	16
,, ,, Welling . .	18	—..T	43
,, st, Kentish Twn.NW	6	36..H	20
Lewisham SE	17	64..T	32
,, hill, Lewishm.SE	17	64..S	32
,, pk,LewishamSE	4	—..U	31
,, rd,Higate.-rd,NW	6	36..F	20
,, ,, Lewishm.SE	4	63..R	31
,, High-road SE	4	63..R	30
,, Jt. Sta, N.K. ry. Lewishm. SE .	4	64..S	31
,, rd.Sta,LewismSE	4	63..S	31
Lexden-road, Acton W .	9	—..M	9
Lexham-gds,Earls Ct.-rd.W	10	51..O	16
Lexington-st, Golden-sq.W	11	45..M	21
Ley-street, Ilford, Essex .	8	—..F	39
Leybourne-av, Ealing W .	9	—..N	6
,, rd,Kentish TNW	6	36..J	20
,, ,, Kew .	14	—..Q	8
,, ,, Leytonne E	7	—..E	34
Leyes-rd, Canning Twn. E.	13	—..M	35
Leyland-road, Lee SE .	18	—..U	34
Leyspring-rd, Leytonste E.	7	—..E	34
Leythe-road, Acton W .	9	—..N	10
Leyton E	7	—..E	31
,, green, E . .	7	—..D	32
,, High-road, E .	7	—..D	31
,, marsh, Leyton E .	7	—..E	28
,, ,, ,, . .	7	40..F	30
,, rd, Stratford E .	7	41..H	32
,, ,, S.Wimbledn.SW	20	—..Z	17
,, square, Peckhm.SE	17	55..Q	27
,, street, Leyton E	7	—..E	31
,, gr.-road, Leyton E.	7	—..D	32
,, pk.-rd, Leyton E .	7	—..F	32
,, ry.-sta, G.E. Rlwy.	7	41..G	32
Leyton ry. sta, Midland Rly.	7	—..E	32
Leytonstone E . . .	7	—..F	33
,, rd, Stratford E .	7	41..H	33
,, ry. sta, G.E. Ry.	7	—..F	33
,, High-road E .	7	—..F	33
Liberia-road, Highbury N	6	38..H	24
Liberty-street, Brixton SW	16	61..R	22
Libra-road, Old Ford E .	12	40..J	30
,, ,, Plaistow E .	13	—..J	34
Library-st, Borough-rd. SE	11	54..O	24
Licensed Victuallers' Asym, Peckham SE . . .	17	55..Q	27
Lichfield-av, Stratford E .	7	41..I	33
,, gr, Finchley N .	1	—..A	16
,, rd, Bethnal-gr. E	12	48..K	29
,, ,, Cricklewd. NW	5	—..G	14
,, ,, Kew . .	14	—..Q	8
Liddington-rd, W. Ham E	12	41..J	34
Liddon-rd, Bickley, Kent .	28	—..Z^2	35
Lidford-rd, Stk. Newng. N	7	38..G	25
Liffler-road, Plumstead .	18	—..P	40
Lifford-rd, Stockwell SW .	16	62..S	23
,, street, Putney SW .	15	59..S	14
Liggatt-road, West Ham E	12	41..J	32
Lightcliffe-rd, Plmrs-grn. N	2	—..A	23
Lightfoot-road, Hornsey N	2	—..C	22
Lighton-rd, Battersea SW .	15	60..T	17
Lilford-rd, Camberwell SE	16	62..S	24
Liian-road, Mitcham .	21	—..Z^2	20
Lilley-la, Mill Hill, Middsx	1	—..A	11
Lillian-road, Castelnau SW	15	58..P	12
Lillie-road, Fulham SW .	15	58..Q	14
Lillieshall-rd, Clapham SW	16	61..S	20
Lillington-st, Pimlico SW .	16	52..P	21
Lillyville-road, Fulham SW	15	58..R	15
Lily-road, Walthamstow E	7	—..D	31
Lilypot-la, Noble-stst. EC .	46	—..L	24
Limburg-rd, Battr.-rise SW	—	60..T	18
Lime-gro, New Malden SW	20	—..Z^1	10
,, ,, Shepherd's B. W	10	50..N	13
,, st, Fenchurch-st. EC	11	46..M	25
,, ,, sq, Lime-street EC	—	46..M	25
,, Tree-av, Ths. Ditton	24	—..Z^4	3
Limehouse causeway E .	12	48..M	30
,, cut E . .	12	48..L	31
,, Rly., G.E.R. E	12	48..M	30
,, ry. st, G.E.R. E	12	48..M	30
,, Workhouse E .	12	48..M	30
Limekiln-lane, Highgate N	6	32..E	20
Limerston-st, Chelsea SW .	15	51..Q	17
Limes-av, Golders-grn. NW	3	—..D	15
,, ,, New Southgte N	2	—..A	21
,, gro, Lewisham SE .	17	64..T	32
,, rd, Croydon, Surrey	26	—..Z^4	24
Limesford-rd, Peckham SE	17	63..T	28
Linacre-rd, Willes.-grn. NW	5	—..H	13
Lincoln-avenue, Wembley	4	—..H	7
,, rd, E. Finchley N	2	—..B	18
,, ,, Sidcup . .	23	—..Y	42
,, ,, S. Norwood SE	27	—..Z^2	27
,, ,, Tottenham N .	3	—..B	27
,, ,, Worc.-pk, Sur.	25	—..Z^5	12
,, st, Bow E . .	12	48..K	30
,, ,, Chelsea SW .	16	52..P	19
,, ,, Leytonstone E	7	—..F	33
Lincolns Inn WC . .	11	45..L	23
,, ,, Fields WC .	11	45..L	22
Lind-road, Sutton, Surrey	29	—..Z^7	17
Linda-st, Battersea SW .	15	60..S	17
Linden-av, Queen's-pk. NW	10	42..J	14
,, ,, Thornton-hth.	26	—..Z^2	23
,, ,, Wembley, Mdx.	4	—..G	8
,, gds, Bayswtr-rd. W	10	43..M	16
,, ,, Chiswick W .	15	—..P	10
,, gro, Nunhead SE .	17	63..T	27
,, rd, Muswell Hill N	2	—..C	20
Lindfield-gds, Hampstd NW	5	35..G	17
,, rd, Castlbar-hl. W	9	..—K	6
Lindley-road, Leyton E .	7	—..F	31
,, st, Whitechapel E	12	47..L	28
Lindore-rd, B'sea.-rise SW .	—	60..T	18
Lindrop-st, Fulham SW .	15	59..R	16
Linds, Lewisham SE . .	4	63..S	31
Lindsey-road, Malden .	25	—..Z^5	12
Linford-road, Ilford . .	8	—..F	41
,, st, S. Lambeth SW	16	61..R	20
Ling-rd, Canning Town E .	13	—..L	34
Lingen-street, Bromley E .	12	49..K	31
Lingfield-av, Norbiton, Sy.	24	—..Z^2	7
,, rd, Wimbledn SW	20	—..Y	14
Lingham-st, Stockwell SW	16	61..S	22
Lingwood-rd, Stmford-hl. N	7	33..D	27
Link-lane, Carshalton, Sur.	30	—..Z^8	21
,, rd, Mitcham, Surrey	26	—..Z^5	19
Linkfield-road, Isleworth .	14	—..R	4
Links-rd, Lr. Tooting SW .	21	—..Z^1	19
Linley-road, Tottenham N	3	—..A	26
Linnell-drive, Hmpstd NW	5	—..D	16
,, rd, Camberwell SE	16	62..R	25
Linora-rd, Walthamstow E	3	—..B	32
Linsey-rd, Bermondsey SE	12	55..O	27
Linslade-rd, Farnborough	30*b*	—..Z^8	40
Lintaine-road, Fulham SW	15	58..Q	15
Linthorpe-rd, Stmfrd-hl. N	7	33..E	26
Linton-grove, W. Norwood	21	—..Y	24
,, rd, Barking, Essex	8	—..I	39
,, street, Islington N	11	38..J	24
Linver-road, Fulham SW .	15	59..R	15
Linzee-road, Hornsey N .	2	—..C	22
Lion-road, Twickenham .	19	—..V	3
,, street, Long-acre WC	11	45..M	22
,, ,, Newington SE	11	54..O	42
,, ,, Poplar E .	12	48..L	31
,, and Lamb-crt,Golden lane EC . . .	—	46..K	24
,, gte-grdns, Richmond	14	—..R	7
Lionel-rd, Brentford, Mx.	9	—..O	7
,, ,, Gunnersbury W	9	—..O	7
Lisbon-st, Blackheath SE .	18	—..Q	34
Lisburn-rd, Hampstead NW	6	36..G	19
Lisford-street, Peckham SE	17	62..R	26
Lisgar-ter, Kensington W .	10	58..O	14
Liskeard-gds, Blackhth SE	18	—..R	34
Lisle-street, Leicester-sq. W	11	45..M	21
Lislesworth, Esher, Surrey	24	—..Z^6	2
Lismore-gds, Kentsh T. NW	6	36..G	19
,, rd, Croydon, Surr.	30	—..Z^8	25
,, ,, Kentish T. NW	6	36..G	19
Lissenden-gds, Highg.-r.NW	6	56..G	20
Lisson-grove, NW . .	11	44..K	18
,, st, Marylbn.-rd, NW	11	44..L	18
Lister-mews, Holloway N .	6	37..G	23
Liston-road, Clapham SW .	16	61..S	20
Litcham-st, Kentish T. NW	6	36..H	20
Litchfield-gds, Willsdn. NW	5	34..H	12
,, rd, Kew . .	14	—..R	8
,, ,, Sutton, Surr.	29	—..Z^7	16
Lithgow-st, Battersea SW .	15	60..S	17
Lithos-rd, Finchley-rd, NW	5	35..H	17
Little Albany-st,Rgt.-p.NW	11	44..J	20
,, Alie-st, Whitechpl. E	12	47..M	26
,, Argyll-st, Reg.-st, W	—	44..M	20
,, Arthur-st,Gldn-la,EC	—	46..K	24
,, Britain, Ridg.-st, WC	—	45..L	21
,, ,, Aldgte-st,EC	11	46..L	24
,, Camden-st,Cm.T.NW	6	37..I	21
,, Church-la, Hmsth. W	15	58..P	13
,, College-pl,Cam.T.NW	6	37..I	21
,, ,, st,Can.st, EC	11	46..M	25
,, ,, ,, West. SW	—	53..O	22
,, Drummond-street, Somers Town NW .	11	45..J	21
,, Ealing, Middlesex .	9	—..O	5
,, ,, la,S.Ealing W	9	—..O	6
,, Earl-st,Shfby.-av,WC	11	45..M	21
,, Essex-st, Strand WC	45	—..M	23
,, Europa-pl, Batt. SW	16	51..Q	18
Little George-st, Minories E	—	46..M	26
,, ,, ,, West. SW	—	53..N	21
,, Heath, Charlton .	18	—..Q	36
,, Ilford-av, Mnr-pk. E	8	—..H	38
,, ,, la, Mnr-pk. E	8	—..G	37
,, James-st, Grays-inn road, WC . .	11	45..K	22
,, Love-la, Wood-st,EC	46	—..L	24
,, New-st, Fetter-la, EC	11	45..L	23
,, Newport-st, Soho WC	11	45..M	21
,, Northampton-street, Percival-st, EC .	11	46..K	24
,, Portland-st,Rg.-st,W	11	44..L	20
,, Pulteney-st, Soho W	11	45..M	21
,, Randolph-st, Camden Town NW .	6	37..I	21
,, Rathbone-pl, Oxfrd-street, W . .	—	45..L	21
,, Russell-st, Blmsb.WC	11	45..L	22
,, St. Andrew-street, Seven Dials WC .	11	45..M	22
,, St. James's-street, St. James's SW .	11	52..N	21
,, Sussex-pl, Hy.-pk.W	—	43..M	18
,, Sutton, Chiswick W	14	—..P	9
,, Sutton-st,Gos.-rd,EC	11	—..K	24
,, Tower-hill, E . .	12	47..M	26
,, Trinity-lane, Upper Thames-street, EC	11	46..M	24
,, Turner-st,Coml-rd.E	12	47..M	27
,, Turnstile, Holbn WC	..	45..L	22
,, White Lion-street, St. Giles WC . .	—	45..M	22
,, Winchester - street, London-wall EC	—	46..L	25
,, Woodcote-la,Cars.Sy	30	—..Z^{11}	20
,, Wormwood Scrubs, Middlesex W .	10	42..K	13
Littlemore-road, Ilford .	8	—..G	40
Littleton-st, Earlsfield SW	20	—..W	17
Littlewood, Lewisham SE .	17	—..U	32
Littleworth, Esher, Surrey	24	—..Z^6	2
,, avenue, Esher .	24	—..Z^7	2
,, Cm.-rd,Esh.Sy.	24	—..Z^6	2
,, rd, Esher, Sur.	28*a*	—..Z^7	2
Livermere-rd, Dalston E .	7	39..I	26
Liverpool-rd, Barking-rd, E	12	49..L	33
,, ,, Islington N .	6	37..H	23
,, ,, Ealing W .	9	—..N	7
,, ,, Leyton E .	7	—..D	32
,, ,, Norbiton .	19	—..Y	8
,, .. Thorn.Hth.Sy	26	—..Z^2	24
,, st, Bishopsgte EC	11	46..L	25
,, ,, Kgs. Crss WC	11	45..J	22
,, ,, New.Cswy SE	11	54..O	24
,, ,, Walw.-rd, SE	16	54..P	25
,, ,, ry st,Bshg.EC	11	46..L	2c
Livingstone-rd, B'sea. SW .	16	60..S	17
,, ,, Hounslow	14	—..S	2
,, ,, N.Sthgte N	2	—..A	22
,, ,, Thornton Hth. Sry	26	—..Z^2	24
,, ,, W. Ham E	12	49..J	32
,, st, N.Wlwch. E	13	—..M	38
Livonia-st, Poland-st, W .	11	45..M	21
Llanover-rd, Sudbury, Mid.	4	—..F	7
,, ,, Woolwich .	18	—..Q	38
Llewellyn-grv, Bermdsey SE	12	55..O	27
Lloyd-park, Walthamstw E	3	—..B	30
,, rd, East Ham E .	13	—..J	37
,, ,, Walthamstow E	3	—..C	29
,, sq, Pentonville WC .	11	45..K	23
Lloyds-av, Fenchurch-st.EC	46	—..M	26
,, ct, Charing Cr-rdWC	45	—..L	21
,, rd, Rosebery-av. EC	11	45..K	23
,, st, Clerkenwell N .	—	45..J	23
Loampit-hill, Lewisham SE	—	63..S	31
,, ,, ,, ,,	17	63..S	31
,, vale, ,, ,,	4	63..S	31
Loanda-st, Haggerston E .	7	39..I	26
Lochaber-road, Lee SE .	17	64..T	33
Lochaline-st, Hammrsth. W	15	58..P	13
Lochinvar-street, Balham .	21	—..V	20
Lochnagar-st, Bromley E .	12	49..L	32
Lock-road, Ham . .	19	—..W	6
Locket-rd, Wealdstne, Mid.	1*a*	—..A	4
Lockhart-st, Bow Comm. E	12	48..K	30
Lockhurst-st, Clapton E .	7	40..G	29
Lockington-st, Batters. SW	16	61..R	20
Locks-lane, Upr. Mitcham	21	—..Z^2	19
Locksley-st, Limehouse E .	12	48..L	30
Lockwood-rd, Bermdsy. SE	12	55..O	27
Locton-street, Old Ford E	7	40..I	30
Loddiges-rd, Hackney E .	7	39..I	28
Loder-street, Peckham SE	17	63..R	28
Lodge-la, Addington, Surr.	30*a*	—..Z^9	31
,, ,, N. Finchley N .	1	—..A	17
,, ,, Plumstead .	18	—..R	42
Lodge-lane, Welling . .	18	—..U	43
,, pl, Regents-pk. NW	11	43..K	18
,, rd, Barking . .	13	—..J	41
,, ,, Carshalton, Sur.	30	—..Z^7	19
,, ,, Croydon, Sur. .	26	—..Z^4	23
,, ,, Hendon NW .	1	—..B	13
,, ,, Plaistow, Kent	23	—..Z	35
,, ,, Regents-pk. NW	11	43..K	18
,, ,, Sutton, Surrey .	29	—..Z^7	16
Lodore-street, Poplar E .	12	49..M	31
Loftie-st, Bermond. Wall SE	12	54..N	27
Loftings-rd, Barnsbury N .	6	37..J	23
Loftus-rd, Shepherds B. W	10	50..M	13
Lollard-st, Kenning-rd. SE	11	53..O	23
Loman-st, Southwark SE .	11	54..N	24
Lomas-st, Ben Jonson-rd E	12	48..L	29
Lombard-ct, Gracech.-st.EC	—	46..M	25
,, rd, Battersea SW	15	60..R	17
,, ,, Woolwich .	18	—..P	35
,, street EC . .	11	46..M	25
,, ,, Fleet-st. EC .	—	45..M	23
Loncroft-rd, Peckham SE .	17	54..Q	26
Londesboro-rd, Stk. New. N	7	38..G	26
London Bridge EC . .	11	46..M	25
London Cemetery, Ilford E	8	—..G	37
,, Docks, Wapping E	12	47..M	27
,, Fields, Hackney E	7	39..J	27
,, Hos, Whitech.-rd.E	12	47..L	27
,, lane, Bromley .	22	—..Z^1	33
,, pl, Hackney E .	7	39..Z	27
,, rd, Brentford, Mx.	14	—..Z	5
,, ,, Bromley .	22	—..Q^1	33
,, ,, Cheam, Surrey	29	—..Z^7	13
,, ,, Clapton E .	7	39..G	27
,, ,, Croydon, Sur.	26	—..Z^5	23
,, ,, East Ham E .	13	—..J	38
,, ,, Forest Hill SE.	22	—..W	27
,, ,, Isleworth .	14	—..R	3
,, ,, Kingston .	19	—..Z	8
,, ,, Mitcham, Sur.	26	—..Z^5	19
,, ,, ,, ,,	25	—..Z^4	17
,, ,, ,, ,,	25	—..Z^2	18
,, ,, Norbury .	26	—..Z^2	22
,, ,, Plaistow E .	13	—..J	34
,, ,, Southwark SE	11	54..O	24
,, ,, Sudbury, Mdx	4	—..G	7
,, ,, Sutton, Surrey	25	—..Z^6	16
,, ,, Tooting . .	21	—..Z^2	19
,, ,, Twickenham .	14	—..T	4
,, st, Comm'cial-rd.E	—	48..M	29
,, ,, Fenchurch-st. EC	11	46..M	26
,, ,, Greenwich SE .	17	—..Q	32
,, ,, Kingston . .	19	—..Z^1	7
,, ,, Paddington W .	10	43..L	17
,, Wall EC. . .	11	46..L	25
,, Bdge.Ry.Sta., City & S. Lon. Ry. .	12	54..N	25
,, Bdge.Ry.Sta, L.B. & S.C. Ry. .	12	54..N	25
,, Bdge.Ry.Sta, S.E. & C. Ry. . .	12	54..N	25
,, Com. Sale Rms. EC	11	46..M	25
,, C.C.Offices, Spring-gds, Westm'r. SW.	11	45..N	21
,, County Hall, Lambeth SE. . .	11	53..N	22
,, County Lunatic As. Hanwell W .	9	—..M	3
,, Hse-yd, St. Pauls Churchyard EC .	—	46..M	24
Lonesome-rd, Up. Mitcham	21	—..Z^2	20
Long Acre, St.Mrtns-la.WC	11	45..M	22
Long Ditton, Surrey . .	24	—..Z^4	5
,, grove, Ewell, Surrey	28*a*	—..Z^9	8
,, ,, road, Epsom .	28*a*	—..Z^1	9
,, lane, Bermondsey SE	12	54..O	25
,, ,, Finchley N .	1	—..A	17
,, ,, S. Norwood,Sur.	27	—..Z^4	28
,, ,, W. Smthfld EC.	11	46..L	24
,, Bridge-rd, Lewish. SE	4	—..U	31
,, Ditton-hill . .	24	—..Z^5	6
Longbeach-rd, Laven.-hl.SW	16	60..S	19
Longbridge-rd, Barking,Es.	8	—..H	41
Longfellow-rd, Bethnal G.E	12	48..K	29
,, ,, Croyd., Sur.	26	—..Z^4	22
,, ,, Walthm. E	7	—..D	30
,, ,, Worcester-pk. Surrey	25	—..Z^5	12
Longfield-av, Castlebar-hl.W	9	—..L	6
,, ,, Hackbge,Sur.	26	—..Z^5	19
,, rd, Cstlebr-hi. W	9	—..L	6
,, ,, Waltham. E .	3	—..C	29
,, st, Wimble.-pk.SW	20	—..V	15
Longford-av, Southall .	9	—..M	1
,, st, Regents-pk.NW	11	44..K	20
Longhedge-la, Up.Edmon.N	3	—..A	26
,, rd, ,, ,,	3	—..A	26
,, st, Battersea SW	16	60..R	19
Longhurst-road, Lee SE .	17	—..U	33
Longlands-pk.-cr, Sidcup .	23	—..X	40
,, ,, rd, ,, .	23	—....	40
,, rd, Halfway-st. Kent . .	23	—..X	40
Longleach-rd, Battersea SW	16	60..S	19
Longley rd, Croydon, Sur.	26	—..Z^5	23
,, ,, Tooting SW .	20	—..Y	18
,, ,, WealdstoneMx	1*a*	—..B	3
,, st, Bermond. SE .	17	55..P	27
Longnor-road, Stepney E .	12	48..K	29
Longridge-rd, Earls-ct, SW	10	51..O	16
Longstone-road, Tooting .	21	—..Y	19
Longton-av, Sydenham SE	22	—..X	26
,, gr, Sydenham SE.	22	—..X	27
Lonsdale-avenue, Wembley	4	—..G	7
,, road, Barnes SW.	15	—..Q	11
,, ,, Kilburn NW	5	—..J	15
,, ,, Qns-pk.NW	10	34..J	15
Lonsdale-rd, S. Norwo'd SE	27	—..Z^2	27
,, ,, Turnham G.W	10	—..O	11
,, ,, Wanstead E .	8	—..D	34
,, ,, Wstbrne-pk.W	10	50..L	15
,, sq. Barnsbury N.	6	37..J	23
Loosebury avenue, Esher .	24	—..Z^7	2
Lopen-road, Edmonton N	3	—..A	26
Loraine mews, Holloway N	6	37..G	22
,, place, Holloway N	6	37..G	22
,, road, Holloway N	6	37..G	23
Lord-st, N. Woolwich E .	13	—..N	37
Lords Cricket Ground, St. Johns Wood NW . .	11	43..J	18
Lordship-hill, Tottenham N	3	—..A	26
,, la, E. Dulwich SE	17	—..U	26
,, ,, Tottenham N .	3	—..A	25
,, pk, Stk. New. N .	7	33..F	
,, rd, Stk. New. N .	7	33..E	25
,, ter, Stk. New. N .	7	33..F	25
,, la, sta, S.E. Ry.	22	—..W	27
Lordsmead-rd, Tottenm N.	3	—..A	26
Lorn-road, Brixton SW .	16	61..R	23
Lorne-road, Finsbury-pk.N	6	32..E	23
,, ,, Forest Gate E	8	—..G	35
,, ,, Walthamstw E	3	—..C	30
,, ,, Wealdstne,Mx.	1*a*	—..A	4
Lorrimore-rd, Walworth SE	16	54..Q	24
,, sq, Walworth SE	16	54..Q	24
,, st, Walworth SE	16	54..Q	24

Lothair-road. INDEX TO STREETS, &c. Manville-road.

	4-in. sht.	9-in. sht.	mar.
Lothair-road, Ealing W .	9	—..N	6
,, ,, Fins.-pk. N	6	32..D	23
Lothbury EC . . .	11	46..L	25
Lothian-road, Brixton SW	16	62..R	23
Lothrop-st, Kensal Grn. W	10	42..J	14
Lots-road, Chelsea SW .	15	51..Q	17
Loubet-street, Tooting SW	20	—..Y	18
Loudoun-rd, St. J'ns Wd.NW	5	35..J	17
,, ,, sta. L.&N.W.R.	5	35..J	17
Loughborough-pk, Brix.SW	16	61..T	23
,, rd, Brix. SW	16	61..S	23
,, st, Kenning-lane SE .	16	53..P	23
,, Jct.Sta,S.E.& C.R. Brixton SE . .	16	62..S	24
Louise-road, Stratford E .	7	41..H	33
Louisville-rd, Up. Tooting	21	—..W	19
Loundoun-road, Ilford .	8	—..D	39
Louvaine-rd, Battersea SW	15	60..T	17
,, st, Stepney E .	12	48..L	29
Love lane, Bickley, Kent .	23	—..Z^2	34
,, ,, Cheam, Surrey .	29	—..Z^8	14
,, ,, Eastcheap EC .	11	46..M	25
,, ,, Mitcham, Surrey	25	—..Z^2	18
,, ,, Morden, Surrey	25	—..Z^4	15
,, ,, Ratcliff E . .	12	47..M	28
,, ,, Tottenham N .	3	—..A	26
,, ,, Wood-street EC	11	46..L	24
,, walk, Camberwell SE	16	62..R	25
Loveday-rd, Ealing Dean W	9	—..M	5
Lovegrove-st, Bermond. SE	17	55..P	27
Lovelace-gds, Surbiton.Sur.	24	—..Z^4	6
,, rd, Surbiton, Sur.	24	—..Z^4	6
,, ,, W. Norwood	21	—..W	24
Lovelinch-st, Deptford SE	17	55..Q	28
Lovells-ct, Paternstr-rowE	—	46..L	24
Loveridge-rd, Kilburn NW.	5	—..H	15
Lovers walk, Finchley N .	1	—..A	13
Lowden rd, Herne-hill SE .	16	62..T	24
Lower Cheam, Surrey .	29	—..Z^8	14
,, Clapton E . .	7	39..G	27
,, Edmonton N . .	3	—..A	27
,, grove, Wands. SW .	15	—..U	16
,, Hook, Surrey. .	28a	—..Z^7	5
,, Mall, Hmsmth W .	15	58..P	13
,, Market, Woolwich .	13	—..P	38
,, Marsh, Lambeth SE	11	53..N	23
,, Mitcham, Mitcham, Surrey . . .	25	—..Z^2	18
,, Norwood SE . .			
,, Morden, Surrey .	25	—..Z^4	13
,, ter, Hampstead NW	5	—..F	17
,, rd, Orpington. .	28	—..Z^6	40
,, ,, Richmond-hill .	14	—..U	7
,, ,, Rotherhithe SE	12	55..O	28
,, ,, St.MaryCray,Kt.	28	—..Z^4	42
,, ,, Sutton, Surrey .	29	—..Z^7	17
,, Streatham .	21	—..Y	21
,, Sydenham SE .	22	—..Y	29
,, Tooting SW . .	20	—..X	18
,, ,, . .	21	—..X	19
,, Addiscombe-road, Croydon, Surrey .	26	—..Z^5	26
,, Ashley-st, Clerken-well EC . . .	11	46..K	24
,, Ashley-st,Clerken. N	11	46..K	24
,, Belgrave-st, Buckingham Pal.-rd. SW	11	52..O	20
,, Berkeley-st, Portman-square W . .	11	44..L	19
,, Bland-st, Gt. Dover-street SE . .	12	54..O	25
,, Boston-rd,Hanwell W	9	—..M	3
,, Camden-rd, Chislehurst, Kent. .	23	—..Z^1	37
,, Chapman-street, St. Georges East E .	12	47..M	27
,, Charles-st, Clknwl.N	11	46..K	24
,, Cherry-gds-st, Bermondsey SE .	12	55..O	27
,, Church-st, Croy,Sur.	26	—..Z^6	23
,, Clapton-rd, Clap. E	7	39..H	28
,, Coombe-st, Croy,Sur.	30	—..Z^7	24
,, court-road, Epsom	28a	—..Z^1	9
,, Cross-rd, Kent.T.NW	6	36..G	19
,, ,, st, Islington N	6	38..J	24
,, Down-rd,Wimble.SW	20	—..Z^1	14
,, East Smithfield E .	12	55..N	26
,, Elmers End, Elmers End, Kent . .	27	—..Z^2	29
,, Evelyn-st, Dept. SE	17	56..P	29
,, Fore-st, Edmonton N	3	—..A	27
,, George-st, Richmd.	14	—..T	7
,, green East, Mitcham Surrey. . .	25	—..Z^2	18
,, green west, Mitcham, Surrey . . .	25	—..Z^2	18
,, Grosvenor-road, SW .	11	52..O	20
,, Gullerhedge-la,Hen.NW	5	—..D	12
,, Ham-road, Norbiton .	19	—..Z	6
,, Hamlet-rd, Walthw. E	3	—..B	31
,, James-st, Golden-sq. W	—	45..M	21
,, John-st, Golden-sq. W	—	44..M	21
,, Kennington-lane, SE .	16	54..P	23
,, Marsh-la, Norbitn, Sur.	24	—..Z^2	8
,, Morden-la, Mordn, Sur.	25	—..Z^4	14
,, Mortlake-rd, Richmnd	14	—..S	7
,, Orchard-st, Claphm SW	16	—..U	21
,, Parkfields, Putney SW	15	59..T	13
,, Park-rd, Peckham SE	17	55..Q	27
,, Porchester-st,Hy.-pk.W	11	44..L	18
,, Queens-rd, Teddington	19	—..Y	3
,, Richmond-rd, Brns. SW	15	—..S	12
,, ,, ,, Mort. SW	14	—..S	9
,, ,, ,, Put. SW	14	—..S	8
,, ,, ,, Put. SW	15	59..S	13
,, Seymour-st,Port.-sq.W	11	44..L	19
,, Sloane-st, Chelsea SW	16	52..P	19
,, Sydenham-st,S.E.R.SE	22	—..Y	30
,, Teddington-rd, Hampton Wick . .	19	—..Z	6
,, Thames-street, EC .	11	46..M	25

	4-in. sht.	9-in. sht.	mar.
Lwr.William-st,S.Jns.W.NW	11	43..J	18
,, Winchester-rd,Catf.SE	22	—..V	30
,, Wood-st, Woolwich .	18	—..P	37
Lowergreen, Esher, Surrey	24	—..Z^5	1
,, la, Esher, Sur.	24	—..Z^5	2
Lowfield-road, Purley, Sur.	30	—..Z^1	22
Lowhall-la, Walthamstw. E	7	—..D	29
,, ,, ,, ,,	7	—..D	30
Lowlands-rd, Harrow, Mid.	1a	—..D	4
Lowman-rd, Holloway N .	6	37..G	23
Lowndes-pl, Belgrve-sq. SW	11	52..O	19
,, sq, Belgravia SW	11	52..N	19
,, st, Belgrve-sq. SW	11	52..O	19
Lownds-av, Bickley, Kent	28	—..Z^2	34
Lowth-rd, Camberwell SE .	16	62..R	24
Lowther-hill, Forest-hill SE	22	—..V	29
,, rd, Higham-hill E	3	—..A	29
,, ,, Norbiton .	19	—..Z	7
,, ,, Walthamstw.E	4	—..B	29
Loxford av, East Ham E .	13	—..J	36
,, lane, Ilford, Essex	8	—..H	40
,, rd, Barking, Essex	8	—..I	39
,, Water, Ilford, Ex.	8	—..H	40
Loxley-rd, Wandswrth. SW	20	—..V	17
Loxton-road, Forest-hill SE	22	—..W	29
Loxwood-rd, Tottenham N	4	—..B	26
Luard-st, Caledonian-rd, N	6	37..I	22
Lubbock-rd, Chislhrst, Kt.	23	—..Z^1	37
Lucas-avenue, Plaistow E .	13	—..J	35
,, road, Penge SE .	22	—..Z^1	28
,, ,, Walworth SE .	16	54..Q	23
,, ,, West Ham E .	12	41..J	32
,, st, Commercial-rd, E	12	47..M	28
,, ,, Deptford SE .	4	63..R	30
Lucerne-rd, Croydon, Sury	26	—..Z^3	24
,, ,, Highbury N .	6	38..G	24
,, ,, Orpington .	28	—..Z^5	40
Lucey-rd, Bermondsey SE	12	55..O	27
Lucian-road, Earlsfield SW	20	—..W	16
Lucien-road, Tooting SW .	21	—..X	19
Ludgate-circus, EC . .	11	45..M	23
,, hill, EC . .	11	46..M	24
,, ,, raily-station, S.E. & C.R.	11	46..M	24
,, square, EC . .	—	46..M	24
Ludlow-rd, Castlebar-hill W	9	—..K	6
Ludwick-rd, Deptford SE .	17	56..Q	29
Lugard-road, Peckham SE .	17	63..R	27
Luke-street, Finsbury EC .	11	46..K	25
Lullington-rd, U.Norwd.SE	22	—..Z^1	26
Lulot-street, Highgate N .	6	—..E	20
Lumber-ct, Seven Dials WC	—	45..M	21
Lumley-street, Oxford-st,W	11	44..M	19
Luna-rd, Thortn. Hth, Sur.	26	—..Z^2	24
,, street, Chelsea SW .	16	51..Q	17
Lunatic Asylum,Banstd.,Sy	29	—..Z^{11}	16
,, ,, Colney H. N	2	—..A	20
Lune-st, Walthamstow E ,	3	—..C	29
Lunham-road, Norwood .	21	—..Z^1	25
Lupton-st, Kentish Tn. NW	6	36..G	21
Lupus-street, Pimlico SW .	16	52..P	20
Lurgan-av, Hammersth. W	15	58..P	14
Lurline-gdns, Battersea SW	16	61..R	20
Lushington-rd, Kens.Ri.NW	10	42..J	12
Luther-road, Teddington .	19	—..X	4
Luton-rd, Walthamstow E	3	—..B	30
,, st, Carlisle-st, NW .	11	43..K	18
,, ,, Plaistow E . .	13	—..L	34
Luttrell-avenue, Putney SW	15	—..T	13
Lutwyche-rd, Forest-hill SE	22	—..W	29
Luxemburg-gds,Hmsmthw	10	58..O	13
Luxor-st, Camberwell SE .	16	62..S	24
Lyall-road, Bow E . .	12	48..J	29
,, street, Eaton-pl. SW	11	52..O	19
Lydden-grv, Earlsfield SW	16	20..V	16
,, road. Earlsfield SW	20	—..V	16
Lydford-rd, Maida-hill W .	10	42..K	15
,, ,, Willes.-grn.NW	5	—..H	14
Lydhurst-rd, Streatham-hi	21	—..W	22
Lydon-road, Clapham SW .	16	61..S	20
Lyford-rd, Wandswth. SW	20	—..V	18
Lyham-road, Brixton SW .	16	—..U	22
Lyme-st, Camden Town NW	6	36..I	21
Lymington-av, Wood-grn. N	2	—..A	24
,, rd, Hamp. NW.	5	35..H	16
Lynch-rd, Wandsworth SW	15	—..U	16
Lyncroft-gardns, Ealing W	9	—..N	6
,, ,, Hamp. NW	5	35..G	16
Lyndal-road, Brockley SE	4	—..U	29
Lyndale-rd, Childs-hill NW	5	—..F	15
Lyndhurst-drive, Leyton E	7	—..E	32
, gds, Barking, Ex.	8	—..I	40
,, ,, Finchley N .	1	—..A	15
,, ,, Hamp, NW .	5	35..G	18
,, grv, Cambrwll SE	17	62..S	26
,, rd, Bowes-pk. N.	2	—..A	23
,, ,, Croydon, Sur.	26	—..Z^3	23
,, ,, Edmonton N	3	—..A	27
,, ,, Hampstd. NW	5	35..G	18
,, ,, Peckham SE	17	62..R	26
,, ,, Wood-green N	2	—..A	23
Lynedoch-st, Kingsld.-rd. N	12	38..J	26
Lynette-ave, Clapham SW .	16	—..U	20
Lynmouth-rd, Stam.-hill N	7	33..E	26
Lynn-road, Ilford . .	8	—..E	40
,, street, Balham SW	16	—..U	20
Lynton-av, Castlebar-hl W	9	—..L	5
,, rd, Acton W .	9	—..L	9
,, ,, Bermondsy. SE	17	53..P	27
,, ,, Croydon, Sury	26	—..Z^4	23
,, ,, Hornsey N .	2	—..C	22
,, ,, Kilburn NW .	10	34..J	15
,, ,, Nw M'ld'n, Sur.	25	—..Z^3	10
Lynwood-rd, U.Tooting SW	21	—..X	19
Lyon road, Harrow, Mdsx.	1a	—..D	4
,, st, Caledonian-rd, N	6	37..I	22
Lyric-road, Barnes SW .	15	—..R	11
Lysia-street, Fulham SW .	15	58..Q	13
Lysias-road, Balham SW .	16	—..U	19
Lytchett-rd, New Bromley	23	—..Z	34
Lytcott-grv, E. Dulwich SE	17	—..Z	26
Lyte-st, Victoria-park E .	12	39..J	28

	4-in. sht.	9-in. sht.	mar.
Lyttleton-rd, Lw. Leyton E	7	41..F	31
Lytton-grove, Putney SW .	15	—..U	14
,, road, Leytonstone E	7	—..D	33
Lyveden-rd, Blackheath SE	18	—..Q	34
Lyveden-rd, Tooting, SW..	20	—..Z	18

M

	4-in. sht.	9-in. sht.	mar.
Maberley-rd, Elmers End, Surrey	27	—..Z^2	28
Maberley-rd, Up. Norw'd,SE	22	—..Z^2	26
Mabledon-pl, Euston-rd,WC	11	45..K	21
Mablethorpe-rd, Fulhm SW	15	58..Q	14
Mabley st, Homerton E .	7	40..H	29
Macaulay-rd, Claphm SW	16	61..S	20
,, ,, E. Ham E .	13	—..J	33
Macclesfield-rd, S.NorwdSE	27	—..Z^3	27
,, st, City-rd EC	11	46..I	24
,, ,, Soho W.	11	45..M	21
McDermott-rd, Peckhm.SE	17	62..S	26
Macdonald-rd, Chapel End	3	—..A	32
,, ,, Forst.-gte.E	8	—..G	34
,, ,, Nw.SthgteN	2	—..A	19
McDowall-rd, Cmbwell. SE.	16	62..R	24
Macduff-rd, Battersea SW	16	60..R	19
Mace-st, Bethnal-green E .	12	47..J	28
Macfarlane-rd, Hmrsmthw	—	50..M	13
Macfarren-pl, Marylbne NW	11	44..K	19
Machell-road, Nunhead SE	17	63..S	28
Mackay-road, Clapham SW	16	61..S	20
Mackenzie-road, Penge .	22	—..Z^2	28
McKerrell-rd, Peckham SE	17	62..R	27
Mackeson-rd, Hampstd NW	6	36..G	19
Macklin-st, Drury-lane WC	11	45..L	22
Macks-road, Bermond'y SE	12	55..O	27
MacLaren-st, L. Clapton NE	—	40..G	29
Maclean-street, Brockley SE	4	—..U	29
McLeod-road, Abbey-wood	13	—..P	42
Maclise-rd, W. Knsngtn. W	10	50..Q	14
McNeil-rd, Camberwell SE .	16	62—R	25
Macoma-road, Plumstead .	18	—..Q	39
Macroom-road, Maida-hl. W	10	42..J	15
Maddin-rd, Lr. Sydenhm SE	22	—..X	29
Maddox-st, Regent-st. W .	11	41..M	20
Madeira-avenue, Bromley .	22	—..Z^2	33
,, rd, Leytonst'ne E.	7	—..F	33
,, ,, Mitcham, S'ry.	26	—..Z^2	19
,, ,, Streatham ;	21	—..Y	21
Madeley-road, Ealing W .	9	—..L	7
Madras-place, Holloway N	6	37..H	23
,, road, Ilford, Essex .	8	—..G	39
Madrid-road, Barnes SW .	15	58..Q	12
Mafeking-av, Brntfrd, Mdx.	14	—..P	7
,, ,, East Ham E	13	—..J	36
,, av, Seven Kings	8	—..E	40
,, rd, Canning T. E	12	49..K	33
,, ,, Tottenham N	3	—..B	27
Magdala-road, Isleworth .	14	—..S	5
,, ,, Up. HollowyN	6	—..F	20
Magdalen hospital, Strthm.	21	—..W	21
,, rd, Wndswth SW .	17	20..V	17
,, st, Brmndsy. SE .	12	45..N	25
Magenta-road, Woolwich .	18	—..P	39
Magnolia-road, Chiswick W	14	—..P	9
Magpie alley, Whitefriars-street, EC	—	45..M	23
Magpiehall-lane, Bromley, Kent	28	—..Z^4	36
Maida-hill West W .	10	43..K	17
,, vale NW . . .	10	43..J	17
Maiden-lane, Queen-st, EC	—	46..M	24
,, ,, Covent-gdn.WC	11	45..M	22
,, ,, railway station, N.L. railway	6	37..I	21
,, road, Stratford E	7	41..I	33
Maidenhead-ct, Aldersgate street EC. . . .	—	46..L	24
Maidenstone-hi, Grnwch.SE	4	64..R	31
Maidman-st, Mile End-rd.E	12	48..K	29
Maidstone-rd, Nw.Sthgte N	2	—..A	21
,, st, Gldsmths-rw.E	—	39..J	27
Maitland-gds, Twickenham	19	—..V	4
,, road, Penge SE .	22	—..Q^1	28
,, pk.-rd,HmpstdNW	6	36..H	19
,, ,, vil,HmpstdNW	6	36..H	19
Majendie-road, Plumstead	18	—..P	39
Maize-row, Limehouse E .	12	48..M	40
Major-road,Bermndsy, SE .	12	55..O	27
,, ,, Stratford E .	7	41..H	32
Malabar-street, Millwall E	12	56..O	30
Malbrook-road, Putney SW	15	—..T	13
Malcolm-rd, Wimbledon SW	20	—..Y	14
Malden, Surrey. . .	25	—..Z^1	10
,, cr, Kentish Tn. NW	6	36..H	20
,, green, Malden, Sy.	25	—..Z^5	11
,, hill, Nw.Malden,Sy.	25	—..Z^2	11
,, rd, Kentish Twn.NW	6	36..H	19
,, ,, Nw. Malden, Sy.	25	—..Z^2	10
,, hill-gardens, New Malden, Surrey	25	..—Z^2	11
Maldon-rd, Acton W . .	9	—..M	10
,, ,, Carshalton, Sy.	—	—..Z^7	20
,, ,, Lr. Edmonton N	3	—..A	27
Maley-avenue, W. Norwood	21	—..W	24
Malham-rd, Forest-hill SE .	22	—..V	28
Mall, The St. James's SW .	11	53..N	31
,, rd, Hammersmith W	15	58..P	13
Mallard-st, S. Hackney E .	7	40..H	30
Mallinson-rd, Battersea SW	16	60..T	18
Mallard-street, Chelsea SW	15	51..P	17
Mallow-street, City-rd. EC	11	46..K	25
Malmains way, Bromley .	27	—..Z^3	31
Malmesbury-rd, Bow E .	12	48..J	30
,, ,, Cann'g T.E	12	49..L	33
Malpas-road, Brockley SE .	4	63..S	29
Malt-st, Old Kent-rd. SE .	—	55..Q	27
,, ,, Percival-street EC	11	46..K	24
Malta-road, Leyton E .	7	—..E	30
,, street, Clerkenwell EC	11	46..K	24
Maltby-st, Bermondsey SE	12	54..O	26

	4-in. sht.	9-in. sht.	mar.
Malton-road, Malden. .	25	—..Z^6	12
Malton-street, Plumstead .	18	—..Q	40
Malva-rd, Wandsworth SW	15	—..U	16
Malvern-avenue, Hale End	3	—..A	32
,, rd, Croydon, Sy..	26	—..Z^3	23
,, ,, Dalston E .	7	39..I	27
,, ,, Hornsey N .	2	—..B	23
,, ,, Kilburn NW .	10	42..J	15
,, ,, Leytonstone E	7	—..F	33
,, ,, Long Ditton,Sy	24	—..Z^5	7
,, ,, Plaistow E .	13	—..J	36
,, ,, Tottenham N	3	—..B	27
Malwood-road, Balham SW	16	—..U	20
Malyons-rd, Lewisham SE .	4	—..U	31
Manaton-road, Peckham SE	17	62..S	27
Manby-grove, Stratford E .	7	41..H	33
,, park, Stratford E .	7	41..H	33
,, street, Stratford E	7	41..H	33
Manchester-av, Aldersgate street EC	—	46..L	24
,, rd, Cubitt Tn. E	17	57..P	32
,, ,, Notting-hl.W	—	50..L	14
,, ,, Thrntn. Hth	26	—..Z^2	24
,, ,, Tottenham N	7	33..D	25
,, square W. .	11	44..L	19
,, st, Mnchstr-sq.W	11	44..L	19
,, ,, Grays Inn road WC. . . .	11	45..K	22
Manchuria-rd, Clapham SW	16	—..U	19
Mandalay-rd, Clapham SW	16	—..U	20
Mandeville-pl,Wigmore-st.W	—	44..L	19
,, st, Clapton E .	7	40..G	29
Mandrake-rd,U.Tooting SW	20	—..W	18
Mandrell-road, Brixton SW	16	—..U	22
Manette-rd,Chng Crs.-rdWC	—	45..L	21
Manfred-road, Putney SW .	15	59..T	15
Manilla-street, Millwall E .	12	56..N	30
Manisty-street, Poplar E .	12	49..M	32
Mann-street, Walworth SE.	17	54..P	25
Mannoch-rd, Wood-green N	2	—..B	24
Manor gds, Holloway-rd. N.	6	37..F	22
,, ,, Merton SW .	20	—..Z^1	15
,, gr, Beckenham .	22	—..Z^2	31
,, ,, Old Kent-rd.SE	17	55..Q	28
,, ,, Richmond. .	14	—..S	8
,, ,, Lee SE. .	17	—..U	33
,, la, Rotherhithe SE .	17	55..P	28
,, ,, Sutton, Surrey .	29	—..Z^7	16
,, park, Essex E. .	8	—..H	36
,, ,, Lee SE . .	17	—..U	33
,, place, Hackney E .	7	33..H	27
,, ,, Paddington W	10	43..K	17
,, ,, Sutton, Sy. .	29	—..Z^7	16
,, ,, Walwth-rd.SE	16	54..P	24
,, rd, Beckenham .	22	—..Z^2	30
,, ,, Bowes-park N .	2	—..A	22
,, ,, Brockley-rd. SE	4	63..S	30
,, ,, Canning Twn E	12	49..K	33
,, ,, Carshalton, Sy.	30	—..Z^7	19
,, ,, Castlebar-hill W	9	—..L	5
,, ,, Forest-hill SE .	22	—..W	28
,, ,, Greenhill, Mdx.	1a	—..C	5
,, ,, Higham-hill E .	3	—..A	29
,, ,, Leyton E . .	7	—..E	31
,, ,, Manor-park E .	8	—..G	38
,, ,, Merton SW .	20	—..Z^1	14
,, ,, Norwood SE .	26	—..Z^2	26
,, ,, Plumstead SE .	18	—..P	40
,, ,, Richmond. .	14	—..S	8
,, ,, Sidcup, Kent .	23	—..X	41
,, ,, Stamford-hill N.	7	33..E	25
,, ,, Teddington. .	19	—..X	4
,, ,, Tottenham N .	3	—..A	27
,, ,, Twickenham .	19	—..V	2
,, ,, West Ham E .	12	41..J	33
,, ,, W. Moulsey, Sy.	24	—..Z^2	2
,, street, Chelsea SW .	16	52..P	18
,, ,, Clapham SW	16	61..S	21
,, ,, Woolwich,Kt.	18	—..Q	38
,, way, Beckenham .	27	—..Z^2	30
,, ,, Lee SE .	17	64..T	33
,, ,, N. Woolwich E	13	—..M	38
,, ct.-rd, Hanwell W .	9	—..L	3
,, pk. cemetery E .	8	—..G	36
,, ,, rd, Chslehst,Kt.	23	—..Z^1	39
,, ,, ,, E. Finchly N	2	—..B	17
,, ,, ,, Sutton, Sy.	29	—..Z^7	16
,, ,, ,, Willsdn. NW	5	—..J	11
,, ,, railway station, G.E. Ry. .	8	—..G	36
Manor way station railway North Woolwich E .	13	—..N	38
Manorgate-road, Norbiton	19	—..Z	8
Manresa-road, Chelsea SW	16	51..P	18
Mansel-rd, Wimbledon SW	20	—..Y	14
Mansell-gdns, Acton W .	10	—..N	10
,, st, Aldgate E .	12	47..M	26
Mansion House-st, Ham. W	10	58..O	13
Mansfield-rd, Croydon, Sy.	30	—..Z^8	24
,, ,, Hampstd.NW	6	36..G	19
,, ,, Ilford, Esx..	8	—..F	38
,, ,, Walthmstw.E	3	—..C	30
,, st, Kingsl'd-rd.E	12	39..J	26
,, ,, Portland-pl.W	11	44..L	20
Mansford-st, Hackney-rd.E	12	47..J	27
Mansion House EC . .	11	46..M	25
,, ,, place, Mansion House EC . .	11	46..M	25
Mansion house-street, EC .	—	46..M	25
,, ,, railway sta. District Rly. . . .	11	46..M	24
Mansion House-st, Kennington-pk.-rd. SE .	16	53..P	23
Manson-pla, S. Knsngtn SW	—	51..O	17
Manstone-rd, Cricklewd. NW	5	—..G	15
Mantell-street, Islington N	11	37..J	23
Manthorp-road, Woolwich.	18	—..P	39
Mantilla-road, Up. Tooting	21	—..X	19
Manton-road, Plumstead .	13	—..P	41
Mantle-road, Brockley SE .	—	53..S	29
Mantua-st, Battersea SW .	16	60..S	18
Manville-rd, Upr. Tooting	21	—..W	19

Manwood-road. INDEX TO STREETS, &c. Milford lane.

4-in. 9-in.
sht. sht. mar.
Manwood-road, Brockley SE 4 —..U 30
Mape-st, Bethnal-gr.-rd. E. 12 47..K 27
Mapesbury-rd, Kilburn NW 5 34..H 14
Maple-rd, Leytonstone E 7 —..D 33
„ „ Penge SE . . 22 —..Z¹ 27
„ „ Surbiton, Surrey 24 —..Z⁸ 6
„ st, Tottenhm-ct-rd.W — 44..K 21
Mapledene-road, Dalston E 7 39..I 27
Maplestead-rd, Up. Tulse-hl 21 —..V 22
Maplethorpe-rd, Croydon . 26 —..Z³ 23
Mapleton-rd, Wandswthsw 15 —..U 16
Maplin-st. Mile End-rd. E. 12 48..K 30
Marathon-av, Golders-gn.NW 1 —..C 15
Marble arch, Hyde-park W 11 44..M 19
„ „ ry. sta., Central London Railway . 11 44..M 19
Marcellus-rd, Hornsey-rd.N 6 32..F 22
March-road, Twickenham. 14 —..U 4
Marchant-st, Deptford SE. 17 56..Q 29
Marchmont-rd, Carshalton, Surrey . . . . 30 —..Z⁹ 20
Marchmont-rd, Richmond. 14 —..T 7
„ st,Bernrd-st.WC 11 45..K 22
Marchwood-cr, Ealing W . 9 —..L 6
Marcia-rd, Bermondsey SE 17 54..P 26
Marcus-st, Wandsworth SW 15 —..U 16
„ „ West Ham E 12 41..J 33
Mardale-road, Edmonton N 3 —..A 27
„ st, Shphds Bsh. W. 10 50..N 13
Marden-rd, Bermondsey SE 12 55..O 27
Marder-road, Ealing W . 9 —..N 5
Mare-court, Cheapside EC . — 46..M 24
„ street, Hackney E . 7 39..I 28
Maresfiel-gds, Hmpstd. NW 5 35..H 17
Margaret-st, Cavendish-sq.W11 44..L 20
„ st, Hackney E . 7 39..H 28
„ „ Clerkenwell WC 11 45..K 23
Margaretting-rd, Wanstead park E . . . . 8 —..F 36
Margate-road, Brixton SW 16 —..T 22
Margery-kp-rd,Fors't-gte.E 8 —..H 34
Margravine-gds,Hmsmth W 15 58..P 14
„ rd, Hmsmth.W 15 58..P 14
Margaretta-ter, Chelsea SW 16 51..P 18
Maria-st, Bethnal-green E. 12 47..J 27
„ „ Kingsland-rd. N 12 46..J 26
„ „ Millwall E . 12 56..O 30
Marigold-st, Brmndsy. SE. 11 55..O 27
Marine-st, Bermondsey SE 12 55..O 27
Marion-road, Mill Hill NW. 1 —..A 12
Marius-road, Balham. . 21 —..W 19
Marjorie-gro, Battersea SW 16 60..T 19
Mark-lane EC . . . . 12 46..M 26
„ road, Wood Green N] 2 —..A 24
„ street, Finsbury EC . 11 46..K 25
„ „ Stratford E . 7 41..I 33
Market-st, Jermyn-st. SW. — 45..M 21
Markhouse-av, Wlthmstw E 7 —..D 29
„ pl, Wlthmstw E 7 —..D 30
Mark.lane station EC. . 12 46..M 26
Market-pl, E. Finchley N . 2 —..B 18
„ „ Oxford-street W 11 44..L 20
„ rd, Caledonian-rd.N 6 37..H 22
„ „ Richmond . 14 —..S 8
„ st, Barnsbury N . 6 37..H 22
„ „ Bermondsey SE 12 54..N 25
„ „ East Ham E . 13 —..J 37
„ „ Edgware-roadW 11 43..L 18
„ „ Finsbury EC . — 46..L 25
„ „ Holloway N . 6 37..H 22
„ „ Mayfair W . — 44..N 20
„ „ Poplar E . . 12 48..M 31
„ „ Woolwich . 18 —..P 38
Markfield-rd, Tottenham N 3 —..C 27
Markham-sq, Chelsea SW . 16 52..P 18
„ street, Chelsea SW 16 52..P 18
Markhouse-rd, Waltham. E 7 —..D 30
Marl-st. Wandsworth SW . 15 60..T 16
Marlborough-gate, Bayswater-road, W . . . — 43..M 17
Marlborough-cres, Bedford-park W. . . . 10 —..O 10
Marlborough-ga, St. James' SW . . . . . 11 52..N 21
Marlborough-hi, St. John's Wood NW . . . 5 35..I 17
Marlborough-hill, Wealdstone, Middlesex . . 1a —..B 4
Marlborough-house, St. James's SW . . . . 11 52..N 21
Marlborough-la, Charlton . 18 —..Q 35
„ pl, St. John's Wood NW . . . 10 35..J 17
Marlborough-rd, Bedford park W . . . . 10 —..O 10
Marlborough-rd, Berm'y SE 17 55..P 27
Marlboro'-rd, Bowes.pk. N. 2 —..A 22
Marlborough-rd,Brmly,Kt. 23 —..Z³ 35
Marlborough-rd, ChingfordE 3 —..A 31
„ „ ChiswickW 14 —..P 9
„ „ Croyd, Sy. 30 ..—Z⁹ 24
„ „ Dalston E 7 39..I 27
„ „ Ealing W 9 —..N 7
„ „ Frst.-gteE 8 —..I 35
„ „ Holl'wy N 6 32..F 22
„ „ LwishmSE 17 64..T 32
„ „ LytnstneE 7 41..G 33
„ „ S. Wimbledon SW 21 —..Z¹ 18
„ „ Old Kent rd SE . 17 55..P 27
„ „ Richm'nd 14 —..U 7
„ „ St. Johns-Wood NW 10 35..J 17
„ „ S. Wimbledon SW . 20 —..Z 18
„ „ Wmblnsw 20 —..W 15
„ „ U. Holloway N . 6 32..E 22
„ „ Upton E . 8 —..I 35
„ „ Wealdstone Middlsx. 1a —..B 4
Marlborough-sq, Chelsea W 16 51..P 18
„ st, Grnwch SE 17 57..P 32
„ rd. sta., Met. Railway. 5 35..I 17
Marler-rd, Forest-hill SE . 22 —..W 29
Marloes-rd, Kensington W 10 51..O 16
Marlow-rd, Homerton E . 7 40—H 29
„ „ S. Norwood SE 27 —..Z² 27
Marlton-st, E. Grnwch SE. 17 57..P 34
Marmadon-rd, Plumstead . 18 —..P 40
Marmion-rd, Battersea SW 16 60..T 19
Marmont-road, Peckham SE 17 62..R 27
Marmora-rd, Honor Oak SE 17 —..U 28
Marne-st, Queens-park W . 10 42..J 14
Marner-street, Bromley E . 12 49..K 31
Marney-road, Battersea SW 16 60..T 19
Marnock-road, Brockley SE 17 —..U 29
Maroon-street, Stepney E . 12 48..L 29
Marquess-rd, Canonbury N 6 38..H 24
Marquis-rd, Camden Twn NW 6 37..H 21
„ „ Finsbury-pk.N 6 32..E 23
Marriott-rd, Finsbury-pk.N 6 32..E 23
Marryatt-rd, Wimbledon SW 20 —..X 14
„ st, Hmrsmth W . 15 58..P 13
Marsala-rd, Lewisham SE 4 63..T 31
Mardsen-rd, E. Dulwich SE 17 62..T 26
„ st, Kentish T'n NW 6 36..H 19
Marsh-hill, Homerton E . 7 40..H 29
„ lane, Low Leyton E 7 —..F 30
„ „ Stanmore, Mx. 1a —..A 7
„ place, Putney SW . 15 59..S 13
„ Farm-rd, Twick'm . 19 —..V 3
„ Gate-lane, Bow E . 12 41..J 31
Marshall-rd, Lewisham SE 17 64..T 32
„ st, Golden-sq. W . 11 44..M 21
„ „ Southwark SE 11 54..O 24
Marshall's-rd, Sutton, Sy. 29 —..Z⁷ 16
Marshalsea-rd, Borough SE 11 54..N 24
Marsham-st, Westmnstr SW 11 53..O 21
Marshfield-st, Isle of Dogs E 12 57..O 32
Marsland-rd, Newington SE 16 54..P 24
Martell-road, W. Dulwich . 21 —..X 24
Marten-rd, Chapel End E . 3 —..A 31
Martha-road, Wanstead E 8 —..D 35
„ street, Shadwell E 12 47..M 28
Martin-rd, Victoria Dock E 13 —..M 34
„ street, Stratford E 7 41..I 32
Martindale-rd, Balham SW 21 —..V 20
„ „ Can'g T'n E 13 —..M 34
„ „ E. Sheen SW 14 —..T 9
Martins-la, Cannon-st. EC. 11 46..M 25
Martin-st, Bermondsey SE. 12 55..O 27
Martletts-court, Bow-st. WC — 45..M 22
Marville-road, Fulham SW. 15 58..Q 15
Mary-place, Notting-hill W 10 50..M 14
„ st, Canning Town E 12 49..L 33
Mary Ann-st, Deptford SE 17 56..Q 30
„ „ N. WoolwichE 13 —..N 37
Marygold-st, Bermond. SE. 12 55..O 27
Maryland-pk, Stratford E . 7 41..H 33
„ point, Stratford E 7 41..H 33
„ rd, Wood-green N 2 —..A 23
„ „ Stratford E . 7 41..H 32
„ sq. Stratford E . 7 41..H 33
„ st, Stratford E . 7 41..H 33
„ Point rly. sta., G.E. Rly. . . . . 7 41..H 33
Marylands-rd, Maida-hl. W 10 43..K 16
Marylebone NW. . . . 11 44..K 18
„ la, Oxford-st W 11 44..L 20
„ road, NW . . 11 44..L 18
„ ry. sta., G.C.Ry 11 44..K 18
„ st, Maryl'b'new— 44..L 19
„ Workhouse, Marylebone-rd, W. . . 11 44..L 19
Maryon-park, Charlton . 18 —..P 36
„ rd, Charlton. . 18 —..P 36
Marys-road, Plaistow E . 13 —..J 35
Masbro'rd, W. Kensingtonw 10 50..O 14
Mascotte-road, Putney SW. 15 59..S 14
Maskell-road, Earlsfield SW 20 —..X 16
Mason-st, Walworth SE . 17 54..P 25
„ „ Woolwich . . 18 —..P 37
Masons-av. Basinghall-st.EC— 46..L 25
„ „ Wealdstne.Mx. 1a —..B 4
„ hl, Bromley, Kent 28 —..Z³ 34
„ Green-la, Ealing W 9 —..K 8
Massinger-st, O. Kent-rd.SE 17 54..P 25
Maswell-park, Hounslow. 14 —..S 2
Matcham-rd, LeytonstoneE 7 41..G 33
Matham-gr, E. Dulwich SE. 17 62..T 26
„ rd, East Moulsey. 24 —..Z² 7
Matheson-rd, Kensington W 10 58..O 15
Matilda-street, Islington N 6 37..I 23
„ st, O. Bthnl-gr.-rd.E12 47..J 27
Matlock-lane, Ealing W . 9 —..M 6
„ road, Leyton E . 7 —..D 32
„ street, Stepney E 12 48..L 29
Matthews-st, Battersea SW 16 60..R 18
„ pk-rd, StratfordE 7 —..I 34
Matthias-rd, Stk. Nwngtn.N 7 38..G 25
Mattison-rd,Finsbury-pk.N 6 —..D 24
Matlock-lane, Ealing . 9 —..M 6
Maud-pl, S. Lambeth SW . 16 53..Q 22
„ road, Leyton E . 7 —..G 32
„ „ Plaistow E. . 13 —..J 34
„ st, Canning Town E 12 49..L 33
Maude-gdns, Walthamstw.E 3 —..C 29
„ rd, Camberwell SE. 16 62..R 25
Mauleverer-rd, Brixton SW 16 —..T 22
Maurice-av, Wood Green N 2 —..A 24
Mauritius-st, E. Grnwch SE 17 57..P 33
Maury-rd, Stk. Nwngtn. N. 7 33..F 27
Mauve-street, Bromley E . 12 49..L 31
Mavelstone-rd, Widmore . 23 —..Z¹ 36
Mawbey-rd, O. Kent-rd. SE 17 55..P 26
„ st, S. Lambeth SW 16 53..Q 22
Mawson-lane, Chiswick W . 15 —..P 11
Maxey-road, Plumstead. 18 —..P 39
Maxilla-gds, N. Kens'g'n W 10 42..L 14
Maxted-park, Harrow . 1a —..D 4
„ road, Peckham SE. 17 62..S 23
Maxwell-rd, Walham-gr. SW 15 51..Q 16
May-road, Low Leyton E . 7 —..F 30
„ st, W. Kensington W 15 58..P 15
Mayall-road, Brixton SE . 16 61..T 23
Maybury-gds, Wisdn.gr.NW 5 34..H 12
„ st, Lr. Tooting SW 21 —..Y 18
Mayes-rd N., Wood-gr'n N 2 —..A 23
Mayfair, W. . . . . 11 44..N 20
„ avenue, Ilford . 8 —..F 38
Mayfield-av, Chiswick W . 10 —..O 11
„ rd, Acton W . 9 —..L 9
„ „ Croydon, Sy. 30 —..Z⁹ 25
„ „ Dalston E . 7 39..I 26
„ „ Higham-hill E 3 —..A 29
„ „ Hornsey N . 6 32..D 23
„ „ Merton SW . 20 —..Z 15
„ „ Sutton, Surrey 29 —..Z⁸ 17
Mayflower-rd, Stockwell SW 16 61..S 22
Mayford-road, Balham . 21 —..V 19
Maygood-st, Islington N . 11 37..J 23
Maygrove-road, Kilburn NW 5 —..H 15
Mayhill-road, Charlton . 18 —..Q 34
Maynard-rd, R'th'rh'the SE 12 55..O 29
„ „ W'lthstw. E . 3 —..C 32
Mayo-road, Croydon, Sy. . 26 —..Z² 24
„ „ Willesden NW . 5 —..H 11
„ „ Wembley . . 4 —..F 6
Mayola-road, Clapton E . 7 39..G 28
Mayow-road, Sydenham SE 22 —..X 28
Mays Hill-rd, Brmley, Knt 27 —..Z³ 33
Maysoule-rd, Battersea SW 15 60..T 17
Mayton-strret, Holloway N 6 32..F 22
Mayville-rd, Leytonstone E 7 —..F 33
„ st, Stk. Nwgton E. — 38..G 25
Maze-hill, Greenwich SE . 17 57..Q 33
„ pond, Southwark SE 12 54..N 25
„ „ ter, Borough SE — 54..N 25
„ road, Kew . . . 14 —..Q 8
„ hill ry. sta. Greenwich SE. . . . . 17 57..Q 33
Mazenod-av, Kilburn NW 5 —..I 16
Mead-la, Seven Kings, Esx 8 —..E 41
„ place, Hackney E . 7 39..H 28
„ „ Croydon, Sy. . 26 —..Z³ 24
„ rd, Chislehurst, Kent 23 —..Z 38
„ row, Westminster Bridge-road, SE. . 11 53..O 23
Meadow-la, Mitcham, Sy. . 26 —..Z⁸ 19
„ road, Bromley . 22 —..Z³ 33
„ rd, S. Lambeth SW 16 53..Q 22
„ „ Merton SW . 20 —..Z 17
„ „ Sutton, Surrey 29 —..Z⁷ 17
„ walk, Ewell, Sy. . 29 —..Z⁸ 10
Meadowcourt-road, Lee SE 17 —..T 33
Meads-road, Edgware, Mx. 1a —..A 8
„ „ Stk. Nwgtn.N 12 —..B 24
Meadvale-rd, Castlebar-hl.W 9 —..K 6
Meadway, Hampstead NW 5 —..D 16
Meakin-rd, Manor-park E 8 —..H 37
Meards-street, Soho W . — 45..M 21
Meath-gds, Bethnal-green E 12 48..K 29
„ road, Ilford, Essex 8 —..G 39
„ „ West Ham E . 12 41..J 33
Mecklenburg-square, WC . 11 45..K 22
Mecklenburgh-st, Mecklenburgh-square WC . . — 45..K 22
Medburn-st, Somers T'n NW 11 37..J 21
Medfield-st, Rochmpt'n SW 15 —..U 12
Medhurst-rd, Bethnal-gr. E 12 48..J 29
Median-road, Clapton E . 7 39..G 28
Medina-road, Holloway N . 6 32..F 22
Medora-road, Brixton SW . 16 —..U 22
Medland-st, Limehouse E . 12 —..M 29
Medlar-st, Camberwell SE. 16 62..R 24
Medusa-road, Catford SE . 4 —..U 31
Medway-rd, Bethnal-gr. E 12 48..J 29
„ st, W'stm'nster SW 11 53..O 21
Medwin-street, Brixton SW 16 61..T 22
Meeks-road, Chelsea SW . 15 51..Q 17
Meeson-road, Stratford E 7 41..I 33
Meeting Hse.la, Pckh'm.SE 17 62..R 27
Mehetabel-rd, Homerton SE 7 39..H 28
Melbourne-av. Bowes-pk. N 2 —..A 23
„ „ Ealing Dn W 9 —..M 5
„ gr, E. Dlwch SE 17 62..T 26
„ pla, Strand WC 11 45..M 22
„ rd, CarshaltonSy.30 —..Z⁸ 20
„ „ East Ham E 13 —..J 37
„ „ Ilford, Essex 8 —..F 39
„ „ Leyton E . 7 —..E 31
„ „ Merton SW . 20 —..Z¹ 15
„ „ Wlthstw.WE 3 —..B 30
„ sq, Stockwell SW 16 61..R 23
Melbury-gds, Wimbled'n SW 20 —..Z 12
„ rd, Addison-rd. W 10 50..O 15
Melford-road, Dulwich SE. 22 —..V 27
„ „ Ilford, Essex . 8 —..F 40
„ „ Leytonstone E 7 —..F 33
„ street, Plaistow E 13 —..K 34
Melfort-road, Norbury . 21 —..Z² 22
„ „ Thornton Hth 26 —..Z² 23
Melina-pl, St. Johns-wd NW 10 43..K 17
„ rd, Shepherds Bshw 10 50..N 12
Melior-st, Bermondsey SE. — 54..N 25
Melling-street, Plumstead . 18 —..Q 40
Mellish-street, Millwall E . 12 56..O 31
Mellison-road, Tooting SW 20 —..Y 18
Mellows-rd, Carshalton Sy. 30 —..Z⁸ 21
Melody-rd, Wandsworth SW 15 —..T 17
Melon-road, Peckham SE . 17 62..R 26
Melrose-av, Cricklew'd NW 5 —..G 13
„ „ Lr. Str'th'm SW 21 —..Z¹ 20
„ „ Norbury, Sy. . 26 —..Z² 22
„ gds, Putney SW . 15 —..U 14
„ „ New Malden . 25 —..Z² 10
„ „ W. Kns'g'n W 10 50..N 13
„ road, Barnes SW . 15 —..R 11
„ „ Merton SW . 20 —..Z¹ 15
„ „ Wandsworth SW 15 —..U 15
„ „ Wood-green N 2 —..A 24
„ ter, Shep. B.-rd, W — 50..N 13
Melton-road, Tottenham N 3 —..C 26
Melton-st, Euston-sq. NW. 11 45..K 21
Melville-av, Croydon, Sy.. 30 —..Z 26
„ road, Barnes SW . 15 —..R 11
„ av, Walthamstow E 3 —..B 30
„ „ Willesden NW 5 —..I 10
Melvin-road, Penge SE . 22 —..Z³ 27
Memorial-av, Canning T'n E 12 49..K 33
Mendip-rd, Battersea SW . 15 60..S 17
Mendora-road, Fulham SW 15 58..Q 15
Menelik-rd, Hampstead NW 5 —..G 15
Menotti-st, Bethnal Gr'n E 12 47..K 27
Mentmore-ter, Hackney E 7 39..I 27
Meon-road, Acton W . . 9 —..N 10
Mepham-st, W't'rloo-rd. SE 11 53..N 23
Mercer-st, Long-acre WC . 11 45..M 22
Mercers-road, Holloway N 6 37..F 21
Merchant-street, Bow-rd. E 12 48..K 30
Merchiston-rd, Catford SE 22 —..W 32
Merchland-rd, New Eltham Kent . . . . 23 —..W 39
Meredith-road, Barnes SW 15 —..R 12
„ st, Clerkenwell EC 11 46..K 23
„ „ Plaistow E . 13 —..K 34
Mereway-rd, Twickenham 19 —..V 3
Merivale-road, Putney SW 15 59..S 14
Merlin-rd, Wanstead-pk. E 8 —..F 36
Merritt-road, Brockley SE 4 —..U 29
Merrick-sq, Borough SE . 11 54..O 25
Merriam-av, Chingford E 3 —..A 32
Merritt-road, Brockley SE 17 —..U 29
Merrivale-rd, Harrow, Msx 1a —..D 3
Merrow-st, Walworth SE . 17 54..P 25
Mersey-rd, Walthamstow E 3 —..B 30
Mersham-rd, Thornton Heath, Surrey . . 26 —..Z³ 24
Merthyr-road, Barnes SW . 15 58..P 13
Mertins-road, Nunhead SE 17 —..T 28
Merton SW. . . . . 20 —..Z 16
„ av, Chiswick W . 10 —..O 11
„ bridge, Merton SW 20 —..Z 17
„ lane, Highgate N . 6 31..E 19
„ rd, Kensington W. 10 51..O 16
„ „ Merton SW . 20 —..Z 15
„ „ Norwood SE . 26 —..Z³ 26
„ „ St. J'ns-wd. NW 5 36..I 18
„ „ Wandsworth SW 15 —..U 15
„ „ Wimbn-pk. SW 20 —..V 15
„ Abbey sta, Mrtnsw 20 —..Z 14
Merton Hall-rd, Merton SW 20 —..Z 14
„ Pk. sta, Merton SW 20 —..Z 15
Mervan-road, Brixton SW. 16 61..T 23
Mervyn-road, Ealing . 9 —..N 5
Messaline-road, Acton W . 9 —..L 10
Messeter-place, Eltham . 18 —..U 37
Messina-av, Kilburn NW . 5 —..I 15
Meteor-st,Clphm. Com.NSW 16 60..T 19
Methuen-pk, Muswell-hill N 2 —..B 20
Met. Asy. Bd. Hospital, Belmont, Sutton . . 29 —..Q¹⁰ 6
Metropolitan Cattle Market, Islington N . . 6 37..H 22
Metropolitan Meat Mkt., W. Smithfield EC. . . 11 46..L 24
Mexfield rd, Wndsworth SW 15 59..T 15
Meymott-st, Blckfr'rs-rd SE 11 54..N 23
Meynell-crescent, Hackney E 7 39..I 28
„ rd, S. Hackney E 7 40..I 29
Meyrick-rd, Battersea SW . 15 60..S 17
„ „ Willesden NW. 5 34..H 12
Miall-road, Sydenham SE . 22 —..X 29
Micheldever-road, Lee SE. 17 —..U 33
Middle-row, Kensal-Gr. W 10 42..K 14
„ lane, Hornsey N . 2 —..C 22
„ „ Epsom . . 29 —..Z¹¹ 10
„ pl, Gt. Queen-st. WC— 45..L 22
„ row, Old-street EC. — 46..K 24
„ street, Dalston E . 7 39..G 26
„ „ Long-la. EC — 46..L 24
„ New-st, Fetter-la EC — 45..L 23
„ Temple-lane, EC . 11 45..M 23
Middlesborough-rd, Edmonton N . . . . 3 —..A 27
Middlesex-st, Aldgate E . 12 46..L 26
„ County Lunatic Asylum, Wandsworth SW 20 —..W 18
Middlesex Sessions House, Westminster SW . . — 53..N 21
Middleton-rd,Camden-rd. N — 37..G 22
„ „ Dalston N . 7 39..I 26
„ „ Hmpstd. NW 5 —..D 16
„ st, Bethnal G. E 12 47..J 27
Midhurst-av, Muswell-hl.N 2 —..B 19
„ road, Ealing W 9 —..N 5
Midland rly. ter. NW . . 11 45..J 22
„ road, Leyton E . 7 —..E 32
„ rd, St. Pancras NW 11 45..J 22
„ terrace, Acton NW 10 —..K 11
„ „ Cricklew'd NW 5 —..F 14
Midmoor-road, Balham SW 21 —..V 20
„ „ Wmbledns W 14 20..Z 14
Milborne-gr, W. Brmptn SW — 51..P 17
Milbourne-la, Claremont,Sy 28a —..Z⁷ 1
Mildenhall-rd, Clapton E . 7 39..G 28
Mildmay-gr, Mildmay-pk.N 7 38..H 25
„ park N . . . 7 38..H 25
„ pk. rly. sta.,N.L.Ry 7 38..H 25
„ rd, Mildmay-pk. N 7 38..H 25
„ st, Mildmay-pk.N 7 38..H 25
Mildred-court, Poultry EC 11 46..M 25
Mildreds-road, Lee SE . 22 —..V 33
Mile End E. . . . . 12 47..K 29
„ „ road E . . . 12 48..K 29
„ „ rly. sta., District & L.T.S.R. E . . . 12 A48..K 29
Miles-lane, Mitcham. . 25 —..Z² 18
„ „ Up. Th'mes-st.EC— 46..M 25
„ road, Epsom . . 28 —..Z¹¹ 10
„ „ Hornsey N . 2 —..B 22
„ st, Hammersmith W 15 58..O 12
„ „ Vauxhall SW . 16 53..Q 22
Milespit-hill, Mill Hill NW. 1 —..A 13
Milford-lane, Strand WC . 11 45..M 23

Milford-road. INDEX TO STREETS, &c. **Myron-place.**

	4-in. sht.	9-in. sht.	mar.
Milford-rd, Ealing Dean W	9	—..M	5
,, ,, Twickenham	14	—..T	5
,, st, S. Lambeth SW	16	61..S	20
Milk-street, Cheapside EC .	11	46..L	24
,, ,, N. Woolwich E	13	—..N	38
,, yard, Shadwell E .	12	47..M	28
Milkwood-rd, Herne-hill SE	16	—..T	24
Mill-hill NW	1	—..A	13
,, ,, brcks, Mill-hill NW	1	—..A	15
,, ,, grove, Acton W .	9	—..N	9
,, ,, la, Bowes-park N .	2	—..A	24
,, ,, road, Acton W .	9	—..N	9
,, ,, sta, G.N.Rly. NW .	1	—..A	15
,, ,, ,, G.N.Rly. NW .	1	—..A	15
,, ,, ,, Mid. Rly. NW .	1	—..A	11
,, ,, pk. rly. sta, Met. Ry	9	—..N	8
,, lane, Brixton-hill .	21	—..V	22
,, ,, Carshalton, Sy. .	30	—..Z^{7}	19
,, ,, Kilburn NW .	5	—..G	15
,, ,, Waddon, Surrey	26	—..Z^{6}	22
,, ,, Woolwich . .	18	—..P	38
,, place, Limehouse E .	12	48..M	29
,, road, Epsom, Surrey .	29	—..Z^{11}	11
,, ,, Lewisham SE .	4	63..S	31
,, ,, Merton SW .	20	—..Z	17
,, ,, New Hampton .	19	—..X	1
,, row, Kingsland-rd. N .	12	38..J	26
,, street, Bermondsey SE	12	55..N	26
,, ,, Hanover-sq. W	11	44..M	20
,, ,, Kingston. .	19	—..Z^{1}	7
Millais-road, Leyton E .	7	41..G	32
Millbank, Westminster SW	11	53..O	22
Millbrook-road, Brixton SW	16	61..S	23
Miller-rd, S. Wimbledon SW	20	—..Y	17
Millfield-lane, Highgate N .	6	31..F	19
,, road, Edmonton N	3	—..A	25
Millfields-road, Clapton E .	7	39..G	28
Millicent-rd, Wlthamstw. E	7	—..E	30
Millstream-rd, Brmondsy SE	12	55..O	26
Millwall, Poplar E . .	12	56—O	30
Millwall Docks, Millwall E	12	56..O	31
,, ,, sta, G.E. rly, Millwall E . .	12	56..O	31
Millwall Junction rly. sta, G.E. Railway .	12	49..M	31
Millman-st, Guilford-st, WC	11	45..K	22
Milman-rd, Kensal Gr. NW	10	34..J	14
Milmans-street, Chelsea SW	16	51..Q	17
Milner-rd, Canning Town E	12	49..K	33
,, ,, Kingston . .	24	—..Z^{2}	6
,, ,, Merton SW .	20	—..Z	16
,, ,, Mitcham, Surrey	25	—..Z^{3}	17
,, square, Islington W	6	38..I	23
,, street, Chelsea SW .	11	52..O	18
Milnthorpe-rd, Chiswick W	14	—..P	10
Milo-rd, East Dulwich SE .	17	—..U	26
Milson-rd, W. Kensingtn W	10	50..O	14
Milstead-st, Brixton SW .	16	—..U	22
Milton-av, East Ham E .	8	—..I	26
,, ,, Highgate N .	6	32..D	21
,, ,, Willesden NW .	5	—..I	10
,, gr, Up. Holloway N	6	32..F	21
,, park, Highgate N .	6	32..D	21
,, road, Acton W. .	9	—..M	10
,, ,, Carshalton Sy	30	—..Z^{8}	20
,, ,, Croydon S'y.	26	—..Z^{5}	25
,, ,, Deptford SE .	17	56..Q	29
,, ,, East Sheen SW	14	—..S	10
,, ,, Kingston .	24	—..Z^{2}	6
,, ,, Hanwell W .	9	—..L	4
,, ,, Hendon NW .	5	—..D	12
,, ,, Herne Hill SE	16	—..U	23
,, ,, Highgate N .	6	32..D	21
,, ,, Mill Hill NW .	—	—..A^{1}	12
,, ,, Old Ford-rd E	12	40..J	30
,, ,, Plaistow E .	13	—..J	34
,, ,, S.Wmbledn.SW	16	20..Y	16
,, ,, Sto. Newgn N	7	38..G	25
,, ,, Sutton, Sur'y	25	—..Z^{6}	15
,, ,, Tottenham N	2	—..B	24
,, ,, U. Edmton. N	3	—..A	26
,, ,, Walthmstw E	3	—..C	31
,, ,, Wndswrth SW	21	—..V	17
,, ,, Wealstn. Mx.	—	—..B	4
,, st, Cripplegate EC .	11	46..L	25
,, ,, S. Lambeth SW	16	61..R	21
,, court-rd, New Cross road SE	17	56..Q	29
Milverton-gds, Seven Kings, Essex .	8	—..F	41
,, rd, Willesden NW	5	—..I	14
Milward-st, Whitechapel E	12	47..L	27
,, ,, Woolwich	18	—..Q	38
Mimosa-street, Fulham SW	—	59—R	15
Mina-road, Bermondsey SE	17	54..P	26
,, ,, Merton SW .	20	—..Z	15
Minard-road, Catford SE .	22	—..W	32
Mincing-la, Fenchurch-st EC	11	46..M	25
Minden-road, Penge SE .	22	—..Z^{2}	27
Minehead-rd, L. Strthm SW	21	—..Y	22
Mineral-street, Plumstead	18	—..P	40
Minerva-road, Kingston .	19	—..Z^{1}	7
,, st, O. Beth.-gr.-rd E	12	47..J	27
Minet-av, Harlesden NW .	10	—..J	11
Minford-gds, W. Kensgtn W	10	50—N	13
Minories E.	12	46..M	26
Minster-rd, New Bromley .	23	—..Z	34
,, ,, Kilburn NW .	5	—..H	15
,, ,, Tottenham N .	7	—..D	25
Mint, The, Tower-hill E .	11	47..M	26
,, rd, Carshalton, Sur.	30	—..Z^{7}	19
,, street, Borough SE .	11	54..N	24
Mintern-street, Hoxton N .	11	46..J	25
Mirabel-road, Fulham SW .	15	58..Q	15
Miranda-rd, Up. Holloway N	6	32..E	21
Miriam-road, Plumstead .	18	—..P	40
Mistears-bldgs, Rthrhte. SE	12	—..N	29
Mitcham Surrey . .	25	—..Z^{2}	18
,, common, Surrey	26	—..Z^{3}	20
,, lane, Streatham .	21	—..Z^{1}	20
,, park, Mitcham .	25	—..Z^{3}	18
,, rd, Croydon, S'y.	26	—..Z^{4}	21

	4-in. sht.	9-in. sht.	mar.
Mitcham-rd, Lr Tooting SW	20	—..Y	18
,, st, St. Lukes EC .	11	46..K	24
,, rly sta, L.B. & S.C. Railway .	25	—..Z^{3}	18
,, Jct. rly. sta, L.B. & S.C. Railway . .	26	—..Z^{3}	19
Mitchell-st, St. Lukes EC .	11	46..K	24
Mitchley-rd, Tottenham N	3	—..B	27
Mitford-rd, Up. Holloway N	6	32..F	22
Mitre-court, Fleet-street EC	—	45..M	23
,, ,, St. John-st. EC	—	46..L	24
,, ,, Wood-st EC .	—	46..L	24
,, square, Aldgate EC .	—	46..M	26
,, street, Aldgate EC .	11	46..M	26
,, ,, Waterloo-rd SE.	11	53..N	23
Moat-place, Stockwell SW .	16	61..S	22
Modbury-st, Kentish T'n NW	6	36..H	19
Moffat-road, L. Tooting SW	20	—..X	18
,, ,, Nw.Sthgate. N	2	—..A	22
,, ,, Thornton Hth	21	—..Z^{2}	25
,, ,, Thrntn Hth S'y	26	—..Z^{2}	24
Mogden-lane, Isleworth .	14	—..T	4
Molesey-pk.-rd, W. Moulsey Surrey	24	—..Z^{3}	1
Molesworth, Lewisham SE	4	64..S	31
,, st, Lewishm SE	17	64..T	31
Molyneux-st, Edgware-rd W	11	44..L	18
Mona-road, Hatcham SE .	17	63..R	28
Monahan-avenue, Purley .	30	..—Z^{11}	22
Monck-st, Westminster SW	11	53..O	21
Moncrieff-st, Peckham SE .	17	62..R	27
Monega-road, Manor-pk. E	8	—..H	36
Moness-street, Poplar E .	12	49..L	32
Moneyer-street, Hoxton N	11	46..J	25
Monier-road, Old Ford E .	7	40..I	30
Monivea-road, Beckenham	22	—..Z^{1}	30
Monk-street, Woolwich .	18	—..P	38
Monkton-st, Kennington SE	11	53..P	23
Monkwell-street, EC . .	11	46..L	24
Monmouth-crt, Whitcomb-street WC .	—	45..M	21
,, rd, Bayswtr W.	—	43..L	16
Monnery-rd, Up. Hlwy. N .	6	37..F	21
Monnow-rd, Bermondsey SE	17	55..P	27
Monsell-rd, Finsbury-pk N	6	32..F	24
Monsey-street, Stepney E .	12	48..L	29
Monson-road, Deptford SE	17	55..Q	28
,, ,, Harlesden NW	10	42..J	12
Monster, The, Pimlico SW.	—	52..P	20
Montagu-pla, Montagu-sq W	11	44..L	19
,, sq, Marylebone W	11	44..L	19
,, st, Montagu-sq W	11	44..L	19
Montague-av, Brockley SE	4	63..T	30
,, close, Borough, High-street SE . .	12	46..N	25
Montague-crt, Lt Britain EC	—	46..L	24
Montague-gds, Acton W .	9	—..M	8
,, ,, Carshalton, Sy	30	—..Z^{7}	20
,, pl, Bedfrd-sq. WC	11	45..L	41
,, ,, Poplar E	12	49..M	30
,, rd, Castlebar-hl W	9	—..L	5
,, ,, Clapton E .	7	39..H	27
,, ,, Croydon, Sy	26	—..Z^{5}	23
,, ,, Edmonton N	3	—..A	28
,, ,, Hendon NW	5	—..D	12
,, ,, Hornsey N .	2	—..C	22
,, ,, Hounslow .	14	—..R	1
,, ,, Leytonstne E	7	—..F	33
,, ,, Merton SW .	20	—..Z	16
,, ,, Richmond .	14	—..T	7
,, ,, S. Hackney E	7	40..H	30
,, ,, Tottenham N	3	—..B	27
,, st, Russell-sq. WC	11	45..L	22
Montana-rd, Wimbledn SW	20	—..Z^{1}	13
Montclare-st, Bethnal-gr. E	12	47..K	26
Monteagle-av, Barking, E'x	8	—..I	39
Monteith-road, Old Ford E	7	40..I	30
Montem-rd, Forest Hill SE	22	—..V	29
,, ,, N. Malden Sy	25	—..Z^{2}	10
,, st, Finsbury-pk. N	6	32..E	22
Montenotte-rd Crch End N.	6	—..D	21
,, ,, Hornsey N	2	—..D	21
Montford-pl, Up. Kennington-lane, SE	11	53..P	23
Montgomery-rd, Edgeware Middlesex . . .	1a	—..A	8
Montgomery-rd, S. Acton W	9	—..O	9
Montholme-rd, Batt'rs'a SW	16	—..U	18
Montolieu-gdns, Putney SW	15	—..T	13
Montpelier-rise, Hendon NW	5	—..D	14
,, rd, Blackhth SW	17	64..S	33
,, ,, Ealing W .	9	—..K	7
,, ,, Croydon Sy.	30	—..Z^{10}	23
,, ,, KntshTn. NW	6	37..G	21
,, ,, Peckham SE	17	63..R	27
,, ,, S.Knsgtn SW	11	52..O	18
,, ,, Sutton, Sur	29	—..Z^{7}	17
,, ,, W. Ealing W	9	—..K	6
,, row, Blckhth SE	17	—..S	33
,, st, Bmptn-rd SW	10	52..O	18
,, ,, Walworth SE	—	54..Q	24
,, sq, S. Knsgtn SW	11	52..O	18
,, vale, Blckhth SE	17	64..S	33
Montreal-rd, Ilford, Essex	8	—..E	39
Montrell-rd, Streatham-hill	21	—..V	22
Montrose-av, Queens-pk NW	10	34..J	15
,, gr, Sudb'ry, Mdx	4	—..H	7
,, rd, Finchley N .	1	—..A	17
,, ,, Wldstn. Mdx. .	1a	—..A	4
Montserrat-rd, Putney SW.	15	59..T	14
Monument London Bdge EC	11	46..M	25
,, st, Lndn Br. EC	11	46..M	25
Moody-street, Mile End E .	12	48..K	29
Mooltan-st, Fulham SW	—	58..Q	15
Moor-lane, City EC . .	11	46..L	25
,, ,, Hook, Surrey .	28a	—..Z^{7}	7
,, Mead-rd, Twickenhm	14	—..U	5
,, street, Soho W . .	11	45..M	21
Moore-pk.-rd, Fulham SW	15	51..Q	16
,, street, Chelsea SW .	11	52..O	19
Mooreland-road, Bromley .	22	—..Z^{1}	33
Moorfield-rd, Orpington, Kt	28	—..Z^{4}	41

	4-in. sht.	9-in. sht.	mar.
Moorfields EC . . .	11	46..L	25
Moorgate-pl, Mrgte-st, EC .	—	46..L	25
,, st, EC . .	11	46..L	25
,, ,, buildings EC .	—	46..L	25
,, ,, rly. station EC	11	46..L	25
Mora-road, Cricklewood NW	5	—..G	13
Morant-street, Poplar E .	12	48..M	30
Moray-rd, Finsbury-pk N .	6	32..E	23
,, ,, Tollington-pk N	6	32..F	23
Morches-place, Putney SW	15	59..S	13
Mordaunt-rd, Harlesden NW	5	—..I	10
,, st, Stockwell SW	16	61..S	22
Morden, Surrey. . .	25	—..Z^{1}	15
,, common, Surrey .	25	—..Z^{4}	13
,, gr, Lewisham SE .	4	63..S	31
,, hill, Lewisham SE	4	64..S	31
,, park, Surrey .	25	—..Z^{1}	15
,, rd, Blackheath SE	18	—..S	34
,, ,, Merton SW .	20	—..Z^{1}	16
,, ,, Mitcham, Sy.	25	—..Z^{2}	17
,, st, Lewisham SE .	4	63..R	31
,, sta, Wimbledon & Croyd. Ry., Merton SW	20	—..Z^{1}	16
Morden Wharf-rd, Greenwich SE . . .	12	57..O	33
Morecambe-st, Wlwrth SE	16	54..P	24
Moreland-rd, Battersea SW	16	—..U	18
,, st, Finsbury-pk N	6	32..E	23
,, ,, Goswell-rd EC	11	46..K	24
Morella-rd, Wndswth.Co. SW	16	—..U	18
Morers-road, Leyton E .	7	—..E	32
Moresby-rd, Up. Clapton E	7	33..E	27
Moreton-gds, S. Knsgtn SW	—	51..P	17
,, place, Pimlico SW	16	52..P	21
,, rd, Croydon, Sur.	30	—..Z^{8}	25
,, ,, Stamford-hl N	7	33..D	25
,, street, Pimlico SW	16	52..P	21
Morgan-road, Holloway N	6	37..H	23
,, ,, Nw. Bromley	22	—..Z	33
,, st, Barking-road E	12	49..L	34
,, ,, Bow E . .	12	48..K	29
Morgans-lane, Tooley-st. SE	12	54..N	25
Morieux-rd, Lea Brdge-rd E	7	—..E	30
Moring-road, Tooting .	21	—..X	19
Morland-av, Croydon, Sur.	26	—..Z^{5}	25
,, rd, Croydon, Sur.	26	—..Z^{5}	25
,, ,, Ilford, Essex .	8	—..F	38
,, ,, Penge SE .	22	—..Q^{1}	28
,, ,, Sutton, Surrey	29	—..Z^{8}	17
,, ,, W'lth'mst'w E	7	—..D	29
Morley-av, Edmonton N ..	3	—..A	27
,, ,, Wood Green N	2	—..A	23
,, ,, Barking . .	13	—..J	39
,, road, Leyton E .	7	—..E	32
,, ,, Lewisham SE	4	64..T	31
,, ,, Twickenham	14	—..U	6
,, ,, West Ham E	12	41..J	34
,, ,, Woolwich .	18	—..P	34
Morning-lane, Hackney E .	7	39..H	28
Mornington-av, W. Ken. W	—	58..P	15
,, cres, Regents-park NW	11	36..J	20
Mornington-cres. station, Hampstead-road NW .	11	—..J	20
Mornington-pl. Cmdn T'n W	11	36..J	20
,, rd, Bow E .	12	48..K	30
,, ,, Lytnstne E	7	—..E	33
,, ,, New Cross-rd SE .	4	—..R	30
,, ,, Regents-pk NW .	11	36..J	20
,, st, Cmdn Tn NW	11	36..J	20
Morpeth-man. Victoria SW	11	52..O	20
,, rd, Victoria-pk E	12	39..J	28
,, st, Bethnal Gr. E	12	47..K	28
,, ter, Victoria SW	11	52..O	20
Morris-av, Manor-park E .	8	—..H	37
,, road, Bromley E .	12	48..L	31
,, street, Battersea SW	16	60..S	19
Morrison-av, Tottenham N	3	—..A	26
Morshead-rd, Maida-hill W	10	43..K	16
Mortham-st, West Ham E .	12	41..J	33
Mortimer-mkt, Tottenham-court-road WC .	—	45—K	21
Mortimer-rd, Castlebar-hl W	9	—..L	6
,, ,, De Beauvoir Town N .	7	38..I	26
,, ,, Kilburn NW .	5	35..I	26
,, ,, Kensl-rise NW	10	42..J	14
Mortimer-st, Cvndish-sq. W	11	44..L	20
Mortlake, SW . . .	14	—..R	9
,, rd, Ilford, Essex	8	—..H	39
,, ,, Kew . .	14	—..Q	8
,, ,, Mortlake SW	14	—..R	8
,, sta., L.&S.W. rly Mortlake SW	14	—..S	10
Morton-gds, Carshalton, Sy	30	—..Z^{7}	20
,, rd, Mitcham, Sur'y	25	—..Z^{3}	17
,, ,, Nw. North-rd. N	7	38..I	25
,, ,, Stratford E .	7	41..I	33
Morval-road, Brixton SW .	16	—..U	23
Morville-st, Tredegar-rd. E	12	48..J	30
Moscow-rd, Bayswater W	10	43..M	16
Moselle-av, Wood Green N	2	—..A	23
,, street, Tottenham N	3	—..A	26
Moss-st, Bethnal Green E .	12	48..J	29
,, Hall corner, N. Finchley N	1a	—..A	17
,, Hall-gr, N. Finchl'y N	1	—..A	17
Mossbury-rd, Battersea SW	16	60..S	18
Mossington-rd, Rthrhthe SE	17	55..P	28
Mosslea-road, Bickley .	28	—..Z^{4}	36
,, ,, Penge SE .	22	—..Z^{1}	28
Mostyn-avenue, Wembley	4	—..G	8
,, gds, Queens-pk. NW	10	42..J	14
,, road, Bow E .	12	48..J	30
,, ,, Merton SW	20	—..Z^{1}	15
,, ,, Stockwell SW	16	61..R	23
Motcomb-st, Wilton-crs. SW	11	52..O	19
Motley-st, S. Lambeth SW.	16	61..R	20
Motspur-pk, Malden, Sry .	25	—..Z^{4}	11
Mottingham, Kent . .	23	—..W	35

	4-in. sht.	9-in. sht.	mar.
Mottingham-la, Mottingham, Kent.	23	—..V	35
,, rd, Eltham SE.	18	—..U	35
Moundfield-rd, Stamford-hill, N	7	33..D	27
Mount-avenue, Chingford E	3	—..A	31
,, ,, Ealing W .	9	—..K	6
,, ,, Southall .	9	—..L	1
,, road, Hendon NW .	5	—..D	12
,, ,, New Malden .	24	—..Z^{2}	9
,, ,, Willesden NW	5	—..F	13
,, st, Berkeley-sq. W .	11	44..M	19
,, ,, Bethnal Green E	12	47..K	26
,, ,, Earlsfield SW .	20	—..W	16
,, ,, Whitechapel E .	12	47..L	27
,, ,, Woolwich . .	18	—..P	36
Mt. Adon-pk. Dulwich SE	22	—..V	26
MountArarat-rd, Richmond	14	—..T	7
,, Ash-rd, Sydnh'm SE	22	—..X	27
Mt. Ephraim-la, Streatham	21	—..X	21
,, ,, rd, Streatham	21	—..W	21
Mountgrove-rd, Highbury N	6	—..F	24
Mount Nod-rd, Streatham	21	—..W	22
,, pk.-av, Croydon .	30	—..Z^{1}	23
,, ,, ,, Harrow, Mx	4	—..E	3
,, ,, cres, Ealing W .	9	—..L	7
,, ,, rd, Ealing W.	9	—..L	7
,, ,, ,, Roxeth, Mx.	4	—..F	3
Mount Pleasant, Rosebery-av. WC	11	45..K	23
,, ,, Ilford, Ex	8	—..H	39
,, ,, hl, Cptn. E	7	38..F	28
,, ,, rd, Castle-bar-hill W . . .	9	—..K	6
Mount Pleasant-la, Upper Clapton-rd. E. . .	7	33..F	28
Mount Pleasant-road, Finsbury-park N . . .	6	32..E	23
Mount Pleasant-road, Higham-hill E . .	3	—..A	29
Mount Pleasant-road, Lewisham SE . . .	4	—..U	31
Mount Pleasant-road, New Malden . . .	24	—..Z^{1}	10
Mount Pleasant-road, Tottenham N . . .	3	—..B	26
Mount Pleasant-road, Willesden NW . . .	5	—..I	13
Mount Pleasant-vil, Stroud Green N . . .	6	32..D	22
Mount Vernon, Hmpstd. NW	—	35..G	17
Mountfield-road, Ealing W	9	—..L	7
,, rd, East Ham E	13	—..K	37
,, ,, Finchley N	1	—..B	16
,, ,, Streathm-hi	21	—..W	22
,, ,, Tottenham N	7	33..D	27
Mountford-pla, Kennington-lane SE . . .	16	53..P	23
Mountgrove-road, Leyton E	7	—..E	32
Mount View-rd, Crouch-hl. N	6	32..D	22
Movers-lane, Barking .	13	—..J	40
Mowbray-rd, Br'ndsb'ry NW	5	—..H	15
,, ,, U. Norw'd SE	22	—..Z^{2}	26
Mowlem-st, Victoria-pk. E	12	39..J	28
Moylan-road, Fulham SW .	15	58..Q	14
Moyser-road, Streatham SW	21	—..Y	20
Mozart-street, Maida-hill W	10	42..K	15
Muddy-lane, Southall .	9	—..L	1
Muir-st, N. Woolwich E .	13	—..N	37
Muridown-av, E. Sheen SW	14	—..S	10
Muirkirk-road, Catford SE	22	—..W	32
Mulberry-st, Com'cial-rd. E	12	47..L	27
Mulgrave-place, Woolwich	18	—..P	38
,, rd, Croydon, Sy.	30	—..Z^{7}	24
,, ,, Fulham SW .	15	58..Q	15
,, ,, Neasden NW	5	34..G	12
,, ,, Sutton, Sur'y	29	—..Z^{8}	15
Mulkern-rd, Up. Hollow'y N	6	32..E	21
Mumford-ct, Milk-street EC	—	46..L	24
Muncaster-rd, Clapham SW	16	—..T	19
Mundania-rd, Cmberwell SE	17	—..U	27
Mundford-road, Clapton E.	7	33..F	28
Munster-road, Fulham SW	15	59..R	15
,, ,, Fulham SW	15	58..Q	14
,, ,, Teddington	19	—..Y	5
,, sq, Regents-pk. NW	11	44..K	20
Munton-rd, N. Kent-rd, SE	11	54..O	24
Murchison-road, Leyton E.	7	—..F	31
Muriel-street, Islington N .	11	37..J	23
Murillo-road, Lee SE . .	17	64..T	32
Murray-road, Hounslow .	14	—..T	1
,, ,, S. Ealing W .	9	—..Q	6
,, ,, Wimbledn. SW	20	—..Y	13
,, st, Camden sq. NW	6	37..H	21
,, ,, Shoreditch N .	11	46..J	25
Murton-st, St. Lukes EC .	11	46..K	24
Musard-road, Fulham W .	15	58..P	14
Muschamp-rd, E. Dulwh. SE	17	62..S	26
Muscovy-ct, Trinity-sq. E	—	46..M	26
Museum-st, Bloomsbury WC	11	45..L	22
Musgrave-cres, Fulham SW	—	60..R	16
Musgrove-rd, Nw. Cross SE.	17	63..R	28
Musjid-rd, Battersea SW .	16	60..S	18
Muswell-av, Muswell-hl. N.	2	—..B	20
,, -hill N	2	—..B	20
,, ,, Cottages, Muswell-hill N .	2	—..B	20
,, ,, pl, Mus.-hi. N	2	—..B	20
,, rd, Muswell-hill N	2	—..B	20
,, ,, ,, ,,	2	—..B	20
,, hill ry. station " .	2	—..C	20
Mutton Brook. Finchley NW	1	—..B	16
,, la, Sudbury, Mdx.	4	—..F	5
Myatt-rd, N. Brixton SW .	16	62..R	23
Myatts-pk, N. Brixton SW	16	62..R	23
Mycenae-rd, Blackheath SE	18	—..Q	34
Myddelton-sq, Pntonvl EC	11	45..J	23
,, st, Clerkenw. EC	11	45..K	23
Myddleton-rd, Hornsey N	2	—..B	22
Myra-street, West Ham E.	12	41..J	33
Myrdle-st, Commrcl.-rd. E	12	47..L	27
Myron-pl, Lewisham SE .	17	64..S	32

Myrthe-road. INDEX TO STREETS, &c. **North Mill Field.**

4-in. sht. *9-in. sht.* *mar.*
Myrthe-road, Acton W . 9 —..M 10
Myrtle-gds, Hanwell W . 9 —..M 3
,, gr, L. Sydenham SE 22 —..Y 28
,, rd, N. Hampton . 19 —..Y 2
,, ,, Sutton Surrey . 29 —..Z^{7} 16
,, ,, Walthamstw. E. 7 —..D 30
,, street, Hoxton N . 11 46..J 25
Mysore-rd, Battersea SW . 16 60..T 19
Myton-road, W. Dulwich . 21 —..X 24

N

Nadine-street, Charlton . 18 —..Q 35
Nading-rd, Lewisham SE . 17 63..S 31
Nags Head-ct, Goldn-la, EC — 46..K 24
Nailour-st, Caledonian-rdN 6 37..H 22
Nairn-street, Bromley E . 12 49..L 32
Nanette-rd, Hmmersmthw 15 58..Q 13
Nansen-rd, Battersea SW . 16 60..S 19
,, ,, West Ham E . 12 41..J 32
Napier-av, Fulham SW . 15 59..S 15
,, rd, Bromley, Kent. 28 —..Z^{3} 34
,, ,, Croydon, Surrey 30 —..Z^{9} 24
,, ,, East Ham E . 13 —..J 38
,, ,, Isleworth . 14 —..S 4
,, ,, Kensington W . 10 50..O 15
,, ,, Leystonstone E. 7 41..G 33
,, ,, Queens Park NW 10 42..J 13
,, ,, Sudbury, Mdx . 4 —..H 7
,, ,, Tottenham N . 3 —..B 26
,, ,, West Ham E . 12 41..J 33
,, street, Deptford SE 17 56..Q 30
,, ,, Hoxton, N . 11 46..J 25
Napoleon-rd, Twickenham 14 —..U 5
Narboune-av, Clapham SW 16 —..U 20
Narboro'-st, Fulham SW . 15 59..S 16
Narcissus-rd, West Hampstead NW . . . 5 35..G 16
Narford-road, Clapton E . 7 33..F 27
Narrow-st, Limehouse E . 12 48..M 29
Nascot-st, N. Knsngtn. W . 10 42..L 13
Naseby-rd, U. NorwoodSE 21 —..Z^{1} 25
Nasmyth-st, Hammers. W. 10 50..O 12
Nassau-rd, Barnes SW . 15 —..R 11
,, ,, Tottenham N 7 —..D 26
,, st, Berners-st, W . 11 44..L 21
Nassington-rd,Hmpstd. NW 6 36..G 19
Natal-rd, Ilford, Essex . 8 —..H 39
,, ,, N. Southgate N . 2 —..A 22
,, ,, Streatham . . 21 —..Y 21
,, ,, Thornton-hth. Sy 26 —..Z^{2} 24
National Gallery, Trafalgar-square WC . . . 11 45..M 21
National Gallery of British Art, Westminster SW . 16 53..P 22
Natural Histy Museum, S. Kensington . . 11 51..O 17
Naval-row, Poplar E . 12 49..M 32
Navarino-road, Dalston E 7 39..H 27
Navarre-road, East Ham E 13 —..J 37
,, st, Bethnal-gr, E . 12 46..K 26
Navy-street, Clapham SW 16 61..S 21
Naylord-rd, Peckham SE . 17 55..Q 27
Neal-street, Long-acre WC. 11 45..L 22
Nealdon-st, Stockwell SW . 16 61..S 22
Neasden NW . . . 5 —..G 11
,, la, Willesden NW. 5 —..H 11
Neate-st, Camberwell SE . 17 54..Q 26
Neckinger, Bermondsey SE 12 55..O 26
,, st, Brmondsy SE 12 55..O 26
Necropolis-sta, Westminster-bridge-road SE . 11 53..O 23
Neeld-cres, Hendon NW . 1 —..C 13
Nelgarde-rd, Catford SE . 22 —..V 30
Nelldale-rd, Rotherhithe SE 17 55..P 28
Nelson-grove, Merton SW . 20 —..Z 16
,, ,, rd, Merton SW20 —..Z 16
,, rd, Bromley, Kent 28 —..Z^{3} 35
,, ,, East Ham E . 13 —..J 38
,, ,, Hale End E . 3 —..A 31
,, ,, Hornsey N . 6 32..D 22
,, ,, Hounslow . 14 —..U 1
,, ,, Merton SW . 20 —..Z 16
,, ,, New Malden, Sy 25 —..Z^{3} 10
,, ,, Merton SW . 20 —..Z 16
,, sq. Blackfriars-rd.SE 11 54..N 24
,, st, Canning Town E 12 49..M 33
,, ,, City road, EC . 11 46..K 24
,, ,, East Ham E . 13 —..J 37
,, ,, East Ham E . 13 —..J 38
,, ,, Greenwich SE . 17 57..Q 32
,, ,, Bethnal Green E — 47..J 27
,, ,, Whitechapel E . 12 47..L 27
,, ,, Woolwich . 13 —..O 38
Nelsons dck, RotherhitheSE — 56..N 30
,, row, Clapham SW 16 61..T 21
Nemoure-road, Acton W . 9 —..M 9
Nepean-st, Roehampton SW 15 —..U 12
Neptune-st, Rotherhithe SE 12 55..O 28
,, ,, S. Lambeth SW 16 53..Q 22
Nether-street, Finchley N . 1 —..A 16
Netheravon-rd, Chiswick W 15 —..P 11
Netherbury-road, Ealing W 9 —..N 6
Netherby-rd, Forest-hill SE 22 —..V 28
Netherford-rd, Clapham SW 16 61..S 20
Netherhall-gds,Hmpstd.NW 5 35..G 17
Netherton-gr, Chelsea SW . 15 51..Q 17
,, rd, Tottenham N 7 33..D 25
,, ,, Twickenham 14 —..T 5
Netherwood-st, Kilburn NW 5 —..H 15
,, rd, W.Knstnw 10 50..N 14
Netley-rd, Brentford, Mdx 14 —..P 7
,, ,, Newbury-park, Ilford, Essex 8 —..D 40
,, ,, Walthamstow E 3 —..C 30
,, street, Maida-hill W 10 43..K 16
,, st, Regents-pk. NW 11 44..K 20
Nettleton-ct, Ald'gate-st.EC — 46..L 24
,, rd, New Cross SE . 4 63..R 29
Neuchatel-rd, Forest-hill SE 22 —..W 29

4-in. sht. *9-in. sht.* *mar.*
Nevada-st, Greenwich SE . 17 —..Q 32
Neve-street, Bow E . 12 48..J 31
Nevern-place, Earls-ct, SW 15 51..P 16
,, rd, Earls-court SW — 58..O 15
,, sq. Earls-court SW 15 51..P 16
Neville-rd, Croydon, Sur'y 26 —..Z^{4} 25
,, ,, Upton E . . 8 —..I 35
,, st, Fulham-rd SW . 16 51..P 17
Nevill-rd,Stk.Newington N 6 38..F 26
,, ,, Kingston . 19 —..Z^{1} 8
,, ,, Stk. Newgtn. N 7 38..F 26
Neville-road, Upton E . 8 —..I 35
Nevills-crt, Fetter-lane EC. — 45..L 23
Nevis-rd, Upr. Tooting SW 21 —..W 19
New Brentford, Middlesex 14 —..P 5
,, Charlton, Kent SE . 18 —..P 35
,, court, Carey-st, WC . — 45..L 23
,, ,, Cloth Fair EC . — 46..L 24
,, ,, St. Swithins-la EC 11 46..M 25
,, ,, The Temple EC . — 45..M 23
,, ,, W. Smithfield EC — 46..L 24
,, Cross SE . . . 4 63..R 29
,, Cut, Lambeth SE . 11 53..N 23
,, Eltham, Kent . . 23 —..W 38
,, End, Hampstead NW 5 35..F 17
,, Hampton, Middlesex 19 —..X 1
,, Malden, Surrey . 25 —..Z^{3} 10
,, rd, Brentford, Mdsx . 14 —..P 6
,, ,, Carshalton, Surrey 25 —..Z^{6} 18
,, ,, Claygate, Surrey . 28a —..Z^{10} 3
,, ,, Commercial-rd E . 12 47..L 27
,, ,, Esher,Surrey . 24 —..Z^{6} 2
,, ,, Grove-pk, Kent . 23 —..Y 35
,, ,, Hackbridge, Sur. 26 —..Z^{5} 20
,, ,, Hayes, Kent . 27 —..Z^{5} 33
,, ,, Hook, Surrey . 24 —..Z^{6} 6
,, ,, Hornsey N . . 2 —..C 22
,, ,, Mitcham, Surrey . 26 —..Z^{5} 19
,, ,, Norbiton . . 19 —..Z 8
,, ,, S. Lambeth SW . 16 61..R 21
,, ,, Tottenham N . 3 —..A 26
,, ,, Walthamstow E . 3 —..B 33
,, ,, Wood Green N . 2 —..A 24
,, ,, Woolwich . . 18 —..P 38
,, Southgate . . 2 —..A 21
,, sq. Lincolns Inn WC . 11 45..L 23
,, street, Bishopsgate EC 12 46..L 26
,, ,, Canning T'n E 12 49..L 33
,, st, Kenngtn-pk.-rd.SE 16 54..P 23
,, ,, St. J'ns Wood NW 11 43..J 18
,, ,, square, Shoe-la EC — 45..L 33
,, ,, St. Martins-la. WC 11 45..M 22
,, ,, Upr. Baker-st. W . 11 44..K 19
,, Town, St. Mary Cray, Kent . . . 28 —..Z^{4} 42
,, Turnstile, High Holborn WC . . — 45..L 22
,, Barn-st, Plaistow E . 13 —..L 34
,, Basinghall-street EC . — 46..L 25
,, Beckenham sta., S.E. & C. Rly. . . 22 —..Q^{1} 29
,, Bond-st, Oxford-st. W 11 44..M 20
,, Brent-st, Hendon NW 1 —..C 13
,, Bridge-st, Blackfriars EC . . . 11 46..M 23
,, Broad-street EC. . 11 46..L 25
,, Burlington-st, Regent street W . . 11 44..M 20
,, Castle-st, Whitechpl E 12 47..L 26
,, Cavendish-st, Portland-place W . 11 44..L 20
,, Charles-st, City-rd. E 11 46..J 24
,, Church-rd, Cmbwl. SE 17 54..Q 25
,, ,, st, Bermondsey SE . 12 55..O 27
,, City-road, Plaistow E 13 —..K 35
,, Compton-st, Charing Cross-road WC . 11 45..M 21
,, Coventry-st, Leicester square W . . — 45..M 21
,, Cross-rd, New Crosss E 4 63..R 29
,, ,, sta., L.B. & S.C. Rly., New Cross SE 4 63..R 29
New Eltham & Pope-st., rly. sta., S.E. & C.Rly. . 23 —..W 38
New Gravel-la, Wapping E 12 47..M 28
,, Homesdale-rd, Bckley 28 —..Z^{3} 35
,, Inn yd, Curtain-rd.EC 12 46..K 26
,, Kent-road, EC . . 12 54..O 25
,, King-st, Deptford SE 17 56..Q 30
,, Kings-rd, Fulham SW 15 59..R 15
,, London-st, Crutchedfriars EC . . 11 46..M 26
,, North-road, Hoxton N 11 38..J 25
,, ,, st, Theobalds-road WC . 11 45..L 22
,, Oxford-street WC . 11 45..L 21
,, Palace yard, Westminster SW. . 11 53..N 22
,, Park-rd, Streatham . 21 —..V 21
,, Portland-rd, Norbiton Surrey . .. 24 —..Z^{2} 7
,, Quebec-st, Portman-square W . . — 44..L 19
,, River-cres, Palmers Green N 2 —..A 24
,, ,, Head, Rosebery av. EC . 11 45..K 23
,, Scotland-yard, Westminster SW. . 11 53..N 22
New Sthgate Sta., G.N.R.. 2 —..A 20
New-st. sq., Fetter-ln, EC — 45..L 23
New Turnstile, H.Hlbn.WC — 45..L 22
,, Union-st, Moorfds EC 11 46..L 25
,, Wanstead, E . . 8 —..D 34
,, Wharf-rd, N . . — 37..J 22
Newark-rd, Croydon, Sur. 30 —..Z^{8} 24
,, st, Whitechpl, E . 12 47..L 27
Newburgh-road, Acton W 9 —..M 9
Newburn-st, Kenningtn SE 16 53..P 22
Newbury-rd, Brmly. Kent. 27 —..Z^{2} 34
,, ,, Hale End E . 3 —..A 32

4-in. sht *9-in. sht* *mar.*
Newbury-rd, Harlesden NW 5 34..I 12
,, ,, Ilford . . 8 —..D 40
,, st, Long-la, EC . — 46..L 24
,, pk ry-sta, G.E.R. 8 —..D 40
Newby-place, Poplar E . 12 49..M 31
,, st, S. Lambeth SW . 16 61..S 20
Newcastle-st, Cubitt-tn. E 17 57..P 32
,, ,, EC . . — 46..L 23
Newcomen-rd, B'tsea. SW . 15 60..S 17
,, ,, Lytnstne. E 7 41..F 33
,, st, S'thw'rk SE 12 54..N 25
Newgate street, EC . . 11 46..L 24
Newick-road, Clapton E . 7 39..G 28
Newington-butts, Ngtn SE 11 54..O 24
,, c'sew'y, Sthwk. SE 11 54..O 24
,, cr, Newington SE 16 54..P 24
,, gr, Kennington-park road SE 16 54..P 24
,, ,, Stk. NwngtnN 7 38..H 25
,, ,, -rd, Dalston N 7 38..H 25
Newland-rd, Hornsey N . 2 —..B 22
,, st, Silvertown E 13 —..N 37
Newlands-pk, Sydenhm SE 22 —..Y 28
,, rd, Hornsey N 2 —..B 22
,, ,, Norbury . 21 —..Z^{2} 22
,, house Asylum, Up. Tooting . 21 —..X 19
Newlyng-rd, Tottenh'm N 3 —..A 26
Newman-st, Battersea SW 16 60..S 18
,, ,, Oxford-st W . 11 45..L 21
Newmans-ct, Cornhill EC . 11 46..M 25
,, row, WC : . — 45..L 23
Newnham-pk, Wood-gr, N 2 —..A 23
Newport-court, Soho WC . — 45..M 21
,, road, Barnes SW 15 58..Q 12
,, ,, Leyton E . 7 —..F 32
,, st, Lambeth SE 11 53..O 22
Newquay-rd, Rushey-gr SE 22 —..W 31
Newry-rd, Twickenham . 14 —..T 5
Newstead-road, Lee SE . 22 —..V 33
Newton-avenue, Acton W 9 —..N 9
,, av, Muswell-hill N 2 —..A 20
,, gro, Bedford-pk W 10 —..O 10
,, rd, Bayswater W . 10 43..L 16
,, ,, Leytonstone E 7 41..H 33
,, ,, Tottenham N . 3 —..C 27
,, ,, Willesden NW 5 —..F 13
,, ,, Wimbledon SW 20 —..Z 14
,, st, Canning Tn. E 12 49..M 33
,, ,, High Hlbn. WC 11 45..L 22
,, ,, Hoxton N . 11 38..J 25
Nibthwaite-rd, Harrw, M'x 1a —..C 4
Nicholas-la,Kg.Willm-st.EC 11 46..M 25
,, pa,Kg.Willm-stEC 11 46..M 25
,, street, Hoxton N 11 46..J 25
,, st, Mile End E . 12 47..K 28
Nicholay-rd, Up. Hlwy. N . 6 32..E 21
Nicholl-sq, Aldersgte-s EC — 46..L 24
Nichols-sq, Hackney E . 12 47..J 26
Nicholson-rd, Croydon, Sy 26 —..Z^{5} 26
Nicoll-rd, Harlesden NW . 5 —..I 11
Nicosia-rd,Wndswth.-cnSW 20 —..V 18
Nigel-road, Manor-park E 8 —..H 36
,, ,, Peckham SE . 17 62..S 27
Nightingale-gro, Lew. SE . 17 —..U 32
,, lane, Balham SW 16 —..U 19
,, ,, Bickley, Ken 28 —..Z^{2} 35
,, ,, Greenwich SE 17 64..R 32
,, ,, Hornsey N . 2 —..B 22
,, ,, L'nd'n Dks. E 12 47..M 27
,, ,, Richmond-hl. 14 —..U 7
,, ,, Wapping E . 12 55..N 27
,, pla, Woolwich . 18 —..Q 38
,, rd, Carshal. Sy . 25 —..Z^{6} 18
,, ,, Clapton E . 7 39..G 27
,, ,, Harlesden NW 10 42..J 12
,, ,, W Moulsey, Sy 24 —..Z^{2} 1
,, ,, Wood Green N 2 —..A 22
,, row, Carshalton . 25 —..Z^{6} 18
,, square, Balham . 21 —..V 19
,, vale, Woolwich . 18 —..Q 38
Nile-road, Plaistow E . 13 —..J 35
,, street, Hoxton N . 11 46..J 25
Nimrod-rd, Streatham SW 21 —..T 20
Nine Elms-lane, Wandsworth-road SW . . 16 53..Q 21
Nine Elms-sta, S.W.R. SW 16 53..Q 21
Ninhams-wd, Farnboro . 30b —..Z^{7} 37
Nisbet-st, Homerton E . 7 40—H 29
Nithdale-rd, Plumstead E 18 —..Q 38
Niton-road, Richmond . 14 —..S 8
,, st, Fulham SW . 15 58..Q 14
Noble-st, Clerkenwell WC . — 45..K 23
,, ,, Gresham-st, EC . 11 46..L 24
Noel-park, Wood Green N 2 —..A 23
,, pk-rd, Wood Green N 2 —..B 23
,, pk and Wood Green Ry. Sta., G.E. Ry. 2 —..A 23
,, road, Acton W . 9 —..L 10
,, street, Berwick-st W 11 45..L 21
Noel-street, Islington N . 11 38..J 24
Nonsuch-park, Surrey . 29 —..Z^{8} 12
,, place, Cheam, Sy. 29 —..Z^{8} 14
Norbiton, Surrey . . 24 —..Z^{2} 8
,, ,, . . 19 —..Z 7
,, av, Kingston . 19 —..Z^{1} 8
,, Common, Surrey 24 —..Z^{2} 8
,, Sta, Norbiton . 19 —..Z^{1} 8
Norbury, SW . . . 21 —..Z^{2} 21
,, av, Norbury SW . 21 —..Z^{2} 23
,, ct.-rd, NorburySW 26 —..Z^{2} 22
,, hill, Norwood SE. 21 —..Z^{1} 23
,, park, Surrey . 26 —..Z^{2} 22
,, rd, Thornton-Hth, Surrey . . 26 —..Z^{2} 24
,, Ry. Sta, L.B. & S.C. Railway . . 21 —..Z^{1} 22
Norcott-road, Clapton N .. 7 33..F 27
,, ,, Twickenham 19 —..V 3
Norfolk-av, Tottenham N . 7 33..D 26
,, cres, Edgware-r,W 11 44..L 18
,, rd, Dalston E . 7 39..G 26

4-in. sht. *9-in. sht.* *mar.*
Norfolk-rd, East Ham E . 13 —..J 38
,, ,, Essex-road N . 7 38..H 25
,, ,, Seven Kings 8 —..E 41
,, ,, Essex-road N 6 38..H 25
,, ,, St. J. Wood NW 6 55..I 18
,, ,, S.Wmbldn. SW 10 20..Z 18
,, ,, Thornton Hth, Surrey . . 26 —..Z^{2} 24
Norfolk-rd, Westbne-gr, W — 43..L 16
,, sq, Hyde Park W 11 43..L 18
,, street, Mile-end E. 12 47..K 28
,, ,, Park-lane W 11 44..M 19
,, ,, Strand WC . 11 45..M 23
,, House-rd, Streatm 21 —..X 21
Norland-gds, Notting hi. W 10 50..M 14
,, rd, Notting hi. W. 10 50..N 14
,, sq, ,, ,, . 10 50..N 14
Norlington-rd, Leyton E . 7 —..E 32
Norman-av, Twickenham . 14 —..U 5
,, ,, Wood-green N 2 —..A 24
,, ,, west,Wood-grN 2 —..A 24
,, ,, Bow E . . 12 48..J 29
,, ,, Croydon, Sy. 26 —..Z^{3} 23
,, ,, East Ham E . 13 —..K 37
,, ,, Greenwich SE. 17 56..Q 31
,, ,, Ilford E . . 8 —..H 39
,, ,, Leytonstone E 7 —..F 33
,, ,, Ilford . . 8 —..H 39
,, ,, Merton, SW . 20 —..Z 16
,, ,, Sutton, Surrey 29 —..Z^{7} 15
,, ,, Tottenham N 3 —..C 26
,, st, Chelsea SW . 16 52..P 18
,, ,, St. Lukes EC . — 46..K 24
,, ,, Leytonstone E 7 —..F 33
Normanby-rd, Neasden NW 5 34..G 12
Normand-rd, W. Kensington SW . . . 15 58..P 15
Normandy-pl,N.BrixtonSW 16 61..R 23
Normanfield-av,Hmpn.Wk 19 —..Z 6
Normanhurst-rd,Brxtn.SW 21 —..— 22
Normanton-rd, Croydon Sy — 30..Z^{8} 25
,, st, Forest-hl.SE 22 —..W 29
Norris-rd, Bow Common E 12 48..K 31
,, st, Haymarket SW . — 45..M 21
Norroy-road, Putney SW . 15 59—T 14
North-av, Carshalton . 29 —..Z^{9} 19
,, ,, Castlebar-hill W. 9 —..L 5
,, Bank, Regents-p.NW 11 43..K 18
,, Brixton,StockwellSW 16 61..R 23
,, Cheam, Surrey . 25 —..Z^{5} 14
,, drive, Tootng. Com. 21 —..X 20
,, end, Croydon, Sy . 26 —..Z^{5} 24
,, ,, Fulham SW . 15 58..P 14
,, ,, Hampstead NW 5 31..E 17
,, ,, W. Kensngtn. W 10 58..O 14
,, Finchley N . . 1 —..A 18
,, gte, Regents-Pk, NW 11 36..J 18
,, grove, Highgate N . 6 31..E 20
,, ,, Tottenham N. 3 —..C 25
,, hill, Highgate N . 6 31..D 19
,, Kensington W . 10 42..L 14
,, lane, Teddington . 19 —..Y 3
,, pk, Croydon, Surrey 26 —..Z^{4} 23
,, ,, Eltham . . 18 —..U 37
,, pla, Wandsworth SW 15 59..T 15
,, ,, Acton W . 10 —..M 10
,, ,, Clapham SW . 16 —..T 21
,, ,, Ealing W . . 9 —..O 6
,, ,, Edgware, Mdsx. 1 —..A 9
,, ,, Highgate N . 6 31..D 20
,, ,, Holloway N . 6 37..H 22
,, ,, Ilford, Essex .. 8 —..E 40
,, ,, Richmond . 14 —..S 8
,, ,, S. WimbledonSW 20 —..Y 16
,, ,, Surbiton, Surrey 24 —..Z^{3} 6
,, ,, Walthamstow E. 3 —..B 32
,, row, Oxford-street W 11 44..M 19
,, ,, Park-lane W . 11 44..M 19
,, side, Clphm. Com.SW 16 60..T 51
,, ,, Wndswth.Cm.SW 15 60..T 17
,, st, Barking Essex . 8 —..I 39
,, ,, Carshalton, Surry 29 —..Z^{7} 18
,, ,, Clapham SW . 16 61..S 20
,, ,, Edgware-rd, NW. 11 43..K 18
,, ,, Isleworth . 14 —..R 4
,, ,, Lambeth SE . 11 53..O 23
,, ,, Mile-end E . 12 47..K 28
,, ,, Plaistow E . . 13 —..J 35
,, ,, Poplar E . . 12 48..M 31
,, ,, Shadwell E . 12 47..M 28
,, ,, Stockwell SW . 16 61..S 22
,, ,, Victoria-park E . 12 39..J 28
,, ,, Westminster SW. 11 53..O 22
,, ,, Woolwich E . 13 —..O 35
North Acton sta, Acton W 9 —..K 10
,, Audley-st, Oxford-street W . . 11 44..M 19
,, Bank-road, Chapel End E , . . 3 —..A 32
,, Birbeck-rd, Leyton E 7 41..G 32
,, ,, ,, Leytonstne E 7 41..G 32
,, Bruton-mews, Berkeley-square W . 11 44..M 20
,, Common-rd, EalingW 9 —..M 7
,, Cross-rd,E.Dlwch SE 17 —..T 26
,, Dulwich sta., S.L. rly., E. Dlwch SE. 16 —..U 25
,, Ealing sta.,Met.Dis rly., Ealing W . 9 —..L 8
,, End, Fulham SW . 15 58..P 15
,, ,, rd, Fulham SW 15 58..P 15
,, ,, ,, Golders Gr. NW . 5 —..E 16
,, ,, ,, Hmpstd.NW 6 31..E 17
,, Field-rd, Stamford-hill N . . . . 7 33..E 26
,, Grafton-rd, Pl'st'wE 13 —..J 34
,, Greenwich sta., Cubitt Town E . . 17 57..P 32
,, James-st, Peck'm SE 17 62..S 27
,, Mill Field, Clapt'n E 7 39..F 28

North Pole-road. INDEX TO STREETS, &c. **Osterley-lane.**

	4-*in.* *sht.*	9-*in.* *sht.* *mar.*
North Pole-rd, N.Knsngnw	10	42..L 13
,, Portman-mws, Portman-square W .	11	44..L 19
,, view, Castlebar-hl.W	9	—..K 6
,, villas, Camden-sq.NW	6	37..H 21
,, Wood, Highgate N .	6	31..E 18
,, Woolwich E . .	13	—..N 38
,, ,, road, Victoria Docks E .	13	—..N 35
,, Sur. Indus. Schools, Upr. Norwood SE	22	—..Z^2 26
,, Torridge-rd, Croydon, Surrey .	26	—..Z^3 23
,, View-rd, Hornsey N	2	—..B 22
,, ,, ,, Wimbledon SW .	20	—..Y 13
,, Western Hospital, Hampstead NW .	5	36..G 18
,, Wharf-rd, Padgtn W	10	43..L 17
,, Woolwich-road E .	12	49..M 34
,, ,, rd, Victoria Docks E	13	—..N 35
,, ,, rly. sta., N. Wlwch E..	13	—..O 38
Northam-st, Lewisham SE.	4	63..S 31
Northampton Institute, Clerkenwell EC .	11	45..K 23
,, pk, N .	7	38..H 25
,, rd, Croyd.Sy	26	—..Z^6 26
,, ,, Exmouth street EC	11	45..K 23
,, sq, Clerkenwell EC .	11	46..K 24
,, st, Percival-street EC	11	46..K 24
,, ,, IslingtonN	6	33..I 24
Northanger-rd, Lr. Streatham SW . . .	21	—..Z^1 21
Northbank-rd, Croydn. Sy.	26	—..Z^3 24
Northborough-rd, Norbury	21	—..Z^2 22
Northbrook-rd, Bowes-pk.N	2	—..A 22
,, ,, Ilford, Esx	8	—..F 38
,, ,, Lee SE .	17	—..T 32
Northcliff-rd, Edmonton N	3	—..A 27
Northcote-av, Ealing W .	9	—..M 7
,, pk.-rd, Acton W	10	—..M 10
,, ,, ,, Hornsey N	2	—..C 22
,, rd, Battersea SW	16	60..T 18
,, ,, Croydon, Sy	26	—..Z^4 24
,, ,, Isleworth .	14	—..T 4
,, ,, Sidcup .	23	—..X 40
,, ,, Twickenham	14	—..T 5
,, ,, WlthmstwE	3	—..C 29
,, ,, Willesden NW	5	—..I 11
Northcott-av, Wood Gr'n N	2	—..A 22
Northcroft-road, Ealing W	9	—..N 5
Northdown-st, Pntnville N	11	45..J 22
Northend, Hampstead NW	6	31..E 17
Northern-road, Plaistow E	13	—..J 35
Northey-st, Limehouse E .	12	48..M 39
Northfield, Wandsworth SW	15	59..T 15
,, av,Ealng Dean W	9	—..M 5
,, road, Ealing W .	9	—..N 5
,, ,, Stmfd.hl.N	6	33..E 26
,, rly. sta., Met. Ry.	9	—..N 5
Northfields-road, Acton W	9	—..K 9
Northolme-rd, Highbury N	6	38..G 24
Northolt-rd, Harrow, Mdx	4	—..F 2
,, sta., G.W.R., Mdx	4	—..H 1
Northport-st., Shoreditch N	11	38..J 25
Northstead-rd, Tulse Hill	21	—..W 23
Northumberland alley, Fenchurch-street EC . .	—	46..M 26
Northumberland-av, Charing Cross SW .	11	45..N 22
Northumberland av, Wanstead E. . . .	8	—..F 36
Northumberland-gr, Tottenham N . . .	3	—..A 27
Northumberland-pk, Tottenham N . . .	3	—..A 27
Northumberland-pl, Bayswater W . . .	10	43..L 16
Northumberland-rd, Leyton-street E . . .	7	—..E 30
Northumberland-st, Marylebone W . . .	11	44..L 19
Northumberland-st, Poplar E	12	48..L 31
Northumberland-st, Strand WC	11	45..M 22
Northunger-rd, Streatham	21	—..Z^1 21
Northway-rd, Croydon, Sy	26	—..Z^4 26
,, ,, Denmark hl. SE	16	62..S 24
Northwick-rd, Gr'nhill, Mx	1*a*	—..C 5
,, ter, St. John's Wood NW . . .	10	43..K 17
Northwold-rd,Stk.Nwgtn.N	7	33..F 27
,, ,, U. Clptn. E	7	33..F 27
Northwood-rd, Catford SE.	22	—..W 29
,, ,, Highgate N	6	32..D 20
Norton Folgate, Bishopsgate E. . .	12	46..L 26
,, gardens, Norbury .	21	—..Z^2 21
,, road, Wembley .	4	—..H 7
Norway Dock, Rthrhth. SE	12	56..O 29
,, yard, Rthrhth. SE.	12	56..O 29
Norwich-rd, Forest Gate E	8	—..H 34
,, ,, Thornton Hth Surrey .	26	—..Z^2 24
,, st, Fetter-lane EC	—	45..L 23
Norwood SE	26	—..Z^3 25
,, cemetery, W. Norwood . .	21	—..X 24
,, green, Middlesex	9	—..O 1
,, pl, Limehouse E	12	48..M 30
,, rd, Herne-hill SE	21	—..V 23
,, ,, W. Nrwd SE .	21	—..W 23
,, jct. ry. sta., L.B. & S.C. Rly. .	26	—..Z^3 26
,, New Town .	21	—..Z^1 24
Notson-rd, S. Norwood SE	27	—..Z^3 27
Notting Hill W. . .	10	50..M 15
Notting Hi.-sta, G.W. Rly. North Kensington W .	10	42..L 14
Notting Hill Gate station, Notting Hill W . .	10	43..M 16
Notting Hill High-st., Notting Hill W . .	10	50..M 15
Nottingham-pl, Mybne-rdW	11	44..K 19
,, rd, Croydon, Sy	30	—..Z^7 24
,, ,, Isleworth .	14	—..R 4
,, ,, Leytonst. E	7	—..D 32
,, ,, WndswthsW	20	—..V 18
,, st, Mylebne-rdW	11	44..L 19
Nova-road, Croydon, Sy .	26	—..Z^5 23
Novar-rd, N. Eltham, Kent	23	—..W 38
Novello-street, Fulham SW	15	59..R 15
Noyna-rd, Up. Tooting SW	21	—..W 19
Nugent-rd, Finsbury-pk N	6	32..E 22
,, ter, S. Johns-wd NW	10	43..J 17
Nun-crt, Aldermanbury EC	—	46..L 24
Nunhead SE	17	63..S 28
,, cem., Peckham SE	17	63..T 28
,, cres, Peckham SE	17	62..S 27
,, gn, Peckham SE	17	63..S 27
,, gro, Peckham SE	17	63..S 27
,, lane, Peckham SE	17	62..S 27
,, rly. sta,(Nunh'd SE	17	63..S 28
Nursery-road, Brixton SW	16	61..T 22
,, rd, Croydon, Sy .	26	—..Z^2 24
,, ,, Merton SW .	16	—..Z^1 16
,, ,, Sutton, Surrey	29	—..Z^7 16
,, st, Clapham SW .	16	61..S 20
,, ,, Tottenham N .	3	—..A 26
,, ,, Walworth SE .	17	54..P 25
Nutbourne-st, Queens-pk W	10	42..J 14
Nutbrook-st, Peckham SE	17	62..S 26
Nutfield-road, Croydon, Sy	26	—..Z^2 23
,, ,, E. Dulwich SE	17	—..T 26
,, ,, Leyton E .	7	41..G 32
Nutford-pla, Edgware-rd W	11	44..L 18
Nuthurst-avenue, Brixton	21	—..W 22
Nutley-ter, Hampstead NW	5	35..H 17
Nuttall-st, Kingsl'nd-rd N	12	38..J 26
Nutwell-st, L. Tooting SW	20	—..Y 18
Nye-street, Poplar E .	12	49..M 31
Nynehead-st, Deptford SE	17	56..Q 29
Nyon-road, Forest Hill SE	22	—..W 29

O

	4-*in.* *sht.*	9-*in.* *sht.* *mar.*
Oak-gro, Cricklewood NW	5	—..G 14
,, ,, Penge SE . .	22	—..Z^2 28
,, lane, Finchley N .	1	—..A 18
,, ,, Hounslow .	14	—..T 3
,, ,, Limehouse E .	12	48..M 30
,, ,, Nw. Southgate N	2	—..A 22
,, ,, Tottenham N .	3	—..C 25
,, ,, Twickenham .	14	—..U 4
,, rd, Canning Town E .	12	49..L 33
,, ,, Chelsfield, Kent .	30*b*	—..Z^9 41
,, street, Ealing W .	9	—..M 7
,, village, Kntsh Tn SW	6	36..G 19
,, villas, Kntsh. Twn.SW	6	36..G 19
,, grove-road, Penge SE	22	—..Z^2 27
,, hl.-gds, Surbiton, Sy	24	—..Z^4 6
,, ,, pk, Hampstead NW	5	35..G 17
,, of Honor-hill SE .	17	—..U 28
Oakbank-rd, Herne Hill SE	16	62..T 24
Oakbury-road, Fulham SW	15	59..S 16
Oakcroft-rd, Lewisham SE	17	64..S 32
Oakdale-road, Leyton E .	7	—..F 32
,, ,, Streatham .	21	—..Y 22
,, ,, Tottenham NW	7	33..D 25
,, ,, Upton E .	8	—..I 35
Oaken-la, Claygate, Surrey	28*a*	—..Z^7 3
Oakfield-rd, Clapton E .	7	39..G 27
,, ,, Croydon, Sy .	26	—..Z^5 24
,, ,, Finchley N .	1	—..A 17
,, ,, Golder's-gr NW	1	—..C 15
,, ,, Higham-hill E	3	—..A 29
,, ,, Hornsey N .	6	32..D 23
,, ,, Ilford, Essex	8	—..G 39
,, ,, Penge SE .	22	—..Z^1 27
,, ,, Plaistow E .	13	—..J 36
Oakford-av, Up. SydnhmSE	22	—..X 27
,, ,, Kent. Twn. NW	6	36..G 20
Oakham-street, Chelsea SW	16	51..P 18
Oakhill-av, Hampstead NW	5	—..G 16
,, rd, Becknhm, Kent	27	—..Z^2 31
,, ,, Surbiton, Sy .	24	—..Z^4 6
,, ,, Sutton, Surrey .	25	—..Z^6 16
,, ,, Wandsworth SW	15	59..T 15
,, way, Hampstead NW	5	—..G 17
Oakhurst-gr, E. Dulwch SE	17	62..T 26
Oakington-av, Wembley .	4	—..F 8
,, rd, Maida Hi. W	10	43..K 16
Oakland-gro, Shep. Bush W	10	50..M 12
,, rd, Bromley .	22	—..Z^1 33
,, ,, Cricklew'd NW	5	—..G 14
,, ,, Hanwell W	9	—..N 4
,, ,, Hanwell W	9	—..M 4
,, ter, Ilford, Essex	8	—..F 39
Oaklea-passage, Kingston	19	—..Z^1 7
Oakleigh-rd, Oakleigh-pk N	2	—..A 19
,, ,, Oakleigh-pk N	2	—..A 20
,, ,, Pinner, Mdx.	1*a*	—..A 1
Oakley-avenue, Ealing W .	9	—..L 8
,, cres, Chelsea SW .	16	52..Q 18
,, ,, City-road EC	—	46..J 24
,, rd, Bromley, Kent	28	—..Z^6 36
,, ,, De B'voir-tn. N	7	38..I 25
,, ,, Harrow, Mid. .	1*a*	—..C 4
,, ,, Islington N .	6	38..I 25
,, ,, S. Norwood SE	—	—..Z^3 27
,, sq, Camden Tn. NW	11	37..J 21
,, street, Chelsea SW	16	51..P 18
,, ,, Lambeth SE	11	53..N 23
Oakmead-road, Balham .	2	—..V 19
Oaks-lane, Newbury-park, Ilford, Essex .	8	—..D 40
Oaks-rd, Shirley, Surrey .	30	—..Z^7 27
Oakthorpe-rd, Bowes-pk N	2	—..A 23
,, ,, Plmrs-grn. N	2	—..A 24
Oaktree-rd, S Johns-wd NW	11	43—K 18
Oakwood-av, Beckenham .	27	—..Z^2 31
,, ,, Mitcham .	20	—..Z^1 17
,, ,, Purley . .	30	—..Z^{11} 23
,, crt, Kensington W	10	50..N 15
,, gro, Sevn. Kgs., Ex	8	—..F 41
,, rd, Cottnhm-pkSW	20	—..Z 12
Oatfield-road, Orpington .	28	—..Z^5 40
Oat-lane, Noble-street EC	—	46..L 24
Oatland-rise, Wlthmstw. E	3	—..B 29
Oban-road, Barking .	13	—..J 40
,, ,, Norwood SE .	26	—..Z^2 25
,, street, Bromley E .	12	49..L 32
Oberstein-rd, Battersea SW	15	60..T 17
Ocean-street, Stepney E .	12	48..L 29
Ockenden-rd, Essex-rd N .	7	38..H 25
Ockley-road, Streatham .	21	—..X 21
Octavia-st, Battersea SW .	16	60..R 18
Odell-st, Bermondsey SE .	17	54..P 26
Odessa-rd, Forest-gate E .	7	41..G 34
Odessa-rd,Harlesden-gr,NW	10	42..J 12
,, st, RotherhitheSE	12	56..O 30
Odger-st, Battersea SW .	16	60..R 19
Offerton-rd, Clapham SW .	16	61..S 21
Offley-road, Brixton SW .	16	53..Q 23
Offord-rd, Barnsbury N .	6	37..I 23
Oglander-rd, Peckham SE .	17	62..S 26
Ogilby-street, Woolwich .	18	—..P 37
Ohio-road, Plaistow E .	12	49..L 33
Oil-hill-lane, Kingston . .	19	—..Z^1 7
Oil-mill-lane, Norbiton, Sy	24	—..Z^2 7
Okeburn-rd, U. Tooting .	21	—..T 19
Okehampton-rd,Wlsdn NW	5	34..I 14
Olaf-street, Notting-hill W.	10	50..M 14
Old Bailey EC . .	11	46..L 24
,, Castle-st, Whtechpl. E	12	47..L 26
,, Change, Cheapside EC.	11	46..M 24
,, Deer-pk.-gds,Richmnd	14	—..S 7
,, Devonshire-rd, Balham SW . . .	21	—..V 20
,, Bethnal-green-road E .	12	47..J 27
,, Bond-st, Piccadilly W.	11	44..M 20
,, Broad-street, EC .	11	46..L 25
,, Brompton-rd, S. Kensington SW . .	15	51..P 17
,, Burlington-st,Bond-s,W	11	44..M 20
,, Castle-st,Whitechpl. E.	12	47..L 26
,, Cavendish-st,Oxfrd-s,W	11	44..L 20
,, Church-rd, C'mrcl.-r.E.	12	—..M 29
,, Claygate-la, Esher, Sy.	24	—..Z^6 4
,, Compton-st, Soho W .	11	45..M 21
,, Devonshire-rd,Blhm.SW	21	—..V 20
,, Dover-rd,BlackheathSE	18	—..R 34
,, Ford-road, Bow E .	12	40..J 29
,, ,, ,, .	12	47..J 28
,, ,, ,, .	12	48..J 31
,, ,, ry.-sta, N.L.R. .	12	48..J 20
,, Gravel-la, Wapping E	12	55..N 27
,, Jewry, Cheapside EC .	11	46..L 25
,, rd, Lee SE .	17	—..T 33
,, ,, Rotherhithe SE	17	55..P 18
,, sq, Lincoln's Inn WC .	—	45..L 23
,, st, St. Lukes EC .	11	46..K 25
,, town, Clapham SW .	16	61..S 20
,, ,, Croydon, Sy .	26	—..Z^6 23
,, Kent-road, SE . .	17	55..P 26
,, ,, rd Ry.-Sta,S.L.R	17	55..Q 28
,, Mill-road, Plumstead .	18	—..Q 40
,, Montague-st,Whtchl.E	12	47..L 26
,, Nichol-st, Bethnal-gr.E	12	47..K 26
,, Oak-la, Acton W .	10	—..L 11
,, ,, ,, Harlesden NW	10	—..J 11
,, ,, ,, Sta, G.W. Rly Acton W .	10	—..K 11
,, ,, road, Acton W .	10	—..M 11
,, Palace-la, Richmond .	14	—..T 6
,, ,, yd, Wstmnstrw.	11	53..O 22
,, Paradise-st,LambethSE	11	53..O 22
,, pk.-av, Balham SW .	16	—..U 19
,, ,, rd, Palmers-gr, N .	2	—..A 23
,, ,, ,, Plumstead .	13	—..Q 41
,, Portsmouth-rd, SW .	12	20..V
,, Pye-st, Westmstr. SW	11	53..O 21
,, Quebec-st, Oxford-stW	11	44..M 19
,, Queen-st, WstmnstrsW	11	53..N 21
,, River Chase,Twicken.	14	—..U 4
,, Scotland-yd, SW .	11	45..N 22
,, Serjeants-inn, Chancery-lane EC .	—	45..L 23
,, Sta.-hill, Chislehirst .	23	—..Z^1 37
,, Swan-la,U.Thames-s,EC	11	46..M 25
,, Woolwich-rd, E Greenwich SE . . .	17	57..P 33
Oldfield-rd, Acton W .	10	—..N 11
,, ,, Bromley, Kent.	28	—..Z^3 36
,, ,, Rotherhithe SE	17	55..P 28
,, ,, Stk.Nwngtn.N	7	38..F 26
,, ,, Willesden NW .	5	—..H 11
,, ,, Wimbledon SW	20	—..Y 14
Old-hill, Upper Clapton N	7	33..E 27
Oldridge-road, Balham .	21	—..V 19
Olga-st, Bethnal-green E .	12	48..J 29
Oliffe-street, Cubitt Tn. E	12	57..O 32
Olinda-rd, Stamford-hill N	7	33..D 26
Oliphant-st, Queen's-pk. W	10	42..J 14
Olive-rd, Cricklewood NW	5	—..G 13
,, ,, Plaistow E . .	13	—..K 35
,, ,, S. Wimbledon SW	20	—..Z 17
Oliver av, Norwood SE .	26	—..Z^2 26
,, gr, Norwood SE .	26	—..Z^2 26
,, rd, Leyton E .	7	41..F 31
,, ,, Sutton, Surrey .	29	—..Z^7 17
,, ,, Walthamstw. E	3	—..C 32
Olivette-street, Putney SW	15	59..S 14
Ollerton-rd,Nw.Southgte.N	2	—..A 21
Olmar-st, Old Kent-rd, SE.	17	55..Q 26
Olven-rd, Plumstead SE .	18	—..Q 39
Olympia, W. Kensington W	10	58..O 14
Ommaney-rd, Nw.Cross SE	4	63..R 29
Ondine-rd, E. Dulwich SE.	17	62..T 26
One Tree-hill, Forest-hillSE	17	—..U 28
Onega-yd, Rotherhithe SE.	12	56..O 29
Ongar-road, Fulham SW .	15	51..P 16
Onra-rd, Leyton-street E .	7	—..E 31
Onslow-avenue, Richmond	14	—..T 7
,, cres S KensingtnSW	11	51..O 17
,, gds, Carshalton,Sy.	—	30..Z^9 20
,, ,, Muswell-hill N .	2	—..C 20
,, ,, S.Kensingtn.SW	16	51..P 17
,, pl, S. Kensingtn.SW	—	51..O 17
,, rd, New Malden .	25	—..Z^2 11
,, ,, Richmond .	14	—..T 7
,, sq, S. KensingtnSW	16	51..P 17
Ontario-st, Southwark SE .	11	54..O 24
Opal-st, Kenningtn-pk.r,SE	16	53..P 23
Opera-arcade, Pall Mall SW	—	45..M 21
Oppidants-rd,Primrse-hl.NW	6	36..I 19
Opthalmic Hospital SE .	11	54..O 23
Orange-st, Bthnl-green-r E.	12	47..K 26
,, ,, Southwk-b-r.SE.	11	54..N 24
,, ,, Leicester-sq.WC.	11	45..M 21
Orb-street, Walworth SE .	17	54..P 25
Orbain-road, Fulham SW .	15	58..Q 14
Orbel-st, Battersea SW .	16	60..R 18
Orchard-av. Church-end N.	1	—..B 16
,, ,, New Malden .	25	—..Z^1 10
,, grove, Beckenham	27	—..Z^2 30
,, hi, Lewisham SE .	4	63..R 31
,, place, Blackwall E.	12	49..M 33
,, rd, Blackheath SE	17	64—S 32
,, ,, Brentford, Mdx	14	—..P 6
,, ,, Bromley-Kent	23	—..Z^1 35
,, ,, Farnborough .	30*b*	—..Z^8 38
,, ,, Highgate N .	6	32..D 20
,, ,, Hook, Surrey .	24	—..Z^6 6
,, ,, Kingston .	19	—..Z^1 7
,, ,, Richmond SW .	14	—..S 8
,, ,, Plumstead SE .	18	—..P 40
,, ,, Richmond .	14	—..S 8
,, ,, Shep. Bush W	10	50..N 12
,, ,, Sidcup . .	23	—..X 40
,, ,, Sutton, Surrey	29	—..Z^7 15
,, ,, Twickenham .	14	—..T 5
,, ,, Welling .	18	—..S 42
,, st, Essex-road N	7	38..H 25
,, ,, Poplar E .	12	49..M 31
,, ,, Oxford-st. W .	11	44..L 19
,, ,, Walthamstw E	3	—..C 29
,, ,, Wandswth SW	15	59..T 16
,, ,, WestminsterSW	11	53..O 21
,, ,, Woolwich .	13	—..O 37
OrdeHall-st, G Orm'd-st WC	11	45..K 22
Ordell-road, Bow E . .	12	48..J 30
Ordnance-rd, Cang. Twn. E	11	49..L 33
,, ,, Greenwich SE	12	57..O 33
,, ,, S. Jhn's-wdNW	5	35..I 18
,, ,, Woolwich .	18	—..Q 38
Oregon-av, Manor-park E	8	—..G 37
Orford-rd, Walthamstow E	3	—..C 31
,, st, Chelsea SW .	11	52..O 18
Oriel-rd, Homerton E .	7	40..H 29
Oriental-road, Silvertown E	13	—..N 33
,, street, Poplar E .	12	48..M 30
Orison-road, Plumstead .	18	—..P 40
Orkney-st, Battersea SW .	16	60..R 19
Orlando-road, Clapham SW	16	61..S 20
Orleans-road, Up. Hlwy. N	6	32..E 22
,, ,, Twickenham	14	—..U 5
,, ,, U. Norwood	21	—..Z^1 25
Orleston-road, Holloway N	6	37—H 23
Orme-sq, Bayswater-rd, W	—	43..M 16
Ormeley-road, Balham .	21	—..V 20
Ormiston-rd, E. Grnwch SE	18	—..P 34
,, ,, Shep. Bush W	10	50..M 12
Ormond-avenue, Hampton	19	—..Z 1
,, rd, Finsbury-pk. N	6	32..E 22
,, ,, Richmond .	14	—..T 6
Ormonde-rd, Mortlake SW	14	—..S 9
,, ter, NW . .	6	36..I 19
Ormsby-st, Kingslnd-rd. E	12	38..J 26
Ormside-st, Peckham SE .	17	55..Q 28
Ornan-rd, Hampstead NW	5	35..H 18
Orpingley-rd, Hornsey-rd N	6	32..F 23
Orpington, Kent . .	23	—..Z^5 42
,, sta, S.E. & C. Ry	28	—..Z^6 40
Orris-road, Upton E .	8	—..I 34
Orsett-street, Lambeth SE	16	53..P 22
,, ter, Westb'ne-ter. W	10	43..L 17
Orthopaedic-hos., Gt. Portland-street W . .	11	44..K 20
Orwell-road, Bow E . .	12	48..K 31
,, ,, Plaistow E .	13	—..J 35
Osbaldeston-rd,Up Clptn N	7	33..E 27
Osberton-road, Lee SE .	18	—..U 34
Osborn-place, Spitalfields E	12	47..L 26
,, st, Whitechapel E .	12	47..L 26
Osborne-rd, Acton W .	9	—..N 9
,, ,, Stroud-gr., N	6	32..E 23
,, ,, Forest Gate E	8	—..H 35
,, ,, Hackny. Wck E	7	40..H 30
,, ,, Leyton E .	7	—..F 31
,, ,, Norbiton .	19	—..Z 7
,, ,, Palmers-gr. N	2	—..A 23
,, ,, S. Hackney E	7	40..H 30
,, ,, Thornton Hth	21	—..Z^2 24
,, ter, S Lambth. SW	16	53..Q 22
Osbourne-rd, Willes.-gr NW	5	—..H 13
Oscar-street, Deptford SE	4	63..R 30
Oseney-crest, Kntsh.Tn NW	6	37..H 21
Osgood-av, Farnborough .	30*b*	—..Z^8 40
Osman-road, Edmonton N	3	—..A 27
,, ,, Tottenham N	7	33..D 25
Osmond-gds, Carshaltn, Sy	30	—..Z^7 20
Osnaburgh-st, Eust-rd. NW	11	44..K 20
Ospringe-rd, Kent. Twn NW	6	36..G 21
Ossian-rd, Stroud-green N	6	32..D 22
Ossington-st, Bayswater W	10	43..M 16
Ossory-rd, Old Kent-rd SE	17	55..Q 26
Ossulton-st, Somers Tn NW	11	45..J 21
Ostade-road, Tulse Hill SW	21	—..V 22
Osterley-lane, Osterley, Mid	9	—..O 1

	4-in. sht.	9-in. sht.	mar.
Princes-rd, Kew . .	14	—..Q	8
,, ,, Lewisham SE.	17	64..S	32
,, ,, Merton SW .	20	—..Z^{1}	17
,, ,, Mortlake SW	15	—..S	10
,, ,, Norbiton .	19	—..Z	8
,, ,, Notting-hill W	10	50..M	14
,, ,, Penge SE .	22	—..Z^{1}	28
,, ,, Richmond .	14	—..T	7
,, ,, Teddington .	19	—..X	2
,, ,, Wimbledon SW	20	—..Y	15
,, ,, Wmbldn-pk SW	20	—..V	14
,, ,, Woolwich .	18	—..Q	38
,, sq, Bayswater W	10	43..M	16
,, ,, Kennington SE	16	53..P	23
,, ,, S George E. E	12	47..M	27
,, st, Bank EC .	11	46..L	25
,, ,, Hanover-sq W	11	44..M	20
,, ,, Rotherh'the SE	12	55..N	28
,, ,, Westminstr SW	11	53..N	21
PrinceArthur-rd,Hmpstd NW	5	35..G	17
,, Cons.-rd, S. Ken. SW	11	51..O	17
,, Ed.-cres, Plaistow E	13	—..M	36
,, ,, rd, Hackney Wick E .	7	40..H	30
,, G'rge's-av, Raynes-park SW . .	20	—..Z^{1}	13
,, Geo-rd,StkNwngtn.N	7	38..G	26
,, Reg.-la, Vict. Dk. E	13	—..K	35
,, of W-cr, Kt. Tn. NW	6	36..H	20
,, ,, gt, Hyde-pk W	11	52..N	18
,, ,, rd, B'tsea SW	16	60..R	19
,, ,, ,, Cng. Tn E	13	—..M	35
,, ,, ,, Kt. Tn NW	6	36..H	19
,, ,, ,, Sutton, Sy	25	—..Z^{6}	17
,, ,, ,, Vic. Dk. E	13	—..M	35
,, ,, ter,Knsngtn W	—	51..N	16
Princelet-st, Spitalfields E	11	47..L	26
,, ,, Spitalfields E	12	47..L	26
Princes-row, Westmstr. SW	—	52..O	20
,, st, Cavendish-sq W	11	44..L	20
,, pk-av, Gldr's-gr NW	1	—..C	15
Princess-rd, Croydon, Sy.	26	—..Z^{4}	24
,, ,, East Sheen SW	15	—..S	10
,, ,, Finsbury-pk N	6	32..F	24
,, ,, Ilford . .	8	—..F	41
,, ,, Kilburn NW .	10	43..J	16
,, ,, Norwood, SE	26	—..Z^{3}	25
,, ,, Reg.-park NW	6	36..I	19
,, st, Oxford-st W .	11	44..L	20
,, ,, Edgware-rd NW	11	43..K	18
,, May-rd,StkNwgtnN	7	38..G	26
Princesses-walk, Kew .	14	— Q	7
Princethorpe-rd,Sydnhm.SE	22	—..X	28
Princeton-st, Bedford-rwWC	11	45..L	22
Printing House-la, Q. Victoria-street EC . .	—	46..M	24
Printing House-sq, Q. Victoria-street EC . .	—	46..M	24
Priolo-road, Charlton .	18	—..Q	35
Prior-street, Greenwich SE	4	64..R	31
Priory-av, Hornsey N .	2	—..B	22
,, gds, Turnham-gr W	10	—..O	11
,, grove, Clapham SW	16	61..R	21
,, ,, W.Brmptn SW	15	51..P	17
,, la, Lee SE . .	17	64..T	33
,, ,, Roehampton SW	15	—..T	11
,, rd, Acton W .	9	—..N	10
,, ,, Barking, Essex	8	—..I	40
,, ,, Hornsey N .	2	—..C	21
,, ,, Kew . .	14	—..Q	8
,, ,, Kilburn NW .	5	35..I	16
,, ,, Plaistow E .	13	—..J	36
,, ,, S. Lambeth SW	16	61..R	21
,, ,, Tottenham N	7	—..D	25
,, ,, Turnham-grn W	10	—..O	11
,, ,, Walthamstow E	3	—..C	30
,, st, Bromley E .	12	49..K	31
,, ,, Camden Tn. NW	6	36..I	20
,, pk-rd, Kilburn NW	5	—..I	15
Prioto-road, Charlton .	18	—..Q	35
Priscilla-road, Bow E .	12	48..K	31
Pritchard's-rd, Hckny-rd E	12	47..J	27
,, ,, Hackney E	12	39..J	27
Priter-rd, Bermondsey SE	12	55..O	27
Probert-road, Brixton SW	16	61..T	23
Probyn-road, Tulse-hill .	21	—..W	23
Proctor-street, Plumstead	13	—..Q	41
Promenade, Ealing Dean W	9	—..M	5
,, Hanwell W .	9	—..M	4
Prospect-hill, Walthmstw E	3	—..C	31
,, pla, Surbiton, Sy	24	—..Z^{3}	5
,, ,, Woolwich .	18	—..P	36
,, rd, Walthmstw. E	7	—..D	30
,, st, Brmndsy SE	12	55..O	27
,, ter, Grays Inn-road WC .	11	45..K	22
Prospero-road, Up. Hlwy N	6	32..E	21
Protheroe-road, Fulham SW	15	58..Q	15
Prout-grove, Neasden NW	5	—..G	11
,, road, Clapton E -	7	39..F	28
Provost-rd, Haverstk-hl NW	6	36..H	19
,, street, Hoxton N	11	46..J	25
Prudent-pas, King-st EC	—	46..M	25
Prujean-sq, Old Bailey EC	—	46..L	24
Prusom-street, Wapping E	12	47..N	28
Prussia-pla, Mitcham, Sy.	25	—..Z^{2}	18
Pudding-la, Eastcheap EC	11	46..M	25
Pulborough-rd, Wndswth SW	20	—..V	15
Pulford-street, Pimlico SW	16	53..P	21
Pulroso-rd, Stockwell SW	16	61..S	22
Pulteney-st, Barnsbury-rdN	6	37..I	23
Pump-court, Temple EC .	—	45..M	23
Punderson-pl, Beth-gr-rd E	12	47..K	27
Purchase-st, Somers Tn NW	11	45..J	21
Purley, Surrey . .	30	—..Z^{11}	23
,, Bury-av, Purley .	30	—..Z^{11}	24
,, downs, Surrey .	30	—..Z^{11}	24
,, knoll, Purley, Sy.	30	—..Z^{11}	22
,, rise, Purley, Surrey	30	—..Z^{11}	22
,, road, Croydon, Sy.	30	—..Z^{9}	24
,, dwns-rd, Purley, Sy	30	—..Z^{10}	24
,, Oaks-rd, Purley, Sy	30	—..Z^{10}	25
Purley, Oaks ry. sta, L.B. & S.C. Ry.	30	—..Z^{10}	24
,, Pk-rd, Purley, Sy.	30	—..Z^{10}	23
,, Ry. Sta, L.B. & S.C. Railway .	30	—..Z^{11}	23
Purrett-road, Plumstead .	13	—..Q	41
Purser's Cross-rd, Flhm SW	15	59..R	15
Purves-rd, Kensal-grn. NW	10	42..J	13
Putley-road, Plaistow E .	30	—..L	35
Putney, Kensal-green SW	15	59..T	14
,, Bridge SW . '	15	59..S	14
,, com, Putney SW .	15	—..S	13
,, heath, SW . .	20	—..V	13
,, hill, Putney SW .	15	59..T	14
,, Bge-rd, SW . .	15	59..S	14
,, ,, ,, Wndswth SW	15	59..T	15
,, ,; Ry Sta, Flm SW	15	59..S	15
,, h'th-la, Putney SW	15	—..U	14
,, Lr.-com, Putney SW	15	—..S	13
,, Pk-av, Putney SW	15	—..S	12
,, ,, la, Putney SW .	15	—..S	12
,, sta, L. & N.W. Rly., Putney SW	15	59..T	14
,, Vale-cem, Wimbledon-common SW	20	—..W	12
Pym-street, Chelsea SW .	16	51..P	18
Pymmes-brk, Palmer's-gr N	2	—..A	24
,, pk, Edmonton N	3	—..A	26
,, rd, Nw. Sthgte N	2	—..A	22
Pyrland-rd, Highbury N -	7	38..G	25
,, ,, Richmond .	14	—..U	7
Pyrmont-gro, W. Norwood	21	—..X	23
,, rd, Chiswick W .	14	—..P	8
,, ,, Ilford, Essex	8	—..F	39

Q

	4-in. sht.	9-in. sht.	mar.
Quadrant, Regent-st. SW .	11	45..M	21
,, rd, Canonbury N	6	38..I	24
,, ,, Thntn.-h, Sy.	26	—..Z^{3}	23
,, st, Canning Tn. E	12	49..L	33
Quaggy-road, Lewisham SE	17	—..U	32
Quainton-st, Kingsbury NW	5	—..F	10
Quaker-st, Spitalfields E .	11	37..K	26
Quality-ct, Chancery-la WC	—	45..L	23
Quarrendon-st, Fulham SW	15	59..R	16
Quarry-rd, Wandsworth SW	15	—..U	17
Queen Mary-av, Plaistow E	13	—..M	36
Quebec Pond, Rthrhth SE	12	56..O	29
,, road, Ilford, Essex .	8	—..E	39
,, ,, Upton E .	8	—..I	34
,, st, Marylebone-rd W	11	44..L	19
Queen-sq, Aldersgate-st.EC	—	46..L	24
,, ,, Bloomsbury WC	11	45..K	22
,, st, Camden Twn NW	6	36..I	21
,, ,, Mayfair W .	11	44..M	20
,, ,, Cheapside EC .	11	46..M	24
,, ,, Croydon, Sury .	30	—..Z^{7}	24
,, ,, Edgware-road W	11	44..L	18
,, ,, Goodmayes, Ex	8	—..F	43
,, ,, Greenwich SE. .	17	57..Q	32
,, ,, Hammersmith W	15	58..P	13
,, ,, Up. Edmonton N	3	—..A	26
,, ,, Woolwich . .	18	—..P	27
,, Adelaide-rd,PengeSE	22	—..Q^{1}	28
,, Anne-street W .	11	44..L	20
,, Annes-gr,Bdfrd-pk.W	10	—..O	10
,, ,, av,Brmly Kt.	27	—..Z^{2}	33
,, ,, gds, Bedford-park W .	10	—..O	11
,, ,, ga, Wstmr SW	11	53..N	21
,, Elizabth-rd,Kngstn	19	—..Z^{1}	7
,, ,, ,, Walthamstow E .	3	—..B	29
,, Elzabth-st,BmdsySE	12	55..N	26
,, Elizabeths walk, Carshalton, Surrey	30	—..Z^{7}	21
,, Elizabeths walk, Stk Newington N	7	33..E	25
,, Margarets-grove, Mildmay-pk. N	7	38..H	25
,, Victoria-st, City EC	11	46..M	24
Queenhithe, Up. Th.-st. EC	11	46..M	24
,, Dock, Upper Thames-street EC . .	11	46..M	24
Queens-av. Finchley N .	1	—..A	17
,, ,, Greenford .	9	—..K	2
,, ,, Muswell-hill N	2	—..B	20
,, ,, Willesden NW :	5	34..H	12
,, cres, Kntsh Tn. NW	6	36..H	19
,, Drive, Th. Ditton	24	—..Z^{4}	4
,, gds, Ealing W .	9	—..K	6
,, ,, Paddington W	10	43..M	17
,, gate,S.Knsngtn SW	10	51..N	17
,, Hall, Lnghm-pl. W.	11	44..L	22
,, Head-st, Islingtn N	6	38..I	24
,, park NW . .	10	34..J	14
,, pk.sta,N.W.Ry.NW	10	42..J	15
,, pla, Clapham SW .	16	61..S	20
,, rd, Barking, Essex	8	—..I	39
,, ,, Battersea SW .	16	52..Q	20
,, ,, Bayswater W .	10	43..M	16
,, ,, Beckenham .	22	—..Z^{2}	29
,, ,, Ealing W .	9	—..L	7
,, ,, Croydon, Sy .	26	—..Z^{4}	24
,, ,, Dalston E .	7	39..I	26
,, ,, E. Moulsey, Sy	24	—..Z^{3}	3
,, ,, E. Wickham .	18	—..S	42
,, ,, Finchley N .	1	—..A	17
,, ,, Finsbury-pk. N	6	32..F	24
,, ,, Forest-hill SE .	22	—..W	27
,, ,, Hendon NW .	1	—..C	13
,, ,, Hounslow .	14	—..R	1
,, ,, Ilford . .	8	—..D	39
,, ,, Ilford, Essex .	8	—..F	39
,, ,, Leytonstone E	7	—..E	33
,, ,, Mitcham, Sury	25	—..Z^{2}	17
,, ,, Morden . .	25	—..Z^{2}	16
,, ,, Mortlake SW .	15	—..S	10
,, ,, Nw Malden, Sy	25	—..Z^{3}	11
Queens-rd, Nw Southgate N	2	—..A	22
,, ,, Norbiton .	19	—..Z	8
,, ,, Norwood SE .	27	—..Z^{2}	27
,, ,, Peckham SE .	17	63..R	28
,, ,, Plaistow E .	13	—..J	35
,, ,, Richmond .	14	—..U	7
,, ,, St. Jns Wood NW	5	35..I	17
,, ,, S. Lambeth SW	16	61..S	20
,, ,, S. Norwood SE	27	—..Z^{2}	27
,, ,, Sutton, Surrey	29	—..Z^{7}	17
,, ,, Teddington .	19	—..Y	3
,, ,, Twickenham .	14	—..U	4
,, ,, Walthamstow E	7	—..D	30
,, ,, Walworth SE .	17	54..Q	25
,, ,, West Norwood	21	—..Y	24
,, ,, Wimbledon SW	20	—..Y	15
,, street, Stratford E	7	41..H	32
,, ter, Isleworth .	14	—..S	5
,, ,, S. Jns Wd. NW	10	35..J	17
,, walk, Ealing W .	9	—..K	6
,, wood, Muswell-hl N	2	—..C	20
,, ,, Welling .	18	—..U	40
,, Club-gds, W. Kensington SW. .	15	58..P	14
,, Gate-gds, S. Kensington SW. .	10	51..O	17
,, Gate-pl,S.Knsgtnsw	10	51..O	17
,, ,, ter,S.Knsgtnsw	10	51..O	17
,, Head pas., Paternoster Row EC .	—	46..L	24
,, Mead-rd, Brmly Kt	27	—..Z^{2}	33
,, pk. &W. Kilburn sta, N.W. rly. Queens-pk NW.	10	42..J	15
Queens-rd, sta, Bayswtr W.	10	43..M	16
,, ,, sta, S.W. rly., Battersea SW	16	61..R	20
,, ,, W. Wlthmstw E	7	—..D	30
,, st eet-place EC .	—	46..M	24
Queensberry-pl, S. Kens.SW	—	51..O	17
Queensborough, Byswtr W	10	43..M	17
,, ter, Bayswater-rd. W . . .	10	43..M	17
Queensbury-st, Canonb y N	6	38..I	24
Queensdale-rd, Nottg-hl W	10	50..N	14
Queensdown-rd, Clapton E	7	39..G	27
Queensland-rd, Holloway N	6	37..G	23
Queensmill-rd, Fulham SW	15	58..Q	13
Queensthorpe-rd,Sydhn.SE	22	—..X	28
Queenswood-rd, Sydhm.SE	22	—..X	29
Quemerford-rd, Holloway N	6	37..G	22
Quentin-road, Lee SE. .	17	64..T	33
Quernmore-rd, Hornsey N .	6	32..D	23
Querrin-street, Fulham SW	15	59..S	16
Quex-road, Kilburn NW .	5	35..I	16
Quick-road, Chiswick W .	15	—..P	10
Quickett-street, Bow E .	12	48..K	30
Quicks-road, Merton SW .	20	—..Z	16
Quill-lane, Putney SW .	15	59..S	14
Quilp-st, Southwark Bdg.-road SE. . . .	11	54..N	24
Quilter-street, Hackney E	12	47..K	27
Quinton-ave, Merton SW .	20	—..Z^{1}	14
,, st, Earlsfield SW .	20	—..W	17

R

	4-in. sht.	9-in. sht.	mar.
Rabbits-rd, Manor-pk. E .	8	—..G	37
Raby-rd, New Malden, Sy.	25	—..Z^{2}	10
,, st, Salmon-la, E	12	—..M	29
Rackham-st, N. Knsngtn W	10	42..L	14
Racquet-ct, Fleet-street EC	—	46..M	23
Racton-road, Fulham SW	15	58..Q	15
Radbourne-rd, Balham SW	21	—..V	21
Radcliffe-rd, Croydon, Sry	26	—..Z^{6}	26
Radford-rd, Lewisham SE	17	—..U	32
Radipole-road, Fulham SW	—	59..R	15
Radleigh-road, Finchley N	1	—..A	17
Radley-road, Tottenham N	3	—..A	26
Radlex-road, Leyton E .	7	—..E	31
Radnor-avenue, Greenhill .	1a	—..C	4
,, gds, Twickenham .	19	—..V	4
,, pla, Hyde-park W.	11	43..L	18
,, road, Harrow, Msx	1a	—..C	4
,, ,, Queens-pk.NW	5	—..I	14
,, ,, Twickenham	19	—..W	4
,, st, Chelsea SW .	16	52..P	18
,, ,, Finsbury EC .	11	46..K	24
,, ,, Peckham SE .	17	55..Q	26
Radstock-st, Battersea SW	16	51..Q	18
Raeburn-st, Brixton SW .	16	61..T	22
Raglan-gds, Wembley .	4	—..G	8
,, rd, Bromley, Kent	28	—..Z^{3}	35
,, ,, Walthamstow E	3	—..C	32
,, ,, Woolwich .	18	—..P	39
,, st, Kentish T'n NW	6	36..H	20
Rahere-st, Goswell-road EC	11	46..K	24
Railton-road, Brixton SW .	16	61..T	23
,, ,, Herne-hl SE	16	—..U	24
Railway-gro, Deptford SE	17	56..Q	29
,, cots, WillesdenNW	10	—..J	11
,, pl, Bethnal-gr. E	12	47..K	28
,, ,, Fnchrch-st. EC	—	46..M	26
,, road, Teddington	19	—..X	3
,, st, Barnes SW .	15	—..S	11
,, ,, Bromley E .	12	49..L	31
,, ,, Chadwell Hth Essex	8	—..E	43
Rainbow-st, Camberwell SE	17	54..Q	25
Rainham-rd, Kensal Gr.NW	10	42..J	14
Rainton-road, Charlton SE	18	—..P	34
Rainville-rd, Hmrsmth W.	15	58..Q	13
Raleana-road, Blackwall E	12	57..N	32
Raleigh drive, Esher. .	24	—..Z^{7}	2
,, gdns, Brixton SW .	16	—..U	22
,, road, Hornsey N .	2	—..B	23
,, ,, Penge SE .	22	—..Q^{1}	28
,, ,, Richmond .	14	—..S	8
,, street, Islington N .	11	38..J	24
Ralph-street, Southwark SE	11	54..O	24
Ramillies-st, Oxford-st. W.	—	44..L	21
Rampayne-st, Westmr. SW	16	53..P	21
Ramsay-vil, Forest-gate E	8	—..G	34
,, rd, Acton W. .	9	—..N	10
,, ,, Forest Gate E	8	—..G	34
,, ,, Leytonstone E	7	41..G	34
Ramsden, Orpington, Kent	28	—..Z^{5}	42
,, rd, Balham SW .	16	—..U	19
,, ,, Nw Sthgte N	2	—..A	19
Ramsey-road, Hendon NW	5	—..D	12
Ramsgate-st, Dalston E .	7	39..H	26
Randall-st, Battersea SW .	16	60..R	18
Randel-pla, Greenwich SE	17	—..Q	31
Randells-road, Islington N	6	37..I	22
Randolph Crest,Maida-hl W	10	43..K	17
,, gds, Kilburn NW	10	43..J	16
,, rd, Maida-hill W	10	43..K	17
,, ,, Victoria Dk.E	13	—..M	35
,, st, Camden T.NW	6	37..I	21
Ranelagh-av, Barnes SW .	15	—..R	12
,, ,, Fulham SW .	15	59..S	15
,, Drive, Twicknm	14	—..T	5
,, gds, Chelsea SW	16	52..P	19
,, ,, Fulham SW	15	59..S	15
,, ,, Ilford, Esx	8	—..E	38
,, par, Barnes SW .	15	—..R	12
,, rd, Ealing W .	9	—..N	7
,, ,, East Ham E.	13	—..J	38
,, ,, Harlesdn NW	10	—..J	11
,, ,, Leytonstone E	7	41..G	33
,, ,, Pimlico SW .	16	52..P	21
,, ,, Sudbury, Mdx	4	—..H	7
,, ,, Tottenham N	3	—..B	26
,, ,, W'brne-pk.W	10	43..L	16
,, ,, West Ham E	12	41..J	33
,, ,, Wood Gr. N .	2	—..A	23
Rangemoor-rd, Tottenm N	3	—..C	26
Rangers-gds, E. Sheen SW	14	—..U	9
Rangoon-st, Crutched Friars EC	—	46..M	26
Rankin-st, Shepherds B. W	10	—..N	11
Rannoch-st, Hmrsmth W .	15	58..P	13
Ransom-road, Charlton .	18	—..P	35
Ranston-st, Lisson-gro, NW	11	43..K	18
Ranuld-rd, Hampstead NW	5	—..G	15
Ranwell-st, Old Ford-rd. E	12	40..J	30
Raphael-st, Knightsbge SW	11	52..N	18
Rashleigh-st, S. Lamb'th SW	16	61..S	20
Rastell-av, Streatham SW .	21	—..W	21
Ratcliff E	12	47..M	28
,, sq, Com'cial-rd. E	12	48..M	29
,, rd, Forest Gate E	8	—..H	35
Rathbone-pla, Oxford-st. W	11	45..L	21
,, st, Canning Tn.E	12	49..L	33
Rathcoole-av, Hornsey N .	2	—..C	23
,, gds, Hornsey N.	2	—..C	23
Rathfern-road, Catford SE	22	—..W	30
Rathgar-avenue, Ealing W	9	—..M	5
,, road, Brixton SW	—	62..S	24
Rathmore-rd, Charlton SE.	18	—..P	35
Rattray-road, Brixton SW	16	—..T	23
Raveley-rd, Bow Comn. E	12	48..K	31
Raveley-st, Kentish Tn.NW	6	36..G	21
Raven-road, Whitechapel E	12	47..L	27
,, st, Whitechapel E .	12	47..L	27
Ravenhill-road, Plaistow E	13	—..J	35
Ravenna-road, Putney SW.	15	59..T	14
Ravensbourne-gds, Castle-bar-hill W	9	—..L	5
,, pk, Catf'd SE	22	—..V	30
,, River, Lewisham SE	4	63..S	31
,, ,, Kent	28	—..Z^{3}	34
,, rd, Catf'd SE	22	—..V	29
,, ,, Rvsbrne	22	—..Q^{1}	32
,, ,, Twickm	14	—..T	5
,, sta, S.E. & C.Rly. .	22	—..Q^{1}	32
Ravensbury Path, Mitcham, Surrey. . .	25	—..Z^{2}	17
,, rd, Earlsfd. SW	20	—..W	16
Ravenscar-rd, Lg. Ditton .	24	—..Z^{5}	7
,, ,, Surbiton .	24	—..Z^{5}	7
Ravnscrt-gds, Hmrsmth W.	10	58..O	12
,, la, Hmrsmth W .	10	58..O	12
,, pk, Hmrsmth W .	10	50..O	12
,, ,, rd,Hmrsmth W	10	58..O	12
,, ,, rly.sta.Met.Rly	10	58..O	12
,, ,, rly. sta, Hmrsmth W .	10	58..O	12
,, sq. Hmrsmth W .	—	50..O	12
Ravenscroft-av, HendonNW	5	—..D	15
,, rd, Cng Tn. E .	13	—..L	34
,, ,, Chiswick-pk. W. .	9	—..O	10
,, ,, Penge . .	22	—..Z^{2}	28
,, st,Hckny rd.E	12	47..J	26
Ravensdale-rd, Stmfd-hl. N	7	33..D	26
Ravensdon-st, Kennington park-road SE. . .	16	53..P	23
Ravenshaw-st,Hmpstd NW	5	34—H	15
Ravenhurst-av, Hendon NW	1	—..B	13
Ravenslea-road, Balham .	21	—..V	19
Ravenstone-rd, Balham SW	21	—..W	19
,, ,, Hendon NW	5	—..D	12
,, ,, Hornsey N	2	—..B	23
,, ,, Lytnstne E	7	41..G	33
Ravenswood-rd, Balham .	21	—..V	20
,, ,, Croyd., Sy.	26	—..Z^{6}	23
,, ,, Wlthmstw E	3	—..C	31
Ravensworth-rd, Queens-park NW . . .	10	42..J	13
Rawleigh-road, Merton SW	20	—..Z^{1}	14
Rawlings-street, Chelsea SW	11	52..O	18
Raydon-st, Highgate N .	6	32..F	20
Rawstorne-st, Goswell-rd. EC.	11	46..K	23
Ray-street, Clerkenwell EC	11	46..K	23
Rayleigh-rd, Canning Tn. E	12	49..K	32
,, ,, W. Kensgtn.W	10	50..N	14
Raymead-av, Thornton H.	26	—..Z^{3}	23
Raymede-st, Kensal-gr. W.	10	42..K	14

	4-in. sht.	9-in. sht.	mar.
Raymond-bgs, Grays Inn WC	11	45..L	23
,, rd, Plaistow E .	13	—..J	35
,, ,, Wimbledn SW	20	—..Y	14
Raymth-rd, Rthrhth SE .	17	55..P	27
Rayners-road, Putney SW	15	—..T	14
Raynes-pk, Wimbledon SW	25	—..Z^2	13
,, ,, sta., L. & S.W. Railway, Raynes-pk. SW	20	—..Z^1	13
Raynham-av, Edmonton N	3	—..A	27
,, rd, Edmonton N	3	—..A	27
,, ,, Hmrsmth W	10	58..O	12
,, ter, Edmonton N	3	—..A	27
Rays-av, Edmonton N .	3	—..A	28
,, road, Edmonton N .	3	—..A	28
Reading-lane, Hackney E .	7	39..H	27
,, rd, Sutton, Surry	29	—..Z^7	17
Reaston-st, New Cross SE .	17	63..R	28
Rebecca-ter, Rthrhithe SE	12	55..O	28
Reckitt-road, Chiswick W .	15	—..P	10
Record Of., Chancery-la WC	11	45..L	23
Recovery-st, Lr. Tootg SW	20	—..Y	18
Recreation-gds, Richmond	14	—..S	7
Recreation Gd, Acton W .	9	—..N	9
,, ,, Addiscombe Croyd. Sry.	26	—..Z^5	23
,, ,, Barking, Ex	8	—..H	39
,, ,, Bcknham, Kent .	27	—..Z^2	29
,, ,, Brentford, Middlesex	14	—..P	6
,, ,, Carshaltn	25	—..Z^6	18
,, ,, Chiswick W	15	—..P	11
,, ,, Croyd. Sy	26	—..Z^4	24
,, ,, Fairfield-rd Croydon, Sy	26	—..Z^6	25
,, ,, Grange-rd, Selhurst SE	26	—..Z^2	25
,, ,, Leyton E .	7	41..G	32
,, ,, Norwd SE	26	—..Z^3	26
,, ,, Plashet E .	8	—..I	36
,, ,, Poplar E .	12	49..M	32
,, ,, Sanderstd, Surrey .	30	—..Z^9	24
,, ,, Thornton Heath, Surrey	26	—..Z^2	23
,, ,, Wapping E	12	55..N	27
,, ,, West Ham lane E .	7	41..I	33
,, road, Bromley	22	—..Z^2	33
Rectory-gro, Clapham SW	16	61..S	20
,, ,, Woolwich .	18	—..P	37
,, la, Lr. Tooting SW	21	—..Y	19
,, ,, Sidcup . .	23	—..Y	42
,, place, Woolwich .	18	—..P	38
,, rd, Barnes SW .	15	—..R	12
,, ,, Beckenham .	22	—..Z^2	30
,, ,, Fulham SW .	15	59..R	15
,, ,, Hornsey N .	2	—..C	22
,, ,, Manor-pk. E .	8	—..H	37
,, ,, Walthamstow E	3	—..C	31
,, ,, Stk. Newgtn N	7	39..F	26
,, ,, Sutton, Surrey	25	—..Z^6	16
,, ,, ry. sta., G.E.R.	7	39..F	27
,, square, Stepney E	12	48..L	29
Reculver-rd, Rothrhthe SE.	17	55..P	28
Red-hill, Chislehurst, Kent	23	—..Y	38
,, ,, Edgware, Mdsx. .	1	—..A	10
,, lane, Claygate, Surrey	28*a*	—..Z^7	4
,, Berry-gr, Up. Sydenham SE . .	22	—..X	28
,, Cross-st, Barbican EC	11	46..L	24
,, Lion-crt, Fleet-st. EC	—	45..L	23
,, ,, ,, Watling-st. EC	—	46..M	24
,, ,, la, Shooter-hill .	18	—..R	37
,, ,, Mkt, White Cross street EC. . .	—	46..L	24
,, ,, pla, Barking, Ex	8	—..I	39
,, ,, road, Surbiton .	24	—..Z^5	7
,, ,, sq, High Hibrnwc	11	45..K	22
,, ,, st, Clerkenwell EC	11	46..K	23
,, ,, ,, Hgh Hlbn WC	11	45..L	22
,, ,, ,, Richmond .	14	—..T	6
,, ,, ,, Wapping E .	12	55..N	27
,, ,, ,, Woolwich .	18	—..P	38
,, ,, yd, Holborn WC.	—	45..L	22
,, Lodge-rd, W. Wickm.	27	—..Z^4	32
Post-hl, Herne-hill SE	16	—..T	25
Redan-st, W. Kensingtn W	10	50..O	14
Redbourne-av, Finchley W	1	—..A	16
Redbridge-la, Wanstd. Esx	8	—..D	37
Redcliffe-gds, Ilford, Esx.	8	—..E	38
,, ,, S. Kensington SW. .	15	51..P	16
,, rd, S.Kensingtn SW	15	51..P	17
,, sq, S.Kensingtn SW	15	51..P	16
,, st, W. Brmptn SW	—	51..P	16
Redclyffe-rd, Upton-pk. E.	13	—..J	36
Redcross-st, Barbican EC .	11	46..L	24
,, ,, Borough SE .	11	54..N	24
Reddins-rd, Peckham SE	17	55..Q	26
Reddons-road, Beckenham	22	—..Q^1	29
Redesdale-st, Chelsea SW .	16	52..P	18
Redfern-rd, Harlesden NW	5	—..I	11
Redfield-la, Cromwell-rd. SW	10	51..O	16
Redford-rd, East Ham E .	13	—..J	38
Redgrave-road, Putney SW	15	59..S	14
Redhill-st, Regents-pk. NW	11	44..J	20
Redington-rd, Hmpstd NW	5	35..F	16
Redmans-rd, Stepney-gr. E	12	47..L	28
Redmead-la, Wapping E .	12	55..N	27
Redmore-rd, Hmrsmth W .	10	58..O	12
Redriffe-rd, Rotherhithe SE	12	56..O	29
,, ,, West Ham E	12	41..J	34
Redruth-road, Lee SE .	17	—..T	33
Redstone-road, Hornsey N	2	—..B	21
Redvers-rd, Wood Gr. N .	2	—..A	23
Redwald-rd, Lr. Clapton E	7	40..G	29
Reedham-st, Peckham SE .	17	62..S	26
Reedholm-vils, Highbury N	—	38..G	25
Reedworth-st, Kennington road SE.	16	53..P	23
Reeves-road, Bromley E .	12	48..K	31
Reform-road, Merton SW .	20	—..Z	16
,, row, Tottenham N	3	—..A	27
,, st, Battersea SW .	16	60..R	19
Regency-sq, Kennington SE	—	53..P	23
,, st, Acton NW .	10	—..K	11
,, ,, Westminstr SW	11	53..O	21
Regent-rd, Herne-hill SE .	16	—..U	23
Regents-row, Hackney E .	12	39..J	27
Regent-sq, Grays I.-rd. WC	11	45..K	22
,, street W . .	11	44..M	20
Regents Canal, Regents-pk NW . . .	11	43..J	18
,, ,, Dock, Limehouse E .	12	48..M	29
,, pk., Marylebne NW	11	44..J	19
,, ,, rd, Primrose-hill NW	6	36..I	19
,, ,, ,, Church End Finchley N .	1	—..B	15
,, ,, ry. sta., Bakerloo Rly. .	11	44..K	20
,, ,, ter, Oval-rd, NW	6	36..I	20
Regina-rd, Ealing Dean W	9	—..M	5
,, ,, Finsbury-pk. N	6	32..E	23
Reginald-rd, Deptford SE .	4	63..R	30
Reidhaven-rd, Plumstead .	18	—..P	40
Reigate-rd, Epsom, Surrey	29	—..Z^{10}	11
,, ,, Ilford . .	8	—..F	41
Reighton-road, Clapton E .	7	33..F	27
Relf-road, Peckham SE .	17	62..S	27
Remington-st, City-road N	—	46..J	24
Rendel-rd, Victoria Dck E	13	—..M	34
Rendlesham-rd, Clapton E	7	39..G	27
Renfrew-rd, Lr. Kennington-lane SE .	16	54..P	23
,, ,, Norbiton .	19	—..Z	9
Renmuir-st, Tooting SW .	20	—..Y	18
Rennell-st, Lewisham SE .	4	64..S	31
Rensburg-rd, Wlthmstw E	7	—..D	29
Renters-hl, Golders Gr. NW	5	—..E	15
,, lane, Hendon NW	5	—..D	14
Rephidim-st, Brmndsy SE	—	54..O	25
Replingham-rd, Sthflds SW	20	—..V	15
Reporton-rd, Fulham SW .	15	58..Q	14
Repton-street, Stepney E .	12	48..L	29
Reservoir-rd, Brockley SE	—	63..S	29
Retcar-street, Highgate N .	6	—..F	20
Retreat-place, Hackney E .	7	39..H	28
,, rd, Surbiton, Sury	24	—..Z^4	7
Revelon-road, Brockley SE	4	63..S	29
Revelstoke-rd, Wimbledon park SW	20	—..W	15
Reventlow-rd, New Eltham Kent	23	—..W	38
Reverdy-rd, Bermndsy SE.	17	55..P	26
Reynolds-road, Acton W .	9	—..N	10
,, ,, Peckham SE	17	—..T	28
,, ,, Stratford E	7	41..I	33
Rhea-st, N. Woolwich E .	13	—..N	37
Rhodes-street, Holloway N	6	37..H	23
,, W.R. Limehouse E	12	48..M	30
Rhodesia-rd, Leyton E .	7	—..F	32
,, ,, Stockwell SW	16	61..S	22
Rhodeswell-rd, Limehouse E	12	—..L	29
Rhyl-st, Kentish Twn NW	6	36..H	19
Rhyme-road, Lewisham SE	4	64..T	31
Ribblesdale-rd, Hornsey N	2	—..C	23
,, ,, Strthm SW	21	—..T	20
Ricardo-street, Poplar E .	12	48..M	31
Rich-st, W. India-Dk.-rd. E	12	48..M	30
Richard-st, Com'cial-rd. E	12	47..M	27
,, ,, Islington N .	11	37..J	23
,, ,, Long-lane SE .	12	54..N	25
Richardson-rd, W. Ham E.	12	41..J	33
,, st, Brmndsy SE	11	54..N	25
Richbell-pl, Lambs Conduit-street WC . .	—	45..L	22
Richborough-rd, Cricklewood NW	5	—..G	14
Richford-rd, West Ham E	12	41..J	34
,, st, Shep. Bush W	10	50..N	13
Richmond, Surrey .	14	—..T	7
,, av, Merton SW	20	—..Z^1	14
,, ,, Morden .	25	—..Z^4	16
,, ,, Willesden-Green NW	5	—..H	13
,, Bdge, Richmnd	14	—..T	6
,, cres, Islington N	6	37..I	23
,, ga, Richmnd-hl	14	—..U	7
,, gr, Richmond	14	—..T	6
,, gr, Surbiton, Sy	24	—..Z^4	7
,, hill, Richmond	14	—..T	7
,, ,, Surrey .	14	—..U	7
,, pk, Surrey .	19	—..W	8
,, ,, rd, E. Sheen SW	14	—..T	10
,, ,, ,, Norbiton	19	—..Z	7
,, rd, Cottenham-park SW .	20	—..Z^1	12
,, ,, Dalston E .	7	39..I	27
,, ,, Ealing W .	9	—..N	7
,, ,, Earls-crt. SW	15	51..P	16
,, ,, Forest-gt. E	8	—..H	35
,, ,, W.Knsgtn W	10	50..N	14
,, ,, Ilford, Esx.	8	—..G	39
,, ,, Isleworth .	14	—..S	5
,, ,, Islington N	6	37..I	23
,, ,, Leytons. E	7	—..F	32
,, ,, Nw Sthgte N	2	—..A	22
,, ,, Norbiton .	19	—..Z	7
,, ,, Plaistow E	13	—..J	34
,, ,, Thornton Heath, Sy	26	—..Z^2	23
,, ,, Ttnhm N .	7	33..D	26
,, ,, Twicknhm	14	—..U	5
,, ,, Wlthmstw E	7	—..D	30
,, ,, Wanstead E	8	—..F	34
,, ,, W.Knsgtn W	10	50..N	14
,, ,, Westbourne grove W .	10	43..L	16
,, sta, L.& S.W. Ry. Richmnd	14	—..S	7
Richmond-st, City-rd. EC	11	46..K	25
,, ,, Edgware-rd NW . .	10	43..K	17
,, ,, St. Lukes EC	11	46..K	24
,, ter, Knsngtn W	10	50..N	14
,, ,, S.Lmbth SW	16	53..Q	22
,, ,, Whthall SW	11	53..N	22
Riddlesdown-rd, Purley, Sy	30	—..Z^1	23
Rideout-st, Woolwich, Knt	18	—..P	37
Ridge-rd, Hornsey N. .	6	32..D	23
,, ,, Lr. Streathm SW	21	—..Z^1	20
,, ,, Sutton, Surrey .	25	—..Z^5	14
Ridgmount-gds, Gower-st. WC	11	45..L	21
Ridgway, Wimbledon SW .	20	—..Z	13
,, gds, Wimbldn SW	20	—..Z	13
,, pl, Wimbledn SW	20	—..Y	14
,, rd, Spring-grove Middlesex. .	14	—..Q	3
,, The, Friern Barnet N . .	2	—..A	19
Ridgmount-st, Gower-st. WC	11	45..L	21
Rigdale-st, Old Ford E .	12	48..J	31
Riding House-st, Regent-street W . . .	11	44..L	20
Ridings-road, Wimbledon	20	—..X	10
Ridley-avenue, Ealing W .	9	—..N	5
,, rd, Bromley . .	27	—..Z^2	33
,, ,, Dalston E. .	7	39..H	26
,, ,, Forest-gate E .	8	—..G	35
,, ,, Hrlsdn-grn. NW	10	34..J	12
,, ,, Plaistow E .	13	—..M	35
,, ,, Wimbledon SW	20	—..Z	16
Ridsdale road, Anerley SE	22	—..Z^1	27
Riffel-rd, Cricklewood NW	5	—..H	13
Rigault-road, Fulham SW	15	59..R	14
Riggeley-rd, Harlesden NW	10	42..J	12
Riggindale-rd, Streathm SW	21	—..Y	21
Rignold-rd, Camberwell SE	16	62..R	25
Riles-road, Plaistow E .	13	—..J	34
Riley-rd, Queen's-pk. NW .	10	42..J	13
,, st, Bermondsey SE	12	54..O	26
,, ,, Chelsea, SW .	16	51..Q	17
Rinaldo-street, Balham .	21	—..V	20
Ringcroft-st, Holloway N .	6	37..H	23
Ringford-rd, Wndswth SW	15	—..U	15
Ringmer-av, Fulham SW .	15	59..R	14
Ringstead-rd, Catford SE .	22	—..V	31
,, ,, Sutton, Sy.	29	—..Z^7	17
Ringwood-rd, Ilford .	8	—..D	38
,, ,, Wlthmstw E	7	—..D	30
Ripley-rd, Canning Tn. E .	13	—..L	35
,, ,, Svn Kngs, Esx	8	—..F	41
Ripon-rd, Plumstead .	18	—..Q	38
Ripple-lane, Barking .	13	—..K	42
,, road, Barking .	13	—..J	38
,, ,, Barking, Esx	8	—..I	39
Ripporth-rd, Old Ford E	7	40..I	30
Rippotsen-rd, Plumstead .	13	—..P	41
Riseldine-rd, Brockley SE	17	—..U	29
Risinghill-st, Pentonville N	11	45..J	23
Risingholme-rd, Wealdstne	1*a*	—..A	4
Ritches-rd, West Green N	2	—..C	24
Ritchie-rd, S. Norwood SE	27	—..Z^4	27
Ritchings-av, Wlthmstw E	3	—..C	29
Ritherdon-rd, Up. Tooting	21	—..W	19
Ritson-rd, Dalston E .	—	39..H	27
,, ,, Tottenham N .	2	—..C	24
Kitter-st, Woolwich, Kent.	18	—..Q	38
Rittoms-lane, Kingston .	19	—..Z^1	7
River-av, Th. Ditton, Sy.	24	—..Z^4	4
,, Brent, Greenford .	9	—..K	3
,, Crane, Twickenham	19	—..V	2
,, Cray, Kent . .	23	—..Z^1	42
,, ,, Kent . .	28	—..Z^3	42
,, Ember, East Molesey, Surrey . .	24	—..Z^4	2
,, lane, Petersham .	19	—..V	6
,, Mole, Surrey . .	24	—..Z^2	3
,, pk-rd, Wood-gren. N	2	—..A	23
,, rd, Holloway N .	6	32..F	22
,, ,, N. Woolwich E .	13	—..L	42
,, Roding, Ilford, Es. .	8	—..F	37
,, st, Bromley E . .	12	48..L	31
,, ,, Clerkenwell EC .	11	45..J	23
,, ,, Putney SW .	15	59..S	14
,, ter, Greenwich SE .	12	57..O	33
,, view-gro, Chiswick W	14	—..Q	9
,, ,, rd, Chiswick W	14	—..Q	9
,, Wandle, Earlsfld SW	20	—..V	16
,, ,, Mitcham, Sy	26	—..Z^5	19
,, ,, Mitcham, Sy	25	—..Z^3	17
Rivercourt-rd, Hmrsmth W	10	58..O	12
Riverdale-rd, Plumstead .	18	—..P	40
,, ,, Twickenham	14	—..T	6
Riverhall-st, S Lambth SW	16	53..Q	21
Riversdale-rd, Highbury N	6	38..F	24
Riverside, Twickenham .	19	—..V	5
Riverview-gds, Twicknhm	19	—..W	4
Rivington-st, Shoredtch EC	11	46..K	25
Roach-road, Old Ford E .	7	40..I	30
Roan-street, Greenwich SE	17	57..Q	31
Roberts-rd, Chapel End E	3	—..A	31
Robert-st, Adelphi WC .	11	45..M	22
,, ,, Davies-street W	11	44..M	20
,, ,, Guilford-st. WC	11	45..K	22
,, ,, Hampstd.-rd NW	11	44..K	20
,, ,, N. Woolwich E	13	—..N	38
,, ,, Plumstead SE .	18	—..P	39
,, ,, Woolwich SE .	18	—..P	37
Robertson-st, S. Lmbth. SW	16	61..S	20
Robeson-st, Limehouse E .	12	48..L	30
Robin Hood-ct, Shoe-la EC	—	45..L	23
,, ,, ,, Milk-st EC	—	46..L	24
,, ,, la, Poplar E .	12	49..M	32
,, ,, ,, Sutton, Sy	29	—..Z^7	15
,, ,, ,, Wimbledon-com. SW	20	—..X	10
,, ,, rd, Wimbledon-common SW	11	20..X	11
,, ,, yd, Leather-lane, EC	—	45..L	23
Robinson-rd, L. Tooting SW	20	—..Y	18
,, ,, Beth.-grn. E	12	47..J	28
Robsart-street, Brixton SW	16	61..S	23
Robson-road, W. Norwood	21	—..X	24
Rochdale-rd, Plumstead SE	18	—..P	42
,, ,, Walthmstw E	7	—..E	30
Roche-road, Norbury .	21	—..Z^2	22
Rochelle-rd, Beckenham .	27	—..Z^3	30
,, st, Bethnal-grn. E	12	47..K	26
Rochester-av, Plaistow E .	13	—..J	35
,, pla, Camdn Tn NW	6	36..H	21
,, rd, Camdn Tn. NW	6	36..H	21
,, ,, Carshalton, Sy.	29	—..Z^7	18
,, row, Westmstr. SW	11	52..O	21
,, sq, Camdn Tn. NW	6	37..I	21
,, ter, Camdn. Tn NW	6	36..H	21
Rochford-st, Hvrstk-hill NW	6	36..G	19
Rock-hill, Sydenham SE .	22	—..X	26
,, road, Homerton E .	7	40..G	29
Rockbourne-rd, Lewshm SE	22	—..W	28
Rockhall-rd, Cricklewd. NW	5	—..G	14
Rockingham-st, Newington Causeway SE . .	11	54..O	24
Rockland-road, Putney SW	15	59..T	14
Rockley-rd, W.Knsngtn W	10	50..N	14
Rock Mount-rd, Norwd. SE	21	—..Z^1	25
Rodborough-rd, Golder's-green NW . . .	5	—..E	16
Roden-street, Holloway N	6	37..F	22
,, ,, Ilford, Essex	8	—..G	38
Rodenhurst-rd, Claphm SW	16	—..U	21
Roderick-rd, Hampstd. NW	6	36..G	19
Roding-road, Clapton E .	7	40..G	29
Rodmere-st, E Grnwch. SE	17	57..P	33
Rodney-pla, Nw Knt-rd SE	11	54..O	24
,, rd, Hackney E .	7	39..G	27
,, ,, Nw Malden, Sy	25	—..Z^3	10
,, ,, Walworth SE .	17	54..P	25
,, st, Pentonville N .	11	37..J	23
,, ,, Woolwich .	13	—..O	38
Rodway-rd, Rochmptn. SW	15	—..U	12
Rodwell-rd, E. Dulwich SE	17	—..U	26
Roe-grn, Kingsbury NW .	1	—..C	10
Roehampton, SW . .	14	—..U	12
,, la, Rochmptn SW	15	—..T	12
,, vale, Putney SW	20	—..W	11
Rokeby-road, Brockley SE	4	63..S	30
,, st, West Ham E .	12	41..J	33
Rokesly-av, Hornsey N .	2	—..C	22
Roland-gdns, Kensgtn. SW	15	51..P	17
,, -rd, Walthmstw. E	3	—..C	32
Rolfe-road, Charlton .	18	—..P	36
Rolleston-rd, Croydon, Sy.	30	—..Z^9	24
Rollins-street, Deptford SE	17	55..Q	28
Rolls-st, Battersea SW .	16	60..R	19
,, bldgs, Fetter-lane EC	—	45..L	23
,, cres, Canning Town E	12	49..K	32
,, road, Bermondsey SE	17	55..P	26
Rollscourt-av, Herne-hl SE	16	—..U	24
Rolph-road, Bromley E .	12	48..K	31
Rolt-street, Deptford SE .	17	56..Q	29
Rolls-passage, WC . .	—	45..L	23
Roma-rd, Walthamstow E	3	—..B	29
Roman-rd, East Ham E .	15	—..L	37
,, ,, Barnsbury N .	6	37..H	22
,, ,, Ilford, Essex .	8	—..H	39
,, ,, Old Ford E .	12	48..J	29
,, ,, Turnham Gn W	10	—..O	11
,, ,, Up. Norwood .	21	—..Y	25
,, Bath-st, Nwgte-st EC	—	46..L	24
Rommany-rd, W Norwood	21	—..X	24
Romberg-rd, Up. Tooting	21	—..X	19
Romford-road, E . .	8	—..H	35
Romilly-rd, Finsbury-pk N	6	32..F	24
Romney-rd, Greenwich SE	17	57..Q	32
,, st, Westmstr. SW	11	53..O	21
Romola-road, Norwood-rd	21	—..V	23
Rona-rd, Hampstead NW .	8	36..G	19
Ronald-st, Ratcliff E .	12	47..M	28
Ronalds-rd, Holloway-rd N	6	37..H	23
Rondu-rd, Cricklewood NW	5	—..G	14
Ronver-road, Lee SE .	22	—..V	34
Rood-la, Fenchurch-st EC	11	46..M	25
Rook-street, Poplar E .	12	48..M	31
Rookfield-av, Muswell-hill N	2	—..C	21
Rookstne-rd, Lr. Tootg. SW	20	—..Y	18
Rookwood-rd, Stamfrd-hi N	7	33..D	27
Rope-wlk, E. Greenwich SE	17	57..P	33
,, yd-rails, Woolwich .	13	—..O	38
Ropemaker-st, Finsbury EC	11	46..L	25
Ropemaker's-fields, Limehouse E	12	48..M	30
Roper-street, Eltham .	18	—..U	37
Ropery-st, Bow-common E	12	48..K	30
Rosaline-rd, Fulham SW .	15	58..Q	14
Rosary-gds. Old Brompton-road SW . . .	15	51..P	17
Rosaville-road, Fulham SW	15	58..Q	15
Roscoe-st, Bunhill-row EC	11	46..K	25
,, ,, Canning Tn. E .	12	49..M	33
Rose-crt, Golden-lane EC .	—	46..K	24
,, ,, Gt. Tower-st EC	—	46..M	26
,, hill, Sutton, Surrey .	25	—..Z^5	16
,, mount, Carshalton, Sy	30	—..Z^8	20
,, street, Long Acre WC	—	45..M	22
,, & Crown-crt, Foster-lane EC . . .	—	46..L	24
Rosebank-av, Sudbury .	4	—..G	4
,, gr, Walthmstw E	3	—..B	30
,, rd, Hanwell W .	9	—..N	4
,, ,, Leyton E .	7	—..D	31
,, ,, Roman-rd E	12	48..J	30
Roseberry-pla, Dalston E .	7	39..H	26
Rosebery-av, Farngdn-rd EC	11	45..K	23
,, ,, Manor-pk. E	8	—..H	37
,, ,, Thorntn-hth	21	—..Z^2	24
,, ,, Tottenhm. N	3	—..A	27
,, gds, Ealing W .	9	—..L	5
,, ,, Fnsbry.-pk N	6	—..D	24
,, ,, Hornsey N .	2	—..C	22
,, rd, Alexr.-pk. N	2	—..A	21
,, ,, Cheam, Sy. .	29	—..Z^8	15

Stephen-street. INDEX TO STREETS, &c. **Taniwha-terrace.**

	4-in. sht.	9-in. sht.	mar.
Stephen-st, Tott. Crt-rd. WC	11	45	L 21
Stephendale-rd, Fulham SW	15	59	S 16
Stephens-rd, West Ham E	12	41	J 33
Stepnenson-st, Cng. Twn E	12	49	L 33
Stepney E.	12	47	L 28
,, causeway, Commercial-rd. E	12	—	M 29
,, gr. Mile End-rd. E	12	47	L 28
,, ry. sta, G.E.Ry. E	12	48	M 29
,, wrkhse, Bromly E	12	49	K 31
,, green ry. sta. E	12	47	K 28
,, high-st, Stepney E	12	48	L 29
Sterling-rd, Tottenham N	3	—	A 27
Sterndale-rd, W. Kens. W	10	50	O 13
,, ,, S. Lmbth SW	16	61	R 21
Sterne-st, Shepherds Bsh W	10	50	N 13
Sternhold-av, Strthm-hl SW	21	—	W 21
Sterry-st, Bermondsey SE	12	54	N 25
Stevenage-rd, E. Ham E	8	—	I 28
,, ,, Fulham SW	15	59	R 13
Stevens's-la, Claygate, Sy.	28a	—	Z^8 4
Steventon-road, Acton W	10	—	M 11
Stew-la, Up. Thames-st. EC	—	46	M 24
Steward-st, Spitalfields E	12	46	L 26
Stewart-road, Leyton E	7	41	G 32
Stewart-st, Isle of Dogs E	12	57	O 32
Stewarts-grove, Chelsea SW	16	51	P 18
,, la, Battersea SW	16	61	R 20
,, rd, S. L'mbeth SW	16	61	R 20
Steyne-road, Acton W	9	—	M 9
Stibbington-st, Smrs Tn. NW	11	37	J 21
Stile Hall-gds, Chiswick W.	14	—	P 8
Stillington-st, Wstmnstr SW	11	52	O 21
Stillness-rd, Forest-hill SE	17	—	U 29
Stirling-rd, Acton W	9	—	O 9
,, ,, New Malden	25	—	Z^2 10
,, ,, Plaistow E	13	—	J 35
,, ,, Stockwell SW	16	61	S 22
,, ,, Wealdstone, Mx	1a	—	A 4
Stock Exchange, Throgmorton-street EC.	11	46	L 25
,, street, Plaistow E	13	—	K 34
,, Orchard-cres, Hlwy N	6	37	G 22
,, ,, st, Hlwy N	6	37	H 22
Stockdale-rd, S. Lmbth SW	16	61	R 21
Stockfield-rd, Strthm-hill	21	—	W 22
Stockholm-rd, Deptford SE	17	55	Q 28
Stockmar-rd, Hackney E	7	39	H 28
Stockton-st, Edmonton N	3	—	A 27
Stockwell SW	16	61	S 22
,, gr, Stockwell SW	16	61	S 22
,, rd, Stockwell SW	16	61	S 22
,, ry. sta., Stockwell SW	16	61	R 22
,, st, Greenwich SE	17	—	Q 32
,, pk.-cres, Stockwell SW.	16	61	R 22
,, ,, rd, Stockwell SW	16	61	R 22
Stodart-road, Penge SE	22	—	Z^2 27
Stoke Newington N	7	38	F 26
,, ,, Common Stoke Newington N	7	33	F 26
Stoke Newington-rd, Stoke Newington N.	7	39	G 26
Stokenchurch-st, Fulhm SW	15	59	R 16
Stondon-pk, Brockley SE	4	—	U 29
Stone bldgs, Linclns Inn WC	—	45	L 23
Stonebridge bridge, Tot. N	3	—	C 25
,, pk, Wlsdn NW	5	—	I 10
,, rd, Totthm N	3	—	C 26
Stonecot-hill, Morden, Sry.	25	—	Z^5 14
Stonecutter-st, Farringdon street EC	..	45	L 23
Stonefield-st, Islington N	6	37	I 23
Stoneham-rd, U. Clapton E	7	33	F 27
Stonehill-rd, Chiswick W	14	—	P 8
,, ,, East Sheen SW	14	—	T 10
Stoneleigh-drive, Malden	25	—	Z^5 12
,, st, Notting-hl. W	10	50	M 14
Stoneleys-rd, Tottenham N	3	—	B 26
Stones-road, Epsom	29	—	Z^{11} 10
Stoney-av, Walthamstw E.	3	—	C 29
,, la, Houndsditch E	—	46	L 26
,, ,, Tooley-st, SE	12	54	N 25
,, st, Southwark SE	12	54	N 25
Stoneyfield-la, Up. Hale, Middlesex	1	—	A 10
Stonor-rd, Kensington W	—	58	O 15
Stoney-la, Houndsditch E	—	46	L 26
Stopford-road, Plaistow E	13	—	J 34
Store-road, N. Woolwich E	13	—	O 37
,, st, Tott.Crt.-rd. WC	11	45	L 21
Storey-rd, Walthamstow E	3	—	C 30
,, st, N. Woolwich E	13	—	N 38
Storey's-ga, Westminstr SW	11	53	N 21
Storks-rd, Bermondsey SE.	12	55	O 27
,, ,, Stratford E	7	—	I 34
Stormont-rd, Lav.-hill SW	16	60	T 19
,, ,, Highgate N	6	31	D 19
Story-st, Caledonian-rd. N	6	37	I 22
Stour-road, Old Ford E	7	40	I 30
Stowage, Deptfrd Creek SE	17	56	Q 31
Stowe-rd, Shepherds B. W	10	50	N 12
Stracey-rd, Forest Gate E	8	—	G 34
,, ,, Harlesden NW	5	—	I 10
Stradella-rd, Herne-hill SE.	16	—	U 24
Strafford-rd, Twickenham.	14	—	U 5
,, street, Millwall E	12	56	N 30
Strahan-road, Bow E.	12	48	J 29
Straights mth, Grnwch SE	—	64	Q 31
Strand WC.	11	45	M 23
,, on-the-Green, Chiswick W.	14	—	P 8
,, rly. sta, Picad'y Ry	11	45	M 23
Stratford-gro, Putney SW	15	59	S 14
,, pl, Cmdn Twn NW	6	37	I 21
,, ,, Islington N	6	37	I 22
,, ,, Oxford-st. W.	11	44	L 20
,, rd, Acton W	9	—	N 9
,, ,, Bromley E	12	48	K 31
,, ,, Hendon NW	1	—	C 14
Stratford-rd, Kensington W	10	51	O 16
,, ,, Plaistow E	13	—	J 34
,, ,, Thrntn H. Sy	26	—	Z^2 23
,, New Town E	7	41	H 33
,, mkt ry., sta, G. E. Railway	7	41	I 32
,, ry. sta, G.E. Rly.	7	41	I 32
Strathblane-rd, Btrsea SW	16	60	T 18
Strathbrook-rd, Lwr Streatham SW	21	—	Z^1 22
,, ,, Streatham	21	—	Z^1 22
Strathearn-rd, Sutton, Sry.	29	—	Z^7 15
Strathern-rd, Wmbldn SW	20	—	X 15
Strathfield-gds, Barking, Ex	8	—	I 40
Strathleven-rd, Brixton SW	16	61	T 22
Strathmore-rd, Crydn, Sry	26	—	Z^4 24
,, gds, Knsngtn W	—	43	M 16
,, rd, Wimbledon park SW	20	—	W 15
Strathray-gds, Hmpstd NW	5	35	H 17
Strathville-rd, Earlsfield SW	20	—	V 16
Strathyre-av, Norbury, Sy.	26	—	Z^2 22
Stratton-st, Piccadilly W	11	44	M 20
Strattondale-st, Cubitt Tn E	12	57	O 32
Strattondale-st, Isle-of-D. E	12	57	O 32
Strauss-road, Acton W	10	—	N 10
Strawberry-hl, Twcknham.	19	—	W 4
,, la, Hckbdge, Sy	26	—	Z^6 19
,, vale, Twcknhm	19	—	W 4
Strawberry hill sta, L. & S.W. Rly., Twickenham	19	—	W 3
Streamlet-pl, Bickley, Knt	28	—	Z^2 34
Streatfield-av, E. Ham E	13	—	J 37
,, st, B'rd'tt-rd. E	12	40	L 30
Streatham SW	21	—	X 21
,, cemetery, Streatham SW.	20	—	X 17
,, com, Strthm SW	21	—	Y 22
,, ,, ,, ,,	21	—	Z^1 21
,, gr, Str'th'm SW	21	—	Z^2 22
,, ,, ,, ,,	21	—	Z^1 23
,, hl, Brixton SW	21	—	W 22
,, pl, Brixton SW	21	—	V 22
,, rd, Lr.Tootg SW	21	—	Z^2 19
,, Com. rly. sta., L.B.&S.C.R. SW	21	—	Z^1 21
,, High-rd, Streatham SW.	21	—	Y 21
,, hl. rly. sta, L. B. & S.C.R. SW	21	—	W 22
Streathbourne-rd, Upper Tooting SW	21	—	W 19
Streatley-gds, Barking, E	8	—	I 40
,, rd, Kilburn NW	5	—	I 15
Stretton-rd, Croydon, Sry.	26	—	Z^4 25
Strickland-st, Deptford SE	—	63	R 30
Strode-road, Fulham SW	15	58	Q 14
,, ,, Tottenham N	3	—	B 26
,, ,, Willesden NW	5	34	H 12
Strone-road, Forest-gate E	8	—	H 36
Stronsa-rd, Shepherds B. W	10	—	N 11
Stroud-green, Croydon, Sy	27	—	Z^5 27
,, rd, Forest Gate E	8	—	G 34
,, ,, S. Norwood SE.	27	—	Z^4 27
,, gr.-rd, Fnsby-pk. N	6	32	E 23
,, ,, sta, Fnsby-pk. N.	6	32	D 23
Strutton-grd, Wstmnstr SW	11	53	O 21
Strype-st, Middlesex-st. E	—	46	L 26
Stuart-road, Acton W.	9	—	M 9
,, ,, Croydon, Sry.	26	—	Z^3 24
,, ,, Nunhead SE	17	—	T 28
,, ,, Weald. Mdsx.	1a	—	A 4
,, ,, Wmbldn-pk. SW	20	—	W 15
Studdridge-st, Flham SW.	15	59	R 16
Studholme-st, Peckham SE	17	62	R 27
Studland-st, Hmrsmth W.	10	58	O 12
,, rd, L. Sydn'm SE	22	—	Y 28
,, ,, Norbiton	19	—	Y 7
Studley-av, Hale End E	3	—	A 32
,, rd, Clapham SW	16	61	R 22
,, ,, Forest Gate E	8	—	I 35
,, Grange-rd, Hnwl W	9	—	N 4
Stukeley-road, Upton E	8	—	I 35
Stumps-hill, Beckenham	22	—	Z^1 30
Sturgeon-rd, Newington SE	16	54	P 24
Sturock-pk.-rd, Wlthmstw E	3	—	C 29
Sturry-street, Poplar E	12	48	M 31
Styles way, Bromley.	27	—	Z^3 31
Styman-street, Hoxton N	11	46	K 25
Sudbourne-rd, Brixton SW	16	—	T 22
Sudbrooke-rd, Balham SW.	16	—	U 19
Sudbury, Middlesex	4	—	G 4
,, avenue, Wembley	4	—	G 6
,, hl, Sdbry, Mdsx.	4	—	F 4
,, ,, station, Mdx.	4	—	G 4
,, & Harrow-rd. ry. sta, G.C.Rly.	4	—	G 5
,, & Wembley ry. sta, L.& N.W.R.	4	—	G 7
,, Town ry. sta., District Rly.	4	—	H 5
Sudely-street, Islington N	11	46	J 24
Sudlow-rd, Wandsworth SW	15	59	T 15
Suffield-Hatch, Chingford E	3	—	A 31
,, rd, Chingford E	3	—	A 31
,, ,, S. Norwood SE	27	—	Z^2 27
,, ,, Tottenham N	3	—	C 26
Suffolk-la, Up. Thms-st. EC	11	46	M 25
,, rd, Dalston E	7	39	I 27
,, ,, Foots Cray	23	—	Z 42
,, ,, Norwood SE	26	—	Z^2 26
,, ,, Plaistow E	13	—	K 34
,, ,, Seven Kings, Ex	8	—	D 41
,, ,, Tottenham N	7	—	D 25
,, st, Forest Gate E	8	—	H 34
,, ,, Pall Mall E. SW	11	45	M 21
,, ,, Poplar E	12	48	L 31
,, ,, Rotherhithe SE.	17	55	P 28
Sugar Loaf-ct, Leadenhall st, EC	—	46	M 26
,, ,, ,, U.T.-st. EC	—	46	M 24
Sugden-rd, Lavender-hl. SW	16	60	T 19
Sugden-rd, Long Ditton	24	—	Z^5 4
Sulgrave-rd, ShphdsBsh. W	10	50	N 13
Sulina-rd, Brixton-hill SW	21	—	V 22
Sultan-road, Penge SE	22	—	Z^2 28
,, st, Camberwell SE	16	54	Q 24
Sumatra-rd, W. Hamps. NW	5	—	G 15
Summer-hl, Chislehurst, Kt	23	—	Z^1 37
,, rd, E.Moulsey, Sy	24	—	Z^2 3
Summerfield-av, Finchley N	1	—	A 17
,, ,, Queens-pk NW	10	34	J 15
Summerhill-rd, W. Gr'n N	3	—	D 25
Summerley-st, Earlsfield SW	20	—	W 16
Summers-lane, Finchley N.	1	—	A 18
Summerstown, Tooting SW	20	—	X 17
Summit-rd, Wlthmstow E	3	—	C 31
Sumner-pl, S. Knsgton SW	11	51	O 17
,, rd, Croydon, Surry	26	—	Z^5 23
,, ,, Harrow. Mdsx.	1a	—	D 3
,, st, Southwark Bdg road SE.	11	46	N 24
,, ,, Peckham SE	16	62	R 26
,, ,, S. Croydon, Sy.	26	—	Z^5 23
Sun-court, Cornhill EC	—	46	M 25
,, ,, Milton street EC	—	46	L 25
Sun-lane, Charlton SE	18	—	R 34
Sun-st, Finsbury EC	11	46	L 25
,, ,, Liverpool-street EC	—	46	L 25
Sunderland-rd, Forest-hl SE	22	—	W 28
Sundorne-road, Charlton	18	—	P 35
Sundridge-av, Bromley, Kt	23	—	Z^{13} 35
,, rd, Croydon, Sy	26	—	Z^5 26
Sunfields-pl, Charlton SE	18	—	R 34
Sunningdale-av, Barking	13	—	J 39
Sunningfields-rd, Hndn NW	1	—	B 13
Sunny-gds, Hendon NW	1	—	B 13
Sunning-hl-rd, Lwisham SE	—	63	S 31
Sunny Side, Wimbledon SW	20	—	Y 14
Sunnybank, Norwood SE	26	—	Z^2 26
Sunnycroft-rd, Hounslow	14	—	R 1
Sunnydene-st, Sydnhm SE.	22	—	X 29
Sunnyhill-road, Streatham	21	—	X 22
Sunnyside-rd, Ealing W	9	—	M 6
,, ,, Edmonton N	3	—	A 27
,, ,, Ilford, Essx.	8	—	G 39
,, ,, Leyton E	7	—	E 30
,, ,, Teddington.	19	—	X 3
,, ,, Up. Hllwy N	6	32	E 21
Sunray-av, Herne Hill SE	16	62	T 25
Sunwell-st, Peckham SE	17	62	R 27
Surbiton, Surrey	24	—	Z^3 6
,, cres, Surbiton, Sy	24	—	Z^2 6
,, rd, Surbiton, Sy.	24	—	Z^2 6
,, rly. sta., L. & S.W. Railway	24	—	Z^3 6
,, hl.-pk, Srbtn, Sy.	24	—	Z^3 7
,, ,, rd, Srbtn, Sy.	24	—	Z^2 6
Surrey Canal, Deptford SE.	17	56	P 29
,, Commercial Docks, Rotherhithe SE	12	56	N 29
,, cres, Chiswick W	14	—	P 8
,, gro, Bermondsey SE	17	54	P 25
,, lane, Battersea SW	16	60	R 18
,, road, Nunhead SE	17	—	T 28
,, row, Blckfrrs-rd SE	11	54	N 24
,, sq, Walworth SE	17	54	P 25
,, st, Croydon, Surry	26	—	Z^6 24
,, ,, Plaistow E.	13	—	K 35
,, ,, Strand WC.	11	45	M 23
,, la, S. Battersea SW.	16	60	R 18
Susannah-street, Poplar E	12	49	M 31
Sussex-gds, Hyde-park W	10	43	M 17
,, grove, Brixton SW	16	61	T 23
,, pl, Hyde-park W	11	43	M 18
,, ,, Leadenhl-st. EC.	—	46	M 26
,, ,, Regents-pk. NW	11	44	K 19
,, ,, S. Knsngtn SW	—	51	P 16
,, rd, Brixton SW	16	61	T 23
,, ,, Croydon, Surrey	30	—	Z^8 25
,, ,, Harrow, Mdsx..	1a	—	C 3
,, ,, Holloway N	6	32	F 22
,, ,, New Malden, Sy	25	—	Z^2 10
,, ,, East Ham E	13	—	J 38
,, ,, Sidcup	23	—	Y 42
,, sq, Hyde-park W	11	43	M 18
,, street, Pimlico SW	16	52	P 20
,, ,, Plaistow E	13	—	K 35
,, ,, Poplar E	12	48	M 30
Sutcliffe-rd, Plumstead	18	—	Q 40
Sutherland-av, Cstlebr-hl W	9	—	L 5
,, ,, Maida-va W	10	43	K 16
,, gds, E. Shn SW	15	—	S 10
,, gr, Wands. SW.	20	—	U 15
,, pl, Bayswtr W.	10	43	L 16
,, rd, Cstlebr-hl W	9	—	L 5
,, ,, Chiswick W	15	—	P 10
,, ,, Croydon, Sy	26	—	Z^5 23
,, ,, Putney SW.	15	—	U 14
,, ,, Roman-rd E	12	48	J 30
,, ,, Tottnhm N	3	—	A 27
,, ,, Wimbledon park SW.	20	—	V 15
,, sq, Walwrth SE	16	54	P 24
,, st, Pimlico SW	16	52	P 20
,, ter, Pimlico SW	16	52	P 20
Sutterton-st, Calednin. rd N	—	37	H 22
Sutton, Surrey.	29	—	Z^7 15
,, gro, Sutton, Surry	29	—	Z^7 17
,, lane, Chiswick W	14	—	P 9
,, rd, Canning Twn E	12	—	L 34
,, ,, Coppetts-rd. N.	2a	—	A 19
,, st, Belvedere-rd SE	11	53	N 23
,, ,, Soho-square W.	11	45	L 21
,, ,, Com'cial-rd. E	12	47	M 28
,, ct-rd, Chiswick W	14	—	P 10
,, ,, ,, Sutton, Sry	29	—	Z^8 16
,, downs-rd, Surrey	29	—	Z^{10} 16
Swaby-rd, Wandsworth SW	20	—	W 17
Swaffield-rd, Wndswrth SW	15	—	U 16
Swain-road, Croyden, Sury	26	—	Z^3 24
Swains-lane, Highgate N	6	31	F 20
,, ,, S. Wmbldn SW	20	—	Z 18
Swales-street, Poplar E	12	48	M 31
Swallow-pl, Oxford-st. W	—	44	L 20
,, st, Piccadilly W	11	44	M 21
Swallowfield-rd, Charlton	18	—	P 35
Swan-la, Rotherhithe SE	12	55	N 28
,, ,, Up. Thames-st EC	11	46	M 25
,, mead, Bermond. SE	12	54	O 25
,, st, Minories E	11	47	M 26
,, ,, Borough SE.	11	54	O 24
,, ,, Goodmans flds E.	12	47	M 26
,, ,, Isleworth	14	—	S 5
,, walk, Chelsea SW	—	52	Q 19
Swanage-rd, Wndswrth SW	15	—	U 17
Swanscoe-rd, Chiswick W	15	—	P 11
Swanscombe-st, Cng. Tn. E	12	49	L 33
Swansea-pl, Shoreditch E	12	46	J 25
Swaton-road, Bow E.	12	48	K 31
Sweet-briar-wlk, Edmntn N	3	—	A 26
Sweetenham-pl, Plumst'd	18	—	P 39
Swete-street, Plaistow E	13	—	K 34
Swift-street, Fulham SW	15	59	R 15
Swinbrook-rd, N.Knsngtn W	10	42	L 15
Swinderby-rd, Sudbury, Mx	14	—	H 7
Swindon-st, Shphds Bsh W	10	50	M 13
Swingate-la, Plumstead SE	18	—	R 40
Swinnerton-st, Homerton E	7	40	H 29
Swinton-st, Grays I.-rd. WC	11	45	K 22
Swiss-ter, St. Jhns Wd. NW	5	35	I 17
,, Cottage sta, Met. Railway NW	5	35	H 17
Sybourne-st, Wlthmstw E	7	—	E 30
Sycamore-gr, Nw Maldn SW	20	—	Z^1 10
,, st, Old-street EC	—	46	K 24
Sydenham-av, Sydnhm SE	22	—	Y 27
,, hl, Sydnhm SE	22	—	W 27
,, park SE	22	—	X 27
,, rise, Forest-hl SE	22	—	W 27
,, rd, Croydon, Sy	26	—	Z^5 24
,, ,, Sydnhm SE.	22	—	Y 28
,, sta, Sydnhm SE	22	—	Y 28
,, hill-road SE	22	—	X 27
,, ry.sta., S.E. & C.Railway	22	—	X 26
,, pk.-rd, Up. Sydenham SE	22	—	X 28
Sydner-rd, Stoke Nwgtn N	7	39	G 26
Sydney-av, Bowes-park N	2	—	A 23
,, ,, Milton-st. EC	—	46	L 25
,, pl, Fulham-rd. SW	16	51	P 17
,, ,, Wardour-st. W.	—	45	M 21
,, rd, Ealing Dean W	9	—	M 5
,, ,, Hornsey N	2	—	B 23
,, ,, Muswell-hill N	2a	—	A 20
,, ,, Raynes-pk SW.	20	—	Z^1 14
,, ,, Sidcup	23	—	X 40
,, ,, Sutton, Surrey	29	—	Z^7 15
,, st, Canning Tn E	12	49	M 34
,, ,, Chelsea SW	16	51	P 18
Sylvan-av, Mill-hill NW	1a	—	A 11
,, grove, Peckham SE	17	55	Q 27
,, hl, Upr. Norwood	21	—	Z^2 25
,, rd, Forest Gate E	8	—	H 34
,, ,, Norwood SE	22	—	Z^2 26
,, villas, Bowes-pk. N	2	—	A 23
Sylvester-rd, Dalston E	7	39	H 27
,, ,, Walthmstw E	7	—	D 30
,, ,, Wembley	4	—	G 6
Symonds Inn, Chncry-la WC	—	45	L 23
Symons-street, Chelsea SW	16	52	P 19
Synagogue-pl, Whitechpl. E	12	47	L 27
Syon-lane, Osterley, Mdsx.	14	—	P 4
,, park, Brentford	14	—	Q 5
,, vista, Kew	14	—	Q 7

T

	4-in. sht.	9-in. sht.	mar.
Tabard-st, Southwark SE	12	54	O 25
Tabernacle-st, City-rd. EC	11	46	K 25
Tabley-road, Holloway N	6	37	G 22
Tabor-gro, Wimbledon SW	20	—	Z 14
,, rd, Hammersmith W	10	50	O 13
Tachbrook-st, Pimlico SW	16	52	P 21
Tadema-road, Chelsea SW	15	51	Q 17
Tagg-st, Bethnal-green E	12	47	J 28
Tait-road, Croydon, Surry.	26	—	Z^4 25
,, street, St. Georges E	12	47	M 27
Talbot-av, E. Finchley N	2	—	B 18
,, ct, Eastcheap SE	—	46	M 25
,, gro, Notting-hill W.	10	50	L 14
,, rd, Bromley	28	—	Z^2 34
,, ,, Carshalton	30	—	Z^7 19
,, ,, Ealing Dean W.	9	—	M 5
,, ,, East Ham E	13	—	J 38
,, ,, Forest Gate E	8	—	G 34
,, ,, Highgate N	6	31	D 19
,, ,, Isleworth	14	—	S 4
,, ,, Norwood SE	26	—	Z^3 25
,, ,, Sudbury, Mdsx.	4	—	H 7
,, ,, Tottenham N	3	—	C 26
,, ,, Twickenham	19	—	V 3
,, ,, Westbrne-pk. W	10	42	L 15
,, ,, Willesden NW	5	—	H 11
,, sq, Hyde-park W	—	43	L 17
Talfourd-pl, Peckham SE	17	62	R 26
,, road, Peckham SE	17	62	R 26
,, ,, Welling	18	—	S 42
Talgarth-rd, W. Knsngtn W	15	58	P 14
Tallis-st, Victoria Embankment EC.	11	45	M 23
Talma-road, Brixton SW	16	61	T 23
Talwin-road, Bow E	12	48	K 31
Tamar-street, Charlton	18	—	P 36
Tamworth-la, Mitcham, Sy	26	—	Z^1 20
,, ,, Up. Mtchm.	21	—	Z^2 19
,, pk, Mitcham, Sy	26	—	Z^1 20
,, rd, Croydon, Sy	26	—	Z^6 23
,, st, Fulham SW	15	58	Q 15
Tan House-st, Hmrsmth W	10	58	O 13
Tanfield-rd, Croydon, Srry	30	—	Z^7 24
Taniwha-ter, Wdfrd-rd. E	8	—	G 35

Tankerton-road. INDEX TO STREETS, &c. Tonsly-hill.

4-in. sht. 9-in. sht. mar.
Tankerton-rd, Lng Ditton. 24 —..Z^{5} 7
,, ,, Surbiton . 24 —..Z^{5} 7
Tankerville-rd, Streatham. 21 —..Z^{1} 21
,, ,, Sutton, Sy. 29 —..Z^{7} 17
Tanner-st, Barking, Essex. 8 —..I 39
,, ,, Bermondsey SE 12 54..N 26
Tanners End, Edmonton N 3 —..A 26
,, hill, Deptford SE . 4 63..R 30
Tannsfield-rd, Lr. Sydnhm SE 22 —..Y 28
Tanswell-st, Lambeth SE . 11 53..N 23
Tantallon-road, Balham . 21 —..V 19
Tanza-rd, Hampstead NW. — 36..G 19
Tapley-strete, Bromley E . 12 49..L 31
Taplow-street, Islington N. 11 46..J 24
Tappesfield-rd, Nunhead SE 17 63..S 28
Tarbert-rd, E. Dulwich SE 17 —..T 26
Tarling-street, Shadwell E. 12 47..M 28
Tarn-street, Newington SE 11 54..O 24
Tasman-road, Stockwell SW 16 61..S 22
Tasso-rd, W. Kensingtn SW 15 58..P 14
Tate Gallery, Grsvnr-rd. SW 16 53..P 22
,, road, Silvertown E . 13 —..N 37
,, ,, Sutton, Surrey. 29 —..Z^{8} 15
Tatnell-street, Brockley SE 4 —..U 29
Tattersall's, Knghtsbdg SW 11 52..N 19
Tatum-road, Willesden NW 5 —..H 10
Taunton-road, Lee SE . 17 —..U 33
Tavistock-av, Wlthmstw E 3 —..B 29
,, cres, Westbourne park W. . 10 42..L 15
,, gro, Croydon, Sy 26 —..Z^{5} 24
,, pl, Tvstck-sq WC 11 45..K 21
,, rd, Croydon, Sy. 26 —..Z^{5} 24
,, ,, Hllwy-rd. N 6 37..F 22
,, ,, Leytnstne E. 7 41..G 33
,, ,, Westbourne-park W. . 10 42..L 15
,, ,, Stratford E . 7 41..I 33
,, sq, Bl'msb'ry WC 11 45..K 21
,, st, Covent-garden WC . . 11 45..M 22
Taviton-st, Euston-rd WC . 11 45..K 21
Taybridge-rd, Lvndr-hl. SW 16 60..S 19
Taylor-rd, Carshalton, Sry 30 —..Z^{7} 19
Taylors-la, Up. Sydnhm SE 22 —..X 27
,, ,, Willesden NW . 5 —..H 11
Teale-st, Bethnal Green E 12 47..J 28
Tebworth-rd, Tottenham N 3 —..A 26
Tedworth-gds, Chelsea SW. 16 52..P 18
,, sq, Chelsea SW . — 52..P 18
Teddington, Middlesex . 19 —..Y 5
,, Cemetery, Teddington . . . . 19 —..X 3
Teddington and Bushy-pk. rly. sta, L. & S.W. Ry., Teddington . . . 19 —..Y 4
Teddington-pk.-rd, Teddington . . . 19 —..Y 4
Teesdale-rd, Leytonstone E 7 —..D 33
,, st, Hackney-rd. E 12 47..J 27
Teeyan-road, Croydon . 27 —..Z^{5} 26
Teignmouth-rd, Crcklwd NW 5 —..H 14
Telegraph-hill, Brockley SE 4 63..S 29
,, rd, Claygate, Sy 28a —..Z^{7} 4
,, st, Mrgate-st. EC — 46..L 25
Telferscot-rd, Strtham SW 21 —..V 21
Telford-av, Str'th'm-hl SW. 21 —..W 21
,, rd, N. Knsngtn W. 10 42..L 14
,, ,, Walthamstow E 3 —..C 29
Temperley-road, Balham . 21 —..V 19
Templar-rd, Homerton E . 7 39..H 28
,, st, Camberwell SE 16 62..R 24
Templars-av, Hendon NW 5 —..D 15
Temple, The, Fleet-st, EC . 11 45..M 23
,, av, Victoria Embankment EC . 11 45..M 23
,, Bar . . . . — 45..M 23
,, Chambers, Tudor-street EC . . — 45..M 23
,, Fortune, Hendon NW . . . 1 —..C 15
,, la, Whitefriars EC — 45..M 23
,, Pier, Victoria Embankment WC . 11 45..M 23
,, rd, Cricklew'd NW 5 —..G 13
,, ,, Croydon, Sury 30 —..Z^{7} 24
,, ,, Ealing W . 9 —..O 6
,, ,, Epsom . . 28a —..Z^{11} 9
,, ,, Hounslow . 14 —..S 2
,, ,, Kew . . 14 —..R 8
,, ,, S. Acton W . 9 —..O 9
,, ry. sta, Dist. Rly. 11 45..M 23
,, st, Dalston E . 7 39..H 26
,, ,, Hackney-rd. E 12 47..J 27
,, ,, Leytonstone E 7 41..G 33
,, ,, Newington SE. 11 45..O 24
,, Fortune-hl, Hampstead NW 1 —..C 16
,, ,, la, Hmpstead NW . . 5 —..D 16
,, Mills-la, Leyton E 7 40..G 31
,, ,, rd, Hckny E 7 40..H 30
,, Sheen, E. Sheen SW 14 —..T 9
Templeton-av, Chingfrd E. 3 —..A 31
,, pl, Earls-ct. SW 15 51..P 16
,, rd, Tottenhm N 7 —..D 25
Templewood-av, Childs-hill NW . . . . . 5 —..F 16
Tenby-road, Stratford E . 7 41..H 33
Tench-street, Wapping E . 12 55..N 27
Tenda-st, Bermondsey SE . 17 55..P 27
Tenham-av, Streatham SW 21 —..W 21
Tenison-st, Lambeth SW . 11 53..N 23
Tennis-court. Holborn WC — 45..L 23
Tennison-rd, S. Norw'd SE 26 —..Z^{3} 26
Tennys-rd, Walthamstow E 7 —..D 30
Tennyson-av, E. Ham E . 8 —..I 37
,, rd, Drayton-gr. W 9 —..M 4
,, ,, Edmonton N 3 —..A 26
,, ,, Kilburn NW. 5 —..I 15
,, ,, Mill-hill NW 1a —..A 12
,, ,, Penge SE . 22 —..Z^{1} 28

4-in. sht. 9-in. sht. mar.
Tennyson-rd, S. Wmbldn SW 20 —..Y 16
,, ,, Stratford E . 7 41..I 33
,, st, S. Lmbth SW 16 61..S 20
Tent-st, Bethnal Green E . 12 47..K 27
Tenter-st, Moorfields EC . 11 46..L 25
,, ,, Spitalfields E . 12 46..L 26
,, ,, E. Gdmns fields E 12 47..M 26
,, ,, N. Gdmns fields E 12 47..M 26
,, ,, S. Gdmns fields E 12 47..M 26
,, ,, W. Gdmns fields E 12 47..M 26
Tenterden-gr, Hendon NW. 1 —..B 14
,, st, H'novr-sq. W 11 44..M 20
Terminus-pl, Victoria SW . 11 52..O 20
Terrace, The, Barnes SW . 15 —..R 11
,, rd, Hackney E . 7 39..I 28
,, ,, Plaistow E . 13 —..J 35
Terrapin-road, Tooting . 21 —..W 20
Terrick-rd, Wood Green N. 2 —..A 22
Terront-rd, Tottenham N . 2 —..C 24
Tetcott-road, Chelsea SW . 15 51..Q 17
Tetford-road, Hendon NW. 5 —..D 12
Tetherdown-pl, Muswell-hl N 2 —..B 20
,, rd, Muswell-hl N 2 —..B 20
Tetley-street, Poplar E . 12 49..M 31
Teviot-street, Bromley E . 12 49..L 31
Tewkesbury-rd, Totten'm N 7 33..D 25
,, ter, Nw Southgate N . 2 —..A 21
Tewson-road, Plumstead . 18 —..P 40
Thackeray-av, Tottenhm N 3 —..A 27
,, rd, East Ham E 13 —..J 36
,, st, S. Lmbth SW 16 61..S 20
Thame-rd, Kent Twn, Sry. 24 —..Z^{2} 3
Thames-pl, Limehouse E . 12 48..M 30
,, side, Kingston . 19 —..Z 6
,, st, Greenwich SE . 17 57..Q 31
,, ,, Hampton . 19 —..Z 1
,, ,, Kingston. . 19 —..Z 1
Thames-st, Rotherhithe SE 12 55..N 28
,, subwy, Twr-hl, EC 12 46..M 26
,, tunnel, Wapping E 12 55..N 28
,, Ditton raily-sta., L. & S.W.R. . 24 —..Z^{4} 3
Thane-villas, Holloway N . 6 32..F 23
Thanet-st, St. Pancras WC 11 45..K 22
Tharp-road, Wallington . 30 —..Z^{8} 21
Thavies-inn, Holborn EC . — 45..L 23
Thayer-st, Manchestr-sq, W 11 44..L 19
Thayers F.-rd, Beckenham 22 —..Z^{2} 29
The Approach, Orpington 28 —..Z^{6} 40
,, Arcde, S. KnsgtnSta, SW 10 51..O 18
,, Avenue, Acton W . 10 —..O 11
,, ,, Alexndra-pk, N 2 —..A 21
,, ,, Beckenham . 22 —..Z^{2} 31
,, ,, Bickley, Kent 28 —..Z^{2} 36
,, ,, Blackheath SE 17 64..S 33
,, ,, ,, 18 —..R 34
,, ,, Brixton SW . 16 61..T 22
,, ,, Brondesbry NW 5 34..I 14
,, ,, Castlebr-hl, W 9 —..L 5
,, ,, Cheam, Surry 29 —..Z^{8} 13
,, ,, Chingford E . 3 —..A 32
,, ,, Esher . . 24 —..Z^{7} 3
,, ,, Greenwich SE 17 —..Q 32
,, ,, Hornsey N . 2 —..B 23
,, ,, Kew . . 14 —..R 8
,, ,, Lee SE . . 18 —..U 34
,, ,, Palmers-gr, N 2 —..A 22
,, ,, Tottenham N 3 —..B 26
,, ,, Twickenham . 14 —..T 5
,, ,, Upr Norwood 21 —..Y 25
,, ,, Wallngtn, Sur 30 —..Z^{8} 19
,, Barons, Twickenham . 14 —..U 5
,, Baulk, Wmbldn-pk SW 20 —..V 15
,, Berrylands-av, Surbtn 24 —..Z^{3} 7
,, Broadway, Hackney E 7 39..I 27
,, ,, Wmbldn SW 20 —..Y 15
,, Brook, Brentfrd, Mdx 14 —..P 6
,, Causway, Claygte, Sy 28a —..Z^{8} 3
,, ,, Mitchm, Sy 25 —..Z^{2} 18
,, ,, Wndswth SW 15 59—T 16
,, Chase, Clapham SW . 16 61—S 20
,, Circus, Greenwich SE . 17 —..Q 32
,, Common, Ealing W . 9 —..M 7
,, ,, Hayes, Kent 27 —..Z^{6} 33
,, Copse, Petersham . 19 —..V 6
,, Crescent, Barnes SW . 15 —..R 11
,, ,, Belmont . 29 —..Z^{1} 15
,, ,, Croydn, Sur. 26 —..Z^{4} 25
,, ,, Sidcup . 23 —..Y 38
,, ,, Surbitn, Sur. 24 —..Z^{3} 6
,, ,, Tottenhm N 7 33..D 26
,, ,, Wlthmstw E 7 —..D 29
,, ,, Wmbdln SW 20 —..X 15
,, Crest, Hendon NW . 1 —..C 14
,, Cross, Tottenham N . 3 —..B 26
,, Downs, Wimbledn SW 20 —..Z 13
,, Drive, Banstead, Sury 29 —..Z^{11} 15
,, ,, Hendon NW . 5 —..D 15
,, ,, Ilford, Essex . 8 —..E 38
,, ,, N. End, Fnchly N 1 —..B 15
,, ,, Orpington . 28 —..Z^{6} 40
,, ,, Sydenham SE . 22 —..Y 27
,, ,, Thorntn-hth, Sy 26 —..Z^{2} 24
,, ,, Walthamstw E 3 —..B 31
,, ,, Wimbledon SW 20 —..Z 13
,, Gardens, Peckham SE 17 62..S 27
,, Glebe, Blackheath SE . 17 64..S 33
,, ,, Herne-hill, SE . 16 62..S 25
,, Grange, Acton W . 10 —..M 11
,, ,, Brmndsey SE 12 54..O 26
,, ,, Wimbledn SW 20 —..Y 14
,, Green, Bushy-park . 19 —..Z^{1} 3
,, ,, Carshaltn, Sur. — —..Z^{6} 18
,, ,, Farnboro', Knt 30b —..Z^{8} 37
,, ,, Grnstd-gr, Knt 30b —..Z^{8} 40
,, ,, Mortlake, SW . 14 —..S 10
,, ,, Stratford E . 7 41..H 33
,, ,, Sutton, Surrey 25 —..Z^{6} 16
,, ,, Tottenham N . 3 —..B 26
,, ,, Twickenham . 19 —..V 3
,, ,, W. Wickhm, Kt 27 —..Z^{5} 31

4-in. sht. 9-in. sht. mar.
The Grove, Brentford, Mdx 14 —..P 6
,, ,, Dulwich . . 21 —..V 25
,, ,, Ealing W . 9 —..M 7
,, ,, Greenford . 9 —..L 2
,, ,, Hmmrsmsth W 10 50..Q 13
,, ,, Hampstead NW 5 35..F 17
,, ,, Hendon NW . 5 —..D 15
,, ,, Highgate N . 6 31..E 19
,, ,, Isleworth . 14 —..R 3
,, ,, Mitcham, Surr. 25 —..Z^{3} 17
,, ,, Muswell-hill N 2 —..B 21
,, ,, Spring-gr, Mdx 14 —..Q 2
,, ,, Stratford E . 7 41..I 33
,, ,, Wandswrth SW 15 —..U 16
,, ,, ,, 15 —..U 17
,, ,, Boltons, West Bromptn SW 15 51..P 16
,, Hyde, NW . . 1 —..C 11
,, Knoll, Beckenham . 22 —..Z^{2} 31
,, Lake-rd, Wimbledn SW 20 —..Y 15
,, Lawns, Shphds Bush W 10 50..N 13
,, Link, Walthamstow E 3 —..C 29
,, Mall, Ealing W . . 9 —..L 7
,, ,, Kensington W . 16 43..M 16
,, Mount, New Malden . 25 —..Z^{2} 11
,, ,, Sydenhm-hl, SE 22 —..X 27
,, New River, Bowes-pk, N 2 —..A 22
,, ,, Plmrs-gr. N 2 —..A 24
,, Oaks-pk, Epsom, Surr. 29 —..Z^{11} 18
,, Oratory, Brmptn-r, SW 11 52..O 18
,, Orchard, Bedfrd-pk W 10 —..O 10
,, ,, Hampstd NW 1 —..C 16
,, Paragon, Brixton-hill 21 —..V 22
,, Park, Carshalton, Sur. 25 —..Z^{6} 18
,, ,, Ealing W . . 9 —..M 7
,, ,, Golders-grn, NW 5 —..E 16
,, ,, Hendon NW . 1 —..C 14
,, ,, Sidcup . . 23 —..Y 38
,, ,, Streatham . . 21 —..Y 22
,, Pavement, Claphm SW 16 61..T 21
,, ,, ,, 16 61—T 20
,, Platt, Putney SW . 15 59..S 14
,, Point, Greenwich SE . 4 64..R 31
,, Retreat, Catford SE . 22 —..V 31
,, ,, Thrntn-hth, S. 26 —..Z^{2} 24
,, Ride, Nw Brentfd, Mx 9 —..O 5
,, Ridge, Child's-hill NW 5 —..F 15
,, Ridgeway, Gldrs-gr. NW 5 —..E 15
,, Ridgway, Sutton, Sur. 29 —..Z^{8} 17
,, Riding, Goldrs-grn, NW 5 —..E 15
,, Rose walk, Purley . 30 —..Z^{10} 21
,, Rough, Cheam, Surrey 29 —..Z^{8} 13
,, Rush, Merton SW . 20 —..Z^{1} 15
,, Rythe, Littleworth, Sy 24 —..Z^{6} 3
,, Sanctuary, Wstmnstr SW 11 53..O 21
,, Steyne, Acton W . 9 —..M 9
,, Slade, Plumstead . 18 —..Q 40
,, Slip, Osterley-pk, Mdx 14 —..P 1
,, Square, Carshalton . 30 —..Z^{7} 19
,, ,, Isleworth . 14 —..S 5
,, Terrace, Chiswick W . 10 —..O 11
,, ,, Knngtn-pk, SE 10 53..Q 23
,, ,, Kew . . 14 —..Q 7
,, Tower, EC . . . 12 46..M 26
,, Vineyard, Richmond . 14 —..T 7
,, Warren, Esher, Surrey 24 —..Z^{6} 1
,, Wrythe, Carshltn, Sur. 25 —..Z^{6} 18
Theberton-st, Islington N . 6 37..I 23
Theobald-rd, Walthmstw E 7 —..E 30
,, st, Nw Knt-rd, SE 12 54..O 25
Theobalds-rd, Croydn, Sur. 26 —..Z^{6} 23
,, ,, WC . . 11 45..L 22
Theodore-rd, Hendon NW . 1 —..B 11
,, ,, Lewisham SE 17 —..U 32
Therapia-rd, For'st-hl-rd. SE 17 —..U 27
Thesiger-rd, Penge SE . 22 —..Q^{1} 28
Thetfrd-rd, Nw Malden, Sy 25 —..Z^{3} 10
Theydon-rd, Clapton E . 7 33..F 28
,, ,, Grve-rd, Bow E 12 48..J 29
,, st, Wlthamstw E 7 —..E 30
Thicket-rd, Anerley SE . 22 —..Q^{1} 27
,, ,, Sutton, Surrey 29 —..Z^{7} 17
Third-av, Acton W . . 10 —..M 11
,, ,, Kensal-green W . 10 42..J 14
,, ,, Maida-hill W . 10 42..K 15
,, ,, Manor-park, E . 8 —..G 37
,, ,, Plaistow E . 13 —..K 34
,, ,, Walthamstow E 3 —..C 31
,, rd-east, Woolwich . 18 —..P 37
,, ,, west, Woolwich . 18 —..P 37
Thirlmere-rd, Muswell-hl, N 2 —..A 20
,, ,, Streatham . 21 —..X 21
Thirsk-rd, Battersea SW . 16 60..S 19
,, ,, Norwood SE . 26 —..Z^{2} 25
Thirth Cross-rd, Twcknhm 19 —..V 3
Thistle-gr, W. Bromptn SW 15 51..P 17
Thistlewaite-rd, Clapton E 7 39..G 28
Thomas-st, Grosvenor-sq, W 11 44..M 20
,, ,, Woolwich . 18 —..P 38
Thompson-rd, E. Dulwch SE 17 —..U 26
Thorn-gr, Leyton-road, E . 7 41..H 32
Thornburn-sq, Brmndsy SE 17 55..P 27
Thornbury-rd, Claphm SW 16 —..U 21
,, ,, Osterley-pk . 14 —..Q 3
,, av, Spring-grove 14 —..Q 3
Thornby-road, Clapton E . 7 39..F 28
Thorncliffe-rd, Clapham SW 16 —..U 21
Thorncombe-rd, Hrne-hl, SE 16 —..T 25
Thorncroft-rd, Sutton, Sur. 29 —..Z^{7} 16
Thorndean-st, Earlsfield SW 20 —..W 16
Thorne-rd, S. Lambeth SW 16 53..Q 22
,, st, Barnes SW . 15 —..S 11
,, ,, S. Lambeth SW 16 53..Q 21
Thornfield-rd, Shepds. B.W. 10 50..N 13
Thornford-rd, Lewisham SE 17 —..U 32
Thorngate-rd, Maida-hi, W 10 43..K 16
Thorngrove-rd, Plaistow E 13 —..J 35
Thornhill-cres, Barnsbry N 6 37..I 23
,, rd, Croydon, Sur. 26 —..Z^{5} 24
,, ,, Islington N . 6 37..I 23
,, ,, Leyton E . 7 —..F 31
,, ,, L. Ditton, Sy 24 —..Z^{5} 7

4-in. sht. 9-in. sht. mar.
Thornhill-sq, Barnsbury N 6 37..I 22
Thornhills-rd, T. Ditton, Sy 24 —..Z^{4} 4
Thornlaw-rd, W. Norwood 21 —..X 23
Thornsbeach-rd, Catford SE 22 —..W 31
Thornsett-rd, Earlsfield SW 20 —..W 16
,, ,, S. Norwood SE 27 —..Z^{2} 27
Thornton-av, Chiswick W . 10 —..O 11
,, ,, Streatham . 21 —..W 21
,, heath, Surrey . 26 —..Z^{2} 23
,, hi, Wimbledn SW 20 —..Z 14
,, rd, Croydon, Sy 26 —..Z^{4} 22
,, ,, E. Sheen SW 14 —..S 10
,, ,, Ilford E . 8 —..G 38
,, ,, Leyton E . 7 —..F 32
,, ,, Streathm SW 21 —..V 21
,, ,, Wimbldn SW 20 —..Z 14
,, st, Stockwell SW 16 61..S 23
,, heath raily-sta, L.B.& S.C. Rly 26 —..Z 23
Thornville-st, Deptford SE 63 4..R 30
Thornwood-road, Lee, SE . 17 —..U 33
Thorny-hedge-road, Gunnersbury W 9 —..O 9
Thorold-rd, Ilford, Essex . 8 —..F 39
,, ,, Wood-green E 2 —..A 22
Thorpe-rd, Barking, Essex 8 —..I 40
,, ,, Chapel-end E . 3 —..A 32
,, ,, East Ham E . 13 —..J 37
,, ,, Forest-gate E . 7 —..G 34
,, ,, Norbiton . . 19 —..Z 7
,, ,, Tottenham N . 7 33..D 26
,, ,, Walthamstow E 3 —..A 31
Thorpedale-rd, Hrnsy-rise N 6 32..E 22
Thorpe-hall-rd, Chapel-end E 3 —..A 32
Thorparch-rd, S. Lambth SW 16 61..R 21
Thorpebank-rd, Shep-.bh. W 10 50..M 12
Thorpewood-av, Sydnhm. SE 22 —..W 27
Thorverton-rd, Childs-hl NW 5 —..F 14
Thrale-road, Streatham . 21 —..T 20
Thrawl-st, Spitalfields E . 12 47..L 26
Threadneedle-street EC . 11 46..M 25
Three Colts-st, Limhouse E 12 48..M 30
,, ,, la, Bethnal-g. E 12 47..K 27
,, Cranes-l, U. Thms-s. EC — 46..M 24
,, Herring-court, Red-cross-street EC . — 46..L 24
,, Mills-la, Bromley E 12 49..K 31
, Tons-pas, Patnsr-sq EC — 46—L 24
Throckmorton-rd, Vic. D. E 13 —..M 35
Throgmorton-avenue, EC . 11 46..L 25
,, street, EC . 11 46..L 25
Throwley-rd, Sutton Sy. . 29 —..Z^{7} 16
Thurlby-road, Wembley . 4 —..H 7
,, rd. W. Norwood . 21 —..X 23
Thurleigh-rd, Balham SW . 16 —..U 19
Thurlestone-rd, W. Norwd 21 —..X 23
Thurloe-pl, S. Kensingtn. SW 11 51..O 18
Thurlow-gds, Sudbury, Mx 4 —..G 7
,, hill, Dulwich SW . 21 —..W 24
,, rd, Hampstead NW 5 35..G 17
,, st, Walworth SE . 17 54..P 25
,, pk.-rd, Dulwich . 21 —..W 24
,, sq, S. Knsingtn. SW 16 51..O 18
Thurso-st, Streatham SW . 17 —..X 17
Thurstan-rd, Wimbledon SW 20 —..Z 12
Thurston-rd, Lewisham SE 4 63..S 31
Thyra-gr, N. Finchley N . 1 —..A 17
Tibbatts-road, Bromley E 12 48..K 31
Tiber-street, Islington N . 6 37..I 22
Tichborne-court, Holborn — 45..L 22
Tidal Basin ry. sta, G.E. Ry. Victoria Docks E . 12 49..M 34
Tideswell-road, Putny SW. 15 59..T 13
Tidey-st, Bow-common E . 12 48..L 30
Ticpigs-lane, Hayes, Kent 27 —..Z^{6} 33
Tierney-road, Streatham . 21 —..V 21
Tilbrigge-road, Ilford . 8 —..F 41
Tilbury-road, East Ham E 13 —..J 37
Tilia-road, Clapton E . — 39..G 28
,, street, Plumstead SE. 18 —..Q 40
Tillotson-road, Ilford . 8 —..E 38
Tilson-road, Peckham SE . 17 54..Q 26
,, ,, Tottenham N 3 —..A 27
Tilney-street, Park-lane W 11 44..N 19
Tilton-street, Fulham SW . 15 58..Q 15
Timbercroft-la, Plumstead 18 —..Q 40
Tindal-st, N. Brixton SW . 16 62..R 23
Tintagel-cres, E. Dlwch. SE 17 62..T 26
Tintern-rd, Wood-green N 2 —..A 24
,, street, Brixton SW. 16 61..T 22
Tinto-rd, Canning Town E 13 —..L 34
Tipthorpe-rd, Battersea SW 16 60..S 19
Tirlemont-rd, Croydon, Sy. — 30..Z^{9} 24
Titchborne-st, Edgware-r. W 11 44..L 18
Titchfield-st, G. Tichfild-st W 11 44..K 20
,, ter, Regnts-p. NW 11 36..J 18
Titchwell-rd, Wandswth SW 21 —..V 17
Tite-street, Chelsea SW . 16 52..P 19
Tiverton-road, Hounslow 14 —..R 2
,, ,, Tottenham N. 7 33..D 25
Tivoli-road, Crouch-end N 2 —..C 21
,, ,, W. Norwood SE . 21 —..Y 24
Tobin-st, Notting-hill W . 10 50..M 14
Tokenhouse-yd, Lothbry EC 11 46..L 25
Tollet-street, Mile-end E . 12 47..K 28
Tollington-pk, Finsbry-pk. N. 6 32..E 23
,, pl, Finsbury-p. N 6 32..E 22
,, rd, Holloway N 6 37..G 23
Tolmers-sq, Hampstd-rd NW — 44..K 21
Tolverne-rd, Cttnhm.-pk. SW 20 —..Z^{1} 13
Tolworth, Surrey . . 24 —..Z^{5} 8
,, common, Surrey 24 —..Z^{5} 7
,, pk, L. Ditton . 24 —..Z^{5} 7
,, rd, Long Ditton. 24 —..Z^{5} 7
,, ,, Surbiton . 24 —..Z^{5} 7
,, pk.-rd, Surbiton 24 —..Z^{5} 7
Tomlins-grove, Bow E . 12 48..K 30
,, ter, Limehouse E 12 48..L 29
Tonbridge-st, Kings-cr. WC. 11 45..J 22
Tonsley-hi, Wandsworth SW 15 59..T 16
,, rd, Wandswrth SW 15 59..T 16
Tonsly-hill, Wandsworth SW 15 60..T 16

Tonsly-place. INDEX TO STREETS, &c. Upton-road.

Street	4-in. sht.	9-in. sht.	mar.
Tonsly-pl, Wandsworth SW	15	60..T	16
Tooke-street, Millwall E .	12	56..O	30
Tooks-ct, Cursitor-st. EC .	—	45..L	23
Tooley-street, SE . .	12	54..N	25
Tooting-common, SW .	21	—..X	19
,, grove, Tooting SW	20	—..Y	18
,, Bec Asy.U.Ttngsw	21	—..X	19
,, ,, com, Ttng SW	21	—..W	20
,, ,, rd, Tootg. SW	21	—..W	19
,, High-st,Tootingsw	21	—..Y	18
,, Junctn. ry. sta., L.B. & S.C.R.sw	21	—..Z^1	19
Toots Wood-rd,Bromly,Kt	27	—..Z^3	32
Topsfield-rd, Hornsey N .	2	—..C	22
Tor-gdns, Kensington W .	10	51..N	16
Torbay-rd, Willesden-laNW	5	—..I	15
,, st, Kentish Tn. NW	6	36..J	20
Tormount-road, Plumstead	18	—..Q	40
Tornburgh-av, Waltham. E	3	—..B	29
Toronto-av,Manor-park E .	8	—..G	37
,, rd, Ilford, Essex .	8	—..E	39
,, ,, Leytonstone E	7	41..G	32
Torquay-st, Harrow-rd, W.	—	43..L	16
Torr-road, Penge SE . .	22	—..Z^1	28
Torrens-road, Brixton SW	16	—..T	22
,, ,, Stratford E .	7	41..H	33
Torriano-av, Kentish T. NW	6	37..H	21
Torridon-rd, Catford SE .	22	—..W	32
Torrington-pk,N.Finchly.N	1a	—..A	18
,, pl,Trring.-sq.WC	11	45..K	21
,, sq, BloomsbyWC	11	45..K	21
Tothill-st, Westminster SW	11	53..O	21
Totnes-rd, Canning Twn. E	13	—..L	34
Tottenhall-rd, Bowes-pk, N	2	—..A	23
Tottenham N	3	—..A	26
,, cmtry,Tottm N	3	—..A	26
,, gr, TottenhmN	3	—..B	26
,, la, Hornsey N .	2	—..C	22
,, mrsh, Tottm.N	3	—..A	28
,, pk, Tottnhm N	3	—..A	25
,, rd, De Beauvoir Twn. N	7	38..H	26
,, ,, Wlthmstw E	3	—..C	30
,, Hale ry-st., G. E.Ry,Tm. N	3	—..B	27
,, st,Tot.-ct.-r.WC	11	45—L	21
,, court-rd, WC .	11	45..K	21
,, ,, ,, ry-sta., Cent. Lond. Ry	11	45..L	21
Totterdown-st, L.Tootg SW	20	—..X	18
Totteridge-rd, Battersea SW	15	60..R	17
Totton-rd, Thorn.-hth, Sur.	26	—..Z^2	23
Totty-st, Bethnal-green E .	12	48..J	29
Toulon-st, Camberwell SE .	16	54..Q	24
Tournay-rd, Fulham SW .	15	58..Q	15
Tower Bridge	12	54..N	26
,, gdns, Twr of Lon.EC	12	46..M	26
,, ,, rd, Tottenm N	3	—..A	25
,, hill, Twr of Lond. EC	12	46..M	26
,, hl,Little,Twr Lon. E	11	47..M	26
,, of London, EC .	11	46..M	26
,, road, Twickenham .	19	—..W	4
,, Royal, Cannon-st. EC	—	46..M	25
,, Stairs, Tower-hl, EC	12	46..M	26
,, st,G.S.Andrws-st,WC	11	45..M	21
,, ,, Hackney E .	7	39..I	27
,, ,, Waterloo-rd, SE .	11	53..O	23
,, Wharf, E . .	12	47..M	26
,, Bdge-rd, Brmndsy SE	12	54..O	25
,, Hamlets-rd,F.Gate E	7	—..H	34
Townmead-rd, Fulham SW	15	60..S	17
Town Hall-gdns,Wd. Grn N	2	—..A	23
Townley-rd, E.Dulwich SE	16	—..U	25
Townsend-la, Kingsbry NW	5	—..D	11
,, rd, Richmond .	14	—..S	7
,, ,, Tottenhm N	7	33..D	25
,, st, Walwrth SE	17	54..P	25
Townshend-rd, S.Jns W.NW	5	35..I	18
,, ter, Richmond	14	—..S	7
Towton-rd, W. Dulwich SE	21	—..W	24
,, ,, ,, SW	21	—..W	24
Tracey-st, Kenngton-rd, SE	16	53..P	23
Tradescant-rd, S. Lmbth.SW	—	53..Q	22
Trafalgar-rd, Dalston E .	7	39..I	26
,, ,, Greenwich SE	17	57..Q	32
,, ,, Merton SW .	20	—..Z	16
,, ,, O.Kent-rd,SE	17	55..Q	26
,, ,, Twickenham	19	—..V	3
,, sq, WC . .	11	45..M	21
,, ,, Chelsea SW .	16	51..P	18
,, ,, Peckham SE .	—	62..R	27
,, ,, Stepney E .	12	48..L	29
,, st, Walwth-rd,SE	16	54..P	24
Trafford-rd, Croydon, Surr.	26	—..Z^3	22
Tranmere-rd, Earlsfield SW	20	—..W	17
Tranquil-vale, Blackhth SE	17	64..S	33
Tranton-rd, Bermndsey SE	12	55..O	27
Travers-road, Islington N .	—	37..F	23
Treadgold-st, N. Knsgtn W	10	50..M	14
Treadway-st, Hackny-rd, E	12	47..J	27
Treasury, Whitehall SW .	11	53..N	22
Treaty-road, Hounslow .	14	—..S	1
Trebovir-rd, Earls-crt, SW	15	51..P	16
Tredegar-square, Bow E .	12	48..K	30
,, road, Bow E .	12	48..J	30
,, terrace, Bow E .	12	48..K	30
Trederwen-st, Dalston E .	7	39..I	27
Tree-road, Victoria Dck, E	13	—..M	35
,, walk, Purley ; .	30	—..Z^{10}	24
Trefoil-rd, Wandsworth;SW	15	—..T	17
Tregarvon-rd, Battersea SW	16	60..T	19
Tregenna-st, Brixton SW .	16	—..U	22
Trego-rd, Hackney Wick E	7	40..I	30
Tregothnan-rd, Stockwl SW	16	61..S	22
Tregunter-rd, Hale End E .	3	—..A	33
,, ,, W.BromptnSW	15	51..P	16
Treherne-rd, N.Brixton SW	16	61..R	23
Trehurst-street, Clapton E	7	40..G	29
Trelawn-road, Brixton SW	16	—..T	23
,, ,, Leyton E .	7	—..G	32
Trellis-street, Bow E .	12	48..J	30
Tremadoc-rd, Clapham SW	16	61..T	21
Tremaine-road, Penge SE .	22	—..Z^2	27
Trent-avenue, Ealing W .	9	—..N	6
,, road, Brixton SW .	16	—..U	22
Trentham-st, Sthfields SW	20	—..V	15
,, ,,Wlmbdn-pk,SW	20	—..V	15
Treport-st, Wandsworth SW	15	—..U	16
Tresco-road, Peckham SE .	17	63..T	27
Tresham-av, Clapton E .	7	—..G	28
,, ,, Homerton E .	7	39..G	28
Tresillian-rd, Brockley SE .	4	63..S	30
Trvanion-rd,W.Knsngtn SW	15	58..P	14
Trevelyan-rd, Leytonstne E	7	41..G	33
,, ,, Tooting SW .	20	—..Y	18
Treverton-st, Kensal-gr. W	10	42..K	14
Treville-st, Roehmpton SW	15	—..U	12
Trevor-rd, Wimbledon SW	20	—..Z	14
,, sq, Knightsbdge SW	11	52..N	18
Trewence-rd, Cottn-pk, SW	20	—..Z^1	13
Trewint-st, Earlsfield SW .	20	—..W	16
Trewsbury-rd, Sydenhm SE	22	—..Y	28
Trig-la, Up. Thames-st, EC.	—	46..M	24
Trigon-grove, Kenngtn SW	16	53..Q	22
Trigon-rd, Kennington SW	16	53..Q	22
Trilby-rd, Forest-hill SE .	22	—..W	28
Trim-street, Deptford SE .	17	56..Q	30
Trinder-rd, Finsbury-pk N	6	32..E	22
Tring-avenue, Ealing W .	9	—..M	8
Trinity-av, Brixton SW .	16	61..T	22
,, ,, E. Finchley N .	2	—..B	18
,, crt, Lit. Britain EC	—	46..L	24
,, hse, Tower-hill EC	12	46..M	26
,, rd, Dulwich SE .	21	—..V	23
,, ,, E. Finchley N .	2	—..B	18
,, ,, Penge SE .	22	—..Z^1	28
,, ,, Rotherhithe SE	12	56..N	30
,, ,, Wandsworth SW	15	—..U	17
,, ,, S. Wmbldn. SW	20	—..Y	16
,, ,, Wood-green N	2	—..A	22
,, sq, Borough SE .	16	61..T	22
,, ,, Brixton SW .	11	54..O	24
,, ,, Tower Hill EC .	12	46..M	26
,, st, Bor. High-st SE	11	54..O	24
,, ,, Canning Twn E	12	49..L	34
,, ,, Islington N .	11	37..J	23
,, ,, Leytonstone E .	7	41..F	33
,, ,, Woolwich .	13	—..O	36
,, Church-passage, Fetter-lane EC .	—	45..L	23
Tritton-rd, W. Norwood SE	21	—..X	24
Trossach-rd, E Dulwch SE	17	—..T	25
Trott-st, Battersea SW .	16	60..R	18
Troughton-road, Charlton	18	—..P	35
Trouville-rd, Clapham SW	16	—..U	20
Trulock-rd, Tottenham N .	3	—..A	27
Trumans-rd, St. Newgtn N	7	38..G	26
Trump-st, Cheapside EC .	—	46..M	24
Trumper's-crsng, G.W. Ry.	9	—..N	3
Trumpington-rd, Forest-gate E - . .	7	41..G	34
Trundley's-rd, Deptford SE	17	56..P	29
Truro-road, Wood-green N	2	—..A	22
Trussley-rd, Hmrsmth W	10	50..O	13
Tuam-road, Plumstead .	18	—..Q	39
Tubbs-rd, Harlesden NW .	10	42..J	12
Tucker-st, Canning Tn. E .	12	49..L	33
Tudor-grove, Hackney E .	7	39..I	28
,, pla, Tott. Ct.-rd WC	—	45..L	21
,, rd, Beckenham, Kt.	27	—..Z^2	31
,, ,, Hackney E .	7	39..I	28
,, ,, Hale End E .	3	—..A	31
,, ,, Norbiton . .	19	—..Z	8
,, ,, Plaistow E .	13	—..J	36
,, ,, Norwood SE .	27	—..Z^4	27
,, st, New Bdge-st EC	11	45..M	23
Tufnell-pk-rd, Holloway N	6	37..G	21
,, ,, ry. sta, Hllwy N	6	36..C	2
Tufton-st, Westminster SW	11	53..O	21
Tugela-rd, Croydon, Sy. .	26	—..Z^4	24
,, street, Catford SE .	22	—..W	30
Tuilerie-st, Hackney-rd E .	12	47..J	27
Tulse-hill, SW	21	—..V	23
,, ,, ry. sta., L.B. & S.C. Rly. .	21	—..W	23
Tulsemere-rd, W Dlwch SE	21	—..W	24
Tulsemore-rd, W Dlwch SW	21	—..W	24
Tun-passage, Ivy-lane EC .	—	46..L	24
Tunis-rd, Shepherd's B. W	10	50..M	13
Tunley-rd, Up. Tooting SW	21	—..W	19
,, ,, Willesden NW .	5	—..I	11
Tunmarsh-la, Plaistow E .	13	—..K	35
Tunnel-av, E Greenwch SE	12	57..O	33
,, pier, Wapping E .	12	55..N	28
,, rd, Rotherhithe SE	—	55..N	28
Tunstall-rd, Brixton SW .	16	61..T	22
,, ,, Croydon, Sy.	26	—..Z^5	25
Turin-rt, Bethnal Grn-rd E	12	47..K	27
Turkey-street, Brixton SW	16	—..U	23
Turks-rd, Twickenham .	14	—..T	5
,, row, Chelsea SW .	16	52..P	19
Turle-rd, Finsbury-park N	6	32..E	22
,, ,, Norbury . .	21	—..Z^2	21
Turnant-rd, Tottenham N	2	—..A	24
Turnbull-road, Plaistow E	13	—..L	35
Turner-road, Lee SE . .	17	64..T	33
,, st, Cmmercl.-rd E	12	47..L	27
Turners-rd, Limehouse E .	12	48..L	30
,, wd, Hampstd. NW	6	31..E	17
Turney-road, Dulwich .	21	—..V	25
Turnham Green ry. sta, Met. Dist. Railway .	10	—..O	11
Turnmill-st, Clerkenwll EC	11	45..K	23
Turnpike-lane, Hornsey N	2	—..B	23
Turnville-rd,W.Knsngtn SW	15	58..P	15
Turpington-lane, Bickley .	28	—..Z^4	36
Turret-grove, Clapham SW	16	61..S	20
Turtle-road, Streatham SW	20	—..W	16
Turton-rd, Sudbury, Mdx.	4	—..G	7
Tuscan-road, Plumstead .	18	—..Q	40
Tuskar-st, E. Greenwch SE	17	57..Q	33
Tussaud's Ex., Baker-st W	—	44..K	19
Tustin-st, Old Kent-rd SE	17	55..Q	28
Tweedmouth-rd, PlaistowE	13	—..J	35
Tweedy-road, Bromley .	22	—..Z^2	33
Twickenham, Middlesex .	19	—..V	4
,, cemty,Twckhm	19	—..V	1
,, pk, Twickhm.	14	—..T	5
,, rd, Isleworth	14	—..R	4
,, ,, Leyton E .	7	—..F	32
,, ,, Teddgtn. .	19	—..X	4
,, ry st, L. & S.W. Ry.,Twckhm	14	—..U	4
Twisden-rd, Kent. Tn. NW	6	36..G	20
Twyford-av, Ealing W .	9	—..M	8
,, crescent, Acton W	9	—..M	8
,, road, Ilford .	8	—..H	39
,, st, Islington N .	6	37..I	22
,, Abbey ry. sta., G.W. Ry. .	9	—..J	7
Tyas-rd, Canning Town E	12	49—L	33
Tyers-street, Lambeth SE .	16	53..P	22
Tylecroft-road, Norbury .	21	—..Z^2	21
Tyler-st, E. Greenwich SE	17	57..P	33
Tyler's-court, Wardour-stW	—	45..M	21
Tynemouth-rd, L. Ttng SW	21	—..Z^1	19
Tylney-rd, Forest-gate E .	8	—..G	35
Tylney-rd, Widmore, Kent	28	—..Z^3	35
Tyndall-road, Leyton E .	7	—..F	32
Tyneham-rd,Lavendr-hl SW	16	60..S	19
Tynemouth-rd,Tottenhm.N	3	—..C	27
,, st, Chelsea SW	15	60..R	17
Tynte-street, Homerton E	7	40..H	29
Type-court, Milton-st, EC .	—	46..L	25
Tyrrell-rd, E. Dulwich SE .	17	—..T	27
Tyrwhitt-rd, Brockley SE .	4	63..S	30
Tysoe-st, Wilmington-sqWC	—	45..K	23
Tyson-road, Forest-hill SE	22	—..Y	28
Tyssen-rd,Stke Newingtn.N	7	39..F	26
Tytherton-rd,U.Hollowy.N	6	37..F	21
U			
Udney-pk.-rd,Teddington	19	—..Y	4
Uffington-rd, W. Norwood	21	—..X	23
,, ,, Willesden NW	5	34..I	12
Ufford-st, Blackfriars-rd.SE	11	53..N	23
Ufton-gr, Southgate-rd. N	7	38..I	25
,, rd, Downham-road N .	7	38..I	25
Uganda-st, L. Tooting SW	21	—..X	18
Ullathorne-rd,Streathm.SW	21	—..X	20
Ulleswater-rd,Palmers-gr.N	2	—..A	22
Ullin-street, Bromley E .	12	49..L	31
Ullin-street, Bromley E .	12	49..L	31
Ullswater-rd,Norwood-r.SE	21	—..W	23
Ulster-ter,Regents-pk. NW	11	44..K	20
Ulundi-rd, Greenwich SE .	17	57..Q	33
Ulverscroft-rd,E.DulwchSE	17	—..U	26
Ulverston-rd, Chapel-end E	3	—..A	32
Ulysses-rd, Hampstead NW	5	—..G	15
Umberston-st,Commerc-r.E	12	47..M	27
Umbria-st,Roehamptn SW	15	—..U	12
Umfreville-rd,Finsbury-p.N	6	32..D	24
Undercliff-rd,Lewisham SE	4	63..S	31
Underhill-rd, Dulwich SE .	22	—..V	27
Underwood-st, Whitechl. E	12	47..L	27
,, ,, Shoreditch N	—	46..J	25
Undine-st, L. Tooting SW .	20	—..Y	18
Union-ct, Old Broad-st. EC	—	46..J	25
,, gr, Clapham SW .	16	61..R	21
,, lane, Brentford .	14	—..R	5
,, rd, Bermondsey SE	12	55..O	27
,, ,, Bromley- Kent .	28	—..Z^3	36
,, ,, Clapham SW .	16	61..S	21
,, ,, Croydon, Surrey	26	—..Z^4	24
,, ,, Holloway N .	6	37..G	21
,, ,, Leytonstone E .	7	41..G	32
,, ,, Millwall E . .	12	56..O	30
,, ,, New Southgate N	2	—..A	22
,, ,, NwngtnCswy.SE	11	54..O	24
,, ,, Rotherhithe SE .	12	54..O	27
,, ,, Stratford E .	7	41..I	33
,, ,, Sudbury, Midx.	4	—..H	7
,, ,, Walthamstow E	7	—..D	30
,, ,, West Dulwich .	21	—..W	25
,, sq, Southwark SE .	11	54..O	24
,, ,, Islington N .	11	38..J	24
,, st, Borough SE .	11	54..N	24
,, ,, Clapham SW .	16	61..S	21
,, ,, Cmmercl-rd. E	12	47..L	27
,, ,, Croydon, Surrey	26	—..Z^6	24
,, ,, Gt.Titchfield-s.W	11	44..L	20
,, ,, Hackney-road, E	12	46..K	26
,, ,, Moorfields EC .	11	46..L	25
,, ,, Pimlico-road SW	16	52..P	19
,, ,, Poplar E . .	12	49..M	32
,, ,, West Ham E .	12	41..J	32
,, ,, Woolwich . .	13	—..O	38
,, Workhse.Croydn.Sy	26	—..Z^4	24
,, ,, Farnboro'Kt	30	—..Z^7	37
University Col.Gower-st.WC	11	45..K	21
,, rd,S.WimbldnSW	20	—..Z	17
,, st,Tot.-ct.-rd.WC	11	45..K	21
Unwin-road, Peckham SE	17	55..Q	26
Upcerne-road, Chelsea SW	15	51..Q	17
Upcott-street, Deptford SE	17	55..Q	28
Uphall-road, Ilford E .	8	—..H	39
Uphalt-avenue, Ilford .	8	—..G	38
Upham-pk.-rd,Chiswick W.	10	—..O	11
Upland-rd, Croydon, Sy .	—	30..Z^8	24
,, ,, E. Dulwich SE	17	—..T	27
Uplands-road, Hornsey N .	2	32..D	23
Upney-la, Barking, Essex .	8	—..I	41
Upper Brighton-rd,Surbitn	24	—..Z^4	6
,, Clapton E . .	7	33..E	27
,, Court-road, Epsom	28a	—..Z^{10}	9
,, Edmonton N . .	3	—..A	26
,, Garden-st,PimlicoSW	—	53..P	21
,, green Mitcham, Sy .	25	—..Z^2	18
,, grove, Selhurst SE .	26	—..Z^3	25
,, ,, Norwood SE .	26	—..Z^3	25
,, James-st,Golden-s.W	—	44..M	21
,, Hale, Middlesex .	1	—..A	10
,, John-st,Golden-s.W.	—	44..M	21
Upper Hill, Richmond .	14	—..T	6
,, Holloway-Station N	6	32..F	21
,, Mall,Hammersth. W	15	58..P	12
,, Market, Woolwich .	18	—..P	38
,, Marsh, Lambeth SE	11	53..O	23
,, Mitcham . .	21	—..Z^2	19
,, Norwood . .	21	—..Z^1	25
,, Parkfields,Putny.SW	15	59..T	13
,, pk.-pl,Dorset-sq.NW	11	44..K	19
,, Pool . . .	12	55..N	26
,, road, Plaistow E .	13	—..K	34
,, Shirley, Surrey .	30a	—..Z^7	28
,, street, Islington N .	11	38..J	23
,, St. Martin's-lane, Long Acre WC .	—	44..M	22
,, Sydenham SE . .	22	—..X	27
,, Tooting . . .	21	—..X	19
,, Addison-g.Knsgtn.W	10	50..N	14
,, Ashby-st,Gosw.-r.EC	—	46..K	24
,, Baker-st,Reg.-pk.W	11	44..K	19
,, Bedford-pl, Russell-square WC . .	11	45..K	21
,, Belgrave-st, Eaton-square SW . .	11	52..O	19
,, Belsize-ter,HmpstdNW	6	35..H	18
,, Berkeley-st, Portman-square W .	11	44..L	19
,, Beulah-hl, Norwood	21	—..Z^2	25
,, Bland-s,G.Dover-sSE	12	54..O	25
,, Brook-st, Gros.-sq. W	11	44..M	19
,, Chadwell-st, Pentonville EC . . .	11	45..J	23
,, Chapman-st, SE .	12	47..M	27
,, Charles-st, Northhampton-square EC	11	46..K	24
,, Charlton-st, Fitzroy-square W . .	11	44..K	20
,, Cheyne-rw, ChelseaSW	16	51..Q	18
,, Clapton-rd, U ClaptnE	7	33..E	27
,, Dorset-st, Bryanston-square W .	11	44..L	18
,, E. Smithfield E .	12	47..M	26
,, Elmers-end, Elmers-end, Kent . .	27	—..Z^4	29
,, Elmers End-road, Elmers-end, Kent .	27	—..Z^3	29
,, Fenton-st, Com.-rd E	12	47..M	27
,, Grange-rd, Berm. SE	17	54..P	26
,, Gloucester-pl, Dorset-square NW . .	11	44..K	19
,, Grosvenor-street, W .	11	44..M	19
,, Grotto-rd, Twicken. .	19	—..V	4
,, Ground-st, Blckfrs SE	11	45..M	23
,, Grove-rd, Hounslow	14	—..S	1
,, Gutter Hedge-lane, Hendon NW . .	5	—..D	13
,, Ham-rd, Norbiton .	19	—..Y	6
,, Hamilton-ter, St. John's-wood NW .	10	43..J	17
,, Holl'w'y sta, Mid. Ry. N	6	32..F	21
,, Hornsey-rse,U.Hlwy N	6	32..E	22
,, Kennington-lane, Kennington SE .	16	53..P	22
,, Manor-st, Chelsea SW	16	51..P	18
,, Marsh-la, Surbiton,Sy	24	—..Z^2	7
,, Marylebone-street, W	11	44..L	20
,, Montagu-st, Montagu-square W . .	11	44..L	19
,, North-st, Poplar E .	12	48..M	31
,, Orchard-st, Brixton .	21	—..V	22
,, Park-place, Dorset-square NW .	11	44..K	19
,, ,, rd, Hampstd NW	6	36..H	19
,, ,, ,, Nw Sthgte N	2	—..A	21
,, ,, st, Islington N .	6	37..I	23
,, Parkfield-rd, Putney SW	15	—..T	13
,, Phillimore-gds,KnstnW	10	50..N	15
,, Quebec-yd, RthrhthSE	12	56..O	29
,, Porchester-st, Edgware-road W . .	—	43..L	18
,, Rathbone-place, W .	11	45..L	21
,, Richmond-rd, Barnes SW	14	—..S	9
,, ,, ,, Mortlke SW	14	—..S	9
,, ,, ,, Putney SW	15	—..T	14
,, Russell-st,Brmndsy SE	12	54..O	25
,, Seymour-st, Edgware-road, W .	11	44..M	18
,, Smith-st, Northampton-square EC .	—	46..K	24
,, Sydenham Sta, S.E. & C.R. . . .	22	—..X	26
,, Teddington-rd, Hampton Wick . .	19	—..Z	6
,, Thames-street EC .	11	46..M	24
,, Tollington-pk, Finsbury-park N . .	6	32..E	23
,, Tooting-park SW .	21	—..W	19
,, ,, road, SW .	20	—..X	18
,, Tulse-hill, BrixtonSW	21	—..V	22
,, Walthamstow-road, Walthamstow E .	3	—..B	32
,, Westbourne-terrace, Harrow-road W .	11	43..L	16
,, William-st, S. John's Wood NW . .	11	43..J	18
,, Wimpole-st, MylbneW	—	44..L	20
,, Winchester-st, Pentonville N . .	11	37..J	22
,, Woburn-pla, Euston-road WC . .	11	45..K	21
Upperton-rd, Plaistow E .	13	—..K	35
,, ,, Sidcup, Kent	23	—..Y	41
Upstall-st, Camberwell SE	16	62..R	24
Upton, E , . . .	8	—..I	35
,, av, Upton E .	8	—..I	34
,, lane, Upton E .	8	—..I	35
,, park-rd, Upton E	8	—..I	35
,, rd, Thornton-hth .	21	—..Z^2	24
,, ,, Upton E . .	8	—..I	35
,, ,, Woolwich .	18	—..Q	39

[96]

4-in. sht. — 9-in. sht. — mar.

Woodgrange pk ry. sta, G.E. Ry. . 8 —..H 36
Woodhayes-rd, Wmbldn SW 20 —..Z 13
Woodheys-rd, Wlsdn NW . 5 —..H 11
Woodhouse-gro, E. Ham E 8 —..I 36
  „ rd, Leytnstn E 7 41..F 33
  „ N Fnchly N 1 —..A 18
Woodhurst-rd, Acton W . 9 —..M 10
  „ Plumstead 13 —..P 41
Woodville-rd, Bowes-pk. N 2 —..A 23
Woodland-gds, Muswell-hl N 2 —..C 20
  „ hil, Norwood . 21 —..Y 25
  „ ri, Muswell-hl N 2 —..C 20
  „ rd, Croydon, Sy 26 —..Z² 23
  „ Putney SW . 15 59..T 15
  „ Up. Norwd. 21 —..Y 25
  „ st, Dalston E . 7 39..H 26
Woodlands, Isleworth . 14 —..R 3
  „ av, Finchley N 1 —..A 17
  „ Finchley N 1 —..A 17
  „ Wanstead E 8 —..F 35
  „ gro, Isleworth . 14 —..R 3
  „ pl, E Grnwch SE 17 57..Q 33
  „ rd, Barnes SW . 15 —..S 11
  „ Bickley, Kt. 28 —..Z² 37
  „ Farnborough 30b —..Z² 41
  „ Harrow, Mx 1a —..C 4
  „ Ilford, Esx. 8 —..G 39
  „ Isleworth . 14 —..R 3
  „ Walthmstw E 3 —..B 32
  „ st, Lewishm. SE 22 —..V 32
  „ pk-rd, Grnwh SE 17 57..Q 33
  „ Tottnhm N 2 —..C 24
Woodlawn-rd, Fulham SW 15 58..Q 14
Woodlea-rd, Stk Newngtn N 7 33..F 25
Woodmansterne-rd, Purley, Surrey . . 30 —..Z¹⁰ 23
Woodnook-rd, Streathm SW 21 —..Y 20
Woodpecker-rd, Nw Cross E 17 56..Q 29
Woodquest-av, Herne-hl SE 16 —..U 24
Woodriffe-rd, Leytonst. E 7 —..E 33
Woods M., Park-street W . 11 44..M 19
  „ rd, Peckham SE . 17 62..R 27
Woodside, Croydon, Sy. . 26 —..Z² 26
  „ Wimbledon SW . 20 —..Y 15
  „ av, Muswell-hl N 2 —..C 20
  „ Th. Ditton . 24 —..Z² 2
  „ Woodside SE 27 —..Z² 27
  „ Wdsde-pk N 1 —..A 17
  „ cres, Sidcup . 23 —..X 40
  „ gds, Tottnhm N. 3 —..N 26
  „ gn, S. Norwd. SE 27 —..Z² 27
  „ Wdsde-pk N 1 —..A 17
  „ la, Woodsde-pk N 1 —..A 17
  „ park, N . 1 —..A 17
  „ rd, Nw Maldn SW 20 —..U 10
  „ Norbiton . 19 —..Z 6
  „ Plaistow E . 13 —..L 35
  „ Sidcup . 23 —..X 40
  „ S Norwd. SE 27 —..Z² 27
  „ Sutton, Sy. . 25 —..Z² 16
  „ Wood-grn. N 2 —..A 23
  „ & S. Norwood ry sta, S.E.&C.Ry 27 —..Z⁴ 27
  „ Grange-rd, Woodside-pk N . . 1 —..A 17
  „ pk-rd, Wdsde-pk N 1 —..A 17
  „ sta, G.N.R. N 1 —..A 17
Woodsome-rd, Hghgte-rd NW 6 36..F 20
Woodstock-av, Hendon NW 5 —..E 15
  „ rd, Carshalton 30 —..Z² 19
  „ Chapel E E 3 —..A 32
  „ Croydn, Sy 30 —..Z² 24
  „ Fnsbry-pk N 6 32..E 23
  „ Golder's green NW . 5 —..E 15

Woodstock-rd, L.Dittn, Sy 24 —..Z⁶ 5
  „ Poplar E . 12 48..M 31
  „ ry-sta, N. S.W. Jnc. Ry 10 —..N 11
  „ Trnhm-grw 10 —..O 11
  „ Wlthmstw E 3 —..B 32
  „ WKnsgtn W 10 50..N 14
  „ st, Cann. Tn E 12 49..L 33
  „ Oxford-st W — 44..M 20
Woodvale-av, Norwood SE 1 —..A
Woodvale-av, Norwood SE 26 —..Z² 26
Woodville-av, Finchley N . 1 —..A 17
  „ gds, Ealing W . 9 —..L 7
  „ gro, Tottenhm N 3 —..C 25
  „ rd, Blckhth SE . 18 —..R 34
  „ Ealing W . 9 —..L 7
  „ Hendon NW. 5 —..D 14
  „ Leytnstne E 7 —..E 34
  „ StkNwngtn N 7 38..H 25
  „ Thrntn H.Sy 26 —..Z² 24
  „ Wlthmstw E 3 —..C 30
  „ Wood-gr. N 2 —..A 23
Woodwarde-rd, E.Dlwch SE 16 —..U 25
Woollett-street, Poplar E 12 48..M 31
Woolmer-rd, Edmonton N. 3 —..A 27
Woolmore-street, Poplar E 12 49..M 32
Woolpack-road, Hackney E 7 39..H 28
Woolsey-st, Whitechapel E 12 47..L 28
Woolstone-rd, Forst-hl SE. 22 —..W 29
Woolwich, Kent . . 18 —..O 39
  „ arsenal, Plmstd. 18 —..Q 38
  „ station 18 —..P 38
  „ cemetry, Plmstd 18 —..R 41
  „ com., Woolwich 18 —..O 37
  „ dck.-yd, Wlwch 18 —..O 37
  „ station 18 —..P 37
  „ rd, Grnwch SE. 17 57..P 33
  „ Woolwich . 18 —..P 35
Wootton-rd, Willesden NW 5 —..F 14
  „ st, Wtrloo-rd. SE 11 53..N 23
Worbeck-road, Penge SE . 22 —..Z² 27
Worcester-park, Surrey . 25 —..Z⁴ 10
  „ rd, Higham-hl E 3 —..A 29
  „ Manor-pk. E 8 —..G 37
  „ Sutton, Sy.. 29 —..Z² 15
  „ Wmbldn SW 20 —..Y 15
  „ st, Pimlico SW . 16 52..P 21
  „ Sthwrk-st. . 11 54..N 24
  „ pk. ry. sta., L. & S.W. Rly. . 25 —..Z¹ 11
  „ rd, Malden. 24 —..Z² 9
Wordsworth-av, E. Ham E 8 —..I 37
  „ rd, Crshltn, Sy 30 —..Z² 20
  „ Penge SE 22 —..Z² 28
  „ StkNwgtn N 7 38..G 26
  „ Wldstn Mx 1a —..B 4
Worfield-st, Battersea SW . 16 52..Q 18
Worgrove-st, Balham SW . 21 —..V 19
Workhouse, Albany-rd. SE 17 54..P 25
  „ High-rd, Leytonstone E. 7 41..G 33
  „ Rotherhithe SE 12 55..O 28
  „ rd, Thames Ditton, Sy. 24 —..Z⁴ 4
Worlds End-psge,Chlsea SW — 51..Q 17
Worlidge-st, Hamrsmth. W 15 58..P 13
Worlingham-rd, East Dulwich SE. . . 17 62..T 26
Wrmholt-rd, ShphrdsBsh W 10 50..M 12
Wormington-rd, Knsl-gr.W 10 42..K 14
Wormwood Scrubs W . . 10 42..K 12
  „ st, Bishopsgate street EC . 11 46..L 25
Woronzow-rd,St.Jns W. NW 5 35..I 18
Worple-av, Wimbledon SW 20 —..Z 14
  „ rd, Cottnhm-pk.SW 20 —..Z¹ 13

Worple-rd, Isleworth . 14 —..T 4
  „ Wimbledon SW 20 —..Z 14
  „ w. Wmbldn SW 20 —..Z¹ 13
  „ way, Richmond . 14 —..T 7
  „ N. Mrtlke. SW 15 —..S 10
  „ S. Mrtlke. SW 15 —..S 10
Worship-st, Finsbury EC . 11 46..K 25
Worslade-road, Tooting SW 20 —..X 17
Worsley-rd, Leytnstne. E . 7 41..G 33
  „ Hampstead NW 5 35..G 18
  „ Bridge-road,Lowr Sydenham SE . 22 —..Y 30
Worthington-rd, Croydon, Sy. 26 —..Z² 22
Wortley-rd, Croydon, Sy.. 26 —..Z² 22
  „ Plashet E . 8 —..I 36
Worton-lane, Isleworth . 14 —..S 4
Wotton-road, Deptford SE 17 56..Q 30
Wragby-rd, Leytonstone E 7 41..G 33
Wray-cres, Finsbury-pk. N 6 32..E 22
Wren-rd, Camberwell SE . — 62..R 25
Wrentham-av, Qns-pk.NW 10 34..J 14
Wrestlers-ct, Camomle-st.EC— 46..L 25
Wrexham-rd, Old Ford E . 12 48..J 31
Wrigglesworth-rd,Dptfrd.SE 17 55..Q 28
  „ st,Hatcham SE . 17 55..Q 28
Wrights-ally,Wimbledn.SW 20 —..Z 13
  „ la, Kensington W. 10 51..O 16
  „ rd, St. Stephens-road E . 12 40..J 30
Wrotham-rd, CmdnTn. NW 6 37..I 21
Wrottesley-rd, Hrsldsn. NW 10 34..J 12
  „ Plumstead 18 —..Q 39
Wroughton-rd, Bttrsea SW 16 —..U 19
Wrythe-la, Carshalton, Sy. 25 —..Z¹ 17
Wyatts-la, Walthamstow E 3 —..B 32
Wyatt-road, Highbury N . 6 38..F 24
  „ Upton E . 8 —..I 34
  „ pk-rd, Brixton SW. 21 —..W 22
Wyche-gro, Croydon, Sry. 30 —..Z² 24
Wycliffe-rd, Battersea SW 16 60..S 19
  „ Leyton E . 7 41..H 32
  „ Wimbledon SW 20 —..Z 16
Wycombe-rd, Tottenham N 3 —..A 27
Wye-street, Battersea SW . 16 60..S 17
Wyeshall-rd, Edmonton N. 3 —..A 25
Wyfold-road, Fulham SW . 15 58..Q 14
Wyke-green, Middlesex . 14 —..P 3
  „ rd, Old Ford E . 7 40..I 30
  „ Raynes-park SW 20 —..Z¹ 13
Wylen-st, Brockley SE . 22 —..W 22
Wymering-rd, Maida-hl. W 10 43..K 16
Wymond-street, Putney SW 15 59..S 13
Wyncliff-rd, Blackburn SE. 18 —..Q 35
Wynhdam-cres Jnctn.-rd.N 6 36..F 21
  „ pl,Brynstn-sq.W 11 44..L 19
  „ rd,CmberwellSE 16 54..Q 24
  „ Ealing W . 9 —..N 5
  „ Norbiton . 19 —..Y 7
  „ Plashet-gr.E 8 —..I 36
  „ st,Marylebn-rd W 11 44..L 19
Wynell-road, Forest-hill SE 22 —..X 29
Wynford-rd,Caldnian-rd.N. 11 37..J 22
Wynne-road, Brixton SW . 16 61..S 23
Wynnstay-gds,Kensingtnw — 51..O 16
Wynatt-st, Goswell-rd. EC 11 46..K 24
Wythes-road, Silvertown E 13 —..N 36
Wyvil-road, S. Lambeth SW 16 53..Q 22
Wyvis-street, Bromley E . 12 49..L 31

Y

Yabsley-street,Blackwall E 12 57..N 32
Yalding-rd,Bermondsey SE 12 55..O 26

Yatton-street, Bromley E . 12 49..L 31
Yeldham-rd,Hmrsmth W . 15 58..P 13
Yelverton-rd, Battersca SW 15 60..R 17
Yeo-street, Bromley E . 12 48..L 31
Yeoman-st, Rotherhithe SE 17 56..P 29
Yeomans-rw,Brmptn-rds SW 11 52..O 18
Yeovil-place, Battersea SW 16 61..R 21
Yerbury-rd, U. Holloway.N. 6 37..F 21
Yester-rd, Elmstead, Kent 23 —..Z 36
Yew-grove,Cricklewood NW 5 —..G 14
Yewfield-rd, Harlesden NW 5 —..H 11
Yewtree-rd, Beckenhm.Kt. 27 —..Z² 29
Yonge-park, Holloway N . 6 32..F 23
York-buildings, Adelphi WC — 45..M 22
  „ gate, Regents-prk. W 11 44..K 19
  „ grove, Peckham SE . 17 63..R 28
  „ place, Baker-street W 11 44..L 19
  „ Battersea SW . 16 60..S 17
  „ Strand WC — 45..M 22
  „ rise, Highgate-rd. NW 6 36..F 20
  „ rd, Acton W . 9 —..L 10
  „ Battersea SW . 15 60..S 17
  „ Brentford, Mdx . 14 —..P 6
  „ Commercial-rd. E. 12 48..M 29
  „ Croydon, Surrey . 26 —..Z⁴ 23
  „ Ealing W . 9 —..N 6
  „ Edmonton N . 3 —..A 27
  „ Hendon NW. 5 —..D 12
  „ Ilford, Essex . 8 —..F 38
  „ Kings Cross N . 11 45..J 22
  „ Lambeth SE . 11 53..N 22
  „ Leyton E . 7 —..F 32
  „ New Southgate N . 2 —..A 22
  „ Norbiton . 19 —..Z 7
  „ S. Wimbledon SW 20 —..Y 16
  „ Sutton, Surrey . 29 —..Z² 15
  „ Teddington . 19 —..X 3
  „ Tulse-hill . 21 —..X 23
  „ Upton E . 8 —..I 36
  „ Walthamstow E . 7 —..D 29
  „ Wandsworth SW . 15 59..T 14
  „ Wealdstone . 1a —..A 3
  „ square, Stepney E . 12 48..M 29
  „ st, Woolwich E. . 13 —..O 36
  „ Adelphi WC . 11 45..M 22
  „ Canning Town E 12 49..L 33
  „ Covent-garden WC 11 45..M 22
  „ Hackney-road E. 12 47..J 27
  „ Jermyn-street SW 11 45..M 21
  „ Mitcham, Surrey . 26 —..Z⁴ 19
  „ Portman-sqare W 11 44..L 19
  „ Twickenham . 19 —..V 4
  „ Walworth-road SE 16 54..P 24
  „ Westminster SW . 11 52..O 21
  „ west, Stepney E . 12 48..M 29
  „ terrace, Clapham SW 16 61..S 21
  „ Regents-park NW 11 44..K 19
  „ road, rly. sta, G.N.R. 11 37..J 22
Young-st, Kensington W . 10 51..N 16
  „ Victoria-D.E E . 13 —..M 34
Youngs-rd, Ley-st. . 8 —..D 40
Yukon-road, Balham . 21 —..Y 20
Yuletide-rd, Harlesden NW 5 —..H 11

Z

Zampa-rd, Rotherhithe SE. 17 55..P 28
Zennor-road, Balham . 21 —..V 20
Zennoria-st, E. Dulwich SE — 62..T 26
Zetland-street, Bromley E. 12 49..L 31
Zion-road, Croydon, Surry. 26 —..Z² 24
Zoological Gds,Rgnts-pk NW 11 36..J 19

PRINCIPAL LONDON CLUBS.

NOTE.—The marginal squares are given to show position for convenience of reference, but the Clubs are not named on the map.

	mar.
Aero of the United Kingdom, Royal, 166 Piccadilly W	11..N 20
Aeroplane, Savoy Hotel, Strand	11..M 22
Albemarle, 37 Dover-street W	11..M 20
Albert, 46 Gerrard-street W	11..M 21
Alexandra, 12 Grosvenor-st. W	11..M 20
Alliance, 61 Curzon-street, Mayfair W	11..N 20
Almack's, 20 Berkeley-street W	11..M 20
Alpine, 23 Savile-row W	11..M 20
Amateur Camping, 4 New Union-street EC	11..L 25
American Universities, 68 Pall-mall SW	11..N 21
Amherst, Amhurst-road, Stoke Newington N	7..G 27
Argyll, 52 Russell-square WC	11..K 22
Army and Navy, 36 Pall-mall SW	11..N 21
Army and Navy Bridge, 139 Victoria-street SW	11..O 21
Arthur's, 69 & 70 St. James's-street SW	11..N 21
Arts, Ltd., 40 Dover-street W	11..M 20
Athenæum, 107 Pall-mall SW	11..N 21
Athenæum Chess, Whittington avenue EC	11..M 25
Austral, Ltd., 45 Dover-st. W	11..M 20
Australasian, 24 St. Mary-axe EC	11..L 26
Authors', 2 Whitehall-court SW	11..N 22
Auto Cycle Union, 18 Down-street W	11..N 20
Automobile, Royal, Pall-mall SW	11..N 21
Bachelors', 7 and 8 Hamilton-place W	11..N 19
Badminton, 100 Piccadilly W	11..N 20
Baldwin, 79A Pall-mall SW	11..N 21
Baltic Exchange Golf, 16 Great St. Helens EC	11..L 25
Bar Golf, 2 Tanfield-court EC	11..M 23
Bath, 34 Dover-street W	11..M 20
Bath (Ladies'), 16 Berkeley-street W	11..M 20
Bayswater, 1 St. Stephen's-square W	10..L 16
Beaufort, 34 Soho-square W	11..L 21
Beefsteak, 9 Green-street WC	11..M 21
Belgravia, 21 St. George's-square SW	16..P 21
Berkeley Bridge, 247 Knightsbridge SW	11..N 18
Billiards Control, Gt. Windmill House W	11..M 21
Blenheim, 26 King-street, St. James's	11..N 2
Boodles', 28 St. James's-street SW	11..N 21
Brewers, 8 Victoria-street SW	11..O 21
British Canoe Association, 1 Water-lane, Gt. Tower-st. EC	11..M 25
British Empire, 12 St. James's-square SW	11..M 21
British Motor Boat, Princes-buildings, Coventry-street W	11..M 21
Brompton, 154 Brompton-road SW	11..O 18
Brooklands Automobile Racing, Carlton House, Regent-street W (office)	11..M 21
Brook's, 60 St. James's-st. SW.	11..N 20
Burlington Bridge, 2 Savile-row W	11..M 20
Burlington Fine Arts, 17 Savile-row W	11..M 20
C. A. Golf	
Calanda, 35 St. George's-square SW	16..P 21
Caledonian, 30 Charles-street, St. James's-square SW	11..M 21
Camberwell, Peckham and Dulwich Conservative, 1 Hanover-park, Peckham SE.	16..R 25
Camberwell Conservative, 1 Brunswick-square SE	16..R 25
Canonbury Tower, Canonbury-place N	6..H 24
Caravan, 358 Strand WC	11..M 22
Carlton, 94 Pall-mall SW	11..N 21
Cavalry, 127 Piccadilly W	11..N 20
Centaur, 39 Shaftesbury-av. W.	11..M 21
Chelsea, 147A Fulham-road SW.	15..Q 16
Chelsea Arts, 143 Church st. SW	16..P 6
Chelsea Conservative, 193 Kings-road SW	16..P 18
Chelsea Football and Athletic, Stamford-bridge SW	15..Q 16
City Athenæum, 3 Angel-ct. EC	11..L 25
City Carlton, 24–27 St. Swithins-lane EC	11..M 25
City Liberal, Walbrook EC	11..M 25
City of London, 19 Old Broad-street EC	11..L 25 11..L 25
City of London Chess, 7 Grocers' Hall-court, Poultry EC	11..M 25
City Union, Ltd., 19 London-wall EC	11..L 25
City University, 50 Cornhill EC	11..M 25
Civic, 6 Northumberland-av. WC	11..M 22
Clapham Constitutional, Ltd., 370 Wandsworth-road SW	16..R 21
Cobden, Broadway-court SW	11..L 23
Cocoa Tree, 64 St. James's-street SW	11..N 21
Colonial Institute, Royal, Northumberland-avenue WC	11..M 22
Connaught, Marble Arch W	11..M 19
Conservative, 74 St. James's-street SW	11..N 20
Constitutional, Northumberland-avenue WC	11..M 22
Coventry, 21 Denman-street W	11..M 21
Cruising, Royal, 1 Bolton-st. W	11..M 20
Crystal Palace, Crystal Palace SE.	21..Y 26
Cyclists' Touring, 280 Euston-road	11..K 21
Devonshire, 50 St. James's-street SW	11..N 20
Dutch, 31 Sackville-street W	11..M 21
East India United Service, 16 and 17 St. James's-square SW	11..M 21
Eccentric, 21 Shaftesbury-av. W	11..M 21
Effra Conservative, 89 Effra-road, Brixton SW	16..T 23
Eldon, 3 Cursitor-street EC	11..L 23
Eleusis, 180 King's-road SW	16..P 18
Emerson, 19 Buckingham-st. Strand WC	11..M 22
Empress, 35 Dover-street W	11..M 20
Engineering Golf, 5 Victoria-street SW	11..O 21
Enterprise, 57 Leadenhall-st. EC	11..M 25
Esperanto, St. Bride's Institute EC	11..L 23
Essex County Cricket, County Ground, Leyton E	7..F 32
Farmers', 2 Whitehall-court SW	11..N 22
Fencing, 7 Cleveland-row SW	11..N 21
Fitzjohn Bridge, 136 Finchley-road NW	5..E 16
Fly Fishers', 36 Piccadilly W	11..N 20
Fulham Conservative, 2–6 Shorrolds-road SW	16..P 18
Garden, Exhibition Gardens, Shepherd's Bush W	10..M 13
Garrick, 15 Garrick-street WC	11..M 22
German Athenæum, 19 Stratford-place W	11..L 20
Golfers', Whitehall-court SW	11..N 22
Green Room, 46 Leicester-sq. WC	11..M 21
Gresham, Gresham-place EC	11..M 25
Grosvenor, 68A Piccadilly and 1A Dover-street W	11..M 20
Grosvenor, 200 Buckingham Palace-road SW	11..N 19
Guards', 70 Pall-mall SW	11..N 21
Gun, Wood-lane, Notting Hill W	10..M 13
Hackney Conservative, 10 Lower Clapton-road NE	7..H 28
Hackney Reform, "The Eagles," 52 Well-street NE	7..I 28
Hampden Residential, 13 Phœnix-street, St. Pancras NW	11..J 21
Hampstead Constitutional, Holly-bush-hill NW	6..G 17
Highbury and Finsbury Park Conservative, 1 Prah-road, Finsbury Park N	6..F 23
Holborn Cycling, 14 Bedford-row WC	11..L 22
Hurlingham, Fulham SW	15..P 13
Hurst Park, 83 Piccadilly W	11..N 20
Imperial Colonial, 84 Piccadilly W	11..N 20
Imperial Social (Ladies'), 6 Lexham-gardens SW	10..O 16
Institute, 4 Corbet-court, Gracechurch-street EC	11..M 25
International, 22A Regent-st. SW	11..L 20
Irish, 28 Charing Cross-rd. WC	11..M 21
Isthmian, 105 Piccadilly W	11..N 20
Junior Army and Navy, Horse Guards-avenue SW	11..N 21
Junior Athenæum, 116 Piccadilly W	11..N 20
Junior Berkeley, 35 Albion-st. W	11..M 18
Junior Carlton, 30 Pall-mall SW	11..N 21
Junior Conservative, 44–44 Albemarle-street W	11..M 20
Junior Constitutional, 101–4 Piccadilly W	11..N 20
Junior Naval and Military, 96 & 97 Piccadilly W	11..N 20
Junior United Service, 11 Charles-street, St. James's-square SW	11..M 21
Kempton Park, 23A St. James's-street SW	11..N 21
Kennel, 2 Savile-row W	11..M 20
Kensington Ladies', Granville-mansions, Penywern-rd. SW	15..P 16
Ladies' Alpine, Gt. Central Hotel W	11..K 18
Ladies' Army and Navy, 2 Burlington-gardens W	11..M 20
Ladies' Athenæum, 31 Dover-street W	11..M 20
Ladies' Automobile, Claridge's Hotel W	11..M 20
Ladies' Empire, 69 Grosvenor-street W	11..M 20
Ladies' Imperial, 17 & 18 Dover-street W	11..M 20
Ladies' Kennel, 156 Regent-st. W	11..L 20
Ladies' Park, 32 Knightsbridge	11..N 18
Ladies' Town and Country, Mortimer-mansions, Mortimer-street W.	11..L 20
Ladies' University, 4 George-street, Hanover-square W	11..M 20
Lambeth Carlton, Ltd., 376 Coldharbour-lane SW	16..T 23
Leander Boat, Riverside, Putney SW	15..T 15
London Athletic, Stamford Bridge, Fulham SW	15..Q 16
London County, 81 & 82 Holland-park W	10..O 15
London Fencing, 7 Cleveland-row SW	11..N 21
London Model Yacht, Kensington-gardens W	10..M 16
London Rowing, Embankment, Putney SW	15..T 15
London Sketch, 79 Wells-st. W	11..L 21
London Yacht, Royal, 30 St. James's-street SW	11..M 20
Loughborough and Herne Hill Constitutional, 197 Coldharbour-lane SE	16..T 23
Ludlow, 24 Leicester-square W	11..M 21
Lyceum (Ladies'), 128 Piccadilly W	11..N 20
Maccabeans, 22 Old-square WC.	11..L 22
Managers', 5 Wardour-street W	11..M 21
Mariners', 5 Arlington-street W.	11..N 20
Marlborough, 52 Pall-mall SW	11..N 21
Marlborough Lawn Tennis, 26 Marlborough-place, St. John's Wood	10..J 17
Marylebone Cricket, Lords' Cricket Ground NW	11..J 18
Masonic, 3 St. James's-st. SW	11..N 21
Middlesex Gun, 178 New Bond-street W (office)	11..M 20
Mildmay Radical, 34 Newington-green N	6..H 25
Minima Yacht, 1 Water-lane EC	11..M 24
Motor, 8 Coventry-street W	11..M 21
Motor Union, 1 Albemarle-st. W	11..M 20
Municipal and County, 4 Whitehall-court SW	11..N 22
National, 1 Whitehall-gdns. SW	11..N 22
National Liberal, Whitehall-place SW	11..N 22
National Sporting, 43 King-st. Covent Garden WC	11..M 22
Naval and Military, 94 Piccadilly W	11..N 20
New, 4 Grafton-street, Piccadilly W	11..N 20
New Bridge, 18 Wellington-court, Knightsbridge SW	11..N 18
New Century (Ladies'), Hay-hill, Berkeley-square W.	11..M 20
New County, 21 Hanover-sq. W	11..M 20
New Era, 67 Curzon-street, Mayfair W	11..N 20
New Oxford and Cambridge, 68 Pall-mall SW	11..N 21
New Reform, 10 Adelphi-ter. WC	11..M 22
New University, 57 & 58 St. James's-street SW	11..N 21
New Victorian (Ladies'), 30A Sackville-street W.	11..M 21
Norfolk-square Nurses, 51–53 Norfolk-square, Hyde-pk. W.	10..L 17
N. Camberwell Progressive, 352 St James's-road SE	16..S 23
Northern Counties, 2 Savile-row W	11..M 20
Onslow Bridge, 5 Harrington-road SW	11..O 17
O.P., Adelphi Hotel WC	11..M 22
Oriental, 18 Hanover-square W	11..M 20
Orleans, 29 King-street, St. James's SW	11..N 21
Oxford and Cambridge, 71–76 Pall-mall SW.	11..N 21
Oxford and Cambridge Musical, Reynold's House, 47 Leicester-square WC	11..M 21
Park Bridge, 4A Marlborough-gate SW	11..J 17
Park Gates, 15 Grosvenor-cres., Hyde Park Corner SW	11..N 19
Patriotic, 65 Old Broad-street	11..L 25
Peckham Liberal, 24 Elm-gr. SE	17..S 26
Pioneer, 5 Grafton-street W	11..M 20
Playgoers', Cranbourn-street WC	11..M 21
Polyglot, 4 Southampton-row WC	11..L 22
Poplar Constitutional, 1 Newby-place E	12..M 31
Portland, 9 St. James's-sq. SW	11..L 20
Portman, 26 George-street, Hanover-square W	11..M 20
Pratt's, 14 Park-place, St. James's SW	11..N 20
Press, 6 Wine Office-ct., Fleet-street EC	11..M 23
Press Golf, 2 Whitefriars-st. EC	11..M 23
Primrose, 4 & 5 Park-place, St. James's SW	11..N 20
Prince's, 197 Knightsbridge SW	11..N 18
Prince's Skating, 245 Knightsbridge SW	11..N 18
Public Schools, 13 Albemarle-street W	11..M 20
Queen's, Ltd., Comeragh-rd. West Kensington W	15..P 14
Railway, 92 Victoria-street SW	11..O 21
Raleigh, 16 Regent-street SW	11..M 21
Ramblers', 217 Knightsbridge SW	11..N 18
Ranelagh, Barnes SW	15..R 11
Ranelagh Sailing, Embankment, Putney SW	15..T 15
Reform, 104 Pall-mall SW	11..N 21
Reformers', Ltd., 7 St. Agnes-place SE	16..P 23
Rehearsal, 29 Leicester-sq. WC	11..M 21
Road Club, Carlton House SW	11..N 21
Royal Societies', 63 St. James's street SW	11..N 20
St. Andrew's House, 31A Mortimer-street W	11..L 20
St. George's Chess, 2 Savile-row W	11..M 20
St. George's Conservative, 32 Churton-street SW	16..P 21
St. James's, 106 Piccadilly W	11..N 20
St. James and Soho, 46 & 47 Frith-street W	11..M 21
St. John's Wood Arts, 28 Finchley-road NW	5..E 16
St. Pancras Reform, 15 Victoria-road NW	2..H 20
St. Stephen's, 1 Bridge-st. SW	11..N 22
Sandown Park, 4 St. James's-street SW	11..N 21
Savage, 6 & 7 Adelphi-terrace WC	11..M 22
Savile, 107 Piccadilly W	11..N 20
Sesame, 29 Dover-street W	11..M 20
Shuttleworth, Fye-foot-lane EC	11..M 24
Slade, 76 Charlotte-street W	11..L 21
Smithfield (Incorporated), 12 Hanover-square W	11..M 20
S. Kensington Conservative, 33 Hogarth-road, Earl's Court SW	15..P 16
S. Norwood Constitutional, 10 South Norwood-hill SE	21..Z[1] 25
Sphinx, 11 Arundel-street WC	11..M 23
Sports, 8 St. James's-square SW	11..N 21
Stanley Ward Conservative, 419 King's-road SW	16..P 18
Surrey County Cricket, Kennington Oval SE	16..Q 23
Sword, 1 Durham House-street, Strand WC	11..M 22
Thames Rowing, Riverside, Putney SW	15..T 15
Thames Yacht, Royal, 7 Albemarle-street W	11..M 20
Thatched House, 86 St. James's-street SW	11..N 21
The Pilgrims', Savoy Hotel WC	11..M 22
The Twentieth Century, Ltd., 25–29 Stanley-gardens W	10..O 10
Three Arts, 19A Marylebone-rd.	11..K 19
Tower Hamlets Conservative, Beaumont-square E	12..L 28
Toynbee Art Students', Toynbee Hall, Whitechapel E	11..L 26
Travellers', 106 Pall-mall SW	11..N 21
Turf, 85 Piccadilly W	11..N 20
Union, Trafalgar-square SW	11..M 21
United Arts, 35 Dover-street W	11..M 20
United Bank and Law, 21 Southampton-buildings WC	11..L 23
United Empire, 117 Piccadilly W	11..N 20
United Service, 116 & 117 Pall-mall SW	11..N 21
United Sports, 4 Whitehall-court SW	11..N 22
United University, 1 & 2 Suffolk-street, Pall-mall-east SW	11..M 21
United Wards of the City, Bush-lane House EC	11..M 25
University, 16 Victoria Park square NE	7..I 29
Vaudeville, 98 Charing Cross-road WC	11..M 21
Vesta Rowing, Riverside, Putney SW	15..T 15
Victoria, 18 Wellington-st. WC	11..M 22
Victoria (Ladies'), 145 Victoria-street SW	11..O 21
Water-Colour Society of Art, Royal, 5A Pall-mall-east SW	11..M 21
Wellington, 1 Grosvenor-pl. SW	11..N 19
Wells, 24 Old Bond-street W	11..M 20
Welsh, 4 Whitehall-court SW	11..N 22
Wembley Park Polo, 556 Oxford-street W	11..L 20
Western, 1 Penywern-road SW	15..P 16
West Indian, Howard Hotel, Norfolk-street WC	11..M 23
West Islington Unionist, 33 Thornhill-square N	6..I 23
West Kensington, Mornington-avenue, West Kensington	10..N 14
Westminster Conservative, 38 Great Smith-street SW	11..O 21
Westminster, Ltd., 3 Whitehall-court SW	11..N 22
Whitefriars, Anderton's Hotel, Fleet-street EC	11..M 23
Whitehall, Princess-street SW	11..K 18
White Heather (Ladies'), 69–71 Longridge-road, Earls Court SW	10..O 16
White's, 37 St. James's-street SW	11..N 21
Windham, 13 St. James's-sq. SW	11..N 21
Working Men's College, Crowndale-road, Camden Town NW	11..I 21
Writers', 10 Norfolk-street, Strand WC	11..M 22
Yorick, 29 & 30 Bedford-street, Strand WC	11..M 22

Four-inch
Scale Maps

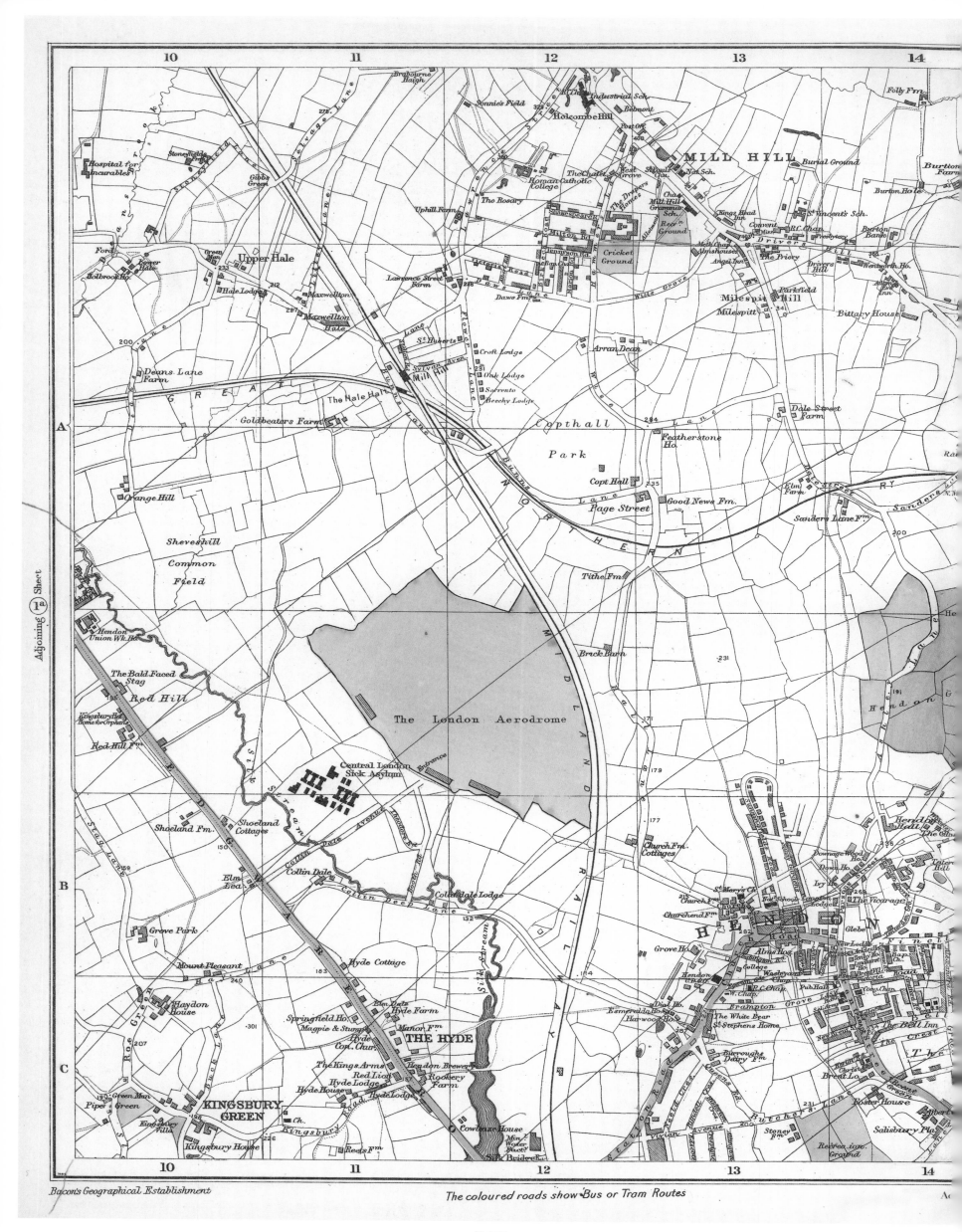

The coloured roads show Bus or Tram Routes

Bacon's Geographical Establishment

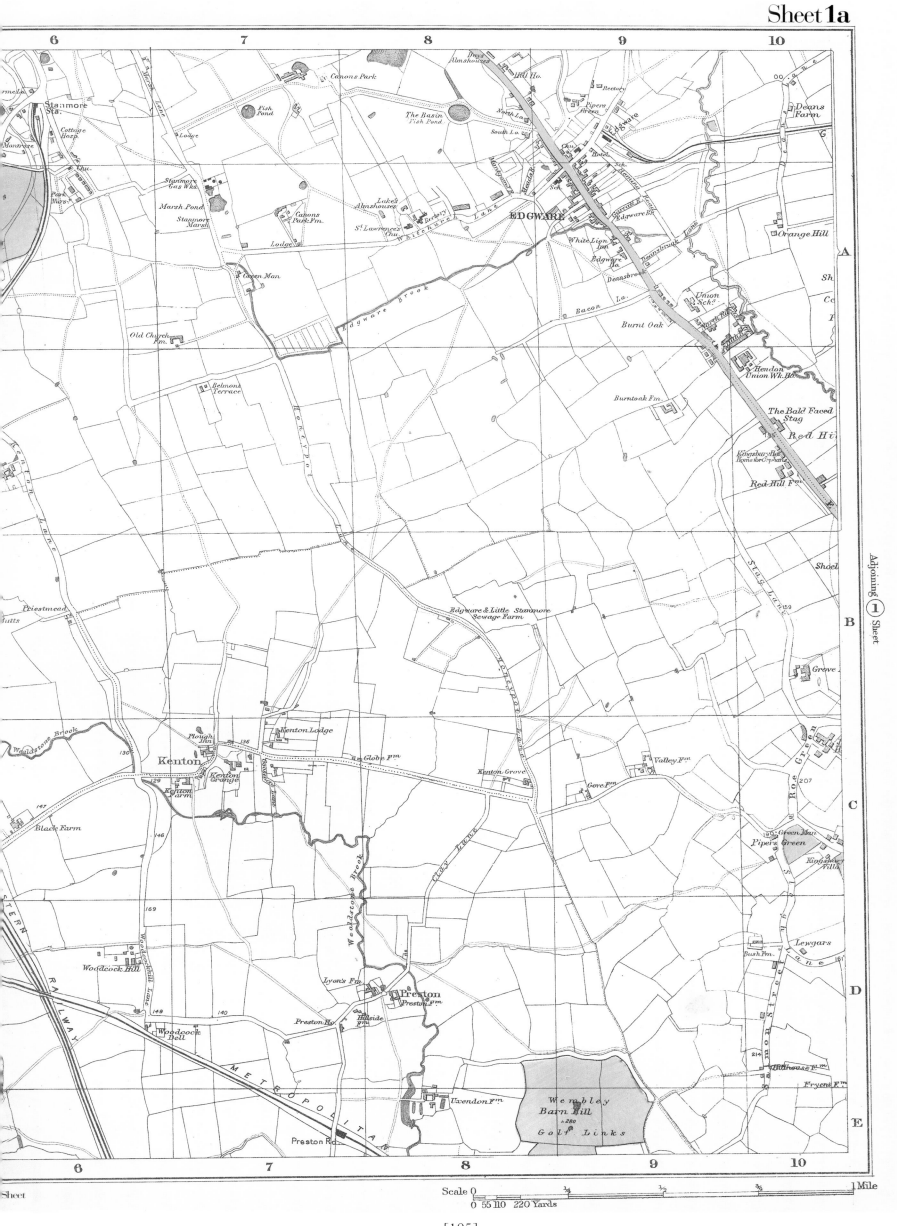

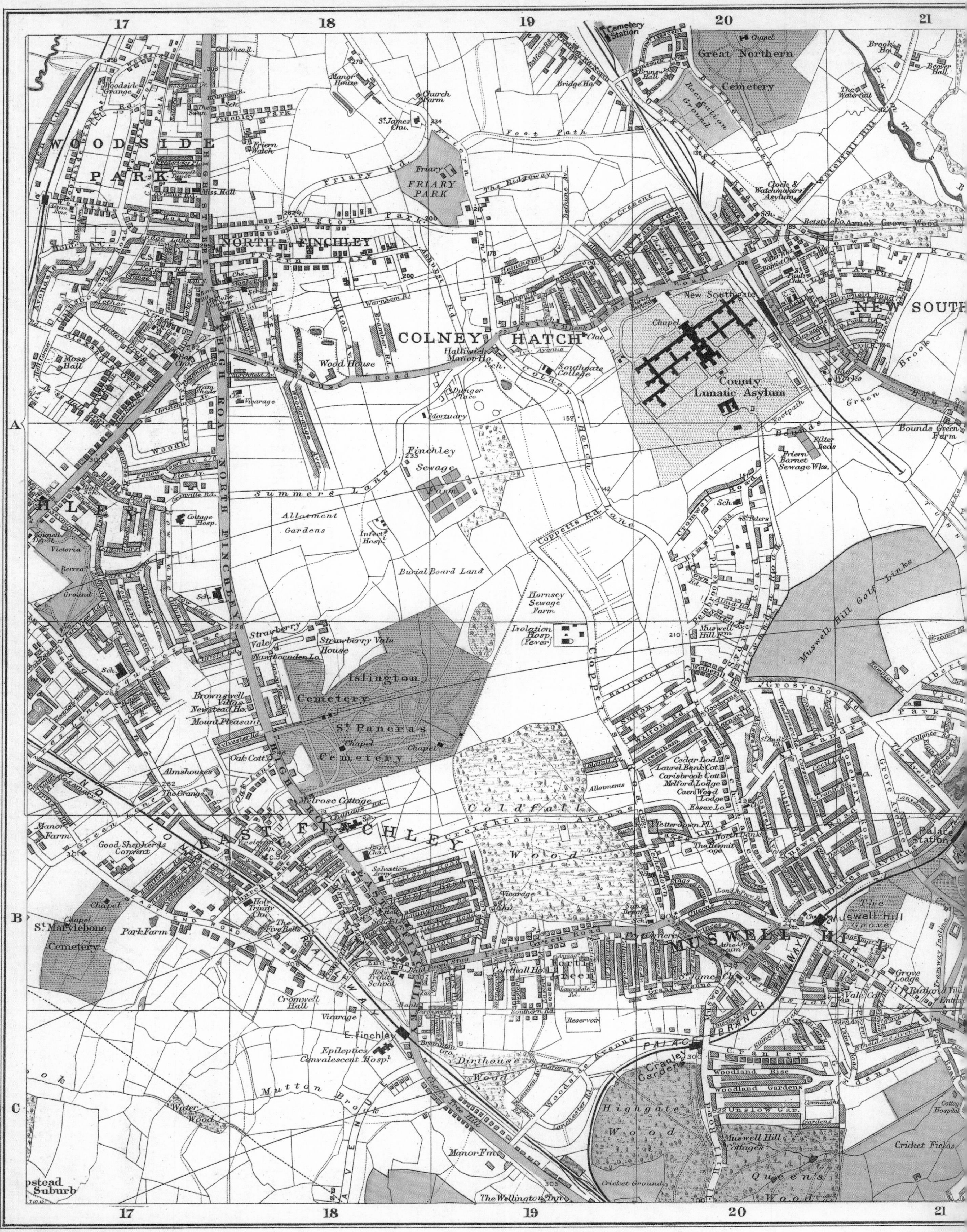

Cemetery Station

Great Northern

Cemetery

Brook Ho.

The Waterfall

Clock & Watchmakers Asylum

WOODSIDE PARK

Woodside Grange

Manor House

Church Farm

St. James Chu.

Friary Rd.

FRIARY PARK

Foot Path

The Ridgeway

Betstyle Lo. Arno's Grove Wood

NORTH FINCHLEY

COLNEY HATCH

Wood House

Halliwick Manor Ho.

Southgate College

New Southgate

Chapel

NEW SOUTH

Moss Hall

Dagger Place

Mortuary

County Lunatic Asylum

Bounds Green Farm

Filter Beds

Friern Barnet Sewage Wks.

A

Finchley Sewage Farm

HLEY

Cottage Hosp.

Victoria

Recrea Ground

Summers Lane

Allotment Gardens

Infect Hosp.

Burial Board Land

Hornsey Sewage Farm

St. Peters

Isolation Hosp. (Fever)

Muswell Hill Golf Links

Muswell Hill Farm

Strawberry Vale

Strawberry Vale House

Hawthornden Lo.

Islington Cemetery

Brownswell Villas

Newstead Ho.

Mount Pleasant

St. Pancras Cemetery

Chapel

Coldfall Wood

Cedar Lodge

Laurel Bank Cot.

Carisbrook Cot.

Melford Lodge

Caen Wood Lodge

Essex Lo.

Grosvenor Rd.

Palace Station

Almshouses

The Grange

Oak Cott.

Melrose Cottage

EAST FINCHLEY

Wood

The Hermitage

Manor Farm

Good Shepherds Convent

Holy Trinity Chu.

Salvation Army

Vicarage

MUSWELL HILL

Muswell Hill Grove

Grove Lodge

B

St. Marylebone Cemetery

Chapel

Park Farm

Holy Trinity School

The Five Bells

Coldhall Ho.

Reservoir

Vale Cot.

Cromwell Hall

Vicarage

E. Finchley

Epileptics Convalescent Hosp.

Dirthouse Wood

Cripplegate Tree Hill

Cranley Gardens

Woodland Rise

Woodland Gardens

Highgate Wood

Muswell Hill Cottages

C

West Wood

Mutton Brook

Manor Fm.

The Wellington

Cricket Ground

Queens Wood

Cricket Fields

Cottage Hospital

22 23 24 25 26

PALMERS GREEN

Hazelwood Ho.
St Johns Cn.
Slanners Almsho.
Windsor Rd.
Osborne Rd.
The Limes
Nursery
Huxley Farm
Ivy Cottage
Huxley Flour Mills

BROOMFIELD PARK
Broomfield House
Cricket Ground
Broomfield Farm
Gravel Pit
The Lodge
Palmers & Southgate
Hill Ho.
Sch.

Wyerhall Nursery
Strand Un. Millfield Ho. School
West Hall

Oakthorpe
Fire Sta.
Chequers Green
Ford
Pymmes Brook
Strand Works

Cock Inn
Chapel
Trinity Aven.
Melbourne A.
Kelvin Av.
Belsize Aven.
St. Michael
Tottenhall Road
Eley's Farm
Edmonton Union Workhouse

BOWES PARK
Maryland
Sylvan Villa
Woodside Road
Clayhill Farm
Devonshire Hill Lodge
EDM

Bowes
C.S.
Cottage Hosp.
Ch.
New River
White Hart Lane
Tent Farm
White Hart Lane Potteries
Devonshire Parade
Brick Fields
St Katharine Training College (Ladies)
Creighton

WOOD GREEN
Town Hall Gardens
Band Stand
Town Hall
Nightingale
Trinity Rd.
Fountain
Home & Colonial Train. Coll.
Tottenham Park
The Moselle
Tottenham Cemetery
Allhallows Chu.
The Priory

Banquet Hall
Wood Green Common
Wood Green Station
Printed Almsho.
Convent Chu.
New Road
Ch.
Engineering Wks.
Lordship Lane
Broadwater Farm
Tower Gardens Rd.
Risley Avenue

ALEXANDRA PARK
Pavilion
Race Course
Gas Works
Allotment
The Avenue
DOWNHILLS PARK
West Green Rd.
WEST GREEN
Hall
GER

HORNSEY
Water Works
The Grove
St Joseph R.C.
P.O.
Hornsey
Recreation Ground
Seven Sisters
North Eastern
Almsho.
Sub Depot

Scale 0   ¼   ½   ¾   1 Mile
0 55 110   220 Yards

Adjoining (3) Sheet
ing (6) Sheet

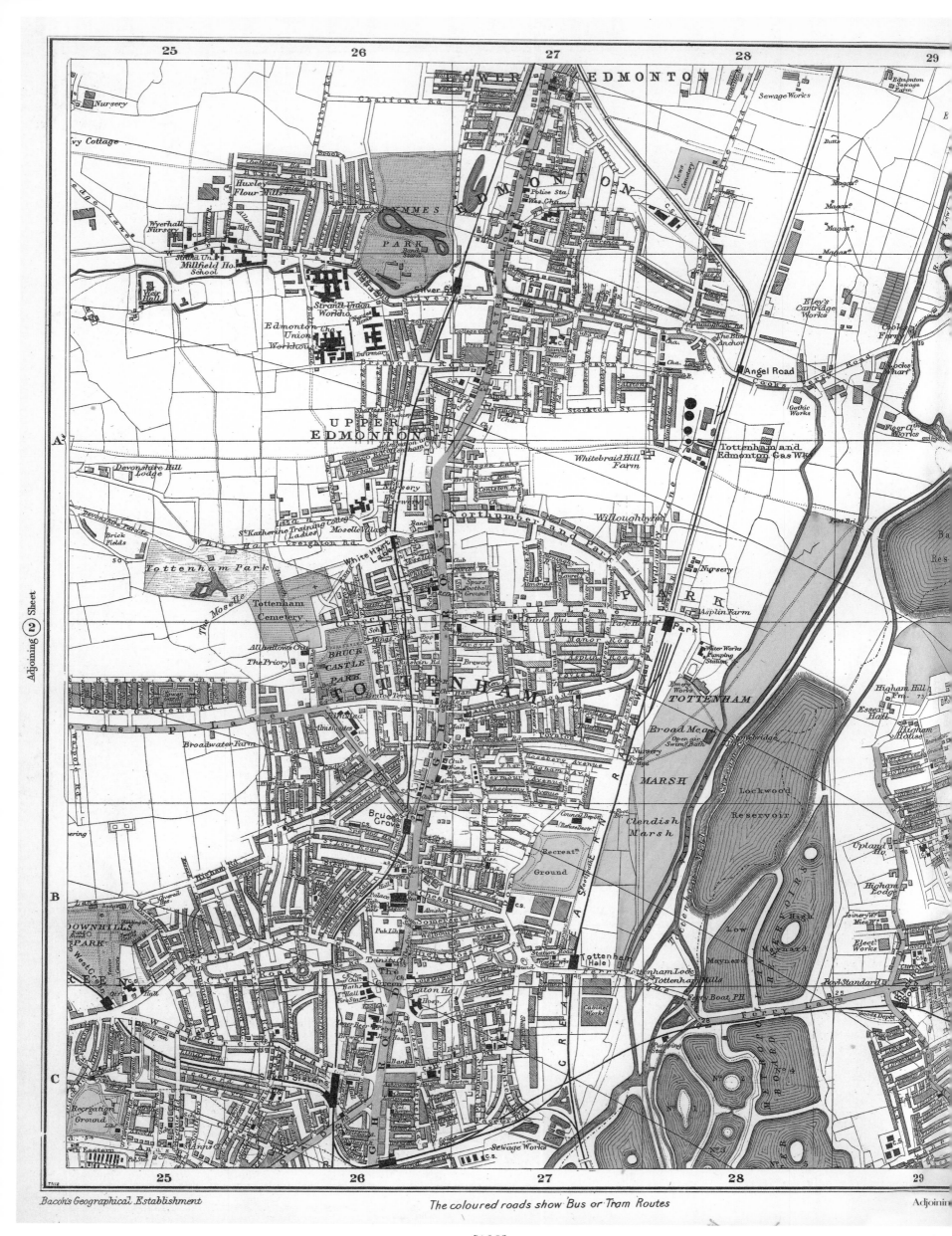

Adjoining 12 Sheet

LOWER EDMONTON

EDMONTON

UPPER EDMONTON

TOTTENHAM

Tottenham Park

The Moselle

Tottenham Cemetery

BRUCE CASTLE PARK

DOWNHILLS PARK

GREEN

Lockwood Reservoir

Clendish Marsh

MARSH

Broad Mead

Tottenham (Hale)

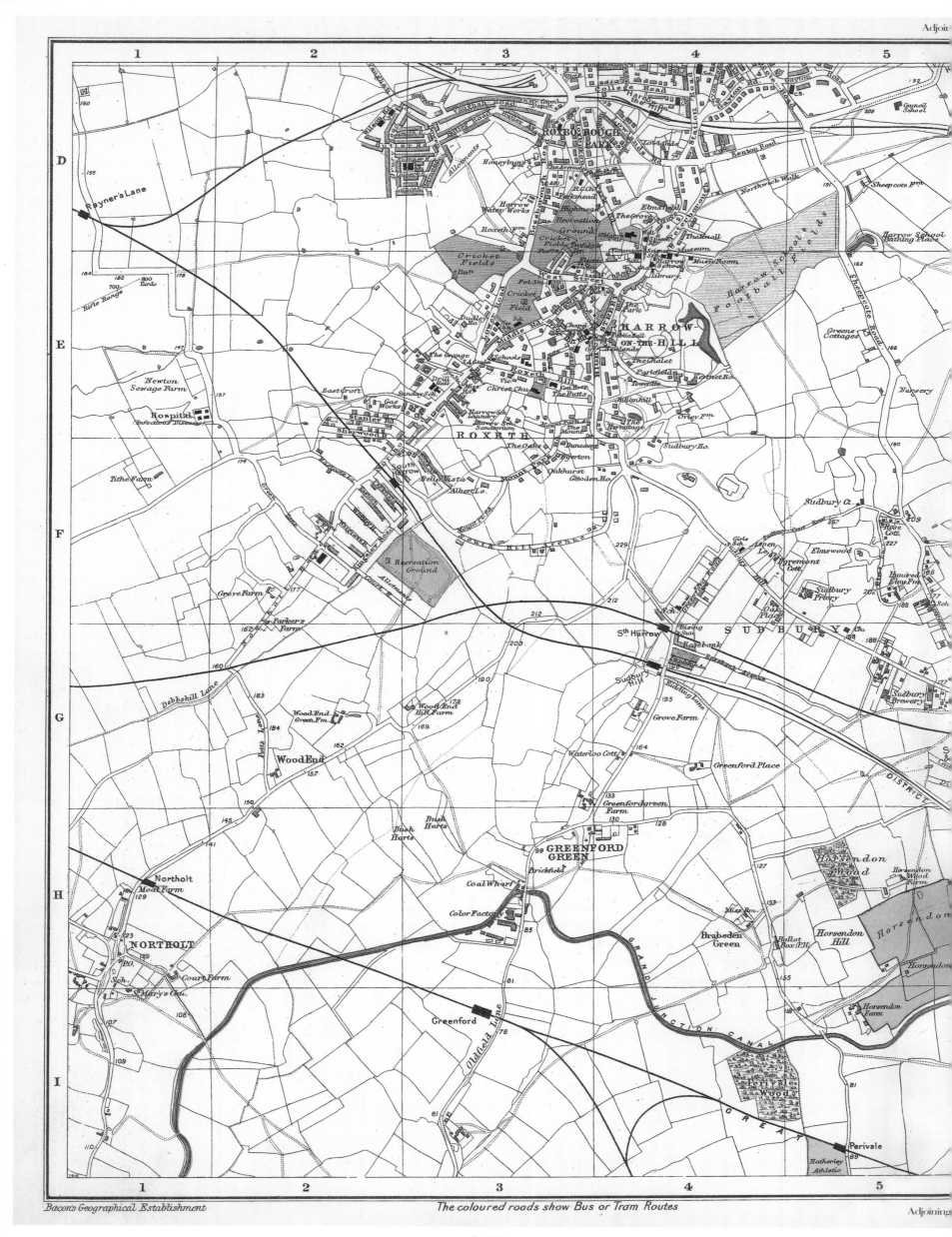

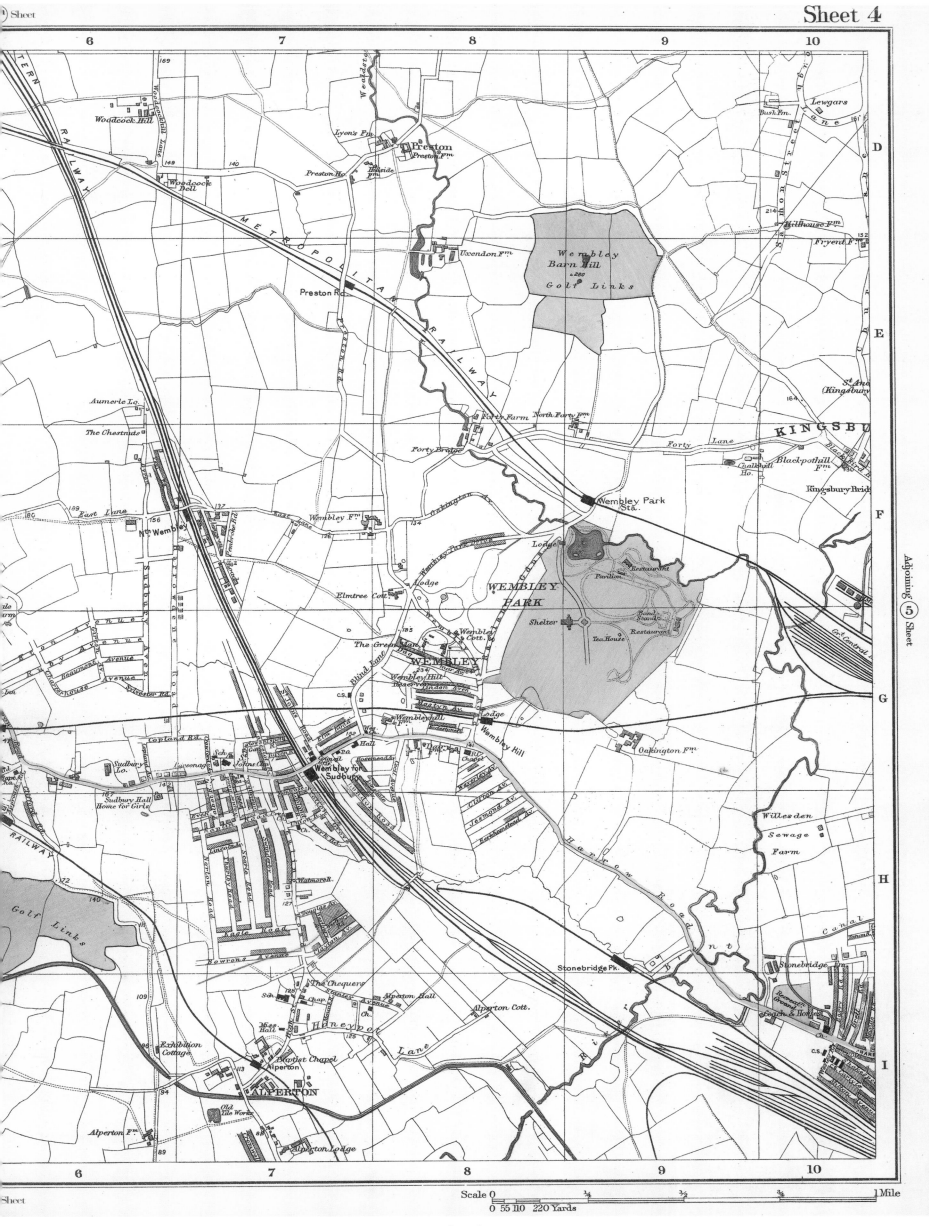

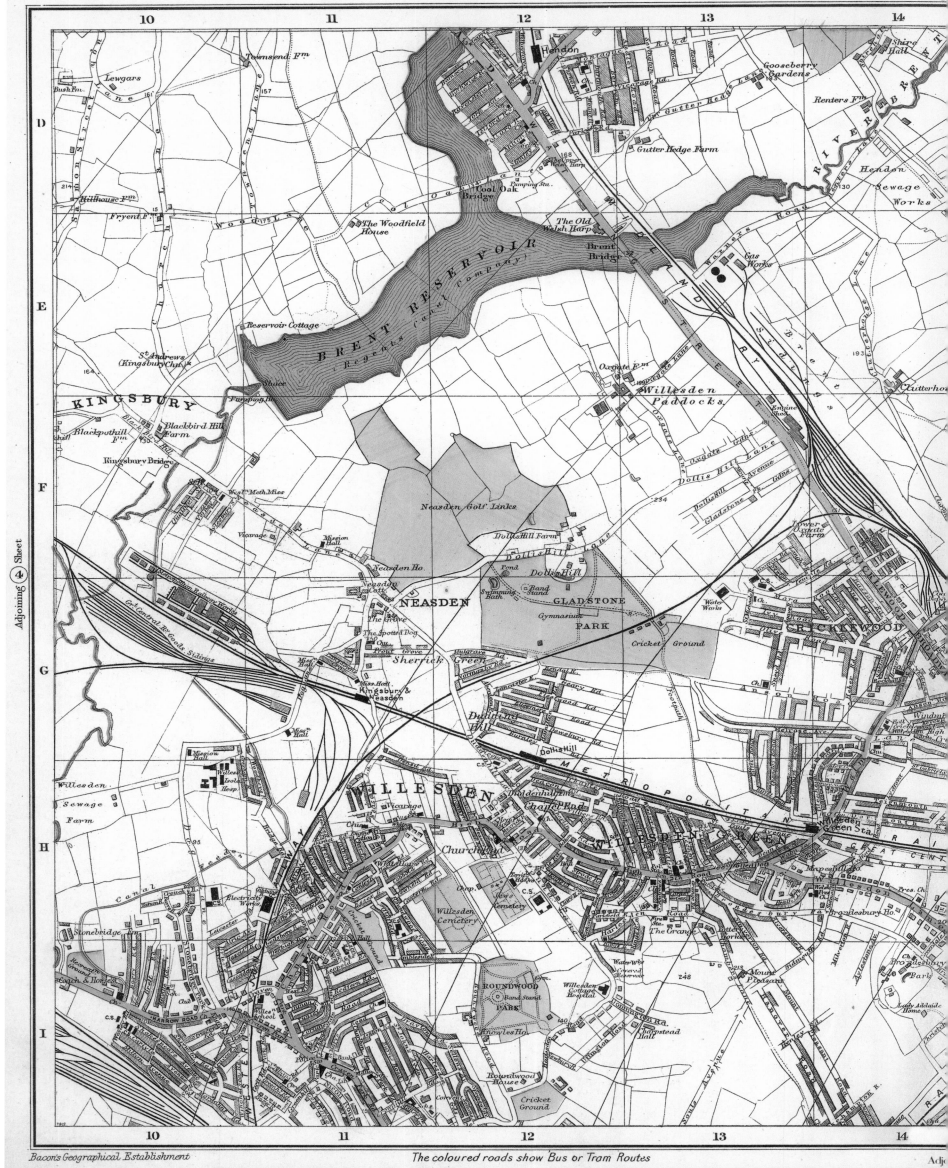

Bacon's Geographical Establishment

The coloured roads show 'Bus or Tram Routes

Adjo

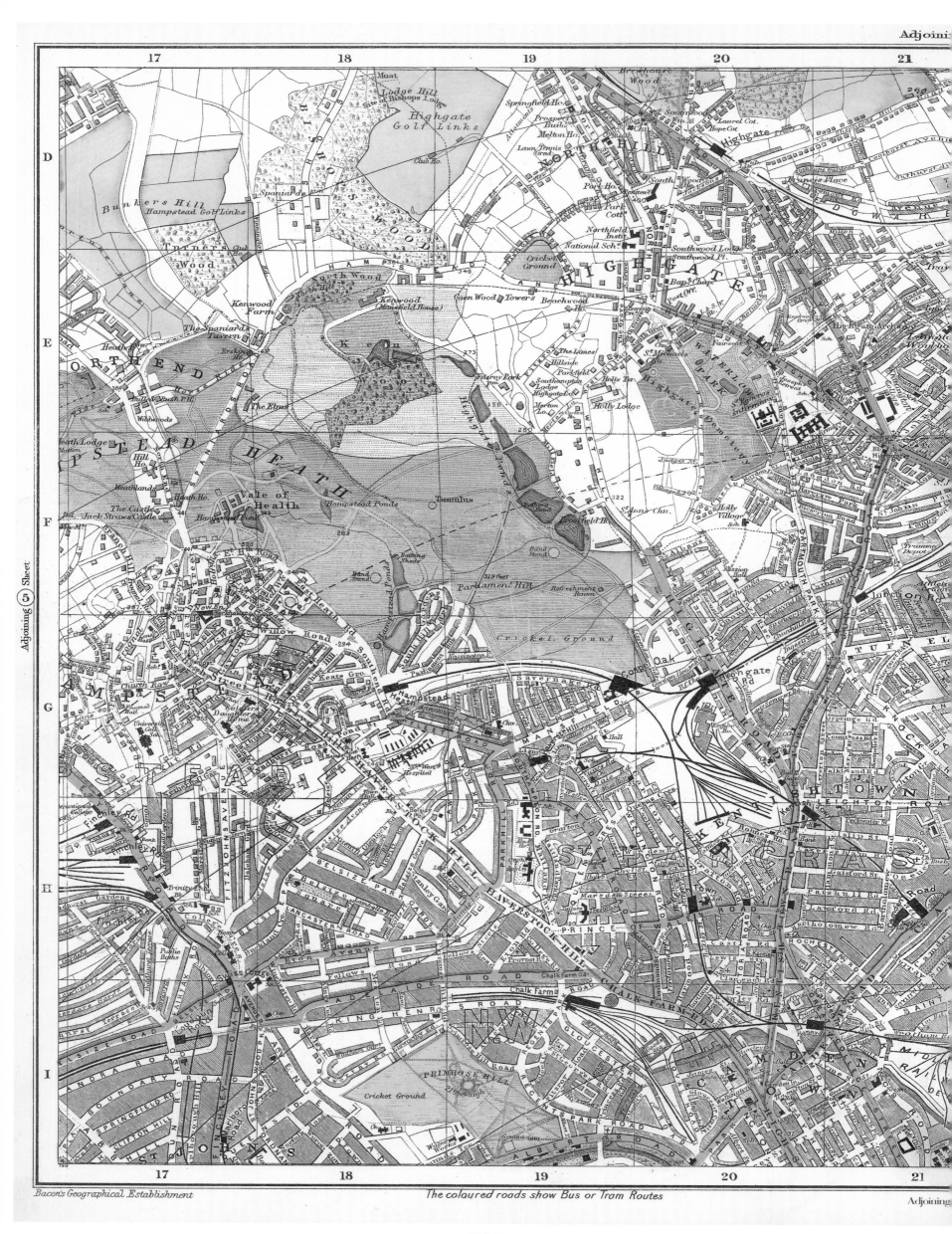

CROUCH END

FINSBURY PARK

Cricket Ground

American Gardens

Boating Lake

Refreshment Ho.

Band Stand

Finsbury Park

Metropolitan Water Board Works

Board Works

Metropolitan Water

Abbey Park Cemetery

CLISSOLD PARK

Clissold Park

Mount Pleasant

Crouch Hill

Hornsey Road

Upper Holloway

SEVEN SISTERS RD.

PARK ROAD

HOLLOWAY ROAD

ISLINGTON

HIGHBURY

Aubert Park

Highbury Park

NEW PARK

Highbury

CANONBURY

BALLS POND RD.

SAINT PAUL'S ROAD

DALSTON

Maiden Lane

GREAT NORTHERN RAILWY

RICHMOND ROAD

COPENHAGEN

Stamford Hill

St. Ann's Rd.

Harringay Pk. Sta.

D

E

F

G

H

I

22   23   24   25

Scale 0   ¼   ½   ¾   1 Mile
0 55 110   220 Yards

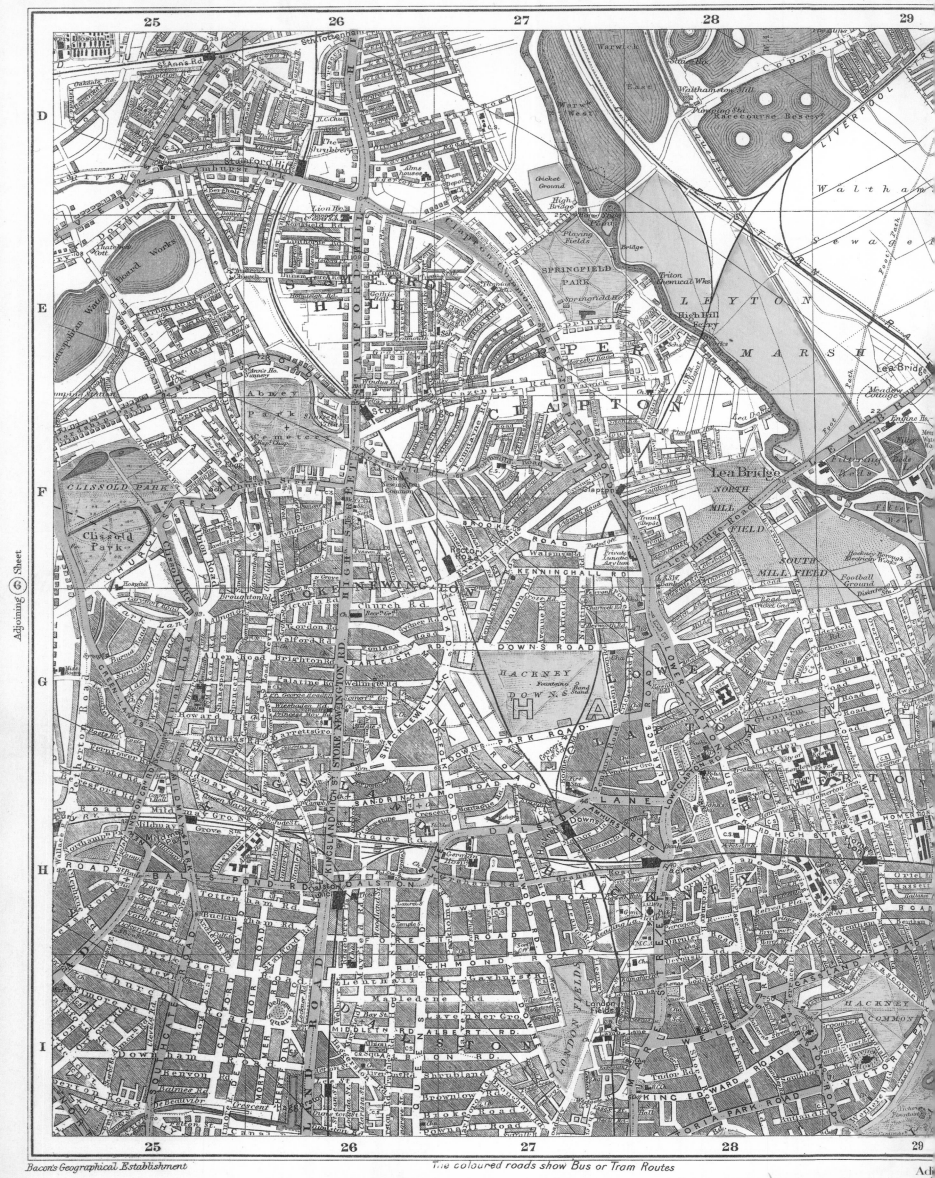

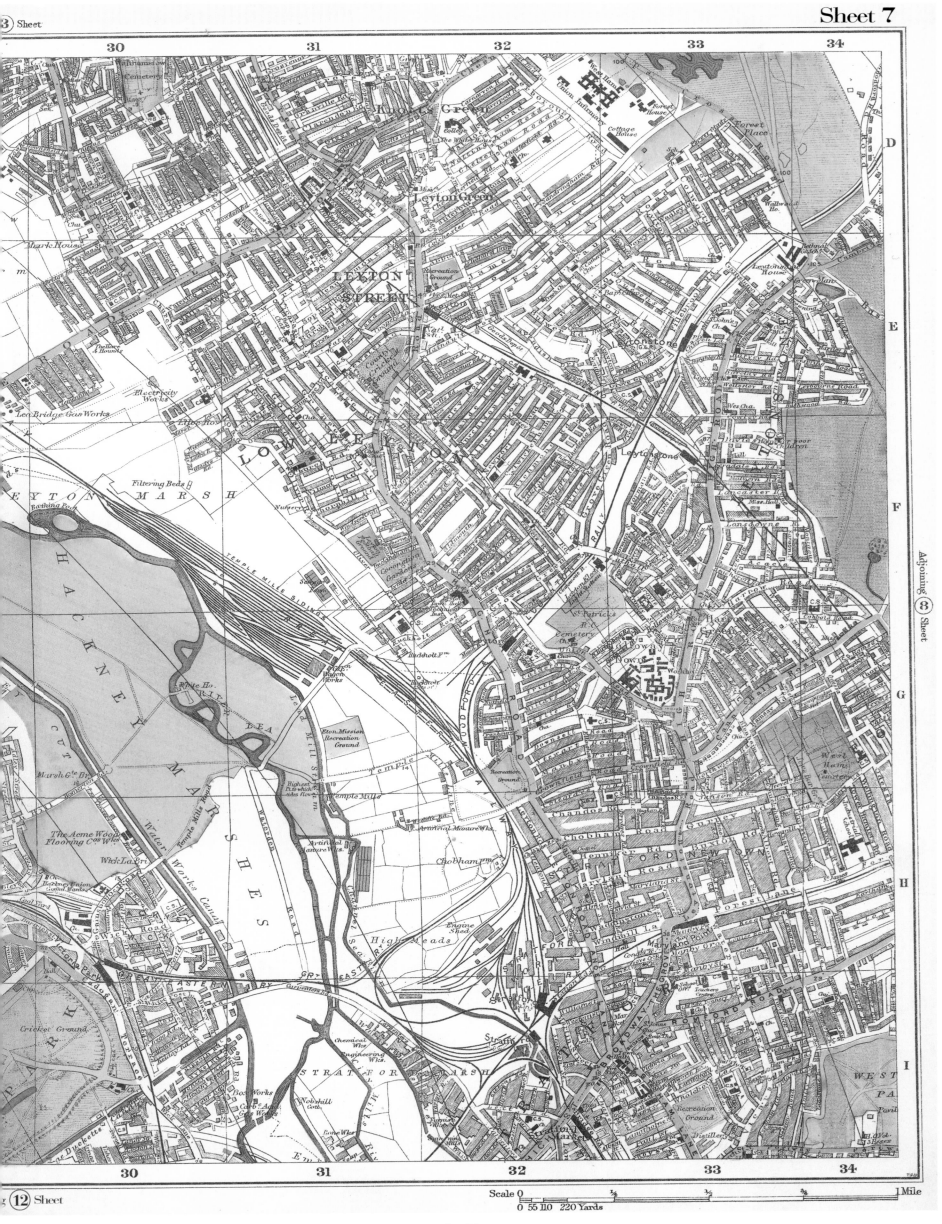

Scale 0 — ¼ — ½ — ¾ — 1 Mile
0 55 110 220 Yards

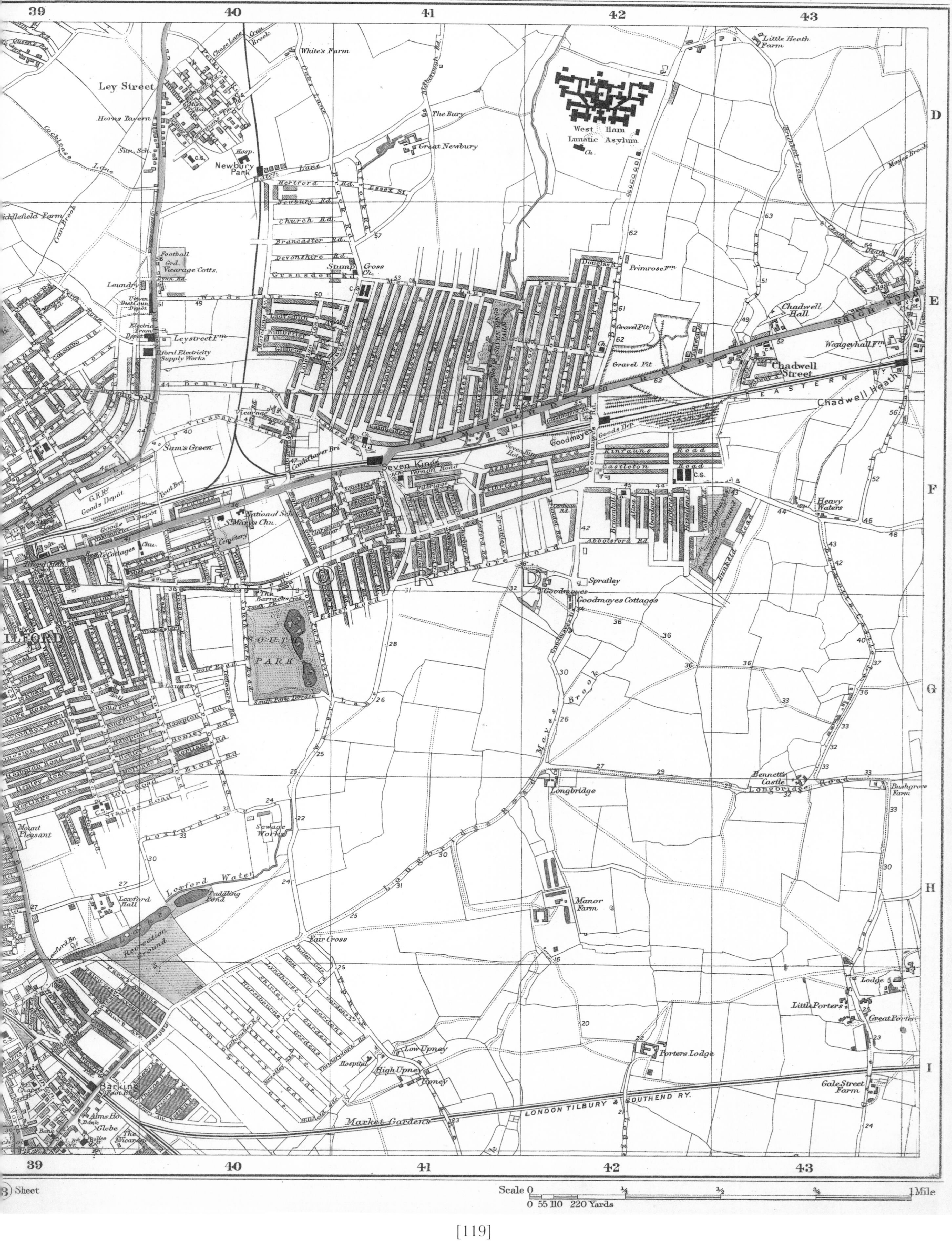

39 40 41 42 43

Ley Street

White's Farm

Little Heath Farm

Horns Tavern

The Bury

West Ham Lunatic Asylum

Cockle Lane

Great Newbury

Ch.

D

Newbury Park

Hertford Rd.

Newbury Rd.

Church Rd.

Brancaster Rd.

Devonshire Rd.

Cross Ch.

Douglas

Primrose Fm

Moyes Brook

Stump

Gransden Rd.

C.S.

Chadwell Heath

63

62

Middlefield Farm

Football Grd.

Vicarage Cotts.

Laundry

Urban Dist Coun Depot

Electric Tram Depot

Ley street Fm.

Ilford Electricity Supply Works

Gravel Pit

Gravel Pit

Chadwell Hall

Wangeyhall Fm

HIGH ROAD

Chadwell Street

56

E

Benton Rd.

Vicarage

Vicarage

ROMFORD

Seven Kings Road

Goodmayes

Goodmayes Goods Dep.

Kintauns Road

Castleton Road

C.S.

Heavy Waters

G.E.R. Goods Depot

Coach

Cauliflower Bri

Seven Kings

National Sch

St Mary's Chu.

Cemetery

Abbotsford Rd.

Spratley

Goodmayes

Goodmayes Cottages

F

ILFORD

The Barracks cross

SOUTH PARK

Goodmayes

Barking Rd.

Mayes Brook

Bennett's Castle

Longbridge Road

Bushgrove Farm

G

Mount Pleasant

Henley Road

South Pk Terrace

Sewage Works

Longbridge

Loxford Hall

Loxford Water

Paddling Pond

Lake Recreation Ground

Manor Farm

H

Fair Cross

Lodge

Little Porters

Great Porters

Barking

Low Upney

High Upney

Upney

Hospital

Porters Lodge

Gale Street Farm

I

Market Gardens

LONDON TILBURY & SOUTHEND RY.

39 40 41 42 43

PERIVALE

GREENFORD

SOUTHALL

FROGMORE
GREEN

Norwood
Green

HANWELL

DRAYTON
GREEN

EALING
DEAN

LITT
EALI

Brent Valley
Golf Links

London
County
Lunatic Asylum

GRAND JUNCTION CANAL

Osterley Park

Scale 0   ⅛   ¼   ½   ¾   1 Mile

0   55   110   220 Yards

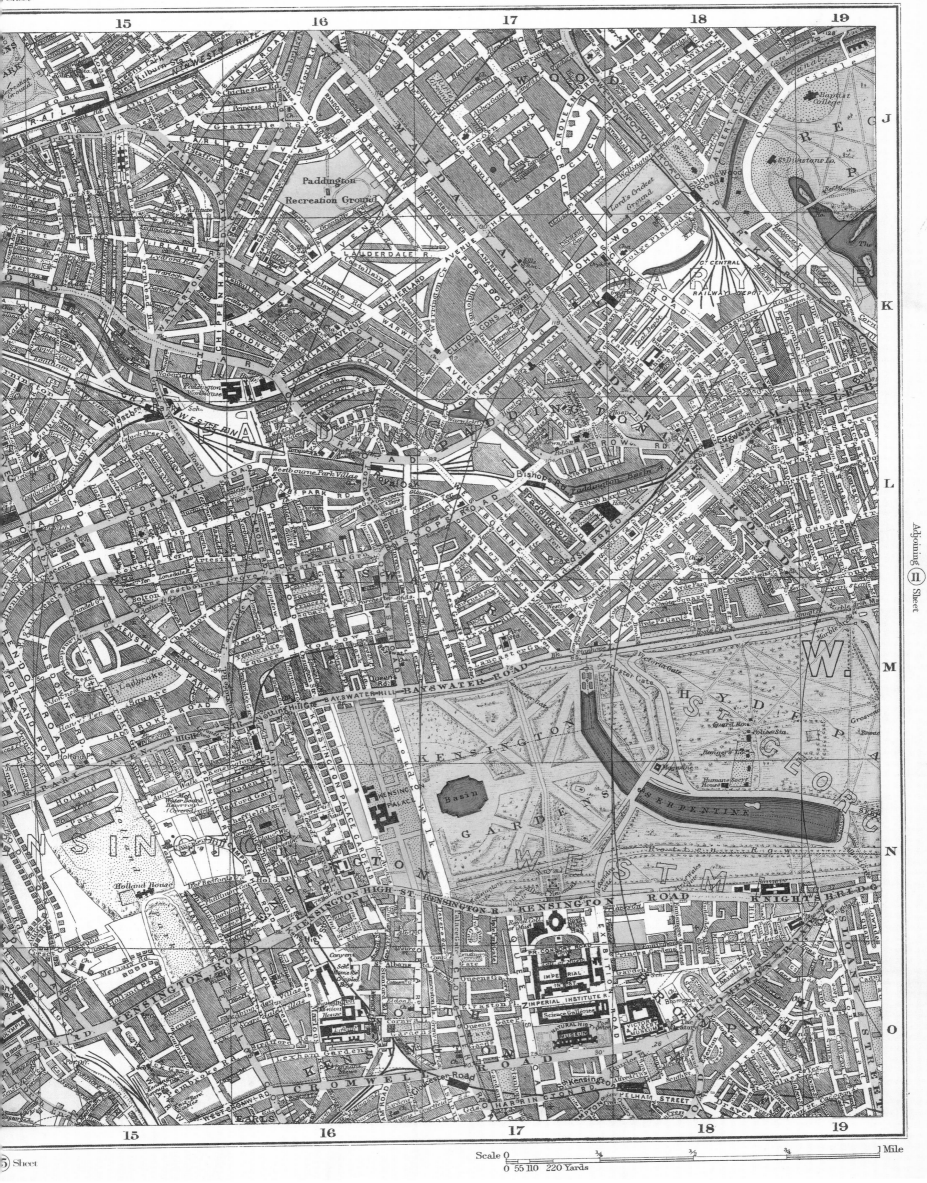

Adjoining (11) Sheet

Scale 0   ¼   ½   ¾   1 Mile

0 55 110   220 Yards

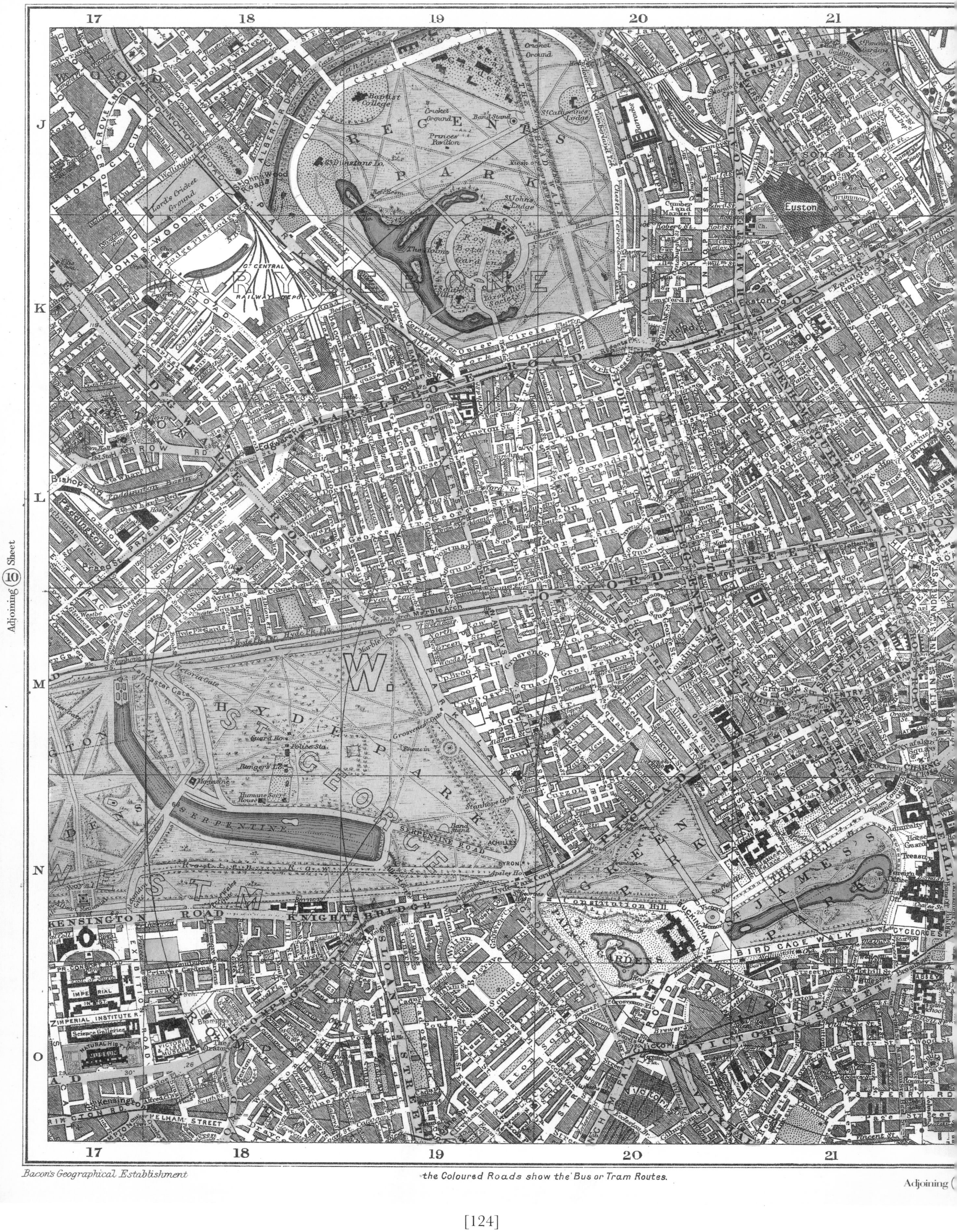

17   18   19   20   21

J

K

L

M

N

O

Adjoining ⑩ Sheet

REGENT'S PARK

MARYLEBONE

Lord's Cricket Ground

Baptist College

Cricket Ground

Band Stand

St Katharine's Lodge

Cumberland Lodge

Euston

St John's Lodge

Roy. Botanic Gardens

The Holme

Zoological Society

HYDE PARK

W.

Marble Arch

Hyde Park Place

Lancaster Gate

Victoria Gate

Guard Ho.

Police Sta.

Ranger's Lo.

Magazine

Humane Socy.

House

THE SERPENTINE

SERPENTINE ROAD

Band Stand

Achilles

Byron

Apsley Ho.

Stanhope Gate

Grosvenor Gate

Fountain

OXFORD STREET

GREEN PARK

ST JAMES'S PARK

Constitution Hill

Buckingham Palace

Buckingham Gardens

BIRD CAGE WALK

Admiralty

Horse Guards

Treasury

KENSINGTON ROAD

KNIGHTSBRIDGE

WESTM'R

Imperial Institute

Science Galleries

Natural Hist. Museum

Imperial Inst.

Victoria Museum

PELHAM STREET

EXHIBITION ROAD

17   18   19   20   21

Bacon's Geographical Establishment

the Coloured Roads show the 'Bus or Tram Routes.

The Coloured Roads show the 'Bus or Tram Routes.

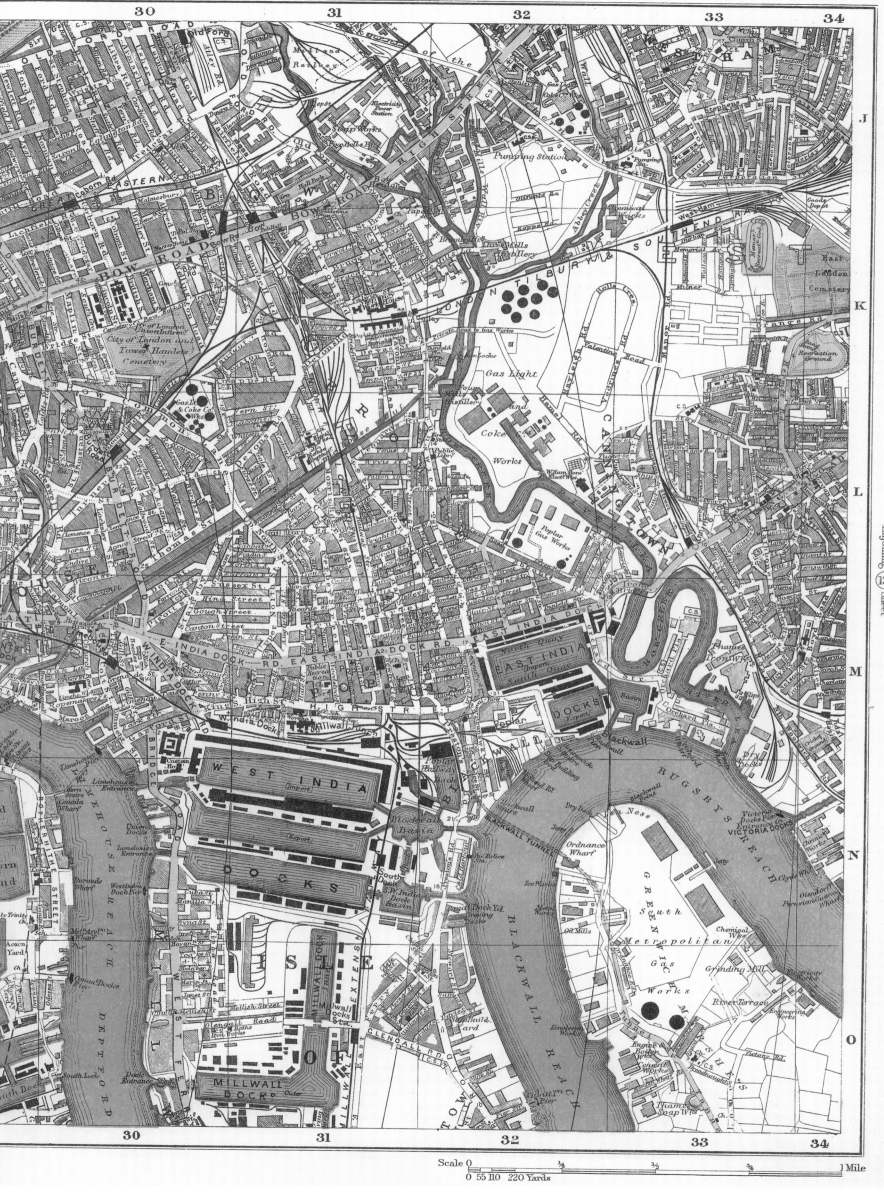

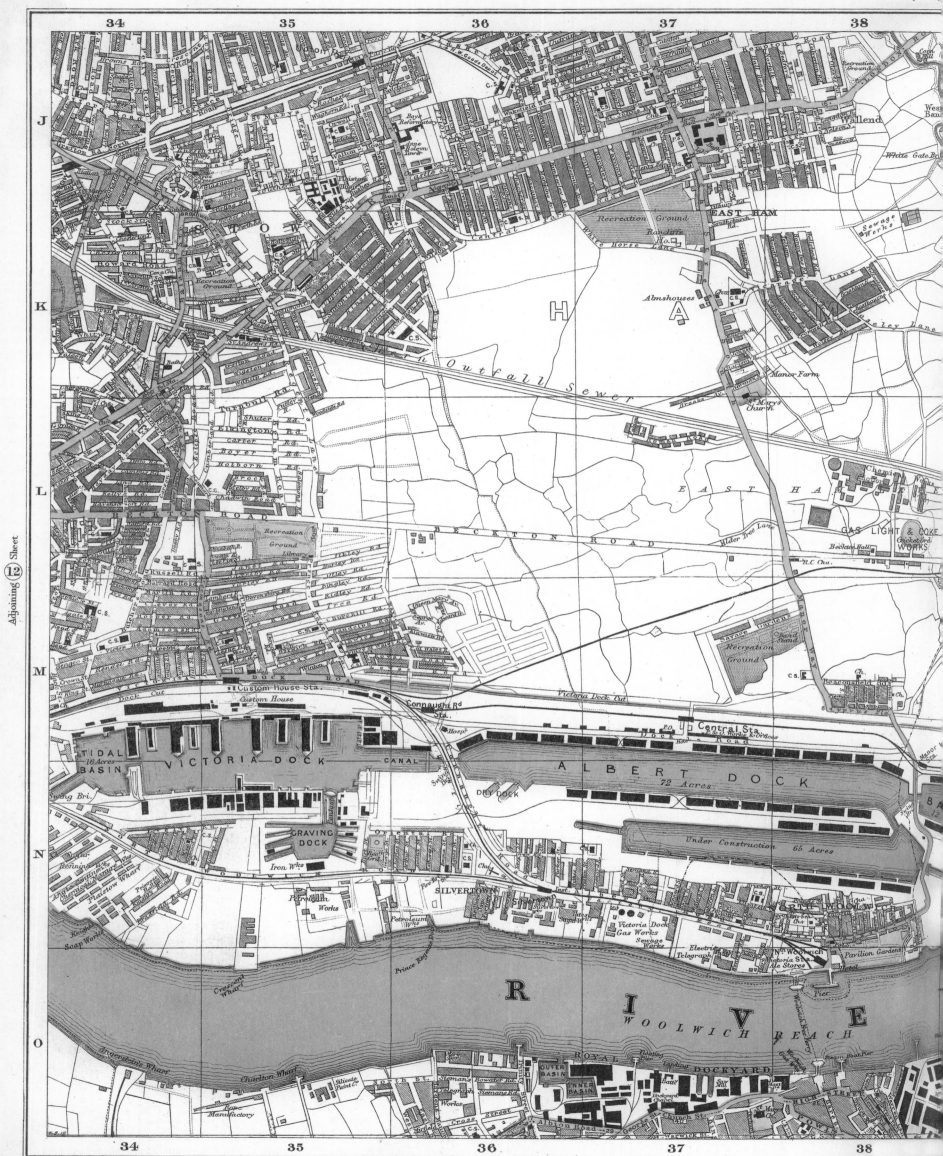

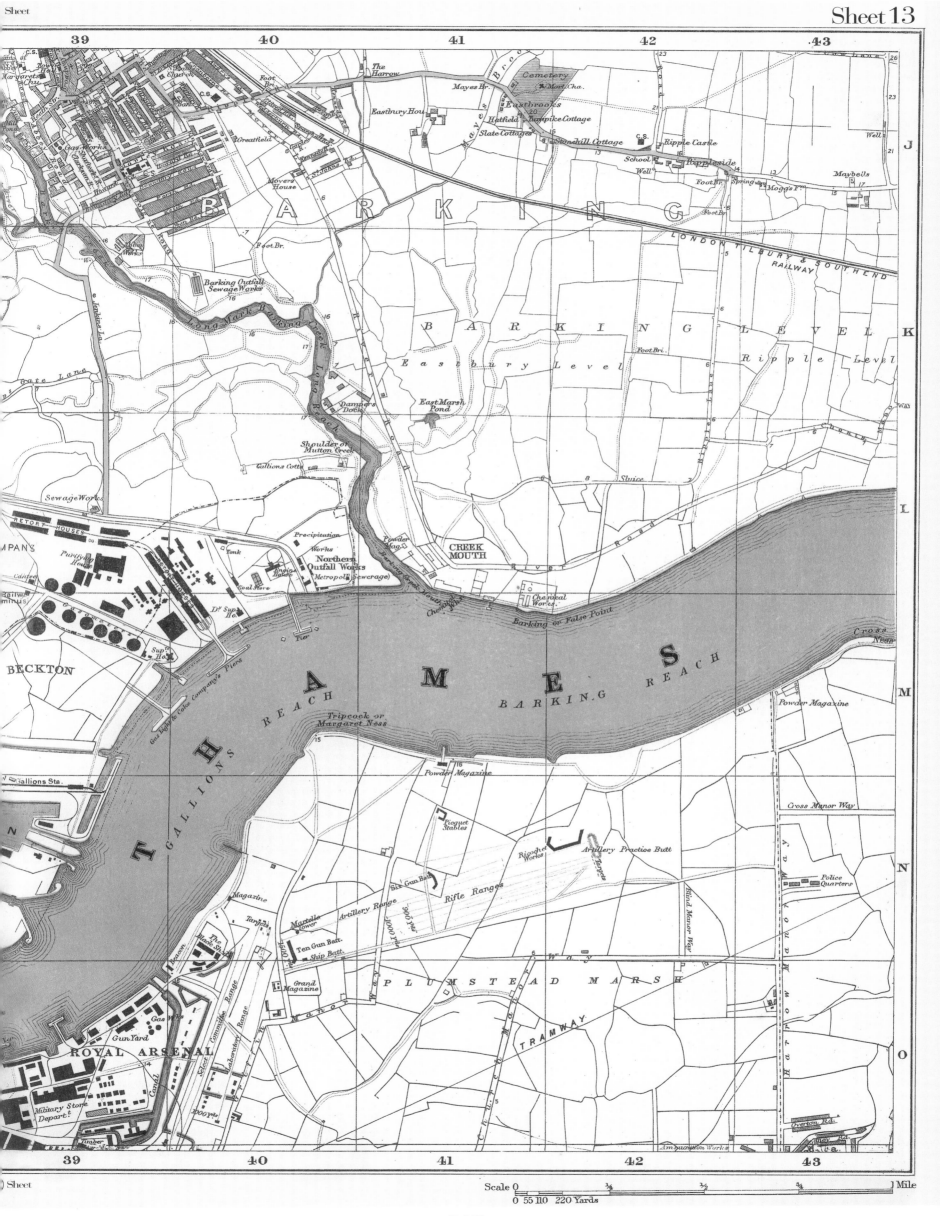

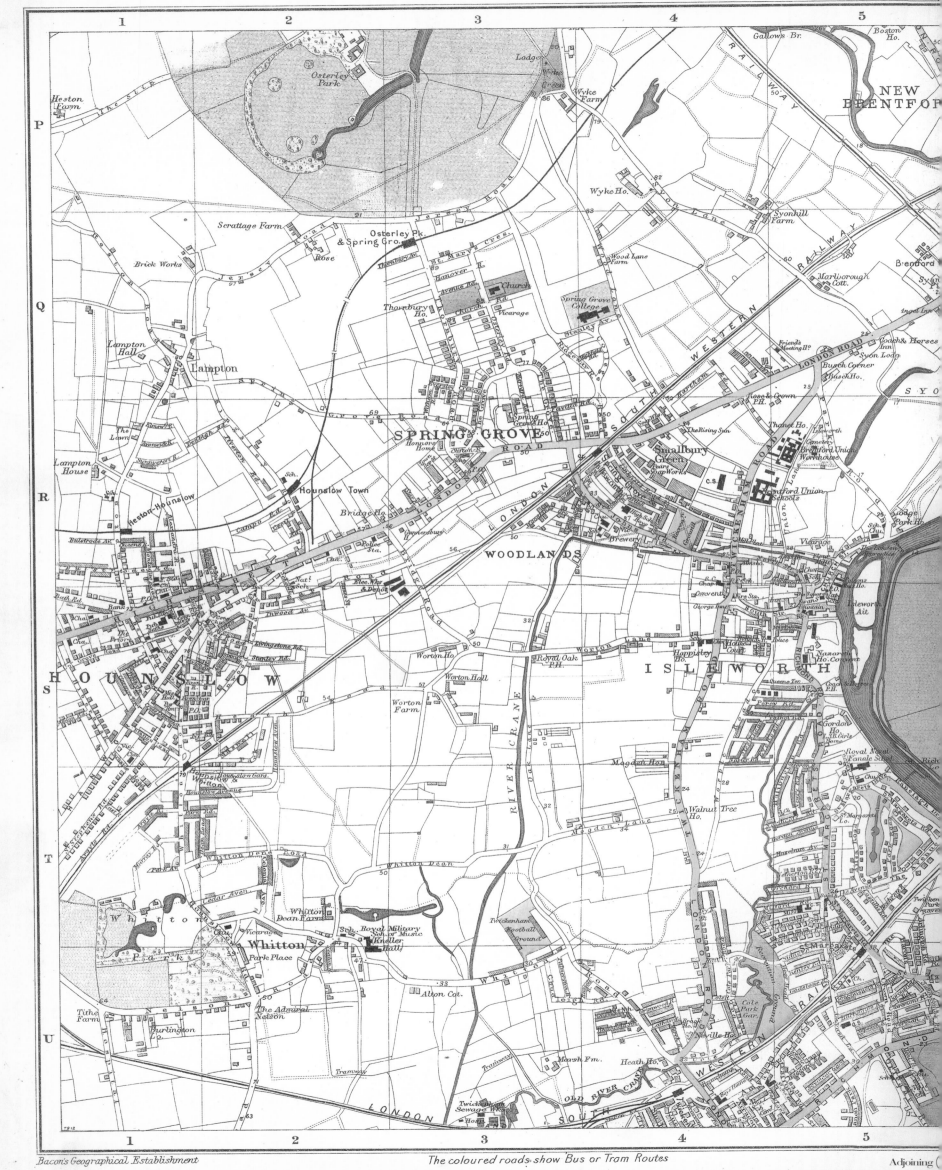

Bacon's Geographical Establishment. The coloured roads show Bus or Tram Routes Adjoining

[130]

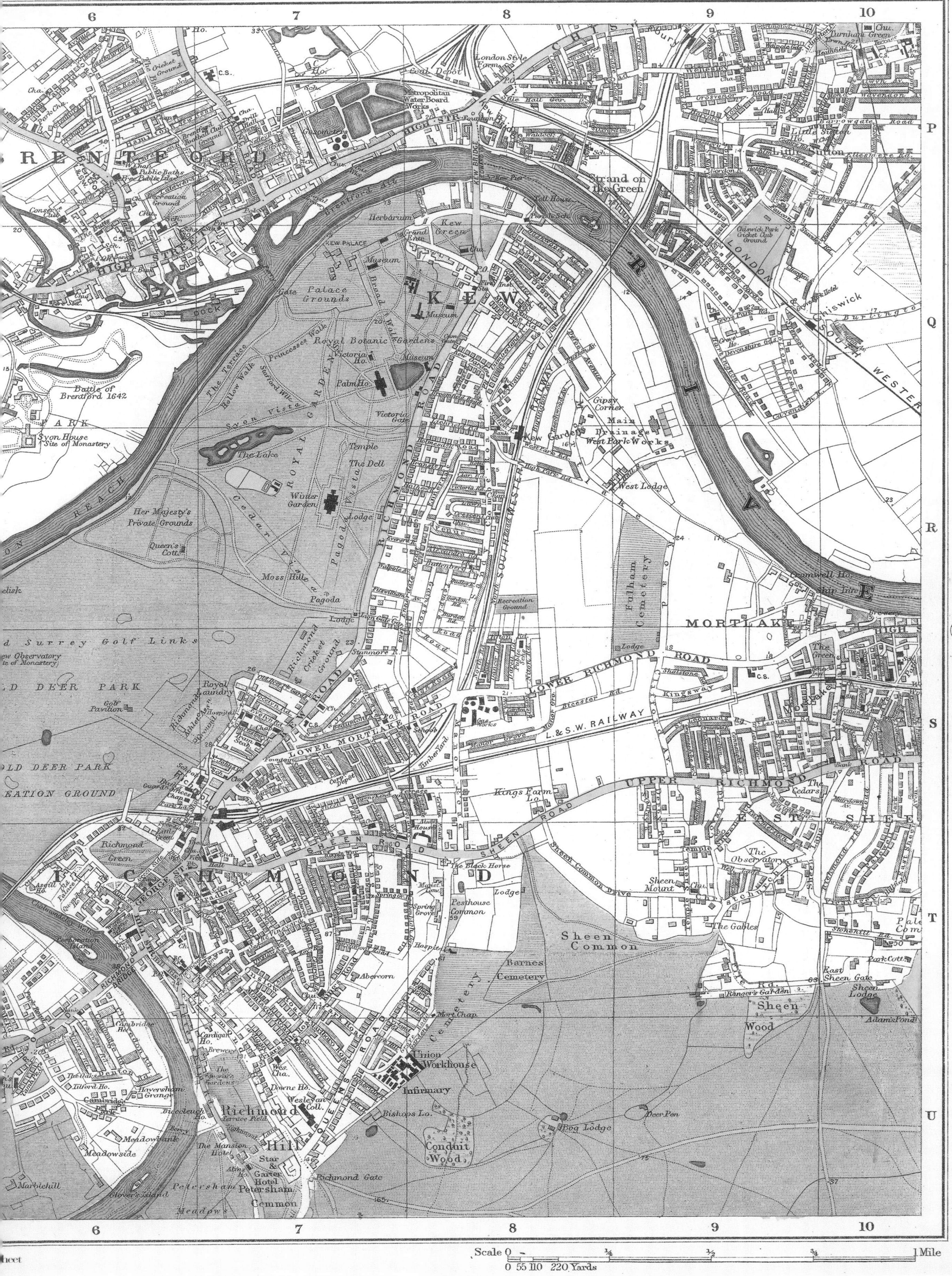

P Q R S T U

6 7 8 9 10

BRENTFORD

Battle of Brentford 1642
Syon House
Site of Monastery
PARK
ION REACH

KEW
Kew Palace
Palace Grounds
Museum
Herbarium
Royal Botanic Gardens
Victoria Ho.
Palm Ho.
Victoria Gate
Temple
The Dell
Winter Garden
Lodge
ROYAL GARDENS
The Terrace
Hollow Walk
Princesses Walk
Syon Vista
Cedar Vista
Pagoda Vista
The Lake
Her Majesty's Private Grounds
Queen's Cott.
Moss Hills
Pagoda

Kew Green
Grand Ent.
Grand Ent.
Museum

Strand on the Green
Kew Bridge
Toll House
Coal Depot
Metropolitan Water Board Works
London Style Farms

Chiswick Park Cricket Club Ground
South WESTERN
Chiswick
Burlington
Sutton
Grosvenor

Gipsy Corner
Main Drainage West Park Works
Kew Gardens
Bank
West Lodge
Fulham Cemetery
Cromwell Ho.
MORTLAKE
The Cedars

RICHMOND ROAD
L. & S.W. RAILWAY
SOUTH WESTERN RAILWAY

Old Surrey Golf Links
New Observatory
Site of Monastery
OLD DEER PARK
Golf Pavilion
Royal Laundry
Royal Observatory
Richmond Cricket Ground
Richmond Hospital
Recreation Ground

LOWER MORTLAKE ROAD
LOWER RICHMOND ROAD
Kingsway
Shalstone
Nicaster Rd.
Kings Farm Lo.

UPPER RICHMOND ROAD
EAST SHEEN
C.S.
Stonehill
The Gables
East Sheen Gate
Sheen Lodge
Adam's Pond
Sheen Wood
Park Cott.

RICHMOND
Richmond Green
GEORGE ST.
Richmond Bridge
Cambridge
Brewery
Wesleyan Coll.
Union Workhouse
Infirmary
Bishops Lo.
Richmond Hill
Star & Garter Hotel
Richmond Gate
Petersham Common
Terrace Field
The Mansion Hotel

SHEEN ROAD
The Black Horse
Springs
Spring Grove
Pesthouse Common
Hospital
Abercorn
QUEENS ROAD

Sheen Common
Sheen Common Drive
Sheen Mount
The Observatory
Barnes Cemetery
Mort. Chap.
Conduit Wood
Deer Pen
Bog Lodge
Ranger's Garden

Marble Hill
Glover's Island
Petersham Meadow
Buccleuch Park
Meadowside
Meadowbank

Adjoining 15 Sheet

Scale 0 — ¼ ½ ¾ 1 Mile
0 55 110 220 Yards

Bacon's Geographical Establishment   The Coloured Roads show the 'Bus or Tram Routes.   Adjoinii

[132]

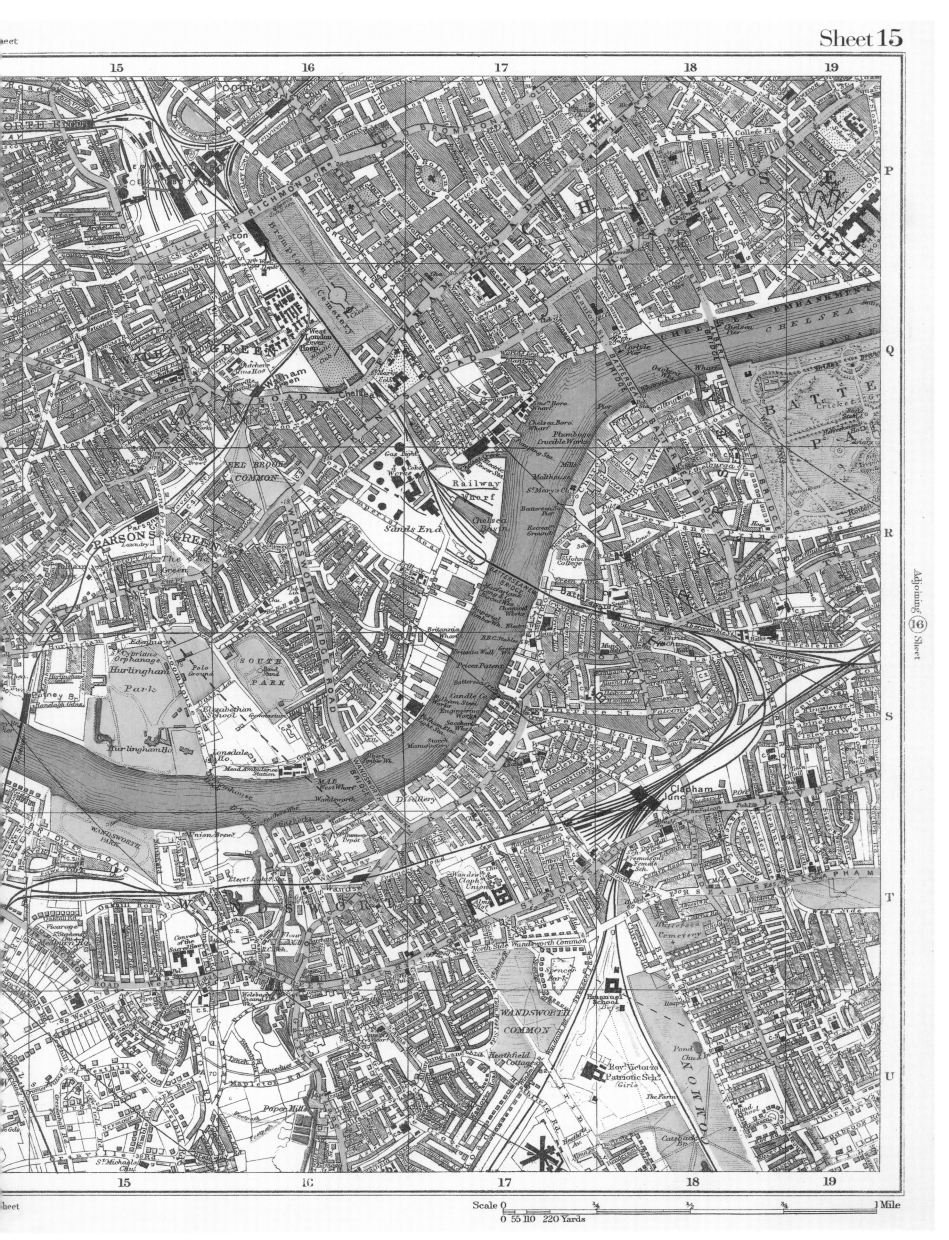

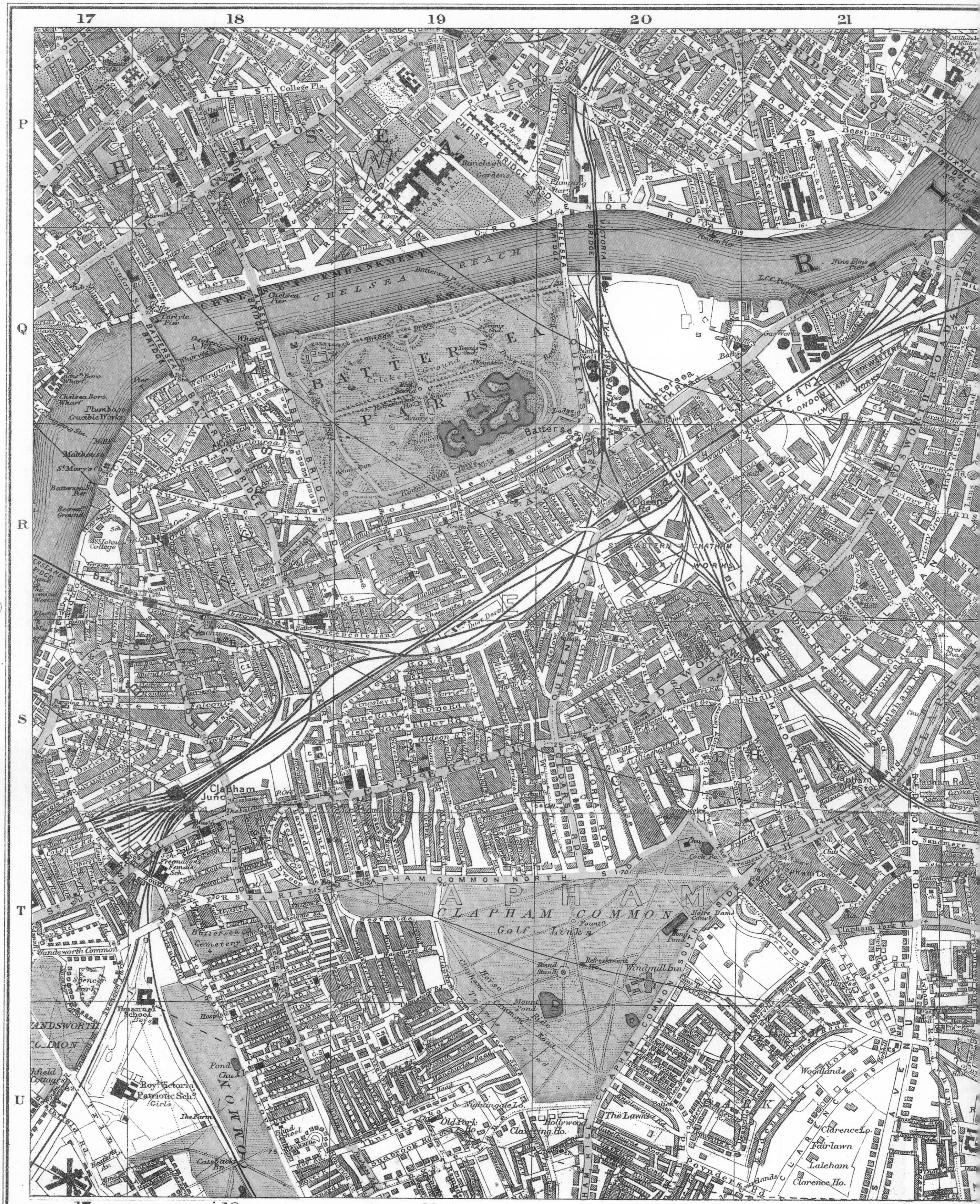

17 18 19 20 21

P

Q

R

S

T

U

17 18 19 20 21

BELGRAVIA

College Pla.

CHELSEA BRIDGE

Ranelagh Gardens

CHELSEA HOSPITAL

CHELSEA EMBANKMENT

Cheyne

Chelsea Pier   CHELSEA REACH   Battersea Park Pier

Nine Elms Pier

L.C.C. Pumping

R

Battersea Pier

Oakley Wharf

2nd Boro. Wharf

Chelsea Boro. Wharf

Plumbago Crucible Works

Gas Works

BATTERSEA   PARK

Cricket Ground

Tennis Ground

Sub Station

Malthouse

St Mary's Ch.

Battersea Sq.

Rearm Ground

St John's College

Battersea

Queen's

SOUTH EASTERN & CHATHAM

WORKS

Clapham Junc.

Freemasons Female Sch.

Battersea Cemetery

Wandsworth Common

Roy. Victoria Patriotic Sch. (Girls)

The Farm

WANDSWORTH COMMON

Hospital

CLAPHAM COMMON NORTH

CLAPHAM   COMMON

Golf   Links

Notre Dame Conv.

Cock Pd.

Refreshment Ho.

Band Stand

Windmill Inn

Mount Pond

Clapham Park

Long Pond

Pond Chase Ho.

Old Park

Hollywood

Clapham Rd.

The Lawns

Woodlands

Clarence Lo.

Fairlawn

Laleham

Clarence Ho.

Adjoining (17) Sheet

Scale 0 ¼ ½ ¾] Mile
0 55 110 220 Yards

Bacon's Geographical Establishment

The Coloured Roads show the Bus or Tram Routes.

Adjoining

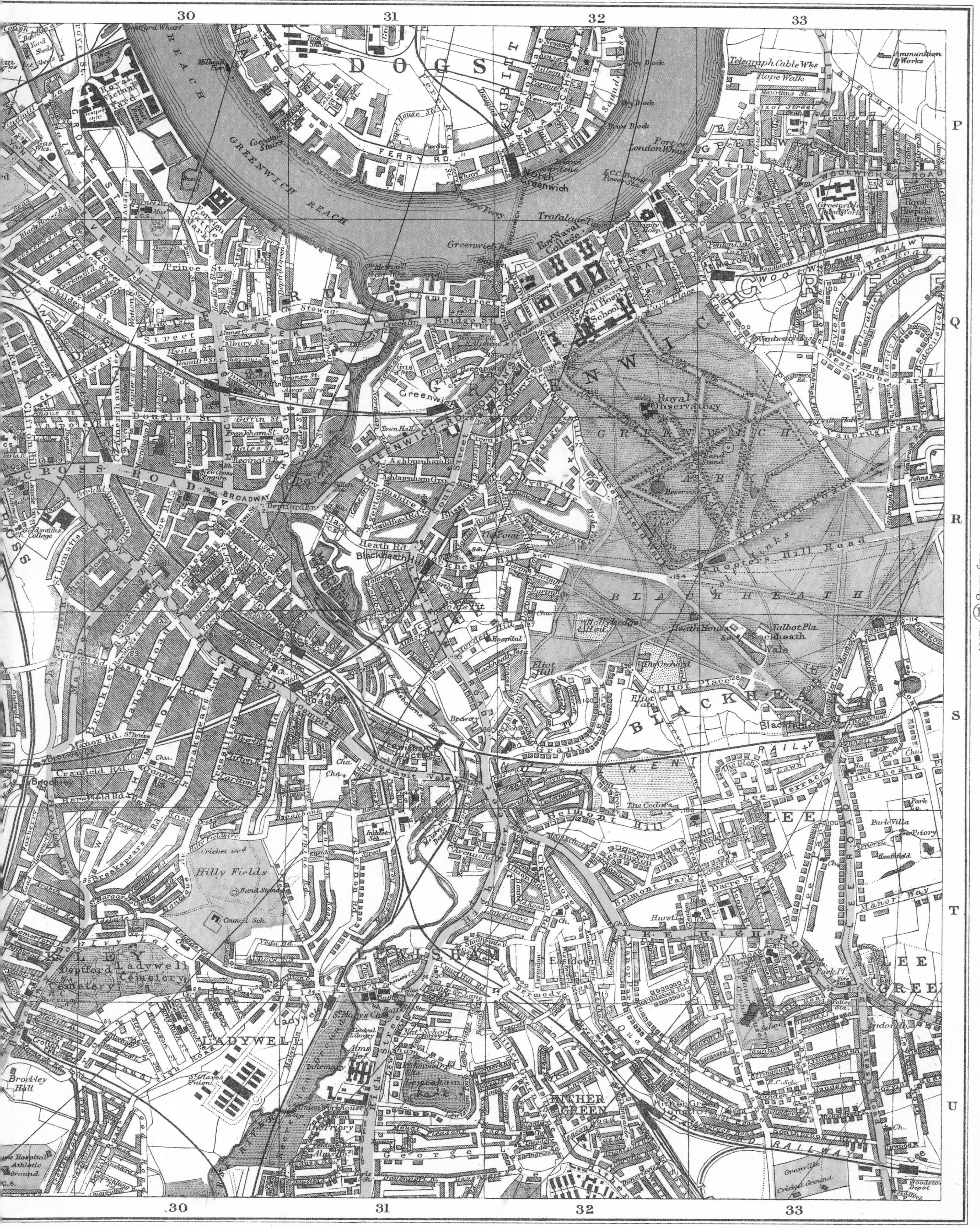

30   31   32   33

P

Q

R

S

T

U

ISLE OF DOGS

GREENWICH REACH

Millwall Dock

Deptford Wharf

FERRY RD.

North Greenwich

Greenwich Pier

Trafalgar Rd.

Roy. Naval College

Royal Hosp. School

GREENWICH PARK

Royal Observatory

Band Stand

Reservoir

WOOLWICH ROAD

Greenwich Union Works

Royal Hospital Cemetery

Telegraph Cable Wks

Rope Walk

Ammunition Works

Westcombe Park

Port of London Wharf

DEPTFORD

NEW CROSS ROAD

Goldsmiths' College

Prince St.

Clifton Hill

Douglas St.

Giffin St.

Deptford Broadway

BLACKHEATH ROAD

Heath Rd.

Blackheath

The Point

GREENWICH HIGH ROAD

Town Hall

Ashburnham Gro.

Devonshire Rd.

Hilly Fields

Cricket Grd.

Band Stand

Council Sch.

BROCKLEY

Deptford & Ladywell Cemetery

LADYWELL

St. Mary's Ch.

LEWISHAM

Brockley Hall

BLACKHEATH

Holly Hedge Ho.

Heath House

Heath Vale

Talbot Pla.

Blackheath Vale

Eliot Hill

Eliot Place

The Orchard

The Cedars

LEE

Park Ho.

Park Villa

The Priory

Heathfield

Belmont Hill

Dacre St.

Manor Way

LEE HIGH ROAD

LEE GREEN

HITHER GREEN

Brewery

Lewisham

Ladywell

Union Workhouse

NORTH KENT RAILWAY

BLACKHEATH & LEE RAILWAY

LEE ROAD

Cricket Ground

Woodstock Works

Hospital Athletic Ground

Scale 0   ¾   ½   ¾   1 Mile

0   55   110   220 Yards

Adjoining 18 Sheet

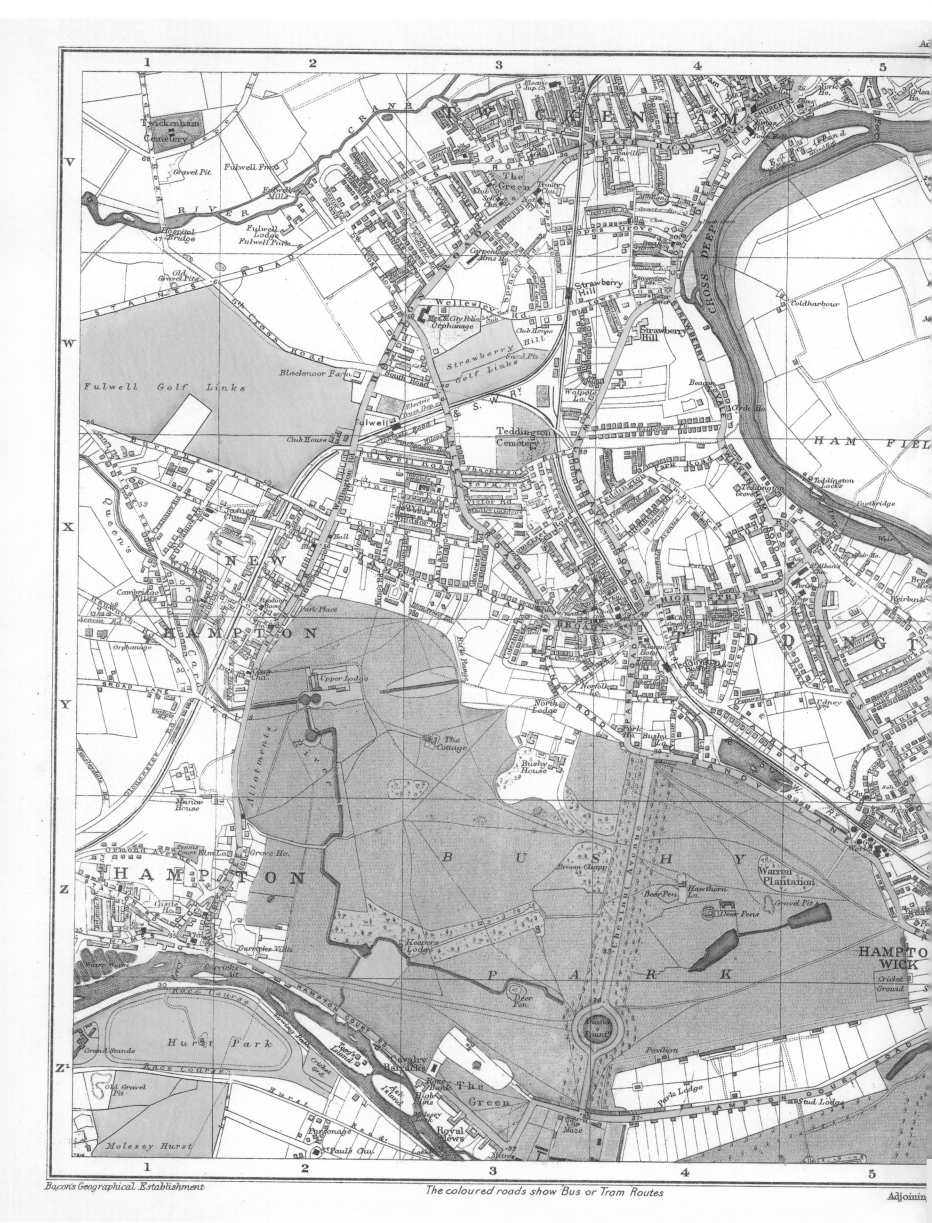

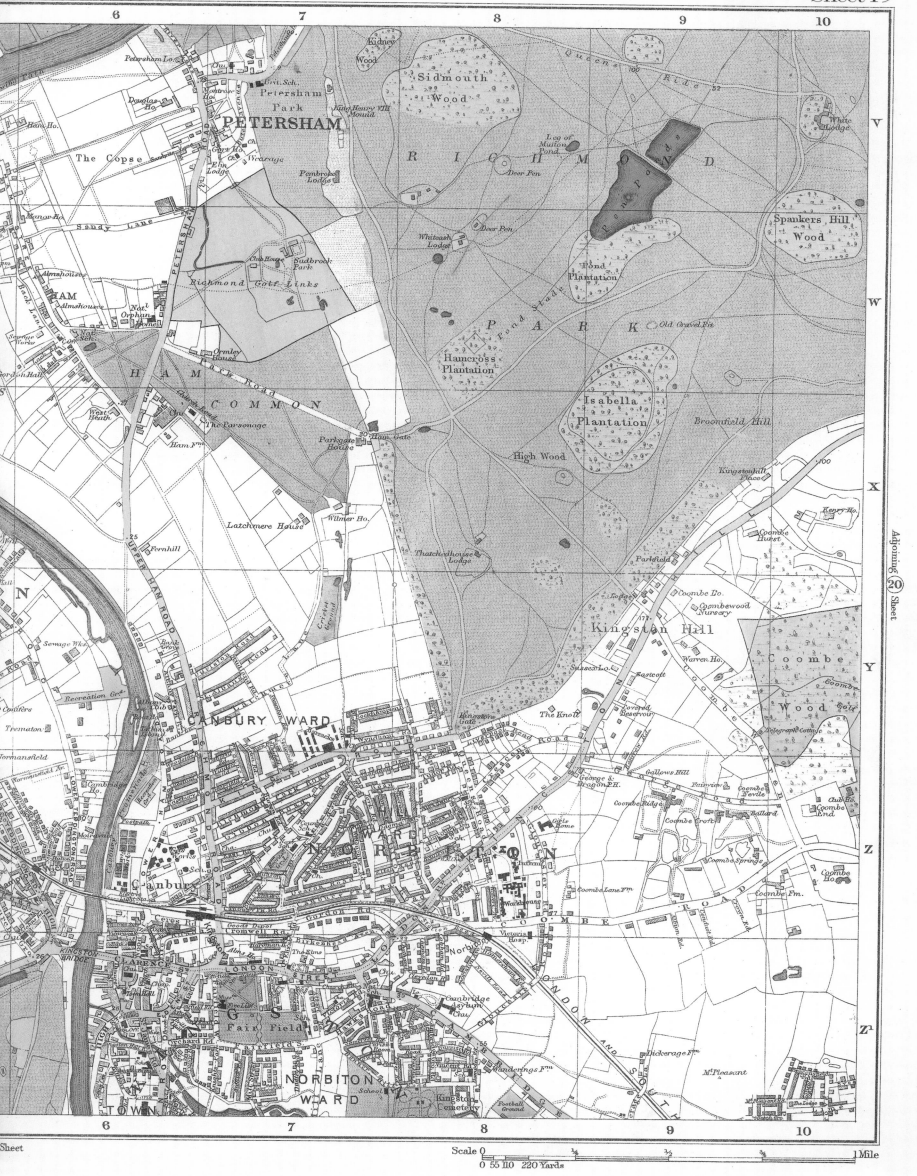

Scale 0   ¼   ½   ¾   1 Mile

0   55   110   220 Yards

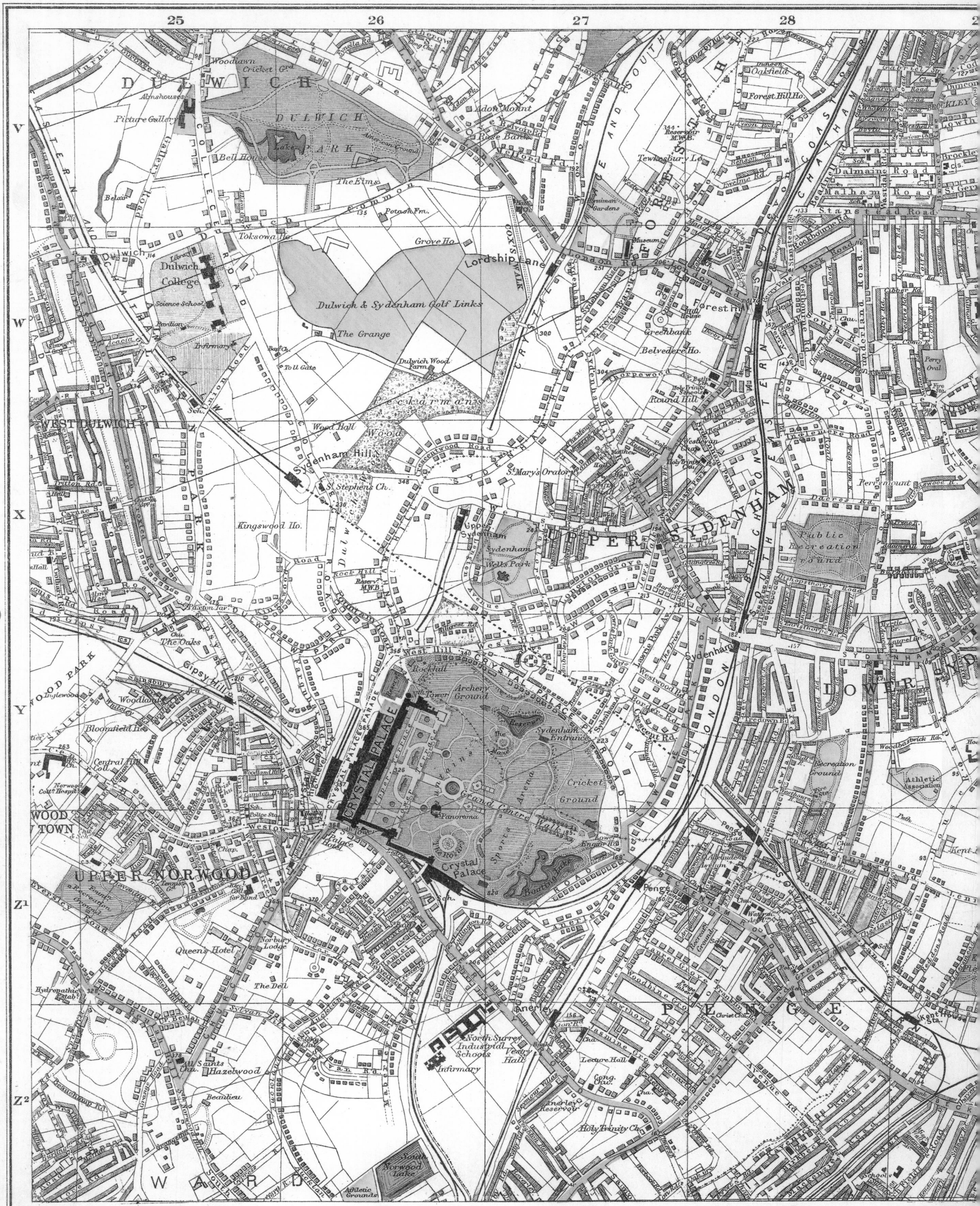

25 26 27 28

DULWICH

Woodlawn Cricket Grd.

Almshouses
Picture Gallery
DULWICH PARK
Lake
Bell House
Belair
The Elms
Potash Fm.
Toksowa Ho.
Grove Ho.
Lordship Lane
Dulwich College
Science School
Pavilion
Infirmary
Dulwich & Sydenham Golf Links
The Grange
Dulwich Wood Farm
WEST DULWICH
Wood Hall Wood
Sydenham Hill
St Stephens Ch.
Kingswood Ho.
Rock Hill Reservr. MWB.
Upper Sydenham
Sydenham Wells Park
UPPER SYDENHAM
FOREST HILL
Forest Hill Ho.
Horniman Gardens
Museum
Forest Hill
Greenbank
Belvedere Ho.
Round Hill
St Mary's Oratory
Perry Oval
Public Recreation Ground

Adjoining 21 Sheet.

WOOD PARK
Inglewood
Gipsy Hill
Woodland
Bloomfield Ho.
Central Hill Coll.
Norwood Cott. Hospl.
WOOD TOWN
UPPER NORWOOD
Queen's Hotel
The Bell
Hydropathic Estabt.
All Saints Ch. Hazelwood
Beaulieu

CRYSTAL PALACE PARADE
Rockhill
Nth Tower
Archery Ground
CRYSTAL PALACE
Sydenham Entrance
The Maze
Grand Centre Walk
Panorama
Sports Arena
Cricket Ground
Palace Ho.
Crystal Palace
Rockhills

LOWER SYDENHAM
Athletic Association

Penge
PENGE
Anerley
North Surrey Industrial Schools
Vestry Hall
Infirmary
Lecture Hall
Cong. Ch.
Anerley Reservoir
Holy Trinity Ch.

South Norwood Lake
Athletic Grounds

WARD

25 26 27 28

Bacon's Geographical Establishment. The coloured roads show Bus or Tram Routes. Adjoining

[146]

34   35   36   37

V

Horn Park

W

MOTTINGHAM

Mottingham Farm

Eltham & Mottingham

Royal Naval School   Chapel

Greenwich Workho.

St Augustine Chu.

GROVE PARK

Chinbrook Rd   Chinbrook Road

X

Grove Park Sta.

Lower Marvels Wood

Model Farm

Chapel Farm   Cricket Ground

Marvels Wood

Coldharbour Farm

Hillside

Y

Sundridge Park

Sundridge Hall

Golf Links

Elmstead Wood

White Horse Hill

Elmstead Court
Elmstead Lodge

Red Hill

Ball's Farm

Garden Wood

Warstan

Cranmore Place

Oakwood

Chislehurst West

Z¹

Plaistow

Club House

Cemy

High Grove

SUNDRIDGE

Rockpit Wood

Elmstead Gr.

Elmstead Woods

Cherrywalk Wood

Oakwood

Camden Wood

WARD

Elmstead Golf Links

Silho

Waldert Cott.

Beecharoft

Chislehurst Golf Links

CAMDEN PARK

Logshill Wood

Park View

Braemar Lodge

Ellesmere Marvelstone

Elmstead Wood

Bullers Wood

Lubbock Road

Christ Ch.

Claverley

Hillside

Ragglewood

Z²

NEW BROMLEY

Cricket Ground

The Acacias
Keystone
Rothwell
Stoneleigh

Logs Hill

Merlwood

Lower Camden

Oakleigh

Woodclyne

BICKLEY

Widmore Green

Bickley Hall

Chislehurst Sta.

Birch Wood

WIDMORE

Palace Farm

Widmore House

BICKLEY PARK

34   35   36   37

Bacon's Geographical Establishment   *The coloured roads show 'Bus or Tram Routes*   Adjoining

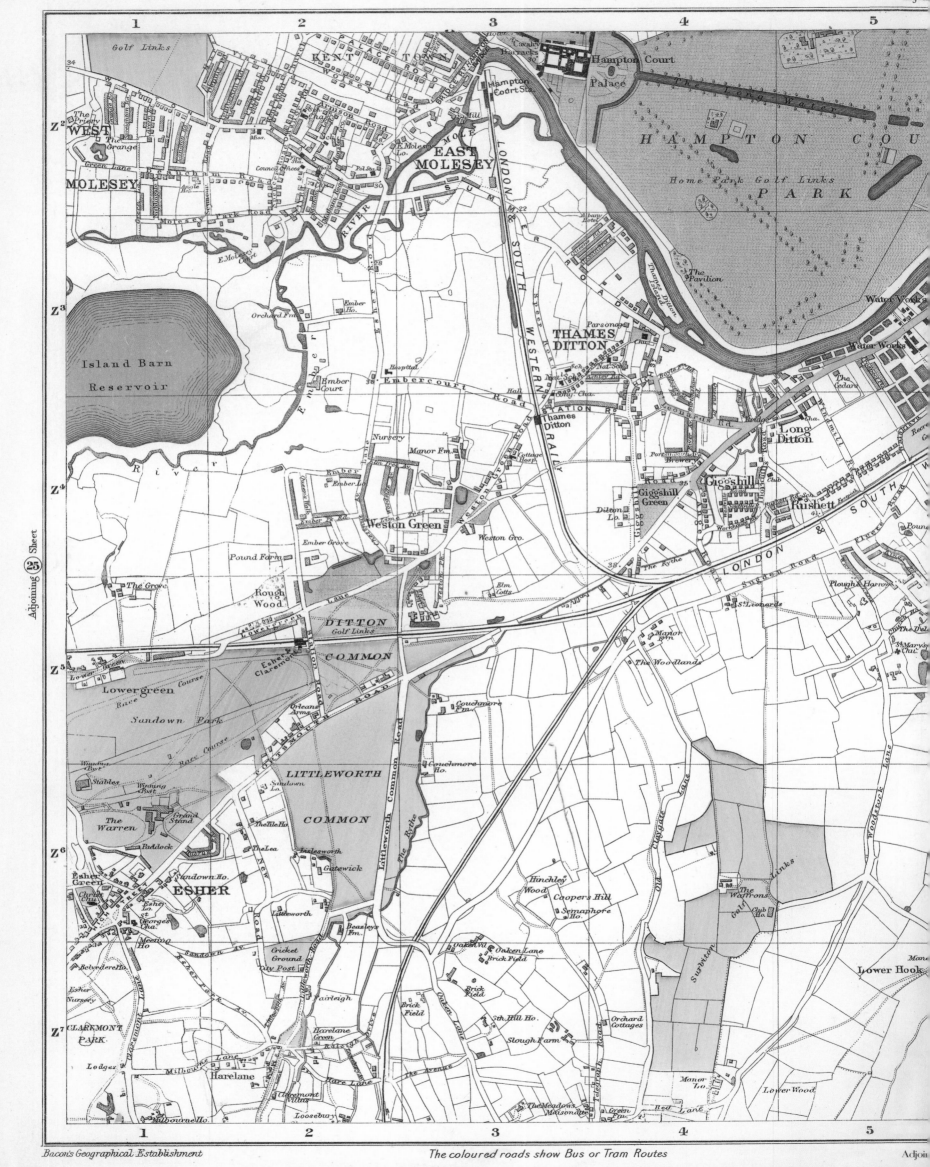

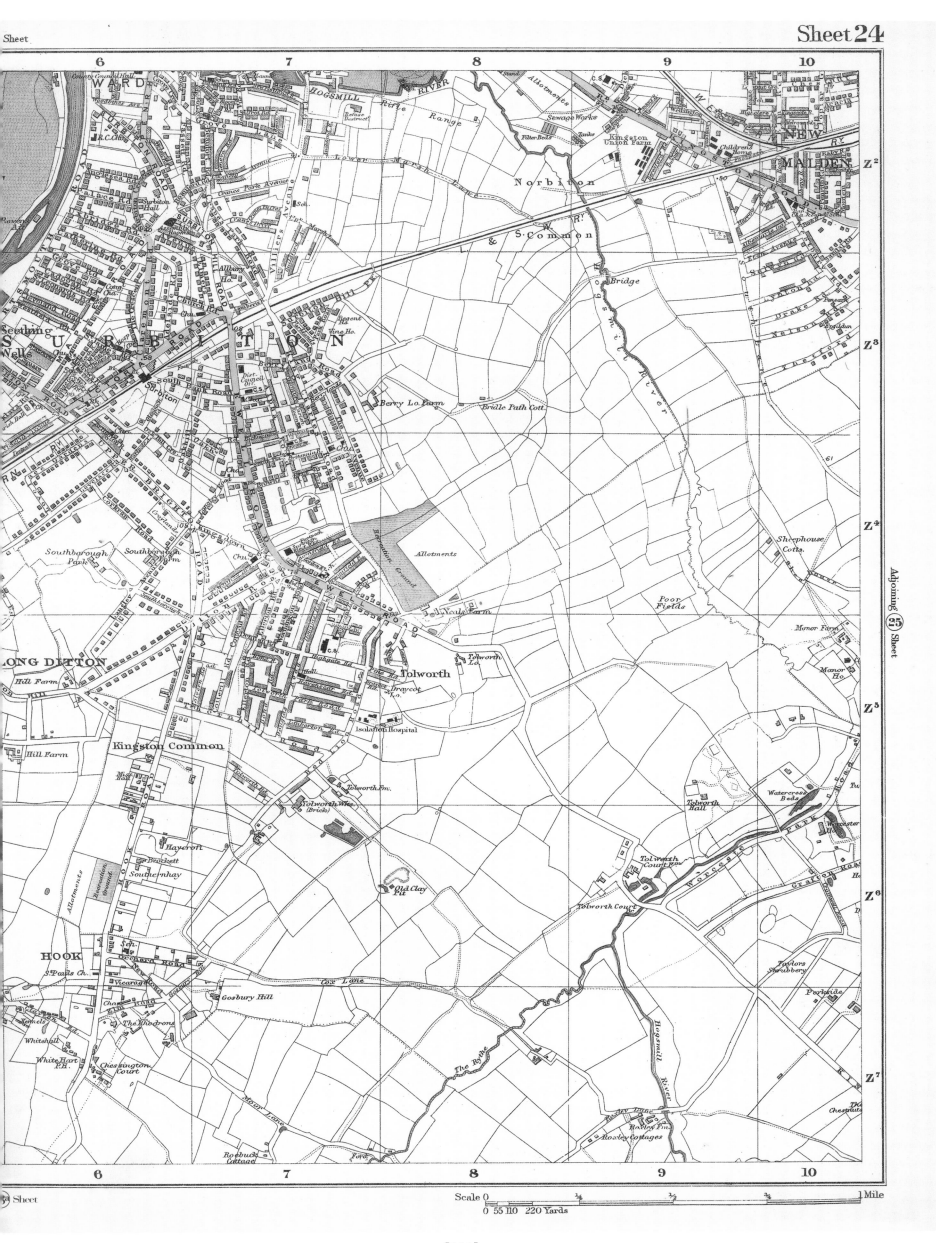

Z²

Z³

Z⁴

Z⁵

Z⁶

Z⁷

Adjoining 25 Sheet

Scale 0 ¼ ½ ¾ 1 Mile

0 55 110 220 Yards

Z² NEW MALDEN

Z³

Z⁴

Z⁵

Z⁶

Z⁷

10 11 12 13 14

Beverley Park

West Barnes

West Barnes Farm

RAYNES PARK

St Saviour's Ch. Parish Hall

Vicarage Ho. Greville Ho.

Pavilions Playing Fields

Satara

West Barnes Park

West Barnes Terrace

Golf Links

Cannon Hill Ho.

Cannon Hill

Chestnut Cottage

Cherry Wood

Cricket Ground

Norbiton Pottery

C.S.

Burlington Rd

Blagdon Farm

Dudley Lodge

Ivy Ho.

Bijou Villas

Malden Golf

Bluehouse Farm

East Cott.

West Cott.

Lower Morden Farm

Coombsfield

Rednor Ho.
Wilton Ho.
The Firs
Elmhurst

The Grange

The Rookery

Firgrove

Motspur Farm

Motspur Park

Battersea New Cemetery

Mort. Chap.

Lower Morden

Peacock

Sheephouse Cotts.

Newhouse Farm

Morden Common

Taylor's Cott.

Upper Green
The Plough

MALDEN

Epsom Sewage Farm

Brick Works

Manor Farm

Fullbrooks

Manor Ho.

Back Green

Malden Green

Worcester Park

Meth. Chap.

Small Pox Hospital

St Anthony's Hosp.

NORTH CHEAM

Park Fm.

Tunstall Ho.

Great Avenue

WORCESTER PARK

Watercress Beds

Worcester Park

Worcester Court

Tennis Ground

Cemetery
Ch.

Harrybrowe
Copthorne

Cheam Common

Brocks
Pyrotechnic
Works

Dancer Dick Wood

Bridge Wood

Poplar Place

Lower Fm. Ho.

Pottery Wks. Hosp.

Queen Vic. Dwl.
The Birches

Londesborough Ho.
The Priory

Taylors Shrubbery

Avenue Wood

White Cott.

Parkside

Astbury

Coldharbour Fm.

Sparrow Fm.

Z⁷

Chesterfield Ho.

Railway Wood

Sparrow Plantation

Lodge

The Chestnuts

Sparrow Plantation

10 11 12 13 14

Bacon's Geographical Establishment. The coloured roads show Bus or Tram Routes Adjoining

[152]

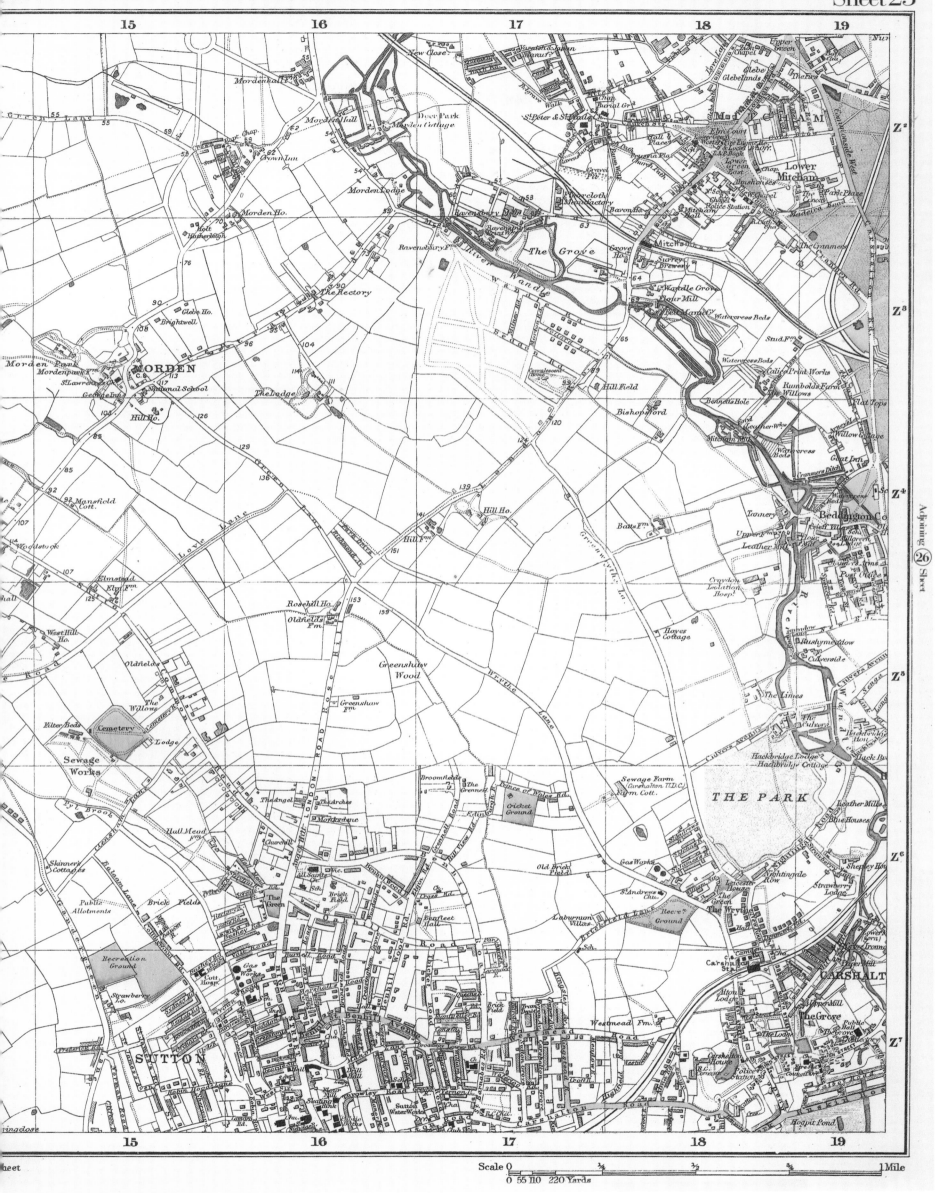

Scale 0 ¼ ½ ¾ 1 Mile

0 55 110 220 Yards

[153]

Nursery
Temple's Cottage
Pollardshill
Wood

Upper Green
Chapel
Glebelands
The Firs
The Croft
Tooting Bec
Golf Links

Z²
MITCHAM
Jesmond
Gravel Pit

St Peter & St Paul
Elm Court
Lower Green East
Tamworth Lodge
India Rubber Works

Lower Mitcham
Shop
Park Place
Madeira Road

Police Station
N. School
Chapel
R. Cath. Chapel

The Grove
Mitcham
Surrey Brewery
The Cranmers
Ravensbury Arms
Blue Houses
Windmill

Z³
Grove Ho.
Waddle Grove
Flour Mill
East Mead
Watercress Beds
Pound
Croydon Rd.

Princes
Golf Links
MITCHAM COMMON

Watercress Beds
Stud Fm.
Calico Print Works
Mitcham Junction
Princes Golf Club Ho.

Hill Field
Rumbolds Farm
The Willows
Flat Tops

Bishopsford
Benedis Hole
Leather Wks
Willow Cottage

Z⁴
Mitcham Mill
Watercress Beds
Goat Inn
Cranmers Ditch
School
Beddington
Nursery
LONDON, BRIGHTON

Tannery
Watercress Beds
Beddington Corner
Old Queens Head
The Poplars

Bails Fm.
Upper Fm.
Leather Mill
Flour Mill
North Fm.
Pimms Cottage

Croydon Isolation Hosp.
Brewers Arms
Post Office
Borough Hospl

Sewage Farm
Grassmere

Hayes Cottage
Lower Fm.

Z⁵
Meadow Lane
Rushymeadow
Culverside
Culvers Avenue
New Road
Long Shaw

The Limes
Cardboard Factory

The Culvers
Hackbridge Hou.
Old Red Lion
Hackbridge Sta.
Sewage Fm.

Z⁶
Hackbridge Lodge
Hackbridge Cottage
Hack Bridge
Hackbridge
Leather Mills
Blue Houses
Watercress Beds

THE PARK
Working Mens
Beddington Park
Park Fm.

Sewage Farm (Carshalton U.D.C.)
Farm Cott.
Female Orphan Asylum

Gas Works
Nightingale Row
Leicester House
Shepley Hou.
St Mary
BEDDING

St Andrews Chu.
The Green
The Wrythe
Strawberry Lodge
Mill Pond
Paper Mill

Laburnum Villas
Recre. Ground
Wallington Bridge
Wallington House
The Elms
Brewery
CROYDON RD.
Manor

Z⁷
Westmead Fm.
Carshalton Sta.
Upper Mill
CARSHALTON
Ironworks
Nat. Sch.
The Rectory
Chalkpit Cott.
Queenswood
Beddington Place

Alton Lodge
The Grove
The Lodge
Conder Gds.
Greenwood Gds.

Carshalton House
Police Station
WALLINGTON
Norton Gardens
Cemetery

Hospit Pond
The Demesne
BRIGHTON & SOUTH COAST

Bacon's Geographical Establishment.   The coloured roads show Bus or Tram Routes

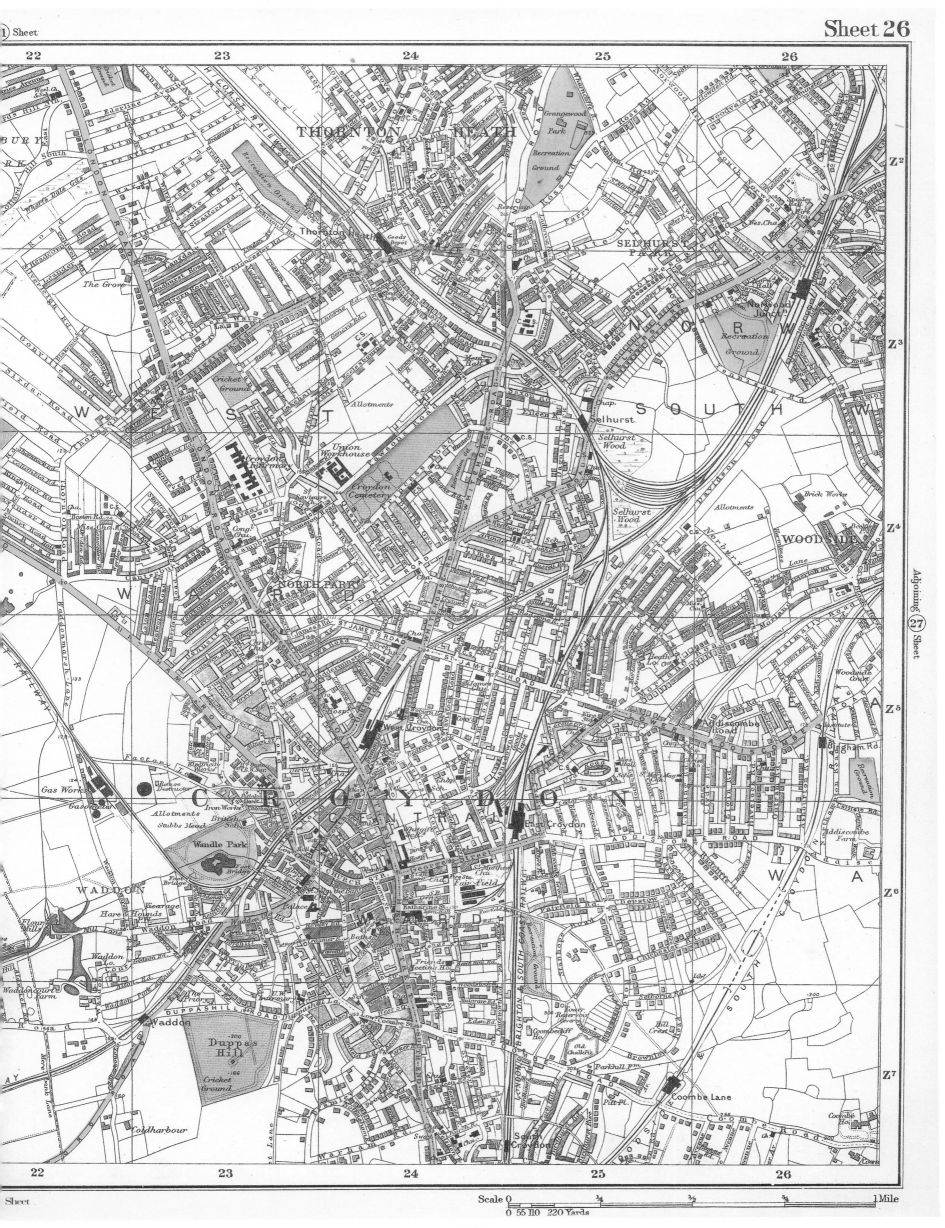

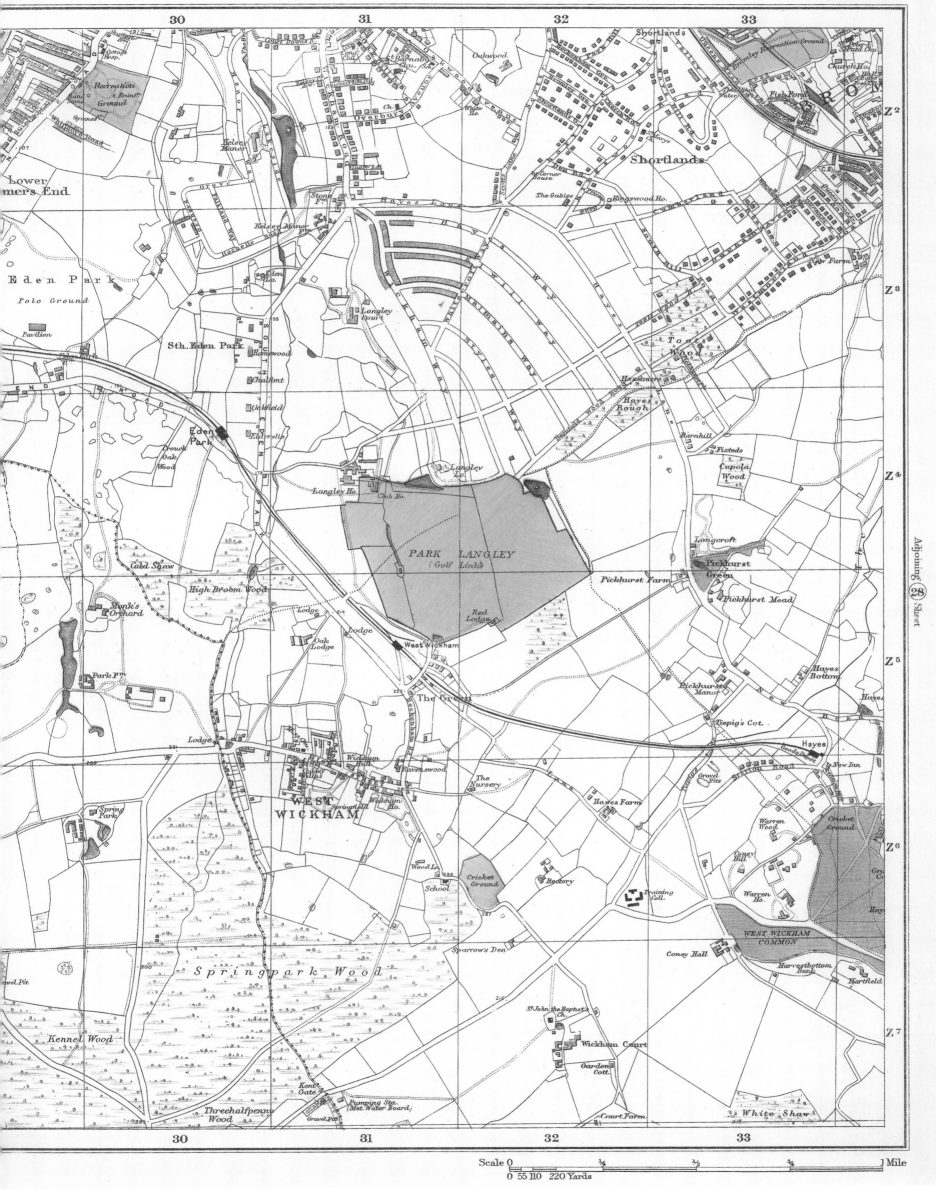

Bacon's Geographical Establishment

The coloured roads show 'Bus or Tram Routes

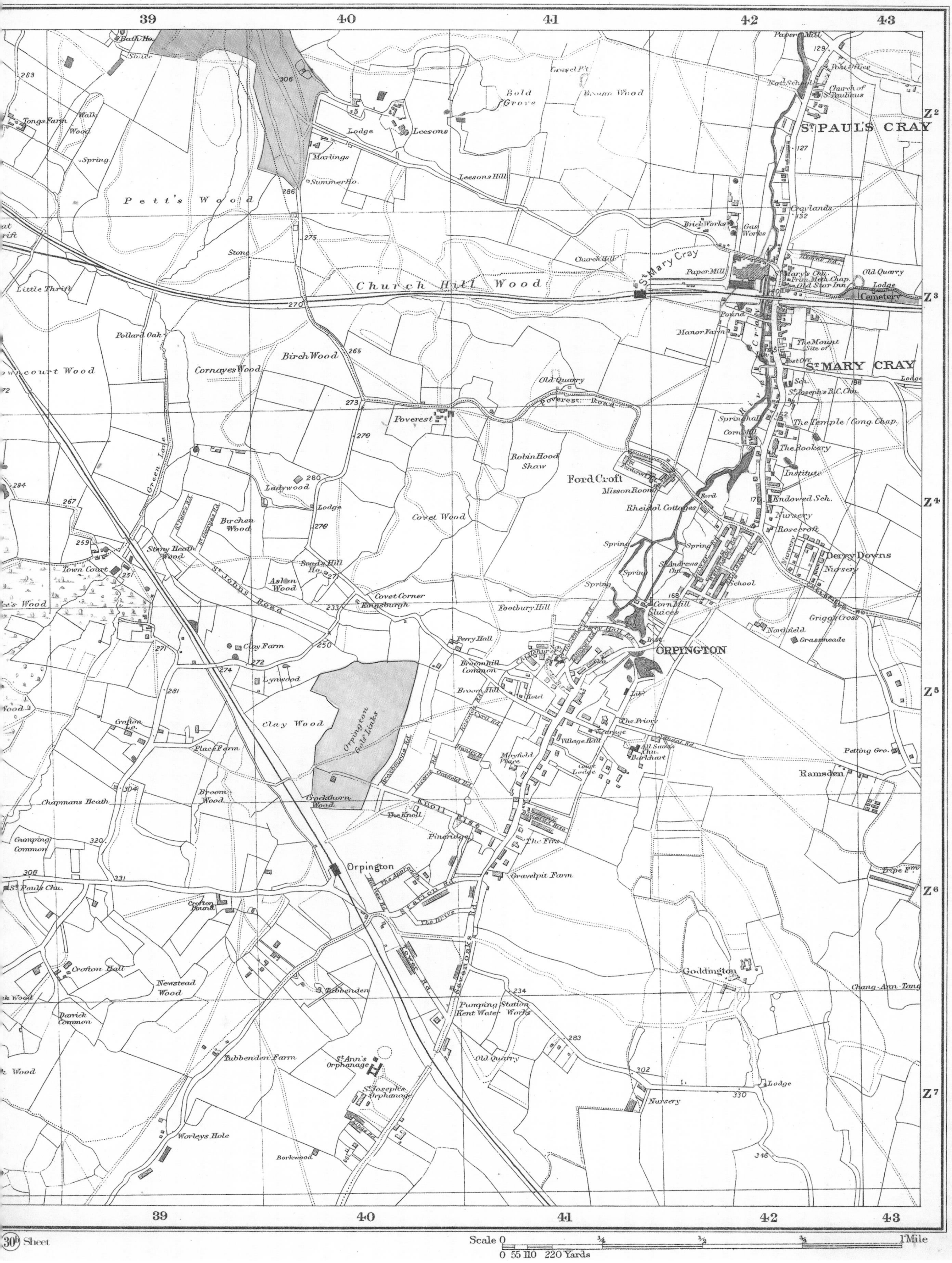

Sheet

39 40 41 42 43

Bath Ho.

Tongs Farm
Walk Wood

Spring

Little Thrift

Pett's Wood

Gravel Pit

Bold Grove

Brown Wood

Paper Mill 129

Post Office
Nat. School
Church of St Paulinus

Z2

St PAULS CRAY

127

Lodge
Leesons

Marlings

Summer Ho.

Leesons Hill

Church Hill

St Mary Cray

Paper Mill

Craylands 132

Brick Works
Gas Works

Mary's Chu.
Prim. Meth. Chap.
Old Star Inn

Church Hill Wood

270

275

Stone

Z3

Cemetery
Old Quarry
Lodge

Pollard Oak

Birch Wood 265

Cornayes Wood

273

Poverest

Poverest Road

Old Quarry

Robin Hood Shaw

Ford Croft

Mission Room

Rheinol Cottages

Spring

Manor Farm

Pound

The Mount
Site of

Post Off.

St MARY CRAY 198

Lodge

St Joseph's R.C. Chu.

Springhall

Corn Mill

The Temple Cong. Chap.

The Rookery

Institute

Endowed Sch. 170

Nursery

Rosecroft

Z4

279

Ladywood

280

Lodge

Covet Wood

270

259

Town Court 251

Stony Heath Wood

Birchen Wood

St Johns Road

Ashton Wood

Send's Hill Ho. 257

Covet Corner

Engsburgh

233

250

Spring

Spring

St Andrews Chu.

School

Footbury Hill

Spring

Spring

168

Corn Mill Sluices

Perry Downs

Nursery

Griggs Cross

Norefield

Grassmeade

Z5

284

267

's Wood

Wood 9

Clay Farm

272

271

274

Lynwood

281

Clay Wood

Orpington Golf Links

Crofton Lo.

Place Farm

Perry Hall

Broomhill Common

Broom Hill

Knoll Rise

Hotel

ORPINGTON

Church St

Inn

The Priory

Village Hall

Mayfield Place

Court Lodge

All Saints Chu.

Barnhart

Grange

Ramsden

Petting Gro.

304

Chapmans Heath

Broom Wood

Crockthorn Wood

The Knoll

Pineridge

The Firs

Gravelpit Farm

Gramping Common

320

306

331

St Pauls Chu.

Crofton Pound

Orpington

The Approach

Z6

Newstead Wood

Derrick Common

Tubbenden

Tubbenden Farm

St Ann's Orphanage

St Joseph's Orphanage

Pumping Station
Kent Water Works

234

Old Quarry

283

302

330

Goldington

Chang-Ann Tang

Lodge

Nursery

Z7

Worleys Hole

Borkwood

346

Scale 0 ¼ ½ ¾ 1 Mile

0 55 110 220 Yards

300 Sheet

[159]

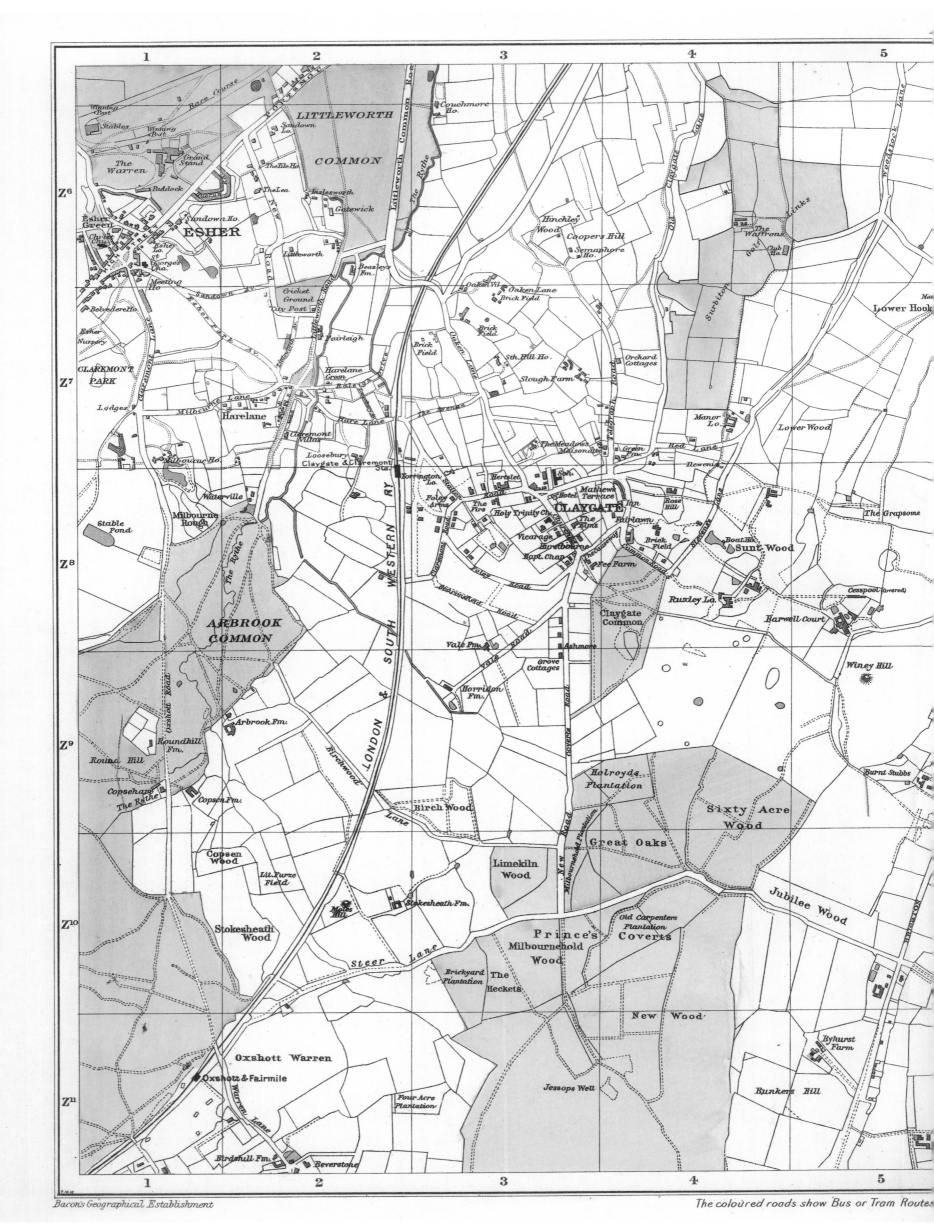

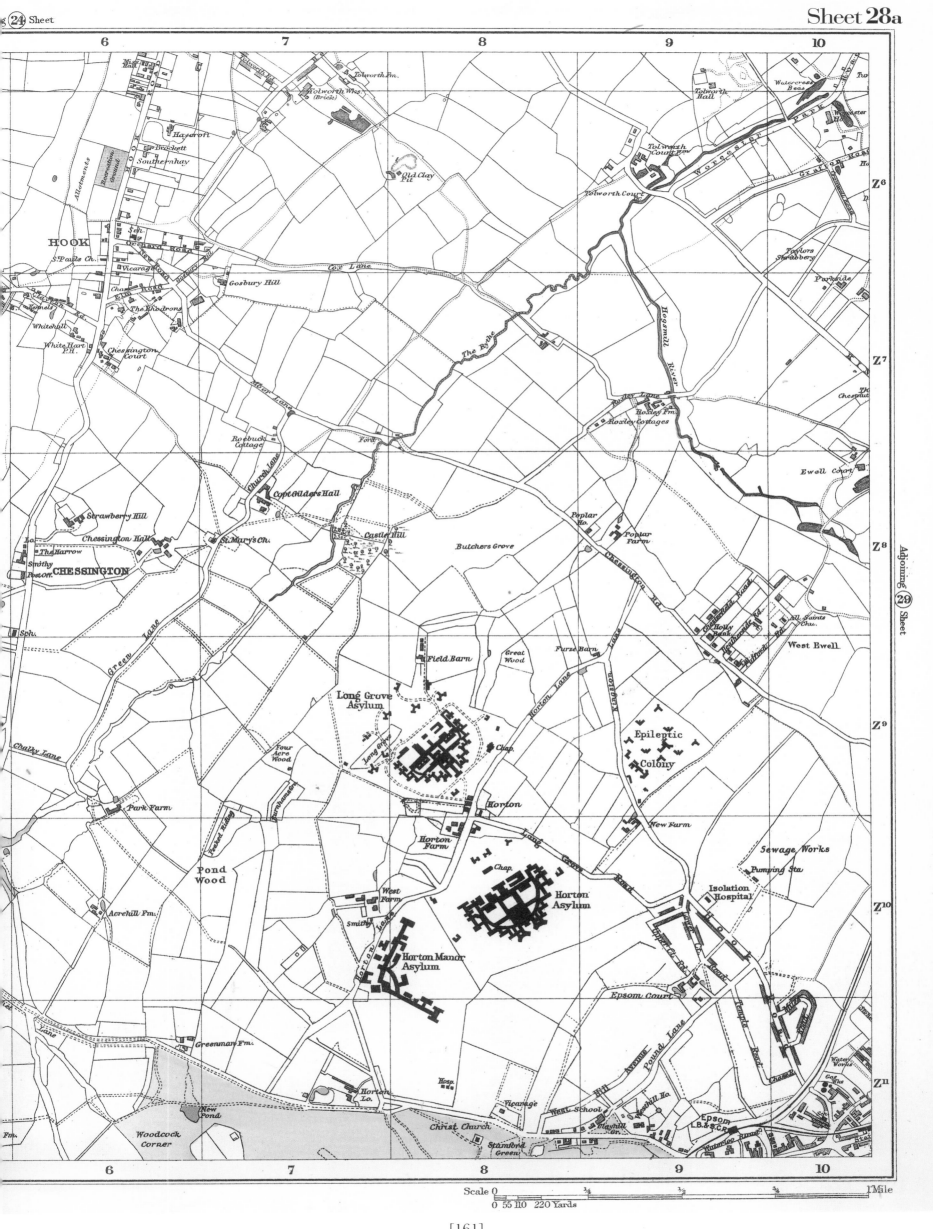

Scale 0   ¼   ½   ¾   1 Mile

0 55 110   220 Yards

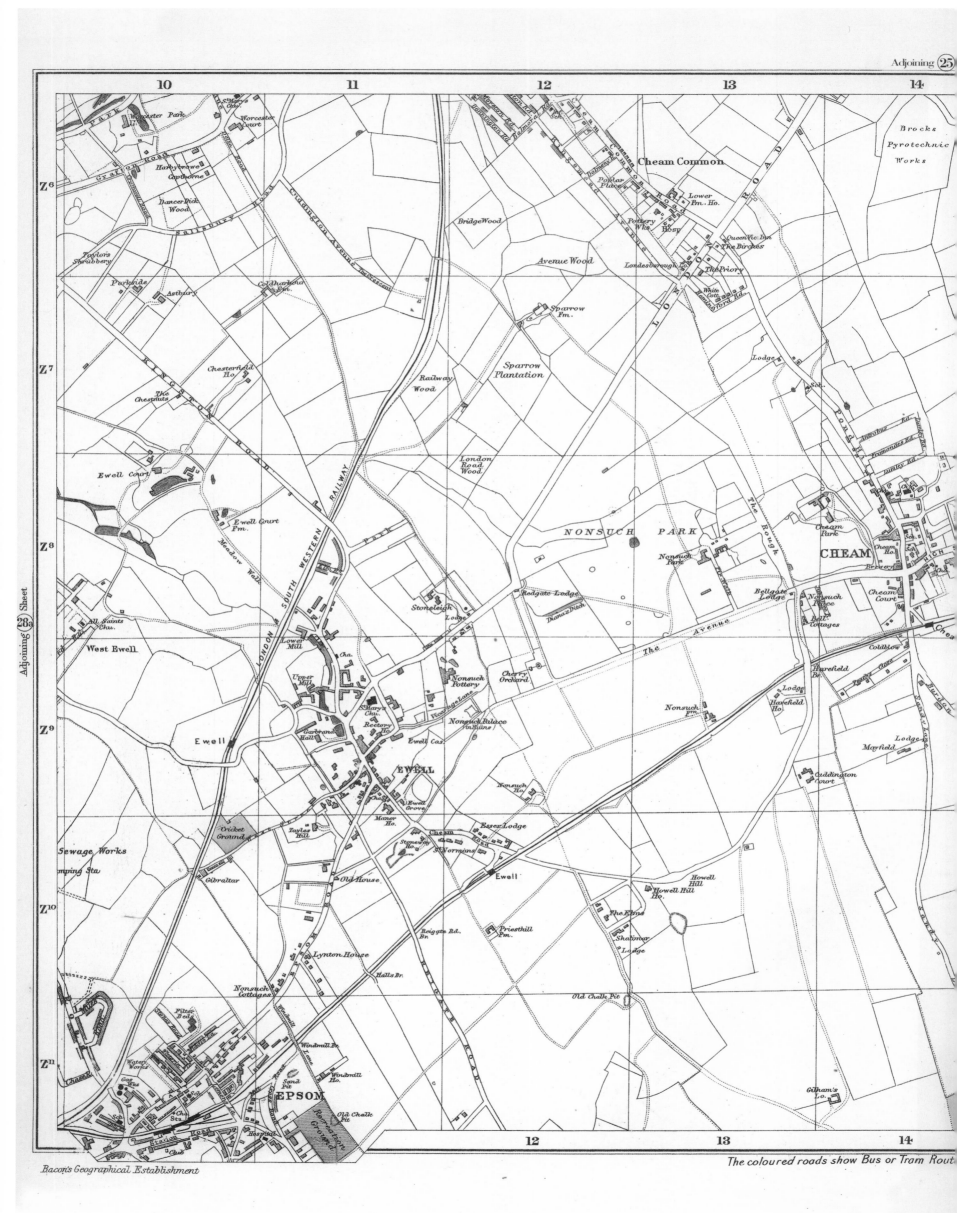

Bacon's Geographical Establishment

The coloured roads show Bus or Tram Rout

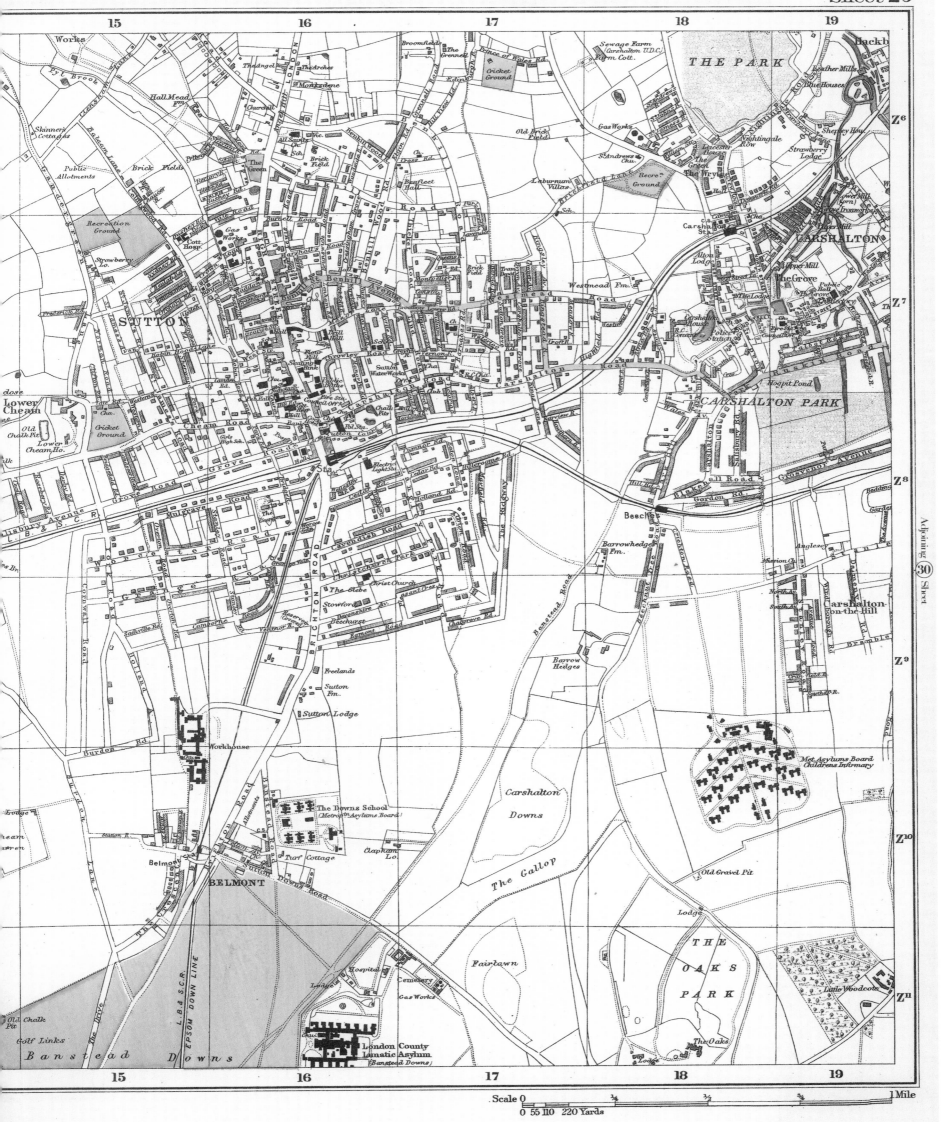

Scale 0   ¾   ½   ¾   1 Mile

0 55 110 220 Yards

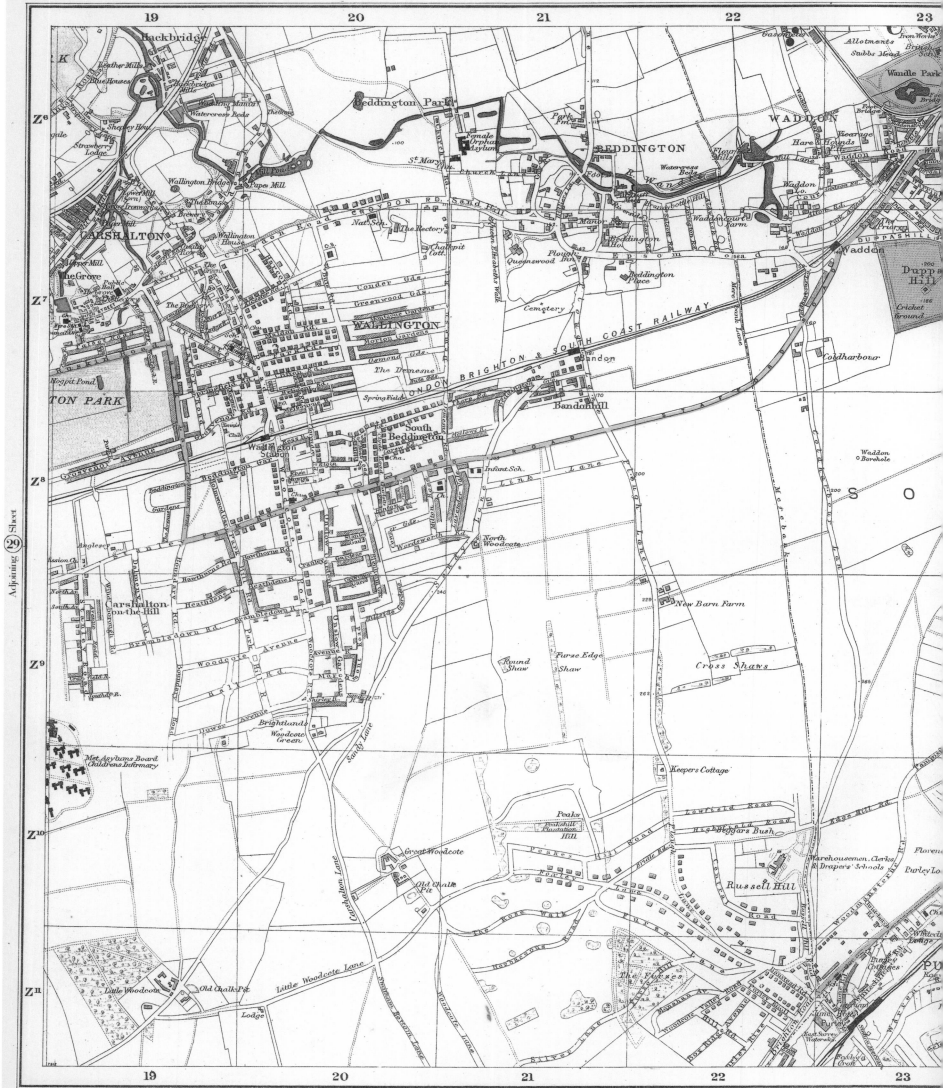

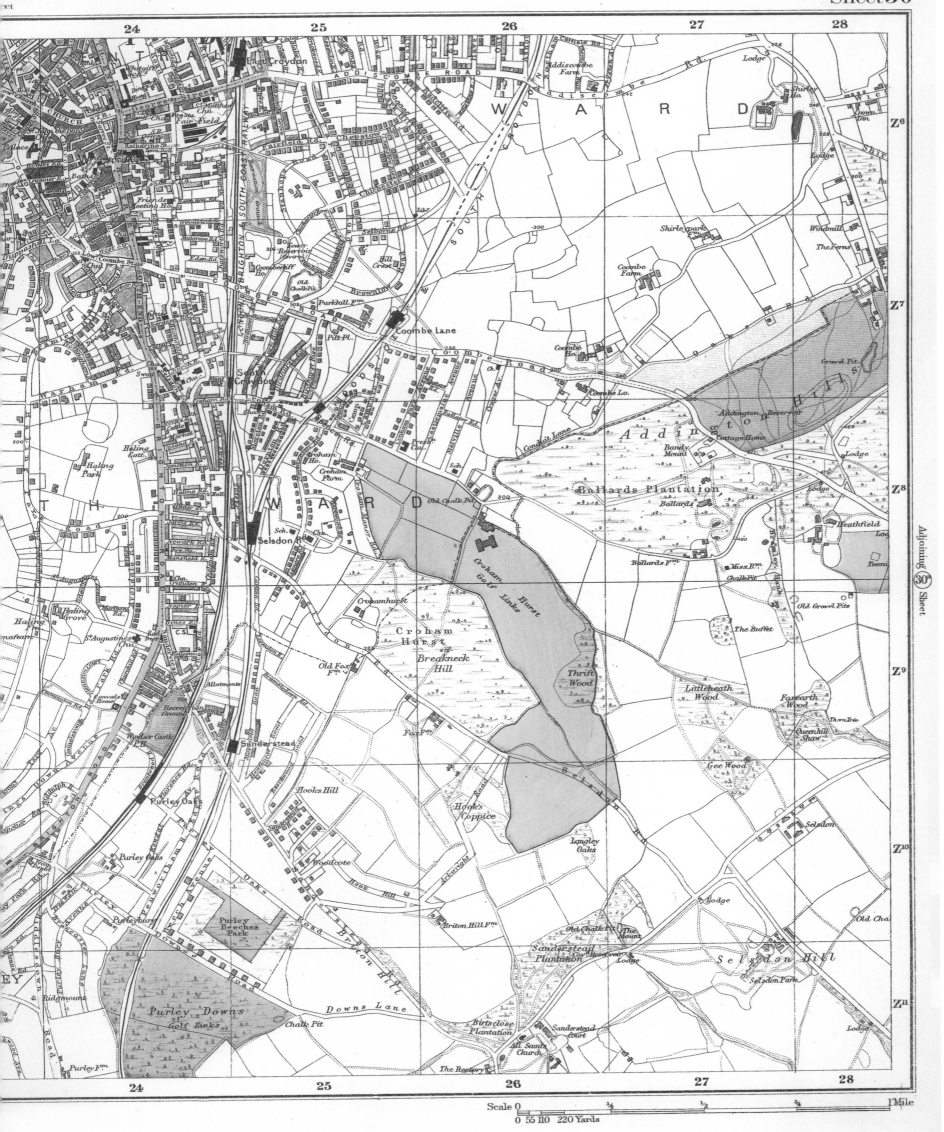

Adjoining (30) Sheet

Scale 0   ¼   ½   ¾   1 Mile

0   55   110   220 Yards

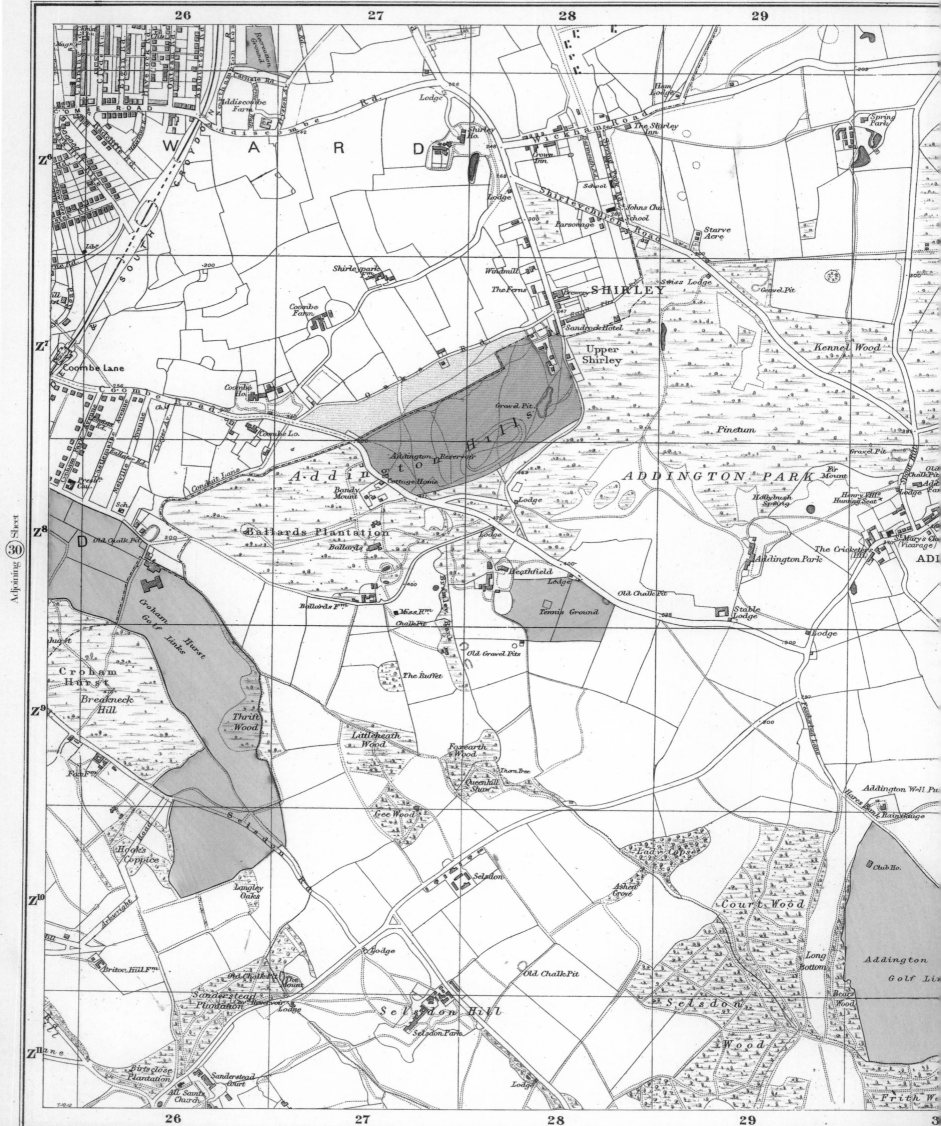

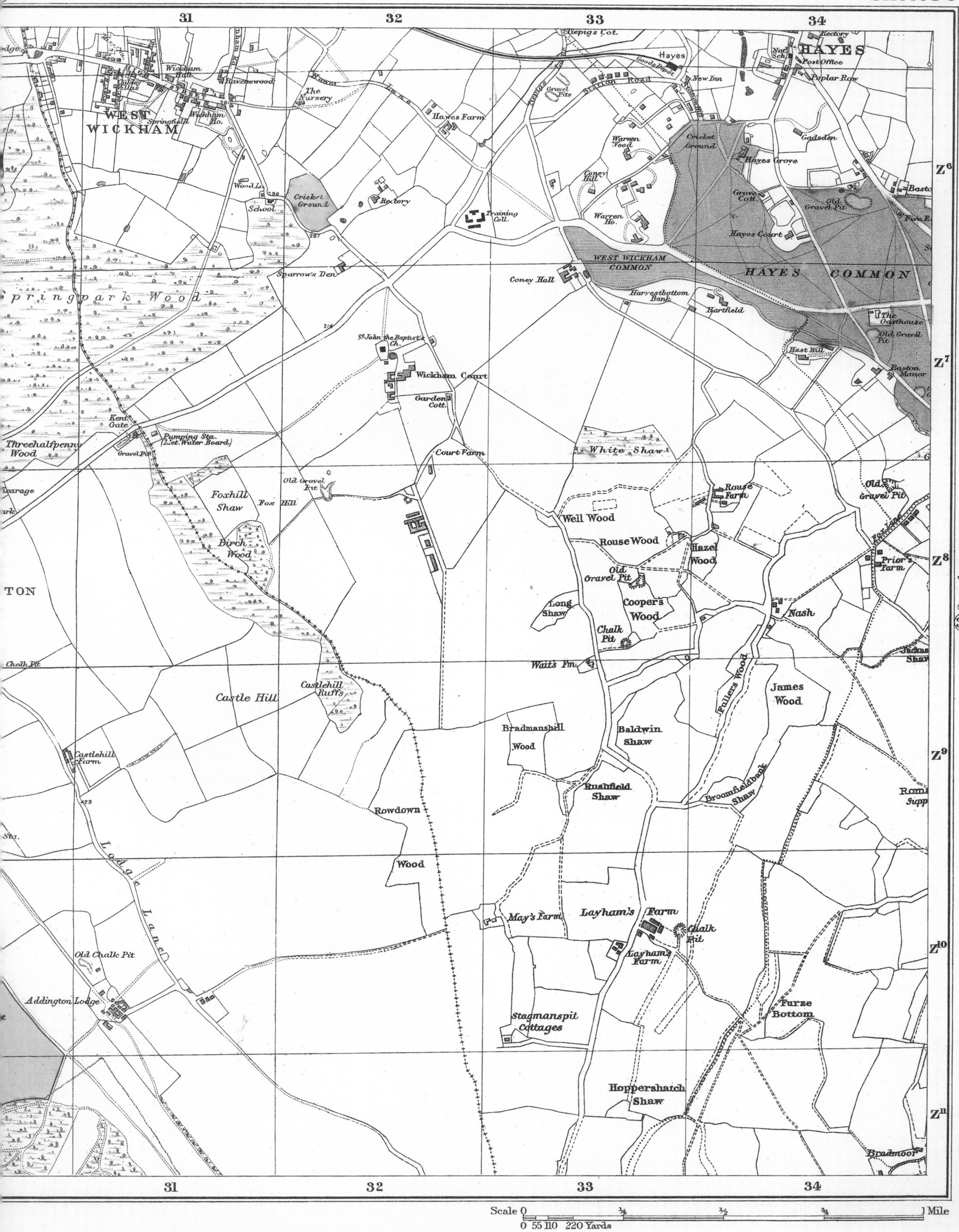

31 32 33 34

Riepigs Cot.
HAYES
Rectory
Nat. Sch.
Post Office
Poplar Row
New Inn
Hayes
Goods Depot
Gravel Pits
Station Road
Lodge
HAYES
WICKHAM
Wickham Hall
Ravenswood
The Nursery
Hayes Farm
Warren Wood
Cricket Ground
Gadsden
Hayes Grove
WEST
WICKHAM
Springfield
Wickham Ho.
Coney Hill
Grove Cott.
Old Gravel Pit
Baston
Z 6
Warren Ho.
Hayes Court
Wood La.
Cricket Ground
School
Rectory
Training Coll.
WEST WICKHAM COMMON
HAYES COMMON
Five E.
Sparrow's Den
Coney Hall
Harvestbottom Bank
Hartfield
The Oasthouse
Old Gravel Pit
Springpark Wood
St. John the Baptist's Ch.
Hast Hill
Z 7
Wickham Court
Baston Manor
Kent Gate
Pumping Sta. (Met. Water Board)
Garden Cott.
Threehalfpenny Wood
Gravel Pit
Court Farm
White Shaw
Old Gravel Pit
Rouse Farm
Old Gravel Pit
TON
Foxhill Shaw
Fox Hill
Old Gravel Pit
Well Wood
Rouse Wood
Hazel Wood
Fox Wood
Z 8
Birch Wood
Prior's Farm
Old Gravel Pit
Long Shaw
Cooper's Wood
Nash
Chalk Pit
Wait's Fm.
Jackas Shaw
Castle Hill
Castlehill Ruffs
James Wood
Fullers Wood
Z 9
Bradmanshill Wood
Baldwin Shaw
Castlehill Farm
Rushfield Shaw
Broomfieldbank Shaw
Rom Supp
Rowdown
Wood
Layham's Farm
Chalk Pit
Z 10
May's Farm
Layham's Farm
Old Chalk Pit
Furze Bottom
Addington Lodge
Stagmanspit Cottages
Hoppershatch Shaw
Z 11
Bradmoor
Lodge Lane
Chalk Pit

31 32 33 34

Scale 0   ¼   ½   ¾   Mile
0 55 110   220 Yards

[167]

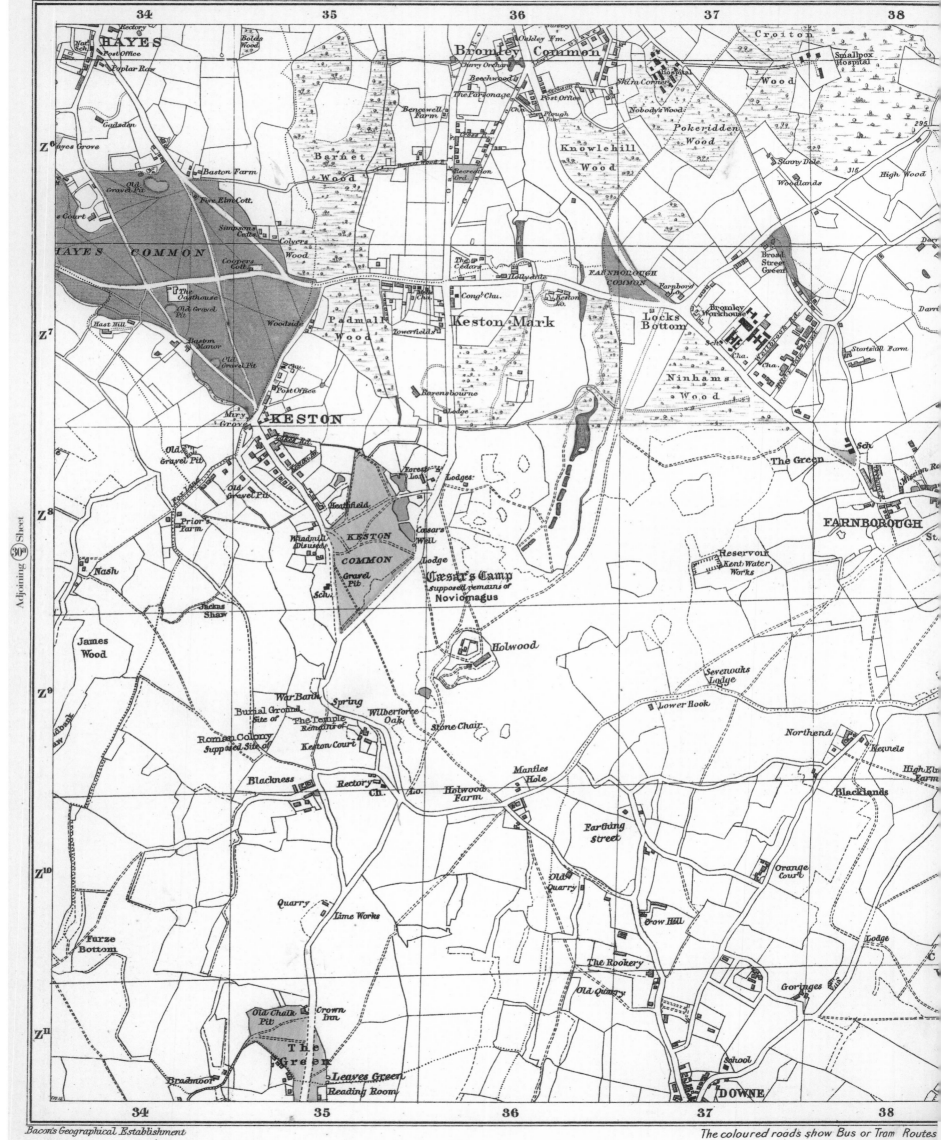

Bacon's Geographical Establishment

The coloured roads show Bus or Tram Routes

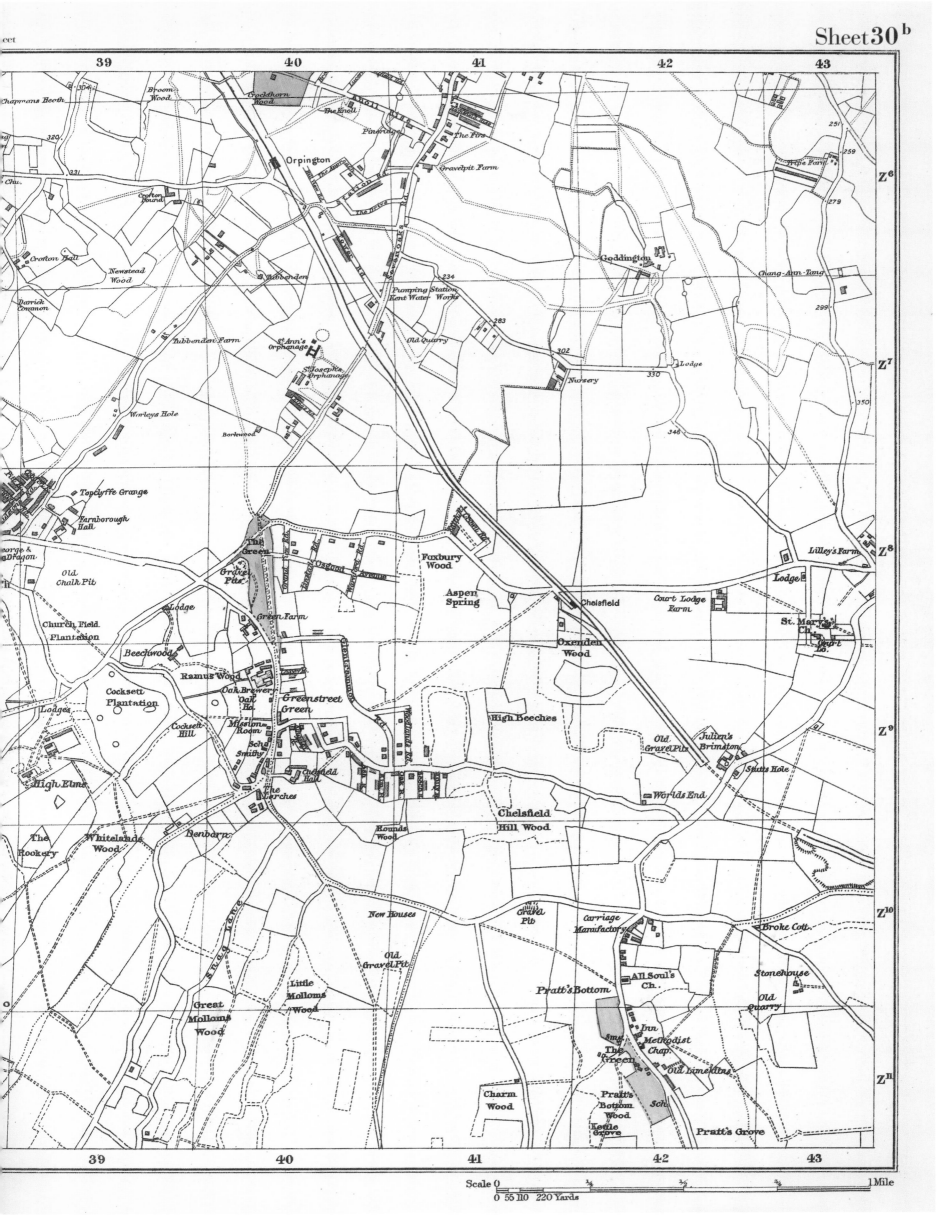

Scale 0   ¼   ½   ¾   1 Mile

0   55   110   220 Yards